Interpretation a M ethod

Interpretation and Method

Empirical Research Methods and the Interpretive Turn

Edited by

Dvora Yanow and
Peregrine Schwartz-Shea

M.E.Sharpe

Armonk, New York
London, England

Library of Congress Cataloging-in-Publication Data

Interpretation and method : empirical research methods and the interpretive turn / edited by Dvora Yanow
and Peregrine Schwartz-Shea.
    p. cm.
 Includes bibliographical references and index.
 ISBN-13: 978-0-7656-1463-6 (pbk. : alk. paper)
 ISBN-10: 0-7656-1463-4 (pbk. : alk. paper)
 1. Political science—Methodology. 2. Political science—Research—Methodology. I. Yanow, Dvora. II.
Schwartz-Shea, Peregrine, 1955–

JA71.I575 2006
320'.072—dc22

2005025001

Printed in the United States of America

The paper used in this publication meets the minimum requirements of
American National Standard for Information Sciences
Permanence of Paper for Printed Library Materials,
ANSI Z 39.48-1984.

♾

BM (c)	10	9	8	7	6	5	4	3	2	1
BM (p)	10	9	8	7	6	5	4	3	2	

. . . human behavior always comes with meaning,
with intentions and purposes.
That is to say, the way others see and react to what you do
is powerfully affected by what they think you mean,
what you are trying to do
and why.
So if the social scientist wants to describe the sequence of the interaction,
he cannot omit what it means to the actors.
He studies not just behavior
but action.
Sam Beer, "Letter to a Graduate Student" (2005)

As a culture, we were aware of the seals and the walruses on top of the ice,
but we didn't know what they were doing underneath the ice.
Joe Seungetuk
Inupiaq artist/writer
Address to the Public Administration Theory Annual Conference
University of Alaska-Anchorage, June 19, 2003

CONTENTS

ACKNOWLEDGMENTS

Our collaboration all started with a curiosity—and a concern—about what the present generation of doctoral students was learning in the methods classroom and how textbook authors and publishers were treating the notion of "methods." This led us, in the 1999 Seattle meeting of the Western Political Science Association (WPSA), to tour the book display room to see what was being marketed to conferees. That, in turn, led to a conference paper the following year in San Jose and to a subsequent effort to condense a narrative content analysis of twelve textbooks into ten pages for *PS: Political Science and Politics.* We are grateful to our San Jose co-panelists Martha Feldman and Sandra Kensen and respondent Janet Flammang and to those who showed up for the morning session, including the late Rita Mae Kelly, Kirstie McClure, and Jane Bayes. Their lively engagement with methodological matters encouraged us to think that others might find questions of method and truth claim justifications as intriguing as they had become to each of us. We are particularly thankful to the *PS* editor who turned down that manuscript, and especially to the acerbic review finding our essay to be a "polemic under the garb of some sort of analysis" in an argument that had been "lost over 40 years ago."

Our bemused outrage at these comments spurred us on to develop a more fully reasoned article for *Political Research Quarterly* and a subsequent Interpretive Research Methods workshop at the 2003 WPSA. We were tremendously gratified by the turnout, but even more so by the comments we received, from both faculty and students, long after we had returned to our respective homes. Our thanks to the participants in that event and to our WPSA colleagues Bill Haltom (that year's local arrangements chair), Tim Kaufman-Osborn (president and program chair), and Betty Moulds (executive director) for making it happen. The enthusiastic response to both article and workshop convinced us that the time was right to pull together the volume you hold in your hands.

Identifying authors who could write engagingly, who were involved with empirical research, and who were grappling with methodological issues—which for us meant not just tools and techniques but the philosophical questions that make tools and techniques matter—was not easy. For both of us, this project has been an education beyond our own subfields. One of us (Dvora) felt as if she were earning her second doctorate. We are indebted to Ido Oren for directing our attention to many interesting scholars in the field of international relations, some of whom became chapter authors; and to Joe Soss, Mary Hawkesworth, Patrick Jackson, and Robert Adcock for helpful suggestions that widened the net even further. Ed Schatz, Ernie Zirakzadeh, and Ted Hopf posted methodologically related comments to various Internet lists that helped sharpen the focus of the book.

We thank the authors of the chapters collected here, both for their patience with our editorial requests, suggestions, and demands and for teaching us a great deal about topics and ways of thinking new to us. Harry Briggs was patient in other ways, and his editorial guidance and vision were always very helpful. Our thanks, too, to Jessica Taverna for her word-processing wizardry in preparing the manuscript, and to Amy Odum for her supportive guidance in the production of the book.

Dvora adds: Most of the work thinking through the scope and shape of the book was done while I was on sabbatical, sitting in Lauren Edelman's office as a visiting scholar at the Center for the Study of Law and Society at the University of California, Berkeley's Boalt Hall School of Law. Laurie not only set in motion my stay at the center; she also kindly made a place for me there while she took her own sabbatical leave elsewhere. I extend my thanks as well to members of the center—then-director Bob Kagan, associate director Rosann Greenspan, Malcolm Feeley, Jonathan Simon, KT Albiston, Kristen Luker—and other visiting scholars that year—Liz Borgwardt, Hila Keren, Ron Harris—along with Eleanor Swift at Boalt, for their gracious hospitality and for making time in their busy schedules to talk about evidence, methods, and other matters. In addition, I am enormously grateful for the colleagueship of two scholars who are commencing their academic careers: Robert Adcock, who was a sounding board for many of my thoughts, directing me to the history and sociology literatures and catching my imprecisions in word choice; and Tim Pachirat, for supremely intelligent, thoughtful, and humane critique in all of our wide-ranging conversations. And my thanks to Peri, for her enthusiasms and cautions, for bringing perspectives from both research and teaching that kept the project on course and unfailingly complemented my own quite different background and reading practices.

And Peri says: I owe a strange debt to colleagues from my early years in the political science discipline, John Orbell, Randy Simmons, and Robyn Dawes, who tutored me in rational choice theory and experiment analysis—giving me the foundation for understanding both the strengths and the limits of those approaches. I want, also, to express my gratitude here to two then–graduate students who first introduced me to feminist scholarship, Debra Burrington and Melanee Cherry, and to other feminist colleagues such as Eloise Buker, the late Rita Mae Kelly, and MaryAnne Borrelli who offered encouragement over the years. More recently, the University of Utah has supported me with two fellowships, a faculty fellowship and the Tanner Humanities Center Aldrich Faculty Fellowship, which provided the time so crucial to my rethinking methodological issues. During the most recent year, my energies would have been much divided without the support of my departmental chair, Ron Hrebenar. Additionally, my departmental colleagues John Francis, Matthew Burbank, and Mark Button provided feedback at critical moments, as have two colleagues from other institutions, Diane Singerman and Valerie Hudson, who provided venues for thinking out loud about the possibilities of new methodological directions. And kudos to my husband, Tim, and my children, Carl and Tierney, for preventing me from being a workaholic. My thanks, of course, to Dvora for her unfailing collaborative skills, her gracious manner, and, above all, those many wonderful intellectual discussions that were part of coediting this project.

Lastly, we owe Robert Adcock the inspiration for the title of this book. He suggested it initially as the name for a listserv created in the winter of 2004–5 as a home for the discussion of methods such as these and the philosophical issues they raise. As the book developed, it seemed an appropriate umbrella for the ideas expressed in these several chapters, and so we have "stolen" it for this project as well. As Robert did then, we acknowledge Hans-Georg Gadamer as the source for these borrowings. We hope our readers will hear in the title the echoes of his work and see it as a mark of our respect for our predecessors and our indebtedness to his, and their, thinking.

INTRODUCTION

WHAT'S "INTERPRETIVE" ABOUT INTERPRETIVE METHODS?

Why designate a set of research tools and procedures "interpretive"? Isn't all science engaged with the interpretation of data? What's "interpretive" about interpretive methods?

It is to the challenge of responding to these sorts of questions that we have set ourselves in this book. Indeed, researchers in all sciences—natural, physical, and human or social—interpret their data. Moreover, the interpretive processes for analyzing texts in what might be called literary social science, such as what is done by historians, political theorists (or political philosophers), and feminist theorists, overlap with those used, for example, in analyzing contemporary governmental and organizational documents. "Interpretive" methodologists make no claim to conceptual exclusivity in their use of that term.

But "interpretation" has a particular meaning at this point in time in methodological discussions concerning empirical social science. Although research methods are often taught and learned as if they were tools and techniques alone, divorced from any methodological context provided by the history of ideas in science and attendant questions concerning the reality status (ontology) of the subject of study and its "knowability" (epistemology), such matters are increasingly being raised for explicit attention and discussion. We take up this concern for such contextualization in this book, focusing on empirical research across the human, or social, sciences.

The challenge of contextualizing methods has been becoming more acutely felt in recent years in response to two not unrelated developments in the philosophy and sociology of science: the so-called interpretive turn, and the increasing cross- or interdisciplinarity of research questions.

THE "INTERPRETIVE TURN" IN THE SOCIAL SCIENCES

As more and more of the work of late-nineteenth- and early- to mid-twentieth-century Continental philosophers became available in English translation, their thinking fueled what became widely known in the latter part of the twentieth century, especially in U.S. writings, as the "interpretive turn" or the "interpretive paradigm" in the social sciences (see, e.g., Burrell and Morgan 1979; Hiley, Bohman, and Shusterman 1991; Rabinow and Sullivan 1979, 1985). The "turn" metaphor developed a life of its own, finding expression also in the linguistic turn (e.g., Rorty 1967; Van Maanen 1995), the rhetorical turn (e.g., D. McCloskey 1985), the narrative turn (see L. Stone 1979a), the historic turn (McDonald 1996), the metaphorical turn (Lorenz 1998), the argumentative turn (Fischer and Forester 1993), the cultural turn (Bonnell and Hunt 1999), even the practice turn (Schatzki, Knorr-Cetina, and Savigny 2001).[1] Yet the implications for empirical human and social science research practices of these philosophical, conceptual, and theoretical turns have only rarely been spelled out, let alone in a way that links them to their ontological and epistemological presuppositions. That is one of our aims in this book.

These various "turns" share not only an orientation toward "taking language seriously" (J.D. White 1992; see also Edelman 1977), but also an overarching appreciation for the centrality of meaning in human life in all its aspects and a reflexivity on scientific practices related to meaning making and knowledge claims. The methodological ideas and the specific methods discussed in these pages have generally been subsumed under the "interpretive" heading because of the interpretive turn, which became a phrase in good currency, and the philosophies that inspired or undergird it. Because those philosophies developed largely in debate with ideas from critical and logical positivisms, and because these ideas inform the so-called scientific method and its reliability and validity criteria, "interpretive" methods and methodologies contend with methodological positivism and with the quantitative methods that enact positivist philosophical presuppositions. The turning, then, is, by and large, twofold: both away from, if not against, the idea of a social scientific practice derived from a model of human behavior abstracted from the physical and/or natural sciences, denuded of the human traits of researchers and researched; and toward a rehumanized, contextualized set of practices. This provides one account of the use of the phrase "human sciences" to refer to psychology, sociology, anthropology, and so on: its emphasis on their meaning-focused and person-centered concerns, as distinct from the more behavioralist connotations of "social sciences."[2]

Much of the work arguing on behalf of interpretive approaches has focused on critiquing the positivist philosophies and ideas that inform the "pre-turn" practices of the social sciences, decrying their limitations and those of their associated methods. Although such critique, well founded in our view, is both warranted and needed, it has had the unintended consequence of establishing a negative tone to the conversation, with authors seemingly always on the attack or in a defensive posture with respect to the contributions of interpretive methods. As a consequence, the positive (in a contributory sense) delineation of interpretive tools and their philosophical grounding has been shortchanged.

We wish not only not to repeat the critique at length, but also to present in a more positive vein the contributions of interpretive methodologies and methods to empirical social science. Part I of this book straddles the two directions of the turning—the turning against and the turning toward: It includes some critique, but that is purposed more to explicate than to be dismissive. Parts II and III detail the turn toward and part IV reflects on the whole enterprise. An impression appears to exist that "interpretive" describes "a type of social science that is only remotely empirical and concerned primarily with problems of meaning or hermeneutics" (Ragin 1987, 3). We are not quite certain what interpretive research Charles Ragin and others might have in mind, but we present work here, particularly the chapters in parts II and III, that is closely, even intimately, empirical and concerned with problems of meaning, conceived of and analyzed hermeneutically or otherwise, *that bear on action as well as understanding*, whether that action is academic-analytic or policy-analytic. Indeed, not only do we see no contradiction between empirical research and meaning-focused analysis, as the book subtitle is intended to suggest; we are also of the view that the central focus of much empirical social science *should be* on problems of meaning. Moreover, as discussed below and in various chapters (especially chapters 2, 5, and 15), the meaning-making activity of human actors is central to understanding causal relationships (although the concept of causality is reconceived on interpretive epistemological and ontological grounds).

We do not see the relationship between interpretive philosophical ideas and research methods as causal or chronological: Philosophical ideas do not necessarily lead to methodological ones or precede them in the timeline of a researcher's analytic or theoretical development. In fact, many social scientists working with interpretive methodologies come to their philosophical presuppositions only *after* extended involvement in empirical research. It is their very grounded, empirically based dissatisfaction with the explanatory power for their research questions of "traditional" quantitative methods, rather than a more general philosophically grounded inquiry, that leads researchers to explore and engage interpretive epistemologies and interpretive-inflected methods. As well, interpretive ideas and orientations have increasingly become part of the "ether" in which contemporary social science debates take place, and they have often been picked up from that context without prior immersion in the philosophical literature.

Yet many issues in empirical research practice do become clearer in light of interpretive presuppositions—once these are articulated. Here is an additional reason for the negative treatment and even outright denigration, in textbooks and elsewhere, of interpretive or so-called qualitative methods: Those of us doing that kind of research have, on the whole, not done a good job of articulating how it is that we do what we do. This is another aim of this book—not only to identify the links between what interpretive researchers do and the ontological and epistemological arguments of interpretive philosophies, but to identify the varieties of interpretive methods and to spell out what deliberations and procedures some of these entail.

MAKING METHODS EXPLICIT

Most researchers using interpretive methods have just set about doing the work, writing the tale, without explicit reflection on their methodological considerations, choices, and decisions. Historians write history; comparativists describe societies and governments and states; organizational studies theorists analyze issues in management practices; policy analysts analyze policies. This makes eminent sense when scholars write to communities with well-established practices of evidentiary proceedings. Increasingly, however, disciplinary and subfield walls are breaking down, and readerly practices bestride such divisions. Here lies a second impulse behind this book.

As long as a researcher is writing for a community of readers sharing the same presuppositions and assumptions, there is little or no need to be explicitly reflective about what was done either in accessing and generating data or in analyzing them, beyond a simple description of settings and sources. But when writing for other interpretive (or meaning or discourse or epistemic) communities, or across communities (as in interdisciplinary and cross-disciplinary work), or within communities with no agreed-upon procedural norms or when such norms are under contestation, explicit statements of methodological concerns and methods procedures become more necessary. The need for explicit statements slides along a continuum; there is no "bright line" indicating where one must come down on the side of methodological disclosure.[3] Relatively more transparency, however, may have a variety of beneficial effects. It enables a more fully developed engagement with methodological positivists (such as, for example, around discussions of objectivity). Over time, more disclosure is likely to provide more insights for improving theorizing about the ways in which researcher positionality may impact the accessing, generating, and analysis of data.[4] And increased methodological transparency, by improving understanding across disciplinary divides, may provide a better foundation for interdisciplinary work and more solid grounds for challenging existing divisions of scholarly inquiry into "fields" and "disciplines," which is at this point in time based as much on organizational inertia as on substantive grounds (Kaufman-Osborn 2006; Klein 1993; D.W. Smith 2003; Wallerstein 1999).

The lack of explicit methodological statements in research writing parallels curricular practices: Unlike the explicit, stepwise, prescriptive training in various forms of quantitative analysis, ethnographic, participant-observer, historical, and textual-analytic methods have, by and large, been taught and learned inductively. Ethnographic and participant-observer research methods in particular have largely been learned through a kind of apprenticeship, through reading others' work in a series of courses and a kind of trial-and-error learning by doing (the "drop the graduate student in the field and see if he swims" sort of teaching). Both teaching and practice entail significant amounts of tacit knowledge (in M. Polanyi's 1966 sense). This is not to say that such researchers have not reflected on their processes, but that they have felt no need to do so in great detail on the written page. As long as they were writing for a community of practice in which methods and their presuppositions were shared *and were accepted as "scientific,"* this was not problematic. The spreading impact of behaviorism on and the growing use of increasingly more complicated statistical methods in the social sciences in the 1970s, however—seen in a range of work-related practices, from position descriptions to publication gatekeeping—coupled with the growth of cross-disciplinary reading and research, has made it increasingly necessary to make such reflection explicit. The lack of such explicitness about their systematicity and the disinclination to situate methods discussions in their philosophical grounding has contributed to the (false) impression that interpretive methods are not serious scholarship: that their procedures are not rigorous or systematic and that their findings are not trustworthy, being little more than "opinion."[5]

Part of our motivation in designing this book has been to make methodological concerns more explicit in a way that is both reflective on (and thereby consistent with one of interpretive methods' own philosophical tenets) and illustrative of what interpretive philosophies and methods have to offer. Combining these two impulses—the drive toward procedural transparency, together with insights garnered from the philosophical mandates of the interpretive turn—leads us to problematize the received wisdom concerning certain terms within "research methods."

Specifically, the several chapters in this book explore the meanings of the concepts of science and scientific reason (Mary Hawkesworth in chapter 2); explanation and causality (Robert Adcock's chapter 3, Mark Bevir in chapter 15); rigor (Dvora Yanow in chapter 4); and generalizability, validity, and reliability (Peregrine Schwartz-Shea's chapter 5). When interpretive researchers and methodological positivists use the same terms but mean different things, without attending to those differences, noncommunicative debates ensue, to the detriment of the subject.[6] It has been thought, and taught, for instance, that interpretive methods lack rigor, do not concern themselves with causality, are not reliable or valid, and so on. Many, if not most, methods textbooks support this view (Schwartz-Shea and Yanow 2002). Discussions of these and other terms in these chapters, however, show that this received wisdom reflects, at times, a construal of their meaning that has been narrowed from their meanings in their earlier or original contexts (e.g., "rigor" in formal logic). This narrowing has led methods discussions in one direction, leaving behind a wide range of analytic methods that are, in point of fact, logically rigorous, concerned with causal relations, and pursuant of research trustworthiness. We appear to have in these contestations a version of partisan battles over ownership of the national flag—except that the defending camp (in this case, those doing qualitative and interpretive work) has by and large accepted the other's (re)definition of important concepts and ceded that terrain, not recognizing that under earlier (if not original) definitions, both (or all) parties' practices would enjoy an equal claim. This capitulation may be due to a lack of training in disciplinary history and in the philosophy of (social) science,[7] as well as to the ahistorical treatments of methods in curricula and in textbooks.

In problematizing these terms, the authors of these chapters return the discussion to earlier meanings underlying their usage. This is not an "original intent" argument—we have no constitution to interpret—but it is an effort to reclaim lost meaning within the philosophy of natural-physical and social-human science. It is our hope here at least to flag the problem of miscommunication due to incompatible terminological meanings as a concern and to suggest that serious attention is needed to concept usage—not that usage is in error, or even "merely" different or idiosyncratic (interpretive researchers are not Humpty Dumpty, making words mean whatever we want them to), but that these meanings represent a shared, collective usage within a community of thought and practice, informed by different philosophical stands. As Schwartz-Shea illustrates with the thought experiment that opens chapter 5, it is shared practices that produce the research *gestalts* that render particular terms intelligible *within* a practice community, but that also make them misunderstood or opaque *across* communities.

SO WHAT'S WRONG WITH "QUALITATIVE"?

"Qualitative" methods as a category and descriptor increasingly do not capture the full range of non-quantitative methods used in empirical social science research, and, in particular, methods of the sort presented here. It seems appropriate, then, to delineate what interpretive research entails by contrasting it with qualitative methods.

Such a discussion rests on an understanding of what is meant by "science" (a point taken up in chapters 1 and 2) and whether there is, or can and should be, only one version of science in the social sciences. Contra Keohane (2003, 11), the "standards of science held up to us by the natural sciences and espoused by economics and psychology" are not the only way to do political and other social sciences; nor is there, for that matter, a single way to do natural science, as Knorr Cetina's (1999) comparative study of particle physics and molecular biology makes clear. Phenomenological approaches are increasingly being heard in economics, especially among European scholars, and, even more strongly, in various subfields of psychology (see, e.g., Atwood and Stolorow 1984). There are established interpretive positions in anthropology and in sociology, as well as a critical theoretical one in the latter. In other areas of these disciplines, as well as in interdisciplinary fields such as organizational studies and urban planning, "qualitative" methods are under increasing pressure to adhere to the characteristics of large 'n' research; in hiring descriptions for faculty positions, "qualitative" increasingly refers to research using focus groups, structured interviews, Q-sort, and other similar techniques, rather than ethnographic, participant-observer, ethnomethodological, semiotic, narrative, and other such approaches. There are differences both in procedure and in rationales for such procedures between these two families of methods, reflecting differences in ontological and epistemological presuppositions. This is what keeps interpretive methods from being a subfield of qualitative methods: The two increasingly do not live under the same philosophical umbrella when it comes to their respective procedural enactments of assumptions about the reality status and knowability of their subjects of inquiry.

The two-part taxonomy of "quantitative" and "qualitative" methods became entrenched during a specific historical moment, with the development of survey research, statistical analysis, and behaviorist theory, and was solidified with improvements in computer processing and the growing capacity to manipulate large amounts of numerical data with increasingly less human effort and involvement. The structural logic of the language of "quantitative" drew "qualitative" into play by counter-distinction: If statistics and "large 'n'" studies (increasingly enabled by computer abilities) were to be understood as quantitative analysis, then "small 'n'" studies using non-statistical methods—field-based observing and interviewing—must be "qualitative" analysis.

What "qualitative" originally designated, then, were the features characteristic of traditional, Chicago School-style field studies of the early- to mid-twentieth century—ethnographies in anthropology departments and participant-observations in sociology departments, as those two separated and carved out distinct turfs, and their extension to political, organizational, and other studies.[8] Such research attends to data of three broad sorts: language (spoken by actors in the situation or written in such forms as organizational correspondence, government documents, or individuals' diaries); acts and interactions (including nonverbal behaviors); and the physical objects used in these acts or in written language (such as governmental buildings, census questionnaires, and organizational mission statements). These three classes of artifact are analyzed to infer the meanings conveyed through them (chapter 1 elaborates on this).

Chief among the features of such work are:

1. word-based modes of accessing and generating data, through observing (with whatever degree of participating; see Gans 1976) extended over time, which immerses the researcher in the language and culture of the study's domain (see Ellen Pader, chapter 8, this volume), and "conversational" or "discursive" (a.k.a. "in-depth" or "unstructured," or even "semi-structured") interviewing, supplemented where appropriate by a close reading of research-relevant documents (see Joe Soss, chapter 6, and Frederic Schaffer, chapter 7, this volume);

2. word-based modes of analyzing word data (rather than "translating" them into numbers for statistical analysis, e.g., see Jutta Weldes, chapter 9, and Dean McHenry, chapter 10, as well as the chapters in part III, this volume); and

3. a richly detailed narrative form of communicating both data and findings, in which tables and figures, when used, supplement and/or illustrate the data and/or analysis—or constitute the data—rather than presenting them in summarized form.

Traditional qualitative methods require a flexible response "in the moment" to observational (including participational) and interviewing circumstances, and so they are not "rigorous" in the literal sense of that word—they do not follow a stepwise course in the way that quantitative studies are described as doing (see chapters 1 and 4 for further discussion). The requisite flexibility also means that the research design often changes in the face of research-site realities that the researcher could not anticipate in advance of beginning the research. For this reason, it is accepted interpretive methodological practice not to begin such a study with a formal hypothesis that is then "tested" against field "realities." Researchers in interpretive modes more commonly begin their work with what might be called informed "hunches" or puzzles or a sense of tension between expectations and prior observations, grounded in the research literature and, not atypically, in some prior knowledge of the study setting. Understanding and concepts are allowed (indeed, expected) to emerge from the data as the research progresses.[9]

Unfortunately, the on-site flexibility and less stepwise research design that characterize traditional qualitative methods have been taken to mean that these methods are not systematic. This is hardly the case, as attention to the care with which settings, interview subjects, and/or research question-relevant documents are identified, considered, and selected; observations and interviews carried out; and analyses conducted will attest (see, e.g., Feldman 1995; Feldman, Bell, and Berger 2003; or Murphy 1980 for further discussion of this point). Neither "qualitative" nor "interpretive" means "impressionistic." Along with procedural systematicity, the work entails a "philosophical rigor" (in Mark Bevir's phrase [2003])—a rigor of logic and argumentation—rather than merely a procedural "rigor." The chapters in parts II and III document the systematicity of interpretive methods.

The difficulty with the "qual-quant" nomenclature, however, goes beyond a misleading understanding of what constitutes "qualitative" research. Increasingly, that term is being used to refer *not* to the traditions of meaning-focused or lived experience-focused research, but to small 'n' studies that apply large 'n' tools (e.g., King, Keohane, and Verba 1994; cf. Brady and Collier

2004). Interpretive methods are not concerned with some of the issues that appear to claim the attention of these and other qualitative researchers following methodologically positivist approaches: establishing concepts to be tested in the field; theory-testing of a priori, deductive theories; problems of measurement and sample size; or building qualitative databases. For interpretive researchers, concepts are embedded within a literature, becoming part of the historical background that forms the context for scholarly thinking; the attempt to specify them once and for all, as universal constructs, violates interpretive presuppositions about the historical locatedness of scholars and actors (as Oren illustrates in chapter 11, this volume). Interpretive researchers also conceptualize theory differently—for some, it is best developed inductively; for others, it is better seen as a "resource" than as an apparatus of causal laws. Word-data, as the chapters here show, need not be translated into numerical indices or measures to achieve legitimacy. Finally, from a constructivist view, building qualitative databases is problematic, because data are seen as being coproduced in and through interactions rather than as objectified, free-standing entities available ("given") for "collection" from the field setting.

Efforts to "improve" the quality (from the point of view of methodological positivism) of meaning-focused studies have brought them under pressure to conform to the validity and reliability criteria that characterize quantitative methods and methodologies. What is problematic here is that quantitative methods are, by and large, informed by positivist philosophical presuppositions, *and their evaluative criteria have grown out of these ontological and epistemological presuppositions*, whereas traditional qualitative methods are informed, explicitly or not, by interpretive philosophical presuppositions and have their own evaluative measures (see chapter 5).

It is the struggle to produce satisfyingly robust data, for instance, *under the requirements of positivist science* that leads King, Keohane, and Verba (1994), for example, to call for increasing the number of observations in order to improve small 'n' studies (see also chapter 5). However, it is a fallacy that small 'n' studies entail a small number of observations: They may entail a small number of research sites—one is not uncommon outside of explicitly comparative work—but field studies of communities or organizations or polities entail large 'n' data points in their sustained observation (with whatever degree of participation) over extended periods of time, often in and of various locations within the research site, extended and repeated conversational interviews, and/or multiplicity of agency, policy, or other documents read and analyzed.[10] One might imagine counting, for example, the large number of hours of engaged observation, the number of conversations held, the number of interactions, and the ensuing number of segments of observation and/or conversation and/or interaction analyzed over the course of the research project—any one of which would yield a large 'n,' indeed. In her study of a single organization—a single 'n' study, by traditional reckoning—sociologist Rosabeth Moss Kanter spent over 120 "personal on-site contact days," during which she conducted over 120 "more than momentary conversations" in which she asked her interlocutors to describe other people (uncounted) and their situations (also not tabulated) (Kanter 1993, 337). This accounting omits the countless hours of observing and "momentary" conversations. In some sense, each one of these constitutes an "observation," although not necessarily as that term is used in quantitative analyses.[11]

The pressure to adopt a more "quantitative" methodology is leading to the growing delimitation of the term "qualitative" to connote methods other than what it initially designated—the sorts of field studies generated by Chicago School-style anthropologists, sociologists, and others and case study developers across the social sciences (e.g., H. Becker et al. 1977 [1961]; Blau 1963 [1953]; Crozier 1964; Dahl 1961; Dalton 1959; R. Kaufman 1960; Lofland 1966, 1969; Powdermaker 1966; Whyte 1955 [1943]). The traditional distinction is a misnomer: "Quants" interpret their data; "quals" count things that they study. But even more than this: The binomial qualitative-quantitative taxonomy has become a placeholder, a surrogate shorthand standing in as a symbolic representation of a much broader issue than the question of who counts. In many senses, "methodology" is usefully seen as "applied ontology and epistemology," and the language of quantitative and qualitative has increasingly become a proxy for differences, largely unarticulated, between positivist and interpretivist philosophical presuppositions concerning the character of social realities and their knowability.

What we are increasingly looking at these days methodologically is, instead, a tripartite division among quantitative, positivist-qualitative, and traditional qualitative methods. The latter have increasingly been termed "interpretive" methods because of their intentional, conscious grounding in or their less explicit but nonetheless recognizable family resemblance to the ontological and epistemological presuppositions of the Continental interpretive philosophies of phenomenology and hermeneutics (and some critical theory) and their American counterparts of symbolic interactionism, ethnomethodology, and pragmatism, among others.[12] Despite differences of specific method, they share a constructivist ontology and an interpretive epistemology. They could as well, then, more fully be called constructivist-interpretive methods; because of the prevalence of the phrase "the interpretive turn" in social science and the cumbersomeness of the doubled term, they are more commonly referred to only as "interpretive" methods, although one also finds reference to "constructivist" or "constructionist" methods.[13]

To understand what is being captured symbolically by "qualitative" and "quantitative," we must go back to the initial purpose of social research: Researchers are making claims to knowledge. To claim that something is knowable entails a related claim in regard to its "reality status." Epistemological and ontological claims are mutually implicating—*and* they implicate methodological choices. If one claims that a door is objectively real (its existence is independent of and external to the observer) and that it is knowable through external ("objective") observation, then methodological positivism's scientific method is a reasonable methodological procedure to choose for establishing and supporting truth claims emerging from research into some aspect of that door.[14] If one can't claim knowledge of an organization or a community on the basis of external observation *alone*, then one needs a different methodology and different methods for producing and supporting knowledge claims.

The "quant-qual" division, in sum, demarcates a distinction between epistemological and ontological claims that rest on positivist philosophical presuppositions and those influenced by schools of thought that put human meaning making at the center of their concerns, which have been subsumed under the term "interpretive." What we have then, in binomial terms, is a "quantitative-interpretive" methods divide.[15]

This binomial becomes especially clear when we separate methods of *accessing* data sources or *generating* data from methods of *analyzing* those data once they are accessed and/or generated. For those human sciences that rule out laboratory or other experimental methods (whether for ethical or for practical reasons, such as the difficulty or impossibility of establishing control groups), data are accessed and generated through observing events and the actors in them (with whatever degree of participation), through talking with those actors about those events, and/or through close readings of documentary and other sources (e.g., film, agency buildings) identified as central to the research question—or some combination of all three. Part II of the book includes discussions of these three modes of generating data.

In our introduction to part II we draw the distinction between accessing and generating data, but we note here our preference for talking about "accessing" data rather than the more widely used "collecting" data. The latter term is laboratory language, in which butterflies or potsherds or other artifacts are physically gathered up and brought back to the lab for analysis; whereas in the nonexperimental, field-based studies[16] conducted in the human sciences, the primary "data" and their sources are left in their locations of origin (or should be). What are brought back are the researcher's copious interview and/or observational notes and/or notes on documents, although copies of documents, interview tapes, and the like may be brought out of the archive or the field.[17] This formulation makes clear that the data of such studies are not the people themselves, or the events and conversations and settings and acts, or even the documents, but rather the researcher's views of these, as encapsulated in her notes. "Data," in this approach, are not things given (*datum, data,* from the Latin "to give"), but things observed and made sense of, interpreted. What is accessed are sources of data; the data themselves are generated, whether by the researcher interacting with visual/tactile/spatial sources or coproduced in conversational and/or participatory interactions. This understanding of "data" as constituted by human researchers' observations renders problematic the creation of databases of interpretive data for other researchers to use. So-called raw data may be the "least interpreted" form (in contrast to succeeding stages in the research process), but the "interpretive moment" cannot be escaped: It colors all stages of the research process, such that human science data are never really "raw" and "unprocessed." Other researchers would be getting processed, not "raw," data—"cooked" and filtered through someone else's interpretive schema.[18]

VARIETIES OF INTERPRETIVE ANALYTIC METHODS

At this point (if not before; see below), "data" in hand, methodologies part company, largely around the question of the legitimacy of "word data." At the epistemological level, methodological positivists posit the superiority of quantitative data over word data. From this perspective, words are *best* translated into numbers for purposes of statistical analysis.[19] Interpretive researchers reject the assumption of the superiority of quantitative data over other forms of data (e.g., sound, visual imagery, built space). They do *not* reject quantitative data per se. Instead, they take an interpretive perspective on numbers: That communities choose to count particular phenomena reveals much about what communities value and the problems that are, or are not, recognized as central to their identities and concerns (see, for example, Czarniawska-Joerges 1992 for an interpretive analysis of budgets).[20] Interpretive researchers, then, respect the form or *genre* of the data, and word data are retained in their original form for purposes of interpretive analysis.

It is common knowledge that there is a wide range of "advanced" methods of statistical analysis: Markov chain Monte Carlo ideal point estimation, multinomial logit analysis and multinomial probit analysis, ARIMA (autoregressive integrated moving average), MANCOVA (multivariate analysis of covariance), and MANOVA (multivariate analysis of variance), cluster analysis, factor analysis, principal components analysis, and more.[21] It is less widely known *outside of the interpretive research community* that there is a broad range of methods for the interpretive analysis of word and other data genres, some of them (e.g., semiotic squares) no less "advanced" or complicated than nonparametric random-effects analysis or Poisson regression. Several of these are explored in part III of the book. To display interpretive methods in all their "infinite" variety, Table I.1 lists here many more than are addressed there; we also note that this table is suggestive and by no means complete.[22]

This variety of analytic methods is suggestive of the fact that all interpretive researchers do not speak with one voice on some of the central philosophical and procedural issues. Interpretive philosophies have only been available beyond the German- (and, to a lesser extent, French) reading world since the mid-twentieth century or so. Their explicit, conscious, and intentional extension into

Table I-1: **Varities of Interpretive Research Methods**

> action research (participatory action research)
> case study analysis
> category analysis
> (social) constructionist/constructivist analysis
> content analysis[1]
> conversational analysis
> critical theoretical analysis (including critical legal studies, critical race theory[2])
> deconstruction
> discourse analysis
> dramaturgical analysis
> ethnographic semantics
> ethnography
> ethnomethodology
> ethnoscience
> feminist analysis
> frame (-reflective) analysis
> genealogy
> grounded theory
> hermeneutics
> life history
> metaphor analysis
> myth analysis
> narrative analysis
> oral history
> participant-observation
> phenomenological research[3]
> poststructural analysis
> science studies
> semiotics
> space analysis
> storytelling analysis
> symbolic interaction
> textual analyses (of various sorts)
> value-critical analysis

1. This refers to word-based content analysis, not incidence rate counts.
2. On critical race theory, see the special issue of *Qualitative Inquiry* on "Critical Race Theory and Qualitative Research" (Lynn et al. 2002).
3. Meaning empirical, not theoretical or philosophical, research.

the world of research methodology, and along with it the effort to argue for the standing of such methodologies and methods in the world of science, began much more recently than that. The internal debates and intellectual arguments are still unfolding. Indeed, one might array the analytic methods listed here along a continuum, from more descriptive to more critical-theoretical (the latter being more explicit in considering the effects of institutional structures and power on individual meaning making). Case study, grounded theory, life and oral histories, and participant-observation analyses—to make a gross generalization—might more commonly be found at the descriptive end; action research, critical theory, deconstruction, discourse, and post-structural analyses might be at the other end; frame and value-critical analyses might be more toward the center on the critical side; and so forth. But the inadequacy of such a distinction is highlighted when one notes that interpretive work of all kinds, in rendering tacit knowledge explicit, makes silenced discourses speak, thereby engaging questions of power. Any interpretive analytic method, in other words, has the capacity to move fully across the descriptive-critical continuum.[23]

What leads a researcher to choose to follow an interpretive or some other path is largely the set of ontological and epistemological presuppositions undergirding the initial shaping of the research question. The linguistic structure of the word does not mean that these *pre*suppositions are necessarily arrived at *prior to* methods. It is equally possible—and, in our experience as researchers, teachers, and readers of others' work, far more likely—that methodological inclinations of whatever sort are arrived at without any conscious attention to their philosophical groundings (especially when graduate programs do not include philosophy of science discussions in core courses). "Presupposition" should be taken in a conceptual or logical sense, then, rather than in a chronological one, to mean what one must suppose—even if one does so un- or subconsciously—about social realities and their knowability in order logically to hold particular methodological positions. A phenomenological approach suggests a way to engage the question, Where do presuppositions come from? They are not necessarily explicitly known, and often not explicitly reflected on or consciously chosen; there seems instead to be a relationship between presuppositional inclinations —toward research that resonates, reflecting personality, type of intelligence (see Gardner 1993), lived experience—and one's choice of field of study and, hence, methods.

Choices are made also within interpretive modes, including between an empirical interpretive path and more philosophical or literary critical interpretive traditions, such as "political theory" in political science and "social theory" in sociology. In drawing a distinction between empirical research analyzed "interpretively" and interpretive textual approaches to canonical thinkers such as Aristotle or Weber, we are not intending to signal that empirical researchers do not theorize or that "theorists" do not engage "real-world" issues. It is, however, our experience as "empirical researchers" who have immersed ourselves in parts of the "theory" world, especially in feminist, critical race, and organizational, public policy, and public administration theories, that the two groups proceed about their theorizing differently: They constitute different epistemic communities, which frame research questions differently, reason arguments differently, and write differently. Clearly, at a conceptual level, there are overlaps: Critical content analysts, to take one example, engage in close readings of organizational, governmental, legal, or other texts that draw on many of the same techniques used by theorists explicating, for instance, foundational texts for their meanings. Yet the reading and writing practices and habits of mind of the two communities are sufficiently different as to render the resulting articles and books qualitatively different in kind. To some extent this is evident in some of the chapters in this volume: Mary Hawkesworth's and Mark Bevir's chapters (2 and 15, respectively) are recognizable as the work of theorists; Pamela Brandwein's and Clare Ginger's chapters (12 and 19, respectively), as the work of empirically oriented researchers, even though both of the latter analyze texts (the one, legal texts; the other, policy texts). Although both editors of this volume find inspiration in the interpretive work of theorists, we have chosen to restrict it to interpretive empirical analysis because it is our sense that *l'analyse du texte* is an accepted practice in theory-oriented fields regardless of philosophical perspective, whereas in empirical fields, such methods as presented here are not widely known, let alone accepted. In addition, we hope that these examples will provide models that might inspire others to do similar work and might provide the means to refute objections that such work isn't "scientific."[24]

Thinking about the connections between textual analysts' and empirical researchers' interpretive work, something very interesting becomes clear in reading the chapters in part II and, especially, part III. Philosophy or theory and method do not seem to be as clearly separable in interpretive work as they are in quantitative work. One can have a full discussion of, say, various statistical findings without having to engage either ontological or epistemological questions.[25] For the authors of chapters in part III, this is hardly the case. It seems that one cannot explain how narratives mean (as Mark Bevir assays in chapter 15) without attending to distinctions between the natural and the human sciences, specifically the connection of beliefs to action. Ido Oren (chapter 11) cannot direct our attention to historical analyses without also engaging questions of epistemology, that is, how researchers understand what it means to do "historical" research. Patrick Jackson (chapter 14) needs to explicate the idea of the double hermeneutic in order to explain what was happening on the floor of the Bundestag. And Pamela Brandwein (chapter 12) must elaborate on insights from science studies concerning knowledge production processes to construct an account of the legal community's receptivity to anachronistic interpretations of court decisions.

There are a number of possible explanations for this general observation. To the extent that quantitative researchers hold positivist presuppositions, they may consider epistemological and ontological issues settled, even irrelevant (perusing the pages of many associational "flagship" journals gives such an impression); and so there is no need to dwell on them in empirical research reports. As important, certain writing traditions discourage or may even preclude epistemological and ontological reflections, because the standard "formula" for writing an "empirical" (read: quantitative) research article does not include such a component. This is evident, for example, in the instructions to authors in the *Publication Manual of the American Psychological Association* (American Psychological Association 2001), which describes a very narrow model of how to present research. The standard methods section, for example, is to consist of a discussion of laboratory methods rather than a broader consideration of methodology, which reasonably could include discussion of epistemological or ontological issues. In contrast, the writing traditions inherited from the Chicago School or encouraged by the ethnographic tradition more generally are much more open ended, allowing and even encouraging scholarly reflection in addition to the "reporting" of findings. As discussed in chapter 5, self-conscious "reflexivity" has emerged as one criterion marking good interpretive research, which explains, in part, its presence in such works. It may also be the case that when there is a dominant method for doing research that is not working for scholars, they may, in a sense, be forced to try to figure out at a "deeper" (i.e., presuppositional) level why that is the case, and this theorizing is worked out in the research writing along with the presentation and analysis of the data. When methodological issues and methods procedures are intertwined in this way, readers from some epistemic communities may experience the writing as more "philosophical" than what they typically associate with "empirical research."

Given all these varieties, we have chosen not to force-fit contributors into our view of interpretive science; and so the chapters at times produce the "wild, messy intercropping" (Tim Pachirat, p. 376, this volume) of interpretive research.

METHODS, METHODOLOGIES, AND PROFESSIONAL PRACTICES: PERSONAL REFLECTIONS

Governmental, legal, organizational, communal, and other social actions and their analysis are a human activity, and human perception is not a "mirror of nature" (Rorty 1979) but an interpretation of it. We have tried to bring together scholars whose work reflects the breadth of interpretive approaches being brought to bear on interesting, important, and relevant concerns of various aspects of human life. We have drawn authors largely from across the subfields of political science, construed quite broadly: not only from international relations, comparative government, American government, and political theory (philosophy), the four subfields that crystallized in the twentieth-century United States as the accepted disciplinary divisions (see Kaufman-Osborn

2006), but also from outside traditional political science: planning, public law, history, area studies, public policy, organizational studies, and public administration. These scholars have formal training in anthropology, urban studies and planning, social theory, and sociology, as well as political science, and hold appointments in schools, departments, and centers of environmental and natural resources, landscape architecture and regional planning, public affairs and administration, Arab studies, and international service, as well as in more standard disciplinary departments. The methodological questions they discuss in their chapters, however, are not restricted by these institutional affiliations and disciplinary boundaries. We asked these authors to reflect on their *own* work, to think about how they had done their research and about the interpretive methodological questions and issues they encountered. Furthermore, we asked them to select one or more epigraphs from published research, theirs or another's, that would serve as a touchstone for the reflective methodological analysis presented in the chapter. These general instructions have, we think, produced methodological discussions that are concrete—grounded, appropriately so, in the lived experiences and struggles of the researchers. We hope, then, that the book brings some answers to our student, practitioner, and faculty colleagues across the disciplines who are themselves seeking direction in interpretive areas. But even more, we hope it challenges and provokes many more questions as to the character of interpretive social science.

This, then, is the additional impetus for preparing this book, and it is a more personal one coming out of our concerns for curricular matters and the future of our several disciplines. One of us was invited a few years ago to meet with a cross-departmental, interdisciplinary group of doctoral students at a large Midwestern U.S. university. Their central and very collective concern, despite divergent departmental affiliations and disciplinary dispersions, was how to get "qualitative" dissertation proposals past their respective committees. What foundations could they use to argue for their work on "scientific" grounds? And then, could they get jobs? And would they be able to get their work published? And, anticipating the future, would they be tenurable?

Both of us have heard such questions again and again over the last few years, in postings to various Listservs, while preparing the Workshop on Interpretive Research Methods in Empirical Political Science held at the 2003 Western Political Science Association conference, and in quiet conversations after conference panels and receptions, in countries in Europe, Latin America, Asia, and the South Pacific, as well as in the United States. In thinking of this book, we have had those, and many other, students in mind, along with the faculty, journal editors, and practitioners (policy analysts, for example) who have shared with us similar concerns. For junior faculty, the problems are publication and promotion and tenure. For senior faculty, it is also the problem of publication and, at times, contending with departmental colleagues who do not value their work when it develops in new directions or who do not wish to hire new faculty with interpretive orientations. For students and faculty alike, the problem is finding a community of scholars with whom one can have an engaged, empathic, and non-defensive conversation. For many journal editors, it is the problem of not knowing what the criteria for good "qualitative" research are or of not knowing who does such work and might be asked to review submissions. For practitioners, along with students and faculty, it is the problem of fighting what often feels like an uphill battle against the entrenched and hegemonic powers of quantitative, positivist-informed research designs and criteria.

Furthermore, in conversations with both graduate students and faculty colleagues in recent years, we have discerned a hesitation, whether out of humility, uneasiness, and/or general reticence, to articulate interpretive philosophical or specifically methodological ideas because they, themselves, were not formally schooled—they seem to mean "credentialed"—in phenomenology or ethnomethodology or semiotics, and so forth. We note that many of those whose work has been central to the philosophical critique of the perceptions and/or foundations of the natural and physical sciences, like Edmund Husserl and Thomas Kuhn, themselves began as scientists—Husserl in mathematics and physics, Kuhn in physics—coming to their philosophical-theoretical positions only through reflection on their own fields and the accepted practices of those fields. This "later-coming" is certainly true of our own intellectual journeys—not that we hold ourselves in the same ranks as those esteemed scholars—as it is of many of those who replied to our 2002 questionnaire as we attempted to develop a database of interpretive researchers in political science: they indicated that they are self-taught, influenced more by their readings or by a chance comment from a colleague or an adviser than by any particular, formal, doctoral curriculum.

This led us to decide to ask each colleague whose work is presented here to write a short, personal reflection describing her or his path to the intellectual position articulated in each chapter. These precede each of the chapters, and they indicate the widely divergent lived experiences through which these scientists have come to their particular practices. What we learn from these narratives, from responses to that database questionnaire, and from our own experience is that it is rarely the case (at least among the social scientific circles within which we travel) that any of us has had formal training—meaning, through degree-focused coursework—in these methods and philosophies. It is far more common, as noted above, for an interpretive researcher studying political or organizational action, social movements, or some other topic to develop those interests and skills out of a dissatisfaction with existing approaches, whether these be the linear rational steps of the policy evaluation model that didn't fit the lived experience of implementing a national public policy, the clash between rational choice stipulations and the feminist theoretical explanations that more closely fit personal experience, or the ahistorical presentism of mathematical models. Some of us experienced this cognitive dissonance as graduate students; others, as junior faculty before receiving tenure; and still others, even after tenure. This personal "turn" tends to be a gestalt shift: Much as one can't entirely reason one's way from seeing a duck to seeing a rabbit,[26] one can't completely think one's way from the elegance of mathematical models to the messiness of ethnographic detail. The fact that the shift happens to different people at different ages suggests that it is not, or not entirely, a developmental stage, unlike the undergraduate shift from thinking in black and white to adding shades of gray (see Perry 1970).

We take this collective experience in an optimistic vein, indicating that all is not lost if departments do not require or even offer an interpretive methods course to their graduate students. At the same time, we mark that curricular neglect or gatekeeping as the negative side of the experience: It is so much more difficult to travel this route on one's own, to struggle to find the sources and fit the pieces of the ideational map together, to locate a community of like-minded scholars, to feel that one is a "real" health studies scholar or sociologist or policy analyst or organizational theorist in a department, or discipline, in which interpretive methodologies are not treated as legitimate ways to do science. Many of the scholars whose work is represented in this book have done just that, but often with a sense of time lost that might have been saved by some earlier intervention. It is for others like us that we have prepared this book.

NOTES

1. Our thanks to Robert Adcock for help in identifying several of these.

2. Another reason for the preference for "human sciences" is the sense that it is a closer rendering of the German *geisteswissenschaften*, as distinct from *naturwissenschaften*, usually translated as "natural sciences." Polkinghorne (1983) discusses its translation and meanings extensively in the appendix (283–9).

3. "Bright line" is increasingly making its way out of the halls of legal discourse. Its origins appear to be obscure. In physics and photography usage, it dates to 1890; the earliest legal usage ("bright line rule") appears to date from the 1970s. This led Ron Harris to think that the term was not imported directly from physics into law; the timing, he thought, might suggest a link between law and economics. Thanks to Hila Keren and to Ron Harris for enthusiastic help trying to source its meaning.

4. This is what Harding (1993) calls "strong objectivity," which means taking positionality into account so that the relationship of knowledge to power can be understood. She argues that the standard, methodological positivist assumption that scholarly position can be ignored produces "weak objectivity" in which power, such as class or gender power, still operates but without accountability.

5. For example, explaining why he excluded social constructivist approaches to policy from his influential *Theories of the Policy Process*, Paul Sabatier writes: "Although it is clear that much of social 'reality' is 'socially constructed,' these [social constructionist] frameworks: (a) leave ideas unconnected to socioeconomic conditions or institutions and (b) conceive of ideas as free-floating, that is, unconnected to specific individuals and thus largely nonfalsifiable" (1999, 11). Our understanding of interpretive research (including social constructionist work), described and illustrated throughout the book, is that, on the contrary, it is thoroughly grounded in specific persons, times, places, conditions, and institutions.

6. We thank Tim Pachirat for initially drawing our attention to this phenomenon of contending methodological camps' using the same terms but meaning different things by them.

7. In her study of the graduate curriculum of fifty-seven political science programs, Schwartz-Shea (2003) found that over half of the programs did not require even minimal exposure to the philosophy of social science.

8. For a history of qualitative methods in sociology and anthropology, see Vidich and Lyman (2003).

9. One of the central, although not always articulated, procedural principles underlying interpretive methods of accessing and generating data (such as observing, with whatever degree of participation) is the extent to which researchers form provisional interpretations based on their own personal responses to the situation(s) under study. The U.S. phenomenologist (albeit better known for his work in developing humanistic psychotherapy) Carl Rogers described this process as first forming inner hypotheses, in a subjective mode of knowing within oneself, about what is going on in the event, "making patterned sense out of [one's] experiencing" from within one's "own internal frame of reference" (1964, 112, 110). This interpretation is then checked in further observation of others' acts and responses and/or in conversation with those others about their experiences and responses, and corroborated or refuted.

10. King, Keohane, and Verba (1994) seem to understand this point. They state: "Although case-study research rarely uses more than a handful of cases, the total number of observations is generally immense. It is therefore essential to distinguish between the number of cases and the number of observations" (52). Yet they go on in chapter 6 to offer advice for increasing the number of observations in small 'n' research. To make sense of this apparent inconsistency requires acceptance of a methodologically positivist framework in which "observation" means, as they state, "*measures* of one or more *variables*" (53; emphasis added). In other words, "observations" do not "count" unless they are in the form of "variables." Moreover, "social inquiry" is restricted to causal inference of a methodologically positivist sort.

11. See the preceding note. Brady and Collier (2004) address many of the limitations of the King, Keohane, and Verba (1994) conceptualization of qualitative methods, although this point about observations is not one they engage.

12. These interpretive schools and methods have family resemblances, in Wittgenstein's sense—as Dosse (1999, xv) noted with respect to contemporary French philosophical schools—but they also have specific differences. Schwandt (2003) makes a similar point about there not being a direct ideational link between phenomenology and methods; rather, he argues, one sees similarities of presuppositions, but with different applications and terminologies in different fields (e.g., the different, and confusing, uses of constructionism in sociology; constructivism in psychology; and both in international relations, but meaning different things; see note 13). At the same time, methodologists are beginning to talk about "phenomenological methods" or "phenomenological approaches" to research and about hermeneutic social science methods (see, e.g., Bentz and Shapiro 1998, chapter 7; Groenewald 2004).

13. We are opting in this book not to draw a conceptual distinction between these two terms, for the reason that the philosophy of science literature that informs our point of view does not draw such a distinction, nor is it predominant in the policy, public administration, and organizational studies fields that are our disciplinary homes. We would be remiss, however, not to note that in comparative politics and in international relations, this distinction appears to be taking root—or, at least, appears to be contested terrain. Daniel

Green (2002), for example, notes that in "constructivist comparative politics," "constructivism" refers specifically to a meeting ground between (social constructionist) agency and Giddens's structuration theory. Moreover, Ted Hopf (2002) draws a taxonomy within international relations (IR) among three different treatments of constructionism. And, as mentioned in the previous note, the two terms are used differently in sociology and psychology. Gergen (1999, 236–37), for instance, distinguishes between the use of constructivism in developmental psychology to mean individuals' mental constructs, inside their respective heads, of their experienced world and constructionists' emphasis on social processes of reality construction. We will not attempt to sort out these definitional and conceptual knots, which are apparently afflicting other fields as well: Hacking identifies a book on the social construction of literacy that concerns "innovative ways of teaching children to read"—it offers, that is, a "'social perspective' on how children learn to read, or don't," rather than treating the idea of literacy as a social construct (1999, 35). We note, then, that our approach is in the same spirit as Patrick Jackson's, who writes: "I utilize this term [social constructionism] rather than the more familiar [in international relations] 'constructivism' in order to signal the fact that my inspiration is the sociological and social theoretical literatures . . . rather than what might be called 'mainstream IR constructivism,'" reflecting the former's concern with "intersubjective negotiations of meaning and processes of social transaction" as distinct from the latter's "causal impact of roles and norms" and debates over "logics of consequences" versus "logics of appropriateness" as "better accounts of social behavior" (2002c, 258, n. 12). See also Hacking (1999) for a detailed parsing of the various meanings of the phrase "social construction."

14. However, as discussed in chapter 1, observation of that door depends on an a priori conceptual framework, as demonstrated most dramatically by Roberson and her colleagues' research (Roberson 2005; Roberson, Davies, and Davidoff 2000) on color perception. This research suggests that the "reasonableness" of a methodologically positivist procedure for counting doors may be self-evident within a single cultural or epistemic community but not necessarily so across interpretive communities.

15. The subtitle of the recently published Brady and Collier volume (2004)—*Diverse Tools, Shared Standards*—illustrates this point: Sharing standards between quantitative methods and qualitative methods in the forms advanced by Brady and Collier is possible because the two modes, in their view, (should) share epistemological and ontological presuppositions.

16. We add "nonexperimental" to distinguish "field studies," understood as ethnographic, participant-observation, or site-based interviewing projects, from "field experiments or natural experiments." On the latter see, for example, Yale University's Summer Program "Designing, Conducting, and Analyzing Field Experiments," sponsored by the Institution of Social and Policy Studies, in operation since 2000.

17. But "collecting" may not even be an accurate representation of what goes on in the natural sciences, nor is the sort of data "collection" done in some of the natural sciences necessarily a good model for all of the physical sciences, such as in physics or astronomy, which study things that are difficult to observe (e.g., atoms, electrons, black holes). As Amann and Knorr Cetina (1990), Latour (1990, 1999), and Lynch and Woolgar (1990a) point out, as often as not it is slices of botanical substances or representational forms of observed things and events, such as maps and diagrams, that are brought back to laboratories, rendered as data, and there transformed into "evidence."

18. We are playing here on the opposition established in the title of Claude Lévi-Strauss's well-known anthropological work *The Raw and the Cooked* (1969). We do not mean to imply that researchers "cook" their data in the sense that accountants might be accused of "cooking"—falsifying—their books, only that from an interpretive perspective there can be no unfiltered data. Kuhn (1970) makes a similar point in noting that things observed do not present themselves as "facts" without some theoretical framework.

19. Formal modelers now appear to share statistical researchers' preference for numerical data over other data forms. In the past, modelers were taken to task by statistical researchers for their reliance on ad hoc examples to "translate" the logic of their models into prose and for their failure to provide "empirical" (i.e., quantitative) data for the testing of their models (D.P. Green and Shapiro 1994). Indeed, the "words" they used *were* from examples drawn from their own heads, rather than having been generated systematically from context-specific documentary or field research, as in interpretive research. Modelers seem to have accepted these arguments that "words" are not good enough as a test of their models. Morton (1999) has sought to close the "gap" between modelers and statisticians by recommending graduate training in both modeling and statistics. The National Science Foundation has funded a number of summer institutes in Empirical Implications of Theoretical Models (EITM) to bring these two groups of scholars together and to "train a new generation of scholars who can better link theory and empirical work" (http://eitm/berkeley.edu). Advanced graduate students and junior faculty are encouraged to apply to the institutes but they should have

"some training in both formal theory and quantitative analysis" (http://eitm/berkeley.edu). According to that same Web site (last accessed June 2, 2005), "researchers use recent advances in game theory and mathematical modeling to develop theoretical models . . . [and then these models] are subjected to the highest standards of [methodologically positivist] empirical research, including statistical analysis, experiments, and case studies."

Despite, or perhaps because of, these efforts, lingering tensions between these scholars were apparent in an extended discussion on the moderated Listserv of the Political Methodology Organized Section of the American Political Science Association. The thread began with a Thursday, March 24, 2005, post with the subject line "H-POLMETH: AJPS Rejection Without Review for Theory Papers." That initial post revealed that one journal appeared to have adopted a policy of not sending out for review purely theoretical articles (i.e., formal models without "empirical," meaning "quantitative," evidence). Some researchers (e.g., Anderson and Simmons 1993) have used field evidence in their tests of the "commons tragedy" model, although the *best* evidence within the modeling community is still conceived of as quantitative in form.

20. By this logic, then, interpretive researchers support efforts to introduce new numerical indices or reconceptualize old ones. For example, scholars advocating for the use of "social indicators" (e.g., T. Atkinson et al. 2002) aim to direct attention to collective matters that are ignored by the gross domestic product (GDP) indicator, such as the unpaid work most often done by women that does not appear in the GDP.

21. We understand that the meaning of "advanced" in this context can be interpreted in a number of ways. For some it is about being more complicated; for others, advanced methods are those that build on methods developed earlier. For example, analysis of variance builds on difference of means (or t-) tests; logistic and log-linear regression build on or adapt ordinary least squares regression to address various "data problems" such as a dichotomous dependent variable, non-linearity, or variables that are all categorical.

22. For additional analytical techniques beyond those mentioned here and in part III, see Creswell (1998a, 6) and P.V. Malone and Chenail (2001, 58).

23. At the philosophical level, critical theorists accused phenomenologists of ignoring the power dimensions of lived experience, in choosing to focus on individual consciousness alone and its capacity for change. As noted in chapter 1, this preoccupation with self to the exclusion of institutions tends to be mitigated when philosophical argumentations are brought into "applied" contexts of organizations, polities, communities, and the like, in which power is harder to avoid.

24. Additionally, this emphasis further contributes to undermining the pernicious fact/value dichotomy. Theorists such as Taylor (1967) and Rein (1976) have contested this ground for some time, but the message has penetrated self-consciously "empirical" fields in an uneven manner. For example, in the graduate curricula of many political science programs, students majoring in the "empirical fields" are often treated differently from those majoring in "political theory." This distinctive treatment reflects a conception of "empirical research" as dealing primarily with "facts," i.e., so-called positive analysis, and of "political theory" as dealing primarily with "normative" issues (values). See the discussion in Schwartz-Shea (2005).

25. As a general observation, we believe this characterization to be accurate, based on our years of participant-observation in the discipline of political science. That said, there are clear exceptions. A veritable cottage industry of critique followed the publication of King, Keohane, and Verba's (1994) methodological text (e.g., Review Symposium 1995). Similarly, Ragin (2000a) has argued that the statistical, regression-based understandings of causality are ontologically implausible. See also chapter 2 of Wendt's (1999) discussion.

26. The "duck-rabbit" is a figure used by Wittgenstein to illustrate the concept of "seeing as." It originated in the work of psychologist Joseph Jastrow. See, for example, http://ist-socrates.berkeley.edu/~kihlstrm/JastrowDuck.htm (last accessed May 20, 2005).

Interpretation and Method

PART I

MEANING AND METHODOLOGY

The chapters in the opening section of this book locate matters of research methods in the context of the ideational history of the human or social sciences, from the perspectives of the sociology of knowledge and the philosophy of science. They engage the "interpretive turn" in social science and seek to explore its implications for thinking about knowledge claims, along with the methodological predispositions and practices best suited to the empirical investigation of human meaning making. Such a perspective entails a degree of reflexivity on the part of the researcher: If one asks how knowledge claims are generated, the role of the researcher—her own a priori knowledge, the filter of his own consciousness—in interpreting observational, conversational, and documentary evidence becomes paramount. And this leads, then, also to a consideration of the role of writing in "worldmaking," the matter of "rigor" in research, and questions of evaluative standards for recognizing "good" interpretive research. These are the central themes explored by the authors of these chapters.

In the opening chapter, Dvora Yanow situates methodological understandings enacted in interpretive empirical methods in the context of their philosophical presuppositions. Her central concern is the question, what does it mean to think interpretively, from the perspective of beliefs about the reality status of the topic of study and its knowability? Looking at the central concerns of phenomenological and hermeneutic philosophies, she identifies some of the ontological and epistemological themes that are central to interpretive research methods—the inevitable role played by researchers' a priori knowledge, their and their research subjects' situatedness in a context, and the interactions and entanglements between consciousness and the action, artifact, and textual embodiments of meaning. Identifying some of the central themes of phenomenology and hermeneutics, she parses their distinct perspectives on human meaning making. Tracing the methodological implications of these philosophies, she finds that what might be significant philosophical distinctions become blurred in empirical research practices. In its totality, her discussion shows that interpretive methodologies and methods stand on their own philosophical grounding: they are not just "remaindered"—lesser, inadequate, "pre-scientific"—versions of methodologically positivist, statistics-based and other so-called quantitative methods.

Mary Hawkesworth looks in greater detail at the positivist presuppositions informing those methods. In chapter 2 she analyzes Popper's attempted rescue of positivism (known as "critical rationalism") as well as subsequent critiques of his position—particularly the logical failure of the falsifiability criterion he posited, his acceptance of the fact/value dichotomy, and his narrow rendering of scientific rationality and reason. As Hawkesworth so vividly expresses it, both positivism and critical rationalism "render reason impotent" (40). By contrast, the alternatives, discussed under the umbrella term of "presuppositionist theories of science," demand reflexivity from scientists and admit (and even require) a more robust understanding of the reasoning ability needed in the consideration and judgment of research quality. In the final section of the chapter, Hawkesworth lays waste to the fact/value dichotomy, demonstrating how conceptions of the political ineluctably color, infiltrate, and ride in on scholarly judgments—no matter the scientists' claims to "objectivity" based on the fact/value dichotomy.

In chapter 3, Robert Adcock takes up the question of generalization from case specifics, looking especially at researchers' understandings of comparative and historical methods. After demonstrating that these understandings are historically situated, Adcock uses the example of James Mahoney and Dietrich Rueschemeyer's *Comparative Historical Analysis in the Social Sciences* (2003a) to analyze modernist (i.e., methodologically positivist) efforts that aim at the "sensible middle ground" between deductive and inductive approaches while simultaneously claiming to provide "contextual knowledge" and to be able to locate "macro causes." Contrasting their approach with the approaches of Clifford Geertz (1995), Reinhard Bendix (1978), and Benedict Anderson (1991), Adcock argues that the latters' interpretive approaches to generalization remain open to contingency, with the result that the particularities of diverse societies' responses to historical change are highlighted rather than "covered" by—flattened, hidden, or subsumed under— a general law.

Generalization is not the only "problem" put to interpretive methodologists by methodological positivism. One of the latter's most common claims is that interpretive research is, and can be, neither rigorous nor objective, given what are perceived to be its procedural "idiosyncrasies" and the researcher's presence in proximity to his observational experience or her interview respondents. Dvora Yanow takes up these claims in chapter 4, arguing that they are commonly based not only on a misunderstanding of interpretive procedures, but also on insufficiently interrogated understandings of what "rigor" and "objective" mean. Making clear the untenable nature of the substance of the charges, Yanow then considers their rhetorical power, arguing that their continued use masks contemporary fears about what it would mean to admit the embodiment of those who claim scientific knowledge through interpretive methods.

Finally, Peregrine Schwartz-Shea shows that when one moves beyond questions of generalization, rigor, and objectivity, interpretive methodologies generate their own criteria for judging the quality of the truth claims. Evaluative criteria, she argues in chapter 5, are—and need to be— specific to the epistemic communities generating the research that they judge. That is, interpretive research should not be held to standards that emerge from, and are logically consistent with, positivist ontological and epistemological presuppositions. Moreover, we should expect evaluative criteria to evolve as research communities respond to the changing world they study, through reinventing and reconstituting themselves, their questions, and their methodologies.

Taken together, these five chapters make the point that interpretive methods will never meet the criteria established for quantitative methods—because each of these modes of generating understanding and claiming it as trustworthy rests on different philosophical grounding. Indeed, ignoring these presuppositional differences is what leads methodologists to try to make qualitative methods fit a methodologically positivist mode, and out of this a split has developed within qualitative methods between researchers who attempt to follow that effort and those who pursue more traditional, meaning-focused, "interpretive" research styles. The chapters in this section lay the conceptual groundwork for the latter, which are then illustrated in the chapters in parts II and III.

CHAPTER 1

THINKING INTERPRETIVELY: PHILOSOPHICAL PRESUPPOSITIONS AND THE HUMAN SCIENCES

DVORA YANOW

I am not a philosopher by training, nor do I read most philosophy easily: Like others who do empirical research, I seem to need more of a grounding in lived experience, and through that I can approach philosophical texts.

After taking a B.A. in politics, I spent three years as a community organizer in a local agency that was part of a national government corporation. My colleagues and I felt that we had a clear national mandate, yet on the ground, it was supremely difficult to get anything done. I wondered why that would be so, and brought that question to my Master's degree work, just at the time that "policy implementation" became a burgeoning field of inquiry. It became clear that in order to understand implementation, I would need to know something about organizations. But in both of these fields, I found all the explanations I was reading—other than Don Schon's arguments about metaphors in policy and organizational processes, and Marty Rein's insistence that the fact-value dichotomy was false—too rational-technical to explain what I had experienced in that very complex work setting.

I was still poking away at that question when I started my Ph.D. program a couple of years later. In the required first semester seminar, we read chapter one of Clifford Geertz's The Interpretation of Cultures, *in which he recounts the story of the Berber tradesman and the wink,[1] arguing for the necessity of "thick description." Like Gretel, I kept following the trail of citations, reading largely in anthropology, human geography, and urban design. I found a wealth of empirical, theoretical, and methodological writings that explored human action in its expressive dimensions—a much broader approach than the rational-technical explanations I found so constraining and so limited in their explanatory power for theorizing what I had lived and studied for three years. The expressive, meaning-focused dimension just wasn't being written about in my main fields of study; and so I continued to read without regard to disciplinary boundaries. Reflecting on my field experience, which, with follow-up interviewing, observing, and document reading, became my case study, I saw that policy implementation could be appreciated as a process through which policy and agency meanings were communicated, and that this was done through three types of artifacts: spoken and written language, certainly, but also acts and objects, such as the agency's buildings. Each of these then led me to other areas of reading. I started trying to piece together the map of Continental and U.S. meaning-oriented schools of thought as I was writing my dissertation. This mapping continued for several years after graduating—in many respects, I'm still reading and learning and filling in gaps in the map. But it all came about because I experienced a misfit between the prevailing theories in my two disciplines and my own lived experience.*

> Believing, with Max Weber, that man is an animal
> suspended in webs of significance he himself has spun,
> I take . . . the analysis of [those webs] to be therefore
> not an experimental science in search of law
> but an interpretive one in search of meaning.
> —Clifford Geertz (1973, 5)

This oft-quoted line from anthropologist Clifford Geertz's *The Interpretation of Cultures* has constituted, for many, the summons to interpretive social science. But that call does not instruct readers directly and explicitly how to analyze those webs of meaning, and the text makes only passing mention (through no fault of the author, who had other purposes in mind) of the vast early- to mid-twentieth-century literature dealing with the tremendously significant components of that sentence: phenomenological analyses exploring the ways in which humans weave not only the social world in which we live but the very identities we construct for ourselves as we live in those worlds; hermeneutic treatises developing ways of interpreting the various sorts of webs woven out of human experience; other philosophical works explaining the relationship between meaning and law, meaning and experiment, meaning and interpretation; and, most crucially, what it might portend in the context of the human sciences to interpret the social world in order to understand not only *what* it means to those for whom specific webs have meaning, but also *how* it means, both to situational actors and to researchers studying those situations.

Reflecting on the problematic of "how" things mean, in the context of doing social science in the spirit of nineteenth- and twentieth-century science, leads rather quickly to the understanding that this is not a matter merely of what "tools" to pick up to strike the nail or to plug the hole in the dike. Rather, we are concerned here, first, with epistemological matters: questions regarding the "knowability" of the subject of study, the capacity of human animals to "generate" or "discover" or "find" or "construct" knowledge about the social webs under their analytic microscopes, and, hence, the character of those claims to knowledge. Moreover, knowing which tool is best suited to the nail or the hole depends on the character of the subject of study, and so epistemological presuppositions themselves rest on the presupposed reality status of that subject. Ontological matters are, then, also a concern: whether the subject of study is considered objectively real in the world, in which case it is believed to be capable of being "captured" or collected, discovered or found, and "mirrored" in theoretical writings, or is considered as socially constructed (in the phrase made widely known through P. Berger and Luckmann [1966]), in which case its character may be apprehended only through interpretation.[2]

Methodological justification, then, cannot be made in the void of ontological and epistemological entailments. A researcher who presupposes that the social world is ontologically constructivist and epistemologically interpretive is more likely to articulate research "questions" that call for constructivist-interpretive methods.[3] These turn a reflexive eye not only on the topic of study but also on the scientist generating or constructing (rather than "discovering" or "finding") that knowledge and on the language she uses in that "worldmaking" (in Nelson Goodman's [1978] term). Such reflexivity might ask such questions as, for example, what the Middle Ages or the Middle East are in the "middle" of—and who "put" them there, and why. It is an approach that sees concepts and categories as embodying and reflecting the point of view of their creators (as Ido Oren, Robert Adcock, and Dean McHenry do in their chapters with respect to political science theorists and Pamela Brandwein, Patrick Jackson, and Ronald Schmidt do in theirs with respect to jurisprudists, political parties, and legislators). In this view, the subject of social scientific study "is not an inert fact of nature . . . merely *there*" (Said 1978, 4) and social scientific theories are not "mirror[s] of nature" (Rorty 1979). All ideas—including those of the natural and physical sciences —have "a history and a tradition of thought, imagery, and vocabulary that have given [them] reality and presence" (to borrow Edward Said's words [1978, 4–5] from the context of Orient and Occident). In this sense, then, social scientific texts do not merely present their subjects through the lenses of their data, but represent and re-present—constitute, construct—them.

The philosophies that developed these concerns emerged in engagement with the critical positivism of the later nineteenth century and the logical positivism of the early twentieth century, through both critique of their perceived shortcomings and positing of what proponents felt was a more logically compelling delineation of the entailments of human social life in constituting Self, Other, and the broader social group. "Interpretive" methodology has since become an umbrella term subsuming several different schools of thought, including those drawing, explicitly or implicitly, on phenomenology, hermeneutics, or (some) Frankfurt School critical theory, along with symbolic interaction and ethnomethodology, among others. Many of these ideas dovetail with late-nineteenth- to early-twentieth-century pragmatism[4] and later-twentieth-century feminist epistemology and research methods (e.g., Falco 1987; Harding 1989, 1990; Hartsock 1987; Hawkesworth 1989; Heldke 1989; Miller 1986; Modleski 1986) and science studies (e.g., Harding 1991, Latour 1987, Longino 1990, Traweek 1988).

This chapter treats, with a rather broad brush, those philosophical presuppositions held in common by several of these schools of thought, which provide conceptual grounding for interpretive methods. Not only do these logically prior, or underlying, notions of social realities and their "knowability" distinguish them from the positivist presuppositions with which they took issue (discussed by Mary Hawkesworth in chapter 2). These philosophical argumentations also provide the methodological principles shared by and manifested in the various interpretive methods of accessing, generating, and analyzing data, for all their other differences. The philosophical terrain encompassed here is vast; discussing it in any detail would require a book-length manuscript itself; and, indeed, many books have been written, both primary sources and secondary analyses, on these questions. If space allowed, other schools of thought could also be more extensively discussed in terms of their influence on and/or manifestations in interpretive research practices, specifically, American pragmatism, toward the more philosophical end of the spectrum of influence (see note 3); ethnomethodology (developed by Harold Garfinkel), also of U.S. origins, toward the more explicitly methodological end; and critical theory (both Frankfurt School and wider ranging), symbolic interactionism (developed by George Herbert Mead and Erving Goffman), and feminist theories in the middle of the continuum (that is, combining both conceptual frameworks and "tools"). In my reading of this history of ideas, the foundational concepts, relationships, and understandings enacted in interpretive research methods are well established in the various philosophical arguments of phenomenology and hermeneutics; the other schools of thought articulate similar ideas, based on similar presuppositions, albeit with different orientations or even, as with Frankfurt School critical theory, in critique. Here, I sketch out the parameters of the arguments as engaged in phenomenology and hermeneutics. Although I am eliding differences that from other perspectives may be crucial, for what I wish to argue those distinctions are less central. My purpose is to show that interpretive methods do not just spring *ab origine*, at whim, but rather have considerable philosophical grounding. I hope to scatter sufficient bibliographical breadcrumbs that a reader curious for greater depth and detail will be able to follow the trail of argument further than space here allows.

TRUTH CLAIMS: EVIDENCE, KNOWLEDGE, AND THE CHARACTER
OF SCIENCE

Textbook discussions of methods (of any sort) rarely begin with reflective inquiry on the practice of science, on the historical situatedness of what it means to "do" science, to "be" scientific. As a result, methods appear to be free-floating tools unmoored in conceptual space (unless one reads also in the philosophy of science literature). But criteria for assessing the knowledge claims made by a study (such as reliability and validity)—indeed, the very act of claiming to know something with some certainty—reflect an understanding of the practice of science that has emerged over the last two centuries, as "science" has parted company from "philosophy" (e.g., natural science from natural philosophy) and developed its own identity. To situate interpretive methods as a scientific undertaking requires a brief excursion into the context of contemporary understandings of science as a practice.

To be "scientific" is, first off, to reflect a particular orientation toward the world in asking certain kinds of questions, and this involves claims making about the subject(s) of study. Built into this questioning practice is, at its core, as a character trait of the profession, an attitude of doubt. A reader of a scientific report can reasonably inquire of its author about the bases for its claims. "How do you know that which you are claiming about this event, or this government, or this organization, or this community? What is the foundation [or 'truth value,' in philosophical language] for your claim(s)?" Since the early 1700s, thanks to Newton, metaphysical accounts to explain an apple falling from a tree, such as Zeus and Hera throwing thunderbolts, are increasingly less likely to be invoked in modern and "modernizing" communities than "scientific laws"—in this case, gravity. Newton's observations and those of other late-fifteenth- to early-eighteenth-century European thinkers, such as Copernicus and Galileo, laid the foundation for a conception of "science" that, for many, replaced religion as the source of certain knowledge. That conception still holds today and actively shapes understandings of what it means to do science or to be scientific.[5]

It rests, first, on the understanding that humans possess powers of reasoning that they can apply *systematically* to the world surrounding them: They need not rely for explanations on the authority of tradition (or charisma, in a Weberian view) vested in religious or monarchic leaders.[6] Second, the application of that reasoning yields a set of "laws" or principles considered to be universal—that is, holding at all places at all times for all persons (i.e., regardless of class or religion, race or gender, paving the way for non-Protestants, non-Europeans, and women to be understood as having personhood). Third, this universality implies a certain regularity or order inhering in natural and physical events (and it is discoverable, point one above). This, in turn, means that these events can be predicted—and, hence, controlled (for more on this history of ideas, see, e.g., Bernstein 1976, 1983; Dallmayr and McCarthy 1977; Rabinow and Sullivan 1979). The extension of this understanding of what "science" entails from the physical and natural world to the social or human world was the foundation of nineteenth-century positivist thought (first as social positivism, reformulated mid-century as evolutionary positivism, and evolving toward the end of the century into critical positivism or empirio-criticism).[7]

The differences among the versions of positivism are not central to the present argument, save for one point that becomes key to the interpretive philosophies that began to develop in engaging critical positivism. In the view of critical positivists, certainty of knowledge could be entrusted only to claims based on the senses (sight, sound, touch, taste, smell); to eliminate error, science had to be limited to sense descriptions of experience. Although this school of thought petered out toward the end of the nineteenth century, a resurgence of related ideas grew in the early twentieth century (especially strong between the two world wars) under the name logical positivism (also known as the "Vienna Circle" because of its proponents' main location; on this history see, e.g., Abbagnano 1967, Passmore 1967, Polkinghorne 1983).[8] It was primarily against the claims of the logical positivists that interpretive philosophies developed (see, e.g., DeHaven-Smith 1988; Hawkesworth 1988; Jennings 1983, 1987; Mary Hawkesworth's chapter in this volume takes up the critique more fully).

Despite disagreements on ontological and epistemological matters, scientists working out of interpretive presuppositions, speaking broadly, share in common with those working out of positivist ones the two central attributes of scientific practice (what it means to "do" science or to "be" scientific) named above: an attitude of doubt, and a procedural systematicity. Where they differ is in how these are enacted. Interpretive scientists share the appreciation for the possible fallibility of human judgment characteristic of post-Popperian science (discussed more fully in chapter 2). Maintaining the attitude of doubt or testability toward their subject matter that derives from this orientation, interpretive researchers enact that doubt in other, nonexperimental ways. They contest the concept of universal and regular generalizability embedded in the notion of "law," although they typically proceed from the assumption that human activity is patterned.[9] They also have a different understanding of what it means to prosecute "rigor" in research (see the discussion in chapter 4); yet interpretive research, following its own canons of practice, is no less systematic than positivist-informed research, which renders the work "methodical" in different ways from that prescribed in the steps of the "scientific method."

The research practices undertaken by scientists conducting their work, knowingly and consciously or not, in ways informed or influenced by interpretive presuppositions enact ideas developed during the first part of the twentieth century in two schools of philosophical thought, phenomenology and hermeneutics. These engaged the same sorts of questions concerning knowledge and social reality that occupied positivist philosophers. Interpretive philosophers argued that the analogy drawn by positivists between the natural and physical worlds and the social world (and calling, therefore, for a single form of scientific practice) is a false analogy. The latter cannot be understood in the same way as the former because of an essential difference between them: Unlike (to the best of our present knowledge) rocks, animals, and atoms, humans make, communicate, interpret, share, and contest meaning. We act; we have intentions about our actions; we interpret others' actions; we (attempt to) make sense of the world: We are meaning-making creatures. Our institutions, our policies, our language, our ceremonies are human creations, not objects independent of us. And so a human (or social) science needs to be able to address what is meaningful to people in the social situation under study. It is this focus on meaning, and the implications of that focus, that the various interpretive methods share.

UNDERSTANDING *VERSTEHEN*: INTERPRETIVE GROUNDING

Phenomenology and hermeneutics took as points of departure first the fact that the researcher's perspective shaped the generation of knowledge, and second that the way to study human actors was through *verstehen*—understanding—as that concept was developed initially by Wilhelm Dilthey and Max Weber.

In addressing the question of how things might be known, early interpretive thinkers (e.g., Johan Gustav Droysen, Georg Simmel, Wilhelm Windelband, and Heinrich Rickert) turned to Kant's central idea that knowing depends on a priori knowledge.[10] The individual was understood to bring prior knowledge to his or her experiences, thereby giving shape to the myriad sensate stimuli (such as light and sound) vying for attention. That is, humans do not perceive the world "bare"—as it is—without some preestablished "conceptual boxes" (Kuhn 1970) or categories of thought structuring that perception and "filtering" various physical sensations.[11] Roberson's research on colors provides an example. It addresses one of the central questions in linguistics concerning whether language structures perception and thought.[12] Roberson and her colleagues (Roberson 2005; Roberson, Davies, and Davidoff 2000) have found, among the groups they have studied, that the respective presence and absence of color terms enables or prohibits the perception of those colors. Furthermore, development of additional terms enables an enhanced awareness of the colors those terms refer to. In other words, the thought categories exist independently of the sensory stimuli. In a conceptual sense, evidence is not manifest in the observational world—it is not "self-evident"; categories of mind are prerequisite to making sense of the phenomenal (empirical) world. If the point holds for elements whose objective reality we take so for granted as part of the physical world, such as colors, how much more is it the case for social scientific constructs such as "democracy" or "community"?[13]

"New" knowledge, then, is understood as being produced not through disembodied reason but through the situated context of the "knower" producing it. Admitting prior knowledge into the realm of scientific inquiry implies a basis for knowledge claims other than the direct physical experience of sensory stimuli. This is not an argument that dismisses the role of the senses in perception—the senses are central to "making" sense. It is, however, an argument that sense making is an historically and socially contextualized process and that the subject of study is itself historically and socially situated. Understanding is not possible from a position entirely outside of the focus of analysis: Prior knowledge is a mediating factor in sense making. This, in turn, is itself implicitly an argument against the understanding of objectivity posited by quantitative methods informed by methodological positivism (see chapter 4). Other interpretive philosophers, such as Rickert, argued further that human values (themselves not sense-based), and not just "sense data," were the appropriate focus of a meaning-oriented social science.

It was in such conversations about the purpose of science and its natural-physical versus human subject matter that the distinction between explanation (or prediction) and understanding emerged. Explanation (*erklaren* in German) was posited to be the method of the natural and physical sciences, understood to entail a description of concepts or objects or processes in terms of their antecedent causes, thereby leading to the discovery of universal, predictive laws. Explanatory processes aim to explain human experiences in terms of natural or physical events external to them—that is, through attending to "objective" events rather than to "subjective" (internal) ones. By contrast, understanding (*verstehen*), posited as the method of the human sciences, was seen as entailing making clear people's interpretations of their own and others' experiences, leading to the discovery of context-specific meaning. *Verstehen*, then, concerns human subjectivity and intersubjectivity as both subjects of and explanations for human action. First developed as a distinction in the mid-1800s by Johan Gustav Droysen, the concepts were elaborated on by Dilthey and Weber writing in the late-nineteenth and early-twentieth centuries, and later by Alfred Schütz (see Beam and Simpson 1984; Burrell and Morgan 1979; Fay 1975; Filmer et al. 1972; Polkinghorne 1988).[14] In Dilthey's framing of it, the method of *verstehen* was to understand material, cultural expressions as the external manifestations of human mind: These could only be understood "in relation to the minds which created them and the inner experience which they reflected" (Burrell and Morgan 1979, 229). Initially comprehended as requiring the reliving or reenacting of the other's experience, *verstehen* was developed by Weber to mean the more detached understanding of the research subject's experience—that is, his or her subjective sense making.

In this approach, the individual is seen as holding membership in a community of meaning, such that his subjective perception and understanding themselves draw on the repertoire of collectively created and sanctioned meanings particular to that community and shared within it by its members. The community's traditions, practices, language, and other cultural elements provide the material out of which individuals craft their meaning making of everyday events. Understandings of "race" and "ethnicity," for example, are specific to political communities and sanctioned and maintained through institutionalized state practices. "Race-ethnic" categories in Australia, for example, are based on language of birthplace, whereas U.S. categories reflect continent of (ancestral) origin (Yanow 2003b). These collective understandings provide the backdrop for individuals' constructions of their own meanings; individual subjectivity, in other words—the contents of individual consciousness (or mind)—is embedded within social practices and collective presuppositions. *Verstehen* denotes the intentional ferreting out by another person of that mental framework—the framework that "stands under" the individual's actions. "Far from being exotic," as Hawkesworth notes (personal communication, May 22, 2004), "*verstehen* underlies our most basic comprehension of others' meanings and actions, such as the 'road rage' that is so comprehensible to commuters." It generates explanation that is context specific, rather than a set of generalized predictive laws.

A central implication of Kant's thinking is that if a knower comes to a study with a priori knowledge, and that shapes or filters what she apprehends, then knowing cannot be said to proceed through direct, unmediated observation alone. Something intercedes or filters between sensory perceptions and sense making. *Verstehen* developed against the notion that the meaning of sense-based "facts," seen by positivists as external to human actors, was readily apparent and could simply be grasped (*Begreifen*, in Weber's terminology) by an external observer. In the reasoning of Weber, Schütz, and others, to the extent that human acts and other artifacts are the projections or embodiments of human meaning, they are not, then, completely external to the world of their creators and of others engaging them (including researchers), and so their meaning must be understood (or interpreted). *Verstehen* is in this sense not "understanding" simply put, but a proactive, intentional, willed effort to understand *from within*—in some instances, not only addressed to the other's meaning, but also to one's own ("the Self," as the German-language writings put it).[15]

With these positions as shared points of departure, phenomenology and hermeneutics emphasize different focuses for study, differing on what each sees as the central locus for the expression of human meaning.

THE MEANING OF MEANING: PHENOMENOLOGY'S LIFEWORLD

> When put under oath in a Canadian court
> to testify about the fate of his hunting lands
> in connection with a case concerning a hydroelectric plant,
> a Cree hunter is reported to have said,
> "I'm not sure I can tell the truth . . .
> I can only tell what I know."
> —*James Clifford* (1986, 8)

Tracing the development of phenomenological thought from its early articulations in Edmund Husserl's writings in the latter part of the nineteenth century to Alfred Schütz's in the mid-twentieth century is tantamount to observing social philosophy develop into social theory and sociology. The further one moves in time, the more grounded the theorizing becomes in explaining human life in all its dimensions. Moreover, reading the work of these two thinkers alone makes it clear that phenomenological philosophy itself diverges epistemologically, although its proponents hold similar ontological presuppositions.[16]

From its inception, phenomenologists argued that meaning making takes place in the "lifeworld" (*Lebenswelt*) of the individual—the bedrock of beliefs against which the very ordinary, mundane moving through one's everyday world, interacting with others, takes place and through which one shapes and reaffirms one's sense of oneself and the elements of one's social world. This was to be the focus of social scientific study. It requires accessing what is meaningful to social, political, cultural, and other groups, and to individuals within them, as well as understanding how meaning is developed, expressed, and communicated. In a phenomenological approach, much of everyday life is seen as consisting of common-sense, taken-for-granted, unspoken, yet widely shared and known "rules" for acting and interacting. It is the articulation of these "rules" that constitutes one of the central concerns of phenomenological analysis and of methods informed by this perspective, such as ethnomethodology and other forms of conversation analysis, symbolic interaction, ethnography, and participant-observation. As the social scientist is herself embedded in that social reality, the analytic problem is to extricate herself sufficiently from that unspoken common sense in order to render it "uncommon," reflect on it, and make sense of it (which is the purchase claimed by ethnographic and participant-observer research for the researcher's standing as "stranger" to the situation being studied; this argument informs the chapters by Joe Soss, Ellen Pader, Clare Ginger, Steven Maynard-Moody and Michael Musheno, and Samer Shehata).

Social realities are seen as "willed into existence through intentional acts" (Burrell and Morgan 1979, 233), through "consciousness" or "mind." Something, in other words, intercedes in the phenomenal experience between sensing and sense-making A knock on the door at different times of day may produce identical sound wave sine curves, but what those sound waves mean differs if the knock comes at two in the afternoon and we are U.S. citizens sitting in a classroom in Hayward, California, in 2005 or if it comes at two in the morning and we are Jews hiding in an attic in Amsterdam in 1944.[17] What we claim as knowledge of social phenomena comes from a willed (or intentional) interpretation of our sense perceptions, not from an uninterpreted registering of them, against the backdrop of preexisting conceptual categories derived from life experience in interaction with others.

Other terms—lens, frame, paradigm, worldview or *weltanschauung*—capture aspects of the same idea as mind or consciousness.[18] Husserl, in his approach to phenomenology, argued that analysis should focus not on the phenomena of lived experience themselves—the objects or events or terms were to be "bracketed" and set aside—but on the perceptual processes or mental constructs humans create in order to make sense of those experiences, what in these other terms might be called the organizing frames or lenses or conceptual boxes that structure perception and comprehension of that reality.[19] This shifts the analytic process from "*What* do you know?" to "*How* do you know [what you claim as knowledge]?" So, for example, in attempting to understand arguments about abortion from "pro-life" and "pro-choice" camps, the researcher or policy analyst would "bracket" the arguments themselves—making no attempt to discern their objective "reality"—and focus instead on their "experienced reality"—on how those arguments are experienced by those making and hearing them and how they become "factual" reality to them, as Luker (1984) did. In this "transcendental" phenomenology, Husserl attempted to transcend experience to focus analysis on "pure" consciousness.

In his approach to phenomenology, Schütz directed inquiry back toward an engagement with lived experience, toward a more "existential" phenomenology in which the individual is engaged in and with a social world. For him, as for Heidegger, experience was about "being in the world," and so its analysis, too, should be about engaging that world rather than bracketing it and setting it aside. It is this set of ideas that has been more productive for interpretive social science and its methods. In this view, each knower comes to his subject with prior knowledge that has grown out of past experience, education, training, family-community-regional-national (and so on) background, and character. These constitute, for each of us, the contexts that give rise to our lifeworld; both lived experience and lifeworld, in turn, shape the way that we understand our "Selves" and the world within which we live (Schütz 1967, 1973). Sense making—interpretation—with respect to a specific event or experience is done through retroactive reflection on that event or experience informed by prior knowledge. It is as if all human actors enact the words attributed, in Yogi Berra's telling, to a baseball umpire speaking about pitched balls crossing the home plate being "balls," or "strikes." "They ain't nuttin' 'til I call 'em."

The point holds, as well, for social scientists with respect to their subjects of study. This renders the researcher, as well as the researched, a situated entity: Meaning making and the specific meaning(s) made by each one are contextualized by prior knowledge and by history and surrounding elements (other events, other experiences), a position shared by critical theorists and echoed in feminist "standpoint theory" (e.g., Hartsock 1987, Hawkesworth 1989). The implication of this argument is not only that universal or cross-case laws are not possible in the same way in which positivist laws claim generalizability (see Adcock's discussion, chapter 3, this volume) but also that social "reality" may be construed differently by different people: The social world we inhabit and experience is potentially a world of multiple realities, multiple interpretations. Discovery of some external, singular reality, a requisite of methodological positivism, is not possible in this view.

The process of sense making is, in this way, iterative: Prior experiences shape one's understanding of new experiences, and new understanding derived from these experiences itself may refine the a priori knowledge brought to bear on subsequent experiences. All knowledge, in this sense, is social knowledge, as Karl Mannheim noted (quoted in Burrell and Morgan 1979); observation and "facts" are theory-laden; and what we take to be objective "facts" may well be shaped, if not affected, by the observer.

The focus on the lifeworld as the core of experience and, hence, of the researcher's analysis positions individual subjectivity at the center. As Bernstein (1976, 145) wrote, describing Schütz's views on this subject:

> A human actor is constantly interpreting his [or her] own acts and those of others. To understand human action we must not take the position of an outside observer who "sees" only the physical manifestations of these acts; rather we must develop categories for understanding what the actor—from his [or her] own point of view—"means" in his [or her] actions. . . . [I]n focusing on action, we can and must speak of its subjective meaning.

It is for this reason that interpretive researchers focus on methods of understanding from the perspective of the actor in the situation. At times, this renders the relationship between the actor's meaning and the researcher's meaning problematic: How do we reconcile the researcher's category construction with the actor's situated meaning? (I return to this point below; see also chapter 4, on faithful rendering, and chapter 5, on evaluative criteria.)

Applied to social situations, phenomenology has been called upon to address not only the individual Self, but Selves in social encounter with one another: how it is that in communal, political, organizational, and other collective settings and encounters, people manage to understand one another without necessarily making explicit the "rules" for living that they, by and large, adhere to. P. Berger and Luckmann (1966, part II) provide an extended and detailed discussion of a hypothetical situation, starting with Persons A and B as aboriginal creators of rules for living in the same setting. Over time, the rules are submerged into unspoken practices, becoming tacit knowledge, creating a sense of "how we do things here." This works well until a third person arrives. New to the situation, Person C does not know the rules, and this requires A and B to make them explicit as they socialize C to the situation they have created and modify that situation and the rules to accommodate C's strengths, talents, and limitations.

Through such interactive processes, members of a group come to use the same or similar cognitive mechanisms, engage in the same or similar acts, and use the same or similar language to talk about thought and action.[20] The shared meanings are public, not private or personal (although the latter may be of interest in psychological studies and other fields less focused on collective action): Each group "has its own sounds, noises, and silences which arouse the attention of its members and have agreed upon significance" (Warner 1959, 455). This is also the process through which institutions are objectified and practices, reified.

Taking off from Berger and Luckmann's book, the notion of "social construction" achieved currency in the human sciences. The creation of intersubjective understanding that they describe there—that which is developed between two (or more) "subjectivities"—was a central concern of their teacher, the phenomenologist Alfred Schütz, in his effort to understand how an individual makes sense of another's acts. This is what is "social" about ontological constructivism: that it has a shared character, developed in the course of living in common, interacting through the medium of political, cultural, and other artifacts in which the meanings embedded in these artifacts come to be known, tacitly, even when such communication is nonverbal.[21]

Were it not for the awkwardness of language, we should rather speak of social *constructing*, rather than social constructions (much like Weick's [1969] distinction between organizing and organization). The gerund captures the dynamism of the process and reserves agency to actors, whereas the noun form excessively reifies process outcomes: "social constructions" have been treated by some, in a most non-phenomenological fashion, as if they were agentless entities, disembodied from their action contexts.[22] This is not to deny the institutionalization and reification that typically occur—the habits of thought and practice that result as constructive acts become mundane, so well described in that section of Berger and Luckmann's work. A phenomenological ontology would remind us, however, and ask us to remind ourselves in the midst of our research and writing of the "as if" character of these institutions; it insists on human agency and, thereby, the possibility of change.

The concept of intersubjectivity, operative in an ontological sense, enables a conceptualization of collective action that is, or may be, otherwise problematic. A student of political, organizational, and social life often wants to make statements not only about individual actors but also about collectivities: states, communities, neighborhoods, departments. The intersubjective character of social "realities"—describing as it does the habits of thinking, the ways of seeing, and the shared meanings submerged therein that knit together members of a group who have been interacting over time—accomplishes what from a more atomistic perspective appears to be an anthropomorphizing sleight of mind. The classic challenge put to analytic philosophy (thinking here of Bertrand Russell or the early Wittgenstein)—what meaning is there in the statement "England declared war"?—provides an example. Such declaration is an act of a single individual; what sense does it make to render it in the collective? Does it mean that "Parliament declared war" or that "Prime Minister Winston Churchill, acting as representative of The Crown, itself standing in for the English people as a whole, declared war"? The phenomenological observation that ongoing interaction leads to communities of interpretation and of practice, while not denying individual differences, enables such statements as "the United States has an immigration policy" or "the department knows how to get its students jobs."[23] The phenomenological concept of intersubjectivity that enables such a conceptualization of collective social reality stands in direct opposition to a methodological individualism that denies the significance, if not the very existence, of historical-cultural-social constructings other than those made through the choices of individuals.

In sum, phenomenology focuses attention on the deeply embedded frameworks of tacitly known, taken-for-granted assumptions through which humans make sense of their lives. Research based on or influenced by a phenomenological outlook seeks to highlight the problematic character of such framings, as Ellen Pader does, for example (chapter 8, this volume), with respect to the everyday concept of "crowding," a taken-for-granted, "commonsensical" assumption about appropriate spatial relations among people sharing a household, which, as a public policy concept, polices all manner of activities and regulations. Phenomenologically inflected methods seek to make explicit the lens or frame or way of seeing—the lifeworld—that makes such perceptions make sense. Reflecting on them and making them explicit potentially enables both understanding and action in their regard.

THE EXPRESSION OF MEANING: HERMENEUTICS AND ARTIFACTS

For hermeneutic scholars, by contrast, among them Dilthey and Gadamer, the focus of social scientific study was to be the cultural artifacts people created and vested with their values, beliefs, and/or sentiments—that is, the material manifestations or objectifications of mind, consciousness, and so on, rather than consciousness itself.

Hermeneutic thinkers focused on the fact that human meaning is not expressed directly. Rather, it is embedded in (or projected onto) artifacts by their creators, and it can be known through interpreting these artifacts. Initially, this meant interpreting the written word: Given its origins as a set of rules for interpreting biblical texts, hermeneutics' initial concern in its application to the social world more broadly was with written artifacts (including, e.g., fiction, poetry, and nonfiction; here is where the linkage between interpretive methodologies and mid- to late-twentieth-century literary theories emerges).[24]

Hermeneutic modes of thought were extended first to text-like objects: other forms of creative expression that were or could be rendered in whole or in part on paper, in two dimensions—art (paintings, drawings, prints), design, drama; subsequently, this grew to include photography, film, and so on, as well as three-dimensional materials, such as sculptures and built spaces (e.g., agency buildings). By even later extension, acts also came to be treated as "text-analogues" (Taylor 1971) under the reasoning that in seeking to understand daily behavior, we treat human acts, too, *as if* they were texts (for example, the act of voting; see also Ricoeur 1971). This greatly expanded the realm of application of hermeneutic methods, to include such things as conversations, speeches, legislative acts (and their transcriptions), and nonverbal communication.[25] Ethnographic, participant-observation, ethnomethodological, and semiotic analyses—indeed, any method that seeks to elicit meaning by rendering spoken words and/or acts as written texts and applying to them forms of textual analysis—are based on this conceptualization of speech, act, and meaning.[26] In this volume, the chapters by Joe Soss and Frederic Schaffer on interviewing, Clare Ginger on environmental impact assessments, Cecelia Lynch and Jutta Weldes on governmental documents, Dean McHenry and Ronald Schmidt on words and categories framing political action, and my own on built space could be seen as examples of hermeneutic analysis. The chapters analyzing the meanings of historical documents—by Ido Oren, Robert Adcock, Mark Bevir, Patrick Jackson, and Pamela Brandwein—could also be seen as forms of hermeneutic analysis.

Kantian notions of a priori knowledge were manifested in hermeneutic thinking in the idea of the hermeneutic circle. The term has been understood as meaning both a process of reasoning

and interpreting, and the community of "readers" (interpreters) engaged in that process and sharing the interpretation of the text under study.[27] As a description of the process of meaning making, it departs from a linear model (such as the steps of the scientific method), instead depicting a
circular, iterative sense making in which initial interpretation starts at whatever point is available
or accessible, with whatever one's understanding is at that point in time. One makes a provisional
interpretation of the text (or other focus of analysis), with the reflexive awareness that one's
interpretation is likely to be incomplete and even possibly erroneous. One then engages the material in further study, at which point one revises one's initial, provisional interpretation. Additional
analysis yields further revised interpretation; and so on and so on.[28]

A slightly different explication of the hermeneutic circle emphasizes the contextual character of
interpretive processes. Much as a word in a sentence needs to be (and is) understood in relation to
the whole sentence (its grammatical structure, other words, the tone and context of utterance), a text
can only be understood within its "con-text," whether this is the author's intent and personal background, the history of the times, other associated or contrasting texts, or something else.[29] The
hermeneutic circularity resides in reading back and forth, iteratively, between text and context. This
process description gave rise to the understanding that "intertextuality"—the way in which one text
invokes another through the repetition of a unique or key phrase, thereby drawing the other text's
meaning into the understanding of the focal one—is operative among text analogues as well. An
agency building might invoke a Greek temple through architectural details, for example, thereby
bringing the meanings associated with antiquity or the classical period into the present context,
affecting how the agency is perceived. This has been common, for instance, in certain periods with
the architectural design of public buildings, such as libraries, courthouses, and museums.

And so it goes, on and on: Further layers of understanding are added as each new insight
revises prior interpretations in an ever-circular process of making meaning. Interpretations are,
therefore, always provisional, as one cannot know for certain that a new way of seeing does not
lie around the corner (the "1491 problem" in respect of certain truth—the certain knowledge in
1491 that the world was flat). There is no more absolute and definitive an end point than there was
a starting point. Certainty rests on other elements (see chapters 4 and 5); finality is only temporal.
This understanding is recapitulated in a vision of scientific research as ongoing and recursive—
and why doctoral students (and others) are commonly directed to conclude their dissertations
with "directions for subsequent research." The hermeneutic circle, then, enacts the attitude of
doubt or testability that is one of the hallmarks of scientific practice.

The idea of the hermeneutic circle could be seen as a conceptual shift from phenomenology's
emphasis on prior *experience* as shaping understanding to the conception of prior *reading* in that
knowledge-shaping role—literally, when working with written texts; figuratively, in considering
hermeneutic applications beyond the literal to text analogues. Gadamer's hermeneutics brings it
closer to phenomenology. One of Gadamer's departures from Dilthey was his observation that
the hermeneutic circle describes all sense making processes in general, not just text-based ones.[30]
For Gadamer, *verstehen* is the process through which researcher and researched come to understand each other's frame of reference, with language playing the central mediating role in interpretation (Burrell and Morgan 1979, 238).

Combining the hermeneutic focus on texts as vehicles for conveying meaning with the phenomenological consciousness that researchers, too, act from an experientially informed standpoint has led to an awareness of the ways in which writing, itself, is a way of world making.
Research designs, formulations of questions, choices of observational sites and persons interviewed,
analytic frames, *and writing* all construct perceptions of the subject of study, rather than objectively
reflecting it. Interpretive research reports increasingly include researchers' reflections on this

process, a practice that itself constitutes a significant departure from positivist-qualitative writing. It has become increasingly common in ethnographic writing to find in methods chapters not only extensive discussion of the physical setting of the research and the political, economic, and/or sociocultural characteristics of the people studied but also reflective descriptions of the researcher and his background and how these might have affected observations, interactions, and what was learned and seen. Diane Singerman (1995), for example, and Samer Shehata (2004; see also chapter 13, this volume), in their respective studies of neighborhoods and organizations in Cairo and Alexandria, reflect on their own researcher-identities at the time as Americans, as female and male, as Jew and as Muslim, as unmarried people of marriageable age, as educated beyond the local norm, and so on. The point of such explicit reflexivity is to examine the ways in which their own "positionality" potentially shapes the ways researchers generate their data and analyses, as Shehata discusses at length in his chapter.

Acknowledging the ways in which writing practices—from what one chooses to reveal about oneself as a researcher to word choice to the construction of a logical argument—create the social reality one is writing about has led several authors to argue that writing, itself, is a method (e.g., Richardson 1994). Some have even argued for the role of their "informants" or study subjects themselves as coauthors or cocreators of the research; among these scholars, some reflect also on the dimensions of power that are inscribed through this process on the setting and/or participants in question (see Behar 1993 for one example). At the very least, such arguments enable us to understand that interpretation does not stop with the experience of an event or its narration. Rather, interpretive moments continue in the writing of research findings, too, a point I will return to below.

What phenomenology seeks to bracket, hermeneutics has made central; where phenomenology focuses on processes of perception, hermeneutics focuses on principles of interpretation. In methodological practices, the distinctions are subtle. Seen from outside the procedural steps of specific methods, from a perspective that seeks to understand the central shift from methodological universalism in search of generalizable principles to contextualized meaning making, the two approaches bear a family resemblance.

PROCESSES OF MEANING MAKING

Neither phenomenology nor hermeneutics engages methods directly (although qualitative methods journal articles and textbooks are starting to discuss "phenomenological research design" and "hermeneutic research methods"). As social philosophies, their concerns were (and continue to be) directly with ontological and epistemological matters. But the orientations of both, and especially their ontological and epistemological questions and positions, undergird the "logics" of interpretive methods (and, one might even say, their ethical concerns as well). That is, a method that focuses on lived experience—such as participant-observation, ethnography, interviewing with that focus, and so on—is phenomenologically inflected; and a method that treats texts and text analogues is hermeneutic in its sense. What these share in common is an orientation to questions of meaning. Although these methods did not develop in any linear, causal sense out of these philosophies, the latter provide grounding—in the form of a clarifying epistemological foundation—for some of the central methodological elements characterizing interpretive research methods.

Issues in the Artifact-Meaning Relationship

Although twentieth-century hermeneutic scholars did not explicitly treat it as such, the relationship between meanings and artifacts is a representational, or symbolic, one: Artifacts come to stand in for, to represent, their embedded meanings. The point is clearest in Goffman's (e.g., 1959, 1974) and Mead's (1934) writings and in the notion of a study of "symbolic interaction," developed in their work.

The representational character of this relationship is at the heart of studies of and arguments concerning language: Are words "transparent" in their meaning, that is, do they equate to what they signify—does the word-meaning reside in the object—or is meaning more a matter of consensus? Foucault (1970, chapter 2), although not customarily grouped with interpretive philosophers, is helpful here. He locates the shift away from seeing words as the mirrors of their signifiers in the passage from the sixteenth century to the seventeenth: "in the sixteenth century, one asked oneself how it was possible to know that a sign did in fact designate what it signified; from the seventeenth century, one began to ask how a sign could be linked to what it signified" (42–43). This is a significant shift, from the analysis of equivalence to the analysis of meaning. The methodological importance lies in the shift in understanding of what it means to interpret symbolic referents. Is one "divining" the preestablished meaning of a sign, much as Joseph interpreted the meaning of the cupbearer's, baker's, and Pharaoh's dreams (*Genesis* 40–41) or as a palm-reader divines the lines on a hand? This would indicate that meanings reside in the objects denoted by signs, that meanings are out there waiting to be "discovered"—hence, the methodological language of "findings." Or are things signified to be understood as (in contemporary language) "constructed" meanings? Foucault drew the distinction in this way:

> Let us call the totality of the learning and skills that enable one to make the signs speak and to discover their meaning, hermeneutics; let us call the totality of the learning and skills that enable one to distinguish the location of the signs, to define what constitutes them as signs, and to know how and by what laws they are linked, semiology; the sixteenth century superimposed hermeneutics and semiology in the form of similitude.[31] (1970, 29)

The hermeneutic symbolic relationship is a dynamic one: each referent to or use of or engagement with an artifact is an opportunity to maintain and reinforce, or revise and change, its underlying meaning (Yanow 1996, 2000). Arguing that meanings cannot be apperceived or accessed directly, but only through interpreting their artifactual representations, leads to the basic methods of accessing sources of data used in interpretive analyses: observing (with whatever degree of participation), a conversational mode of interviewing, and the close reading of documents. These engage the concrete specificities of acts, language, and/or objects—artifacts embodying and expressing the more abstract value, belief, and affective meanings.

For example, casual talk in common everyday encounters rarely explores meanings explicitly. One might strike up a conversation with someone in the grocery store and infer what she values or believes or what is meaningful to him from the words spoken, the tone of voice, and other elements of nonverbal communication, including dress, bearing, gestures, and facial expressions. The point holds for corporate entities as well: Organizations' or governments' beliefs or values are seen as conveyed not only in their written policy statements but also in their nonverbal communication, such as their acts or the acts of their agents (see Lipsky [1980] on street-level bureaucrats being perceived as representing agency policy), or in the programs and spaces designed and/or used for implementing policies (see, e.g., Stein 2004, Yanow 1996). In this vein, Hopf (2002) built an argument about Soviet and post-Soviet identity, at two moments in time, through what might be called a hermeneutic reading of newspapers, popular magazines, high school textbooks, and the like, as well as official state documents. He treated these artifacts as the embodiments of contemporaneous, collective identity elements, reading them as expressive of those collective meanings.

Individuals and collective entities also use language, whether written or spoken, to communicate meaning. When word and deed conflict, we tend to trust the deed as the more "accurate" reflection of what the actor actually means.[32] Asked directly to explain their acts and/or beliefs, research-relevant publics are likely to report what they think the researcher wants to hear, or what they believe is socially acceptable, or simply what they think they believe or value. Governmental or organizational statements, likewise, may express an ideal or desired state of affairs, rather than the experienced values of enacted policies-on-the-ground. The tension between desired states and experienced ones reflects what Argyris and Schon (1974) called "espoused values," as distinct from "theories-in-use" manifested in acts or interactions, a distinction echoed by parents admonishing their children to "Do as I say, not as I do." In this sense, spatial design and other physical artifacts are a form of deed: a nonverbal enactment of underlying values, beliefs, and/or sentiments (the first presupposition).

Researchers seeking to understand human meaning can have direct observational access to artifacts—to what people and organizations do. (I mean this as a statement about capability, not permission.) Meanings cannot be observed directly. We infer meaning(s) from their manifestations in or expressions through the more directly observable, more tangible artifacts that embody them. Analysis proceeds through a constant tacking back and forth in ongoing comparison between the nonverbal data of objects and acts observed and "read" and actors' explicit pronouncements, whether in formal or informal speech or in writing.

This process points to one of the strengths of interpretive research: its utility for studying situations in which the meanings of words and deeds are not or are not likely to be congruent. Such interpretations are customarily treated as provisional, subject to corroboration, or refutation, through further observation and/or conversational interviewing. This is a common use of interviews—for clarifying, corroborating, and/or refuting the researcher's provisional meaning making derived from observation, reading, and/or other conversations, with the same or with other conversants. Because of the word-deed tension, efforts are made to ground such interviewing in the details of lived experience (see Schaffer, chapter 7, this volume).

Interpretive Moments

Related to this is the question of making interpretations: who does it, and when?

Interpretive researchers argue that the meaning they are after is that made by members of the situation; and so one would privilege those members' meaning making over the researcher's. Extreme versions of phenomenology (so judged by many, if not most, empirical researchers, as they border on solipsism; see Burrell and Morgan 1979, 238–40) argue that it is impossible to understand another's meaning without reliving it. This position has been rejected by most in favor of the notion that we live in an intersubjective world in which empathetic understanding of another's meaning is possible. This latter idea is what undergirds ethnographic and participant-observer analyses in particular (and even more so analyses of built space, as noted in chapter 20, this volume): that the researcher draws on a basic commonality of human experience and processes of understanding, and that through learning the language of the setting and its customs, the researcher can acquire sufficient familiarity as to be able to understand events that transpire, while at the same time drawing on sufficient "stranger-ness" to make the accepted, unspoken, tacitly known, commonsensical, taken-for-granted, local "rules" of action and interaction stand out as, in some way, different, thereby opening them up for reflection and examination.[33] This means that researchers are drawing on themselves—their Selves—in significant ways.

One can delineate four interpretive moments over the course of a research project.[34] Assume that we are interested in understanding an event. With a contemporaneous event, initial interpretations are made by persons actually present and observing it, even, perhaps, actively participating in it. This could as well be the researcher, acting as participant-observer, as a member of the community-society-polity-organization under study. In an initial experiential interpretation, the researcher casts herself, implicitly, in an "as if" role—as if she is standing in for the situational member, drawing on their shared humanity as a point of reference, while also drawing on her own stranger-ness, which enables her to see and make explicit what for others is common sense. As noted above, she will want to corroborate, refute, or revise that initial, *provisional* sense making through conversations (interviews) with situational members and/or through further (participant-) observation and/or documentary evidence produced by situational members.

If, on the other hand, the researcher's initial interpretation of the event develops from material conveyed to him by a member—that is, the researcher was not present, whether for reasons of schedule, timing, or access—he will also want to talk to other situational members who were there, so as to access their reports about the event, including their interpretations of it. In this situation as well, the researcher is likely to want to read materials, should they exist and be obtainable, pertaining to the event produced by various other actors in it—contemporaneous newspaper accounts, radio or television program transcripts, diaries and the like, agency memos or correspondence or annual reports, and so on—for similar corroborative purposes. The further removed the event is from the present time, the closer the research moves to historical analysis, resting exclusively on documentary sources if participants are no longer living or otherwise unable to render firsthand reports, however clouded by the passage of time.

Any one of these circumstances presents a second interpretive moment, in which the researcher seeks to make sense of material that is secondary with respect to her firsthand experience of the event. This is what Schütz, Geertz, and others (e.g., Mark Bevir and Patrick Jackson in this volume) mean in characterizing human sense making as interpretations of interpretations, a double hermeneutic (in Giddens's term [1984]). The time and space dimensions of this doubling are captured in what Schütz (1967) called first- and second-order interpretations; methods textbooks refer to the duality as emic-etic;[35] Geertz (1983, 57) termed them "experience-near" and "experience-distant."

Two additional interpretive moments become clear in looking beyond research-site interactions at the research process as a whole. A third comes in the analysis and writing up of accessed and generated data. As noted above, writing itself has increasingly come to be seen as a way of world making, as words are carefully and rhetorically-logically chosen and both data and analysis are shaped into a logical, persuasive account. This perception emphasizes the extent to which writing is, itself, a method—a method of analysis and of discovery, as the researcher combs through observational and interview notes and sees ever newer things.[36]

The fourth interpretive moment is brought into focus by "reader-response theory" from literary studies. This approach to textual analysis took issue with earlier theories as to the locus of textual meaning. These earlier theories had been based on two usually unspoken assumptions fundamental to early communications theories: that meaning is determinate; and that meanings are made and set only by their "senders" (in the systems language of much communications theory) or creators. This led critics to search for meaning in the author's intent (in which case it was the reader's job to ferret out the meaning intended by the author, leading to explorations in authorial biographies, contemporaneous histories, and so forth). Contesting this came the argument that meaning resided in the text itself—the author was "dead" (which meant the reader's job was to analyze the text's rhetorical or poetic devices: metaphors, rhyme scheme, rhythm, and so forth; see, for example, Ciardi 1959). Contending, in turn, with this approach was one that argued that readers were not passive recipients of authors' meanings but active constructors of meaning themselves, bringing their own backgrounds to the texts they read, drawing on these backgrounds as well as on the words of the text in its interpretation. Meaning, in this view, is created out of an interaction between reader and text, or among reader, text, and author's intentions (e.g., Iser 1989).[37] From this perspective, textual meaning is not finite, since each reader hypothetically brings a different experience to the reading, or the same reader, marked by new experiences in the interim, might even "find" a different meaning on two separate readings.

The fourth moment, then, takes place in the reading (or hearing) of the research report. What this highlights is the distinction between "authored" texts and "constructed" texts, and it points to one of the issues in evaluative criteria for research and one of its central dilemmas. As Peregrine Schwartz-Shea notes in chapter 5 of this book, one of the interpretive procedures for dealing with questions of research trustworthiness is to involve situational members in reading the draft research report. The dilemma is how to proceed when that reading is at odds with the researcher's interpretation. Seeing textual meaning as not finite and reading as an interpretive moment suggests a potential reframing of such an encounter, from one in which the researcher dismisses the reading as inherently flawed to one that opens the door to an exploration of rationales (or backgrounds) for different readings. (The procedural implications are explored in that chapter.)

The same layering of interpretation and meaning holds when the subject of interpretation is a (literal) text or a physical artifact, rather than an event. This may be seen in examples from the organizational implementation of public policies (e.g., Ingersoll and Adams 1992, Stein 2004, Swaffield 1998, Yanow 1996; see also Chock 1995, Linder 1995). Not only are legislative and other language and organizational buildings texts (or "texts") that are interpreted by implementers and others acting in the situation for which the text was produced; but those interpretations—in the form of agency language, objects, and acts—themselves become "texts" that are "read," by those actors and others. An act, object or spoken language is interpreted by its "readers"—agency staff, clients, and so forth. And these interpretations come in the form of responses—acts, language, and/or objects—that themselves are then treated as texts and interpreted, prompting further responses. It is in this sense that interpretive methodologists claim that "it" is interpretation or meaning-construction "all the way down."

CONCLUDING THOUGHTS

> [There is a saying] I heard often in prison,
> "if you treat a man human,
> he'll treat you human."
> The staff and prisoners treated me human,
> and I tried to do the same.
> —*Ann Chih Lin* (2000, 189)

The methods of accessing or generating and analyzing data used today in meaning-focused research study both meaning and the artifacts that embody and convey it. Interpretive science's appreciation for the multiplicities of possible meaning and attendant ambiguities has refocused attention on the perspectival, and even rhetorical, character of scientific writing (a concern of feminist theory and science studies also). This has led to an appreciation for the narrative or storied character of both scientific and everyday communication, something noted especially by Maynard-Moody and Musheno in their chapter. Attention to language's persuasive elements brings in considerations of power and power relations, as well as privileged speech and silences in collective, public discourses.

Interpretive philosophies have not been without their critics from within the interpretive end of the epistemological spectrum. Specifically, Frankfurt School critical theorists have charged phenomenology on ontological grounds with an excessive preoccupation with the Self—a kind of disengaged contemplation or philosophical navel-gazing—that ignores the impacts on individuals of institutions and their power. In the critics' view, phenomenologists (appeared to) believe that the self-understanding that can emerge from reflection could override power imbalances and, perforce, lead to change. As they saw it, phenomenological argumentation leads to inattention to questions of power and even a dismissiveness toward the operative reality of institutional, and institutionalized,, power—an undervaluing of the seemingly objective reality of social institutions and the problematics of change (see, e.g., Fay 1975). Critical theorists argue that interpretation's emphasis on understanding meanings is not enough, that understanding needs to be anchored to action (Beam and Simpson 1984).

Whereas this criticism may well pertain at the level of the philosophical writings, and especially the more solipsistic and transcendental ones, it seems less founded when these philosophies are applied to actual practices—in organizations, for example, or social practices or other empirical applications of interpretive methods. Once phenomenology, the particular target of such criticism, is brought into the realm of political and other social realities, theorists must, and do, contend with questions of power in its communal, social, organizational, political, and/or other institutional manifestations. To put the point somewhat differently, DNA science doesn't tell genes what to do; but interpretive social science of necessity engages a social world that acts and responds, to its own meaning making, at least, and potentially to the meaning making of the scientific community; and such action perforce involves interpretive science with issues of power, institutions, and other engaged concerns. As will be clear in the chapters in parts II and III of this book, one can find among interpretive researchers a continuum from the more critical to the less critical (in a critical theory sense; meaning, with greater and lesser explicit attention to and reflexivity about power issues and the social realities of institutions). The critique does not seem applicable to all interpretive research.

In addition, applied to neighborhoods, communities, organizations, states, public policies, governmental decision making, and other empirical settings, interpretive approaches are arguably more democratic in character than analyses informed by methodological positivism: they accord the status of expertise to local knowledge possessed by situational actors, not just to the technical expertise of researchers. Much of the work to date in interpretive policy analysis, for example (e.g., Colebatch and Degeling 1986; Feldman 1989; C. Fox 1990; Hofmann 1995; Jennings 1983, 1987; Maynard-Moody and Musheno 2003; Maynard-Moody and Stull 1987; Yanow 1996, 2003b), appears to be motivated by a desire not only to explain agency performance, but to make it more just, more equitable, more effective. Several theorists (e.g., Dryzek 1990; Hawkesworth 1988; Jennings 1983; Schneider and Ingram 1993, 1997) argue, further, that interpretive analysis presupposes or requires an ethical commitment to a more democratic policy process and analysis.

Interpretation as a method, then, is conducted as "sustained empathic inquiry" (Atwood and Stolorow 1984, 121), in which empathy constitutes an intentional embracing of the other's meaning. Studying the lifeworld of research site members and the political, organizational, and/or communal artifacts they embed with meaning, as hermeneutics would argue, entails a decentering of expertise on the part of the researcher. Accessing local knowledge of local conditions accords legitimacy to those for whom this is their primary experience, their lifeworld. It thereby shifts the researcher's expert role from technical-rational subject-matter expertise to process expertise, in knowing how to locate and access local knowledge and make it the subject of reflection, publicly discussable. It is a radically democratic move within the presently dominant conceptualization of organizational, policy, and other expert-based analyses.

In sum, scientific practices that focus on meaning and meaning making in specific situational contexts and on processes of sense making more broadly are informed by interpretive philosophies and presuppositions. They are concerned with understanding the lifeworld of the actor in the situation(s) being studied, but they also reflect on the problematics of (re)presenting that lifeworld and those meanings, including the role of the researcher as an actor in doing so, and they engage the role of language and other artifacts in constructing and communicating meaning and social relationships in that lifeworld. Research begins from the presupposition that social reality is multifold, that its interpretation is shaped by one's experience with that reality, and that experiences are lived in the context of intersubjective meaning making. The researcher engages these meanings through various methods that allow access to actors' meanings. Interpretation operates at several levels: that of the situational actor *and/or* the researcher experiencing and interpreting an event or setting; of the researcher interpreting conversational interviews with situational actors and situation-relevant documents and extending those interpretations in preparing a report; and of the reader or audience interpreting the written or oral report. In this view, all knowledge is interpretive, and interpretation (of acts, language, and objects) is the only method appropriate to the human, social world when the research question concerns matters of human meaning.

NOTES

The ideas developed in this chapter build on earlier work, including a chapter focused on organizational studies as an interpretive science (Hatch and Yanow 2003). My thanks to Mary Hawkesworth and to Peri Schwartz-Shea for their close critical readings of earlier drafts. All errors of interpretation remain my own.

1. Geertz imagines an exchange in which the muscles of the tradesman's eyelid contract. How should this contraction be understood, he asks: was it an involuntary twitch, or was the tradesman signaling some meaning through an intentional wink? He uses this to illustrate the point that we need much more information—about the character of the events, the persons, the times, and so on—in order to be able to interpret which it was or to consider that it might have had other meanings altogether. This "richer," fuller description is what he characterizes as "thick" description.

2. For these reasons, I avoid talking about the "nature" of the subject of study: From an interpretive ontological perspective there is nothing "natural" about our topics of investigation. Whereas this term (the "nature" of something) may seem like a dead metaphor and my point, a minor linguistic quibble, I believe that source meanings do tend to ride in on the backs of words, even when that knowledge is tacit. I thank Davydd Greenwood for drawing my attention to the metaphoric character of this term.

3. This is itself a delimiting statement: It posits that some subjects of study are more usefully approached through interpretive methodologies and their attendant tools of analysis than others. The dividing line rests with the presuppositions brought to a "research question" by the scientist: Questions about the same research subject may be formulated differently, depending on the epistemological and ontological orientations of the researcher (and, of course, on her education and training—connections that may well be interrelated; see the discussion of presuppositions in the book's introduction). I put "research question" in quotation marks because it has become clear to me that different methodological camps understand this phrase differently. Whereas projects influenced more by methodological positivism treat this phrase literally —for them, a research question is a full-blown statement, a hypothesis—for interpretive researchers, the "question" is more commonly a topic, a puzzle, or a tension that draws their attention, often because of some prior, possibly experiential knowledge that informs their curiosity and suggests that this is an area worthy of research attention. This difference in approach is manifested also in research designs: Interpretive research designs more commonly begin with what might best be called hunches, rather than with hypotheses.

4. William James credited Charles Pierce with the coinage of the term, although Pierce did not like James's formulation of the philosophy and himself called it "pragmaticism" (Menand 2001). George Herbert Mead was a point of contact for James, John Dewey, and Charles Pierce and for some of the Continental philosophers (Menand 2001). The points of similarity are pronounced in Mead's and Dewey's work, among them the emphasis on the context specificity of knowledge and the extent to which the Self is constituted in interaction within society and its themes. See Mead (1934); Menand, relating sources (1997) and history (2001); and Polkinghorne (1983). On James as a precursor to the later Wittgenstein, Merleau-Ponty, and Heidegger, see Connolly (2005, chapter 3): James was arguing against the idea of "a unified world knowable through fixed laws unconnected to any power above nature." S.K. White (2004), indeed, argues that pragmatism creates the possibility of a critical social science.

5. This is not to say that the doing of science originated in Europe at this time. There is ample historical evidence of what would be recognizable today as agronomy, astronomy, and other sciences in ancient Babylon, Egypt, Greece, China, Mexico, Africa, and India and medieval Muslem Spain, all long before Copernicus (see, e.g., Teresi 2002). My intention is not to engage in history of science debates, but to note that contemporary understandings of what "science" entails developed out of Renaissance-era European work.

6. We have, in fact, not only replaced the authority of monarchic or religious knowledge with the authority of science, but vested increasingly more epistemic authority in technical-rational expertise, from physicians to planners to policy analysts, removing science from "just" humans applying their powers of reason based on lived, embodied experience (see, e.g., Jordan [1997] on the authority of obstetricians over women giving birth, or Yanow [2004] in the context of organizational practices and managerial knowledge; Harold Garfinkel's point, in coining the term "ethnomethodology," was that in everyday life, humans engage in just this sort of science-like inquiry). I return to this point below.

7. One might, in fact, reach back to Aristotle to justify these arguments about what constitutes "science," as Alker (1996, chapter 2) does in making a claim for the study of politics as a science. There (76–7), he draws on two distinctions: between *physis* (nature) and *nomos* (law or convention), and among *techne* (craft, art), *episteme* (science), and *phronesis* (translated in the present volume as "practical reasoning"). The three ideal types of Aristotelian political science in Alker's articulation revolve around defining science as the deliberative application of perception, practical reason, and intelligence in the development of systematic knowledge concerning regularities of belief, action, practice, and so on (77–86, passim). The three types he finds in Aristotle's writings are distinguished by the relative place of art, science, and perfection, the latter, as I see it, akin to the nineteenth-century idea of progress as perfectibility that became inextricably interwoven with notions of scientific discovery and the scientific method.

8. The logical positivism of the Vienna Circle philosophers (e.g., Moritz Schlick, Otto Neurath, Kurt Godel, and Rudolf Carnap) is considered by many the intellectual descendant of nineteenth-century positivism (see, for example, Abbagnano 1967), although this linkage of the two sets of ideas is not uncontested.

9. Even chaos theorists are, by implication, arguing that recurrent and widespread chaos is a recognizable pattern.

10. And so interpretive thought of the late-nineteenth to early-twentieth centuries is sometimes referred to as neo-Kantian or, as Kant's ideas were part of the German Idealist movement, neo-Idealist.

11. To the extent that the metaphor of a "filter" suggests simplification, it is misleading. As M. Lynch (1990) notes, there is a transformation going on in this process, a point I do not have space to develop here but hope to have captured somewhat in the rendering of *verstehen* as, among other things, proactive understanding from within. The willed effort may, indeed, be transformative; certainly, sense does not simply present itself.

12. This is known in linguistics as the Sapir-Whorf hypothesis. The well-known story—debunked by Steven Pinsker—that the Eskimos have multiple terms for different kinds of snow is part of this debate. The research of Roberson and her colleagues provides empirical support for the contention that language does structure perception, although this position is by no means uncontested.

13. My thanks to Mary Hawkesworth and Peri Schwartz-Shea for help in articulating this point.

14. That understanding and explanation are separable and that interpretive science does not "explain" are contested ideas that have largely been rejected by interpretivists. The rejection hinges on understanding explanation to mean more than causal or predictive relationships (see the discussion in Mark Bevir's chapter 15, this volume).

15. Parsing the term may help in grasping its meaning. Its precise etymology is, according to the German dictionary *Duden*, unknown. The prefix *ver* means entirely, thoroughly, fully, through (Boris Ewenstein, personal communication, December 21, 2004). *Stehen* is to stand, standing. "Through-standing," then, means

to perceive, to recognize, to grasp with the faculties of the mind; to have a clear conception or sense of something. Under-standing, then, might imply trying to figure out the meanings that stand under—that underlie—the focus of one's analysis. *Verstehen* connotes, in this way, a more active reaching across for meaning than the more passive, hierarchical ordering of the English word. My thanks to Boris Ewenstein for his assistance on this.

16. This section and the next draw on Bernstein (1976), Burrell and Morgan (1979), Dallmayr and McCarthy (1977), Fay (1975), Filmer et al. (1972), Polkinghorne (1983), Schütz (1967, 1973), and D.W. Smith (2003). For an overview of feminist and postmodern theories, see Nicholson (1990).

17. The example derives from one that my Hayward colleague Dick VrMeer used in class.

18. Whereas these other terms can be useful aids to understanding the phenomenological argument, it may be necessary to sound a caution: Unlike a pair of eyeglasses that may be regularly put on and taken off or exchanged for a different pair, phenomenological "lenses" or "frames" are not tools that may be engaged and switched so readily. As I have tried to describe here, they are grounded—rooted, entrenched—in years of socialization and acculturation to a community of meaning, an interpretive community, and individuals are imbued with the "way of seeing" developed within their communities. It is this, for example, that leads to the so-called culture shock experienced by those who sojourn for the first time in cultures not their own. Unhappily for this set of ideas, the popularization of the notion of "paradigm" has led to a widespread understanding that paradigms are easily replaced, something that Kuhn's argument itself does not suggest. The idea that these concepts can be used instrumentally, as Mary Hawkesworth notes—"pick a tool, try it out, discard it if your hypothesis is not confirmed"—is at odds "with the depth, complexity, and tacit nature of the lifeworld, which haunts (and structures) our perceiving" (personal communication, May 22, 2004).

19. Husserl drew on the Greek *epoche,* meaning hold up or set aside, for this method.

20. This both describes the operations of the hermeneutic circle (discussed below) and Kuhn's paradigm, and makes them possible.

21. The ways in which collective knowing is mediated by and through objects is the focus of activity theory, developed out of Leont'iev's analysis of human conduct as object-oriented activity. This is treated in the context of work practice and organizational studies by, e.g., Engeström, Puonti, and Seppänen (2003).

22. See also Hacking's (1999) discussion—the social construction of *what?*—which notes the many ways the phrase has become hackneyed and misused, as if the nouns to which the phrase has been applied—authorship, brotherhood, child television viewers, danger, emotions, etc.—could be socially constructed, whereas it is the ideas about or perceptions of those things, rather than the things themselves, that are collectively fabricated over time.

23. The problem of "personifying" states is Milliken's (2001, 21–23) concern as well, and she develops a parallel theoretical analysis. In the context of organizational studies, see the essays in Nicolini, Gherardi, and Yanow (2003) for various methodological treatments of collective action.

24. In biblical scholarship, hermeneutic rules for textual interpretation were stipulated in talmudic exegesis (those Jewish texts, codified in the sixth century, interpreting the laws of conduct articulated in what the Christian world calls the "Old Testament"). In Christian traditions, hermeneutic rules were developed in the context of the debate between Protestantism and Catholicism over who had interpretive authority: the Church and its representatives, or any layperson trained in hermeneutic rules. Traweek (1988, 160) links these ideas to natural science through the analogy of the Bible to "the book of nature": Physicists, she writes, equating nature with data, use their machines to read and decipher nature-data texts. For primary works in hermeneutics see, e.g., Dilthey (1976) and Gadamer (1976); secondary sources include Bernstein (1976), Burrell and Morgan (1979), and Polkinghorne (1983).

25. This brings us back full circle, ironically enough, to the study of rhetoric and oratory and the ancient Greek sources of political theory. Indeed, Burke's dramatistic literary theory (1969 [1945], 1989), which extends literary analysis to interpretations of everyday life and has been applied widely to social, organizational, and policy acts (see, e.g., Feldman 1995, Gusfield 1989, Yanow 1996), harks back to Aristotle's theories of drama.

26. In many respects, symbolic interaction and ethnomethodology are the U.S. counterparts to the European schools of thought. Both are more explicitly methodological, as noted at the beginning of the chapter, especially the latter, and both combine phenomenology's focus on lived experience with a more semiotic hermeneutics. On ethnomethodological analysis, developed in both its conversation and event analysis forms in the mid-1900s, see Garfinkel (1977); on symbolic interactionist theory, see Mead (1934) and Goffman (1959, 1974). Goffman's work, of course, also draws on dramatistic metaphors.

27. This parallels the two senses in which Kuhn (1970) used the term "paradigm" in reference both to the

shared way of seeing, defining, and researching a scientific "problem" and to the community of scientists seeing the problem in that way. See also Kuhn (1977). Merton (in Merton and Barber 2004, 266–69) briefly discusses the differences between his and Kuhn's uses of "paradigm."

28. I describe my experience of this process in my sense making of the architectural design of the community center buildings, in chapter 20, this volume.

29. This list roughly follows the history of ideas in literary analysis, from seeing meaning as residing in the author's intentions (and hence, his own background); to the so-called "death of the author" period, in which meaning was seen as residing in the text alone (in word choice, alliteration, rhythm, etc.); to the rise of reader-response theory, which argued that the interpretation of texts is influenced by what the reader brings to the reading—or in an interaction among all three elements. See, e.g., Ciardi (1959), Iser (1989), and the discussion below and in note 37.

30. Indeed, this captures a central pedagogical point, especially as articulated by Freire (1972, 1973): that an educator must start with students at the point of their present understanding and move forward from there.

31. These ideas are important both for a philosophy of categories and categorizing and for understanding various of the interpretive methods taken up in part III of this book. The passage continues: "To search for a meaning is to bring to light a resemblance. To search for the law governing signs is to discover the things that are alike" (Foucault 1970, 29). This is, of course, the concern of semiotics (the study of signs and their signifiers; see, e.g., Gottdiener and Lagopoulos [1986], Manning [1977]). There are significant differences between Foucault's thinking and the phenomenological and hermeneutic ideas sketched out in this chapter—he was, for example, very critical of phenomenology as a philosophy and what he saw as its ignoring of power—and I do not mean to appear to be eliding them in citing him here and in such a brief reference. I do not have the space to delve into these differences, which are discussed and debated at length in other works (e.g., Dreyfus and Rabinow 1983, Hoy 1986).

32. Psychological research (e.g., Rosenhan, Frederick, and Burrowes 1968) bears this out.

33. Collins (2001, 108–9) suggests two indicators through which one knows one has succeeded in this: "ceasing to commit *faux pas* during interactions with respondents . . . [and] the nature of conversations . . . if you can get them to listen to you seriously and interestedly when you discuss their subject that means you are getting somewhere. . . ." He is addressing tacit knowledge in practices, but the point holds more broadly.

34. This delineation of four possible interpretive moments in the research process builds on Van Maanen's (1995, 5–23) discussion of three "moments" in ethnography: collecting information, constructing a report, and its reading by various audiences.

35. From the linguistic terms phonemic ("internal" meaning) and phonetic (universal laws).

36. I hasten to emphasize that the discovery is of what the researcher saw—that is, his frames or sense making—in his notes on observations and/or interviews, not of what was "actually" in the experience or setting.

37. Given interpretive methods' treatment of acts and objects as "texts," there is an irony, wholly unintended, in my reference here to Iser's work, since he dismisses the extension of the text metaphor to action. In response to Stanley Fish's comment that his method does not consider the world as a text, Iser noted the "restrictions of the literary text that make it an unsuitable metaphor for reality" (1989, 66–67).

CHAPTER 2

CONTENDING CONCEPTIONS
OF SCIENCE AND POLITICS

Methodology and the Constitution of the Political

MARY HAWKESWORTH

My introduction to political science was atypical in many ways. My earliest course work at the University of Massachusetts and at the University of Sussex was more oriented toward political philosophy and the "New" Political Science advocated by its eponymous Caucus than by behavioralism. Although Georgetown University required all Ph.D. students to complete a two-semester sequence in "Scope and Methods" and "Quantitative Analysis," the faculty was dominated by "traditionalists" who maintained a healthy skepticism of the "behavioral revolution." As a consequence, my "Scope and Methods" course devoted a great deal of time and attention to issues in the philosophy of science. I ingested Hume's analysis of the problem of induction, Popper's critique of positivism, and Feyerabend's critique of critical rationalism before I took my first statistics course.

Halfway through my Ph.D. course work, I spent a summer at the Interuniversity Consortium for Political and Social Research (ICPSR) at the University of Michigan learning advanced quantitative techniques. There I was struck by the gulf between textbook accounts of research design, hypothesis formation and testing, and cautious and tentative conclusions drawn from correlations, and the unfettered confidence in quantitative techniques, the apparent lack of concern about the adequacy of the data to "measure" the political phenomena under investigation, and the insistent focus on strategies to maximize the R^2.

One of the last courses I took in graduate school, "Normative Policy Analysis," sought to explore tacit and explicit biases that structure policy making, policy implementation, and policy interpretation and raised important questions about the role of policy analysts in relation to the tacit presuppositions of "scientific" approaches to policy studies. Max Weber's convictions concerning the "fact/value dichotomy" seemed a particularly inadequate guide for policy analysts concerned with attacks on affirmative action, reproductive freedom, welfare provision, environmental protection, and democratic norms of participation, transparency, and accountability.

My first book, Theoretical Issues in Policy Analysis, *attempted to demonstrate a range of philosophical and empirical flaws in positivist approaches to political science and policy studies and to indicate some of the benefits that might accrue from a postpositivist approach to policy studies. In two editions of the* Routledge Encyclopedia of Government and Politics *(1992, 2003), I have tried to make visible the impact of particular methodologies upon our understandings of the political world. This chapter continues that project.*

❖ ❖ ❖

Etymologically, the term "methodology" arises from the conjunction of three Greek concepts: *meta, hodos*, and *logos*. When used as a prefix in archaic Greek, *meta* typically implied "sharing," "action in common," or "pursuit or quest." *Hodos* was usually translated as "way" but when combined with *logos*, which was variously translated as "account," "explanation," "truth," "theory," "reason," or "word," *hodos* suggests a very particular way to truth that lies at the deepest level of being (Wolin 1981). Bringing the three Greek terms together opens possibilities for a variety of interpretations of methodology: "a shared quest for the way to truth," "the action thought takes en route to being," "a shared account of truth," or "the way a group legitimates knowledge claims." The Greek roots of the term are particularly helpful in highlighting certain facets of methodology. Methodologies are specific to particular communities of scholars and as such political. The appropriate methodology for any particular inquiry is a matter of contestation, as scholars often disagree about the "way to truth." Strategies that are accredited as legitimate means to acquire truth gain their force from decisions of particular humans working within particular academic communities; thus there is a power element in the accreditation of knowledge. Power is never the only factor involved, but neither is it a negligible factor.

Over the course of the twentieth century, specific methodologies have been hailed as the hallmark of particular communities of scholars. As academic disciplines broke off from their progenitors and declared their autonomy, methodology often became the terrain upon which battles were fought. Methodology as a coherent set of ideas about epistemology, strategies of inquiry, and standards of evidence appropriate to a research process or the production of knowledge came to define distinctive disciplines. Disciplines with shared allegiance to particular fields of investigation, epistemological assumptions, and methods of inquiry formed coalitions under broad rubrics such as the natural sciences, the life sciences, the social sciences, the behavioral sciences, and the humanities.

Although scholars within and across disciplines continue to disagree about the appropriate means to produce knowledge, much of the conceptual richness revealed by etymology is masked by standard texts designed to teach the methodology accredited within political science. Given the established power hierarchy within the discipline in the aftermath of the behavioral revolution, "the way" to knowledge has often been presented as if it were uncomplicated, value neutral, and uncontestable.

Logical positivism, a theoretical account of the nature of science advanced by philosophers associated with the Vienna Circle in the early-twentieth century, masked the specificity and the power dimensions of methodology by invoking the unity of science. Indeed, the epistemological assumptions that inform positivism have provided the justification for construing the "scientific" production of political knowledge as immune from politics, values, and subjective bias. Positivist assumptions promised not only an escape from subjectivity and bias, but also to provide analytic techniques that could generate "laws of politics" or at least law-like generalizations that would enable political scientists to explain the existing political world and predict future political developments.

Although the epistemological presuppositions of positivism have been under attack for more than forty years, the political developments of the last decade of the twentieth century have presented a very different kind of challenge to positivist hegemony within political science. None of the major political events of the past decade were predicted or adequately explained by the dominant paradigms developed within political science. Whether one considers the end of the cold war and the collapse of the Soviet system; democratization and globalization; political integration within the European Union and its aspiring member states; regional and genocidal wars in the Balkans and in Rwanda and Burundi; the end of Apartheid in South Africa; the emergence of a global civil society through the development of the Internet and the proliferation of nongovernmental organizations; the reemergence of terrorism on the global scene; the unprecedented international assent to a "war" that is not between states or between factions within a state, but pits a coalition of Western military forces operating under executive order against non-state actors; the Al-Qaeda network, which moves clandestinely within and across national boundaries of multiple states; or the role of the U.S. Supreme Court in determining the outcome of the 2000 U.S. presidential election, political science failed to predict or explain these critical events.

Perhaps then it is time to reconsider the limitations of the positivist assumptions that undergird the dominant research methodologies in political and other social sciences, to challenge overly simplistic versions of empiricism in order to afford social scientists more sophisticated analytic tools.[1] According to certain versions of empiricism, a simple and direct relation exists between knower and known. The senses function as faithful recording devices, placing before the "mind's eye" exact replicas of that which exists in the external world, without cultural or linguistic mediation. Precisely because observation is understood as exact replication, strategies for the acquisition of knowledge are said to be "neutral" and "value free." In this view, scientific investigations can grasp objective reality, because the subjectivity of individual observers can be controlled through rigid adherence to neutral procedures in the context of systematic experiments, logical deductions, and statistical analysis of data.

Empiricist assumptions of this sort have been central to the development of the discipline of political science and to the scientific study of politics in the twentieth century (Finifter 1983; Greenstein and Polsby 1975; King, Keohane, and Verba 1994; Seidelman and Harpham 1985; Tanenhaus and Somit 1967). In the following sections, I will explicate and critique the positivist and Popperian conceptions of science that have profoundly influenced the recent practice of social science, advance an alternative conception of science, and explore its implications for political inquiry. Clarifying and criticizing the methodological presuppositions of the social sciences provides the grounds for challenging the myth of methodological neutrality, identifying new areas for investigation concerning the political implications of particular modes of inquiry, thereby fostering theoretical self-consciousness about the relation of social science to contemporary politics.

CONTENDING CONCEPTIONS OF SCIENCE

Positivism

Within the social sciences, empiricist commitments have generated a number of methodological techniques to ensure the objectivity of scientific investigations. Chief among these is the dichotomous division of the world into the realms of the empirical and the non-empirical. The empirical realm, comprising all that can be corroborated by the senses, is circumscribed as the legitimate sphere of scientific investigation. As a residual category, the non-empirical encompasses everything else—religion, philosophy, ethics, aesthetics, and evaluative discourse in general, as well as myth, dogma and superstition—and is relegated beyond the sphere of science. Within this frame of reference, social science, operating within the realm of the observable, restricting its focus to descriptions, explanations, and predictions that are intersubjectively testable, can achieve objective knowledge. The specific techniques requisite to the achievement of objective knowledge have been variously defined by two conceptions of science that have shaped the practice of social science: positivism and critical rationalism.

On the grounds that only those knowledge claims founded directly upon observable experience can be genuine, positivists adopted the "verification criterion of meaning," which stipulates that a contingent proposition is meaningful if and only if it can be empirically verified (Ayer 1959; Joergenson 1951; Kraft 1952). The verification criterion was deployed to differentiate not only between science and non-science, but between science and nonsense. In the positivist view, any statement that could not be verified by reference to experience constituted nonsense: it was literally meaningless. The implications of the verification criterion for a model of science were manifold. All knowledge was believed to be dependent upon observation; thus any claims, whether theological, metaphysical, philosophical, ethical, normative, or aesthetic, that were not rooted in empirical observation were rejected as meaningless. The sphere of science was thereby narrowly circumscribed and scientific knowledge was accredited as the only valid knowledge. In addition, induction, a method of knowledge acquisition grounded upon observation of particulars as the foundation for empirical generalizations, was taken to provide the essential logic of science.

The task of science was understood to comprise the inductive discovery of regularities existing in the external world. Scientific research sought to organize in economical fashion those regularities that experience presents in order to facilitate explanation and prediction. To promote this objective, positivists endorsed and employed a technical vocabulary, clearly differentiating facts (empirically verifiable propositions) and hypotheses (empirically verifiable propositions asserting the existence of relationships among observed phenomena) from laws (empirically confirmed propositions asserting an invariable sequence or association among observed phenomena) and theories (interrelated systems of laws possessing explanatory power). Moreover, the positivist logic of scientific inquiry dictated a specific sequence of activities as definitive to "the scientific method."

According to this model, the scientific method began with the carefully controlled, neutral observation of empirical events. Sustained observation over time would enable the regularities or patterns of relationships in observed events to be revealed and thereby provide for the formulation of hypotheses. Once formulated, hypotheses were to be subjected to systematic empirical tests. Those hypotheses that received external confirmation through this process of rigorous testing could be elevated to the status of scientific laws. Once identified, scientific laws provided the foundation for scientific explanation, which, according to the precepts of the "covering law model," consisted in demonstrating that the event(s) to be explained could have been expected, given certain initial conditions ($C_1, C_2, C_3, \ldots$) and the general laws of the field ($L_1, L_2, L_3, \ldots$). Within the framework of the positivist conception of science, the discovery of scientific laws also provided the foundation for prediction, which consisted of demonstrating that an event would occur given the future occurrence of certain initial conditions and the operation of the general laws of the field. Under the covering law model, then, explanation and prediction have the same logical form, only the time factor differs: Explanation pertains to past events; prediction pertains to future events.

Positivists were also committed to the principle of the "unity of science," that is, to the belief that the logic of scientific inquiry was the same for all fields. Whether natural phenomena or social phenomena were the objects of study, the method for acquiring valid knowledge and the requirements for explanation and prediction remained the same. Once a science had progressed sufficiently to accumulate a body of scientific laws organized in a coherent system of theories, it could be said to have achieved a stage of "maturity" that made explanation and prediction possible. Although the logic of mature science remained inductive with respect to the generation of new knowledge, the logic of scientific explanation was deductive. Under the covering law model, causal explanation, the demonstration of the necessary and sufficient conditions for an event, involved the deductive subsumption of particular observations under a general law. In addition, deduction also played a central role in efforts to explain laws and theories: the explanation of a law involved its deductive subsumption under a theory; and explanation of one theory involved its deductive subsumption under wider theories.

Critiques of Positivism

The primary postulates of positivism have been subjected to rigorous and devastating critiques (Popper 1959, 1972a, 1972b). Neither the logic of induction nor the verification criterion of meaning can accomplish positivist objectives; neither can guarantee the acquisition of truth. The inductive method is incapable of guaranteeing the validity of scientific knowledge owing to the "problem of induction" (Hume 1975 [1748], 1978 [1739]). Because empirical events are contingent, that is, because the future can always be different from the past, generalizations based upon limited observations are necessarily incomplete and, as such, highly fallible. For this reason, inductive generalizations cannot be presumed to be true. Nor can "confirmation" or "verification" of such generalizations by reference to additional cases provide proof of their universal validity. For the notion of universal validity invokes all future, as well as all past and present, occurrences of a phenomenon; yet no matter how many confirming instances of a phenomenon can be found in the past or in the present, these can never alter the logical possibility that the future could be different, that the future could disprove an inductively derived empirical generalization. Thus, a demonstration of the truth of an empirical generalization must turn upon the identification of a "necessary connection" establishing a causal relation among observed phenomena.

Unfortunately, the notion of necessary connection also encounters serious problems. If the notion of necessity invoked is logical necessity, then the empirical nature of science is jeopardized. If, on the other hand, positivism appeals to an empirical demonstration of necessity, it falls foul of the standard established by the verification criterion of meaning, for the "necessity" required as proof of any causal claim cannot be empirically observed. As Hume pointed out, empirical observation reveals "constant conjunction" (a correlation in the language of contemporary social science); it does not and cannot reveal necessary connection. As a positivist logic of scientific inquiry, then, induction encounters two serious problems: It is incapable of providing validation for the truth of its generalizations and it is internally inconsistent, for any attempt to demonstrate the validity of a causal claim invokes a conception of necessary connection that violates the verification criterion of meaning.

The positivist conception of the scientific method also rests upon a flawed psychology of perception. In suggesting that the scientific method commences with "neutral" observation, positivists invoke a conception of "manifest truth," which attempts to reduce the problem of the validity of knowledge to an appeal to the authority of the source of that knowledge (for example, "the facts 'speak' for themselves"). The belief that the unmediated apprehension of the "given" by a passive or receptive observer is possible, however, misconstrues both the nature of perception and the nature of the world. The human mind is not passive but active; it does not merely receive an image of the given, but rather imposes order upon the external world through a process of selection, interpretation, and imagination. Observation is always linguistically and culturally mediated. It involves the creative imposition of expectations, anticipations, and conjectures upon external events.

Scientific observation, too, is necessarily theory laden. It begins not from "nothing," nor from the "neutral" perception of given relations, but rather from immersion in a scientific tradition that provides frames of reference or conceptual schemes that organize reality and shape the problems for further investigation. To grasp the role of theory in structuring scientific observation, however, requires a revised conception of "theory." Contrary to the positivist notion that theory is the result of observation, the result of systematization of a series of inductive generalizations, and the result of the accumulation of an interrelated set of scientific laws, theory is logically prior to the observation of any similarities or regularities in the world; indeed, theory is precisely that which makes the identification of regularities possible. Moreover, scientific theories involve risk to an extent that is altogether incompatible with the positivist view of theories as summaries of empirical generalizations. Scientific theories involve risky predictions of things that have never been seen and hence cannot be deduced logically from observation statements. Theories structure scientific observation in a manner altogether incompatible with the positivist requirement of neutral perception, and they involve unobservable propositions that violate the verification criterion of meaning: Abstract theoretical entities cannot be verified by reference to empirical observation.

That theoretical propositions violate the verification criterion is not in itself damning, for the verification criterion can be impugned on a number of grounds. As a mechanism for the validation of empirical generalizations, the verification criterion fails because of the problem of induction. As a scientific principle for the demarcation of the "meaningful" from the "meaningless," the verification criterion is self-referentially destructive. In repudiating all that is not empirically verifiable as nonsense, the verification criterion repudiates itself, for it is not a statement derived from empirical observation nor is it a tautology. Rigid adherence to the verification criterion then would mandate that it be rejected as metaphysical nonsense. Thus the positivist conflation of that which is not amenable to empirical observation with nonsense simply will not withstand scrutiny. Much (including the verification criterion itself) that cannot be empirically verified can be understood and all that can be understood is meaningful.

Critical Rationalism

As an alternative to the defective positivist conception of science, Karl Popper advanced "critical rationalism" (1972a, 1972b). On this view, scientific theories are bold conjectures that scientists impose upon the world. Drawing insights from manifold sources in order to solve particular problems, scientific theories involve abstract and unobservable propositions that predict what may happen as well as what may not happen. Thus scientific theories generate predictions that are incompatible with certain possible results of observation, that is, they "prohibit" certain occurrences by proclaiming that some things could not happen. As such, scientific theories put the world to the test and demand a reply. Precisely because scientific theories identify a range of conditions that must hold, a series of events that must occur, and a set of occurrences that are in principle impossible, they can clash with observation; they are empirically testable. Although no number of confirming instances could ever prove a theory to be true due to the problem of induction, one disconfirming instance is sufficient to disprove a theory. If scientific laws are construed as statements of prohibitions, forbidding the occurrence of certain empirical events, then they can be definitively refuted by the occurrence of one such event. Thus, according to Popper, "falsification" provides a mechanism by which scientists can test their conjectures against reality and learn from their mistakes. Falsification also provides the core of Popper's revised conception of the scientific method.

According to the "hypothetico-deductive model," the scientist always begins with a problem. To resolve the problem, the scientist generates a theory, a conjecture or hypothesis, which can be tested by deducing its empirical consequences and measuring them against the world. Once the logical implications of a theory have been deduced and converted into predictions concerning empirical events, the task of science is falsification. In putting theories to the test of experience, scientists seek to falsify predictions, for that alone enables them to learn from their mistakes. The rationality of science is embodied in the method of trial and error, a method that allows error to be purged through the elimination of false theories.

In mandating that all scientific theories be tested, in stipulating that the goal of science is the falsification of erroneous views, the criterion of falsifiability provides a means by which to reconcile the fallibility of human knowers with a conception of objective knowledge. The validity of scientific claims does not turn on a demand for an impossible neutrality on the part of individual scientists; on the equally impossible requirement that all prejudice, bias, prejudgment, expectation, or value be purged from the process of observation; or on the implausible assumption that the truth is manifest. The adequacy of scientific theories is judged in concrete problem contexts in terms of their ability to solve problems and their ability to withstand increasingly difficult empirical tests. Those theories that withstand multiple intersubjective efforts to falsify them are "corroborated," are identified as "laws" that with varying degrees of verisimilitude capture the structure of reality, and for that reason are tentatively accepted as "true." But in keeping with the critical attitude of science even the strongest corroboration for a theory is not accepted as conclusive proof. For Popperian critical rationalism posits that truth lies beyond human reach. As a regulative ideal that guides scientific activity truth may be approximated, but it can never be established by human authority. Nevertheless, error can be objectively identified. Thus informed by a conception of truth as a *regulative ideal* and operating in accordance with the requirements of the criterion of falsifiability, science can progress by the incremental correction of errors and the gradual accretion of objective problem-solving knowledge.

Although Popper subjected many of the central tenets of logical positivism to systematic critique, his conception of "critical rationalism" shares sufficient ground with positivist approaches to the philosophy of science that it is typically considered to be a qualified modification of, rather than a comprehensive alternative to, positivism (Stockman 1983). Indeed, Popper's conception of the hypothetico-deductive model has been depicted as the "orthodox" positivist conception of scientific theory (Moon 1975, 143–87). Both positivist and Popperian approaches to science share a belief in the centrality of logical deduction to scientific analysis; both conceive scientific theories to be deductively related systems of propositions; both accept a deductive account of scientific explanation; both treat explanation and prediction as equivalent concepts; and both are committed to a conception of scientific progress dependent upon the use of the hypothetico-deductive method of testing scientific claims (H. Brown 1977, 65–75; Stockman 1983, 76). In addition, both positivist and Popperian conceptions of science are committed to the correspondence theory of truth and its corollary assumption that the objectivity of science ultimately rests upon an appeal to the facts. Both are committed to the institutionalization of the fact/value dichotomy in order to establish the determinate ground of science. Both accept that once safely ensconced within the bounds of the empirical realm, science is grounded upon a sufficiently firm foundation to provide for the accumulation of knowledge, the progressive elimination of error, and the gradual accretion of useful solutions to technical problems. And although Popper suggested that reason could be brought to bear upon evaluative questions, he accepted the fundamental positivist principle that, ultimately, value choices rest upon non-rational factors.

Most of the research strategies developed within social science in the twentieth century draw upon either positivist or Popperian conceptions of the scientific method. The legacy of positivism is apparent in behavioralist definitions of the field that emphasize data collection, hypothesis formulation and testing, and other formal aspects of systematic empirical enterprise, as well as in approaches that stress scientific, inductive methods, statistical models, and quantitative research designs. It surfaces in conceptions of explanation defined in deductive terms and in commitments to the equivalence of explanation and prediction. It emerges in claims that social science must be modeled upon the methods of the natural sciences, for those alone are capable of generating valid knowledge. It is unmistakable in the assumption that "facts" are unproblematic, that they are immediately observable or "given," and that hence their apprehension requires no interpretation. It is embodied in the presumption that confirmation or verification provides a criterion of proof of the validity of empirical claims. And it is conspicuous in the repudiation of values as arbitrary preferences, irrational commitments, or meaningless propositions that lie altogether beyond the realm of rational analysis (Eulau 1963; Kaplan 1964; Eulau and March 1969; Meehan 1965; Storing 1962; Welsh 1973).

Popper's insistence upon the centrality of problem solving and incrementalism in scientific activity resonates in the works of those committed to a pluralist[2] approach to political analysis (Dahl 1971, Lindblom 1965). Popperian assumptions also surface in the recognition that observation and analysis are necessarily theory laden, as well as in the commitment to intersubjective testing as the appropriate means by which to deflect the influence of individual bias from substantive political analyses. They are manifest in the substitution of testability for verifiability as the appropriate criterion for the demarcation of scientific hypotheses and in the invocation of falsification and the elimination of error as the strategy for the accumulation of knowledge. They are reflected in the pragmatic notion that the existing political system constitutes the appropriate "reality" against which to test hypotheses. They are obvious in the critique of excessive optimism concerning the possibility of attaining "absolute truth" about the social world through the deployment of inductive, quantitative techniques; in the less pretentious quest for "useful knowledge"; and in the insistence that truth constitutes a regulative ideal rather than a current possession of social science. They are conspicuous in arguments that the hypothetico-deductive model is applicable to political and social studies and in appeals for the development of a critical, non-dogmatic attitude among social scientists. Moreover, Popperian assumptions are apparent in a variety of strategies devised to bring reason to bear upon normative issues, while simultaneously accepting that there can be no ultimate rational justification of value precepts. Popperian presuppositions about the fundamental task of social science are also manifest in the pluralists' commitment to a conception of politics premised upon a model of the market that focuses research upon the unintended consequences of the actions of multiple actors rather than upon the particular intentions of political agents (Cook 1985; Lindblom and Cohen 1979; MacRae 1976; Wildavsky 1979).

Postpositivist Presuppositionist Theories of Science

Although Popper's critical rationalism is a significant improvement over early positivist conceptions of science, it too suffers from a number of grave defects. The most serious challenge to critical rationalism has been raised by postpositivist[3] presuppositionist theories of science (Bernstein 1978, 1983; H. Brown 1977; Gunnell 1986, 1995, 1998; Hesse 1980; Humphreys 1969; Longino 1990; Polanyi 1958; Stockman 1983; Suppe 1977). Presuppositionist theories of science concur with Popper's depiction of observation as "theory-laden." They agree that "there is more to seeing than meets the eye" (Humphreys 1969, 61) and that perception involves more than the passive reception of allegedly manifest sense-data. They suggest that perception depends upon a constellation of theoretical presuppositions that structure observation, accrediting particular stimuli as significant and specific configurations as meaningful. According to presuppositionist theories, not only is observation theory-laden, but theory is essential to, indeed constitutive of, all human knowledge.

Within recent work in the philosophy of science, the epistemological and ontological implications of the postpositivist understanding of theory have been the subject of extensive debate. Arguing that the theoretical constitution of human knowledge has ontological as well as epistemological implications, "antirealists" have suggested that there is no point in asking about the nature of the world independent of our theories about it (Laudan 1990). Consequently the truth status of theories must be bracketed. But antirealists have insisted that theories need not be true to be good, that is, to solve problems (Churchland and Hooker 1985, van Fraassen 1980). Metaphysical "realists," on the other hand, have emphasized that even if the only access to the world is through theories about it, a logical distinction can still be upheld between reality and how we conceive it, between truth and what we believe (Harré 1986). Hilary Putnam (1981, 1983, 1988, 1990) has advanced "pragmatic realism" as a more tenable doctrine. Putnam accepts that all concepts are theoretically constituted and culturally mediated and that the "world" does not "determine" what can be said about it. Nonetheless, it makes sense on pragmatic grounds to insist that truth and falsity are not merely a matter of decision and that there is an external reality that constrains our conceptual choices. Following Putnam's lead, "scientific realists" have argued that scientific theories are referential in an important sense and as such can be comparatively assessed in terms of their approximations of truth (Glymour 1980, R. Miller 1987, Newton-Smith 1981).

Although the debates among realists and antirealists about the criteria of truth and the nature of evidence are intricate and complex, both realists and antirealists share convictions about the defects of positivism and accept the broad contours of presuppositionist theories of science. On this view, science, as a form of human knowledge, is dependent upon theory in multiple and complex ways. Presuppositionist theories of science suggest that the notions of perception, meaning, relevance, explanation, knowledge, and method, central to the practice of science, are all theoretically constituted concepts. Theoretical presuppositions shape perception and determine what will be taken as a "fact"; they confer meaning on experience and control the demarcation of significant from trivial events; they afford criteria of relevance according to which facts can be organized, tests envisioned, and the acceptability or unacceptability of scientific conclusions assessed; they accredit particular models of explanation and strategies of understanding; and they sustain specific methodological techniques for gathering, classifying, and analyzing data. Theoretical presuppositions set the terms of scientific debate and organize the elements of scientific activity. Moreover, they typically do so at a tacit or preconscious level and it is for this reason that they appear to hold such unquestionable authority.

The pervasive role of theoretical assumptions upon the practice of science has profound implications for notions such as empirical "reality" and the "autonomy" of facts, which posit that facts are "given," and that experience is ontologically distinct from the theoretical constructs that are advanced to explain it. The postpositivist conception of a "fact" as a theoretically constituted entity calls into question such basic assumptions. It suggests that "the noun, 'experience,' the verb, 'to experience' and the adjective 'empirical' are not univocal terms that can be transferred from one system to another without change of meaning. . . . Experience does not come labeled as 'empirical,' nor does it come self-certified as such. What we call experience depends upon assumptions hidden beyond scrutiny which define it and which in turn it supports" (Vivas 1960, 76). Recognition that "facts" can be so designated only in terms of prior theoretical presuppositions implies that any quest for an unmediated reality is necessarily futile. Any attempt to identify an "unmediated fact" must mistake the conventional for the "natural," as in cases that define "brute facts" as "social facts which are largely the product of well-understood, reliable tools, facts that are not likely to be vitiated by pitfalls . . . in part [because of] the ease and certainty with which [they] can be determined and in part [because of] the incontestability of [their] conceptual base" (Murray 1983, 321). Alternatively, the attempt to conceive a "fact" that exists prior to any description of it, prior to any theoretical or conceptual mediation, must generate an empty notion of something completely unspecified and unspecifiable, a notion that will be of little use to science (B. Williams 1985, 138).

Recognition of the manifold ways in which perceptions of reality are theoretically mediated raises a serious challenge not only to notions of "brute data" and the "givenness" of experience but also to the possibility of falsification as a strategy for testing theories against an independent reality. For falsification to provide an adequate test of a scientific theory, it is necessary that there be a clear distinction between the theory being tested and the evidence adduced to support or refute the theory. According to the hypothetico-deductive model, "theory-independent evidence" is essential to the very possibility of refutation, to the possibility that the world could prove a theory to be wrong. If, however, what is taken to be the "world," what is understood to be "brute data," is itself theoretically constituted (indeed, constituted by the same theory that is undergoing the test), then no conclusive disproof of a theory is likely. For the independent evidence upon which falsification depends does not exist; the available evidence is preconstituted by the same theoretical presuppositions as the scientific theory under scrutiny (H. Brown 1977, 38–48; Moon 1975, 146; Stockman 1983, 73–76).

Contrary to Popper's confident conviction that empirical reality could provide an ultimate court of appeal for the judgment of scientific theories and that the critical, nondogmatic attitude of scientists would ensure that their theories were constantly being put to the test, presupposition theorists emphasize that it is always possible to "save" a theory from refutation. The existence of one disconfirming instance is not sufficient to falsify a theory because it is always possible to evade falsification on the grounds that future research will demonstrate that a counterinstance is really only an "apparent" counterinstance.[4] Moreover, the theory-laden character of observation and the theory-constituted character of evidence provide ample grounds upon which to dispute the validity of the evidence and to challenge the design or the findings of specific experiments that claim to falsify respected theories. Furthermore, postpositivist examinations of the history of scientific practice suggest that, contrary to Popper's claim that scientists are quick to discard discredited theories, there is a great deal of evidence that neither the existence of counterinstances nor the persistence of anomalies necessarily lead to the abandonment of scientific theories. Indeed, the overwhelming evidence of scientific practice suggests that scientists cling to long-established views tenaciously, in spite of the existence of telling criticisms, persistent anomalies, and unresolved problems (Harding 1986; Ricci 1984). Thus it has been suggested that the "theory" that scientists themselves are always skeptical, nondogmatic, critical of received views, and quick to repudiate questionable notions has itself been falsified and should be abandoned.

The problem of falsification is exacerbated by the conflation of explanation and prediction in the Popperian account of science. For the belief that a corroborated prediction constitutes proof of the validity of a scientific explanation fails to recognize that an erroneous theory can generate correct predictions (H. Brown 1977, 51–57; Moon 1975, 146–47). The logical distinction between prediction and explanation thus provides further support for the view that no theory can ever be conclusively falsified. The problem of induction also raises doubts about the possibility of definitive refutations. In calling attention to the possibility that the future could be different from the past and the present in unforeseeable ways, the problem of induction arouses the suspicion that a theory falsified today might not "stay" falsified. The assumption of regularity, which sustains Popper's belief that a falsified theory will remain falsified permanently, is itself an inductionist presupposition, which suggests that the falsifiability principle does not constitute the escape from induction that Popper had hoped for (Stockman 1983, 81–82). Thus despite the logical asymmetry between verification and falsification, no falsification can be any stronger or more final than any corroboration (H. Brown 1977, 75).

Presupposition theorists acknowledge that "ideally, scientists would like to examine the structure of the world which exists independent of our knowledge—but the nature of perception and the role of presuppositions preclude direct access to it: the only access available is through theory-directed research" (H. Brown 1977, 108). Recognition that theoretical presuppositions organize and structure research by determining the meanings of observed events, identifying relevant data and significant problems for investigation, and indicating both strategies for solving problems and methods by which to test the validity of proposed solutions, raises a serious challenge to the correspondence theory of truth. For it both denies that "autonomous facts" can serve as the ultimate arbiter of scientific theories and suggests that science is no more capable of achieving the Archimedean point or of escaping human fallibility than is any other human endeavor. Indeed, it demands acknowledgment of science as a human convention rooted in the practical judgments of a community of fallible scientists struggling to resolve theory-generated problems under specific historical conditions. It sustains an image of science that is far less heroic and far more human.

As an alternative to the correspondence theory of truth, presupposition theorists suggest a coherence theory of truth, premised upon the recognition that all human knowledge depends upon theoretical presuppositions whose congruence with nature cannot be established conclusively by reason or experience. Theoretical presuppositions, rooted in living traditions, provide the conceptual frameworks through which the world is viewed; they exude a "natural attitude" that demarcates what is taken as normal, natural, real, reasonable, or sane from what is understood as deviant, unnatural, utopian, impossible, irrational, or insane. In contrast to Popper's conception of theories as conscious conjectures that can be systematically elaborated and deductively elucidated, the notion of theoretical presuppositions suggests that theories operate at the tacit level. They structure "preunderstandings" and "prejudgments" in such a way that it is difficult to isolate and illuminate the full range of presuppositions that affect cognition at any given time (Bernstein 1983, 113–67). Moreover, any attempt to elucidate presuppositions must operate within a "hermeneutic circle." Any attempt to examine or to challenge certain assumptions or expectations must occur within the frame of reference established by the other presuppositions. Certain presuppositions must remain fixed if others are to be subjected to systematic critique. This does not imply that individuals are "prisoners" trapped within the framework of theories, expectations, past experiences, and language in such a way that critical reflection becomes impossible (Bernstein 1983, 84). Critical reflection upon and abandonment of certain theoretical presuppositions is possible within the hermeneutic circle; but the goal of transparency, of the unmediated grasp of things as they are, is not. For no reflective investigation, no matter how critical, can escape the fundamental conditions of human cognition.

A coherence theory of truth accepts that the world is richer than theories devised to grasp it; it accepts that theories are underdetermined by "facts" and, consequently, that there can always be alternative and competing theoretical explanations of particular events. It does not, however, imply the relativist conclusion that all theoretical interpretations are equal. That there can be no appeal to neutral, theory-independent facts to adjudicate between competing theoretical interpretations does not mean that there is no rational way of making and warranting critical evaluative judgments concerning alternative views. Indeed, presuppositionist theorists have pointed out that the belief that the absence of independent evidence necessarily entails relativism is itself dependent upon a positivist commitment to the verification criterion of meaning. Only if one starts from the assumption that the sole test for the validity of a proposition lies in its measurement against the empirically "given" does it follow that, in the absence of the "given," no rational judgments can be made concerning the validity of particular claims (Bernstein 1983, 92; H. Brown 1977, 93–94; Gunnell 1986, 66–68; Stockman 1983, 79–101).

Once the "myth of the given" (Sellars 1963, 164) has been abandoned and once the belief that the absence of one invariant empirical test for the truth of a theory implies the absence of all criteria for evaluative judgment has been repudiated, then it is possible to recognize that there are rational grounds for assessing the merits of alternative theoretical interpretations. To comprehend the nature of such assessments it is necessary to acknowledge that although theoretical presuppositions structure the perception of events, they do not create perceptions out of nothing. Theoretical interpretations are "world-guided" (B. Williams 1985, 140). They involve both the preunderstanding brought to an event by an individual perceiver and the stimuli in the external (or internal) world that instigate the process of cognition. Because of this dual source of theoretical interpretations, objects can be characterized in many different ways, "but it does not follow that a given object can be seen in any way at all or that all descriptions are equal" (H. Brown 1977, 93). The stimuli that trigger interpretation limit the class of plausible characterizations without dictating one absolute description.

Assessment of alternative theoretical interpretations involves deliberation, a rational activity that requires that imagination and judgment be deployed in the consideration of the range of evidence and arguments that can be advanced in support of various positions. The reasons offered in support of alternative views marshal evidence, organize data, apply various criteria of explanation, address multiple levels of analysis with varying degrees of abstraction, and employ divergent strategies of argumentation. This range of reasons offers a rich field for deliberation and assessment. It provides an opportunity for the exercise of judgment and ensures that when scientists reject a theory, they do so because they believe they can demonstrate that the reasons offered in support of that theory are deficient. That the reasons advanced to sustain the rejection of one theory do not constitute absolute proof of the validity of an alternative theory is simply a testament to human fallibility. Admission that the cumulative weight of current evidence and compelling argument cannot protect scientific judgments against future developments that may warrant the repudiation of those theories currently accepted is altogether consonant with the recognition of the finitude of human rationality and the contingency of empirical relations.

Presupposition theorists suggest that any account of science that fails to accredit the rationality of the considered judgments that inform the choice between alternative scientific theories must be committed to a defective conception of reason. Although the standards of evidence and the criteria for assessment brought to bear upon theoretical questions cannot be encapsulated in a simple rule or summarized in rigid methodological principles, deliberation involves the exercise of a range of intellectual skills. Conceptions of science that define rationality in terms of one technique, be it logical deduction, inductive inference, or empirical verification, are simply too narrow to encompass the multiple forms of rationality manifested in scientific research. The interpretive judgments that are characteristic of every phase of scientific investigations, and that culminate in the rational choice of particular scientific theories on the basis of the cumulative weight of evidence and argument, are too rich and various to be captured by the rules governing inductive or deductive logic. For this reason, *phronesis*, practical reason, manifested in the processes of interpretation and judgment characteristic of all understanding, is advanced by presupposition theorists as an alternative to logic as the paradigmatic form of scientific rationality (Bernstein 1983, 54–78; H. Brown 1977, 148–52).

Presupposition theorists suggest that a conception of practical reason more accurately depicts the forms of rationality exhibited in scientific research. In contrast to the restrictive view advanced by positivism that reduces the arsenal of reason to the techniques of logic and thereby rejects creativity, deliberative judgment, and evaluative assessments as varying forms of irrationality, phronesis constitutes a more expansive conception of the powers of the human intellect. Presupposition theorists suggest that a consideration of the various processes of contemplation, conceptualization, representation, remembrance, reflection, speculation, rationalization, inference, deduction, and deliberation (to name but a few manifestations of human cognition) reveals that the dimensions of reason are diverse. They also argue that an adequate conception of reason must encompass these diverse cognitive practices. Because the instrumental conception of rationality advanced by positivists is clearly incapable of accounting for these various forms of reason, it must be rejected as defective. Thus presupposition theorists suggest that science must be freed from the parochial beliefs that obscure reason's diverse manifestations and restrict its operation to the rigid adherence to a narrow set of rules. The equation of scientific rationality with formal logic must be abandoned. There is no reason to suppose that there must be some indubitable foundation or some ahistorical, invariant method for scientific inquiry in order to establish the rationality of scientific practices. Moreover, the belief that science can provide final truths cannot be sustained by the principles of formal logic, the methods of empirical inquiry, or the characteristics of fallible human cognition. Phronesis constitutes a conception of rationality that can encompass the diverse uses of reason in scientific practices, identify the manifold sources of potential error in theoretical interpretations, and illuminate the criteria of assessment and the standards of evidence and argument operative in the choice between alternative theoretical explanations of events. As a conception of scientific rationality, then, phronesis is more comprehensive and has greater explanatory power than the discredited positivist alternative.

Presupposition theorists offer a revised conception of science that emphasizes the conventional nature of scientific practices and the fallible character of scientific explanations and predictions. Confronted with a world richer than any partial perception of it, scientists draw upon the resources of tradition and imagination in an effort to comprehend the world before them. The theories they devise to explain objects and events are structured by a host of presuppositions concerning meaning, relevance, experience, explanation, and evaluation. Operating within the limits imposed by fallibility and contingency, scientists employ creative insights, practical reason, formal logic, and an arsenal of conventional techniques and methods in their effort to approximate the truth about the world. But their approximations always operate within the parameters set by theoretical presuppositions; their approximations always address an empirical realm that is itself theoretically constituted. The underdetermination of theory by data ensures that multiple interpretations of the same phenomena are possible.

When alternative theoretical explanations conflict, the judgment of the scientific community is brought to bear upon the competing interpretations. Exercising practical reason, the scientific community deliberates upon the evidence and arguments sustaining the alternative views. The practical judgment of the practitioners in particular fields of science is exercised in examining presuppositions, weighing evidence, replicating experiments, examining computations, investigating the applicability of innovative methods, assessing the potential of new concepts, and considering the validity of particular conclusions. Through a process of deliberation and debate, a consensus emerges among researchers within a discipline concerning what will be taken as a valid theory. The choice is sustained by reasons that can be articulated and advanced as proof of the inadequacy of alternative interpretations. The method of scientific deliberation is eminently rational: It provides mechanisms for the identification of charlatans and incompetents, as well as for the recognition of more subtle errors and more sophisticated approximations of truth. But the rationality of the process cannot guarantee the eternal verity of particular conclusions. The exercise of scientific reason is fallible; the judgments of the scientific community are corrigible.

The revised conception of science advanced by presupposition theorists suggests that attempts to divide the world into ontologically distinct categories of "facts" and "values," or into dichotomous realms of the "empirical" and the "normative," are fundamentally flawed (Hawkesworth 1988). Such attempts fail to grasp the implications of the theoretical constitution of all knowledge and the theoretical mediation of the empirical realm. They fail to come to grips with the valuative character of all presuppositions and the consequent valuative component of all empirical propositions. The theoretically mediated world is one in which description, explanation, and evaluation are inextricably linked. Any attempt to impose a dichotomous relation upon such inseparable processes constitutes a fallacy of false alternatives, which is as distorting as it is logically untenable. For the suggestion that "pure" facts can be isolated and analyzed free of all valuation masks the theoretical constitution of facticity and denies the cognitive processes through which knowledge of the empirical realm is generated. Moreover, the dichotomous schism of the world into "facts" and "values" endorses an erroneous and excessively limiting conception of human reason, a conception that fails to comprehend the role of practical rationality in scientific deliberation and that fails to recognize that science is simply one manifestation of the use of practical reason in human life. Informed by flawed assumptions, the positivist conception of reason fails to understand that phronesis is operative in philosophical analysis, ethical deliberation, normative argument, political decisions, and the practical choices of daily life as well as in scientific analysis. Moreover, in stipulating that reason can operate only in a naively simple, "value-free," empirical realm, the positivist presuppositions that inform the fact/value dichotomy render reason impotent and thereby preclude the possibility that rational solutions might exist for the most pressing problems of the contemporary age.

Although the arguments that have discredited positivism are well known to philosophers, they have had far too little impact in the discipline of political science. This is especially unfortunate because the critique of positivism has wide-ranging implications for that field of study. The postpositivist conception of knowledge suggests that theoretical assumptions have a pervasive influence upon the understanding of the political world, accrediting contentious definitions of politics, and validating particular variables while invalidating others. Moreover, positivist assumptions mask the controversial character of evidence adduced and the contestability of accredited strategies of explanation. Thus the postpositivist conception of science opens new areas of investigation concerning disciplinary presuppositions and practices: What are the most fundamental presuppositions of political science? What limitations have been imposed upon the constitution of knowledge within political science? By what disciplinary mechanisms has facticity been accredited and rendered unproblematic? How adequate are the standards of evidence, modes of analysis, and strategies of explanation privileged by the dominant tradition? Have methodological precepts subtly circumscribed contemporary politics?

Questions such as these focus attention upon the political implications of determinate modes of inquiry. The politics of knowledge emerges as a legitimate focus of analysis, for the analytic techniques developed in particular cognitive traditions may have political consequences that positivist precepts render invisible. In circumscribing the subject matter appropriate to "science," restricting the activities acceptable as "empirical inquiry," establishing the norms for assessing the results of inquiry, identifying the basic principles of practice, and validating the ethos of practitioners, methodological strictures may sustain particular modes of political life. For this reason, the positivist myth of methodological neutrality should be supplanted by an understanding of methodology as "mind engaged in the legitimation of its own political activity" (Wolin 1981, 406). Such a revised conception of methodology would enable and require political scientists to examine the complex relations among various conceptions of politics, various techniques of political analysis, and various forms of political life. Focusing on four definitions of politics, the final section of this chapter will attempt to illuminate some of these complex relations.

CONTENDING CONCEPTIONS OF POLITICS

Informed by positivist and Popperian assumptions, political scientists have attempted to restrict their focus to description, explanation, and prediction of events in the political world. They have attempted to devise "value-free" definitions of politics grounded squarely upon observable phenomena. A brief examination of the definitions most frequently invoked by political scientists suggests, however, that each definition is value laden and that each subtly structures the boundaries of the political in ways that have implications for the practice of politics.

The Institutional Definition of Politics

For the first half of the twentieth century, the "institutional definition" of politics dominated the discipline of political science. In this view, politics involves the activities of the official institutions of state (Goodnow 1904; Hyneman 1959). Established by tradition and constitution, existing governmental agencies constitute the focal point of empirical political research. Typically adopting a case-study approach, political scientists examine constitutional provisions to identify the structures of governance and the distribution of powers within those structures in particular nations. Great effort is devoted to the interpretation of specific constitutional provisions and to the historical investigation of the means by which such provisions are subtly expanded and transformed over time. This approach often tends to be heavily oriented towards law, investigating both the legislative process and the role of the courts in interpreting the law. Foreign policy is typically conceived in terms of the history of diplomacy, and domestic policy is understood in relation to the mechanisms by which governments affect the lives of citizens.

Although the focus on the official institutions of state has a certain intuitive appeal, the institutional definition of politics can be faulted for sins of omission. If politics is to be understood solely in terms of the state, what can be said of those societies in which no state exists? If the constitution provides a blueprint for the operations of the state, how are states that lack constitutions to be understood? What can be known about states whose constitutions mask the real distribution of power in the nation? If governments are by definition the exclusive locus of politics, then must we conclude that all revolutionary movements are apolitical? The institutional definition of politics provides neither a neutral nor a comprehensive account of political life. It accredits a particular mode of decision making within the nation-state by stipulative definition. In so doing, it subtly removes important activities from the realm of the political.

Concerns such as these led many scholars to reject the institutional definition of politics as underinclusive. By structuring the focus of political analysis exclusively on the institutions of state governance, this definition fails to encompass the full range of politics. It cannot account for political agents such as political bosses, political parties, and pressure groups operating behind the scenes to influence political outcomes. It excludes all modes of political violence, except those perpetrated by states, from the sphere of the political. It thereby delegitimizes revolutionary activity, regardless of precipitating circumstances. And in important respects the institutional definition of politics narrowly construes the range of human freedom, identifying constitutionally designated mechanisms for social transformation as the limit of political possibility. In addition, the institutional definition of politics fails to do justice to international relations, leaving altogether unclear the political status of a realm in which there exist no binding law and no authoritative structures capable of applying sanctions to recalcitrant states.

Politics as the Struggle for Power

To avoid the limitations of the institutional definition, many political scientists have argued that politics is better understood as a struggle for power (Catlin 1964; Lasswell 1950; Morgenthau 1967; Mosca 1939). Within this frame of reference, individuals participate in politics in order to pursue their own selfish advantage. The central question for political research then is "who gets what, when, how" (Lasswell 1950). Such a research focus necessarily expands political inquiry beyond the bounds of governmental agencies, for although the official institutions of state constitute one venue for power struggles, they by no means exhaust the possibilities. Within the struggle-for-power conception, politics is ubiquitous.

In an important sense, the struggle-for-power definition of politics not only expands the sphere of political research beyond the institutions of state, it also extends political analysis beyond the realm of the empirically observable. The exercise of power often eludes direct observation and the effects of power are more easily inferred than empirically documented. Thus it is not surprising that many political researchers working with the conception of politics as power struggle ground their investigations upon a number of contentious assumptions. Perhaps the most fundamental of these is a conception of the person as a being actuated primarily by the *libido dominandi*, the will to power. Precisely because individuals are taken to be governed by an unquenchable desire for power, politics is said to be essentially a zero-sum game in which competition is unceasing, and domination for the sake of exploitation is the chief objective. But the posited will to power, which constitutes the explanatory key to the inevitable nature of political life, is lodged deep in the human psyche—wholly unavailable for empirical observation. Although proponents of the struggle-for-power definition have claimed simply to be "political realists," it is important to note the circularity that informs their cynical "realism." Politics is defined as a struggle for power "because" human beings are driven by the libido dominandi; but the evidence that people are driven by the libido dominandi is inferred from their involvement in politics.

An unacceptable degree of circularity also infects the response of political "realists" to their critics. Critics have objected that the struggle-for-power definition fails to explain the full range of political phenomena: if politics is merely a competition through which individuals seek to impose their selfish objectives on others, why have values such as equality, freedom, and justice played such a large and recurrent role in political life? With its relentless emphasis upon the pursuit of selfish advantage, the struggle-for-power conception of politics seems unable to account for this dimension of politics. Political "realists," such as Gaetano Mosca, have suggested that appeals to noble principles constitute various forms of propaganda disseminated to mask the oppressive character of political relations and thereby enhance the opportunities for exploitation. According to Mosca (1939), no one wants to confront the naked face of power. Political leaders do not wish to have their selfish objectives unmasked because it will make their achievement more difficult. The masses do not wish to confront their own craven natures. So rulers and followers collude in the propagation of "political formulae"—noble phrases that accord legitimacy to regimes by masking the ruler's self-interest. Whether the appeal be to "divine right of kings," "liberty, fraternity, and equality," or "democracy of the people, by the people, and for the people," the function of the political formula is the same: a noble lie that serves as legitimating myth. Thus political "realists" discount the role of substantive values in politics by unmasking them as additional manifestations of the will to power, a will that is posited and for which no independent evidence is adduced.

Although such a degree of circularity may impugn the logical adequacy of the struggle-for-power conception of politics, it does not mitigate the unsavory consequences of the widespread dissemination of the definition by political scientists. When "science" asserts that politics is nothing more than the struggle for power, the moral scope of political action is partially occluded. If people are convinced that politics necessarily involves the pursuit of selfish advantage, then the grounds for evaluating political regimes is severely circumscribed. In an important sense, the distinction between a good ruler (i.e., one who rules in the common interest) and a tyrant (i.e., one who rules in self-interest) ceases to exist. For if all politics is by definition a struggle for selfish advantage, then what distinguishes one ruler from another cannot be the divergent ends pursued by each. All that distinguishes a "noble statesperson" from an "ignoble oppressor" is the nature of the political formula disseminated. A "good ruler" is simply an excellent propagandist. What distinguishes regimes is not the values pursued, but the ability of the political leaders to manipulate popular beliefs. Within the frame of cynical "realism," it makes no sense to denounce the systematic manipulation of images as an abuse of the democratic process, for manipulation is a constant of political life. What cynical science must denounce is the illusory notion that democracy could be anything more.

The Pluralist Conception of Politics

Pluralists have advanced a third conception of politics that has had an enormous influence upon the discipline of political science. Devised to avoid the shortcomings of both the institutional and the struggle-for-power definitions, that conception conceives politics as the process of interest accommodation. Unlike the cynical insistence that power is the only value pursued in politics, the pluralists' viewpoint argues that individuals engage in politics to maximize a wide range of values. Although some political actors may pursue their selfish advantage exclusively, others may seek altruistic ends such as equality, justice, an unpolluted environment, or preservation of endangered species. Without preemptively delimiting the range of values that might be pursued, pluralists suggest that politics is an activity through which values and interests are promoted and preserved. In contrast to the institutional definition's focus on the official agencies of government, pluralists emphasize that politics is a process of "partisan mutual adjustment" (Lindblom 1965), a process of bargaining, negotiating, conciliation and compromise through which individuals seeking markedly different objectives arrive at decisions with which all are willing to live. In this view, politics is a moderating activity, a means of settling differences without recourse to force, a mechanism for selecting policy objectives from among a competing array of alternatives (Crick 1962).

The pluralist conception of politics incorporates a number of modernist assumptions about the appropriate relation of the individual to the state. Pervaded by skepticism concerning the power of human reason to operate in the realm of values and the concomitant subjectivist assumption that, in the absence of absolute values, all value judgments must be relative to the individual, pluralists suggest that individuals must be left free to pursue their own subjectively determined ends. The goal of politics must be nothing more than the reconciliation of the subjectively defined needs and interests of the individual with the requirements of society as a whole in the most freedom-maximizing fashion. Moreover, presupposing the fundamental equality of individuals, pluralists insist that the state has no business favoring the interests of any individual or group. Thus, in the absence of rational grounds for preferring any individual or value over any other, pluralists identify coalition building as the most freedom-maximizing decision principle. Politics qua interest accommodation is fair precisely because the outcome of any negotiating situation is a function of the consensus-garnering skill of the participants. The genius of this procedural conception of politics lies in its identification of solutions capable of winning the assent of a majority of participants in the decision process.

Pluralists have ascribed a number of virtues to their conception of politics. It avoids the excessive rationalism of paternalist conceptions of politics that assume the state knows what is in the best interests of the citizenry. It recognizes the heterogeneity of citizens and protects the rights of all to participate in the political process. It acknowledges the multiple power bases in society (for example, wealth, numbers, monopoly of scarce goods or skills) and accords each a legitimate role in collective decision making. It notes not only that interest groups must be taken into account if politics is to be adequately understood, but also that competing interests exist within the official institutions of state—that those designated to act on behalf of citizens must also be understood to act as factions, whose behavior may be governed as much by organizational interests, partisanship, and private ambitions as by an enlightened conception of the common good.

Despite such advantages, pluralism, too, has been criticized for failing to provide a comprehensive conception of politics. In defining politics as a mechanism for decision making that constitutes an alternative to force, the interest-accommodation definition relegates war, revolution, and terrorism to a realm beyond the sphere of politics. In emphasizing bargaining, conciliation, and compromise as the core activities of politics, the pluralist conception assumes that all interests are reconcilable. Thus it sheds little light upon some of the most intractable political issues that admit of no compromise (for example, abortion, apartheid, racism, or *jihad*). Moreover, in treating all power bases as equal, pluralists tend to ignore the structural advantages afforded by wealth and political office. The notion of equal rights of participation and influence neglects the formidable powers of state and economy in determining political outcomes. In addition, the interest-accommodation definition of politics has been faulted for ethnocentrism. It mistakes certain characteristics of political activity in Western liberal democracies for the nature of politics in all times and places.

Although the pluralist conception fails to achieve a value-neutral, comprehensive definition of politics, it too has a subtle influence upon the practice of politics in the contemporary world. When accredited by social scientists as the essence of politics, the interest-accommodation conception both legitimizes the activities of competing interest groups as the fairest mechanism of policy determination and delegitimizes revolutionary action and political violence as inherently antipolitical. Even in less extreme circumstances, the pluralist definition of politics may function as a self-fulfilling prophecy, severely curtailing the options available to a political community by constricting the parameters within which political questions are considered.

The pluralist conception of politics presupposes the validity of the fact/value dichotomy and the emotivist conception of values. As a version of non-cognitivism, emotivism is a meta-ethical theory that asserts that facts and values are ontologically distinct and that evaluative judgments involve questions concerning subjective emotions, sentiments, or feelings rather than questions of knowledge or rational deliberation (Hudson 1970). Applied to the political realm, emotivism suggests that moral and political choices are a matter of subjective preference or irrational whim about which there can be no reasoned debate.

Although emotivism has been discredited as an altogether defective account of morality and has been repudiated by philosophers for decades, it continues to be advanced as unproblematic truth by social scientists (MacIntyre 1981; Warwick 1980). And there is a good deal of evidence to suggest that "to a large degree, people now think, talk and act as if emotivism were true" (MacIntyre 1981, 21). Promulgated in the texts of social science and incorporated in pop culture, emotivist assumptions permeate discussions of the self, freedom, and social relations (Bellah et al. 1985). Contemporary conceptions of the self are deeply infused with emotivist and individualist premises: the "unsituated self" who chooses an identity in isolation and on the basis of arbitrary preferences has become a cultural ideal. Freedom is conceived in terms of the unrestrained pursuit of idiosyncratic preferences in personal, economic, moral, and political realms. Moral issues are understood in terms of maximizing one's preferred idiosyncratic values, and moral dilemmas are treated as strategic or technical problems related to zero-sum conditions under which the satisfaction of one preference may obstruct the satisfaction of another preference. Thus the individual qua moral agent becomes indistinguishable from the "rational maximizer" hypothesized by rational choice theory. Respect for other individuals is equated with recognition of their rights to make choices and to pursue their own preferences without interference. Condemnation of the immoral actions of others is supplanted by the nonjudgmental response of "walking away, if you don't like what others are doing" (Bellah et al. 1985, 6). Emotivism coupled with individualism encourages people to find meaning exclusively in the private sphere, thereby intensifying the privatization of the self and heightening doubts that individuals have enough in common to sustain a discussion of their interests or anxieties (Connolly 1981, 145).

Any widespread acceptance of emotivism has important ramifications for political life. At its best, emotivism engenders a relativism that strives "to take views, outlooks and beliefs which apparently conflict and treat them in such a way that they do not conflict: each of them turns out to be acceptable in its own place" (B. Williams 1985, 156). The suspension of valuative judgment aims at conflict reduction by conflict avoidance. By walking away from those whose subjective preferences are different, individuals avoid unpleasant confrontations. By accepting that values are ultimately arbitrary and hence altogether beyond rational justification, citizens devise a modus vivendi that permits coexistence amid diversity.

This coexistence is fragile, however, and the promise of conflict avoidance largely illusory. For the underside of emotivism is cynicism, the "obliteration of any genuine distinction between manipulative and non-manipulative social relations" and the consequent reduction of politics to a contest of wiles and wills ultimately decided by force (MacIntyre 1981, 22, 68). Thus when intractable conflicts arise because avoidance strategies fail, they cannot be resolved through reasoned discourse, for in this view, rational discussion is simply a facade that masks arbitrary manipulation. Thus the options for political life are reduced by definition either to the intense competition of conflicting interests depicted in the pluralist paradigm or to the resort to violence.

The political legacy of emotivism is radical privatization, the destruction of the public realm, "the disintegration of public deliberation and discourse among members of the political community" (Dallmayr 1981, 2). For widespread acceptance of the central tenets of emotivism renders public discussion undesirable (for it might provoke violence), unnecessary (for the real outcomes of decisions will be dictated by force of will), and irrational (for nothing rational can be said in defense of arbitrary preferences). Privatization produces a world in which individuals are free to act on whim and to realize their arbitrary desires, but it is a world in which collective action is prohibited by a constellation of beliefs that render public deliberation impotent, if not impossible. The pluralist conception of politics is not the sole disseminator of emotivism in contemporary societies, but its confident proclamation of interest accommodation as the only viable mode of politics contributes to a form of public life that is markedly impoverished. That it appeals to scientific expertise to confer the "legitimacy of fact" upon its narrow construal of political possibility should be the cause of some alarm to members of a discipline committed to "value-free" inquiry.

The Functionalist Definition of Politics

To escape problems of ethnocentrism and devise a conception of politics that encompasses the political experiences of diverse cultures and ages, in the 1960s behavioral political scientists suggested a new approach that would be both broadly comparative and thoroughly scientific.

Extrapolating from organic and cybernetic analogies, both systems analysis and structural-functionalism conceived politics as a self-regulating system existing within a larger social environment and fulfilling necessary tasks for that social environment (Almond and Coleman 1960; Easton 1971 [1953]; Mitchell 1958, 1967). In this view, politics involves the performance of a number of functions without which society could not exist. The task of political science was to identify these critical political functions, show how they are performed in divergent cultural and social contexts, and ascertain how changes in one part of the political system affect other parts and the system as a whole so as to maintain homeostatic equilibrium. Once political inquiry had generated such a comprehensive understanding of political processes, political scientists could then provide meaningful cross-cultural explanations and predictions. The goal of the systematic cross-cultural study of politics, then, was to generate a scientific understanding of the demands made upon political systems (for example, state building, nation building, participation, redistribution); the nature of the systems' adaptive responses, including the conversion processes that operate to minimize change; and the scope of political development in terms of structural differentiation and cultural secularization, which emerge when the system confronts challenges that surpass its existing capabilities.

Despite its wide popularity, this functionalist conception of politics encountered difficulties with its effort to identify the core political functions without which societies could not survive. Although scholars committed to the functionalist approach generally concurred with David Easton that the political system involves "those actions related to the authoritative allocation of values" (Easton 1971 [1953], 143–44), they disagreed about precisely what those actions entailed. W.C. Mitchell (1958, 1967) identified four critical political functions: the authoritative specification of system goals; the authoritative mobilization of resources to implement goals; the integration of the system (center and periphery); and the allocation of values and costs. Easton (1971 [1953]), as well as Almond and Coleman (1960), offered a more expansive list, including interest articulation, interest aggregation, rule making, rule application, rule adjudication, political recruitment, political socialization, and political communication.

Critics noted that neither enumeration was sufficiently precise to satisfy expectations raised by the model. Neither delineated clearly between the system and its boundaries; neither specified a critical range of operation beyond which the system could be said to have ceased to function; neither explained the requirements of equilibrium maintenance with sufficient precision to sustain a distinction between functional and dysfunctional processes. In short, critics suggested that terminological vagueness and imprecision sustained the suspicion that the putative political functions were arbitrary rather than "vital" or indispensable (Gregor 1968; Landau 1968; Stephens 1969).

In contrast to the promise of scientific certainty that accompanied the deployment of the functionalist conception of politics, the model, critics also pointed out, did not generate testable hypotheses, much less identify "scientific laws" of political life. Critics argued that in marked contrast to the optimistic claims advanced by its proponents, the chief virtue of the functionalist conception was heuristic: It provided an elaborate system of classification that allowed divergent political systems to be described in the same terms of reference. A common vocabulary of analysis enabled comparison of similarities and differences cross culturally (Dowse 1966; Gregor 1968).

Additional limitations were noted by critics of the functionalist conception of politics. The model's emphasis upon system maintenance and persistence rendered it singularly incapable of charting political change. Although traditional modes of political analysis classified revolutions and coups d'état as fundamental mechanisms of political transformation, functionalist analyses could depict such events as adaptive strategies by which the "system" persists. Thus the systems approach blurred important issues pertaining to the character of political regimes and the significant dimensions of regime change (Groth 1970; Rothman 1971).

If functionalist analyses tended to mask political change at one level, at another level they tended to impose an inordinate uniformity upon the scope of political development. Within the functionalist literature, the pattern of development characteristic of a few Western liberal democracies such as the United States and Great Britain was taken as paradigmatic of all political development. Succumbing to a form of "inputism," political scientists proclaimed that certain modes of economic development rendered certain political developments inevitable. The dissemination of capitalist markets would produce strains upon traditional societies, resulting in increasing demands for political participation, which would eventually culminate in the achievement of liberal democracy. Despite the clear ideological content of this projection and despite critics' cogent repudiation of the scientific pretensions of functionalism, this model of development has been repeatedly hailed by political scientists as a matter of indisputable, empirical fact. What is important to note here is not merely that political scientists operating within this tradition have mistaken the political choices of particular communities for the universal political destiny of the species or that their beliefs about the value neutrality of their scientific endeavor have blinded them to the hegemonic aspects of their projections, but also that political scientists have used their leverage as "experts" to advise developing nations to adopt strategies that produce the world prophesied by political science.

Although modernization theory suffered some setbacks in the 1970s and 1980s as a number of "modernizing" democracies in Latin America and Africa were overthrown by military dictatorships, modernization theory was reinvigorated in the 1990s under the rubric of "democratization." Once again political scientists are linking capitalist markets with competitive elections as the key to "democratic consolidation." Like earlier proponents of modernization, consultants currently offering advice on democratic consolidation assume that modern methods of capitalist production and exchange will generate modernist belief systems, including commitments to representative democracy. They suggest that participation in a competitive market economy will promote norms of instrumental rationality, universalism, and egalitarianism, which foster mobility and individual achievement while negating hierarchies rooted in ascriptive status. The rise of individualism will in turn foster demands for increasing political participation and the emergence of multiparty electoral contests.

The assumptions of modernization and democratization theories (i.e., the process is linear, cumulative, expansive, diffuse, and fundamentally occupied with the tradition/modernity dichotomy) offer little insight into the simultaneous emergence of various forms of ethnic nationalism and fundamentalism during the 1990s. Nor do they square well with the possibility that human freedom is compatible with more than one version of modernity. Nevertheless, they do represent yet another instance of the politics of knowledge. Armed with the assumptions of this model of economic and political development, some political scientists are again reshaping the world in their own image.

METHODOLOGY AND THE CONSTITUTION OF POLITICAL LIFE

Under the guise of "value-free empirical inquiry," contemporary political scientists have used scientifically accredited "facts" to supplant political choice. Under the rubric of realism, they have recommended action to enhance the stability of regimes by minimizing "dysfunctional" and "destabilizing" forces such as citizen participation. Under the precept of scientific prediction, they have promoted capitalist market relations as the substance of an inevitable political development. Although implementation of such policy advice is typically justified as another example of knowledge hastening progress, there are good reasons to challenge such optimism. For there is at least as great a likelihood that scientific knowledge will subvert freedom as that it will contribute to undisputed "progress."

Positivist approaches to political science are committed to the belief that definitions are and must be value free, that concepts can be operationalized in a thoroughly non-prescriptive manner, and that research methodologies are neutral techniques for the collection and organization of data. Positivism conceives the political scientist as a passive observer who merely described and explained what exists in the political world. Postpositivism challenged the myth of value neutrality, suggesting that all research is theoretically constituted and value permeated. Illuminating the means by which the conviction of value-free research masks the valuative component of political inquiry, postpositivism questions the fundamental separation between events in the political world and their retrospective analysis by political scientists. In recent years, critical theorists and postmodernists have suggested that this notion of critical distance is yet another myth. Emphasizing that every scientific discourse is productive, generating positive effects within its domain of inquiry, postmodernists caution that political science must also be understood as a productive force that creates a world in its own image, even as it employs conceptions of passivity, neutrality, detachment, and objectivity to disguise and conceal its role (Foucault 1973, 1979). In this period of "democratization," there are good reasons to treat the postmodernists' cautions seriously, for particular methodologies in political science not only construe the political world differently, but also act subtly to promote specific modes of political life.

NOTES

This essay draws upon arguments developed in this author's *Theoretical Issues in Policy Analysis* (1988); "The Science of Politics and the Politics of Science," in Mary Hawkesworth and Maurice Kogan, eds., *Encyclopedia of Government and Politics* (1992); and "Political Science in a New Millennium: Issues of Knowledge and Power," in Mary Hawkesworth and Maurice Kogan, eds., *Encyclopedia of Government and Politics* (2003). I am grateful to Peri Schwartz-Shea and Dvora Yanow for their helpful suggestions to improve an earlier version of the chapter.

1. Empiricism is an old and rich epistemological tradition that dates at least to Aristotle. Many versions of empiricism suggest that the senses can generate reliable knowledge of facts as well as values, and material as well as immaterial reality. This chapter focuses exclusively on versions of empiricism dating from the nineteenth century that severely constrict what the senses can know. Auguste Comte was the first to coin the term "positivism," suggesting that reliable empirical knowledge must eschew metaphysical and theological questions and restrict itself to material domains that can be corroborated by the senses. See his *Course in Positive Philosophy* (1853) and the *System of Positive Policy* (1854).

2. Within political science, "pluralism" has had more than one incarnation. In this chapter, I am using the term as it was defined in the 1960s by scholars such as Harold Lindblom (1965) and Robert Dahl (1971) to refer to a conception of politics as "interest accommodation" and to the endorsement of incrementalist, "trial-and-error," or "satisficing" approaches to political knowledge.

3. The term postpositivist implies theories that (1) have been developed in the aftermath of positivism, (2) incorporate a systematic critique of positivist conceptions of knowledge and science, (3) reject instrumentalist conceptions of theory (i.e., the belief that theories are "tools" consciously created and held, fully explicable, and easily abandoned when falsified), and (4) shift from a correspondence theory of truth to a coherence theory of truth. Although Popper's critical rationalism fits the first criterion and approximates the second, it does not entail the radical break with positivism incorporated in the second two dimensions of postpositivism. Indeed, as noted above, critical rationalism shares sufficient ground with positivism that it is typically considered a qualified modification of, rather than a systematic alternative to, positivism. Similarly Imre Lakatos (1970) tried to preserve the Popperian conception of falsifiability as the ground for the "ratio-

nality of science" while engaging Kuhn's critique of positivism and critical rationalism. Lakatos recognized the critical role played by a scientific research community in shaping a "research program" and the role that presuppositions play in shaping the negative heuristic (inviolable assumptions) and positive heuristic (questions for investigation and accredited methods of inquiry). But like his teacher, mentor, and colleague Karl Popper, Lakatos did not break definitively from an instrumentalist conception of theory or the correspondence theory of truth. Thus neither Popper nor Lakatos fits the definition of "postpositivist" developed here.

4. Lakatos (1976) recognized that scientific theories could not be conclusively falsified and devised several strategies to circumvent this problem. He introduced a distinction between the theory's "hard core" or "negative heuristic," which was not subject to refutation, and its auxiliary hypotheses, which could be falsified. He also argued that the falsification of auxiliary hypotheses need not justify the immediate abandonment of a "useful theory." Instead he recommended that useful theories be allowed to "prove their mettle" over time, that is, that scientists evaluate the "progressive" or "degenerative" nature of the research program by assessing how the theory responds to anomalies (unfulfilled predictions) and unexplained phenomena by introducing modifications in the "protective belt" of auxiliary hypotheses. Although "degenerative" research programs—those whose explanatory power shrinks as ad hoc hypotheses proliferate—ought to be abandoned, "progressive" research programs, which continue to maintain or increase their explanatory power despite falsification of some hypotheses, ought to be preserved.

CHAPTER 3

GENERALIZATION IN COMPARATIVE AND HISTORICAL SOCIAL SCIENCE

The Difference That Interpretivism Makes

ROBERT ADCOCK

My initial thought as an undergraduate at the University of Minnesota was that I had gone to "the U" to train to become a research chemist; but this plan did not survive my introduction to extended lab research, and by my sophomore year I was hunting for alternative endeavors. Supplementing my chemistry major with a second major in political science left my interests something of a hybrid mess. But I settled on graduate school in political science, declaring in my personal statement that my "research interests" lay in "questions about the nature of a 'scientific' approach to the 'political' realm and the role of 'theory' within that approach." Dual interests in political theory and methods, and a specific concern with contentions around "scientific" method, have persisted throughout my graduate training. They have, however, been substantially reshaped and specified.

Early in graduate school I found myself puzzled by the way that debate around whether political science could and should be "scientific" was often conducted among graduate students. Positions on the issue paralleled disagreements over the merit of statistical and formal techniques, with everyone seeming to agree that such techniques seek to model political science on natural science. My own experience was, however, that I had not heard of such techniques as regression when I was a chemistry undergraduate and that my friends who had gone to graduate school in the natural sciences, although learning complex techniques, were not learning the ones taught in our methods courses. The confusion that this situation generated for me cleared up only when I came to recognize that most techniques abused or celebrated in our debates over "science" had not been imported from natural science, but rather had been developed within the social and behavioral sciences. Over time I came to believe that not only most techniques, but also much of the conceptual vocabulary deployed in "methods" conversations—so often seen as efforts to ape natural science—had a similar line of descent. Thus, in studying "validity" with David Collier, I found that my understanding of the issues involved was helped most by tracking the origins of the way social scientists use that concept and by my discovery that these origins mostly lay in psychometrics.

My realization that techniques and concepts at the heart of much contention over "science" in the social sciences were often not derived from the natural sciences was complemented by a belief that I gradually evolved regarding some of the most theoretical stances and arguments deployed in these contentions. I knew that these often drew on the philosophy of science. At one point, this had led me to think that this literature might be the place to go in pursuing my own research concerns. But auditing lectures in the area failed to excite me, and as I quizzed my friends who were pursuing physics Ph.D.s about it, I increasingly came to conclude that practicing natural scientists have little awareness of such philosophy. Judging that natural scientists nevertheless go about their work just fine without referring to philosophers' debates about it, I increasingly found it hard to grasp why I had once thought that the contemporary success of "realists" in the philosophy of (natural) science would help improve my own thinking about social science.

The fizzling of my interest in the philosophy of science combined with my thoughts on the origin of many methodological techniques and concepts to support an emerging belief that the direction from which I wanted to explore "science" and "method" in social science was via the history of social science. This belief fit well with the attitudes I had developed in my study of political theory. As I had learned more about the various approaches within that subfield, I had found myself most attracted to those that came closest in temperament to the work of historians. This consolidation of a personal preference for a certain way of working with texts was the last element pushing me to pursue dissertation research on the history of "method" in social science. My chapter here grows out of that research.

> Certainly it does not now have to be
> argued that the only thorough method of study
> in politics is the comparative and historical.
> —*Woodrow Wilson* (1889, xxxv)

In 1889, Woodrow Wilson, one of the first people to hold a Ph.D. in the study of politics from an American university, published *The State*, which he took to be the first textbook of "comparative politics." Reading Wilson's reflections on the book in his preface (1889, xxxiv–xxxvi), a scholar in today's field of comparative politics would find key parts of the terminology familiar: Beyond the choice of field label, there is Wilson's identification of his approach as a "comparative and historical" one and of his central object of study as "the State." Yet, if a scholar today were to use these terms in the way that Wilson did, colleagues would likely react with confusion, perhaps even concern. Surface similarities here mask a century of intellectual change that, for better or worse, has reconfigured the meanings and practices associated with these terms. For scholars of comparative politics seeking to select and justify an approach for their research, a glance back to Wilson's comparative and historical approach does, however, have its purposes. The contrasts between the practices and aims of Wilson's approach and those propounded today under the label of "comparative historical analysis" may serve at minimum as a reminder that the content of any approach is a contingent product of past legacies, present contentions, and future hopes.

The construction and elaboration of "comparative historical analysis" as a self-conscious approach marks one of the more successful intellectual movements within sociology and political science in recent decades. Pioneers of that movement—such as Theda Skocpol and Dietrich Rueschemeyer—have recently collaborated with younger scholars trained in the approach—such as James Mahoney and Paul Pierson—on the edited volume *Comparative Historical Analysis in the Social Sciences* (Mahoney and Rueschemeyer 2003a). Its contributors reflect upon the evolution of their approach over the last three decades, articulate its distinctiveness, defend its methods, and acclaim its findings. This is a volume liable, I suspect, to leave practicing or aspiring interpretivists ill at ease. The volume's claims as to the need for historical perspective and sensitivity to context will appear familiar. But interpretive social scientists are unlikely to share the conceptions of theory and causal analysis deployed to articulate the aims of comparative historical analysis, nor are they likely to endorse the accompanying efforts to show that this approach can pursue these aims in as systematic and rigorous a fashion as statistical research or formal modeling. Some interpretivist readers, perhaps eager for allies, might ponder discounting these aspects of the volume as strategic rhetoric. But they will likely be disabused of that idea when they find its editors framing "the kind of research considered in this volume" in an explicit contrast with "'interpretive' approaches aimed at uncovering the culturally situated meanings of human behavior" (Mahoney and Rueschemeyer 2003b, 11).

Interpretive scholars might respond to this contrast in any of a number of ways. A key decision is whether to promote, instead, a broader notion of "comparative historical analysis" that would also encompass interpretive studies with a comparative and historical bent. This chapter is premised on the belief that there are important differences here, which should be made more, not less, explicit. Instead of calling for a more inclusive conception, I seek to explicate "comparative historical analysis" as articulated by its proponents and use it as a point of contrast against which to highlight characteristics of an alternative, interpretive approach to comparative and historical social science. In characterizing and contrasting these two approaches, my most important goal is to suggest that a key difference between them centers not upon their accepting or rejecting efforts to see particular developments in a more "general" perspective, but upon how they conceive of the kind of knowledge that such "generalization" sets out to construct. To recognize this difference is not, in itself, to endorse one approach over the other, but rather to recognize grounds upon which scholars may select between them in better accord with their own contingent beliefs as to the kind of knowledge they hope to construct by doing "social science."

This chapter proceeds in two parts. In the first, I sketch some broader trajectories and turning points in the evolution of comparative and historical inquiry within the American social sciences. This material helps me, in the chapter's second part, to characterize the two contemporary approaches of concern and to do so in a way that situates them historically. My historical sketch, which moves from the era of Woodrow Wilson's *The State* up into the 1970s, is crafted with a "genealogical" temperament: I narrate its subject matter as a series of contingent shifts that do not sum up to any overarching direction of "progress" (or "decline"). In these shifts various approaches ebb and flow, and although later approaches may inherit legacies from earlier ones, they do not clearly "build" upon or "progress" beyond them. There are, of course, other ways to plausibly narrate the evolution of comparative and historical social science, and in adopting a genealogical perspective I have had certain concerns in mind. From this perspective, contemporary approaches to comparative and historical social science appear as the contingent outcomes of a succession of events that lack the internal logic of intellectual "progress" that could justify an approach on account of its having prevailed in the course of this succession. Genealogy thereby encourages us to view judgments as to the merits of preserving, remaking, or rejecting an approach as contingent choices that should rest upon recognizing and evaluating, rather than overlooking or hastily dismissing, possible alternatives, even when, and perhaps especially when, that approach has been favored by some of a field's more successful scholars.[1]

BEFORE "COMPARATIVE HISTORICAL ANALYSIS"

As the self-selected label of a consciously distinctive approach, "comparative historical analysis" is a product of the mid- to late 1970s.[2] The lead figure in this development was Theda Skocpol.

She gave the phrase currency as a label for the blend of practices, and ways of thinking about those practices, that she crafted in the work that led up to her 1979 book *States and Social Revolutions*. While drawing significantly on other scholars, Skocpol combined and reshaped the ideas and exemplars that they offered. However, rather than proclaiming its novelty, Skocpol presented "comparative historical analysis" as having "a long and distinguished pedigree" going back to canonized figures such as Alexis de Tocqueville (Skocpol 1979, 36). The approach as it has developed in recent decades is indebted to her, not only with regard to its name, practices, and methodological self-reflections, but also for its self-image regarding how it stands in relation to the intellectual past.

This image is well expressed by the brief positioning sketch with which Mahoney and Rueschemeyer open their introduction to *Comparative Historical Analysis in the Social Sciences*. This sketch has two key elements. First, it asserts the "long and distinguished history" of their approach: Comparative historical analysis is portrayed as central to the work of "the founders of modern social science" (the named exemplars here are Adam Smith, de Tocqueville, and Marx), and as retaining "a leading position" when "social science began to organize itself into separate disciplines in the early twentieth century" (the exemplars here are Otto Hintze, Max Weber, and Marc Bloch). Second, it offers a subsequent trajectory of decline and revival: Comparative historical analysis is portrayed as entering relative "eclipse" by the mid-twentieth century, to the point of being threatened with "permanent decline," but that "neglect" has given way in "recent decades" to "a dramatic reemergence" in which "this mode of investigation has reasserted itself at the center of today's social sciences" (Mahoney and Rueschemeyer 2003b, 3).

As with many sketches of the intellectual past offered by social scientists advancing their contemporary agendas, this sketch offers an image that is somewhat simplistic. Comparative historical analysis is dubiously aggrandized by its narration as the revival of a classic tradition peopled by a few European intellectuals. This narration provides one recent strand of American social science with illustrious predecessors, while bypassing inquiry into how the practices and aims of the contemporary approach might differ from those of the European figures invoked, or whether other past figures and developments, perhaps even some American ones, might not be more relevant for understanding its intellectual roots. Although Mahoney and Rueschemeyer favor a narrow vision of comparative historical analysis when distinguishing it from other approaches within contemporary comparative social science, when sketching predecessors their vision jumps over major differences. Exploring the genealogy of their approach with the same sensitivity for distinctiveness that they apply in dealing with the present yields a different sort of history.

Mahoney and Rueschemeyer's sketch overlooks a wide wave of mid-nineteenth-century conversations that articulated and implemented the belief that a combination of cross-societal comparison and broad historical perspective is the best approach to social science.[3] Exemplified in the diverse work of such European figures as Auguste Comte, Sir Henry Maine, and Johann Bluntschli, these conversations diffused to America, where they had a vital impact on the shape the social sciences assumed during the expansion and transformation of the American academy in the last three decades of the nineteenth century. Telling histories and making comparisons were not, of course, wholly new activities at this time, but the participants in these conversations saw themselves as practicing new, more scientific *methods* of pursuing them. They spoke with pride of their "comparative method," their "historical method," or their "comparative and historical method." They believed, moreover, that methodological advance was producing major intellectual progress. The English scholar Edward Freeman, who coined "comparative politics" as a name for the field of inquiry applying the "Comparative Method" to matters political, exemplified this excited belief. His lectures on the field opened with a ringing declaration: "The establishment of the Comparative Method of study has been the greatest intellectual achievement of our time. It has carried light and order into whole branches of human knowledge which before were shrouded in darkness and confusion" (Freeman 1873, 1). Such discussions formed a key background to the Ph.D. training in "historical and political science" that the new Johns Hopkins University began to offer in the late 1870s. For Woodrow Wilson, one of that program's first graduates, the dominance of the "comparative and historical" method was, as we saw in our epigraph, a given.[4]

Among this wave of figures seeking to combine cross-societal comparison with a broad historical perspective, there was, however, significant diversity. For present purposes, two broad lines of approach may be usefully distinguished. On the one hand, evolutionary positivists, such as Herbert Spencer, took natural science as an epistemological model. Taking all societies—from any time and place—as their domain of study, they constructed general types, distinguished evolutionary stages, and sought natural laws of social evolution considered as a progressive whole. In contrast, developmental historicists, such as Maine, held a more distinctly humanistic conception of comparative and historical studies. Tending to limit the range of their research, they crafted synthetic narratives of the origin, diffusion, and development of institutions across selected groups of historically interconnected societies. This developmental perspective often, in turn, provided background for practically oriented comparative evaluations of contemporary institutions within such a group of societies. It was just this blend of cross-societal historical synthesis and practical evaluation that characterized Wilson's *The State*.

Evolutionary positivism and developmental historicism both diffused from Europe to take solid root in late-nineteenth-century American intellectual life. As such they offer a basic starting point for understanding how subsequent shifts have successively remade comparative inquiry in America. Around the turn of the twentieth century, challenges to these two approaches gained support on both sides of the Atlantic, but the specific agendas that grew at their expense varied. In America the broad trend up into the 1930s was away from cross-societal syntheses—charged with being premature at best and lacking adequate factual support—toward primary research with narrower horizons. Rather than seeking to synthesize such a diverse range of human social experience, new agendas in America carved that experience up into pieces, each to be made the object of its own field of detailed empirical inquiry. For example, where historical and practical inquiry into politics had earlier intertwined in a single conversation, there now emerged two increasingly separate conversations: "historians" studying the past for its own sake, and "political scientists" pursuing practically minded studies of present-day issues of governance (Adcock 2003a). In another fragmentation, "anthropology" and "sociology" became increasingly distinct endeavors as scholars turned away from the search for stages and natural laws of social evolution considered as a progressive whole. No longer taken as an early stage in a schema of progress, "primitive" societies were instead to be sympathetically observed in extended detail by anthropologists, while many sociologists took the social problems and tensions of industrialized society to demarcate their own distinctive field of detailed empirical study.[5]

The decline of developmental historicism and evolutionary positivism was accompanied by shifts in the practice and conception of comparative and historical method(s). Where the two earlier conversations approached comparative and historical endeavors as intertwined, the turn of the century witnessed several examples of the fraying of this intertwining. Thus, among political scientists, those who persisted in comparative endeavors increasingly focused on the present day: The developing subfield of "comparative government" was to offer a far less expansive historical vision than had Wilson's *The State*. Another example of this fraying was found in anthropology, where Franz Boas reconceptualized the "comparative method" of evolutionary positivism not as a counterpart but as a contrast to the "historical method." Treating the former as burdened by fallacies, Boas (1973 [1896]) endorsed the latter as a proper basis for the detailed primary studies of a narrower scope that he and his students were to make a new orthodoxy for American anthropologists.

A different line of movement away from evolutionary positivism was, however, to have a larger import for the long-term fate of cross-societal inquiry in America. The turn of the century saw the beginning of a remaking of positivist social science. Although the belief that natural science provides a model for all scientific inquiry would persist, the content of that model was changing. Nineteenth-century positivists had presupposed the existence of natural laws of social progress when they sought to weld comparative and historical findings together into synthetic schemes. For positivists in the new century, however, explicit notions of "progress" would come to appear laden with subjective meaning and values in a fashion inappropriate to the conceptual structure of rigorous science. In need of a new basis on which to construct knowledge, positivists would increasingly look to the observation and statistical analysis of correlations as a foundation for properly "scientific" social science. An important role inaugurating this transition was played by Franklin Giddings of Columbia University.[6] His *Principles of Sociology* presented the comparative and historical methods as applying a single logic, that of the "method of concomitant variations": both were said to center on the "systematic observation of coherences among phenomena," with "comparative method" focusing on coherences "distributed in space" and "historical method" on coherences "through periods of time." This portrayal was accompanied by the suggestion that these methods "may become precise when they can become statistical" (1896, 64). In succeeding years, as Giddings learned of Galton and Pearson's work pioneering the tools of correlational analysis, his belief in the potential of statistical work deepened. He would come to acclaim the "statistical method" as "an inestimably valuable form of the comparative and historical methods" that promised to "bring our knowledge of society up to standards of thoroughness and precision comparable to the results attained by any natural science" (1904, 175–76).

Giddings' work was a forerunner of a set of epistemological changes that gained momentum over the next generation as social science advocates for the new statistical techniques grew in number and promoted a new image of "scientific method." We can label this shift as the rise of modernism, where "modernism" denotes, as it does in the history of art or architecture, a novel, distinctively twentieth-century perspective.[7] For the idea of a break from the nineteenth century that this label implies, the appeal to the "method of concomitant variations" made by Giddings is especially noteworthy. In this appeal Giddings drew on the account "Of the Four Methods of Experimental Inquiry," in John Stuart Mill's *System of Logic* (1865 [1843]). But in using one of these methods as a model for the logical structure of social scientific inquiries, Giddings made a major departure, for Mill had held that none of the methods was a satisfactory model for social science.[8] Novel in 1896, the belief that a logical reconstruction of experimental inquiry can, and should, provide a model for all scientific inquiry was to become commonly accepted among interwar expositors of scientific method. As already evident with Giddings, this belief developed intertwined with the argument that, when experimental inquiry itself cannot be pursued, the best approximation to the "scientific" kind of knowledge that it models is offered by statistical analysis.

The blend of belief and argument offered by social science proponents of this new view of scientific method was, however, far from sweeping all before it in the interwar years. Much of the empirical thrust that marked American social science up into the 1930s was worked out through the burgeoning of largely qualitative case-study and field research, perhaps most notably associated with the "Chicago School." Many practitioners in these traditions found the threat posed by the modernist vision to their self-image as scientists unconvincing. The threat was more pressing, however, for the few scholars still pursuing projects of cross-societal inquiry. Lacking the credentials to "rigor" that case study and fieldwork practitioners could locate in the careful design and practice of primary data gathering, they reacted to new views of scientific method in either of two ways:[9] 1) rejection in favor of views reminiscent of the nineteenth century; 2) endorsement combined with efforts to bring their comparative endeavor up to modernist standards. These two were not, however, to remain the only responses in the decades ahead.

When we turn from the interwar to the post–World War II period, we find another shift of terrain. As the aftermath of World War II unfolded into the cold war and European decolonization, cross-societal studies acquired attention among American social scientists to an extent they had not enjoyed for decades. High student interest mixed with generous government and foundation funding in the 1950s and 1960s to fuel a burgeoning wave of such studies. These circumstances alone, however, do not account for the confident "scientific" self-understanding that dominated this wave of inquiry. This self-understanding extended beyond the growing large 'n' statistical tradition, exemplified by such projects as *A Cross-Polity Survey* (Banks and Textor 1963) and the *World Handbook of Political and Social Indicators* (Russett et al. 1964). It also permeated studies largely or entirely qualitative in character and studying a small number of societies, or even just one, in a cross-societal perspective. Scientific confidence here drew on a third response to the view of science promoted by modernist epistemology. This response blended partial endorsement with partial reconfiguration. It accepted the belief that a reconstructed logic of experiments could and should provide the model for all scientific inquiry. But, the promotion of statistical analysis that had accompanied this belief was supplanted by arguments holding that, at least under current conditions in the social sciences, non-statistical studies could also constitute cutting-edge exemplars of "science."

A leading role in shaping this reconfigured variant of modernism was played by Talcott Parsons. He combined a sweeping image of the evolution of social science, reconstructions of the work of selected earlier scholars, and a specific line of argument as to how non-statistical, cross-societal inquiry could constitute rigorous science. The image of convergence was central to his project. Its use extended beyond his famous vision of a modern social theory born out of a turn-of-the-century convergence between grand European traditions (Parsons 1937). It also framed an ideal of social science in which refined theory and empirical research come together as mutually supportive partners. Parsons singled out the "broad comparative treatment of total social systems and of large-scale societies" as leading the way toward this convergence (1954a, 12–13).[10] In doing so, he offered a noteworthy framing of the logic of Weber's comparative sociology of religion:

> [B]y the use of the comparative method on the broadest scale, Weber was carrying on *empirical* research which came closer to the logic of the crucial experiment than was the case for the work of almost any of the "empirical" sociologists whose coverage of the supposedly important facts of an empirical field was often much more "adequate" than his. The essential point is that the very breadth of the range Weber covered gave him, since he had a fruitful conceptual scheme, the opportunity to *select out* what for him were the *theoretically crucial* considerations of fact. (1954a, 15–16, italics in original)

This framing incorporates several key moves characteristic of the reconfigured modernist stance that Parsons helped to formulate and promulgate. First, it is accepted that an idealized logic of experimental inquiry provides the epistemological model against which to assess social science practices. Second, it is contended that qualitative cross-societal inquiry can achieve the standards of this model as well or better than alternative approaches. This is combined with a not-so-subtle hint that other approaches, caught in a narrow empiricist interpretation of how to pursue this model, can lose sight of what is really interesting. Third, it is held that scientific success rests here upon the use of a conceptual scheme that focuses attention onto the factors most crucial for the building of theory. In sum, while endorsing much of the view of science that the statistical tradition had crafted in connection with its promotion of new techniques, this stance reconfigures that view by holding that its conception of scientific rigor can also be achieved via, and indeed even requires, the crafting and use of a carefully refined, general theoretical scheme.

The overlaps and divergences between Parsons and the statistical tradition outline the main varieties of the modernist self-understandings that dominated the post–World War II wave of cross-societal inquiry. The shared epistemological standpoint of these understandings did not end debates over method; but it channeled them into contention around how best to produce knowledge of a modernist form that was presupposed to be the "scientific" ideal. Expressions of dissent from the ascendant modernism of the 1950s and 1960s can be found in the work of some individuals (for example, Mills 1959; Moore 1958), but it was only in the 1970s that such dissent would develop into shared new agendas within comparative studies. Those agendas were, however, far from being of one piece: Although some would chart a path beyond modernism, others domesticated earlier lines of dissent into the more contained endeavor of adding new options to the menu of modernist inquiry.

COMPARISON, HISTORY, AND THE PURSUIT OF THE "GENERAL" IN POST-PARSONIAN SOCIAL SCIENCE

> The golden age (or perhaps it was only the brass) of the social sciences when, whatever the differences in theoretical positions and empirical claims, the basic goal of the enterprise was universally agreed upon—to find out the dynamics of collective life and alter them in desired directions—has clearly passed.
> —*Clifford Geertz* (1983, 34)

The leading agendas of comparative inquiry in the 1950s and 1960s testify to the ascendance of modernist social science, as variously interpreted by proponents of statistical analysis and by scholars emphasizing refined theorizing as a source of rigor. Viewed against this background of contained contention, studies from the 1970s appear marked by new departures in two different directions. Some scholars rejected the modernist standpoint: a shift exemplified by the rejection of the "experimental science" model in the opening essay of Geertz's *Interpretation of Cultures* (1973a, 5). Rejection of that model, and of the belief in the methodological unity of the natural and social sciences it embodied, was a basic starting point for the endeavor of interpretive social science,[11] articulated perhaps most influentially by Geertz. Other new departures were marked, in contrast, by their continuing reliance upon a modernist standpoint. Pioneers of new modernist approaches—such as Skocpol (1979) for comparative historical analysis and Popkin (1979) for rational choice—crafted novel ways to pursue knowledge with the same basic epistemological form as that sought by the mainstream of prior decades. Alongside these departures, the cross-national statistical tradition held its ground, though losing some of the excitement it had held in the 1960s. However, the Parsonian agenda of studies conducted in the framework of a refined theoretical scheme of systems and functions declined noticeably. This panorama of comparative inquiry moving into its post-Parsonian period offers us a context of intellectual legacies and contentions against which to explicate the agenda of comparative historical analysis and to explore the contrasting, interpretive approach to comparative and historical social science.

Modernist Epistemology and Comparative Historical Analysis

In setting out to explicate comparative historical analysis,[12] we should be wary of claims about its qualities that, while they might do important rhetorical work for proponents of the approach, do not capture relevant distinctions. Proponents recur, for example, to the claim that this approach focuses on "big questions" of major substantive and normative importance. This claim is, of course, not novel. Indeed, along with the perhaps not unrelated claim of building on a grand European tradition, it parallels the identity that Parsons crafted for comparative inquiry in the post–World War II era. Some interpretive social scientists have, moreover, also found appeal in this self-image of asking big questions and perpetuating the heritage of Weber or other classic European figures. Such parallels may testify to the continuing contemporary vitality of certain strategies of legitimation among social scientists, but they help us little with the task at hand.

A more fruitful starting point is to spell out further the modernist epistemology that comparative historical analysis inherits. Earlier I spotlighted some moments in the genealogy of modernism in American social science: emphasizing the rise of new correlation-based statistical tools, the adoption of ideal reconstructions of experimental inquiry as a model for all scientific inquiry, and the later crafting of a variant of modernism open to the merits of qualitative inquiry. Modernist epistemology grew out of, and remains rooted in, the first two of these developments. Their interplay supported a new interpretation of statistical and experimental inquiry as sharing a single underlying logic: a logic that in turn came to be widely treated as *the* logic of all scientific inquiry. This logic is embodied in the now-familiar methodological language in which talk of "controlled experiments" and "control" groups passes over into talk of "statistical controls" and "controlling for confounding variables." As this logic/language was extended to analyze practices beyond those with reference to which it originated—as, for example, when qualitative cross-societal studies came to be interpreted as approximations to a "crucial experiment" or as setting up "controlled comparisons"—it carried with it the presupposition that such studies, if they are "scientific," must by definition seek to construct knowledge with a modernist form.

What are the characteristic traits of this modernist form of knowledge? First, it is built upon a certain way of interpreting the world: Reality as experienced is mentally carved up into conceptually isolated factors, which are, in turn, conceived of as potentially standing in various possible relationships with one another.[13] Second, knowledge construction is taken to center around the formulation and evaluation of propositions characterizing these relationships (their existence, type, or size, and often also their "causal" direction). Third, generalization—that is, the pursuit of knowledge specifically "general" in character—is taken to denote the subset of this endeavor in which those propositions characterize relationships as recurring across some portion of time and space. Among comparative social scientists working from a modernist standpoint, such generalization has often been equated specifically with formulating and evaluating claims about relationships that are characterized as recurring across more than one macro-societal unit.

Within comparative inquiry, the endeavor to produce knowledge claims with a modernist form has proven compatible with a range of views on further issues. Most important for this chapter, it has not entailed the choice of any specific approach—formal-theoretical, statistical, or qualitative—with which to pursue the endeavor. The agenda of comparative historical analysis arises out of its proponents' efforts, beginning in the 1970s, to articulate and defend a particular stance on this issue. Using criteria that presuppose a modernist goal, they propound a largely, often entirely, qualitative approach comparing the development, during specified periods of their histories, of a limited number of cases framed in macro-societal terms. Comparative historical analysts do not reject a statistical approach outright, but they do reject the belief that statistical techniques, and the large number of cases they require, are necessary prerequisites for the rigorous construction of modernist knowledge. Finally, and crucially, they also reject the belief that a single, refined theoretical scheme is necessary, or even helpful, to the pursuit of this goal.

In support of this stance, comparative historical analysts have sought to specify just how their approach might achieve the rigor that others contend necessitates statistical analysis or a refined theoretical scheme. Attention focused first on the claim that comparative historical analysts could— by careful selection of which societies, and which periods of those societies' histories, to compare —set up inductive analyses that approximate the logic of the methods of agreement and differ- ence as laid out in John Stuart Mill's account of experimental inquiry. More recently, however, proponents of the approach have come to recognize that this claim has serious problems. The volume edited by Mahoney and Rueschemeyer (2003a) testifies to a more recent proliferation of appeals to other techniques—such as Boolean algebra/QCA,[14] fuzzy set logic, Bayesian analysis, pattern matching, process tracing, and causal narrative—as potential sources of rigor. While shar- ing a concern to identify techniques to play this role, comparative historical analysts currently diverge in the details of their responses such that it is problematic to identify the approach today with any single technique or set of techniques.

Commonalities among comparative historical analysts can be better located in their use of two sets of conceptual contrasts, which together construct a common identity for their approach out of a shared sense of what it is not. The rejection of single, refined theoretical schemes offers a revealing entry point here. This rejection served initially to position comparative historical analy- sis in contrast to Parsonian functionalism, which offered not only a contending approach to com- parative social science more generally, but one that also used qualitative, macro-societal, comparative history. Though that tradition is now quite defunct, comparative historical analysts have continued to emphasize this rejection, recently turning to it as a basis on which to contrast their approach with the rising rational choice tradition. While thus emphasizing their rejection of approaches that rely on a single, refined theoretical scheme, comparative historical analysts also insist that they are not atheoretical. They conceptualize their approach as occupying a sensible middle ground between two extremes: overambitious single theories on the one hand, and narrow empiricism on the other. This perceived middle ground involves "a pluralistic approach to theory that allows specific research questions and actual historical patterns to help shape the selection of appropriate analytic frameworks" (Mahoney and Rueschemeyer 2003b, 21). Although we might debate whether this center holds—in the sense that a philosophically satisfactory explication of it can be given—such a debate would be beside the point. The common identity of comparative historical analysts resides not in any extended account and defense of theoretical pluralism, but in a shared presupposition as to that stance's integrity and desirability.

A second set of conceptual contrasts cuts across much of the same terrain as the first, but runs along a somewhat different axis. Rational choice theory is again assigned to a role once filled by Parsonian functionalism: here, the role of an ambitious universalizing theory claiming to apply at all times and places. In conceptualizing this role, comparative historical analysts again pair it off with an opposite extreme and proceed to see their own approach as occupying a sensible middle ground. The opposite extreme—assigned to interpretive/area studies scholars—is portrayed as a particularizing approach uninterested in, or even hostile to, generalization in the modernist vein. The perceived middle ground here is then seen to lie in the pursuit of "mid-range" modernist propositions. This involves formulating and evaluating propositions about recurring relationships among factors, but doing so with the expectation that the range of this recurrence is limited by certain scope conditions. Belief in the distinctiveness and desirability of this variant of modernist social science is fundamental to the common identity of comparative historical analysts. It underpins the self-conception of their approach as one that is "historical" and sensitive to "context." Comparative historical analysts hold it to be ahistorical (and prima facie implausible) to seek or employ theory with a universal form, whether pitched at a macro, micro, or whatever level. This belief supports their practice of combining the modernist endeavor to formulate and evaluate generalizing propositions about recurring relationships with efforts to specify boundaries to that recurrence. For comparative historical analysts, it is these latter efforts that specifically mark out their approach as one that is sensitive to context.

To understand the agenda of comparative historical analysis, it is essential to recognize that its proponents view their approach as occupying a sensible middle ground. Such recognition need not, however, entail endorsement of this image or of the presuppositions upon which it is constructed. Thus, a Parsonian or a rational choice theorist may want to contend that, when push comes to shove, theoretical pluralism is just another take on the long-standing empiricist hostility to the necessary role that an explicit and internally coherent set of theoretical premises must play in any rigorous social science. On the other hand, a large 'n' statistical analyst may contend that mid-range "general" propositions, if they meet modernist standards, differ from "universal" propositions only in presentation, certain factors having been removed from the proposition itself and presented instead in the alternative form of scope conditions. Finally, for an interpretive social scientist, all such methodological contentiousness may appear as much bustle over little, so long as it offers only contained variations upon a modernist vision of social science's agenda.

Interpretive Social Science and the Pursuit of the "General"

The interpretive turn in American social science involved more of a departure than just asserting that the meaningful character of human action matters and merits central attention. This had, after all, been a basic belief of Parsons. Indeed, the modernist stance, in most, if perhaps not all, of its varieties is quite capable of bringing meanings within the reach of its analyses. In order to do so, it approaches meaningful human action in a particular way: Meanings are conceptually isolated from action and then categorized as occupying one position within a broader, abstractly conceived range of possible meanings. Actions are, in turn, understood in relation to a range of possible positions on a similarly isolated action factor. With this conceptual work accomplished, efforts to characterize relationships between positions on the meaning and action factors can begin. The kind of conceptual treatment of meanings that makes such efforts possible is elaborately exemplified in the categorization of possible "value-orientations" constructed by Talcott Parsons and Edward Shils (1951). But similar conceptual work takes place, albeit usually in less sophisticated and self-conscious forms, whenever social scientists seek to bring meanings within the reach of modernist analyses that establish and evaluate relationships between factors.

Interpretive social science stands in basic contrast to such analyses. Interpretivists diverge from modernist practices of knowledge construction at their most basic step: They are skeptical of the act of conceptually isolating factors, without which it is impossible to even formulate the propositions about recurring relationships to which modernists aspire. As an alternative starting point, interpretivists set out to grasp meaning and action together as parts of a complex, situated whole. They inquire into the making, remaking, and implications of meanings as a point of entry for gaining an understanding of such complexes. Their endeavor to interpret meanings involves attending, on the one hand, to the material, social, and cultural setting(s) of those whose meanings they are; and, on the other hand, to the actions through which these settings are made, remade, and sometimes transformed. For interpretive scholars, sensitivity to context involves following through a complex of meaning, setting, and action as it develops in a specific time and place. It is a conception of "context" that diverges markedly from that held by comparative historical analysts. No judgment in favor of one or the other is needed to recognize that, to an interpretive scholar, the claim that a work such as Skocpol's *States and Social Revolutions* is sensitive to context may appear confusing or even mistaken.

Interpretive social science is usually, and correctly, associated with situated efforts to understand the meaningful character that action has for those whose action it is: the characteristic question in such scholarship is, "What do, or did, these people believe themselves to be doing?" Interpretive scholars do not, however, all conceive of the character or purpose of these efforts in the same way. Efforts to understand particular viewpoints might, for example, be seen as an end in themselves, or they may be seen as serving a kind of political/moral engagement that centers on giving voice to marginalized, subaltern viewpoints. Alternatively, some scholars subsume efforts to understand particular viewpoints as an important, but not the only, component of an endeavor to fashion accounts that locate such viewpoints in a broader perspective. Geertz is specifically concerned with this last endeavor when he differentiates between experience-near and experience-distant concepts. In doing so, he does not seek to promote one type of concept over the other, but to explain that, in his efforts to understand concepts that are experience-near for those he studies, his larger goal is to grasp such concepts "well enough to place them in illuminating connection with experience-distant concepts theorists have fashioned to capture the general features of social life" (1983, 57–58).

Geertz's talk of the "general" here is far from tangential. It flags a concern that is basic to his scholarship and that makes his works prominent examples of a strand of interpretive social science marked off by its practitioners' endeavors to locate particular viewpoints in more general perspective. This strand encompasses, though it is not restricted to, interpretive studies that use macro-societal comparisons, such as Reinhard Bendix's *Kings or People* (1978) and several of Geertz's studies (1968; 1983, chapters 6, 8; 1995, chapter 2). The use of this form of comparison makes such works a significant point of reference for comparative historical analysts, who locate the distinctiveness of their own use of macro-societal comparison in terms of a focus on "macro-causal analysis" absent from the work of Bendix and Geertz (Skocpol and Somers 1980; Skocpol 1984). There is indeed a significant contrast here, and in revisiting it below I am not concerned to reject it, but to consider how it looks from another point of view. In reflecting on certain characteristics of the approach of Bendix and Geertz,[15] my aim is not, however, simply to further elucidate this contrast. By drawing out these characteristics, I also hope to illuminate more broadly two ways in which interpretive social scientists may employ a comparative and historical stance in order to locate particular viewpoints in more general perspective, regardless of whether or not they specifically deploy a macro-societal lens in doing so.

Comparative historical analysts draw on a number of presuppositions when, to contrast their approach with that of Geertz and Bendix, they emphasize their own concern with macro-causal analysis. First, they presuppose that there are such things as macro causes; second, that the action of these causes can be represented in the form of modernist propositions about recurring relationships; and, third, that such generalizing propositions can be both carefully formulated and thoroughly evaluated using their own, primarily qualitative approach. The macro-causal inquiry that rests upon these presuppositions treats cross-societal comparison as a way to identify and probe recurring relationships of coexistence or sequence between conceptually isolated macro factors. To anyone who doubts at least one of these presuppositions—which includes, but is not limited to, most interpretive social scientists—this use of comparison may seem misguided for any of a number of reasons. Which, if any, alternative uses of comparison are preferred will depend on the broader standpoint from which such criticism comes. Thus, for example, Charles Tilly (1997) has argued forcefully for redirecting comparative inquiry to focus on formulating and evaluating propositions about recurrent causal mechanisms at more micro levels. However, for interpretive social scientists concerned to construct general perspectives, the preference is, in contrast, for uses of comparison not framed by the notion of recurring connections that remains just as essential for Tilly's stance as it is for macro-causal analysis. To flesh out what this might involve we can turn to the works of Geertz and Bendix for examples of how comparison may be employed in connection with other conceptions of the "general."

A key practice of Geertz and Bendix in this regard pivots around the notion of a problem (a task, a challenge, etc.). By conceptualizing problems with some degree of abstraction, they construct frameworks in which developments in different societies are presented and compared as alternative responses to a common problem. They conceptualize some problems in universal terms. Thus, for example, both conceptualize legitimation as a challenge facing the political authorities in all societies (Bendix 1978, 16–18, 60; Geertz 1983, 142–43). Other problems are conceptualized as general to a certain setting. Thus, for example, in framing a comparative study of authority under kings, Bendix (1978, 4, 7) conceptualizes a "tension between central authority and local government" that he sees as general to the setting of monarchical rule. At whatever level of abstraction it is pitched, Bendix and Geertz wield their problem-centered practice in a way that is distinctively open to contingency. The comparisons they construct with it tend to highlight the range and diversity of particular responses to any one "general" problem. This emphasis is supported by a characteristic way of deploying historical perspective. Bendix and Geertz treat actors as responding to general problems within specific historical contexts, where legacies of the past shape their perceptions, both of the problem itself and of possible responses to it. Such contextual attention to the views of actors is essential here, since for an interpretivist, an account that presents actors as responding to a "general" problem will only be persuasive to the extent that its abstract formulation of that problem can also be unpacked as a redescription of some "particular" concrete problem(s) that those actors see themselves as responding to.

Attending to the use of problems as a conceptual hinge around which comparative and historical contrasts come together within a general perspective illuminates much about the approach of Geertz and Bendix. It has broader ramifications also. By recognizing that their problem-centered practice exemplifies one distinctive way of engaging the general, we are put in a position to explore the broader potential of this mode of engagement for interpretive social science by following up on resemblances to this practice in the work of other interpretivists. Such an exploration is beyond the scope of this chapter, but some hints are possible. We might, for example, turn to Susanne Rudolph's brief for the comparative study of state formation in Asia and note that a conceptualization of a general problem underpins her suggestion as to how the history of North Indian states might be compared with that of China. She suggests, in particular, a comparative history framed around responses to the problem of how to sustain the integration of an empire and its component regional kingdoms (Rudolph 1987, 731). Turning to the domain of more contemporary policy-oriented studies, we might reflect on how the problem-centered practice explored in this chapter relates to the concept of a dilemma that Mark Bevir, Rod Rhodes, and Patrick Weller advocate using in the interpretive study of comparative governance (2003a, 2003b).

A focus on problems is not, however, the only way in which interpretive social scientists may employ a comparative and historical stance in pursuit of a general perspective. A second way of proceeding in this regard is exemplified in Bendix's (1978) and Geertz's (1968) works when they engage with the general as conceived in the form of a "general" movement of history. Here, their initial conceptual move incorporates temporality and change: They envision a process in which certain beliefs and practices originate and then diffuse across societies, changing those societies and, as they do so, undergoing further development themselves. In envisioning such a process, Bendix and Geertz do not assume that the changes that they bring together as moments in a "general" movement all have the same exact shape or converge on an identical outcome. The goal is, as Bendix puts it, to combine "an understanding of a country's historical particularity with its participation in a general movement of history" (1978, 4). Rather than envisioning a general movement of history sweeping away particularities, both scholars envision it as interacting with particularities in each society so as to produce a variety of outcomes. As we saw earlier with regard to problems, a general conception again serves here to help illuminate how legacies of the past play into the shape of developments in different societies.

Some interpretive scholars might, upon considering examples of the ways in which Geertz (1968) and Bendix (1978) envision general historical movements, worry that they perpetuate a long-standing tendency to privilege Europe as an origin point of such movements. This tendency should not, however, be seen as inherent in the notion of a general historical movement. Other possibilities are evident, for example, in Benedict Anderson's *Imagined Communities* (1991), where a general movement of nationalism is envisioned, with European developments appearing not as the origin point but as an intermediary moment of a historical movement that starts in the Americas and ends in Asia. Interpretive scholars may also explore how contemporary accounts of "globalization" link the particular and the general. Alongside some broad similarities in form to Bendix's and Geertz's general historical movements, such accounts are also different enough in their details as to perhaps suggest how this mode of engaging the general might take onboard more complex, multi-origin, and multidirectional notions of "movement."

CONCLUSION

The strand of interpretive social science that I have used Bendix and Geertz to illuminate parallels comparative historical analysis insofar as both approaches employ a comparative and historical stance in pursuit of a general perspective. The approaches differ, however, in whether or not, in doing so, they pursue the "general" in the one specific form—recurring relationships between conceptually isolated factors—that the epistemological standpoint that I have labeled "modernist" sees as central to the agenda of social science. In this chapter I have genealogically situated comparative historical analysis as one variation upon the modernist agenda; and I have, in turn, highlighted some beliefs that bring interpretive scholars together in contrast to that agenda. There is, however, much diversity among interpretive social scientists, and I have been concerned here primarily with explicating one specific strand of interpretive work: comparative and historical scholarship that, while diverging from modernist epistemology, does endeavor to construct and employ general perspectives. My explication has emphasized that the "general" can, in addition to the form of a general relationship, also be conceived of in the form of a general problem, or of a general movement of history.

Because I have drawn the notions of a general problem and a general movement of history from the work of interpretive scholars, it should be evident that both notions may be used to frame engagements with the general that are compatible with interpretive commitments. This does not entail the conclusion, however, that any use of either of these two notions necessitates adherence to an interpretive approach. A broad survey of the ways that these notions have been used would turn up applications by a range of approaches—from developmental historicism to Parsonian functionalism. Such a survey would make possible nuanced consideration of which approaches may use one or both of these notions without conflicting with their commitments, and of how the practices associated with each notion can shift in accord with other aspects of various approaches. Such a survey and consideration reaches well beyond the scope of this chapter, but given my concern with comparative historical analysis, some brief reflections in relation to that one approach do seem called for.

Comparative historical analysts are, by their own reckoning, centrally committed to the pursuit of modernist knowledge claims about recurring relationships—and, specifically, about recurring macro-causal relationships. Can commitment to this one type of generalizing effort be pursued alongside engagement with the "general" as conceived in the form of a general problem or of a general historical movement? I do not see any reason why an appeal to a general problem need prove hard to combine with macro-causal analysis. Indeed, examples of such a combination can be found in some prominent works of comparative historical analysis. Thus, Ruth and David Collier, in their *Shaping the Political Arena* (1991), conceptualize a general problem of how to politically incorporate a rising labor movement, and then use this to frame a macro-causal effort to specify and evaluate propositions about recurring relationships that are suggested by patterns they discern in the variation of responses to this problem within Latin America.

It is, however, more problematic to try to combine the general conceived in the form of a general historical movement with the modernist macro-causal inquiry pursued by comparative historical analysts. Such inquiry employs cross-societal comparison primarily to identify and probe recurring relationships of coexistence or sequence between conceptually isolated macro factors. Such recurrences are, from a modernist standpoint, essential for causal analysis; but they carry weight in this regard only to the extent that the instances that make them up occur independently of one another. This independence stands in direct contrast to the conditions that make cross-societal comparison most useful when the general is pursued in the form of a general historical movement. Here, such comparison serves to help identify and characterize successive moments in the cross-societal diffusion and evolution of beliefs and practices. Cross-societal comparison is hence most effective precisely when developments in one society influence those in another. In sum, the conditions presupposed if cross-societal comparison is to serve modernist macro-causal analysis are directly at odds with those that make such comparisons most useful in recounting a general movement of history.

Although this may at first seem an all-too-abstract methodological point, it takes on added significance when we situate our reflection upon it historically. Our contemporary era is marked by a profusion of interpretations that situate the present as a period of unprecedented, and further deepening, cross-societal interaction of diverse forms involving diverse actors. To the extent that we credit such interpretations, we are pushed to query how far the vision of major changes as occurring at the level of "societies," and doing so independently on a society-by-society basis, remains a plausible ground on which to construct general perspectives about our contemporary world. For social scientists such as Tilly (1997) who remain committed to a modernist agenda, this situation offers compelling reasons why macro-causal analysis should be shelved in favor of searching for recurrent causal mechanisms at more micro levels of analysis. But, if endorsed by comparative historical analysts, such a response calls for a change in the character of their approach so substantial that it might be meaningfully said to bring it to an end. For interpretive social scientists who seek to construct general perspectives, the implications are, however, quite different. A belief that the contemporary world is marked by an increasingly complex web of global interactions calls for adjustments of approach here also, as I have earlier suggested with regard to how general "movements" of history are envisioned. But such shifts would be far from involving the jettisoning of any of the core commitments of an interpretive social science that employs a comparative and historical stance in pursuit of general perspectives.

NOTES

1. In characterizing a "genealogical" approach in this fashion, the exemplar I have most in mind is John Gunnell's *The Descent of Political Theory: The Genealogy of an American Vocation* (1993). While recognizing points of overlap with other proponents of genealogy, such as Foucault (1984), I would emphasize that, in my understanding, viewing a present approach genealogically does not in itself dictate any specific conclusion as to the merits of that approach. One might, in principle, recognize the contingency of an approach, explore and evaluate alternatives to it, and then choose, at the end of this process, to endorse it.

2. The phrase "comparative historical analysis" or close equivalents were used before the mid- to late 1970s. It was only then, however, that the phrase became specifically associated with one particular approach to comparative and historical social science. Previously it was used, when used at all, to refer to any of several such approaches, or to all such approaches. For examples of earlier usage, see Bendix (1968) and Flanigan and Fogelman (1971).

3. For detailed interpretations of most major figures and broad trends within this wave of conversations, see Bock (1956; 1974), Burrow (1966), and chapter 7 of Collini, Winch, and Burrow (1983). My brief sketch here is indebted to these scholars while also drawing on my ongoing dissertation work in this area.

4. For more detail on the dominance and diversity of comparative and historical method among American scholars of politics from the mid-nineteenth up into the early twentieth century, see Farr (2002).

5. This change within sociology is exemplified and promoted in Park and Burgess's *Introduction to the Science of Sociology* (1921), which was foundational for interwar "Chicago School" sociology. Park and Burgess see the history of sociology from Comte to their own era in terms of "the transformation of sociology from a philosophy of history to a science of society," the most recent stage of which consists in the new "period of investigation and research" in which sociologists are "more concerned with social problems than with social philosophy" (1921, 44).

6. On the key role of Giddings and his students William Ogburn and F. Stuart Chapin in the rise of an "objectivist" science of sociology centered on an agenda of statistical analysis, see Bannister (1987). See also D. Ross (1991, 428–48) on the widening influence of "instrumental positivism" in American sociology in the first three decades of the twentieth century.

7. The temporal scope of "modernism," as I use the term, parallels that of such phrases as "modern art" or "modernist literature," rather than the more expansive notions of "modernity" that take the Enlightenment, or even the scientific revolution, as their beginning point. For a wide-ranging exploration of "modernism" in this sense, tracking family resemblances across changes in math and science, through philosophy, into art and literature, see Everdell (1997).

8. For his views on Mill, see Giddings (1896, 54, 64–65). In the 1890s, Durkheim made a parallel departure in his *Rules of Sociological Method*. Like Giddings, Durkheim moved away from Mill to adopt the experiment as a logical model for social science. He also specifically took the "method of concomitant variations" as foundational in this regard (Durkheim 1938 [1895], chapter 6).

9. Examples of both responses are provided within the tradition of comparative work that continued throughout the interwar period at Yale. The first response is exemplified by Albert Keller, who completed the massive synthetic project begun by his mentor William Graham Sumner with the four volumes of the *Science of Society* (Sumner and Keller 1928). The second response is exemplified by George Murdock, who was Keller's student and, later, also a faculty member at Yale. Murdock directed the Cross-Cultural Survey begun in 1937. Conducted under the aegis of Yale's Institute of Human Relations, the survey was a major effort to gather, classify, and analyze a worldwide collection of data, which in 1949 became the better-known Human Relations Area Files project. Murdock's analyses of the data collected by these projects made him a pioneer of cross-national statistical research in American social science.

10. This second image of convergence embodied a specific, modernist conception of "theory" that became widespread in post–World War II social science. On this conception, see the chapter on "empirical theory" in Bernstein (1976).

11. As represented, for example, in Rabinow and Sullivan (1979). For recent reflections on some of the variety of forms of this broad endeavor, see Scott and Keates (2001).

12. My characterization of comparative historical analysis in the next few pages is based on Skocpol (1979, 33–40), Skocpol and Somers (1980), Skocpol (1984), Collier (1998), and Mahoney and Rueschemeyer (2003b).

13. I have spoken of "factors" rather than "variables" in an effort to present modernist epistemology in a way that encompasses a range of scholars—qualitative as well as quantitative—not all of whom specifically favor "variables" talk. If we also recognize flexibility in the manner in which these scholars construct relationships between factors—by focusing, for example, on "configurational" groupings of factors rather than on individual factors considered one by one—both the "case-oriented" qualitative and the "variable-oriented" quantitative approaches contrasted by Ragin (1987) can be recognized as variations upon the modernist standpoint I am sketching.

14. Boolean algebra forms the basis for the specific computational technique of "qualitative comparative analysis" (QCA). QCA has recently been adapted to also incorporate the use of fuzzy set logic (fsQCA). On QCA and fsQCA, see Ragin (2000b) and the Web site www.fsqca.com.

15. In treating Bendix and Geertz together as exemplars of a shared approach, I am following a grouping initially made not by these scholars themselves, but by comparative historical analysts. As such, it does skate over some issues within interpretivism—such as the role of documentary sources versus ethnographic observation in the understanding of particular viewpoints—that might in other contexts lead interpretivists to contrast Bendix and Geertz. My main purpose here, however, is to explicate how interpretive social scientists construct and employ "general" perspectives, and for this purpose, the grouping seems productive, as I hope my discussion illustrates.

CHAPTER 4

NEITHER RIGOROUS NOR OBJECTIVE?

Interrogating Criteria for Knowledge
Claims in Interpretive Science

Dvora Yanow

> "Just now we are an objective people," *The Times* wrote in . . . 1851. . . .
> "We want to place everything we can lay our hands on
> under glass cases, and to stare our fill."
> The word denoted the modern sense of detachment, both
> physical and conceptual, of the self from an object-world . . .
> —*Timothy Mitchell* (1991, 19–20)

> [O]bjectivity grew more important as a scientific ideal and also as a practical necessity.
> . . . [P]rofessional social scientists finally based their claims to competence in social
> analysis on the authority conferred by scientific methods and attitudes. The value of
> objectivity was emphasized constantly in both training and professional practice, until it
> occupied a very special place in the professional ethos. . . . [T]he tension between reform
> and knowledge reappeared as a conflict between advocacy and objectivity.
> —*Mary O. Furner* (1975, 322–23)

> With few exceptions, most social researchers,
> whether they be radical, conservative, or totally apolitical,
> try to convince their readers that their research has been objective.
> —*Stephen Cole* (1976, 224)

Interpretive research is often held to evidentiary standards—criteria, such as rigor or objectivity, that concern the character of material brought in support of a claim——that it cannot possibly achieve, for two reasons. For one, these expectations often reflect substantive misunderstandings of the character of the criteria themselves, definitionally, as well as of what interpretive research entails—what its own procedures are. At the same time, they hold interpretive research to criteria that contradict its own fundamental presuppositions concerning social realities and their "knowability." That is, research deriving from interpretive ontological and epistemological presuppositions is often held accountable to criteria that developed over time out of positivist presuppositions, which interpretive philosophies long ago rejected as inapplicable to human sciences.

As Mitchell shows in the first epigraph, although they have been treated as universals, these terms are, in fact, historically situated.

Aside from their substantive dimension, however, the charges are put to rhetorical use in a gate-keeping fashion designed and/or intended to control the terms of debate and to regulate what research is going to be accorded the status of science.[1] In methodological writings, methods statements, and reviews of interpretive work, a constricted sense of what it means to be rigorous and of what constitutes objectivity is being used to dismiss interpretive work as non-trustworthy and as nonscientific (see C. Lynch 2005). The second epigraph captures a part of this move.

The substantive charges may be engaged by showing either that they misunderstand the character of the research in question or that the criteria themselves are definitionally problematic. But substantive explications on their own cannot dislodge rhetorical arguments from their position of power and control: rhetorical arguments have to be engaged at the level of rhetoric. Their rhetorical character becomes clearer, however, when the substantive misunderstandings and mischaracterizations are brought into focus, and the rhetorical arguments can then be more fully engaged. This chapter explores three types of substantive defense against charges that interpretive research is neither rigorous nor objective—definitional-terminological, procedural, and philosophical-conceptual—returning to the rhetorical element at the end.

I wish to parse the terms rigor and objectivity not as they have been set out by philosophers, logicians, or methodologists but, rather, as they are treated or enacted in methods texts and debates. In their adoption from philosophical sources and implementation in research practices and instructional tools, these two hallmarks of the scientific standing of a research project have taken on ever more restricted (and restrictive) denotations and connotations as the discussion has become ever more focused on tools and techniques (in what has been referred to as "methodism") at a growing remove from characteristics of knowledge processes (and, hence, of "science"). Although there is much to be learned from the philosophy of natural-physical science and social science, in the context of this analysis an inductive approach that starts from social science practice and common usage is of greater utility. It is common usage that arms the debate carried out in the pages of textbooks and methods courses, rather than the more idealized, philosophical discussion, found in philosophy of (social) science books and courses, of principles developed in abstraction from the practices of the physical and natural sciences that are thought to apply both to them and to the human sciences.[2] And it is practice that informs the procedural rebuttal. Knowing how rigor and objectivity are used in common discourse—as seen, for example, in methods textbooks and dictionary definitions—grounds the discussion in ways that starting from philosophy cannot; and such grounding in practice contexts is important because these practices are what enact and perpetuate epistemic communities and their boundaries. Parsing the meanings-in-use reveals the ways in which interpretive work is, in fact, rigorous in a philosophical sense and how its subjectivity need not be seen as non- or anti-scientific.

PARSING RIGOR AND OBJECTIVITY

One of the challenges that interpretivist researchers (and qualitative ones as well) often encounter is the claim that their scholarship is neither rigorous nor objective. Such charges include faulting interpretive researchers for lacking fully formulated hypotheses before beginning field research, hypotheses that identify dependent and independent variables, posit their relationship, and indicate how they are to be measured—in short, all the elements that characterize a prospectus for a quantitative research project.[3] The "goodness" of hypotheses, variables, measurement, and other techniques and tools rests, conceptually, on questions of rigor and objectivity. The two terms exist in a conceptually prior relationship to reliability and validity: the way the latter are operationalized in methods discussions presumes that the data in question have been generated through rigorous and objective research procedures.

Interpretive researchers have countered that such expectations misunderstand their research procedures. A counterargument can be prosecuted, then, in procedural terms, stipulating what it is that interpretive research actually does. But in the process of detailing such an argument—exploring the criteria for being scientific, for example, including, specifically, for generating trustworthy evidence—it becomes clear that, definitionally and terminologically, the two terms are used in various methods textbooks and arguments to mean different things, which makes it difficult to articulate a substantive-procedural defense. Definitionally, interpretive research *is* rigorous, if by that one means the rigor of logic, drawing on a broader understanding of "rigor" than the restricted one that emerges from methodological positivism and textbook "common sense."

Moreover, there is the matter of philosophical differences undergirding the charges. These come from a position that assumes that there is only one way of demonstrating rigor and objectivity—and that is the one informed by positivist ontological and epistemological presuppositions. Philosophically, interpretive work rejects the possibility that a human sciences researcher *can* stand outside the subject of study, which renders positivist-inflected objectivity an inapplicable criterion (although methodological interpretivists could do a better job of making these presuppositions explicit and showing how interpretive methods relate to them, the project of this book).

On Rigor

What does it mean for research to be conducted in a rigorous fashion? Most textbooks do not begin with either definitional statements or philosophical discussions. One typically finds a sentence in the opening section, where the hallmarks of scientific work are enumerated, that simply posits that science is "rigorous." At times, the sentence may suggest one or more antonyms, although they are rarely positioned specifically in opposition to "rigor" itself. Rather, direct, explicit contrast is commonly made between scientific work and metaphysical explanations or casual observation (such as in the statement, "Indeed, the distinctive characteristic that sets social science apart from casual observation . . . ," which appears in King, Keohane, and Verba [1994, 6]).

Absent textbook definitions or classroom discussion, the reader is left to infer what rigor means from the broader context of the textbook's treatment of what constitutes science, as distinct from unscientific ways of knowing. The term is often taken to be a procedural descriptor, characterizing how the researcher goes about accessing (gathering, collecting, generating) and/or analyzing data. Because "rigor" typically occurs in the descriptive textbook phrase "systematic and rigorous," a common inference is that rigorous means "stepwise," inflexible, unyielding. Its opposite, again by inference rather than explicit textbook definition or discussion, is unsystematic, without plan, and chaotic. Formal definitions corroborate this inferred, common sense. "Rigor" means:

1. Strictness or severity (*The American Heritage Dictionary of the English Language*, 4th ed. 2000)[4]
1. Rigidity; stiffness (*Webster's Revised Unabridged Dictionary* 1998)
5. Exactness without allowance, deviation, or indulgence; strictness (*Webster's* 1998)

These give the etymological derivation as "stiff," from the Latin.[5]

Its textbook meaning is adumbrated in procedural distinctions, such as in discussions of "the scientific method," typically introduced shortly after the initial sections on the attributes of science.

The scientific method—it is always named with the definite article, itself implying a procedural unity across all sciences—has traditionally been presented as having five or so steps, as in the following composite example:

1. Identify research problem/
   state hypothesis
2. Prepare research design
3. Collect data
   Observation/measurement/sampling
4. Process/analyze data
5. Draw conclusion(s)/findings[6]

The staged sequencing of steps—they are sometimes presented as a flow chart—enacts the definitional meanings of rigor. Its graphic design suggests that the scientific research process is, indeed, exacting, even rigid, without allowance for deviation. As research based on participant-observation, conversational interviewing, and/or the close reading of documents is not "stiff" and stepwise in this way—a point discussed below—it is, ipso facto, "not rigorous." And the common, rather inchoate textbook descriptions of qualitative and interpretive methods that are found in general textbooks corroborate, by inference, their status as the opposite of rigid, strict, "rigorous" research (see Schwartz-Shea and Yanow 2002).

A defense of interpretive methods on procedural grounds against charges of non-rigor might draw on its definition as meaning "exacting" but look even more to its companion term—systematic—to stake a claim. When interpretive research is done well (meaning according to its own established and accepted procedures), it is, in point of fact, carefully designed and crafted and systematically carried out. Thickly descriptive work is rich in its detail and rigorous in its argumentation. "Interpretive" does not mean "impressionistic." The systematicity, however, is different from that of quantitative methods; interpretive methods have their own procedural criteria. Part of this difference lies in the characteristics that make many interpretive research methods incapable of being rigorous in the other senses of that term—of unyielding and inflexible stiffness. This is especially the case when interacting with people, but the point holds for documentary evidence as well.

The researcher involved in conversational interviewing and observing-participating cannot adhere "rigidly" to a research protocol. Such situations do entail more ambiguities and fewer controls over others' acts (precisely what survey questionnaires are intended to eliminate or surmount). This would hold for any research orientation, such as phenomenologically influenced ones, that accords others the full range of human agency, including legitimating others' local knowledge—their own expertise in their own lived experience. Not only can human responses not be controlled, but the interpretive researcher does not seek to control them, beyond pointing conversations toward explicating that which the researcher is assaying to understand. Document-based research has similar characteristics in that the researcher does not and cannot know ahead of time what she will find in the text. Any single discovery might set the research trajectory off onto another path—to a different set of documents, a different archive, a different geographic location, a different research question. The research has, then, an improvisational quality.

However, much as it is a misunderstanding of improvisational theater to imagine that the whole of a performance is made up on the spot, so is it a misunderstanding of interpretive research to think that procedures are spontaneously generated. Instead, in the same way that improv company members engage in a tremendous amount of preparation in learning their theatrical craft, rehearsing a repertoire of patterns of action and interaction and response for months before going on stage, so, too, interpretive researchers learn the action repertoires of their research craft: how to select "good" research sites—places where they will be more likely to observe what it is that they want to see; how to identify "good" documentary locations or "good" people to chat with; how to "topic talk" with them; and so on. One develops a repertoire of reading, conversational, and/or participatory "moves"—ways of framing a question, of following a lead, of responding to what has just been said, of joining a group engaged in an ongoing conversation (see, e.g., Walsh 2004), of getting oneself invited to meetings, and so on. As with theater, research "improvisation" consists of drawing on that repertoire as the specific situation requires, in the context of one's research role and in keeping with one's personal values: responding appropriately to what someone has just said ("Yes, I had to find a back-alley abortion quack"), to an invitation just delivered ("Hey, let's go shoot some dope"), to a heretofore obscure reference ("File note to myself: Dig up Kerry's Congressional testimony").[7]

Such replies and acts cannot be scripted in advance, as one cannot anticipate what others will say or do; and so, as Katz (2004, 7) notes, this lack of a preestablished research protocol with detailed time- or place-based steps is "not a sign of the [researcher's] regrettable incapacity to plan research." Rather, it means that interpretive research cannot be "strict," without deviation from such a plan; but being adaptive to human response does not mean that the research cannot be, or is not, systematic. This inability to script the research ahead of time relates to another characteristic of interpretive research: the fact that one typically does not start out with developed hypotheses, which one then tests with "field" data, but rather allows one's hypotheses or explanations to emerge from extended immersion in the data themselves. Interpretive research rarely proceeds from a formalized hypothesis because the researcher does not know ahead of time what meaning(s) will be found, expecting them to be generated through (participant-) observing and/or conversational interviewing and/or the close reading of documents. The general "hypotheses"—"hunches" would be a term more characteristic of interpretive procedures—carried by the researcher into the data-generating phase or site are more likely to concern ways in which meaning(s) is (are) communicated than to be specific ideas about things to be explained in the setting under study. Generalization, too, is more likely to concern communicative, meaning-making processes than substantive rules or principles. Interpretive researchers are quite serious about letting the data "speak for themselves," resisting the impetus to rush to premature judgment and analytic closure, and this limits their ability to prespecify operative variables and their measurement. This is the idea that Glaser and Strauss (1967) sought to capture in "grounded theory" see also Locke 2001; Strauss and Corbin 1990). Its very unscriptedness makes writing proposals for interpretive research problematic for granting agencies and committees that see science as always being hypothesis driven.

Modes of analyzing interpretive data are less "improvisational," but here, another characteristic makes it appear on the surface as if they lack systematicity: It can be difficult to make explicit how one goes about making sense of one's data. Formal semiotic analysis is perhaps the most stepwise, procedurally, of all interpretive analytic methods: The steps entailed in setting up semiotic squares, clusters, or chains can be articulated clearly (see, e.g., Feldman 1995; Gottdiener and Lagopoulos 1986). But even here, discovering the connective tissue of meaning often comes as much from a flash of insight as it does from following any elaborated system of rules. As Feldman (1995, 30) emphasizes, it would be more accurate to see the analytic device (e.g., the semiotic square) as a tool for stimulating thought than as itself producing that thought (unlike, for instance, a regression analysis in which the computer generates the findings in the form of the coefficients and R squared).

The most exacting descriptions of forms of interpretive analysis describe a kind of indwelling with one's data: whether using index cards held in the hand or large sheets of paper tacked to the walls, the process entails reading and rereading and reading again—musing, in an abductive[8] way (Locke, Golden-Biddle, and Feldman 2004)—until, in the light of prior knowledge of the theoretical literature or the empirical data, or both, something makes sense in a new way. The experience feels like parts of a thousand-piece jigsaw puzzle suddenly fitting together; but it is no easier to describe how the brain "processes" those pieces of cardboard and makes sense of their concavities than it is to describe how one "sees" metaphoric or categorical or semiotic meaning—we still cannot see inside the black box that is the brain at work making judgments or imagining analytic associations (something not unique to interpretive analysis).[9]

A different way of engaging the "non-rigorous" charge is philosophical. What the procedural focus misses is the philosophical context in which rigor has a particular, technical meaning: that of logic and its deliberations concerning the character of truth.[10] In classical logic, rigor concerns the precision of syntax. In this context, rigor would be defined more formally as containing premises from which conclusions may be derived logically—that is, in which the structural syntax of a set of statements is sufficiently precise as to produce a cogent argument, where "cogent" means well-grounded, convincing, persuasively relevant, appealing to the intellect or to powers of reasoning (see *The American Heritage Dictionary of the English Language*, 4th ed. 2000; *Webster's Revised Unabridged Dictionary* 1998; *Dictionary of the History of Ideas* 2003).[11]

In this sense, then, research is rigorous, definitionally, to the extent that its arguments are constructed logically—that is, where conclusions are adequately supported by the evidence that is presented, such that the reader is persuaded of the cogency of the argument.[12] There is nothing inherent in the character of interpretive research that would prevent it from being rigorous in this sense. Indeed, the rigorousness of the presentation of the argument—its analytic rigor—is one of the criteria against which interpretive research is judged within its own epistemic communities.[13]

This understanding of rigor links to one of the central issues in interpretive methodology, the character of the text produced by the researcher reporting on her analysis. There is a perception that ethnographic and other interpretive scholarship should be undertaken only by "good" writers. Good interpretive writing can be as engaging as good fiction, sometimes with turns of phrase as beautiful as those found in some poetry.[14] But one might say the same about good political theory. What readers are responding to, I believe, is the character of the expositional logic, along with the "music" of the text (word choice, phrasing, sentence rhythm, and so on). Here is analytic rigor: the crafting of a sound argument, in which observations build upon observations, sentences upon sentences, paragraphs and sections upon themselves, until the logic of the whole compels reason to say, Ah, yes, this makes sense as an explanation! And the choice of words and their combinations in sentences, and the combinations of sentences in paragraphs, contribute to this meaning-making process: As Aristotle suggested long ago, rhetorical persuasion appeals to the feelings and to one's sense of rightness in addition to one's sense of logic.[15] Such an understanding of rigor supports the contention in interpretive methodologies that writing itself is an integral part of the researcher's analytic method (see, e.g., Richardson 1990).

On Objectivity

> We commonly do not remember that it is, after all, always the first person that is speaking. . . . I, on my side, require of every writer, first or last, a simple and sincere account of his own life, and not merely what he has heard of other men's lives; some such account as he would send to his kindred from a distant land; for if he has lived sincerely, it must have been in a distant land to me.
> —*Henry David Thoreau,* Walden (1939 [1854], 14)

Thoreau, noting that "[i]n most books, the *I*, or first person, is omitted," asked his readers' indulgence as he followed a different course of action. Over 150 years ago, he put his finger on a tension that befuddles social scientific writing today: To signal "objectivity," the writer uses all manner of circumlocutions that enable her getting around the presence of the first person I (as this writer has just now done); whereas, especially in field research, what is being reported is nothing less than the researcher's I/eye account of what was learned there (including from others' accounts of their own lives). The presence of reflexivity in interpretive methods focuses on the central fact of the researcher herself living "in a distant land" and the ways in which that lived experience shapes her interpretation of others' interpretations of their own metaphorically distant lands. The "I" whose absence was intended to communicate impersonal objectivity is increasingly de rigueur on the written pages of interpretive science, for important philosophical reasons, alluded to by Thoreau.

How does this touted subjectivity comport with scientific demands for objectivity? As with the previous discussion, an explication of the wide range of meanings with which "objective" is used helps clarify the arguments. As with the discussion of rigor, I will explore its entailments from the perspective of its common usage in textbooks and in research practices, rather than starting from philosophical definitions and discussions.[16] These meanings-in-use treat objectivity as an attribute of two different aspects of research practice: as a characteristic of evidence or as a characteristic of the process through which the evidence is produced. The latter includes the character of the person(s) producing the evidence, that is, the acts and attitudes of the researcher and/or the actors in the research setting. The intertwining of evidence and persons blurs ontological and epistemological objectivities, as objectivity refers variously to physical and cognitive-emotional distances, which meanings themselves become intertwined in discussions and debates. Once again, definitional-terminological and procedural stipulations are mutually implicating, and both are enacted in the philosophical distinctions. I take them up in this order.

Definitional Matters

A Focus on Evidence. The most basic dictionary definition draws on the simple linguistic structure of the word, as "of or pertaining to an object" (first definition, *Webster's Revised Unabridged Dictionary* 1998). The antonym invoked by the term's linguistic structure, "subjective," carries a similar basic definition; yet "of or pertaining to a subject" immediately introduces persons into the picture. In a research context, "subjective" evidence, research, or meaning would pertain to either the researcher or a situational actor (that is, it would be "of"—in the sense of "belonging" to, or deriving from—that subject). Who, then, is the creator of meaning that pertains to an object, and, more crucially, what is his relationship to that meaning?

Webster's second definition points toward an answer. It constitutes a metaphoric extension of the basic linguistic construction:

> 2. (Metaph.) Of or pertaining to an object; contained in, or having the nature or position of, an object; outward; external; extrinsic;—an epithet applied to whatever is *exterior to the mind*, or which is simply *an object of thought or feeling* . . . [emphasis added].

This presumes a human actor (or her mind) apperceiving something exterior to her, to which she has directed thought or feeling. There is no reflexivity here: the object is not describing itself or something of its creation; and the human actor is physically, cognitively, and emotionally separate from the object in question.

A Focus on Persons and Processes. The separation between mind and act becomes clear in looking at objectivity's synonyms, all of which characterize various forms of "impersonality":

- detached
- distanced (held at arm's length)
- dispassionate; without emotion
- neutral; without personal judgment
- factual
- value free
- impartial; not taking sides, treating all alike
- fair
- without bias; free from prior conceptions

The conceptual connotations of its antonym are "personal" and "involved" (not distant), "interpreted" (not factual), "biased" (not impartial), "distorted," "prejudiced." Textbook discussions recapitulate these denotations and connotations. To take but one example—there are myriad—and this one from an older anthropology-sociology text oriented toward field research, objective means "to state the characteristics of objects and events as they exist and not to interpret, evaluate, and prejudge them" (Spradley and McCurdy 1972, 13). Hence, to be objective means to reason based on facts, rather than feelings, following the laws of logic, rather than emotion—even though logic is itself an activity of mind and, hence, unobservable.

The synonyms as listed suggest a continuum between physical distance, at the one end, and cognitive and/or emotional distance at the other—between, in other words, body and mind, ontological "objectivity" and epistemological "objectivity." Ontological objectivity posits a reality external, physically, to the observer: The body is separate from the object in question, detached, distanced, held at arm's length. Epistemological objectivity—the cognizant, emoting mind that is separate from the object in question—is captured in the second set of synonyms: dispassionate, without emotion, neutral, value free, impartial, fair, unbiased. "Objectivity," in general methods discussion, posits a link between physicality (bodily presence and proximity) and ways of knowing, including affect, experience, and prior knowledge (as in prejudgment), such that physically distancing the researcher's body from the research situation can and will disengage his cognition and empathy from generating or shaping understanding. In this view, being physically outside of what one is studying enables standing as an epistemological outsider: It is humanly possible (in this view) to know one's subject of study—to observe it, and to describe and make sense of those observations—without influence of any sort on either observation or description (in oral or written narrative). Perceptions of objective reality are completely autonomous from the observing subject, independent from the observing mind—and the act of observing (e.g., the presence of the observer) does not affect that which is being observed.[17]

Several methodological terms bespeak an ontological objectivity. "Data" are "that which are given"; researchers "discover" evidence and produce research "findings." These terms suggest that the patterns "unearthed" through research processes were always there, waiting to be found, rather than constructed by naming. A sense of ontological objectivity underlies what Eugene Webb and his colleagues originally called "unobtrusive measures" of social phenomena (Webb et al. 1981 [1966]): indicators of social status that a researcher could observe and interpret without having to ask questions of those who had created or used them, "found objects," as it were, whose meaning rested entirely in their physical existence.[18]

There is another dimension at play here, however, concerning the reactivity of the objects' users to the way research questions might be articulated (or to any other nonverbal aspect of the interaction with the researcher). What was "unobtrusive" was the researcher's presence; and, indeed, in the second edition the beginning of the book title was changed to *Nonreactive Measures* (Webb et al. 1981 [1966]). The language of nonreactivity emerges from the concern for epistemological objectivity—the extent to which something about the observer's "person" might affect those being observed such that they would alter their acts or behavior or words.[19] In survey research this is articulated as the concern for "interviewer effects": that something in the way a question is asked will affect the response, leading to skewed data (e.g., answers that reflect what the respondent thinks the researcher wants to hear or what is socially acceptable to say); and survey design assays to control for such effects. Terms and concepts such as these rest on a view of science and its theories as holding a mirror up to nature (Rorty 1979).

The Philosophical Critique

Interpretive philosophies reject the human possibility of such social scientific mirroring. In their view, social realities and human knowledge of them are created by human actors through our actions and interactions. We are not and cannot be outside of them: Researchers see and name patterns in other human actions because we are human ourselves, and it is our humanity, first and foremost, that enables such empathetic recognition of human reaction to human experience. But that means that these patterns exist as much in our habits and practices of sight itself (not only as individuals, but as members of communities of knowing and practice, as well; see below) as in what we are seeing. Theories, in this view, do not mirror the social world; they constitute interpretations of it. Being at a physical remove, then, from what we study does not guarantee cognitive-emotional separateness. In fact, interpretive research challenges the idea that understanding is even possible from a position of cognitive externality. Even those forms of research done at something of a physical remove from their topics of study—historical or database analysis—rely, at one point or another, on human understanding to get "inside" the research subject (history, in a projected imagining; databases, in the original survey interaction; see McHenry, chapter 10, this volume, on a related point). And some forms of research, such as space analysis, draw on the researcher's kinesthetic experience, itself requiring physical presence (see chapter 20, this volume).

Central to this argument about the impossibility of physical-cognitive detachment are certain human physical limitations. One is that we do not observe without "filtering" what we see. We categorize as we go along, sorting the multitude of sensorial stimuli into conceptual "mailboxes" that focus and shape attention selectively.[20] Without prior knowledge, without some prior "conceptual boxes" (Kuhn 1970) or "toeholds of the mind" (Vickers, personal communication, January 1981), we could not organize all the stimuli that come at our senses; we would, in a cognitive sense, be "blind" to them.[21] A phenomenological approach suggests that all humans, including researchers, perceive the world of their experiences through "lenses" composed over time from various elements: education and training; lived experience, work/professional, kinesthetic, and otherwise; familial, communal, societal background; personal psychology, temperament, and so forth. Although these lenses may be expanded, researchers' observations may still be shaped, unconsciously, by their theories and other perspectives.[22] As science studies also show, analysis is inherently a shaping of "reality," rather than an exact point-for-point recapitulation of sense data.

Time poses another physical constraint. Even if human sense organs were physically capable of attending to every detail in an observed setting, researchers typically do not have sufficient time to note all these stimuli. We not only see much more than we can take in; we lack the time to read it all or to write it all down.[23]

Research in nonverbal communication suggests yet another dimension of the impossibility of detached knowledge. Although survey researchers continue to refine survey instruments in an effort to minimize interviewer effects, if not to eliminate them outright,[24] research in nonverbal communication, including paralanguage (e.g., tone of voice), personal decor (such as dress), and facial and other gestures suggests that the researcher's mere presence potentially can affect the process of the research—and what's more, the researcher may not know in what ways it has.[25]

The preceding definitional discussion points to the philosophical context for objectivity's concern with what constitutes the mind and whether things exist external to it or are "products" of it. Here is where object (evidence), act/process (its creation), and actor (its creators) begin to be intertwined. The philosophical debate distinguishes between "the real"—what exists in nature, and is therefore understood as having its own reality external to the human mind—and "the ideal"—what exists in or is created by an individual mind in its thoughts or experiences.[26] "Subjective," in this sense, refers to the latter, and "objective" means that which has existence independent of experience or thought.[27] By extension, then, "objective" refers to something that is based on observable phenomena (bracketing the matter of the act of observing) rather than on unobservable thoughts or mind.[28] Following on the real-ideal dichotomy, if something subjective exists only in the mind, it is not real; it is illusory, deriving from one's own consciousness.

The pejorative sense of subjective emerges, then, not only from its connotations of bias but from its connections with the personal, the emotional, and the "non-real." A subjective response is not just (seen as) idiosyncratic and/or potentially unfair due to unfounded prejudice; it is associated with a phenomenological preoccupation with the self, with one's own consciousness and emotional states: a moody self-absorption divorced from engagement with the "real" (objective) world.[29] If a response is emotional, it is non- or irrational; if it does not lie in the realm of the rational, it is, ipso facto, not scientific.

The presumed fact-value dichotomy, seen clearly in public policy studies, draws on this real-ideal distinction, in which values are seen as belonging to the realm of the nonrational and ideal. Since its development in the 1970s, the policy analysis field has been concerned that analysts' values would taint their analyses. The critique of epistemological objectivity also raised questions about policy "objects": were policies themselves value-free? Early on, the possibility of the value-free policy analyst (and hence analysis) was rejected. The initial solution proposed that analysts identify their biases, make them explicit, set them aside, and go about their work. In this vein, they could then separate out policy facts from policy values and avoid attending to the value context within which directly observable acts, objects, and language are situated. The critical rejoinder argued that the so-called fact-value dichotomy was erroneous. From an interpretive perspective, such separation, whether within the analyst or of the policies themselves, is an impossibility, as Hawkesworth (1988, 58–72) pointed out: It institutionalizes facts and values as separate realms, on the one hand treating values as if they were objects that could be separated from their creators-believers and externalized, and on the other, not problematizing the constitution of facts.[30]

The Procedural Defense: Trustworthy Research and Faithful Knowing

The charge that interpretive research is not objective emerges also from conceptions of its procedures that reflect a lack of awareness or misperceptions of what such methods actually involve. One of these is the concern that the researcher is generating idiosyncratically personal knowledge that cannot possibly be trustworthy. The concern is for the outcomes of this perceived idiosyncrasy, including, but not limited to, its potential for bias: Personal knowledge is seen not as neutral to the subject of study, but rather as potentially prejudiced against persons or settings (e.g., for reasons of political ideology or race-ethnicity or class or gender, and so on), resulting in analytic findings that cannot be relied upon as the basis for subsequent research or action (such as policy or administrative actions). Such a view emerges, in particular, concerning the epistemological subjectivity of the person or persons acting as "guide(s)" to knowledge in the situation under study, as well as of the researcher, subjectivities that seemingly appear to be so individualistic as to be idiosyncratic. Part of what detailed descriptions of interpretive methods delineate is the very procedural systematicities that transcend individual idiosyncracies.

Several interpretive research practices intentionally and self-consciously address the oblique, partial sight that characterizes all human observation. (This also forms part of the systematic and reflexive character of the research.) These include the purposive selection of texts, respondents, and/or observational posts that map across times, locations, experiences, and/or interpretive (or epistemic) communities. This comparative "mapping" of views includes "snowball sampling"— not really sampling at all,[31] in which those interviewed are asked to suggest others—as well as a heightened attention to the possibility that the network of personal ties that such recommendations often draw on may create patches of silent or silenced voices in data sources, requiring additional purposive selections to fill these gaps. Similar techniques are used in identifying and selecting documents. The image of the wagon train circling the campfire, each wagon having its own vantage point on the fire (J. Murphy 1980), or the Picassoesque portrait that enables the physically impossible view of the back of the ears and the side of the nose and the front of the forehead all at the same time capture this research ideal.[32]

Single case field research is often comparative in this way, implicitly, if not formally, as is historical analysis, and such comparative vision constrains idiosyncrasy, both of researcher and of "guide" (whether human or textual). The multiple observational "points" encountered and engaged in texts, in activities and events, and in interviews provide endless opportunities for comparison of ideas from different vantages, checking idiosyncratic interpretation. Furthermore, the researcher almost always carries some expectations for what constitutes "normal" or antici-pated activity, often based on what she is accustomed to in her own place or time, and this, too, serves as a comparative anchor. Additional comparison emerges in juggling the familiarity that grows through prolonged exposure with the "stranger-ness" of new encounters. Comparison is also brought to bear through extended observation over time, as well as in attending to the ways in which times of day, days of the week, and seasons of the year influence variability in human activity in the setting. Historical and contemporary text-based research have their own parallels to these comparative elements.

With respect to research "guides," the researcher is constantly alert to wildly idiosyncratic or even mildly divergent sense making by situational actors (including in their textual half-lives as reported meanings linger on long after the researcher has left the field), looking instead, in cases of collective sense making, to discern collective, public meanings rather than individual, private ones. (The obvious exception is studies of key individuals in which personal response is central to the analysis.) Moreover, interpretive researchers rely on a sort of "projective imagination" (Kemper 1990, 95), drawing on personal experiences in all their dimensions (kinesthetic, affective, cogni-tive, and so on) as proxy for understanding others, contextualized by intersubjective knowing, in a comparative context.[33]

Anthropological literature and lore has long been full of cautions about taking this to what was perceived as an extreme: losing the "stranger" aspect of epistemological distance and crossing over—"going native"—in a way that is more projective identification than projective imagina-tion. Much of that discussion has been framed in terms of the costs to objectivity of "losing oneself" in or among the community one is studying, an argument fully rooted in methodological positivism. (The insider/native-outsider distinction is also no longer sounded as much because many more "natives" are now studying their own cultures; see Shehata, chapter 13, this volume.) From an interpretive perspective, by contrast, what is perceived to be lost in this process is the epistemological purchase (rather than any scientific "purity") enabled by prolonging one's "estrangement" from the situation under study such that acts, objects, terms, and events continue to appear unusual or different, thereby continuing to be subjects for inquiry rather than fading into to the world of taken-for-granted commonplaces.[34] Contemporary thinking focuses more on the relative advantages and disadvantages to researcher learning of each phase of the stranger-familiar balance as it changes over time, which also includes a more self-conscious and explicit reflexivity on the processes and changes entailed.[35]

A sociology of the professions view brings into focus a different sort of check on researcher idiosyncrasy. The presumed isolated independence of individual response ignores both professional-social and methodological intersubjectivity developed within academic practitioner communities. Researchers' analyses are contextualized, shaped, and constrained by various aspects of academic practices. The attitude of doubt—the "testability" of traditional research, enacted within interpretive research in researcher reflexivity—is embedded in review processes of various sorts that serve as scientific controls and corrections on more obvious "non-objective" practices (everything from faulty logic, to the [in]appropriateness of methods to research questions, to the ethical malpractice of falsifying data). An extended "apprenticeship" in a doctoral program socializes the new scientist to an epistemic and practice community. These aspects of professional practice instantiate control mechanisms enacted at various times and in various forms: critiques of the researcher's ideas and writing that begin during coursework and continue through conference paper and journal publication vetting and promotion and tenure reviews. Additional review mechanisms are built into interpretive research processes (see Schwartz-Shea, chapter 5, this volume), all of them forms of methodological intersubjectivity designed to ensure that the researcher is not "proving" what he already "knows." Situating research within or in relation to an interpretive community in these ways serves to delimit idiosyncratic interpretations.[36]

This procedural point relates to a philosophical point concerning the certainty of truth claims with regard to the meanings of events, acts, terms, and so on. The character of that certainty lies in the dual sense in which Kuhn (1970; see also Kuhn 1977) used the term "paradigm" in his analysis of scientific practices to designate both the framing of knowledge about or approach to a scientific problem, and the community of scientists sharing that frame. The same intertwined duality is implied in understandings of the "hermeneutic circle" as meaning both the process of interpreting texts and the communal character of that process: that modes of interpreting (or "making") meaning are developed among a group of people—an epistemic community of interpreters, a circle—acting and interacting together in that process, thereby coming to share in the understanding of a problem.

Phenomenological analysis suggests that the two are inseparable: the process by which a problem comes to be framed is the same process that creates the community (of scientists or other interpreters, variously termed an interpretive community, epistemic community, discourse community, community of meaning, community of practice or of practitioners, and so on) that frames it in that way. It is a process of creating intersubjective understandings, in which members come to share a set of practices, knowledge about those practices, knowledge about one another, about how to address new situations, and so on. The resulting interpretive or epistemic community shares a frame, a view of how to approach and interpret new situations (see, e.g., the description of this process in P. Berger and Luckmann 1966, part II; see also Latour 1987).

In this sense, knowing and understanding are subjective processes—understood from the viewpoint of the subject acting (and interacting) in and interpreting the situation; they are not "objective" processes, understood from outside, at a remove, through sense-based observation alone. Phenomenologists and hermeneutic scholars alike emphasize the context specificity of knowledge: It is created *in* a situation, and it is *of* that situation. Knowledge and practice intertwine: Social realities are constructed by the actors in those situations, acting together—that is, the knowing and understanding are also *inter*subjective; and the meanings of these acts can only be understood through interpretation.

The certainty of knowledge about the social world being observed and judgments about the "goodness" of that knowledge rest within the community that has established procedural rules for generating interpretations. There is no external authority—no king, no religious leader, no deity, no universal and independent set of rules—to which one can appeal for verification. There is only the collective sense making of the interpretive community—whether scholars or citizens—observing, interpreting, theorizing, and reporting about these observations in the rhetorical style developed and accepted by that community (see Bruner 1990, Fish 1980, Geertz 1983). This selfsame collective sense making of a research community regulates the interpretive practices of its members, constraining researcher idiosyncrasy and, by implication, ethics.

Aside from apprehension concerning researcher idiosyncrasy, objectivity charges also touch on questions of factual (in)accuracy, reflecting misunderstandings concerning the social character of many "facts." The implied logic is that a lack of physical-cognitive distance leads to bias (the ontological-epistemological link) and, hence, to inaccuracy. This line of reasoning is often used to argue for the mathematicization of observational data as a way of protecting their analysis from such bias. Objectivity, in other words, is equated with numbers (and numbers with facts and truth).

One rejoinder to this argument rests on the questionable facticity and accuracy of measuring and counting. Languages are full of terms now taken to be "objective facts" that have become so through a process of social consensus, over time. Most English speakers, for example, use such indices as "foot," "yard," and "inch" without attending to their (long buried) social origins, much as few people are cognizant of the arbitrary fixing of Greenwich Mean Time.[37] American assumptions concerning the accuracy of vote counts or census tallies were shattered by the 2000 presidential election snafus in Florida or the 1990 and 2000 undercounts of the homeless and other groups. Even voting machines allow room for counting errors, although many presume that machines are more exacting than people.

In reducing words and other forms of evidence to numbers that can be analyzed by computers, statistical analysis appears to eliminate the human factor that is seen as the source of idiosyncrasy, bias, and inaccuracy, such that a second researcher can (in this view) run the same database and/or the same numbers through the computer and come up with an identical analysis. One can, however, certainly point to the many junctures along the words-to-numbers road at which human judgment is operative. A more interesting project is to enumerate the many circumstances in which research on human action *requires* human judgment, such that without it, both accessed data and data analysis may be seriously flawed. In such instances, the more accurate analysis and judgment of human action is likely to come from "subjective" human "readings" of other humans' lives than from "objective" counting. Ironically, in this way, interpretive research restores humans to the centrality from which the Copernican revolution, at the dawn of European science, displaced them. The challenge is to show how that centrality of human judgment can be scientific—systematic and subject to reflection—without the pejorative meanings that attach to subjectivity: that "subjectivity" need be neither idiosyncratic, and certainly not intentionally prejudiced, nor inaccurate.[38]

Given, then, that interpretive researchers are and can be neither physically nor cognitively-emotionally external to what they are studying, but rather are (or claim to get) epistemically "inside" the subject of study and present "social reality" from the perspective of situational members, it seems critical to be able to assess the relationship between members' knowing and the researcher's knowing, including the latter's active role in constructing and shaping the narrative that (re)presents that social reality. The researcher is not a transparent conduit and without analytic agency herself. Indeed, imagining that transparent conduction were even possible would place research back in the realm of "objective truth" generated by a physically and affectively-cognitively external researcher and of theories mirroring reality.

The notion of a "faithful" reading, as an aspect of researcher reflexivity, suggests a way of addressing both sides of this interaction. As Merttens (2004, 27) has written, "An interpretation, to be useful or sensible, rests upon a notion of faithfulness to the text." In the context of interpretive research, this would mean, on the one hand, a faithfulness to texts and text analogues—an engagement with written and spoken texts and narratives, acts, and physical artifacts that grapples with their intended and experienced meanings. This is, after all, what the field researcher implicitly promises on negotiating entry; and it is certainly what situational members look for in reading research reports (and why so-called member checks are suggested as a way of ascertaining that the researcher got it "right").[39] On the other hand, it suggests a faithfulness to the researcher's own theoretical and analytic agency, as well. The interpretation is, in other words, both experientially faithful, seeing and portraying the situation as situational actors (including, at times, the researcher as participant) understood it, and analytically faithful, in keeping with the researcher's theoretical and conceptual "priors" and insights.

Two processes are at play here. One is an "intertextuality," both literal and figurative. Much in the same way that actual texts interpolate phrases and ideas from other texts, the interpretive researcher reads analytically "across" the experienced reality of the situation under study (whether rendered in literal texts or, analogously, in acts and/or physical artifacts, in historical or current ones), drawing on prior knowledge of terms and concepts and theories that may usefully inform that reading. Analyses of organizational or policy metaphors (Edelman 1977, Schon 1979, Yanow 1992a), for example, typically do not find their actors invoking metaphor-talk to describe their language use.[40] It is the researchers themselves who introduce "metaphor" as an analytic device, useful in its ability to enlighten an understanding of the lived experience being described. One may say, then, that the interpretation is faithful not only to the words or acts themselves, on the surface of meaning, but also to the "interior" meanings embedded in words and acts that inform and contextualize them, as felt by situational actors and by the researcher.

The other aspect emerges especially when actor and researcher "faiths" collide. Here is a reading of the research "text"—whether literal text or the social realities being rendered and studied as if they were texts—much in the manner of seeing and reading Wittgenstein's "duck-rabbit."[41] As described by Kuhn (1970, 62–65, and chapter 10, esp. 114–15; see also Law and Lodge 1984, 47–48), with reference also to Bruner and Postman's work, the interpretive process is like a gestalt switch: the insight comes in an "Aha!" moment and, once having seen the thing in that new way, the researcher not only cannot undo that sight, he very often cannot retrace his steps and reproduce how the insight came about and how the "switch" took place. The researcher is then faced with explicating, analogously, concerning the situation under study, how those who live with or in it daily see it as a duck, whereas the researcher sees both duck and rabbit. The sense that a topic has been rendered "faithfully" typically comes when the researcher can make a case for both with analytic rigor.

Lastly, whereas "objectivity" requires that anything knowable be capable of being stated explicitly, interpretive research opens the door to knowledge of things whose enactors cannot articulate them in words but that are observable in their acts or in physical artifacts of their creation and/or usage. Logical positivism, intersecting with the analytic philosophy of Bertrand Russell and the early writings of Ludwig Wittgenstein, argued for an unambiguous correlation between language and its referents, insisting that all knowledge must be rational—the product of reason (rather than emotion) and capable of being made explicit.[42] Michael Polanyi, however, argued that there is a realm of knowability aside from the explicit: "[W]e can know more than we can tell," he wrote (1966, 4; see also M. Polanyi and Prosch 1975).[43] In shifting the focus of study to human meaning, dropping the insistence on the transparent correlation between words and their signifiers, and recognizing the possibility of accessing meanings through their artifactual representations, interpretive science opens to the social reality of tacit knowledge. Ethnomethodological analyses (see, e.g., Charon 1985) illustrate this, for example, in showing how a conversation clearly understandable to its participants is full of "missing" pieces that make it opaque to an onlooker (the stranger-"outsider") who does not share their frame of reference. Participants make sense of situations, events, interactions, and so on by relying on tacit knowledge that is commonly not articulated but is nonetheless shared among members of an interpretive community (think of a family, for instance, or a workgroup; Law and Lodge 1984, 102, provide an example). Studying —indeed, accepting the social reality of—something that is not "directly observable" is, perhaps, the ultimate challenge to objectivity as it is commonly used, whereas interpretive research treats it as part of the social realities it seeks to understand and analyze.

CONCLUDING THOUGHTS: RHETORICAL USES OF ARGUMENTATION

Physical-spatial and cognitive-emotional objectivities intertwine. The positivism-inflected assumption is that physical distance removes social realities from the sphere of the observer's influence: To be physically outside of what is being studied—to hold it at arm's length—is to be not caught up in it cognitively or emotionally; to know without being involved is, metaphorically, to be physically detached. The presumptive ability to "distance" oneself from one's emotions is founded on the Cartesian mind-body duality, with mind as a machine that reasons (much as the Artificial Intelligence field would have it in replicating human reasoning processes in computer programs, especially in robotics) and emotions relegated to the body's netherworld. Neuroscientist Antonio Damasio argues for a more Spinoza-like view, that mind and body are the same substance, intertwining feeling and reason, and that feeling and emotion are central parts in the development of consciousness (see, e.g., Damasio 2001); G. Lakoff and Johnson (1999) argue that cognition is possible only because the mind is embodied. This suggests a new perspective on the blurring of personal life and researcher "distance" in interpretive research. Indeed, this formulation negates the possibility of detachment, the body of necessity dragging the mind along, whether proximate or distant with respect to the experience being studied.

It seems impossible today to conceive of the human sciences researcher standing outside of the context of his study, removed, distant—"objective"—in the mode of the white-coated lab experimentalist observing rats in a maze or cells in a petri dish—herself not constituting (constructing) the idea(s) of the social reality she is studying, if nothing else, through the creation and naming of categories that label and frame the study, thereby highlighting some elements and occluding others. Even non-interpretive social science appears to be coming closer to a different view, seen, perhaps, in reflecting on Charles Ragin's thoughtful description of "fuzzy sets" (2000a, 6–7). The fuzzy set researcher, Ragin says, by contrast with conventional variables analysis, needs "a good base of substantive knowledge" of the subject matter "and a solid grasp of its theoretical relevance"—why it "matters and how it should be assessed" (2000a 7). This is precisely what an interpretive researcher is after.

Yet I suspect that interpretive perspectives will continue to be denigrated and/or denied standing as science.[44] Unlike "reliability," "validity," and the like, neither rigor nor objectivity shows up, typically, in methods statements, whether in books or in research articles. Rare is the author who, in writing, makes such explicit argumentation as "What makes this research objective is my use of . . ." and rarer still the one who argues, "The research reported here is rigorous because. . . ." Yet those claims continue to be made by implication, through the rhetorical use of various elements of a research report: its structure (for example, the inclusion of a methods section), the delineation of particular methods, and discussions of the validity, reliability, generalizability, and so forth of the findings. Implicit in these statements are claims for the rigorousness—this chapter's third epigraph could as well have included this—and objectivity of the research. Although not argued for in methods statements, in their (perceived) absence rigor and objectivity are invoked by reviewers (of journal submissions, grant proposals, etc.), typically to undermine a piece of work that is seen as not adhering to some protocol. Seemingly anticipating such an attack, interpretive (or qualitative) researchers at times themselves mention the "subjectivity" of their findings, either with respect to views reported by "informants" or, less commonly, with respect to the researcher's own subjectivity, perhaps hoping to head it off.

Yet definitional-philosophical-procedural explication—all this interpretive rhetoric—has not held sway against methodological positivism's charges. The subject has been discussed at length, in different fields of thought, for over a century; and still, interpretive research is castigated for—in the accusers' eyes—not being rigorous or objective. That a substantive defense has not been successful suggests that its rhetorical character is what is compelling the debate and that a rhetorical analysis is what is required. What is at stake—what is the locus of fear—that enables these terms to retain their rhetorical power in the face of so much explication? And why would interpretive researchers want to lay claim to those terms (even in equivalent terms holding meanings closer to their own modes of research)? An answer may lie in the relationship posited between rigor in its unvarying, stepwise sense and objectivity's meaning of physical-cognitive distance.

The implicit logic of the charge is that without clearly articulated hypotheses and measurable variables, interpretive research falls short of the rigor and objectivity expected of (social) science, calling into question its truth-, proof-, and/or knowledge-claims because the character of its evidence cannot be properly assessed and the research is not recognizable as scientific. Adhering to explicit, codified, public (known) procedures is presumed to generate knowledge claims that can be regenerated by any researcher following the same procedures. This is what creates "objective" knowledge: It is not the product-property of any single researcher—that would render it "subjective" knowledge, of or pertaining to the researcher-subject. The purpose of "rigorous" method-steps is to contain researchers' behavior; the persistent power of the rhetorical attack—"This research is neither rigorous nor objective"—comes to "punish" transgressors seeking to escape those controls.[45] That the punishment has practical implications, depriving researchers of the means to livelihood (e.g., shutting down avenues of research, closing down possibilities of employment) and of their academic-scientific identity (degrees, positions, publications, and promotions) is what makes the rhetoric so powerful, including in motivating interpretive scholars to seek to reclaim the terms by defining and explicating away their problems.[46]

The relationship between the understanding of rigor as stepwise and unyielding and objectivity as physically and emotionally distant, along with extensive attention to the intricacies of tools and techniques, serves to mask underlying aspects of research that are perceived to be problematic. The terms and the anticipated (or real) accusations work as a "myth," not in the sense of misguided belief but in a structural sense, deflecting attention from elements for which there is no shared consensus or that might undermine a tentative or fragile one (Yanow 1992b). The rigor/objectivity charge blocks a focus on problematic aspects central to the research undertaking: the trustworthiness of its "findings." Attention is being diverted from the claims to knowledge, certainty, and "truth" that make research trustworthy and that support the social status of science—and, most specifically, from our discomfort with the idea that bodies and emotions play a role in generating scientific knowledge.

The myth is that analytic rigor entails logos alone, rather than pathos and ethos as well. "Objectivity"—disembodied reason based on facts (logos), rather than feelings (pathos), following the laws of logic (also logos), rather than emotion (or a moral feeling, ethos)—denies the latter; accepting subjectivity threatens to undermine the separation. Policing research for its rigor and objectivity is either the remnant of an earlier historical battle to establish the scientific bona fides of the several social sciences, or it is a present, real concern to shore up that "scientific" character of their practices among governmental agencies and a broader public as other than commonplace literary, impressionistic, armchair activity. It is as if the acceptance of the all-too-human characteristics of the researcher in the generation and interpretation of data portends the descent of social science back into its amateur roots, if not its even earlier metaphysical antecedents. As Furner (1975, 290–91, 323) notes, "objective," in the new economics, sociology, and political science associations at the end of the nineteenth century, was defined in a special way: "It restricted open public advocacy of the sort that allied [these disciplines] with reforms which threatened the status quo. . . . [A]t least the appearance of objectivity was essential to survival, for without it there was no assurance of professional support in time of need." "Rigorous," "objective" social science would not get mixed up with social reform. "Public sociology" (Burawoy 2005), for instance, is problematic in this view because the sociologist is then no longer "outside"—external to—the social world: she is no longer "objective"; his reformist zeal threatens rigorousness.

Claiming knowledge based on an external authority distances us from these problems and eliminates the messiness that is part of being human; it maintains the illusion of human perfectibility and scientific "progress." The time and energy spent debating tools and techniques—the so-called methodism or methods fetishism—keeps researchers from engaging these other, highly problematic issues. An unyielding procedural "rigor" that enables claims to "objective" knowledge keeps researchers from having to relinquish a shop-worn distinction between body and mind that is increasingly blurred; from seeing that the source of research authority is vested in and regulated by communal discourse; and from being accepting of a knowledge whose character is neither absolute nor universal, but deeply, unremittingly human, and therefore potentially flawed. A human science, "mired" in human fallibility, renders us firmly in our humanity.

It is, in the end, interpretive science's insistence on reflexivity, in the spirit of the testability that is a hallmark of scientific work, within the context of a community of practitioners, that enables researchers to maintain a check on idiosyncratic, biased, erroneous interpretation. Such a reflexive science proceeds with "passionate humility" (Yanow 1997), the recognition that our analyses—indeed, even our prior suppositions—might be wrong, married with conviction in our analytic rigor and faithfulness to self and other, based on methodical, systematic research processes.

NOTES

An earlier version of this chapter was presented at the 2004 American Political Science Association conference (September 2–5). My thanks to Tim Pachirat and Robert Adcock for readings of an earlier draft, that made better sense than I of my woolly thinking and that pushed me to make explicit my tacit knowledge. I cannot imagine better readers. Neither of them, however, should be held to account for faults and flaws that remain.

1. I am indebted to Tim Pachirat for helping me see more clearly the intertwining of substantive and rhetorical arguments.

2. Robert Adcock's influence is reflected in the formulation of this point. My thanks to him and to Tim Pachirat for pushing my thinking on its significance.

3. This may, in fact, be the problem that Steven Maynard-Moody and Michael Musheno ran into in their initial proposal to the National Science Foundation for the research that resulted in their 2003 book and other publications. See chapter 18, this volume, on page 318.

4. All dictionary definitions quoted here were accessed online through the spring and summer of 2004 at http://dictionary.reference.com, which compiles entries from various dictionaries.

5. One seemingly common understanding is that the methodological meaning of rigor comes from rigor mortis, "the need to render events lifeless so that they can be studied 'scientifically'" (Harold Orlans, in a post to the Interpretation & Method listserv, February 28, 2004, http://listserv.cddc.vt.edu/mailman/listinfo/interpretationandmethods, quoted with permission). As far as I can tell, this is not the etymology of the methodological meaning. The fact that many understand it in such a context, however, speaks volumes for the vitality of methodological positivism.

6. There are different variations on the labels for these steps. One of the interesting ones, for interpretive methodological purposes, separates "data processing" from "data analysis" and joins the latter with "interpretation" (Singleton and Straits 1999, 92). Some more recent "qualitative" methods textbooks present research design in a more complex fashion, with internal feedback loops and attention to the fact that hypotheses do not emerge de novo (see, e.g., Marshall and Rossman 1995 or Berg 2001). Some quantitative and general methods textbooks are also demurring from this traditional model. Singleton and Straits (1988, 29; 1999, 28), for example, noting that the "characteristic mode of inquiry that distinguishes scientific research from other forms of research" is referred to by some people as "the scientific method," comment: "But this unfortunate phrase implies a definitive, orderly procedure that simply does not exist in science." Their subsequent treatment of the stages of social research (1999, 92), however, presents a staged sequence much like the one here (albeit with the caveat that it is an idealized model), as do discussions in other texts.

7. "Abduction" was introduced by the pragmatist philosopher Charles Sanders Peirce to refer to a type of reasoning he saw as distinct from both deduction and induction.

8. The difference, however, between research improv and theatrical improv is that field researchers typically learn on the job while engaged in their first research project, whereas theater improv performers have been actually practicing their craft for some time before going out on stage in a formal engagement. If there is any similarity here, it lies in the fact that neophyte improv performers meet their first real audience members at their first performance, and so they are learning on the job, too, much as field researchers are. And there is no doubt that field researchers' responses (to situations, people, and texts) improve with practice. Researchers' prior preparation consists of extensive reading, coursework, paper writing, talking with faculty and student colleagues who have done field research, and so on. It is more an apprenticeship of the mind than of act. I suspect that it is this improvisational character with its ambiguities, openness, and relative lack of control(s) that leads both some persons to engage in interpretive research and others to denigrate it. I find similar implications for administrative and classroom practices (Yanow 2001).

9. The sense-making process entails matching one's interpretive data with the conceptual boxes provided by one's provisional theorizing. As I discuss in the concluding section, it is akin to the pattern matching described by Kuhn (1970).

It does seem, in fact, that something in the physical act of writing observational notes, transcribing interview tapes and notes, shuffling cards and flip charts, and correlating data with an outline in coding is key to the analytic process. Much as one often discovers one's argument in the physical process of writing or typing, interpretive researchers "discover" their analyses in and through various forms of note making. It is this attribute, perhaps, that makes computer programs for "qualitative" data useful, rather than any computer-based operations per se. Louis Agassiz apparently perceived something similar when, commenting on a student's progress in studying a preserved fish, he said, "a pencil is one of the best of eyes" (L. Cooper 1945, chapter 7. "How Agassiz Taught Professor Scudder").

10. Rigor is also a term in mathematical reasoning, in which it shares with formal logic an attention to logical processes of deduction, especially in establishing mathematical proof.

11. The commonsensical understanding of rigor as "stepwise" may derive from this sense. The definitions risk becoming circular in their use of "logic" and "valid," and so it might be worth reminding ourselves that logic (from the Greek "logos," meaning "reason") is a system of reasoning whose study focuses on the structure of propositions as distinguished from their content. That is, "formal" logic is the logic of forms or structures of language.

12. This formulation invokes the old problem in analytic philosophy of the tension between formal logic and substantive "truth." That is, one can construct arguments in which the logic of the forms of statements is valid—the conclusions do, indeed, derive from the premises—but the content of the statements is patently absurd.

13. Mark Bevir (2003) has referred to what I take to be the same characteristic as "philosophical rigor." By derivation, this definition of structural rigor evolves to a more procedural methodological one, albeit one closer in sense to the structural definition than to the previous definition: Rigor means adherence to procedures that have been generally accepted as leading to correct conclusions. The defense of interpretive research in these terms is the same as the defense presented there: Good interpretive research adheres to accepted procedures. The difficulty is that these procedures have not, by and large, been explicated in ways accessible to those outside of the epistemic communities conducting such research.

14. Taste in such matters is highly individualistic. My personal list includes the writings of Clifford Geertz (e.g., 1973a, 1983) and John Van Maanen (e.g., 1978).

15. I thank Tim Pachirat for enabling me to see these aspects of my argument. As he reminded me, McCloskey (e.g., 1985) has also noted this in the context of writings in economics. The essays in Simons (1989) explore various social science fields. The ways in which researchers' writing itself can constitute the subject being studied has been treated by Clifford and Marcus (1986), Geertz (1988), Golden-Biddle and Locke (1993), Van Maanen (1988), and Yanow et al. (1995).

16. The concept has been debated and discussed at length. See, e.g., Bernstein (1983), Bevir (1999), Latour (1999), and M. Weber (1946). For a treatment oriented toward language and objectivity, see Lakoff and Johnson (1980), chapters 25–26.

17. This is the point that Werner Heisenberg argued against in the context of physics research, named the "uncertainty principle": that, in quantum mechanics, the act of measuring the physical characteristics of one entity (such as the speed of particles in motion) itself potentially alters the behavior of the very things and processes one is observing, thereby affecting the knowledge the researcher could claim. This was enacted in human terms in the stage set for the San Francisco production of Michael Frayn's play *Copenhagen* (1998). Heisenberg went to Copenhagen during World War II to visit the senior physicist Niels Bohr, with whom he had studied prior to the war, for some purpose related to the development of the atomic bomb. No record of their meeting has, so far, been discovered; the play script speculates as to what transpired. The scene design has the two men, walking in the woods to escape having their conversation overheard by Nazis, who, they assume, have bugged Bohr's home, move around and around in a circular space bordered by a high wall that serves as the foundation for on-stage bleacher seating. It is as if the audience members seated in the risers are observing the interaction of two human atoms, whose words and deeds bounce off each other in unpredictable—and, today, unknown—ways.

18. For instance, laundry hanging from a line might be "read" for purposes of socioeconomic class or some other analysis—how many items of what category of clothing or linens, in what condition (having holes, marked by repairs), and so on—without having to talk to the person who hung the wash or the one who owns it.

19. Indeed, in the introduction to the 2000 reissue of the book, Schwartz and Sechrest (2000, xi–xii) wrote: "As we review the references to Webb et al., we reach the conclusion that it [the book] clarified a pervasive problem in social science research and that it proposed a plausible remedy. . . . The problem was one of validity." The solution required "a new mind-set in planning and carrying out research," one that drew on multiple methods and creativity in going beyond conventional data-gathering techniques.

20. Kuhn (1970, 5) described research during the "normal science" phase as "a strenuous and devoted attempt to force nature into the conceptual boxes supplied by professional education." Latour (1999) takes issue with the language of "filter," commonly used in this context, which he sees as implying a passive acceptance of external reality. I think this problem is resolved by conceptualizing the process as a "sorting"

of inputs into a set of slots or boxes, representing the categories that the individual (researcher or otherwise) is attuned to at any given moment. The slots change—we drop some, add new ones, alter existing ones—as understanding changes; and in this and the sorting processes, we actively filter our observations, which in turn shapes the world of social realities.

21. Here is where the linguistic argument enters in, that without words, we would be unable to "see" things. The argument is being advanced in empirical research with color terms (Roberson 2005) and number terms (Gordon 2004).

22. This effect on theoretical formulation has been documented in analyses of metaphors of social theory (e.g., R.H. Brown 1976) and in feminist studies of medical and other natural sciences historically, for example in conceptualizations of the fetus, of women's internal organs, and of women's health that were shaped by images or theories of the male bodily norm (see, e.g., Tuana 1989).

23. As a rule of thumb, researchers plan on twice the amount of time for note taking as they spend observing or interviewing (i.e., one hour of conversational interviewing requires, on average, two hours for writing up one's notes on the interview; transcribing from an audio- or videotape can require much more, depending on the kind of transcription equipment one has, the level of detail one wants to note, etc.).

24. For example, by attending to word choice, question order, and training in presentation skills and processes, or through (e-)mailed questionnaires that eliminate human contact altogether (although they have a lower rate of return). These techniques and others are detailed in survey design textbooks and sections of general textbooks.

25. At the other end of the spectrum from such efforts to "contain" the researcher and delimit interactions is the argument that the actors in the situation under study are coproducers of evidence along with the researcher (see, e.g., Behar 1993).

26. This is the subject area of the philosophy of mind. See, e.g., Sellars (1997) for an overview of the debates. Latour (1999) has an interesting discussion from a science studies perspective.

27. These meanings, however, have not been constant over time. An essayist for *Webster's Revised Unabridged Dictionary* (Trendelenburg, 1998 edition, accessed at http://dictionary.reference.com) notes: "In the Middle Ages, subject meant substance, and has this sense in Descartes and Spinoza. . . . Subjective is used by William of Occam to denote that which exists independent of mind; objective, what is formed by the mind. . . . Kant and Fichte have inverted the meanings. Subject, with them, is the mind which knows; object, that which is known; subjective, the varying conditions of the knowing mind; objective, that which is in the constant nature of the thing known."

28. This begs the question of who is doing the observing. The medical definition of objective, however, takes point of view into account: "1. Based on observable phenomena; presented factually. 2. Indicating a symptom or condition perceived as a sign of disease by someone other than the person affected" (*The American Heritage Stedman's Medical Dictionary* 2002, http://dictionary.reference.com/search?q=objective; [accessed October 31, 2005 4th ed.]). Subjective, by contrast, means "Of, relating to, or designating a symptom or condition perceived by the patient *and not by the examiner*" (*The American Heritage Dictionary of the English Language*, 4th ed. 2000; emphasis added). Following this definition, to the extent that interpretive analysis is "based on observable phenomena"—even if it is an interpretation of those phenomena, much as a symptom or condition would be perceived in analysis as a sign of something else—such research is, definitionally, objective as long as the interpretation is made by someone other than the person experiencing the condition! This in effect eliminates autoethnography, such as that of Greenhalgh (2001), as well as interaction between patient and physician in negotiating the diagnosis, which is a central issue in contemporary medical practice.

29. Herein lie the roots of the difficulties of accommodating a public sociology (e.g., Burawoy 2005) or an engaged political science within the framework of academic science (the "ivory tower").

30. See, e.g., Rein (1976). This line of argument dovetailed with the growing view in both public policy and public administration, especially in implementation studies, that the politics-administration dichotomy was an oxymoron: Rather than seeing politics, and, hence, values, as restricted to the pre-administrative policy-framing and legislative phases, administrative acts came to be seen as themselves fraught with politics, much as organizational acts were increasingly seen as political (see, e.g., Fox 1990, Nakamura 1990, Pressman and Wildavsky 1973, and Yanow 1990, in implementation studies; Pfeffer 1981 in organizational studies).

31. My argument that these methods do not constitute "sampling" is based on the latter's close association with statistical science, where it is defined and used as "a set of elements drawn from and analyzed to estimate the characteristics of a population" (*American Heritage Dictionary*, accessed at http://

dictionary.reference.com on December 16, 2004). What interpretive research does is not sampling in the sense that researchers make no claim for statistically scientific estimation, and its usage in an interpretive context glosses this distinction, as well as the ways in which "representativeness" means different things in these different contexts. As my coeditor notes, many qualitative and interpretive researchers "will use phrases like snowball sampling or purposive sampling (say, across organizational divisions) without necessarily claiming 'representativeness' in the traditional statistical sense—though they might claim an enhanced validity, say, in that second example" (personal communication, December 17, 2004). Although I agree with this observation, in keeping with my broad concern for more reflexivity concerning interpretive methods, I would like to see researchers engage this question of representativeness more explicitly, rather than using the word rhetorically to make scientific claims.

32. Locke, Golden-Biddle, and Feldman (2004) use the vivid example of seeing a sculpture in a museum, where the viewer walks around and around, and around again, studying the piece from various angles.

33. The divergences between the researcher's and others' responses themselves, however, could well be data for analysis. Behar (1993) provides an example of a different sort, in which one "ordinary" (i.e., not elite) individual's life is the subject of analysis; but here, that personal narrative is presented as an example of methodological co-construction of family and communal events and experiences, and used as a lens through which to explore them. In drawing on personal experience, interpretive researchers are (or should be) acutely aware of the ways in which present experience is shaped by prior experience and traits that are not necessarily universalizable.

34. Some forms of action research might be seen as requiring the researcher to "go native" in an identification with the actors in the situation under analysis. As practiced in some areas of political science (notably public policy analysis), in sociology, and in organizational studies, it appears to move close enough to advocacy that some challenge its standing as science altogether. I do not have space here to give this the attention it deserves.

35. The Geertzian terminology for emic-etic distinctions—experience-near, experience-distant (Geertz 1973)—draws on this intermingling of ideas concerning physical-spatial and cognitive-emotional proximities. Knowing-understanding is a matter of experiential proximity; and different physical distances lead to different qualities of experience.

36. As Lipsky (1980) noted with respect to street-level bureaucrats, academics—field researchers in particular—work out of the range of direct supervision. This does not mean there are not controls, however. It just moves the controls from directly hierarchical ones to more indirect, professional associational ones. That does not mean that the controls are any less powerful, however.

The downside of such controls, as Kuhn (1970) noted, is that this leads to theoretical and intellectual conservatism that dampens the introduction of new ways of thinking. This is why, as he also notes, innovative ideas are more likely to come from newer members of the scientific communities and from others on their margins.

37. This is the institutionalization process P. Berger and Luckmann (1966) describe in part II. There is a wonderful story about how U.S. railroads achieved a "universal" spacing between the rails, that traces its origins back through English carriages to Roman caissons and the distance between the two horses pulling them. For related discussions, see Scott (1998).

38. Bevir (1999) comes close to arguing for such a subjective definition of objectivity. In his view, objectivity rests on a theory's grounding in pure (unmediated) experience, which is to say on pure facts. But rejecting the possibility of pure experience leaves certainty (knowledge, truth) grounded in subjectivity "because our observations do not record reality neutrally but rather make sense of reality through a theoretical understanding, therefore, our knowledge must depend at least in part on us. Because experience contains human elements, knowledge must contain human elements, and because we cannot eradicate these human elements, objectivity must be a product of our behaviour, not just our experiences. We must portray objectivity as a product of a human practice" (Bevir 1999, 97). To the extent that theoretical understanding is a property of a scientific or epistemic community, the subjectivity is collective: an intersubjectivity. "Objectivity," in other words, is a property of a community of interpretation and practice.

39. This is one of the arguments against doing "undercover" or disguised research, which introduces deceptive practices into an implicitly honest and above-board relationship.

40. Unlike M. Jourdain in Molière's play, *Le bourgeois gentilhomme*, who discovered that he had been speaking prose all along. In organizational studies, however, as analytic terms from organizational culture came into wider and wider circulation and currency, executives and managers did begin to speak of rituals, ceremonies, symbols, metaphors, and the like and to institute them in their organizations.

41. I am indebted to the discussion in Monk (2004, esp. 39–42) for helping me articulate this connection.

42. As noted above, this positioned moral and value statements, for example, beyond the realm of science because they were seen as products of emotion, rather than reason.

43. His example of bicycle riding illustrates this: If you know how to ride a bicycle, you know which way to turn the front wheel when falling to the right; otherwise, you would always be falling and could not claim to hold that knowledge. But most bicycle riders asked this question cannot articulate their knowledge. Furthermore, even if they could, they could not write a manual naming all the rules for riding a bicycle. Moreover, even if they could write such a manual, no novice could read it, get on a bicycle, and ride off without falling—absent learning the "tacit knowledge" (in this case, of a kinesthetic sort) that experienced riders know but cannot articulate.

44. I take as evidence of this several sections of the 2004 report on "Scientific Foundations of Qualitative Research" (Ragin, Nagel, and White 2004).

45. In fact, Lakoff and Johnson's claim that objectivity concerns self-control (1999, 277) sheds another light on this argument concerning the uses of "objectivity" to control researchers' behaviors—namely, that its rhetorical usage for control purposes stems from a fear of bodies being "out of control." I do not have the space here to develop this implication of these two arguments.

46. The fact that many political science doctoral students and junior faculty fear to self-identify when posting to the Perestroika list—indeed, the existence of that group at all, as an outlet for constructive criticism of the American Political Science Association—attests to the power of these controls.

CHAPTER 5

JUDGING QUALITY

Evaluative Criteria and Epistemic Communities

PEREGRINE SCHWARTZ-SHEA

In graduate school, I decided to pursue the area of "research methods" because I thought it would help me to do better research. In my experience, having to teach a topic forces me to clarify my own understanding. I also thought that enthusiasm about teaching research methods would assist me in obtaining a job; and, indeed, I did end up teaching "Quantitative Methods" in both of the positions for which I was hired. This decision to teach methods proved pivotal to my intellectual journey in ways that I would never have anticipated in 1982.

Over the course of many years teaching research methods, I changed texts several times for various reasons, but the language to which students were introduced remained constant: operationalization of independent and dependent variables; hypothesis construction and tests of statistical significance; the grounds for causal inference (time order, association, and non-spuriousness); and criteria for evaluating empirical research—in other words, the reliability and validity of operationalized concepts and the internal validity and generalizability of results. Clearly, this was the way to do "empirical" research in the social sciences. I was completely puzzled, then, as I became interested in feminist research (which insisted on the observer's standpoint, a direct challenge to universality and objectivity) and philosophy of social science and experienced the disconnect between what I had been teaching and what I was hearing in conference panels on these topics. Specifically, if positivism was so discredited, why was this not reflected in the many research methods texts I had perused and used?

My training in rational choice theory had equipped me with the faith that abstract theory could be married to empirical research to produce objective, grand theory—the physics of the social sciences. Reading interpretive work and feminist philosophy of social science shook that faith. I first gave up on the possibility of a grand theory applicable to all historical epics and cultures, then on rigid notions of objectivity. But still, research "standards" were the rope that kept me from falling into the abyss of "postmodern relativism." Reading interpretive research engendered mixed emotions—an excitement at the possibility of doing research in new ways, and fear: "How do I evaluate such work? I thought I knew what knowledge was and, instead, the meaning of knowledge is contested!" It was as if the rules of academia had shifted underneath me, and in my disorientation I grasped at "standards" as a way of understanding my identity as an academic.

The language learned in quantitative methods courses not only disciplines researchers but imprisons them. The desire to better answer such questions as "On what grounds does one distinguish 'good' from 'bad' interpretive research?" is what brought me to write this chapter.

I feel nervous when researchers claim that their accounts of reality are far too rich and complex to be expressed as measurement.
—*APSA Political Methodology Section e-mail list participant* (February 2003)

With methods, as with people, if you focus only on their limitations you will always be disappointed.
—*Ian Shapiro* (2002, 612)

Consider the following thought experiment. Imagine that you are a traditionally trained political scientist, steeped in what might be called the "variables gestalt," which encompasses, among other things, a commitment to measurement, hypothesis testing, and causal analysis. You have been asked to review a manuscript comparing two government agencies, based on interpretive scholarship. I construct the thought experiment using political science because the interpretive epistemic community is not as well established in that discipline as it is in some other social sciences, making this a plausible scenario.[1] But the scenario could as well hold for sociology or organizational studies or any other social scientific area of study.

Setting aside epistemological and ontological presuppositions, as well as choices of the particular theoretical lens informing your work (e.g., realism versus neorealism in international relations theory or rational choice theory versus political psychology in American politics), when you sit down to read an empirical study, you bring with you a set of standard expectations about the logic of research, as well as a developed, discipline-directed set of critical reading skills honed through training in your field. You are expecting to encounter independent and dependent variables (whose operationalization can be critically assessed); you are expecting to see causal reasoning and perhaps a causal model (the internal logic of which you know how to evaluate); you are expecting to find statistical analysis—be it a regression equation, ANOVA, or some other technique (you might even turn immediately to the tables, before reading any of the text, in order to see what sort of analysis is involved); and you are trained to assess the appropriateness of techniques as a function of nominal, ordinal, or interval-level data, to know whether underlying statistical assumptions are met, and so on. Over time, you have become quite practiced at reading and critiquing research conducted within this gestalt, and your application of evaluative criteria is almost second nature. A particular reading experience results from these expectations and practices; its particularity is evinced by the fact that both graduate and undergraduate students must acquire these critical reading skills.

The interpretive study you have been sent as part of the peer review process is based on sixteen months of participant-observation, numerous supplementary in-depth interviews, and document analysis. The manuscript offers a radically different reading experience: None of the variables have been operationalized in the ways to which you are accustomed—in fact, what the variables are is not even clear, let alone which ones are dependent and which are independent; no causal model is offered; there are no tables reporting statistical analyses; there is no discussion of generalizability.

In short, given your customary reading experience, this study is unrecognizable as a piece of scientific research: It does not fit your sense of what rigorous, objective research looks like. Your standard set of evaluative criteria simply does not apply, and you question whether such research qualifies as social science. Your experience is similar to that of the e-mail list participant quoted in the first epigraph: the "rich and complex" data reported in the study make you "nervous." What sort of evaluation can you, would you, send to the journal editor or to the author? As Shapiro implies (in the second epigraph), if you are unaware or dismissive of research gestalts other than your own, you will clearly be disappointed in this manuscript. To assess it on its own terms, you must reorient yourself, recognize the legitimacy of such a study as science, and ask, "What are the strengths of interpretive methodologies? What are the purposes of this kind of research?" Such a reorientation is essential to understanding the interpretive gestalt and the evaluative criteria associated with it.

One of the obstacles encountered by those seeking to strengthen interpretive epistemic communities in political science, sociology, and similarly constituted disciplines is the allegation that there are no criteria for judging the quality of interpretive research—the "anything goes" charge. This allegation is disputable in light of the substantial, growing body of literature spanning several social science disciplines that addresses the question of appropriate criteria for judging interpretive research. In this chapter I assess this body of work. My purpose is to provide researchers new to interpretive research with a vocabulary that they can use and discuss with (and convey to) those interested in participating in and strengthening interpretive epistemic communities within their respective disciplines.

The scholarly enterprise is built on the exercise of judgment. Whether it is assessing a dissertation, evaluating a manuscript in the peer review process, or judging a research proposal for funding, scholars sit in judgment of others and, likewise, submit their own scholarship to such judgment. There are consequences of these judgments: some proportion of graduate students fails to receive degrees, some manuscripts are never published, and many research proposals go unfunded. Although individuals make these judgments, they do so in the context of a complex structure of competing yet overlapping intellectual communities defined in numerous, crosscutting ways, that is, in terms of discipline, subject matter, national and continental identities, research and funding networks, and diverse understandings of the purposes of research and scholarship.

These distinct communities have been characterized as epistemic communities (Alston 1989, Knorr Cetina 1999), and it is particular epistemic communities that are—or should be—the arbiters of research quality for any given study. Despite periodic declarations of the necessity and superiority of a single episteme (E.O. Wilson 1998, Laitin 2003)[2], multiple epistemic communities define the landscape of the social sciences,[3] and a diversity of approaches, rather than a unitarian hegemony, is arguably a more appropriate measure of progress or maturity in the social sciences (Dryzek 1986, 1990; Rule 1997). To fully understand these communities' judgments, one must understand each one's particular research gestalt—that bundle of shared epistemological and ontological presuppositions, theoretical commitments, research goals, evaluative criteria, and methodological and reading practices. This is not a simple task, for despite explicit methodological training in many disciplines, much learning is still craft based; that is, novices often learn by reading exemplars and by collaborating with senior researchers, in an apprenticeship-type arrangement similar to that of the craft guilds. In such learning by doing, by immersion, assumptions are not always made explicit. Instead, they form a background knowledge that knits practices together into a coherent whole. Without that background knowledge, a simple listing of evaluative criteria, although useful in displaying a particular vocabulary, does little to communicate a research gestalt because the terms are a kind of shorthand for the ontological and epistemological positions informing the community's practices. But once one is steeped in that gestalt, once its positions and habits of mind become second nature, then the relevant evaluative criteria for assessing the quality of a particular study take on a self-evident character.

In what follows, I offer a very brief characterization of the interpretive gestalt as grounding for understanding the interpretive criteria literature. Next, I briefly review two classic texts that launched the development of this literature. The heart of the chapter then examines the evolving debate on how best to think about criteria for interpretive research. In the concluding section I return to the broader framework of epistemic communities and the burden of scholarly judgment.

UNDERSTANDING THE INTERPRETIVE RESEARCH GESTALT

Specifying the components of a research gestalt is a tricky business, for no single set of attributes is shared by all who consider themselves as conducting interpretive research. That said, as the thought experiment was meant to illustrate, distinctions between research gestalts can meaningfully be made, and these differences have significant consequences for applying evaluative criteria to any particular study. These caveats noted, I provide a brief, and necessarily incomplete, characterization of the interpretive gestalt.

There are two key, interrelated parts of the interpretive gestalt that are essential to grasping it and understanding how it differs from a variables gestalt. First, a central goal of interpretive techniques is understanding human meaning making; issues of causality are not necessarily excluded but are understood much differently by different gestalts (more on this later). Being attuned to meaning making involves a recognition of, and sensitivity to, the ambiguities of human experience; researchers presuppose that meanings are negotiated and constructed, and they often deliberately investigate efforts to promulgate or resist particular meanings, at the same time that they explore the variation of meanings across context—what Soss (chapter 6, this volume) calls "indexicality."[4] Additionally, many interpretive researchers emphasize that actors may "know more than they can tell" (M. Polanyi 1966, 4), what Polanyi termed "tacit knowledge." Such knowledge need not be explicitly articulated in order to be used. For example, M.R. Schmidt (1993) describes grouters' unstated "feel" for grouting, which made them suspect structural problems with a dam that went undetected by engineers. Similarly, Flyvbjerg (2001) describes tugboat operators' "local knowledge" of a coastline that enables them to bring a large ship into port. Documenting the existence and use of tacit knowledge and local knowledges helps to revalue and preserve them in an increasingly rationalized social world (T. Mitchell 1991, J.C. Scott 1998). A related emphasis in much interpretive research is on the extent to which actors may not be fully aware of the ways in which taken-for-granted assumptions underlie their meaning-making activities. By studying the symbols, rituals, stories, and other artifacts through which actors make sense of their worlds, researchers seek to reveal the intricate, evolving connections between taken-for-granted understandings and human activities and practices. Such "revelations" can make possible new understandings and evaluations of the status quo, enabling human growth and change.

Second, interpretive researchers maintain a sensitivity to the "form" of the data: much of it is word data from such sources as interviews, documents, observational field notes, and the like; increasing attention is being given to imagery and sound (Bauer and Gaskell 2002), as well as to architectural space and objects (Harper 2003; Yanow, chapter 20, this volume). Some of the data may be in numerical form, although from an interpretive perspective, numerical data tend to be "read" and treated in different ways than from quantitative perspectives (see, e.g., Czarniawska-Joerges 1992), and they are not viewed as superior to other forms. Rather, the distinct forms of data encode and enact diverse human practices, a classic hermeneutic and anthropological insight. In this sense, numbers and indexes manifest the human propensity to count and, particularly in contemporary society, the respect accorded the (seeming) precision of numbers.

Altogether, the data *retained in their diverse forms*—what might be termed the genres of the data—constitute the complex human meaning-making enterprise, which interpretive methods are particularly suited to studying. Respecting the various genres of data enables interpretive researchers to offer holistic, multifaceted understandings of human experience—not only of the human love of numbers and words, but of the ways in which sight, sound, and embodiment make possible and limit human activities, practices, and meaning making. To be clear, researchers from the variables gestalt also study space, objects, documents, and human meanings, but their approach is to "*trans*-form" data into numbers, whenever possible, in order to be able to apply statistical analytic techniques in the ways and for the purposes illustrated in the thought experiment.[5] It is for these reasons that the experience of reading interpretive empirical research (in all its voluminous complexity, as attested to in this volume) is usually a very different one from reading variables-based research. How, then, should interpretive research be judged?

THE BEGINNINGS OF THE "CRITERIA LITERATURE": CLASSIC TEXTS

In the late 1970s and the early 1980s, scholars began to articulate and develop the criteria implicit in qualitative-interpretive[6] research practices as distinct from those used in the variables gestalt. Two texts are recognized as "classics" in the development of this literature (Creswell 1998b), and they serve as useful benchmarks for understanding its evolution. Miles and Huberman's *Qualitative Data Analysis: A Sourcebook of New Methods* (1984) and Lincoln and Guba's *Naturalistic Inquiry* (1985) were among the first to present fully articulated responses to skepticism (much of it coming from researchers influenced by positivist understandings of scientific practices) concerning the scientific character of qualitative methods, and these texts are much cited in the literature on evaluative criteria.

Although Miles and Huberman did not add a full-fledged discussion of evaluative criteria until their second edition (published in 1994), their 1984 text is notable because it focuses on qualitative data *analysis*, the stage most maligned by methodological positivists as unreliable and subject to bias. Indeed, Miles and Huberman accept this critique and seek to develop "reliable and valid" methods of analysis for "word data." Their chapters on coding provide a variety of techniques (e.g., writing memos; pattern coding; time, role, and effects matrices) for what they term "data reduction"—by which they mean the process of "selecting, focusing, simplifying, abstracting, and transforming" word data (1984, 21). As they emphasize, data reduction need not mean quantification because "[q]ualitative data can be reduced and transformed in a variety of ways: through sheer selection, through summary or paraphrase, through terms being subsumed in a larger pattern and so on" (1984, 21). The Miles and Huberman text, then, is traditional in its emphasis on coding, but it still deserves being labeled "qualitative-interpretive" because of the authors' healthy skepticism of quantification and their emphasis on qualitative data analysis as a meaning-making enterprise built primarily on the analysis of word data retained in their contexts of origin.[7]

In contrast to Miles and Huberman, Lincoln and Guba (1985) chart what they term a "postpositivist" approach, and, in their chapter on assessing the quality of interpretive research, they explicitly reject the possibility of "universal criteria," that is, criteria understood as applying to the evaluation of the methods used in all research gestalts. The four evaluative criteria they propose as appropriate to interpretive research are *parallel* to the four criteria rooted in methodological positivism with whose critique their analysis begins. So, for example, instead of the

Table 5.1

Interpretive Approaches to Evaluative Criteria: The Classic Texts

Criterion	Terms used in methodological positivism[1]	Lincoln and Guba (1985): parallel terms[2]	Miles and Huberman (1994): parallel and *new terms*
Truth value	Internal validity	Credibility	Internal validity/credibility/ *authenticity*
Applicability	External validity/ generalizability	Transferability	External validity/ transferability/*fittingness*
Consistency	Reliability	Dependability	Reliability/dependability/ *auditability*
Neutrality	Objectivity	Confirmability	Objectivity/confirmability[3]
			Utilization/application/ action[4]

Sources: The first three columns are taken from Erlandson et al. (1993, 133), who replicate Lincoln and Guba's (1985) approach to evaluative criteria. The sets of terms in the fourth column are the subheadings under which Miles and Huberman discuss what they call "Standards for Quality" (1994, 278–80).

[1]Lincoln and Guba (1985) refer to the "conventional paradigm" rather than to "methodological positivism."
[2]Lincoln and Guba (1985) refer to their approach as "naturalistic inquiry" rather than as "interpretive."
[3]Miles and Huberman (1994) offered no new terms for this criterion.
[4]Miles and Huberman (1994) added a fifth criterion that was not present in the earlier discussion of Lincoln and Guba (1985).

criterion of "internal validity," which emerges from positivist concerns, they propose a reconfigured and renamed "credibility" criterion as more appropriate to interpretive research. Nevertheless, a positivist influence is still apparent in their work: As subsequent scholars argued, establishing a parallel set of terms meant accepting positivist presuppositions about what matters in scholarly research. (Lincoln herself later accepted this critique of parallelism and offered reconceptualized criteria [1995] in lieu of the earlier ones.)

In their second edition, Miles and Huberman (1994) introduced a discussion of "standards for quality." They adopted the approach of Lincoln and Guba, listing both the methodologically positivist terms and Lincoln and Guba's interpretive terms; but they added a third set of possible criteria for three of the four original ones. For example, they added "authenticity" to rival "internal validity" and "credibility" in response to criteria literature published after the 1985 Lincoln and Guba text, most notably in Guba and Lincoln (1989), which argued for "authenticity" as more appropriate for qualitative research than "validity." Perhaps sensitive to the emerging criticism of the initial Lincoln and Guba approach, Miles and Huberman added a fifth set of criteria as well—"Utilization/Application/Action"—arguing that this set is "an essential addition to more traditional views of 'goodness'" (1994, 280). Table 5.1 traces the beginnings of the debate about criteria for judging interpretive-qualitative research quality as reflected in these texts, portending the proliferation of criteria that followed in subsequent years.

CRITERIA: AN EVOLVING DEBATE

A decade ago we noted (in Huberman and Miles [1983]), that qualitative researchers shared no canons, decision rules, algorithms, or even any agreed-upon heuristics to indicate whether findings were valid and procedures robust. That situation is changing, but slowly. . . . And when we read the research reports, they are most often heavy on the "what" (the findings, the descriptions) and rather thin on the "how" (how you got to the "what"). We rarely see data displays—only the conclusions. . . . Researchers are not being cryptic or obtuse. It's just that they have *a slim tradition to guide their analytic moves*, and few guidelines for explaining to their colleagues what they did, and how.

—*Miles and Huberman* (1994, 262, emphasis added)

There is a "deep structural tension" (Bensel 2003, 103) within epistemic communities reflected in the literature on evaluation criteria. Evaluative standards aid in the production and judgment of research quality, but they may also constrain innovation. Some methodologists, such as Miles and Huberman, emphasize the enabling side of criteria and their potential for improving scholarly production, communication, and judgment. Others, such as Wolcott (1990), eschew the discussion of criteria altogether, characterizing it as a distraction that neither guides nor informs research (cf. Schwandt 2001). Most scholars working on this issue seem to accept the pragmatic necessity of criteria, but they are suspicious of approaches that take positivist-informed standards as the operative template. Instead, they seek to develop new criteria consistent with interpretive presuppositions. This latter perspective has led within the last decade or so to a flourishing of terminology and classification schemes as scholars seek to develop new visions of what it means to do and evaluate scholarly research in an interpretive mode. Table 5.2 displays this variety as developed in the work of methodologists following the two classics.

The works presented in this table were selected because of the prominence of the author(s) as judged by extensive citations of their work in the criteria literature and, as important, because these texts demonstrate the evolution of this literature over time. Note, first, the variability in the number of terms produced by each of the studies summarized here: Lincoln and Guba (1985), used here as a baseline, introduced four interpretive criteria; Eisner (1991) argues for three criteria; Maxwell (1992) describes five; Lather (1993) and Riessman (1993), four each; Lincoln (1995), eight; and Brower, Abolafia, and Carr (2000), three. Also notable are the changes in terminology across time, particularly the change in Lincoln's perspective: In 1985 (coauthoring with Guba) she promoted the use of four criteria that parallel positivist terms, whereas by 1995 she is arguing for the use of eight different criteria as more appropriate to interpretive presuppositions.

Part of what emerges in this literature in the early 1990s (something that Miles and Huberman [1994] pick up on with their inclusion of the "utilization/application/action" criterion set) is the concern that research should be used not only to solve problems identified by privileged, elite decision makers, but also to challenge inequalities in society (such as Lincoln's "sharing of privileges" and "voice" criteria and Brower, Abolafia, and Carr's "criticality" criterion, noted in Table 5.2). The addition of this sort of rationale has not been uncontroversial. For example, Atkinson, Coffey, and Delamont (2003, 156) argue that this development "conflates" judging the scientific adequacy of a research project with political, ethical, and other kinds of concerns. Such disagreement is likely to continue. Judgments of scientific inclusion ("This study is 'good' research") and exclusion ("This research is 'junk' science") are made through the application of evaluative criteria; but decisions about inclusion and exclusion are *themselves* political (i.e., judging that political and ethical concerns are best excluded as irrelevant to scientific adequacy is *itself* a political decision)—making the line between "political" and "nonpolitical" criteria difficult to draw.

Table 5.2

Interpretive Approaches to Evaluative Criteria: Selected Later Texts[1]

Study	Lincoln and Guba	Eisner	Maxwell	Lather	Riessman	Lincoln[3]	Brower, Abolafia, and Carr
Year	1985	1991	1992	1993	1993	1995	2000
Criteria[2]	Credibility	Structural collaboration	Descriptive validity	Ironic validity	Persuasiveness	Epistemic community standards	Authenticity
	Transferability	Consensual validation	Interpretive validity	Paralogic validity	Correspondence	Positionality	Plausibility
	Dependability	Referential adequacy	Theoretical validity	Rhizomatic validity	Coherence	Community purpose	Criticality
	Confirmability		External validity/ generalizability	Situated/ embedded validity	Pragmatic use	Voice	
			Evaluative validity			Critical subjectivity	
						Reciprocity	
						Sacredness	
						Sharing of privileges	
Number of terms	4	3	5	4	4	8	3

[1]Lincoln and Guba (1985) is one of two classic texts that serve as a baseline for comparison with later interpretive criteria writings. The six other texts presented here were selected based on the prominence of the author(s) as judged by extensive citations of their work in the criteria literature, as well as to illustrate the evolution of this literature over time.

[2]Terms are listed in the order discussed by the authors.

[3]Terms represent my words summarizing full-sentence explication.

At an operational level, attempting to specify techniques that can be used to verify whether evaluative criteria have been met produces a dizzying array of terminology, as Table 5.3 illustrates.

The scholars presented in this table interpret the link between techniques and criteria in quite different ways. For example, Erlandson et al. (1993) replicate practically all of the Lincoln and Guba (1985) techniques, although, without explanation, they omit "negative case analysis" from techniques for verifying "credibility" and add "purposive sampling" to the techniques for establishing "transferability." Brower, Abolafia, and Carr (2000) connect their techniques to criteria different from those named by the other authors, listing "authenticity," "plausibility," and "criticality." And Miles and Huberman (1994), in contrast to the others, do not connect techniques, which they call "tactics," to any specific criteria at all.[8]

Surveys of the literature, such as Creswell's (1998a), deal with this cacophony by advising novice researchers to know the criteria and techniques within the specific interpretive tradition they are using; his text includes biography, phenomenology, grounded theory, ethnography, and case study research. Although this may be sound advice in many ways, it suggests that these research practices are entirely separate and unrelated, ignoring the commonalities among methods deriving from their shared ideational grounding (see Yanow, chapter 1, this volume). It is this common ground that constitutes the interpretive research gestalt described above, lending these practices collectively a character that is different from variables gestalt practices and, hence, rendering them unrecognizable to the researcher in the hypothetical scenario with which the chapter opened. My claim is not that the interpretive gestalt is strictly delimited, but that it identifies and recognizes a set of research practices and understandings that facilitate communication across various research traditions, that lead to the sort of reading habits described in that scenario, and that demarcate them from others. In short, I contend that the terminological proliferation in the criteria literature gives a misleading impression of interpretive research practices as fragmented and disjointed, whereas from an ontological and epistemological perspective they are characterized more by agreement than by cacophony.

Making clear that these methods do share common ground requires understanding how the literature got into the thicket of criteria and technique.[9] One explanation for the multiplicity of interpretive criteria is the dominant understanding established by methodological positivism of what constitutes "scientific" research in the social sciences. Against this seemingly hegemonic backdrop, interpretive researchers working on developing appropriate evaluative criteria face a dilemma: either to reclaim and redefine recognized, methodologically positivist terms in order to communicate with researchers across the board (as well as with outsiders perceived to hold funding purse strings—this is Morse and Richards's [2002] position)[10] or to invent new terms that better fit research conducted within an interpretive gestalt, thereby improving discussion among members of that epistemic community (Miles and Huberman's [1994] position)[11]. Although both strategies are reasonable responses to the marginalized position of interpretive research, their simultaneous pursuit contributes to the terminological complexity apparent in Tables 5.1 through 5.3.

A second explanation for the apparent multiplicity of interpretive criteria is varying and inconsistent usage of the terms "criterion" and "technique." The appellation "criterion" implies an overarching principle, whereas "technique" implies a means of achieving that principle. Most authors are internally consistent as they build new taxonomies, but reading *across* studies one does not find consistency: what one author calls a "criterion," another calls a "technique." As taxonomies have accumulated over time, the potential confusion for novice researchers rises exponentially—concealing the commonalities that may be more apparent to researchers experienced in the interpretive gestalt. In sum, when asked the question, what are the appropriate standards for evaluating an interpretive study? or what are the guidelines for conducting a high-quality

Table 5.3

Criteria and Techniques in Selected Literature
(where relevant, techniques are listed below their associated criterion)

Study	Lincoln and Guba	Erlandson et al.[1]	Miles and Huberman[2]	Brower, Abolafia, and Carr	Additional terminology[3]
Year	1985	1993	1994	2000	Date varies
Criteria and techniques	*Credibility* • Prolonged engagement • Persistent observation • Triangulation • Peer debriefing • Negative case analysis • Referential adequacy • Member checks • Reflexive journal *Transferability* • Thick description • Reflexive journal	*Credibility* • Prolonged engagement • Persistent observation • Triangulation • Peer debriefing • Referential adequacy • Member checks • Reflexive journal *Transferability* • Thick description • Reflexive journal • Purposive sampling	Following up surprises Making if-then tests Triangulation Looking for negative evidence Representativeness Feedback from informants Researcher effects Checking the meaning of outliers Ruling out spurious relations	*Authenticity* • Detailed description of data collection procedures • Thick, copious description • Represent natives' view of the world *Plausibility* • Description of research methods • First person plural pronoun • Normalize the atypical • Smooth contestable findings	Trustworthiness (Lincoln and Guba 1985; Riessman 1993; Finlay and Gough 2003); Social implications (Thomas 1993) Individual perceptions: Testing out with others (Moustaka 1994) Replication; Validation (Seale 1999) Rigor (Morse and Richards 2002) Evidentiality; Veracity (Atkinson, Coffey, and Delamont 2003)

Dependability		Dependability	Criticality
• Dependability audit	Checking out rival explanations	• Dependability audit	• Unique impressions
• Reflexive journal		• Reflexive journal	• Reexamine taken for granted assumptions
	Replicating findings		
Confirmability		Confirmability	• Analysis of both front stage and back stage
• Confirmability audit	Weighing the evidence	• Confirmability audit	
• Reflexive journal		• Reflexive journal	
	Using extreme cases		

[1]Erlandson et al. (1993) replicate almost all of the Lincoln and Guba (1985) techniques but neglect to mention their deletion of negative case analysis as a technique for verifying "credibility."

[2]Miles and Huberman (1994) use the term "tactics" rather than "techniques."

[3]Some of these terms are treated by authors as criteria, others as techniques, the confusion noted in the text.

interpretive study?, reading the criteria literature suggests that there is little consensus. I show, however, that a different approach reveals considerable commonalities, commonalities indicative of the interpretive gestalt.

AN INDUCTIVE APPROACH TO A SET OF CRITERIA

A skeptic might argue that the apparent lack of consensus displayed in Tables 5.1–5.3 does not much matter to research practice. But many within the interpretive epistemic community may well concur with Miles and Huberman that "shared standards are worth striving for" (1994, 277) because shared standards facilitate scholarly communication and judgment, and that means, presumably, that they should be clear and coherent. Stepping back from this seemingly reasonable presumption, one might still question whether such "striving" reveals an unstated, positivist faith in the possibility of a coherent taxonomy of a universalistic, Platonic nature. This is the conclusion of J.K. Smith and Deemer (2003) who, in their analysis of the criteria literature, self-consciously refuse to provide any recommendations of particular criteria or any taxonomies such as those presented in the texts discussed above. Instead, they argue that there cannot, and never should, be a *definitive* list of evaluative criteria. They reject the possibility of any universal, unchanging taxonomy as ahistorical *and* as inconsistent with the epistemological and ontological presuppositions of interpretivism. A definitive list, they argue, is inconsistent with interpretive skepticism concerning the possibility and usefulness of universal knowledge; research is an historically situated endeavor, and the criteria literature should reflect this situatedness. They also argue that an ahistorical approach makes the discussion of research quality too abstract. The meanings of criteria are "ever subject to constant reinterpretation" as they are applied to concrete studies (J.K. Smith and Deemer 2003, 445).

Smith and Deemer's fundamental insight is that the criteria literature should not be chasing the mirage of the perfect, timeless taxonomy. Yet they acknowledge that having some slowly evolving list of criteria offers a pragmatic place to begin the assessment of research, a point of entry into the hermeneutic conversation about the quality of any particular interpretive study, with additions or deletions emerging in response to new thinking, new practices, and changing research priorities. What Smith and Deemer do not do is to take the next step: assess which of the plethora of criteria and techniques should constitute the first entries in that evolving list. Perhaps they resist this step because of its political implications of scientific inclusion and exclusion and, as important, because they would have to find grounds on which to justify their decisions—bringing back the specter of a timeless, universal taxonomy. One way out of this conundrum is to step back from a normative, a priori, deductive approach and, instead, to develop a list that draws, inductively, on what is taught and used most widely, as an indicator of accepted interpretive practices. Although I agree that epistemic communities develop and change, for any particular period of time it should be possible to name a core list of criteria and techniques provisionally useful for the pragmatic work of judging the quality of interpretive research, yet always subject to revision.

In analyzing the cacophony of terms displayed in Tables 5.2 and 5.3, it is possible to ask which ones are used and taught most often. What is it about a particular term (whether identified as criterion or as technique) that adds to its "in-use" attractiveness? And, as important, how does that term reflect and construct interpretive practices? In addition to analyzing the textbooks represented in those tables for answers to these questions, I examined some twenty-five other social science methods textbooks, skimming the textbooks' tables of contents and criteria chapters (where they existed) and inspecting the indexes for relevant terms, using what might be called an "index test" for the prevalence of the terms.

Admittedly, drawing on texts is an imperfect indicator of teaching and research practices. I have no indicators for their course adoption, and even that is a weak indicator of how they are used in coursework. Indeed, it might be argued that the particular terms I identify are prevalent in texts solely because of their rhetorical character, rather than because they are the ones most widely used in empirical research. For these reasons, the list offered is a suggestive, rather than a definitive, representation of usage in contemporary interpretive empirical research. At the same time, their rhetorical character, the intuitive appeal of a term, is part of what I analyze below on the grounds that this quality is vital to understanding criteria usage within an epistemic community.[12]

Seven terms or concepts emerged from this analysis and, based on the index test, were divided into "first-order" and "second-order" terms or concepts.[13] The four terms I am calling first-order are ubiquitous in the criteria literature and are readily found in text indexes: *thick description, trustworthiness, reflexivity,* and *triangulation.* The three concepts I deem second-order—*informant feedback/member checks, audit,* and *negative case analysis*—are widespread in their usage, although they lack the ubiquity of the first four in that no single term has emerged that captures the amalgam of research practices and expectations each of these concepts represents. Instead, diverse terminologies and practices are associated with each of them, and these are my labels for designating the ideas associated with each concept. For example, one might find "negative case analysis" in some indexes, "outlier analysis" in others, and "rival explanations" in still others, depending on disciplinary traditions or idiosyncratic factors. The practices to which these three terms refer, however, are described in many of the texts, and they can be encapsulated, for present purposes, in these particular labels.

First-Order Terms: Thick Description, Trustworthiness, Reflexivity, and Triangulation

"Thick description," Gilbert Ryle's term borrowed by Clifford Geertz (1973a) to characterize ethnographic writing, has taken on the aura of a "standard" by which to recognize and judge interpretive research; it is part of what scholars have come to expect when reading an interpretive study. The term has come to refer to the presence in the research narrative of sufficient detail of an event, setting, person, or interaction to capture context-specific nuances of meaning such that the researcher's interpretation is supported by "thickly descriptive" evidentiary data. The subtext of this wealth of detail is the provision of evidence that the researcher was, in the original case of ethnography, actually present on-site, an eyewitness to the events, setting, and interactions described. The term can be extended to assessing other methods, such as historical or document analysis, because its purpose is not an exhaustive listing of details but a nuanced portrait of the cultural layers that inform the researcher's interpretation of interactions and events—supporting the researcher's claim, for instance, that what she saw was a "wink" and not a "blink," in Geertz's famous example, borrowed, also, from Ryle (Geertz 1973a, 6–7); or, in the case of document analysis, supporting Jackson's (chapter 14, this volume) claim that "Western Civilization" (*Abendland*) had particular, strategic meanings in post–World War II German politicians' debates over reconstruction.

"Trustworthiness," introduced by Lincoln and Guba (1985) and now used widely, is an umbrella term that captures the broad problem that research needs to be seen as trustworthy—that is what the concerns for "reliability" and "validity" are all about. It offers a way to talk about the many steps that researchers take throughout the research process to ensure that their efforts are self-consciously deliberate, transparent, and ethical—that they are, so to speak, enacting a classically "scientific attitude" of *systematicity* while simultaneously allowing the potential *revisability* of their research results. As a tool of assessment, it facilitates discussion of criteria for judging the overall quality of a research study and the degree to which others—scholars, laypeople, policy actors—can build on its analysis.

"Reflexivity," the third term, has diverse roots. "Reflection" and "reflexivity" are central themes in phenomenology and critical theory, respectively. This practice entered the criteria literature through Lincoln and Guba's (1985) recommended technique of keeping a "reflexive journal," defined as "a kind of diary in which the investigator on a daily basis, or as needed, records a variety of information about the *self* (hence the term 'reflexive') and *method*" (Lincoln and Guba 1985, 327, emphasis in original). This recommendation institutionalized a practice long recognized in ethnographic and participant-observer research; it received renewed attention from feminist philosophers of science (Harding 1991; E. Anderson 1995) and methodologists (Reinharz 1992), who drew critical attention to the gendered nature of research selves. The connotations of this term, then, have grown far beyond Lincoln and Guba's connecting it to daily diary writing to suggest an overall scholarly attitude, that is, a keen awareness of, and theorizing about, the role of the self in all phases of the research process. The literature developing this concept in relation to interpretive research is extensive (Schwandt 2001), such that "reflexivity" has become an expected characteristic of interpretive work. Texts have been written on its philosophical status (Bartlett 1992), the role of emotion therein (Carter and Delamont 1996), and practical techniques for accomplishing it (Finlay and Gough 2003).

Finally, "triangulation" is understood, most broadly, as trying to understand a phenomenon using at least three different analytic tools. The term has its origins in the use of trigonometry for the purpose of surveying, whether on land or sea. In this usage, it is a method of locating an unknown point using two known points at the vertices of a triangle. It is notable as one of the few techniques endorsed by both positivist and interpretive methodologists. Adapted for social science research within variables-oriented methods, it has the status of a supplementary technique and commonly refers to the use of multiple indicators in operationalizing a complex concept (W.L. Neuman 1997), although it also increasingly refers simply to the use of different methods for accessing and generating data in the same study (Jones and Olson 1996). Qualitative methods texts now routinely distinguish among several types of triangulation, including multiple data sources (persons, times, places), multiple methods of access (observation, interviews, documents—this is the most commonly understood meaning), multiple researchers (such as teams of ethnographers studying a single site), and even multiple theories or paradigms in a single research project (for an example, see Papa, Auwal, and Singhal 1995).

What accounts for the widespread acceptance of these four terms? I suggest that their rhetorical character, while communicating substantive concerns, is a major factor explaining their appeal. "Thick description" gains some of its power from its silent partner, the "thin description" of numerical indexes such as the Gross Domestic Product, summary tables reporting regression results, or Arthur Banks's Cross-National Time-Series Data Archive (critiqued by McHenry, chapter 10, this volume). "Thick description"—the "piled up structures of inference and implication" (Geertz 1973a, 7)—implies the use of words, adjectives even, in such a way that readers expect to read about, *and researchers are given permission to impart*, the "lived experiences" of the people they study. Seemingly quite simple on the face of it, thick description communicates a standard for research practice easily understood by both the scholars producing the research and those reading it.[14] By contrast, Lather's (1993) "rhizomatic validity" is less likely to attract widespread usage quickly because "rhizomatic" is not transparent in its reference and does not readily bring to mind a desired practice.

"Trustworthiness" draws rhetorical power from its relational quality: If "I trust you" or "I trust this study," it follows that something more can be done than would otherwise be the case. For example, if "I trust you," we can pursue a project together. Likewise, if the results of a study are judged trustworthy, they can be implemented or built upon. Another part of this term's appeal is its consistency with interpretive presuppositions. As Riessman observes, "'Trustworthiness' not 'truth' is a key semantic difference: The latter assumes an objective reality; the former moves the process into the social world" (2002, 258). "Trustworthiness" captures researchers' very human longing to produce research for a social purpose (even if that purpose is furthering academic research rather than immediate real-world applicability). Indeed, the first Lincoln and Guba criteria text (1985) applied this general term to both positivist and interpretive research. It rivals the positivist standards of "validity and reliability" in its clarity while, at the same time, emphasizing the humanistic aspect of interpretive research.

As a noun, "reflexivity" can be a bit opaque, but the term builds on the verb "to reflect," an act of contemplation associated with the familiar activity of keeping a diary, which, in everyday parlance, implies not simply recording events but thinking about one's "self" in relation to "others." In scholarly activity, this criterion encourages a research practice in which the researcher understands him- or herself to be the means, the instrument used, to produce the research product. This understanding, in turn, demands specific efforts to document and analyze this role. Some commentators (Atkinson, Coffey, and Delamont 2003, 195; Ellis and Bochner 2003) decry "hyper-reflexivity" as indicative of scholarly navel-gazing or solipsism (autoethnography,[15] in particular, has been indicted for such excesses); but, as a general criterion, what reflexivity communicates is that researchers cannot expect to hide behind "third-person," omniscient exposition—the so-called view from nowhere or God's-eye view (Haraway 1988, Harding 1993). The term's success may be due to its implied and easily understood admonition "to reflect on one's research role." It, too, is consistent with interpretive presuppositions that the meanings of language and action are not self-evident in life or research and must, therefore, be robustly analyzed.

"Triangulation" implies a multidimensionality to the research process, a connotation that may have contributed to its widespread acceptance as an evaluative criterion within the interpretive gestalt. That is, multidimensionality is consistent with the interpretive sensitivity to the various forms or genres of data and to the possibility of complexity and richness that comes from working across genres. Methodological discussions of triangulation emphasize this richness by noting not only the extent to which data from multiple sources, methods, researchers, and/or paradigms present possibilities for corroboration, but also that they are likely to bring to light inconsistent and even conflicting findings (Hammersley and Atkinson 1983; Mathison 1988). And so, although its multidimensionality attracts researchers, this fuller understanding of triangulation also compels researchers committed to trustworthiness to grapple with, rather than discount, inconsistent and conflicting findings. Rather than embracing the ideal of parsimony, called for by methodologically positivist research methodologies, interpretive researchers argue that simplicity should be "an empirical finding rather than a theoretical commitment" (H. Becker 1998, 44).[16]

Second-Order Concepts: Informant Feedback/Member Checks, Audit, and Negative Case Analysis

By comparison with the four first-order terms just discussed, the three second-order concepts are much more clearly "techniques" addressing the "how to" of achieving trustworthy research. Each one invokes a set of methods for answering three questions commonly put to researchers:

1. "How do you know that your study's 'representations' are *recognizable* by the people you studied? How does the reader know 'these words,' 'these views,' are theirs, rather

than yours?" *Informant feedback/member checks* is a specific way that researchers test their own meaning making by going back to, and asking for feedback from, those studied.

2. "How exactly did you do this research?" Anticipating an imaginary *audit* leads researchers to prepare for it by keeping detailed records of their research procedures.

3. "How does the reader know that you didn't look *only* for confirmatory evidence?" *Negative case analysis* represents a set of techniques through which researchers check their own preliminary meaning making by searching for evidence that would challenge those initial ideas.

These labels and their cognates reflect and construct interpretive research practices in different ways, incorporating aspects of the four first-order terms in the rich overlay of ideas that makes up the interpretive gestalt.

"Informant feedback" and "member checks," terms of anthropological and sociological origin, both respond to the first set of questions. Both of them recommend that the researcher go back to the people studied for an assessment of whether the researcher has "got it right." They involve techniques for assessing the connections between the researcher and the situational actors who, together, coproduce the data that are analyzed. As methodological discussions illustrate (e.g., Emerson and Pollner 2002; Miles and Huberman 1994, 275–77), this is a complex endeavor for many reasons, but the impulse behind the technique is indicative of the interpretive gestalt. Whether data are accessed and generated through prolonged field research, in-depth interviewing, or document analysis, the recommended procedure of going back to "members" is based on recognition of the potential for a gulf in understanding between the researcher and "others." Going back to "others" is more than the journalistic practice of "fact-" or "quote checking" (which implies that there is a singular social reality that can be captured by the reporter); it is a fuller recognition that what "others" have to offer may be quite complex, for example, their tacit knowledge, insider vocabularies, and/or positioned understandings of an event, organization, or policy, any of which the researcher may or may not have grasped. The charge is not to take members' meanings for granted, as well as to guard against projecting contemporary meanings onto the past or personal meanings onto another group.[17]

Reflexivity, one of the first-order criteria, assists with "informant feedback/member checks" because it helps the researcher to theorize the potential gulf between self and others, drawing on a variety of factors that constitute, and potentially divide, human experience, including educational attainment, social class, race, gender, profession, and historical period. Whether the researcher conducts an in-depth interview with a single mother on welfare (as in Soss 2000), completes months of participant-observation in the field offices of the Bureau of Land Management (Ginger 2000), or pores over nineteenth-century court cases (Brandwein 1999), both "reflexivity" and "informant feedback/member checks" caution researchers to go back again to check their "constructions" of meaning against those of the actors studied (Lincoln and Guba 1985, 315).[18]

There are a number of reasons why members' reactions to researchers' constructions may be quite mixed, but one of the most significant is that the researcher is positioned between study participants and potential audiences, and the two groups may have quite different interests in a study's implications. For example, the study results might be used to assist participants or they might provide new means for their subjugation. How the researcher deals with this in-between positioning depends not only on the identity and power of the studied group but on the researcher's purpose, which can vary from a commitment to "giving voice" to a marginalized group (e.g., the homeless), as in some action research (see, for instance, Wang, Cash, and Powers 2000); to presenting a group's distinctive worldview for policy makers (e.g., medical students, as in H. Becker et al. 1977 [1961], or addicts, as in Burns 1980); to providing a critical, even potentially emancipatory, perspective on group meanings and practices, as in some feminist research (see Pierce 1995, on litigation lawyers, and D. Kaufman 1989, on religiously orthodox women). What this discussion reveals is that the technique of "informant feedback/member checks" is entangled with some of the more recent interpretive criteria, such as "voice" or "authenticity" and "critical subjectivity" or "criticality" (see Lincoln 1995 and Brower, Abolafia, and Carr 2000 in Table 5.2); with other techniques, such as front-stage and back-stage representation (see Brower, Abolafia, and Carr 2000 in Table 5.3); and with the concern, mentioned earlier, about whether such criteria are inappropriately "political."

Whatever the mix of researcher purpose and the power of the group under study, one possible result is seamless agreement: all group members agree that the researcher has "got it right." Alternatively, and more likely, one or more group members may protest some aspects of the researcher's representations. Such protest (as well as the researcher's purposes and perspectives on the contestation) may be included in the research report and assessed against member quotations and other thickly descriptive elements in a way that shows that the researcher has taken members' meanings seriously, and not just at face value. In Atkinson, Coffey, and Delamont's words, "informants' accounts should neither be endorsed nor disregarded: they need to be analyzed" (2003, 194).

The technique and practice of informant feedback/member checks also bears a family resemblance to what is called "grounded theory" (Glaser and Strauss 1967). Although disagreements have developed between its creators over what this technique entails (Atkinson, Coffey, and Delamont 2003; Creswell 1998b; esp. 148–54),[19] what is germane here is the similarity between the impulse to "go back" to members and the desire to "ground" theory. Both these techniques— though very different in detail, in stage of research when they are undertaken, and so forth— emphasize inductive analysis as a check on researchers' tendencies to forget the gulf between self and others to the possible detriment of faithful constructions of others' meanings and to the possible detriment of theory when it overgeneralizes the ideas of its particular human creators, thereby producing, by implication, "ungrounded" theory. Many methodologically positivist research practices fail to adequately address this gulf. For example, in survey research, participants are not allowed to "talk back" to researchers, to articulate the ways in which the wording of a question fails to capture their concerns, or to articulate an alternative option beyond the limited number from which they are told to choose.[20] In interpretive research practice, the use of "member checks" and "informant feedback" is evidence of a methodological commitment to "getting it right" from the perspective of situational actors' lived experiences.

"Audit," the second concept, refers to a set of practices for documenting study procedures, enabling the researcher to respond to the question, "How exactly did you do this research?" Lincoln and Guba (1985) used the term in their discussion of techniques for demonstrating the criteria of dependability (parallel to reliability) and confirmability (parallel to objectivity). (See Table 5.3.) They give credit for the operationalization of the auditing concept to Halpern (1983), but it was also part of the language of evaluation research that had been developing in public policy analysis throughout the 1970s, when evaluations began to be built in to the policy process. Perhaps no other term better illustrates the disciplining force of criteria, because it may be the anticipation of a critical "audit" of his data and research processes that provokes the researcher to construct "an audit trail," that is, a record as complete as possible of the processes and steps he used to conduct the research. The goal is to make the linkages among researcher decisions, evidence generated, and inferences drawn as transparent as they can be.

The term "audit" has not been much repeated in the criteria literature; its associations with accounting plus the linear notion of a "trail" are a bit at odds with other interpretive language, such as "thick description" and the notion of "immersion" in the field or the data, which imply more synergistic understandings of the research process. Although the term itself has not spread widely, Lincoln and Guba's specific terminology and descriptions codify practices that have been used by researchers in various types of field studies—although perhaps not quite in the ways envisioned by Lincoln and Guba (1985), who describe a full-blown, formal process complete with a written agreement with an outside, paid auditor whose "letter of attestation" assesses a study's dependability and confirmability. Instead, the peer review process typically fulfills the auditor role, and the researcher is expected to provide a detailed record of what has been done in the research process.[21] At least in the ethnographic tradition (Altheide and Johnson 1994), such record keeping has long been a taken-for-granted part of research and writing practices. Reviewers expect to find, as Brower, Abolafia, and Carr put it, a "detailed description of procedures" (2000, 391). For document analysis this expectation has typically been met by providing basic information on selection and authenticity of documents; for interviews, researchers provide information on who was selected, how long and where they were interviewed, interviewing and transcription techniques, the total number of interviews, and other relevant details. The expected background information for participant-observation is yet more extensive, including site selection, length of time in the field, events observed, researcher's role, and so on (see Altheide and Johnson 1994, 491).[22]

Description of the research process in anticipation of a peer review "audit" might be better thought of as meeting a criterion of "transparency" than of reliability/dependability and objectivity/confirmability. This is so because it is now widely recognized in the criteria literature that these latter terms import too much of a positivist conception of research into interpretive criteria. In attempting to parse the concept of reliability, Lincoln and Guba (1985) argued that repeatability of results, a common definition, depends "upon an assumption of naive realism. There must be something tangible and unchanging 'out there' that can serve as a bench mark if the idea of replication is to make sense" (1985, 299). They went on, however, to concede the possibility that human investigators can be careless, and for this reason they suggested "dependability" as a more useful term to identify that problem. Such skepticism of the appropriateness of "reliability" as a standard has continued and grown in interpretive research. Hollway and Jefferson, for example, argue that standard definitions of this term—consistency, stability, repeatability of results—assume that "meanings can be controlled and made identical in successive applications of a question," making reliability an "invalid criterion" from their interpretive perspective on interviewing (2000, 79). Notably, they do not mention the term "dependability" as an alternative; it does not seem to have caught on in the literature as a replacement for "reliability" or as a way to refer to researcher carefulness. "Confirmability" has also not enjoyed widespread usage; rather, the notion of objectivity has received intensive and extensive criticism (see, e.g., Harding 1993). What interpretive researchers emphasize in place of objectivity is reflexivity, which can be assessed by a variety of techniques, including the reflexive journal, reflexive writing practices, member checks, descriptions of research methods, and attention to the researcher role in the generation of evidence, among others.

To sum up discussion of the audit concept, interpretive researchers are committed to, and have written about, techniques for recording and making available their research processes for others' inspection, for addressing the question, "How exactly did you do this research?" Although "audit" is used in the criteria literature and research methods texts to some extent, its use is not ubiquitous but, instead, represents a plethora of practices that enact the goal of "transparency." Because the word "transparency" evokes expectations that researchers willingly lay bare their processes for inspection and critique—the *sin qua non* of peer review—it might be a better term to encompass the reasons interpretive researchers document their research processes. But it is not a term used in the criteria literature or in research methods texts. The literature makes clear that interpretive researchers document their research processes, but such documentation is for purposes other than attaining "reliability" or "objectivity," as those terms' epistemological groundings conflict with interpretive presuppositions about the contextual nature of meaning making over time and the role of the researcher in the research process.

A variety of techniques are intended to enable interpretive researchers to respond to the third question, "How does the reader know that you didn't look *only* for confirmatory evidence?"[23] Collectively, these techniques can be represented by the concept "negative case analysis," used by Lincoln and Guba (1985). Because of its Popperian connotations of falsifiability and a priori deductive theorizing, what needs to be emphasized about negative case analysis is that it relates directly to the researcher's own struggle to make meaning—to make sense of interactions observed in the field, of patterns he or she is seeing in documents or interviews, and/or of possible inconsistencies resulting from triangulation. In these usages, negative case analysis is a technique designed to prevent a researcher from settling too quickly on a pattern, answer, or interpretation; the researcher consciously searches for any evidence—that is, the "negative" or negating case— that will force a reexamination of initial impressions, pet theories, or favored explanations. A slew of related techniques can accomplish the same goal.[24] For example, Miles and Huberman use several phrases to refer to this idea: "checking the meaning of outliers," "using extreme cases," "following up surprises," "ruling out spurious relations," and "checking out rival explanations" (1994, 262). H. Becker (1998, 192–94) talks about "deviant cases." The member checking suggested by Erlandson et al. (1993) and others is intended to accomplish much the same thing. Lincoln and Guba (1985) recommend what they call "peer debriefing," that is, having a colleague critique one's preliminary analysis. Brower, Abolafia, and Carr also list similar techniques to meet their criterion of "criticality": "weighing competing interpretations" and "recognizing and examining competing views or voices" (2000, 391).

Agar's (1986) methodological treatise on ethnographic field research offers a slightly different perspective on researchers' meaning-making processes. While in the field, researchers need to record their initial "breakdowns" in understanding due to their stranger status. As they become more familiar with a setting, what was once "strange" becomes familiar and taken for granted; that is, a state of "coherence" is reached.[25] Coherence can be further tested by researchers' seeking out additional social settings in which to assess their newfound cultural understanding(s). Documenting the transformation from breakdown to coherence, from incidents of cultural awkwardness to smooth navigation of the culture, provides the evidentiary basis for demonstrating that the researcher did not look *only* for confirmatory evidence.[26]

As Agar's work attests, techniques for responding to the third question are quite specific to each data analytic form and even substantive area, making generalizations about techniques and criteria relative to data analysis much more difficult than for the data accessing and generating stage.[27] Part of the difficulty is the sheer number of analytic methods, from semiotics to genealogy to ethnographic semantics (see Table I.1, xx, in the Introduction), in contrast to the comparatively limited number of ways in which data can be accessed (via observation, interviews, or documents).[28] As an example of a specific test developed for historical analysis of documents, Brandwein (see chapter 12, this volume) discusses how the concept of "anachronism" emerged in the Cambridge School as a criterion for assessing researchers' representations and analyses of documents from earlier time periods. For interpretive scholars working in public law and science studies, anachronistic interpretations are poor interpretations because they project contemporary ideas onto historical actors, thereby misunderstanding those actors' meaning making. The anachronism criterion can be used by scholars as a yardstick both in their own research and in evaluating others' research.

Again, there are interconnections between negative case analysis and other techniques and criteria already reviewed. Negative case analysis, like informant feedback/member checks, is aided by reflexivity and, particularly, by the use of a reflexive journal to examine self-other relations as well as the researcher's evolving understandings of purpose and theory (see Soss, chapter 6, this volume, pp. 136–37). An interpretive understanding of triangulation, one of the first-order criteria, similarly pushes the researcher to look for and analyze inconsistencies and contradictions, and the admonition to "thickly describe"—another first-order criterion—heightens researchers' observational skills and the possibilities for detecting the ambiguities, missteps, and covert disagreements among actors in a field setting. In sum, when asked the question, How do I know that you didn't *only* look for confirmatory evidence?, interpretive researchers who follow these procedures can lay out for a reviewer or other reader a number of different techniques employed.

The extent to which these techniques are effective and persuasive depends not only on researchers' careful preparations but also on the character of the audience. The use of any of the techniques reviewed here does not guarantee that readers will be satisfied with the researchers' answers to the three questions commonly put to them. As discussed in chapter 1 (see pp. 20–21 on reader-response theory), interpretive researchers appreciate that they are contributing to a conversation, that there will be another "interpretive moment" because readers bring their own backgrounds and experiences, their own meaning making, to researchers' texts.

BUT WHAT ABOUT CAUSALITY AND GENERALIZABILITY?

As causality and generalizability are a constitutive part of the variables gestalt and are seen, along with reliability and validity, as hallmarks of "scientific" work, a word is necessary concerning their meaning from an interpretive perspective. In their 1985 book Lincoln and Guba discussed causality in terms of "internal validity"—the phrase popularized by Campbell and Stanley's (1963) canonical treatise, *Experimental and Quasi-Experimental Designs for Research*, which has been particularly influential in the fields of education and psychology and has been widely used as the basis for discussion of research design in social science methods texts. Campbell and Stanley held up the true experiment as *the* preferred method for determining causal relationships.[29] They show how the true experiment controls for eight "threats" to internal validity, that is, threats to the claim that a change in the independent or "treatment" variable was responsible for a change in the dependent variable. This mode of thinking about causality is still the modus operandi in a variety of fields, notably mainstream evaluation research, psychology, and medical research. It is an understanding of causality tied to a search for general, predictive laws of human behavior.

Given the interpretivist rejection of the possibility of ahistorical, acultural laws, it is not surprising that some have imputed to interpretive scholars a disinterest in causality (see Gerring's [2003b, 27] question to Clifford Geertz). But, as Geertz's reply clarifies, what is at issue is the *understanding* of causality. The "causal laws" perspective emphasized by Campbell and Stanley (and hegemonic in methods texts) is only one way to think about the concept. Causality is receiving renewed attention in a variety of fields,[30] and interpretive researchers are coming to better understand the ways in which they can reclaim this powerful term on their own ground.

Two interrelated moves are possible. One is to reorient the understanding of causality from general laws to specific cases. Telling quite specific causal stories about how a policy was implemented (as done, e.g., by Pressman and Wildavsky 1973) is not inconsistent with interpretive presuppositions; far from it. This is "Sherlock Holmes causality"—a careful mapping of clues in context, a tracing of connections among events. Interpretive methods lend themselves very well to demonstrating such causality.

The related move, which strengthens the previous one considerably, is to note the role that human meaning making plays in action. Human meaning making and beliefs are understood as "constitutive of actions," and this view of causality can be used to explain not only individual actions (see Jackson's discussion of·the beliefs and strategic actions of key German leaders, chapter 14, this volume) but also the "broad patterns of behavior associated with social movements" (Bevir, chapter 15, p. 285, this volume). In sum, interpretive researchers have a lot to contribute to understandings of causality in ways that broaden the conceptualization of causality beyond the variables-based, explanation-prediction, general law model.

Finally, what of generalizability? Campbell and Stanley introduced the cognate term "external validity" and identified a supposed trade-off in research design: Experiments are strong on internal validity (causal inference) and weak on external validity (generalizability), in their view, whereas surveys are strong on external validity and weak on internal validity. Just as they did with "internal validity," they offered ways to "design away" "threats" to external validity. Lincoln and Guba's (1985) response to Campbell and Stanley was to argue that such thinking about the criterion of generalizability misunderstands the research process and the use of research findings. Whether research findings from a particular study should be "generalized" to another setting should, logically, be the responsibility of the person who seeks to "transfer" those findings to the new setting. (Based on this logic, they rechristened the criterion of "external validity" or "generalizability" as "transferability.") The responsibility of the researcher is to provide sufficient "thick description" so that others can assess how plausible it is to transfer findings from that research study to another setting. It is just such an understanding of, and emphasis on, context— and of the ways in which context and Sherlock Holmes causality are intertwined—that will enable others to build on the research findings they find trustworthy. Consistent with the methodological ferment occurring in contemporary qualitative-interpretive methods,[31] Adcock (chapter 3, this volume) lays out yet other ways in which interpretive scholars may relate particular studies to more general, historical trends and concerns.

CONCLUDING THOUGHTS: EPISTEMIC COMMUNITIES AND JUDGMENT

> "Judgment calls" . . . refers to all of those decisions (some big, some small, but all necessary and consequential) that must be made without benefit of a fixed, "objective" rule that one can apply, with precision, like a template or a pair of calipers. . . . We suggest . . . that a set of rules to replace judgment calls not only would be difficult to fashion, but also would be dysfunctional if we had them.
>
> —*Joseph E. McGrath* (1982, 13–14)

Today, in a number of social science disciplines, the possibility of judgments about research quality based on "a view from nowhere" (Haraway 1988) has been replaced by the understanding that such judgments take place within epistemic communities. Cross-epistemic judgments may sometimes be necessary and even desirable, but, as the thought experiment opening the chapter illustrated, their legitimacy requires a reviewer with an understanding of alternative research gestalts' distinctive practices and purposes. Whether within or across epistemic communities, however, judgment cannot be escaped, and the desire for templates, calipers, and algorithms for judgment may be indicative of the very human fear of shouldering responsibility for consequences, big and small. It is perhaps psychologically easier to point to some list of criteria presumed to be universal than it is to say, "In my judgment, in the context of the practices of this epistemic community, for such and such reasons, this study is inadequate."

If, on the one hand, developing a single set of evaluative criteria is inconsistent with interpretive methodology's context specificity and commitment to historically grounded understanding of the world, and yet, on the other hand, one accepts the necessity of evaluative judgment, how is one to proceed? This chapter offers a list of criteria developed inductively, of value for its brevity, for its historical specificity, and for its connections to interpretive research practices and purposes. As a suggested set of common criteria it offers those working within an interpretive gestalt a starting point for discussion of research quality that should be tied, ultimately, to the specifics of the research question under consideration. Giving reasons for our judgments to the members of our epistemic communities *is* the best that we can do.

NOTES

An earlier version of this chapter was presented in the panel, "What does it mean to do interpretive work? Evaluative criteria and other issues," at the American Political Science Association Annual Meeting, Chicago, IL, September 2–5, 2004. Thanks to Dvora Yanow for organizing the panel and inviting me to participate and for her patient editing and friendly debates on this and other projects.

1. There are numerous indicators of this lack of pluralism in political science, but most relevant to my purpose here is the lack of graduate training in, and in parts of the discipline even awareness of, interpretive methodologies (Schwartz-Shea 2003, 2005). Thus, the interpretive epistemic community in political science still struggles for recognition, whereas disciplines like anthropology, sociology, communication, education, and organizational studies have thriving communities of interpretive scholarship (in some cases, more so in substantive research and theoretical areas than in methods) with journals, funding, and faculty positions on par with other epistemic communities in those fields. I do not mean to suggest that there aren't raging battles over methodology in these disciplines. Rather, interpretive communities have a place at the table, and the fights are among equals or near equals. In contrast, in disciplines like political science the situation of interpretive communities is better described as invisibility or marginalization in the face of hegemony.

2. "This essay thus appeals to the universality of the scientific method rather than to a divisive pluralism" (Laitin 2003, 7). Those arguing that a "mature" discipline has a hegemonic paradigm include Kuhn (1970) and Lakatos (1970).

3. Epistemic communities and their associated research gestalts divide disciplines and cross their boundaries in all of the social sciences, although the degree of pluralism varies notably across disciplines (Klein 1993). One consequence is that, for example, a quantitatively trained sociologist may share more with a mathematician interested in applied statistics than with her feminist departmental colleague who, with his collaborator in cultural studies, examines the political meanings of rap music.

4. Indexicality is "the tendency for a given object, event, phrase, or identity to take on different meanings in different contexts. [Interpretive researchers] don't just want to know what something means, pure and simple, or how a person categorizes the world, always and forever. [They] want to explain [for example] how and why the identity of 'welfare recipient' is significant in one setting but irrelevant in another, a sign of selfishness in one setting and of self-sacrifice in another" (Soss, chapter 6 this volume, p. 139).

5. Within the field of comparative politics, there is a qualitative research tradition known as "comparative historical analysis" (Mahoney and Rueschemeyer 2003a), similar to case study research in other fields and often referred to as "small 'n' research." Even though quantification is not feasible for these comparative case studies, these qualitative researchers speak the language of variables and causal models and endorse goals of prediction and generalizability. See Adcock, chapter 3, this volume, for an analysis of positivist and interpretive approaches to comparative case study research. Researchers across the social sciences who use game-theoretic or formal modeling techniques also share the variables gestalt when it comes to testing the models' implications. For example, see Morton (1999).

6. The term "qualitative-interpretive" is necessary in this context to distinguish this research from qualitative-positivist research. What can be confusing for those reading across disciplines is that the label "qualitative" can mean very different things. For example, in political science, as discussed in note 5, "qualitative" research has most often meant "qualitative-positivist" research. In contrast, in the many fields repre-

sented in the handbook edited by Denzin and Lincoln (2000), the kind of research done under the qualitative label is typically consistent with the interpretive approach emphasized in this volume.

7. As Miles and Huberman emphasize in their introduction, "the data concerned appear in *words*" (1984, 21, emphasis in original). They do suggest converting words to numbers in some cases, but they advise that "this is not always wise. Even when it does look like a good analytic strategy, our counsel is this: keep the numbers, and the words you used to derive the numbers, *together* in your ensuing analysis. That way one never strips the data at hand from the contexts in which they occur" (1984, 21, original emphasis).

8. Among the terms in the last column of Table 5.3, "trustworthiness" is used as a general rubric for the quality of research, Moustakas's "testing out with others" appears similar to the technique of "peer debriefing," and Seale's "replication" and "validation," like Atkinson, Coffey, and Delamont's (2003) use of "evidentiality" and "veracity," appear to be criteria rather than techniques in that they do not directly address the "how to" question.

9. Readers who might be under the impression that such complexity is unique to interpretive criteria debates should consult Adcock and Collier's discussion of the variety of definitions of, and approaches to, "validity" in psychology and political science (2001, esp. 536–38). For more detailed discussion of criteria and techniques, see Schwartz-Shea (2004).

10. Morse and Richards argue that "to claim that reliability and validity have no place in qualitative inquiry is to place the entire paradigm under suspicion; such a claim has ramifications that qualitative inquiry cannot afford, and it diverts attention from the task of establishing useful and usable measures in the qualitative context" (2002, 168).

11. Miles and Huberman, who have been arguing since 1983 for the development of distinct criteria appropriate to qualitative-interpretive work, emphasize that "the problem of quality in qualitative studies deserves attention on its *own* terms, not just as a justification device" (1994, 277, emphasis in original).

12. What I cannot claim to know based on this methodology is the extent to which these selected textbook authors are members of particular *disciplinary* interpretive epistemic communities. That claim would require considerably more research on text usage by discipline. For an example of such research showing the *lack* of recognition of interpretive research in the discipline of political science, see Schwartz-Shea and Yanow (2002).

13. The labels of "first-order" and "second-order" were chosen over two other possible sets of labels for these two categories. I rejected "criteria" and "technique" based on my analysis that these terms could not be coherently distinguished in the literature (Schwartz-Shea 2004). I rejected "primary" and "secondary" because the connotations of these terms imply a normative ordering that does not reflect my intention of describing what I found vis-à-vis my "index test."

14. Atkinson, Coffey, and Delamont argue that the term "thick description" is "dreadfully misunderstood and misrepresented" in that it means more than attention to detail but also "a disciplined appreciation of the over-determination of cultural phenomena" (2003, 114). Although I do not disagree with their analysis, my point is to emphasize the comparative power of the term—the clear way that it evokes a practice—which derives in part from its implicit contrast to the variables research gestalt.

15. Autoethnography "refers to a particular form of writing that seeks to unite ethnographic (looking outward at a world beyond oneself) and autobiographical (gazing inward for a story of one's self) intentions" (Schwandt 2001, 13). It is commonly the use of the researcher's own personal experience with something, e.g., illness, to understand how others might similarly experience it, e.g., interactions with physicians, hospitals, etc. See, e.g., Greenhalgh (2001).

16. There is a striking contrast between the interpretive understanding of triangulation and the term's usage within the variables gestalt. There, triangulation is attractive because of its promise of discovery and precision—the pinning down of a concept (as achieved through composite measures) or the identification of a "true position" (Neuman 1997, 151). In such approaches, corroboration is the theme; the point of triangulation is to use methods that offset each other's weaknesses (Singleton and Straits 1999, 393); this emphasizes consistent findings across methods, and inconsistencies are regarded as problematic. This perspective on triangulation reflects the positivist preference for parsimonious explanations, which are often described as "elegant" and "powerful." For a critique of the argument about "offsetting weaknesses," see Atkinson, Coffey, and Delamont (2003, 144–48).

17. Pader (chapter 8, this volume) argues that, through field research experience, scholars can learn an "ethnographic sensibility" that can improve their reading practices of others' research, as well as of others' experiences, over the lifetime of their careers.

18. Literally "going back" is not always possible, as is most evident in the case of historical research; cost and other barriers (e.g., participant privacy) are impediments in contemporary studies. But researchers have

been innovative in pursuit of the ideal, cross-checking meaning making between participants in a single study or, in the case of historical research, developing additional techniques for assessing researchers' representations from documents of earlier time periods (see Brandwein, chapter 12, this volume).

19. Atkinson, Coffey, and Delamont object to calling "grounded theory" a "technique" (2003, 151), but space precludes recounting the nuance of their argument here.

20. To be sure, there is significant attention to the importance of pretesting surveys to counter such problems and to the use of focus groups to discover the kinds of language most likely used by potential respondents. Underlying these efforts, however, is the assumption that there is a "communication problem" to be *solved* rather than, as in the interpretive approach, an appreciation of the deep contextuality of human meaning-making processes, which neither pre-testing nor focus groups can eliminate. Once the final decisions about question wording have been made, administering a survey enacts a one-size-fits-all logic that perforce ignores individual differences in interpretation of questions and, depending on the scope of the survey, group cultural differences as well. For an example of this latter difficulty, see the discussion in Pader (chapter 8, this volume, pp. 168–70). For a discussion of this issue overall, see Suchman and Jordan (1992).

21. Practices vary by discipline and journal. At a minimum, reviewers can request such information or authors may indicate that such information is available on request. Online publishing provides new ways to promote more widespread access to such background materials, although clear norms have yet to be established.

22. The connection of such practices to other criteria for evaluation is apparent. Documenting one's research process is part and parcel of showing a study's trustworthiness, a way of saying, "I was there and this is what I did," as "thick description" likewise shows.

23. This question sometimes involves an accusation of researcher *bias*—that a researcher is assumed to favor a particular outcome for which, consciously or unconsciously, she garners positive evidence while ignoring the negative cases. This charge comes most often from a positivist perspective that presumes that "word analysis" is somehow less systematic and less objective than quantitative analysis. For a discussion of bias, objectivity, and interpretive methodology, see chapter 4, this volume.

24. Negative case analysis bears a family resemblance to counterfactual analysis (prevalent in the study of international relations and historical research) in that both can be used to check and/or tighten the argument of the researcher. Whereas negative case analysis techniques use existing data to check initial data-based inferences, counterfactual analysis uses imagined scenarios to explore the theoretical logic of the argument. On the need for more rigorous counterfactual analysis, see Fearon (1991).

25. A similar process of moving from "puzzlement" to "insight" can occur in many of the forms of interpretive data analysis, from deconstruction (Clair 1993) to semiotics (Feldman 1995).

26. Agar's methodological advice on what to expect concerning meaning making in the field can be contrasted with the National Science Foundation *Report of the Workshop on the Scientific Foundations of Qualitative Research*. Though laudable in its goal of "making qualitative projects competitive in the NSF review process" (Ragin, Nagel, and White 2004, 3), the executive summary emphasizes that grant supplicants should provide and reviewers should expect to find "*plans to look for and interpret disconfirming evidence*, alternative explanations, unexpected findings, and new interpretations—try to be wrong as well as right" (2004, 17, emphasis in original). It is not so much the specific language or the impulse that is problematic. As discussed, this same impulse is part of the interpretive emphasis on triangulation, reflexivity, and negative case analysis; that is, it is appropriate to seek a complex, in-depth portrait of whatever phenomenon is under study. What is troublesome is the failure to recognize that for interpretive researchers, predicting what will constitute "disconfirming evidence" *at the design stage* is inconsistent with interpretive presuppositions that researchers seek to understand the meaning of others. The NSF requirements put the cart before the horse in stipulating that the researcher should know ahead of time what can only be discovered in the midst of doing research.

27. As discussed in the Introduction to Part III, ethnography is simultaneously a method of data access, generation, *and* analysis.

28. There is a similar diversity of statistical analytic techniques, but these share an epistemological edifice most easily understood in terms of the language of "Type I" and "Type II" errors, in which what the researcher claims is compared to a "true situation in the world" (Neuman 1997, 323). A "Type I" error is made when a researcher claims that a relationship exists in the data when, due to sampling error, that is not the case in the world. A "Type II" error is made when the researcher claims that a relationship does not exist, based on the sample data, when in fact such a relationship *is* the case in the world. This distinction assumes

a "truth" out in the world that is independent of researcher meaning-making processes. In contrast, because interpretive meaning-making processes do not assume an objective (i.e., external) truth, they cannot be evaluated on the basis of how well they capture "truth."

29. Adcock (see chapter 3, this volume) describes the history behind Campbell and Stanley's confident exposition of their approach to causality and generalizability.

30. New formulations of causality can be found in chaos theory and complexity theory, as well as in discussion of causal mechanisms. See Gerring (2000), Ragin (2000b), and Tilly (1995).

31. For a listing of initiatives, see the first paragraph and associated notes from chapter 22, this volume. Additionally, the editors of this volume offered a workshop on "Interpretive Research Methods in Empirical Political Science" at the 2003 Western Political Science Association Meetings and, in 2005, the International Institute for Qualitative Methodology (Canada) sponsored a weeklong workshop titled "Thinking Qualitatively."

PART II

ACCESSING AND GENERATING DATA

Question:
All the cocks in Kasombe Village are white.
Lute Mirla saw a cock in Kasombe Village.
What colour was the cock she saw?

Answers:
Lute Mirla went to the market yesterday to sell two chickens.
Lute Mirla has a sister she goes to see in Kasombe Village.
Ask Lute Mirla when she gets back.
—*Andreas Fuglesang* (1982, 15)

"Access," in the context of traditional field research methods treatises, is typically used in reference to gaining entrée to a research site or person—a community, overseas or domestic; an organization; an archive; a government official. Although we begin this section overview with some discussion of that understanding of access, we are primarily using the term in a different sense. In standard methods textbooks and discussions, the more commonly found phrase is "gathering" or "collecting" data. Yet, as the chapters in this section demonstrate, interpretive data are understood less as being accessed by the researcher, as if they had some ontologically prior, independent existence, like some exotic fruit just waiting for the researcher to come and discover and "pluck" it, than as being "generated"—at the very least by the researcher in conceptual, mental interaction with her documentary materials and observed events. In addition, when research data are generated through interviews or in the physical and nonverbal exchanges between respondents and researcher during participatory interactions, one might speak of the "co-generation" of data. And so we speak here of accessing sources that might enable the generation of data.

ACCESS AS ENTRÉE TO POTENTIAL SOURCES
OF POTENTIAL EVIDENCE

Methods texts treating field research typically discuss "entry" into the field setting. The notion that entry is a problem is curious, as is the use of that language. As Feldman, Bell, and Berger (2003, ix) point out, the language suggests the imagery of a door, and only a single door at that, which needs somehow to be made to open. Although common now across qualitative methods texts, this concept seems to have emerged out of traditional anthropological research and its historical context, in which a researcher—typically from England, France, the United States or some other Western country—sought (and seeks) to conduct research—to observe, to participate, to talk to people—in a village or community in some non-Western location. To do so, researchers often did have the experience of exerting pressure on some barrier—often a colonial administration or, later, perhaps an officer in a Ministry or a prefecture in a non-Western country—for permission to set up shop in some remote location. The Ministry was, for all intents and purposes, a single door that, eventually, usually yielded.[1]

But more than that, a whiff of the colonial heritage out of which late-nineteenth-century anthropology grew and the patronizing or even racist attitudes of that era and those practices seems to attach to the concept of that entryway: Textbooks treat it in a dehumanized fashion, as if it were an inanimate object, with the person seeking entry—the researcher—as the only party having reasoned agency. Those with authority to grant or deny entry are often portrayed, historically at least, as unreasonable, and therefore lesser, human beings. Yet, there are people behind those literal and metaphoric doors. And so Feldman and her colleagues propose that the problem of access be treated as a matter of human relationships that need to be created, fostered, and nurtured in an ongoing fashion over time; and that the researcher needs to have some skill level in such processes (2003, xi). The problem, then, is one of *gaining* access, as their title proclaims, more than entry, more verb than noun. Similarly, those researching documents in archives typically must gain access to those repositories and are faced with somewhat similar issues.

This more human-centered, interactive, process approach dovetails with our articulation of a set of methodological skills used in accessing potential sources that might help generate potential evidence or data, which are distinct from the sets of tools used in analyzing those data once one has them in hand (although we note later that this distinction is largely a heuristic device that does not hold uniformly or universally for all the analytic methods discussed here). Among these methods of generating data is the ability to talk with people: the interview.

"Interviewing" as used in interpretive methods means something other than administering a survey or otherwise following a list of questions that the researcher feels he must cover in their entirety lest the interview be deemed a failure. Chapman (2001) captures the differences in spirit underlying these practices in describing the reactions of his research partner, an economist trained in survey research, and himself, trained as an anthropologist, as they set out to talk to people in an organizational setting. Chapman finds himself completely enthralled with what he is learning from their field research—interviews that last half a day, observations of meetings—while his colleague's attention wanders and he sees little coming out of such "nondirected" research. On their interviewing, Chapman writes: "I think my colleague at the time viewed [what the textbooks call 'unstructured interviews'] as a subset of 'interviews'; I regarded it as a subset of 'talking to people'" (2003, 23). The relationship building that Feldman and colleagues argue for seems paramount in Chapman's comments.

This phase of interpretive research, however, does not necessarily concern gaining access solely for purposes of interviewing, as many modes of interpretive research draw on sources of evidence other than people's talk. Ethnographic, participant-observer, and other methods draw also on observations of what people do, with varying degrees of researcher participation in those acts. Some studies—analyses of work practices or organizational culture(s) come to mind—rely on observations of the physical objects used by people in these acts, including the spaces within which these acts take place and the objects used therein, and they entail analyses of the meanings embedded in, conveyed by, and interpreted through these artifacts (see, e.g., Gagliardi 1990; Rafaeli and Pratt 2005). In addition, historical, deconstructionist, semiotic, frame, and other analyses rely on documents as potential sources of potential evidence.

"Accessing data," then, is shorthand for a wide variety of methods used in generating the data that form the basis for what one analyzes, commonly, with other sorts of methods. Some of the activities that comprise this accessing-and-generating stage may precede negotiating physical access; in some fields, these are rarely included in methods discussions. For example, for certain research projects, the researcher needs to identify the sorts of documents—whether historic or contemporary, legislative or organizational, public or proprietary—that *might* yield information that *might* be relevant to the topic under investigation. Sometimes this can mean identifying and/or locating archives, private libraries, newspaper morgues, or other repositories. For other sorts of studies or other phases of the same study, "identifying and locating" may refer to the individuals one thinks *might* know something about one's subject that *might* be useful to one's analysis. Other studies or phases require similar thinking through of potential settings—"field sites"—that might yield interesting observational data.

The doubled potentiality—will this person, document, or setting be relevant to my study, and if I manage to negotiate access, will what I learn inform my research?—marks this exploratory phase of accessing data. It is an exploration done before efforts to gain actual access can be initiated, with one major class of exceptions. In interpretive research, one source—whether human, documentary, or setting—may, and often does, lead to another; in fact, one typical question closing an interview is, "With whom else should I speak?" And so this identification-and-access process is carried out continually, as contingency is not only anticipated but built into the research design. For this reason, detailing a research plan in advance of carrying out the research has limited utility and efficacy, and often is just not possible or desirable. This is especially the case when research is done in places not well known in advance, especially those at a significant distance such that it is difficult or even impossible to make one or more preliminary scouting trips. Information passed on by predecessors at one's research site may be outdated. And although the internet has made many more sources of information available in advance, its tools and capabilities are not unlimited.

The discussions in these chapters of methods of accessing and generating data begin after these initial determinations of potentiality have been made and after permissions, where necessary, have been secured. What are being accessed are less the data themselves than potential sources of potential evidentiary data. In engaging these data sources through talking to people, observing and/or interacting with them, and/or reading about them and/or their activities, evidence is being generated—collaboratively, in the case of interviews and interactions—that the researcher will analyze and then marshal to make an argument.

TALKING

Interview as a subset of talk, as Chapman put it, denotes a range of talk modes. Various methods textbooks even use the term in reference to "administering" questionnaires. The kind of interviewing interpretive researchers draw on most widely does not follow, in lock-step fashion, a prepared list, survey style, of dozens of questions, and especially not those that can be answered with a single word or checked box. It is a talk mode sometimes referred to as "in-depth" or "open-ended" interviewing.

"Conversation" comes close to capturing the character of interviewing in an interpretive mode. It is an ordinary term—in reporting on one's daily activities, one is more likely to talk about having a conversation than about talking in depth or open endedly. We may well sacrifice the rhetorical power of technical terminology in talking about "conversational interviewing." But these *are* discursive conversations, not interrogations. Many of them do take place in kitchens and living rooms, in community centers and in well-baby clinics, on shop floors and outside corner grocery stores—and not only in offices and other, more formal settings. They are as likely to be chatty exchanges—"informal" interviews—started up by the office water cooler or in the neighborhood watering hole (whether the café or the pub) as set up on the calendar in advance ("formal" interviews).[2] And they can be as much "small talk" as "big" talk—and may, at times, combine both.

The more discursive format has led to such interviews being called "open ended." That terminology positions the concept in opposition to survey questionnaires, whose items are "closed ended." But this linguistic opposition has itself led to a perceptual and conceptual opposition that is problematic—a view that unlike the more structured and rigid procedures of survey research, open-ended interviewing rambles all over the place, with no structure and no direction on the part of the interviewer. In fact, the opposite is far more likely to obtain. Whereas we might construct a continuum of interview genres from more directed to less directed, in interpretive interviewing the researcher does direct the conversation in one way or another, toward some focus or purpose relative to the research question. For that reason, interviewing in an interpretive mode has also been called "purposive conversation."

"In depth" is another term for interviewing in a conversational or discursive mode. It, too, developed to distinguish such methods from survey questionnaires, which are often characterized as being more "superficial" in the extent to which they delve into their subjects' lives. True, interpretive interviewing is intended to explore the meaning(s) of terms and/or situations and/or events and so on to the persons who live with and/or lived through them. One might conceive of experience-based meaning as "deeper" in some way than attitudes or single-sentence opinions. But "in-depth" interviewing seems to grasp as little of the character of such methods as "open-ended" interviewing, both terms having been developed to contrast their practices with surveys more than to capture the style of this mode of interaction itself.

Joe Soss's chapter 6 masterfully reviews some of the nuances in the relationship between interviewer and respondent and the strengths of the conversational approach. The unique context of a conversational interview—an exchange with a focused listener who is eager to devote the time to hear the respondent's views—allows the respondent to reflect on and even explore her own ideas, to reveal not only strong views but also worries, uncertainties—in a word, to engage human vulnerability. So often, everyday human interactions are marked by habitual, unreflective modes of communicating. Conversational interviewing, by contrast, can be a way to lay bare, as Soss argues, human agency—those points at which human beings go along with others' expectations of them and those points at which they resist and, instead, chart an autonomous path.

Soss also analyzes how recognizing others' humanity and agency means coping with the emotional connections and disconnections that arise in this intimate setting. Reflexivity on the researcher's part is essential—reading one's own sympathy or repugnance, knowing when to push an issue forward or when to back off, and analyzing how these emotions and decisions affect the data co-generated in these exchanges. Social, occupational, and political life is filled with emotional content—anger, humiliation, empathy, fear—that can be key to understanding individual and collective, organizational, communal, political, and other action. Conversational interviews can enable the exploration of how people make sense of their emotional experiences and how this sense making connects to action.

The discursive character of interviewing in an interpretive mode is clear in the brief transcript reported by Frederic Schaffer in chapter 7. Despite the fact that the interviewer has been trained in very specific techniques, absent Schaffer's descriptive phrases labeling the kind of questions being asked, the interchange resembles nothing more than a conversation between two persons, one of whom is most interested in what the other has to say about the subject of *demokaraasi/demokrasya*. In another context, one might imagine having a similar conversation with one's immigrant grandmother about her experiences: The curiosity to know is what drives the conversation.

Such conversations are structured, although the structure varies according to the subject and the setting. For some research questions, a chronological structure is most appropriate (in what order did events unfold?). For others, it might be a spatial structure (e.g., what was going on next door as x was happening?), possibly organized horizontally (right to left, or left to right, depending on the culture and/or the question or event), possibly vertically (top to bottom, or vice versa). Time and space are not the only organizing principles for conversational interviews, although they are common ones. An agency-related interview might be structured along organizational lines (authority, hierarchy, power). Gender might be another structuring principle, the demographic or organizational "mapping" of neighborhoods, another.

Schaffer's identification of kinds of questions takes a major step toward detailing what, exactly, goes on in a "client-centered" interview (of the sort developed by Carl Rogers [1951], in a therapeutic context) or in the so-called active listening that derives from it. There are myriad ways in which an interviewer paraphrases what she has just been told, both to signal that she really has been listening, thereby further developing rapport with the person being interviewed, and to communicate, sincerely, what she has understood. Schaffer shows some of the forms such paraphrasing can take. His note 4 is tremendously important on this score: By conveying to our interlocutor what it is that we just understood of what we were told, we check on our interpretations. This is the attitude of testability (or "revisability"), that hallmark of doing science or being scientific, enacted in a very concrete way, as it opens the door to the possibility of learning that we did, in fact, "get it wrong"—we made our own sense, but it was not the sense of the person talking, and that, after all, is what we were after.

Schaffer underscores the importance of context, specifically in the ways that language and act are mutually implicating in the process of learning to make sense of any symbol system. His quote from Wittgenstein on games highlights the difference between coming to a study with concepts and theories already in place versus avoiding the rush to diagnosis and waiting to see whether patterns emerge out of one's immersion in what one is told. This line of thinking positions the researcher methodologically in the language debates of philosophy and linguistics and their applications (e.g., in legal studies): It is a Wittgensteinian position to claim that meaning resides not in the words themselves but in their usage—a position that characterizes interpretive methodologies more broadly, given their focus on context specificity (see, e.g., Valverde 2003).

We want to emphasize that ordinary language interviewing may be used within one's own national or other culture, too. As scholars of organizational culture have noted over the last twenty-five years and more (e.g., Smircich 1983; Ingersoll and Adams 1992), agencies and their divisions or departments establish their own cultures, and language usage is one way in which they demarcate these boundaries. Researchers coming to study organizations within their own national, regional, or other cultures may be as much foreigners to them and their language particularities as Schaffer was studying Senegalese demokaraasi in Woloff. Whatever the setting, interpretive researchers begin not with predefined concepts, but with curiosity to discover how local practices inform local vocabularies—what "native" terms and concepts mean in local usages.

We note that Schaffer's interview is a wonderful example of the claim that interpretive methods are more democratic, in the sense that they acknowledge the interlocutor's expertise in his own situation and the legitimacy of his own local knowledge. The interviewer is respectful of Juan de la Cruz and of Juan's local knowledge of his own experience, his own views, his own language; the interviewer treats Juan as expert on these—which, of course, he is. Conversational interviewers in an interpretive mode long ago gave up on the idea that one could control for "interviewer effects." Even if one could train survey researchers to adhere strictly to the questionnaire protocol—something that is humanly very difficult—one cannot control for the "effects" of nonverbal communication, including tone of voice and other paralinguistic elements, physical characteristics such as hairstyle and posture, facial and hand gestures, and so on. These, too, communicate meaning and are interpreted, whether in keeping with intended meanings or not. The alternative to "control" is to be as reflectively aware as possible of the ways in which one might be affecting the exchange.

Moreover, as Schaffer notes, "nonjudgmental" does not mean "blank" or "passive." Some methodologists argue that it is inhumane and unethical for researchers to withhold their opinions when they feel strongly about something their interlocutors say (on this, see Holstein and Gubrium 1995). Without the constrained response possibilities of a survey, with the focus on understanding meaning rather than on opinion or attitude, and with the format of a conversation, people are far less likely to try to second-guess the interviewer's hidden motives and to reply with a surmised "right" answer. Their views of their own lives, in the end, are what interpretive researchers are trying to get close to. And researchers are always contextualizing what they are told, with other interviews and/or documents and/or their own observations.

OBSERVING

Another central mode of accessing and generating potential data is observing, with whatever degree of participating (Gans 1976). This mode can be used as a stand-alone source of data, or it can be combined with interviewing, in which each method is used to corroborate (or refute) provisional interpretations derived from the other. In researching demographic changes in a neighborhood, it can be as edifying to pay attention to the amount and kinds of laundry hanging on the line, for example, as it is to interview the neighbors.

Ethnographic and participant-observational research rest on observation. (Both may include varying degrees of participation, which itself entails observing, and they may also draw on documentary evidence; as both methods engage people in conversation, they typically do not designate "interviewing" as a separate method.) The two approaches were divided in the United States with the demarcation between sociological ethnography and anthropological ethnography, separating the territory between domestic studies and overseas ones. Within the United States, the "unmarked" names of fields in sociology and other areas that imply "U.S." or "domestic" as a modifier—such as public administration, public policy, urban studies, labor studies, community studies, social problems, organizational studies—tend to use "participant-observer" methods; those fields whose research typically requires facility in a language other than English and an extended sojourn in some "foreign" locale—such as international studies, comparative government, development studies—tend to use "ethnographic" methods. As Katz (2004, 9) describes the difference, anthropological ethnography "has been much more likely to require long term personal planning, travel documents and funding"; whereas sociological study entails a "relatively full and temporally open ended participant observation in the social lives of subjects."

In chapter 8, Ellen Pader develops the idea that it is possible to learn to observe with "an ethnographic sensibility." Ethnography is "the attempt to understand another life world using the self—as much of it as possible—as the instrument of knowing" (Ortner 1996, 281). In such a study, "the whole self physically and in every other way enters the space of the world the researcher seeks to understand." Contemporary ethnographers, as Ortner notes, commit "to producing understanding via richness, texture, and detail rather than parsimony, refinement, and (in the sense used by mathematicians) elegance" (Ortner 1996, 281). This "richness, texture, and detail" is the Geertzian notion of "thickness"—a layering of observations that situates both knower and known in their respective contexts. What Pader means by an ethnographic "sensibility" is entering this world-space and looking beneath its surface not only to find the modes of thinking that shape patterns of activity there, but also to attend to what is, intentionally or otherwise, not being "seen" or spoken about.

Choosing a single chapter to represent such a complex mode of data access and generation was daunting, and, indeed, other chapters in part III (notably Samer Shehata's chapter 13 and Clair Ginger's chapter 19) should also be read for the ways in which they describe observational methods. Pader's chapter accomplishes two things that we wish to underscore. First, she "makes strange" for us the everyday observational processes that ordinary human beings take for granted and that researchers, ordinary humans themselves, have to denaturalize. Learning *how* to look and how to see for scientific purposes can take considerable practice. Second, in recounting examples from her own experiences and from the ethnographic literature, she makes plain how exceedingly difficult this task can be. Her accounts illustrate how easy it can be for policy analysts and other researchers who have *not* developed an ethnographic sensibility to misread others' actions because they have not grasped those others' operating assumptions, often because they have not reflected on and, hence, cannot "see" their own.

Pader's chapter offers a welcome contrast, indeed, a critical corrective, to the sorts of analyses built on a priori assumptions about a universal human nature. Such analyses might be characterized as theory driven, as analyses that attempt to "force fit" observations into the framework generated by a given theory (Kuhn 1970; I. Shapiro 2002) in an attempt to "save" the theory, rather than altering it or developing a new one that would give a better account of the observations. They are found most prominently in economic analyses of public policy and economic and human behavior (e.g., Gary Becker's 1981 exchange theories of marriage and the family). Many analysts (e.g., W. Brown 1988; Charusheela and Zein-Elabdin 2003) have noted that "economic man" is a theoretical perspective that is not only male, but culturally Western, and that its use imposes particularistic, rather than universally held, assumptions on cultures and societies that assume quite different things about human goals and human flourishing, thereby running the risk of misunderstanding and misanalyzing them. Pader's treatment of observation harkens back to the roots of the scientific enterprise in which the curiosity to know about a particular phenomenon meant hours and days of intense, direct observation, *partnered* with theoretical thinking, in a way that allowed theories to emerge out of observational data.[3]

READING

Humans inscribe and communicate what is meaningful to them in the context of their political, social, cultural, organizational, and communal lives in, on, and through a wide range of artifact types. Many analyses, especially in political science, have restricted their understanding of documentary evidence to the literal sense of written records—and even further narrowing that sense, sometimes, to those records produced by governing elites. Public policy studies examine legislative and agency documents; international relations studies look at transcripts of negotiations, for example; public law studies analyze court records and Supreme Court opinions; and so on.

Depending on the research question, however, restricting "documentary" evidence to materials produced and approved by governing elites can be overly limiting. By contrast, for example, in his study of communist and postcommunist Russian identity, Hopf (2002) drew on popular novels purchased at corner kiosks, high school textbooks, the daily press, and other written materials that were widely read at the time. Restricting documentary evidence to written materials alone can also be limiting.[4] Political, social, organizational, and cultural identities and values are embedded also in films, both fictional and documentary; in state-issued postage stamps; in folk songs, especially the genres of labor, military (marching), revolutionary, and women's songs (e.g., Fernandes 2003); in architectural design (e.g., of corporate or governmental buildings; see, e.g., Goodsell 1988; Lasswell 1979; Mosse 1975; Yanow 1993, 1998, and chapter 20 in this volume); in museum exhibits (see, e.g., Luke 2002); and in political cartoons (see Gamson and Lasch 1983). Social scientific research in ethnic studies, urban studies, cultural studies, and other fields that explore films and other aspects of non-textual culture and that treat a broad range of textual materials as repositories and communicators of meaning have expanded the scope of written artifacts that are useful in interpretive empirical research. In historical research, such a reach is not uncommon, although no less innovative. Drawing on such textual materials as travelers' accounts describing world exhibitions, T. Mitchell (1991) uses them to read the layout of streets, the design of schools and the structure of schooling, and other non-textual activities in analyzing the everyday manifestations of colonial power in Egypt and the successful imposition of order. In his subsequent volume, Mitchell (2002), reaches even more broadly for sources of evidence, encompassing the anopheles mosquito, the Nile, the Aswan Dam, and the land (or patterns of land ownership) as nonhuman actors in Egyptian history. Similarly, Darnton uses cats and false teeth as evidence, respectively, in his histories of revolutionary France (1984) and revolutionary America (2003).

The unnecessarily narrow treatment of material culture may emerge from the language of "documents," which is how most methods textbooks treat the residual category after acts observed and individuals interviewed. In political science, this orientation may come from the customary and comfortable practices developed out of its deeply entrenched, long-standing history of treating ancient texts (Plato, Aristotle) and "government documents," ranging from constitutions to statutes to executive edicts—all the accoutrements of governing. More than other social sciences (except, perhaps, legal studies), political science retains a very strong textual hermeneutic orientation, as in its emphasis on constitutional analysis. Yet all social science practices devote time and energy to reading and writing, and so the narrow focus on literal texts may derive quite simply from occupational habits, or even from a failure of imagination. As many well-regarded scholars have broken free from these constraints, however, we are inclined to regard this straitjacketing of inquiry as less "genetic" than learned. And if the latter, it can be unlearned, as imagination is unleashed.

Jutta Weldes's discussion of "high" versus "low" data (chapter 9) expands the range of documentary materials that could yield insights into social, political, and other meanings to include such things as science fiction, film, advertisements, architecture, music, and war memorials, among others. What her chapter makes especially clear is that it is no accident that these data possibilities have been ignored. Conceptions of theory produce conceptions of "appropriate" data; and the state-centric nature of mainstream international relations theory, in her case, as well as the self-conceptions of social scientists as serious people who tackle serious topics, have combined to limit the kinds of questions and associated data admitted to the mainstream. Weldes asked a research question that transgressed these confines, and that question led her to consider the "low data" of popular culture as essential sources for revealing the partial character of elites' understandings of globalization, a limited understanding that, simultaneously, is made possible and plausible by these broader discourses.

In short, her chapter enacts the broadest understanding of "methodology"—revealing the complex ways in which both the framing of research questions depends upon prior theoretical understandings (themselves, as discussed in chapter 1 of this volume, dependent on ontological and epistemological presuppositions) and the questions thus framed, in turn, define what "counts" as evidence. As Kuhn (1970) noted, observation is theory laden. That does not mean, however, that observation is "theory determined," a point made by I. Shapiro (2002), for otherwise, human beings could never learn. Empirical evidence can still be unexpected and can startle the researcher and upset accepted theories and habitual understandings. It is precisely that potential for the proverbial upsetting of the apple cart that renders it so important to broaden the scholarly imagination about what "counts"—not only as social science evidence, but as legitimate social science research questions and topics.[5]

Considering the range of possibilities for evidentiary sources in the context of a hermeneutic philosophy of social science highlights the extent to which the repertoire of human meanings is expressed in various genres, such as the range of artifacts considered by Weldes. The principle of "intertextuality" holds, then, not only across different (literal) texts but across data genres. A researcher unread in the Bible or the Qur'an, for instance, would miss out on the resonances to their audiences of U.S. president George W. Bush's, Israeli prime minister Ariel Sharon's, or Saudi Arabian crown prince Abdullah's speeches. But that researcher would also miss something of significance (or that was significant at the time) in agency and polity meaning in an analysis of the National Aeronautics and Space Administration if he did not know that it named its "Enterprise" spaceships, at many Americans' requests, after the fleet in the science fiction series *Star Trek* (Weldes 2003b).

Admitting of a broader range of evidentiary sources is not simply a matter of imagination; it is also a matter of philosophical presupposition. For a science that focuses on numerical "facts," admitting less bounded, more ambiguously interpreted materials into the realm of "data" is, or can be, a stretch. This predisposition is evident in the common distinction between "hard" and "soft" data, reflecting the perceived centrality of numerical ("hard") data to the enterprise of "true" (i.e., methodologically positivist conceptions of) science.

One of the temptations—we think it an especially American one—in dealing with governmental documents, numerical reports in particular, is to treat them as inherently "honest" or "truthful." Perhaps this is a hallmark of positivist-influenced or ontologically realist research: We think that interpretive researchers, especially those influenced by feminist methods, with their emphasis on standpoint epistemologies (see, e.g., Hartsock 1987), and critical theory, which questions the ties between knowledge and power, are less likely to take government pronouncements on faith and more likely to "lift the rug" and "look beneath the surface." The reflexivity embedded in these approaches leads researchers to question the production of knowledge (including of their own role in that). This questioning may lead to exploring silences in discourse, what is not being said, such as the "hidden transcripts" (J.C. Scott 1990) underlying official pronouncements.

Julia Paley (2001), for example, describes the ways in which residents of a barrio in Chile resisted the efforts of the census taker and administrators of other survey questionnaires. In one case, the respondent registered the fact that his choice of television station depended on context: who else was watching, what was on, and so forth. Not satisfied with the response, the questioner tried again. He met again with a reply that did not satisfy him. At that point, and despite all training to the contrary, the surveyor "fed" the respondent the answers on the sheet. Such situations are familiar to survey researchers, and tremendous efforts are made to train questioners not to yield to such counterpressure. But a second case describes resistance of a different sort. On being asked what sort of electric appliances she had in her house, the respondent told the census taker that she had none, despite the fact that several were visible and even running during the "interview." The respondent later explained to Paley: "Why should I say I have these things when in reality they're no good? The refrigerator is more than twenty years old . . . The television was a gift . . . I didn't purchase it. The washing machine . . . was a [piece of junk] . . . that washed only when I begged it by saying 'please'" (2001, 154). She apparently saw her answers as counterbalancing those of her neighbors, who claimed to have appliances they could not afford because of the symbolic value—the status—they perceived attached to such possession, which would "elevate their image in their own and the census-takers' eyes" (2001, 154).

It would be too simplistic to say that such respondents are "lying," or that governments "lie" through statistics. We see these responses, rather, as an element of the "presentation of self" (Goffman 1959): of the conscious and willing construction of a "front stage" that presents what is perceived, whether by individuals or by governments or by organizations or some other collective, as a desirable persona or image, in an effort to mask a less desirable "back stage."[6]

These are the sorts of issues that Dean McHenry engages in chapter 10. He looks at the three categories for studying political protest that appear in a widely accepted and widely used database, the Cross-National Time-Series Data Archive. These categories—riots, strikes, and demonstrations—were developed by Arthur Banks based on reading the *New York Times* accounts of events in India. But from his own lived experience there, McHenry came to understand that these categories did not adequately identify the multitude of forms of political protest carried out by Indians, for which they had many more than three names. McHenry asks, then, what the widespread adoption of such experience-distant categorical language does for our understanding of events. What sense can we make of the numbers toted up and reported in such databases if the assumptions underlying category definitions are derived from some experience other than the one the researcher is trying to understand—indeed, from one so distant, physically and conceptually, from the subject of study that the analytic categories do not do justice to actors' lived experiences? What sort of faith, interpretive or otherwise, can we place in numerical analyses generated in such fashion?

It is not only geographic distance that produces such conceptual-experiential distortions. Similar discrepancies arise from official—state—statistics that indicate, for example, the number of "traditional birth attendants" trained in the latest obstetrical medical procedures, usage rates of modern delivery tools and of more "sanitary" sterilization techniques for boiling the tools, and so on (Jordan 1989). On the basis of these numbers, the state reports (e.g., to the World Health Organization) on the extent of medical coverage provided to ever increasing numbers of rural communities otherwise not served by hospitals, and perhaps this translates into United Nations funding. But, as Jordan so richly details, at graduation ceremonies certificates are awarded to midwives who had help from staff in taking the written objective tests—which in her view "measure changes in linguistic repertoire and discourse strategies" (1989, 6) more than the degree to which midwives incorporate the training into their repertoires of practice:

> For measuring behavioral effects, simple interviewing [as in a survey] is inadequate. . . . It is not that the midwives lie. . . . As competent social actors, they adjust their way of talking to the person they are talking to. . . . [T]he trainers never appreciate the ways in which the statistics they compile have little to do with reality. They orient to the statistical requirements of the national bureaucracy and when they go out into the communities they carry with them [this] way of looking at the world. . . . (1989, 7)[7]

What is required, in Jordan's view, are detailed observations made "by someone who has the midwives' confidence and is allowed to accompany them on births and pre- and postnatal visits, since the only way one can find out about utilization of what they have learned is to be there on actual occasions of use" (1989, 7). The sorts of analyses Jordan calls for are interpretive in their reflexivity: their willingness to subject numerical sources of evidence to critique, rather than accepting their production at face value. This is the normative heart of McHenry's argument, and it harks back to Kirstie McClure's reading (1999) of the circular legitimation of the science of statistics: the Royal Society of Statistical Science announced itself as the source of its own legitimacy. As T. Mitchell notes in the context of their twentieth-century usage:

> Colonial power had long made use of statistics, whether for administrative needs or to produce a larger "illusion of bureaucratic control." . . . But the circulation of statistics among a "public" . . . enabled them to take on the form of an "objective culture" . . . , [leading to] a divide between two worlds, a sphere of figures, numbers, facts, and trends on the one side, and the world to which these refer on the other. The latter must stand as its opposite, the realm of the material, the real. (2002, 103)

Dean McHenry calls on us to heed such misplaced concreteness[8] and to interrogate the largely unspoken and silent assumptions embedded in its products, along with the processes through which they are produced.

SEPARATING ACCESS FROM ANALYSIS

We wish to underscore what we noted at the beginning of this introduction, that the distinction we are drawing between methods of accessing or generating data and methods of analyzing them is useful for analytic and conceptual purposes, but it does not hold for all methods and can be profoundly misleading in some cases. To take the latter point first: Analysis commences when one begins to conceive of a research project, to frame one's research question, read others' writings on the subject, and design one's study. One may be more or less conscious of this—we urge researchers to be more so—which is one of the reasons why "data analysis" as a formal undertaking typically is listed as a penultimate step, rather than as an initial one. This positioning, too, is a methodological issue, as it posits that analytic activities are performed on data alone, not on one's readings or thought processes. In our view, separating analysis from other research activities is a narrow and limiting construal of what transpires in crafting research—although we borrow it for heuristic purposes.

The other point that warrants articulation is that some methods lend themselves more to the distinction between access and analysis than others. In some it is clear that analysis is a mental activity performed on data in hand (though one need not necessarily wait until the "end" of a data accessing phase to do so). Such is the case with formal semiotic analysis, for example, or category or metaphor analysis, or any other form in which the researcher works primarily (if not exclusively) with word data, whether accessed through documents or through interviewing. In other modes of research, however, it is far more difficult to separate out analytic processes from those entailed in accessing and generating data: Temporally, they are much more intertwined. This is particularly the case for ethnographic, participant-observation, case study, and (participatory) action research. Practitioners of these methods typically do not see themselves as analyzing their data in a fashion that is separate and distinct from what they do in accessing them.

We suggest, with all due respect, that this is one of the practices or habits of mind that has led to a misconstrual that what such researchers do is lacking in rigor. As noted in the introduction to the book, given that these methods are, at this point in academic time, crossing boundaries into disciplinary locales in which their presuppositional grounding is not widely known and/or is not clear, it would be worth the effort for practitioners in such communities to make the tacit knowledge of their practices as explicit as possible. This is what we hope the chapters in this section of the book accomplish with respect to talking, observing, and reading.

NOTES

1. These narratives are fairly common in accounts of anthropological fieldwork through the first half to two-thirds of the twentieth century. For a relatively recent one, see Barley (1983).

2. The possibility of these sorts of informal exchanges has been curtailed by some Institutional Review Board (IRB) policies in the United States. So-called cold calling has been prohibited by some university IRBs, which now require that researchers send possible interviewees written notification informing them about the study before approaching them either on the phone or in person. This renders all conversational interviews "formal." Where instituted, these prohibitions have been uniformly applied to individuals from "vulnerable populations" (e.g., children or prisoners) as well as to professionals, such as university professors or administrators of nonprofit organizations. See Katz (2004) for a discussion of the impacts of local implementation of IRB policies on field research, as well as the IRB-related essays in the special issue of *Qualitative Inquiry* (Cannella and Lincoln 2004), especially Nelson (2004) and Lincoln and Tierney (2004).

3. For an interesting fictionalized account, see S. George's (2002) historical novel, *The Beekeeper's Pupil,* which tells the story of Francis Huber's curiosity, theorizing, and hours of observation that led to his scientific treatise on bee behavior, published in French in 1792.

4. We do not mean by this a criticism of Hopf's work, which we find very creative in its use of materials.

5. When it comes to creativity and imagination about "data," Webb et al.'s 1966 text, *Unobtrusive Measures*, merits recognition. Yet it is not clear that scholars have much taken up their advice. That failure may be due in part to the methodologically positivist underpinnings of their text—particularly evident in the change in title in the 1981 edition to *Nonreactive Measures*—emphasizing a classically positivist concern that the researcher may be a "contaminant." Based on such presuppositions, numerical data are the *best* data, and, indeed, transforming data into numbers is the "objectifying" process meant to protect against the problem of scholarly "bias." Thus, although Webb et al. encouraged researchers to think about data more expansively, an admonition to transform "data" into numbers may be implicit in the book, and this may have precluded its use. In contrast, Weldes's call in chapter 9 for consideration of a greater range of evidence is supported by her interpretive ontological and epistemological presuppositions. Data of various genres can be considered and used by the scholar; interpretive methods do not presuppose that word-data generated through reading documents or novels or viewing portraits must be turned into numbers to constitute legitimate evidence.

6. Such an approach characterizes Murray Edelman's analyses of political language, categories, and numbers (1964, 1977, 1988), especially in the context of their usage in public displays or "spectacles." See also Schram (1995a) on narrating welfare statistics or Gusfield (1981) on drunken driving accident statistics.

7. For an extended critique of the assumptions about human agency, communication, and language use built into survey research, see Suchman and Jordan (1992).

8. The allusion is to Alfred North Whitehead's (1932) "fallacy of misplaced concreteness," noting the attribution of concreteness to numbers or other entities that are, in fact, abstracted from the more concrete experience that they are used to represent.

CHAPTER 6

TALKING OUR WAY TO
MEANINGFUL EXPLANATIONS

A Practice-Centered View of Interviewing for Interpretive Research

JOE SOSS

I'm not sure if I snuck up on this project or if it snuck up on me. I'm fairly certain, though, that some kind of sneakiness was involved: There was no sign of it from a distance. Looking back now, I see a string of conversations and decisions that accumulated piecemeal and in unexpected ways. I also see remnants of plans I thought I had abandoned—ideas that I had once seized upon as dissertation topics; worked out with feverish excitement; presented to my friends as neatly wrapped, rational research designs; and then discarded as worthless. These failed efforts turned out to have worth after all. Many generated ideas that later cropped up as key elements of the project I describe in this chapter.

The seeds of the study were planted in a late-night conversation on the floor of my Madison apartment. I was preparing for a comprehensive exam, and a friend came over to help me get a better handle on "political participation" as a subfield of American political science. By chance, I had just finished reading Donileen Loseke's work on the social construction of domestic violence at women's shelters and had also just come across Felstiner, Abel, and Sarat's classic paper on "naming, blaming, and claiming" in the emergence of legal disputes. At the time, neither seemed especially relevant for my work. But they were full of exciting ideas, and I couldn't stop thinking about them. The more my friend and I talked, the more these ideas crowded in and pushed toward two themes. First, perhaps students of political participation needed to pay more attention to the "everyday" claims people make on governments as they try to solve important problems in their own lives. And second, perhaps explanations of political participation should pay more attention to the ways people classify self and circumstance, and how such classifications may suggest or obscure the possibility of seeking government action. I made up my mind to study marital violence—to investigate the processes by which people become willing to classify themselves as "victims," spouses as "abusers," and circumstances as ones that justify claims on publicly funded shelters, local social services, and judicial institutions.

Then I promptly forgot all about it. Over the next two years, I cycled through lots of unrelated dissertation ideas and began to develop a new interest in welfare politics. I had no plans to pursue this topic in my dissertation until I read a series of feminist writings that identified welfare claiming as an important form of political action by poor women. Suddenly, the conversation on my apartment floor came back to me, and I began to wonder: how do people name their circumstances in a way that suggests it is okay, even sensible, to take on the stigmatized identity of "welfare mother" by making claims on a state agency? This question led to others and, over the course of a year, I became committed to a broad study of the political lives citizens lead in relation to the welfare state. Interestingly, the question of whether my study would be "interpretive" never occurred to me. Because I started with questions about how people construed their world, it seemed sensible to go out and talk with them. And once I began trying to "explain" welfare recipients' choices and actions, I found that the interpretive writings of Geertz, Taylor, and others offered the most helpful models for what I was doing. The chapter that follows is a reconstruction of what I did when I researched my 2000 book, Unwanted Claims. *I suspect it's not what I would have told you if you'd asked me to describe my methodology at the time.*

"You're just a number."
—*Sarah,* client in the Social Security
Disability Insurance (SSDI) program

"I felt like a number."
—*Alissa,* client in the Aid to Families
with Dependent Children (AFDC) program

Sarah and Alissa used similar words, but did they mean the same thing? And what, if anything, did their words signify about the ways they understood and oriented themselves toward state welfare agencies? Throughout 1994 and 1995, I interviewed SSDI and AFDC clients, listening to individuals in each program say that agency workers "treat you like a number" and "you feel like a number."[1] The consistency of language was impressive. Had I treated the words as literal reports of emotion (coding them as "respondent did/did not feel like a number"), my analysis would have suggested no difference across program groups. Alternatively, I might have inferred that clients were using a metaphor to say they had been treated as less than human. But this interpretation, reasonable it may seem, would have been based on nothing but my own intuitive reading and would have led to the same mistaken conclusion: equivalence across groups.

The first approach (coding literal language) would have sidestepped the thorny problem of meaning in order to get on with the task of converting words into a form of data more suitable for variable-based analysis. The second approach would have solved the problem by fiat, imposing a fixed meaning based on my own assumptions about shared common sense. As an empirical matter, however, I wanted to know how *participants* understood their welfare relationships—what conceptual frameworks *they* used to make sense of their encounters with government. I wanted to know where such understandings came from and how they led clients to see particular courses of action as permissible, reasonable, and right. These research goals demanded that questions of meaning be placed at the forefront of empirical research, rather than being pushed to the side or settled on the basis of assumptions I had carried into my fieldwork.

Like any approach to generating social science evidence, the in-depth interviews I conducted were imperfect in many ways and inappropriate for some purposes. One advantage of this method, however, was that it permitted me to treat client statements as more than a series of discrete verbal reports to be coded, each in its own right, and then correlated with one another. It allowed me to pursue the meanings of specific statements by locating them within a broader web of narratives, explanations, telling omissions, and nonverbal cues. The open-ended format of my conversations with clients, and the large bodies of text they produced, made it possible to explore how individual comments fit together as parts of a more meaningful whole. Indeed, the parts and the whole, as I gradually came to understand them, could be used as a kind of commentary on one another. Small, seemingly isolated statements hinted at broader conceptions; their patterns of convergence and discord offered a way to develop, assess, and revise an emerging account of latent understandings. At the same time, as my inferences about broader conceptions took shape, they offered a contextual standpoint for making sense of each individual comment and for linking seemingly unconnected remarks.

Through this process of tacking back and forth (Taylor 1979), I came to see that AFDC and SSDI clients meant different things when they said they "felt like a number." SSDI clients often deployed this phrase while describing the pleasant but uninterested demeanor of the bureaucrats they spoke with in impersonal telephone conversations. When telling a story about such an interaction, clients occasionally acted out the lines of the agency worker with a stiffened back and the voice of a robot. In this group, "feeling like a number" was part of a field of metaphors that included being a "needle in a haystack" and a blip "lost in their computers somewhere." It was almost never accompanied by references to feeling degraded, mistreated, or vulnerable. Rather, clients used the phrase to express their perception of anonymity as participants in the program as well as the ambivalent feelings that accompanied this sense of status. The number metaphor expressed a small lament that clients were not really known "as themselves" in the program. But it also signaled a highly valued sense of privacy from the state (relief that their cases did not seem to be under close surveillance) and a sense of security about equal treatment under program rules (relief that no one seemed to be singled out on a personal basis). I asked Sarah, "What do you mean when you say you're a number?"

> Well, a lot of people say "I feel like a number." Well, you feel like one of millions getting SSDI. So, that means you don't feel like they're watching over you. They can't watch over every single person. . . . [I feel] like they don't single me out. I don't feel like less of a person. I know if I had questions, I can call them on the hot line. And actually, those people are very nice.

When AFDC clients said they felt "like a number," the same words took on a different meaning. In this group, the phrase routinely appeared in stories that turned on themes of humiliation and impotence. When imitating an agency worker, AFDC clients were less likely to strike a robotic pose than to drop into a deep, commanding voice while pointing at me with an index finger. Their explanations of the number metaphor emphasized that being a mere number meant people could do anything to you. And rather than the image of a "needle in a haystack," they offered analogies emphasizing powerlessness, silencing, and vulnerability. Consider Alissa's remarks:

> It's a big system. "Stand in this line." You feel like cattle or something being prodded. That's how I felt. You go all the way through this line to do this, and then this line to do that. It's like a cattle prod. It's like you're in a big mill. I felt like a number, or like I was in a prison system. . . . It feels like you're in a cattle prod. They're the cowboys, and you're a cow. I feel like a cowboy would have more respect for the animals because he knows that the cattle are his livelihood. But these people are like, "I'm helping you. This is something I'm doing for you. So just be quiet and follow your line."

But why worry so much about the meaning of one phrase? The goal of my research was not to show that a single phrase carried two different meanings, nor was it simply to suggest that AFDC clients felt worse about their experiences than did SSDI clients. As Howard Becker points out (1998, 151), efforts to make sense of "strange talk" provide an entry point for explanation, often taking the researcher "right to the heart of how a complex social activity is organized and carried out." I struggled with the meaning of this phrase because it offered an entry point into the specific ways clients *conceptualized* their welfare relationships. Such conceptions were the pivot point for my explanatory analysis. On one side, I sought to show how clients' understandings emerged from experiences with particular types of policy designs and bureaucratic transactions. On the other, I sought to show how these understandings led clients to see particular choices, attitudes, and actions as sensible and, in some cases, natural and inevitable.

The preceding examples are taken from research I conducted for my doctoral dissertation, later published as *Unwanted Claims* (Soss 2000). This chapter makes use of that study, some-times in comparison with other research I have pursued, to explore the strengths, limits, and uses of in-depth interviews for interpretive research. *Unwanted Claims* was built around a set of re-search questions regarding the political lives citizens lead in relation to the U.S. welfare state. Comparing across the AFDC and SSDI programs, I set out to investigate the demands citizens make on government bureaucracies (welfare claiming), the political relationships citizens have with particular types of government agencies and officials (welfare participation), and the conse-quences these relationships have for citizens' broader political orientations and behaviors. In each area of inquiry, I sought to illuminate individuals' reasons for the choices they made and the actions they pursued; I sought to show how these reasons were explicable in light of more basic understandings of identities and circumstances, norms and obligations, the workings of power, the nature of government, and so on; and I sought to show how these understandings, in turn, came to be for the people in my study. In Max Weber's (1978, 4) well-known terms, the project concerned itself "with the interpretive understanding of social action and thereby with a causal explanation of its course and consequences."

My goal in this chapter is not to add to the number of valuable texts that offer how-to instruction on conducting interviews (Gubrium and Holstein 2002; Rubin and Rubin 1995; Spradley 1979) and interpretive analysis (Feldman 1995; Manning 1987; Riessman 1993; Yanow 2000). Instead, I aim to provide something that lies midway between general accounts of interpretive social science (M. Dean 1994; Geertz 1973b; Giddens 1976; Norton 2004a; Taylor 1979; M. Weber 1978) and spe-cific accounts of field research experiences (Kondo 1990; Liebow 1967; MacLeod 1995; Zanca 2000). My goal is to outline a practice-centered view of how interpretive methodologies and inter-view methods can be brought together in a fruitful manner.

To do so, I start by sketching a grounded view of what interpretive methodology might mean in the context of interview research. Rather than emphasizing philosophical paradigms, I address interpretive methodology as "a concrete practical rationality" deployed in a particular research project (Flyvbjerg 2001, 29) and outline some ways to think about this logic-in-use in the context of interview research. Next, I explore interview methods, highlighting their distinctive qualities and asking what might make them more or less "in depth." The third section draws these discus-sions together, offering an assessment of the strengths and limitations of interview methods when researchers take an interpretive approach. Finally, the conclusion offers some reflections on the role of emotion in interpretive interview research.

SO, WHAT MAKES INTERVIEW RESEARCH INTERPRETIVE?

To understand the uses and limits of interviews for interpretive research, one must first clarify what is meant by "interpretive." The key issues here concern *methodology*, not methods per se. A method such as interviewing can offer a better or worse fit for a given methodology, but the label "interpretive" has less to do with one's techniques than with the logic of one's inquiry. As Kenneth Waltz (1979, 13) explains, "once a methodology is adopted, the choice of methods becomes merely tactical." In the research for *Unwanted Claims*, my interpretive methodology drove me toward methods that emphasized time in the field and flexible, detailed conversations with participants. But the interpretive nature of the project did not flow from the specific ways I chose to access data, nor did it arise from the fact that my evidence was primarily "qualitative" rather than "quantitative." To begin with methods or data in this way would be to start too close to the ground; it would put the proverbial cart before the horse.

It can be equally misleading, however, to begin too far from the ground—too far from what we do when we do research. I think of *Unwanted Claims* as an interpretive study. Yet as I pursue this label in relevant literatures, I often find it difficult to map the abstract descriptions onto my work. Some of the most widely assigned essays on methodology (e.g., Guba and Lincoln 1994) seem to imply that an interpretive project is one that is carried out by a particular type of person (an *interpretivist*) whose worldview is defined by a particular epistemological and ontological paradigm (*interpretivism*). This literature is bracing stuff. Packs of scholars take sides in longstanding philosophical disputes and clash over the bedrock beliefs that drive their research. Reflecting on my own work, however, I find it hard to square such accounts with experience.

Most of my work is question driven.[2] I begin with a question about some political phenomenon and then, if I come to see the question as interesting and consequential, I try to specify a methodology that will help me work with it in a fruitful way.[3] As a result, some of my projects follow a more positivist logic while others are more interpretive. As I describe below, the methodology of *Unwanted Claims* differed from my more positivist studies in decisive ways. But as I have moved between projects, picking up one methodology and setting another aside, it has been the logic of my inquiry that has changed. I have not been transformed into a wholly different type of researcher, nor have I been forced to trade in my core beliefs about the nature of knowledge and reality. For this reason, I find it most helpful to apply the label "interpretive" to the logics of specific pieces of research rather than to researchers themselves or to any philosophical first-principles one might attribute to researchers. The interpretive/positivist distinction, in this usage, is a matter of practice rather than identity or worldview. It is a matter of what we assume, require, and do for the sake of a particular inquiry rather than an aspect of who we are or a fixed description of what we believe in general.[4]

This emphasis on "concrete practical rationality" (Flyvbjerg 2001, 29) also underscores that the distinctly interpretive quality of *Unwanted Claims* does not flow in any direct manner from its emphasis on meaning and interpretation. Few political scientists today assert that meanings are inconsequential for what they study, and fewer still deny the need to interpret their data (Yanow 2003c, 9; Adcock 2003b, 16). When I conduct hypothesis testing, statistical research with survey data from the American National Election Study (ANES), I often rely on the seven-point scales the ANES uses to measure racial stereotypes, such as respondents' assessments of "intelligence" among "blacks" and "whites."[5] When I use these measures to produce studies that I view as standard positivist fare, I do not suddenly abandon my assumptions that the social world is a meaningful place, that racial classifications are socially constructed, and that I must interpret my evidence about people's beliefs and emotions. To the contrary, I am centrally concerned with the ways people make sense of the social and political world, and I deploy concepts and theories that are fundamentally about meaning making.[6]

Thus, in my own experience, the interpretive/positivist distinction fares poorly as a way to identify discrete and opposing classes of methods, schools of researchers, world-defining paradigms, or beliefs about the relevance of meaning. Yet in practice, researchers' orientations toward meaning and interpretation—the *priorities* we place on them, the *assumptions* we make about them, the *roles* we assign them in our analysis—vary considerably across research projects. It is in such areas of "concrete practical rationality" that we must look in order to see how interviews were used in *Unwanted Claims* to pursue an interpretive approach to explanation. I will suggest three aspects of the project's methodology that strike me as distinctly interpretive and that shaped the ways I deployed my interview methods.

First, I prioritized skepticism about shared meaning; I was willing to forego some research goals in order to place greater empirical pressure on my assumptions that particular words, actions, objects, people, and events had self-evident or widely shared meanings. In my more positivist research with survey data, I often bracket concerns about the constancy of meaning in order to pursue goals such as correlating attitudes with behaviors and generalizing to specific populations. When ANES respondents state their assessments of black and white "intelligence," some may be thinking of the innate potential of two groups of human beings; others may be making a factual statement about scores on IQ tests; and others may be thinking about educational attainment, or may be rejecting such "book learning" in favor of "common sense and street smarts." Likewise, respondents may draw the boundary between "black" and "white" in different ways or may doubt that such racial categories are meaningful at all. When analyzing survey data, I care about such possibilities, but I cannot do much about them. My research strategy is not designed to facilitate the interrogation of such differences in understanding (beyond the dimension of difference captured by the stereotype scale). This limitation, in turn, can be traced to a deeper methodological decision not to prioritize an empirical account of such interpretive differences as a prerequisite for valid observation and explanation. In such research, I place a high value on the careful pretesting of fixed-format interview questions and then proceed with my analysis on the assumption that respondents are interpreting and answering the questions in reasonably comparable ways.

In the research for *Unwanted Claims*, by contrast, I was centrally concerned with the analytic problems and opportunities that might flow from polysemy. I foregrounded my suspicions that clients might interpret a single interview question in different ways and that a single phrase might mean different things when spoken by different people. I placed these possibilities at the center of my research strategy and designed my interviews to dig into them. Accordingly, I valued tailored, mutually negotiated communication over the controlled, consistent questioning I would prize in a more positivist project (qualitative or quantitative).[7] Although I entered the field with expectations about meaning, my methodology made it an empirical question whether clients interpreted the act of claiming benefits or the experience of sitting in a waiting room in one manner or another. Of course, it is not possible to treat the meaning of every word and object as up for grabs in a research project; the researcher has to make choices about where and how to dig for differences. But one of my key assumptions in this project was that I needed to use my interviews self-consciously and systematically—even if selectively—to uncover unexpected differences in interpretation. The potential for polysemy was central to the ways I judged evidence, approached client and program comparisons, and constructed explanations for individuals' choices and actions.

Second, I placed clients' understandings and sense-making efforts at the forefront of empirical investigation, and I sought to encounter such understandings and efforts on terms plausible to the participants themselves. Because the conceptual worlds of welfare recipients stood at the heart of my study, much of my fieldwork was devoted to assembling coherent accounts of how clients understood relevant phenomena. The goal was not primarily to get detailed reports of behaviors, attitudes, and beliefs—though these tasks were important to me as well. Rather, it was to understand clients' conceptions of how welfare relationships work (and should work), their ways of organizing their program experiences and drawing lessons from them, their notions of what makes it acceptable to claim welfare benefits, their ways of classifying their fellow welfare participants, their images of what government is and does, and so on. As I elaborate below, such understandings were basic to my analytic approach. They were the background premises for clients' choices and actions; they contained the logics that made a host of obscure, seemingly unrelated narratives explicable.

To pursue such understandings, I placed a high priority on encountering clients' conceptions on terms they found plausible and in a language they found familiar. As Jennifer Hochschild (1981, 21) notes, such priorities direct a researcher toward methods that invite "textured, idiosyncratic responses. The researcher must permit—even induce—people to speak for themselves and must be wary of channeling their thought through his or her own preconceptions about what questions to ask, how answers should be shaped, and what coding categories best subdivide the responses." This description captures important aspects of my approach. But here, it is important to emphasize two points.

First, making it a priority to *encounter* participants' understandings on their own terms is not the same as *accepting* participants' descriptions of their understandings. Interviewees can easily misrepresent or misperceive their own conceptions of the world. Likewise, I found that although some aspects of clients' conceptions were consciously held and easily articulated, others were so natural to participants (so much the water in which they swam) that they could hardly be perceived, let alone expressed. They were buried in what Schütz (1967, 74) calls the "taken for granted" of everyday life. To get at them required interrogating the gaps and silences in clients' accounts, the inconsistencies between narratives and declarations, and the unstated major premises of an assortment of incomplete syllogisms (H. Becker 1998, 147–49). Second, *prioritizing* exposure to language that is meaningful to insiders is not the same as *privileging* insiders' concepts over social scientific concepts. Rather, it involves carefully distinguishing the roles of each within our analyses. As Clifford Geertz (1973b) emphasizes, in an interpretive project, we seek to assemble thick descriptions of participants' conceptual worlds so that we can compel them to speak to the social scientific concepts we care about most.[8]

Third and finally, I treated construction of a coherent account of participants' understandings as a prerequisite for adequate explanation and sought to ascertain the sources and consequences of such understandings. All social scientists build explanation out of a dialogue of theory and evidence. But our demands of the evidence—the types of empirical accounts we deem necessary for explanation—vary across projects. In some instances, I deem it adequate to show that relevant variables covary in a theoretically telling manner. For example, I might conclude that differences in state welfare policies can be "explained" by differences in the racial composition of welfare recipients without demanding any direct evidence of lawmakers' intentions (Soss et al. 2001). My approach to explanation in *Unwanted Claims* placed a higher priority on people's conceptual worlds. Throughout the study, I asked why reasonable people found it sensible to choose and act as my interviewees did. I sought out clients' reasons for considering this action more appropriate than that one, for feeling as they did about an institution, for drawing particular conclusions from particular experiences. Charles Taylor captures the basic outline of such an effort to construct the rudiments of interpretive explanation:

> We make sense of action when there is a coherence between the actions of the agent and the meaning of his situation for him. We find his action puzzling until we find such a coherence. . . . This coherence in no way implies that the action is rational: the meaning of a situation for an agent may be full of confusion and contradiction, but the adequate depiction of this contradiction makes sense of it. (1979, 35)

Under the methodology I pursued for *Unwanted Claims*, I assumed such "coherence" was necessary, though not sufficient, for an adequate explanation of the choices and actions under consideration (see M. Weber 1978). Thus, my efforts to "understand" were not a substitute for efforts to "explain" (cf. Hollis and Smith 1990); I aimed to "make understanding a prerequisite of explanation rather than an alternative to it" (Adcock 2003b, 17). One way to think about this methodology is to view participants' understandings and intentions as conditions that mediate the causal effects of other factors in our analysis (Blumer 1956; Lin 1998). C. Wright Mills captures something of this logic when he writes that:

> Men discern situations with particular vocabularies, and it is in terms of some delimited vocabulary that they anticipate consequences of conduct. . . . The vocalized expectation of an act, its "reason," is not only a mediating condition of the act but it is a proximate and controlling condition for which the term cause is not inappropriate. . . . [Yet] the differing reasons men give for their actions are not themselves without reasons. (1940, 904, 906, 907)

As described in the introduction, my interviews revealed that AFDC and SSDI clients differed strongly in the ways they conceptualized their status in welfare relationships. Pressing forward along the explanatory chain, these understandings became the core of my explanation for why SSDI clients were more willing than AFDC clients to assert themselves when dealing with government agencies. They understood their subject position in a way that made assertiveness seem sensible and effective, while AFDC clients saw themselves as vulnerable and impotent actors who would risk a great deal by speaking up. Such understandings gave AFDC clients good reasons to be reticent. The other side of my task was to press backward along the explanatory chain, seeking out Mills's "reasons for reasons." I asked how clients' understandings came to be—their conditions of possibility, their origins in experience, their development through social and personal efforts to make meaning. Ultimately, my explanation emphasized how distinctive institutional designs structured program experiences differently for AFDC and SSDI clients, how participation under these designs fostered different understandings of status in welfare relationships, and how these understandings made it sensible for AFDC clients to adopt a more reticent posture than their SSDI counterparts.

These are the main qualities that lead me to view *Unwanted Claims* as an interpretive rather than a positivist piece of interview-based research: I prioritized and pursued the analytic challenges and opportunities raised by polysemy; I sought to construct accounts of insiders' understandings and sense-making efforts out of empirical materials encountered on terms plausible to the participants themselves; and I treated such accounts of understanding as a necessary cornerstone of my explanatory analysis—as the root of sensible action whose origins and consequences needed to be traced.

SO, WHAT IS AN IN-DEPTH INTERVIEW AND WHAT MAKES IT IN DEPTH?

For some interpretive projects, in-depth interviews will not serve the researcher's purposes as well as other methods for accessing data, such as participant-observation (Eliasoph 1998; Walsh 2004), focus groups (Gamson 1992; D. Hunt 1997), or archival research (B. Schwartz 1987; Doty 1993). So, it is worthwhile to ask what "in-depth interviewing" entails and why we might deploy or forego this method for a particular interpretive project. I take up the first question here, and then turn to the second below.[9]

It is conventional to say that an interview is a conversation pursued for the purpose of gathering information to be used for research purposes (Berg 1998, 57). But what makes an interview "in-depth"? When scholars invoke this adjective, they generally seem to mean "semistructured or unstructured"—formats that provide freedom for probes and follow-up questions as opposed to the structured interviews one might find in a survey or some other study that prioritizes reliability-as-uniformity over flexible, detailed exploration. Fixed-format interviews are, implicitly at least, cast as the "shallow" counterpart in this usage because they forbid researchers from digging in areas that emerge as promising during the course of an interview.[10] By contrast, in the introduction to his classic *Political Ideology*, Robert Lane describes what made his interviews "in-depth" and what made them such a good match for his interpretive goals:

> The conversations were *discursive*; the responses of the men rambled, followed their own trains of thought, gave scope to anecdote and argument, moral comment and rationalization. This had several advantages: it offered insight into connotative meanings of words and phrases, it permitted one to follow the course of associative thinking (something relied upon for clinical insights); it illuminated the mechanisms of argument and evasion employed in dealing with sensitive political material. . . . The conversations were [also] *dialectical*, that is, conversational. There was opportunity for extended probing, for pushing further into the personal meaning of clichés and conventional phrases, for testing whether or not the first impression gained was the correct one, for reflecting back the sense of what was said to clarify the men's own thinking. (1962, 9, emphasis in original)

As these comments suggest, the term "in-depth" is usually invoked to suggest a more "conversational" format. Lane (1962) writes of smoking cigars with his interviewees and of a friendly, comfortable exchange of ideas in a relaxed setting.[11] Kristen Monroe (1996, 19) reports that "it seemed more natural to engage in a conversation with the individuals I interviewed, treating each as I would a new friend rather than as a subject." It is worth unpacking this comparison a bit, taking a moment to consider how in-depth interviews are and are not like everyday conversations.[12]

To be sure, there are some similarities. In an in-depth interview, there is a give-and-take between individuals: Each responds to what the other has said. Because the researcher does not simply move on to the next item on a preset list of questions, an in-depth interview can be as unpredictable as any other conversation. It may veer off into topics irrelevant to the research; it may get emotionally difficult for one person or both; it may get tense or boring or develop a running joke; it may breeze along or stumble into an uncomfortable impasse. Like a conversation, an in-depth interview must be navigated as it unfolds, and this navigation depends on what Berg (1998, 80) refers to as full-channel communication. The interview is not just an exchange of words, but also an exchange of physical gestures, silences meant to signal, uses of voice, tone, and laughter—all of which must be attended to by the researcher. And just like other conversations, in-depth interviews can involve evasion tactics, fronts, lies, emotional manipulation, self-serving frames, and dissemblance. These aspects of the interview are, in their own right, evidence for the researcher. But they are also part of what must be wrestled with and challenged. Like other conversations, in-depth interviews involve dynamics of power, control, and authority (Ng 1996). From the outset, the identities of the researcher and interviewee may imply a status imbalance that cannot be overlooked. In the interview, power and social roles are aspects of the "definition of the situation" that must be mutually negotiated. Accordingly, an in-depth interview can take on a dynamic that feels like an interrogation, an amiable chat between friends, or an instructional session in which interviewees hold privileged knowledge and researchers play the role of the uninitiated student.

On the other hand, an in-depth interview is not *just* like an everyday conversation. To begin with, research interviews can involve people who have only known each other a short time, yet they may address topics that are not normally discussed by relative strangers. Moreover, researchers conduct interviews to acquire specific materials needed for a research project, and this agenda usually leads to departures from the norms of everyday conversation. I sometimes had to abruptly steer the dialogue back to relevant topics (and away from, say, a lengthy digression on a crazy uncle in Ohio). I also had to help my interviewees get comfortable with the idea that it would not be rude, in this context, to hold forth on a topic for fifteen minutes without giving me a turn to talk. In the normal course of events, people have precious few conversations in which they encounter a sympathetic listener who hangs on their every word, encourages them to elaborate for long stretches, and reflects their words back to them in hopes of gaining a more nuanced and complete understanding. Interpretive research, in particular, requires the pursuit of thick descriptions, and this means working hard to encourage elaboration, clarification, reflection, and illustration. In all of this activity, we carry the interview away from normal conversation (Eliasoph 1998).

Thus, the "in-depth" aspects of in-depth interviews make them more conversational than a fixed-format interview but also quite different from everyday conversations. It is also possible to take a wider perspective on what makes interview research more or less "deep." When scholars speak of "in-depth interviewing," they frequently have in mind a series of conversations between a researcher and interviewees. Instead, it may be more fruitful to think of in-depth interviewing as an interconnected, simultaneous set of activities that collectively constitute *a mode of field research*. In field research, the acquisition and analysis of data often occur simultaneously, and what appears to be a single method is often a conjunction of interrelated activities (Emerson, Fretz, and Shaw 1995).[13] In-depth interviewing, from this perspective, can be viewed as a set of simultaneous activities that support and direct one another in the field: discursive and dialectical conversations with interviewees, transcription activities, coding and analysis of data in hand, analytic memo writing, purposive selection of next informants, revision of interview protocols, and so on.

To illustrate with just a single activity from this list, consider transcription. Often a slow, painstaking process, transcription is among the least appreciated aspects of interview research. In some projects, it is left aside until the researcher leaves the field, or is handed off to a paid assistant. In my experience, however, transcription in the field "deepens" the method. In the research for *Unwanted Claims*, transcribing offered an unparalleled opportunity to note and reflect on interviewees' phrases, the organization of their narratives, the salience of one reported experience relative to another, and so on. As a result, transcription sessions were the occasions when some of my most fruitful insights and conjectures took shape. They also offered a unique opportunity to detect problems in my interview technique, reconsider the phrasing of my questions, and reassess the mix of topics I aimed to cover in interviews. Some transcription sessions were nothing but tedious. Others led to the writing of important analytic memos[14] and to significant changes in the ways I pursued future rounds of interviews.

This description of entwined research activities suggests an even broader way to think about in-depth interviewing: as a kind of evolving dialogue between "fieldwork and framework" (Hopper 2003; Sanjek 1990). Here, "fieldwork" refers to all the locally oriented activities the interviewer pursues in the field, both inside and outside actual conversations with interviewees. "Framework" refers to the broader knowledge of theory, history, and social structure that the author brings to bear on interviewees' local, case-specific, and person-specific encounters. As Kim Hopper (2003, 7) notes, fieldwork and framework "relate to one another as context and story, disciplinary backdrop and case-at-hand, history and action." Part of what makes interview research "deep" is immersion in, and pursuit of, this dialogue. While in the field, I shifted between conversations with welfare clients and conversations with the ideas, histories, and empirical claims I found in scholarly writings. Each moved my view of the other to a different place. Successive rounds shifted my standpoint considerably over the course of the project.

Such changes in standpoint are a common theme in the literature on field research, especially in writings on ethnography (Emerson et al. 1995). Sometimes, however, I think this process is discussed in a fashion that is too linear to match my experience. The author enters a strange new setting; the swirl of new social discourse is at first opaque; slowly, the researcher gains some interpretive footing; and at last, after some struggle to master emic understandings, the obscure is made plain. This narrative—I am tempted to call it a Geertzian narrative—captures an important part of what changed over time in my research for *Unwanted Claims*. But its emphasis on progressive enlightenment must be tempered a bit with two observations.

In interpretive research, strangeness has its benefits too. The newly arrived outsider is often able to notice as unusual—and hence draw into analysis—the very things that insiders take for granted. The famous French observers Alexis de Tocqueville and Harriet Martineau were able to see strangeness in the democracy and society of nineteenth-century America, and this made all the difference for their classic analyses. Similarly, the early days of an interview project provide distinctive opportunities based on unfamiliarity. As I became more comfortable with clients' perspectives, I also developed blind spots; I stopped noticing some things at all and started seeing others as unremarkable. After my fieldwork ended, I was pleasantly surprised by some of the long-forgotten observations buried in my earliest journal entries and field notes. Thus, the interviewer's standpoint changes in a complex way over time: the benefits and liabilities of strangeness fade, while the benefits and liabilities of familiarity rise in proportion.

The narrative of progressive enlightenment in the field also misleads in a second way. It understates the importance of systematic analysis after one exits the field. In my experience, the dialogue between fieldwork and framework did not move steadily toward better understandings. I went through periods when *everything* seemed to make sense in terms of some concept I had recently encountered, or when a comment by a particular client seemed like the Rosetta stone of my analysis. Later, everything seemed to make sense in terms of some newer concept or comment. I felt sure that clients saw an experience in a particular way; then I developed doubts; then I returned to a version of my earlier view. To be sure, I understood much more in the final days of my fieldwork than in the early days. But throughout my field experience, and even at its end, I stood in a particular thicket of trees; I was not standing back to view the forest. After my last interview, I felt confident that I knew the story my dissertation would tell. But this confidence was misplaced. Over the next year, as I sorted, sifted, and integrated the materials in a more systematic way, the story changed.

For an interpretive research project, then, in-depth interviewing offers a dynamic method—one that offers flexibility in the interview itself and shifting standpoints over time. It is centered on discursive and dialectical conversations with interviewees. But more broadly, it is an evolving dialogue between fieldwork and framework, mediated by concrete activities of transcription, memo writing, purposive reading of literatures, and the like. It entails simultaneous data collection and analysis, but it remains incomplete without more systematic analysis after exiting the field. In the following section, I will consider some key strengths and weaknesses of in-depth interviews for interpretive research. But before moving on, it is worth noting that I have said nothing about what in-depth interviews mean to the interviewee. An adequate account would require a separate chapter; I will only point to some indications that we should care about this question.

Research methods are expressive acts. The ways we approach the people we study convey messages—both in ways we control and intend and in ways we do not. At one of my interviews, for example, I spent most of the day with an AFDC client and her preteen son, talking about this and that, shoveling the snow off the front walk together, and trying to get to know each other. In the afternoon, when her son brought in the mail, it included a survey from a researcher studying welfare recipients. (Two researchers in one day: what are the chances?) The son opened the self-administered survey and, slipping into the faux-British accent Americans often use to signify pretentiousness, began to pose the questions to his mother. Joining in the fun, she responded with an overdrawn Black English Vernacular, laying it on thick as she gave answers that exaggerated the worst welfare stereotypes. At the end of the charade, they threw the survey in the trash.

Because I sometimes conduct survey research, I felt compelled to ask why the woman had given me so much of her time but would not give a far smaller amount to this other researcher. Her answer was that I "cared enough" to come to her house and see what a day in her life was like, that I was willing to spend my time making lunch with her and getting to know her son. My investment in building rapport and getting to know a participant in my study were, to her, signifiers of respect and caring. The truth is that I did care. But I don't care any less when I work with fixed-format surveys that allow for a larger sample of respondents. What mattered in this instance had little to do with any real difference between this other researcher and myself (an unknowable quantity, in any event); it had to with what our methods symbolized to the person we approached. Moreover, the methods themselves did not inherently mean one thing or the other. Another woman might have viewed my request for a day's time and a lengthy interview as intrusive and presumptuous. The self-administered survey might have been perceived as showing more respect for her privacy and for the fact that she was busy with the work of survival amid poverty.[15] Perhaps this signals an additional element that can make our interviews more or less "in-depth": our efforts to address participants' understandings, not only of the phenomena under study, but also of the research interaction itself. Participants' perceptions of what our methods "say" about the researcher and her or his project can have a major impact on what the researcher "finds" in the field.

IN-DEPTH INTERVIEWS FOR INTERPRETIVE RESEARCH

How, then, do the topics of the two preceding sections fit together? How should we think about the use of in-depth interviews for interpretive research? Without aiming to provide an exhaustive list, I will draw on my experience with *Unwanted Claims* to suggest several important limits and strengths. In addition to interviews, my study included participant-observation in a shelter for homeless families, disability support groups, and welfare agencies. Thus, my point of reference for the discussion that follows is based on a contrast between these two methods in research—others' and my own.

At the outset, it is worth noting that the distinction employed here is something of an analytic fiction. In many projects, fieldwork consists of an evolving blend of interactions with participants that cannot be easily disentangled. A researcher may initially seek to participate and observe in ways that avoid disrupting "natural" interactions in any way; later, she may find it helpful to start asking more direct questions of her informants; then she may press on to informal ethnographic interviews, and eventually she may decide to make the interviews more formal and tape them for transcription. It seems fruitless to seek out the exact point at which one method ends and the other begins. Instead, the discussion that follows contrasts stand-alone ideal types: (a) flexible interviews unaccompanied by participant-observation and (b) participant-observation that seeks to minimize researcher disruption.

The limitations of in-depth interviews are most often discussed in relation to the strengths of mass survey research: the difficulties of using in-depth interview data to assess the reliability of a uniformly asked question, state the frequencies of behaviors and attitudes with precision, estimate parameters in a broader population, apply statistical controls to assess partial correlations, and so on. In an interpretive study, however, these limitations may be so distant from relevant research goals that they do not present the researcher with much reason for concern. Other limitations, though they are often ignored by methods textbooks, come to the fore in a comparison with participant-observation and strike a bit closer to home for interpretive work (see H. Becker and Geer 1957).

First, social processes of meaning making—patterns of conflict and collaboration that produce shared conceptions of reality—are often primary objects of concern in interpretive research (Adcock 2003b, 16). Yet they are singularly difficult to observe with a one-on-one interview. The interview, in a sense, stands outside the stream of interactions we seek to understand and, thus, offers only an indirect basis for accessing them. In the research for *Unwanted Claims*, I asked my interviewees about their efforts to make sense of events with others, and I encountered some relevant details, secondhand, through the stories they told. But my interviews did not provide access to social meaning-making processes in anything like the form I encountered in my ethnographic work at the shelter. They did not allow me to observe everyday language actually being exchanged, to account for the rituals and conformity pressures in group negotiations, or to trace changes in framing over the course of a group discussion (see Walsh 2004). If my interviews captured such things at all, they did so only in retrospect and out of context.

Second, interpretive research concerns itself with meaningful social discourse and, as Geertz (1973b) emphasizes, this discourse is not at all restricted to the verbal realm. Researchers can encounter some nonverbal communication within the interview setting, but interviews do not allow the researcher to freely explore the broader flow of social discourse: behaviors in everyday social interactions, the design and negotiation of built spaces, the deployment of community symbols, the production of artwork, the invocation of documents produced in the name of the collective, and so on. As an interviewer, I could not compare word and deed to seek out the basis of their contradiction or congruence. My window on social discourse was a conversational one. Without my additional participant-observation work, I would never have heard about, let alone observed, a broad range of meaningful behaviors, objects, and settings.

Third, interpretive research is typically concerned with indexicality—the tendency for a given object, event, phrase, or identity to take on different meanings in different contexts. We don't just want to know what something means, pure and simple, or how a person categorizes the world, always and forever. We want to explain how and why the identity of "welfare recipient" is significant in one setting but irrelevant in another, a sign of selfishness in one setting and of self-sacrifice in another. My interviews offered access to such variation, but only up to a point. Clients talked about feeling more ashamed when they first applied for benefits than they felt later; they felt more humiliated when using food stamps in a "normal" grocery than when using them in a grocery located in a really poor neighborhood; and so on. In this manner, I found a number of consistent patterns in clients' reports. But the key word here is *reports*. These were clients' retrospective accounts of shifting meanings and emotional responses. The interviews, taken alone, did not allow me to witness changes in the use and meaning of key constructs across different types of interactions. Context-to-context differences were hard to reach with this method because the method was premised on only one kind of context: a one-on-one conversation with me.

Fourth, interviews provide a particular *kind* of context for accessing participants' understandings. Two features of the context merit special consideration for interpretive research. One, because interviews are one-on-one conversations with a researcher, the researcher's identity and self-presentation are central to the data produced. The welfare recipients I interviewed were not delivering a soliloquy; they were having a conversation with a white man, a Jew, a fellow from the university, that friend of Alissa's, that guy (you know the one) who works over at the shelter . . . a specific person with a social identity that the interviewee made sense of in a particular way.[16] Two, as noted earlier, in-depth interviews provide individuals with a type of audience they may rarely encounter in everyday life: attentive, encouraging, patient, willing to press on vague answers, and eager to clear up confusions. Nina Eliasoph captures the problem in discussing the differences between her ethnographic observations in *Avoiding Politics* and Robert Lane's portrait of political reasoning in *Political Ideology*:

> The results of his respectful, sympathetic interviews offer striking insights into abstract political beliefs and reasoning, but such intimate, therapeutic relationships between interviewers and their subjects may encourage respondents to speak in uncharacteristically serious ways about issues that they usually treat flippantly, or ironically, or do not discuss at all, or discuss in some contexts only for the purpose of showing that they are smart, or discuss in other contexts only to reassure themselves that the world is all right after all. . . . If a curious, open-minded researcher offers free, unjudgmental, unhurried contexts for interviewees to reason aloud . . . most people can *become* thoughtful, reasoning citizens. If given this rare opportunity, almost everyone turns out to have the potential to think about politics. . . . While Americans are able to reason about politics if given the kind of opportunity that the sympathetic, open-minded interview researchers give them, this opportunity almost never presents itself to most Americans. (1998, 19, 151)

The understandings I encountered in my research were ones that emerged through these specific types of interactions. My work as a participant-observer frequently made the effects clear. Shelter residents, a majority of whom were AFDC recipients, talked to one another *and to me* in ways that departed significantly from the detailed, searching conversations I had in my formal interviews. At the shelter, I interacted with residents as the occupant of an actual membership role in the social setting (as a shelter staff member), not primarily as a researcher. Our conversations were grounded in residents' own efforts to meet their needs or their own desires for sociability, not in the topics and goals of my research project. Even after a small amount of such fieldwork, the particularity of the in-depth interview encounter was readily apparent to me.

Thus, the insights and observations I obtained through in-depth interviews were limited by the unusual context of their fabrication and by the specific social identities I represented to participants. But this is not to say that they were false relative to the "real thing" out in the social world or false relative to what recipients would have told a researcher with a different social identity. The issue is more complicated than that. All research activities yield evidence that is *partial*— "partial" in the sense of being fragmentary and incomplete, "partial" in the sense of being ripped out of a more holistic context, and "partial" in the sense of being prone to some bias or another.[17] The understandings people express in everyday interactions—the ones we observe in participant-observation—are molded by conformity pressures, by taboos against certain topics or viewpoints, by strategic efforts to look like something other than a dope or a dupe, and so on (Eliasoph 1998). Relative to this context, a private conversation with an encouraging researcher may offer a space in which individuals find it easier to say certain things they understood but stifled in more public contexts. Likewise, the welfare clients I interviewed might have discussed their experiences differently had they been talking to a Latina researcher who presented herself as a former AFDC recipient. Such a shift would be important, but it would not signify the removal of identity-based biases so much as the substitution of one set for another. The understandings revealed in each context of observation, and in the presence of each researcher, would be partial in their own ways. For interpretive research, what is interesting and important is why such differences emerge, how they reflect the limits and distortions of each investigation, and how comparisons across studies can yield deeper insights and stronger explanations. There is a great deal to be learned from the inconsistencies in what participants reveal in different contexts and to different researchers. I think Ann Lin puts the matter in proper perspective in her study of prison program implementation:

> Clearly prisoners self-censored in their choices of what to mention to me . . . but . . . they may self-censor in the other direction when they talk to male researchers. . . . The more interesting possibility [than the possibility of deception] is that male and female interviewers, especially in a highly gendered environment like the prison, simply "cue" different responses. . . . Interviewing by both sexes allows different themes to emerge, themes that might be absent or less salient if only same-sex interviewing and research were to take place. This means that "lying" should be less our concern than systematic bias, and bias should be evaluated less for how it can be eliminated, than for how it works and what it tells. . . . The only solution is for the researcher to know who she is, not only as someone who affects the research site in particular ways, but also as someone who characterizes it in partial and biased ways. This is less wrong than inevitable, and because of that, suggestions that one can be unbiased should be the most troubling. A good research ethic should allow researchers to discuss how their questions and preoccupations—as well as their personal characteristics and the context of their interactions—affected their research. When researchers confront their own bias with honesty and matter-of-factness, rather than with fear and denial, they push forth knowledge in the understanding that all knowledge is imperfect. (2000, 191, 194)

So what, then, are the primary benefits of in-depth interviews for interpretive research? First, in-depth interviews can be used to pursue questions that are difficult to locate in documentary sources or everyday interactions and to explore such questions in intricate detail. At the shelter for homeless families, for example, interactions with the welfare agency were a common topic of conversation and a significant aspect of observable social transaction. By contrast, I could have worked at the shelter for years without uncovering clients' conceptions of how power works in the broader U.S. political system. As a result, I could not have drawn inferences about how these core political views were built on clients' experiences with welfare bureaucracies and administrators. Conversations on this topic were hard to stumble across because they rarely took place. Even if they could have been located, they would not have allowed for the detailed probing needed to map out clients' conceptions and explore their mixed sentiments.

For many questions that concern students of politics, relevant interactions cannot be readily observed or are, at best, fleeting. The conceptions of interest may be impossible to infer from observable behaviors and may seldom be discussed in the normal course of affairs. To get at these sorts of understandings, we must ask. We must set the agenda, press for sustained discussion, and challenge vague statements for clarification and elaboration. Such asking, pursued informally, can be incorporated into participant-observation research. But it lies in tension with, and can undermine, the goal of observing and participating in transactions *as they would normally occur*. In proposing the injunction "Ask me no (research) questions, I'll tell you no lies," Elliott Liebow explains his participant-observation approach as follows:

> I did ask questions, of course, but these were not questions I brought with me from the outside. They were "natural" questions that arose spontaneously and directly out of the social situation. They were the same sorts of questions that everyone else asked. They were situation-specific questions, not research questions. . . . For participant observation, the value of this injunction [is] that it discourages the researcher from contaminating the situation with questions dragged in from the outside. It allows the different situations under observation to develop according to their own inner logic and according to the needs of participants, not the needs of the researcher. In this way, one comes closer to the ideal of observing behavior as it would have been had the observer not been present. (1993, 321–22)

My own experience leads me to reject the strong version of this injunction: I feel I was quite able to ask shelter residents a few research-related questions during after-hours conversations without disrupting the broader tenor and logic of shelter interactions. But I think Liebow's advice captures an important difference in methods. Research-driven questioning is riskier business in participant-observation research. By contrast, it is a central component of in-depth interviewing —one that makes this method a good fit for interpretive projects in which researchers are concerned with hard-to-locate phenomena.

Second, and perhaps most obvious from the discussion so far, in-depth interviews permit an exceptional degree of flexibility, control, and detail in the pursuit of participants' understandings. In in-depth interviews, we are not hemmed in by the fixed scope, order, and wording of items on a survey questionnaire. With a little care and reassurance, we can push beyond the limits of what is normally appropriate in everyday conversation. By being responsive to informants, we can evade the restrictions imposed by our a priori thinking about which topics are important and what they mean. By being a bit more directive, we can pull the conversation back to issues we need to address, even as we continue to encourage our interviewees to speak in terms that are their own. Throughout the interview, we retain freedom to probe, follow up, challenge, double back, abandon a fruitless line of inquiry, ask if we have understood correctly, or simply express our fascination and ask the interviewee to say more. And crucially, the interview format allows us to record a *verbatim* transcript of the resulting dialogue. Unlike most field notes, such transcripts can precisely capture the ways individuals use words and phrases, organize their narratives, and puzzle through the phenomena under discussion.[18] Thus, both in its process and in its product, the in-depth interview allows researchers to access participants' understandings in an unusually flexible and fine-grained manner.

Third, in-depth interviews are invaluable for recovering and analyzing the agency of individuals. In my research for *Unwanted Claims*, I was centrally concerned with welfare clients as political actors who actively interpret and categorize, choose and take action. Welfare scholarship is chockablock with theories that cast welfare recipients as victims of structural forces, passive objects of social control, products of socialization who simply "enact" a culture-of-poverty script, rational actors who automatically respond to changes in incentives, and "targets" who unfailingly internalize messages conveyed by policy designs. I wanted to explore the agency of such people and to do so in a way that could supply a counterpoint to these well-established stories of constraint. Whether I was examining welfare claiming, welfare participation, or broader forms of political action, my goal was consistent: to explain demand making and quiescence, not just as results of forces acting on welfare recipients, but also as products of clients' own efforts to understand where things stood and how they worked, determine what was appropriate and acceptable, and choose a sensible course of action.

In-depth interviews provided an ideal method for uncovering such agency. In the interviews themselves, clients were positioned as interpreters of their own experiences and tellers of their own tales. They were not only the central focus of their narratives; they were the acting subjects of these narratives. The interviews helped me escape some of the scholarly biases I brought to the field—to recover an image of welfare clients as people who try to read the lay of the land, figure out what will happen next, and take action for good reason. The interviews allowed me to see the people I met as agents acting on their own self-concepts and standards, dreams and aspirations, fears and self-doubts, and histories of accomplishment and disappointment.[19]

Fourth, in-depth interviews offer an excellent way to map the conceptual world of participants in ways that illuminate both coherence and inconsistency. It is not a coincidence that Robert Lane's (1962) classic study of political ideology is known for revealing *both* the integrated belief system ("ideational counterpart to a constitution") that supplied his interviewees with a moral compass for political life *and* the "morselized," fragmented ways his interviewees thought about political events. Jennifer Hochschild's (1981) classic interview study, *What's Fair*, offers a similar pairing. It shines a light not only on the consistent, coherent ways Americans think about distributive justice in different spheres of life, but also on the troubling disconnects in this thinking and on the profound ambivalence Americans experience when they try to sort through their conflicting values and feelings.

Interviews offer a superb way to learn how individuals knit their own conceptions together and put them to use. They can be used to uncover logics of integration (widely shared or idiosyncratic) and sources of disintegration. On both sides of this ledger, the value is that we can explore the *substantive* connections that link beliefs and sentiments. The "connective tissue" sought here is not the same as a conclusion that several attitudes are correlated across cases. Rather, it is grounded in the way each subjective element justifies, supports, or derives from another; the way each casts its shadow on the meaning of another; the way, ultimately, the elements function together as parts of a broader whole. Interviews allow researchers to pursue disjuncture and ambivalence by directly digging into the stuff of mixed sentiment. Inner conflicts bubble to the surface as individuals traverse complex issues. Interviewees may start in one direction, then reverse themselves; they may stop in midstream to say they feel torn; they may sputter and blush when asked to reconcile two of their own statements. If the interviewer is attentive, such moments can be seized as valuable openings for interpretive analysis.[20]

CONCLUSION: ON EMOTION AND THE IN-DEPTH INTERVIEW

In this chapter, I have tried to parse some of the methodological issues that arise when social scientists use interviews for interpretive research. My aim has been to suggest ways of thinking that might be helpful for contemplating the fit between interview methods and interpretive analytic goals. Throughout this essay, however, I have skirted an issue that could have threaded its way through every section. Depending on one's research question, it can be a crucial part of what makes an interview project "interpretive." It can be a key element of what makes interviews "deep." And it can emerge as a major benefit and challenge of the choice to use in-depth interviews rather than some other method of data collection. I am speaking of emotional engagement.

Some interviews are cool, professional interactions. They address low-intensity topics in a dispassionate way, and they need not do otherwise. Interpretive interviews, however, often take up topics *because* they are meaningful to participants and focus on what experiences mean to people at a more personal level. The interview setting itself can sometimes feel like an intimate conversation, and its open-ended format increases the odds that emotional issues will arise. Blee and Taylor (2002, 96) go so far as to say, "Intensive interviews are the best method for probing deep emotional issues."

Their claim may be a bit overstated. In my ethnographic work at the family shelter, for example, I participated in emotionally intense events and had many occasions to reflect on them with shelter residents and staff after hours. The fact that such conversations took place in the kitchen or on the playground, outside an in-depth interview setting, did not prevent me from exploring deep emotional issues. Indeed, the "non-interview" setting may have facilitated the conversations. On the whole, however, I agree that in-depth interviews are a superb forum for exploring emotional issues. They are unusually well suited for broaching emotional issues with care and in privacy, exploring them in a nuanced manner, and doing so in a way that is responsive to signals about when to dig deeper or go no further. In my work for *Unwanted Claims*, these features were key advantages of the interview method. They provided an ideal way to explore the feelings of futility, vulnerability, anonymity, humiliation, shame, pride, and frustration that accounted for so many of the clients' decisions and behaviors.

It is not enough, though, to cite emotional engagement as a "strength" of in-depth interviewing and leave it at that. The navigation of emotion was a persistent theme in my interviews and a defining feature of my field experience. It was central to the reflexivity, human connection, and reciprocal agency that lent an interpretive quality to my project. And in this regard, there were not only opportunities but also risks and challenges.

My interview questions sometimes opened emotional floodgates in ways that I—with no training as a therapist and perhaps too much confidence in my ability to absorb emotionally jarring conversation—was poorly equipped to handle. Starr recounted how, after learning of her acceptance to the SSDI program, she had tried to commit suicide; she felt overwhelmed with hopelessness when she saw an official governmental stamp on her life: "*long-term* disabled." Dizzy, once a proud and popular tavern owner, broke down as he described his anger, depression, and loneliness; he had watched even his most loyal friends drift away as his years of in-house isolation accumulated. Hope told one wrenching story after another about the sexual abuse she endured as a child and the brutal beatings and rapes she suffered as an adult victim of spousal violence. On and on it went, as so many AFDC clients described the desperation of their circumstances, their sadness about the lives they were providing for their children, and their anger at personal humiliations experienced at welfare agencies and grocery stores.

This emotional content, it must be said, was not limited to the sympathetic. Some clients openly expressed hatreds and prejudices that I found repellent. Some engaged in emotional manipulation or described behaviors (for example, toward their children) that I found upsetting. The emotional dynamics of the interviews, like the human beings themselves, varied tremendously. But in one way or another, they consistently presented challenges for a new researcher who was unsure how to "appropriately" respond to the high level of emotional intensity in interview encounters. I am hesitant to give advice on this matter; it feels presumptuous. But for what they are worth, I will share three injunctions that I find helpful to repeat to myself when I conduct this type of research.

Know your limits. Acknowledge that there are limits to what you can provide your interviewees and what you can absorb without doing harm to yourself. When raw emotions poured out, I tried to listen to interviewees in an open and accepting way, and I did my best to be supportive and patient. But I am neither a therapist nor a trained social worker. I did not have the skills or resources to provide what people needed. I could not do much to help them cope with, let alone change, their life circumstances. And amateurish efforts by a well-meaning researcher— misplaced intervention or blundered counseling—could easily have made matters worse. For all these reasons, I consider it essential to respect the limits of what I can offer an interviewee.

The other side of this coin is that each of us is limited in the emotional stress we can absorb. I came home from some interviews wiped out, feeling like I had been kicked in the stomach. I went through stretches of sleepless nights. At times, I experienced a deep sadness about what I had heard, anger at people and institutions I saw as responsible, frustration at my inability to effect change, guilt about my privileges and the time I fiddled away on a doctoral dissertation. Eventually, I learned that part of the field research process was learning how to acknowledge and deal with my own potential for burnout and depression. Deadlines be damned, I sometimes took long breaks between interviews and asked for leave at the shelter. I sometimes changed the order of upcoming interviews because the next in line seemed like it might be particularly difficult. In retrospect, I wish I had done more of this. I wish I had paid closer attention to my own signals and been more willing to take such breaks. It would have been good for me, for the people around me, and for my research project.

The researcher role is a human role. When we do research, we continue to be a person just like any other.[21] Interpretive interviews bring this fact to the fore, making the human connections we experience in everyday life a salient element of the research process. As a counterpoint to the difficult emotional material I am focusing on here, it is worth saying that this is part of what makes interviewing such a joy and such a satisfying way to do research. For all the hard moments described in the preceding paragraphs, my field experiences included far more highs than lows, many more good times than bad.

The point I mean to highlight, however, has to do with how we respond to emotional intensity in an in-depth interview. The decision to conduct an in-depth interview is a decision to share an experience with another person, and there are times when the human element has to take precedence—that is, times when we should view our navigation of the interview through a human lens rather than a research lens. It is okay to turn the tape recorder off; our research can wait. In fact, it will probably survive just fine if we decide not to press forward with a particular line of questioning in a particular interview. And although we should not try to take on the role of therapist, we can and should offer the same support and compassion we would extend if the situation occurred outside a research context. To be sure, just as in the rest of life, we sometimes botch the job. My response to an emotional outpouring was sometimes pitifully clumsy. I stammered a reply that conveyed little aside from the fact that I did not know what to say, and I felt all the worse for it afterward. But perfection cannot be the goal in such situations. The best we can offer, and the least we should offer, is a fallible but genuine effort to engage the people we interview as human "ends in themselves" rather than mere means for achieving our research goals (Cassell 1980, Reinharz 1992).

Emotions can advance rather than threaten good research. In the toughest emotional periods of my field research, the concept of "reflexivity" ceased to be an abstract methodological matter for me. I could see clearly that my questions were affecting my interviewees; their emotions and stories were having deep effects on me; and all of this was affecting my research. For some readers, this statement will seem like nothing remarkable—only a description of interpretive research in practice. But for others, all this talk of emotion will sound alarm bells about the loss of objectivity and the risk of sympathetic capture. These are important concerns, but they are unlikely to get us very far if they are framed in a way that makes emotional indifference a precondition for exacting and trustworthy analysis. The issue is not whether emotion is present or absent; it is how emotions affect our research.[22] Rather than holding our research hostage to amorphous anxieties about the loss of detachment, we should be specific about how and when intense emotions can pose a threat to good research. I think strong emotions pose a problem in three general types of circumstances: (a) if the researcher develops an unchallengeable attachment to a preferred methodological or theoretical approach, (b) if the researcher becomes personally invested in a particular portrayal of participants' understandings or a particular answer to their research question, or (c) if the research experience evokes such intense emotions for the researcher that she or he is personally harmed or cannot confront important tasks needed to complete the research project.

All three circumstances are problematic, but none is a *necessary* outgrowth of research that involves direct, responsive interaction with the intense emotions of interviewees. A reflexive engagement with the people one is studying is not at all the same as allowing one's emotions to direct the answers to research questions. To the contrary, emotional engagement can supply a powerful motivation to get one's explanations "right" and an essential means for accomplishing this goal. Emotions are storehouses of knowledge, compasses for navigating the world, and basic expressions of the meanings we attach to political objects and events. Had I not engaged emotion in an open and responsive way, I would have given up a crucial channel for accessing clients' conceptual worlds and a basic process for developing interpretive explanations. Whatever flaws my eventual analysis contained, it would have been far less trustworthy if I had retreated from emotion and steadfastly sought to protect my study from its intrusion.

Strong emotion was a periodic outcropping in my research experience. A large number of interviews were not particularly emotional at all. They were interesting and fun, or even a little dull in some cases. The point I want to end with, however, is the great potential for in-depth interviews to facilitate access both to participants' emotions and to emotional issues related to one's research topic. Social scientists study people who commit atrocities and people who survive them. We study activists who mobilize around horrifying problems and who feel tremendous passion for what they do. Emotions and emotional issues are central to social and political life, so we need methods to explore them. Interviews are superb for this purpose. They bring emotion to the surface, in ways we intend and ways we do not. It is here that we find some of the most distinctive, most fruitful, and most difficult aspects of using in-depth interviews for interpretive research.

NOTES

1. Unless otherwise noted, all quotations are drawn from interviews conducted for the research that appears in Soss (2000). All names are pseudonyms chosen by the interviewees themselves.

2. The distinction between method-driven and problem-driven research has become a common reference point in debates about methodological pluralism in American political science (see I. Shapiro 2004). I avoid this terminology here because prevailing usage tends to rely on a somewhat naive treatment of "problems" that ignores (a) the social and political construction of what constitutes a problem and (b) the crucial roles that normative and empirical theories—and related methods—play in this constructive process (see Levi 2004, Norton 2004b). The term used here, "question driven," is perhaps a little too capacious, but it has the twin virtues of being less beholden to the "problem vs. method" distinction and more faithful to the flow of my research experience. Most of my empirical research originates in my question asking. And in fact, these questions are often directed at the way a "problem" has been framed.

3. The rough outline of a methodology is usually implicit in the way I've asked my initial question. Yet although it may be present in tacit form, the methodology is not fully specified by the question. Its broad orientation is defined, but its precise form is not predetermined. Thus, the challenge is to refine the inchoate, not to "find the best choice" on some abstract checklist of methodological options.

4. In addition, I think Andrew Abbott (2001) makes two crucial points about this distinction. First, in practice, the labels "interpretive" and "positivist" signify relative differences within particular scholarly contexts. We cannot identify a set of absolute traits (A, B, and C) that are shared by all interpretive works and that are wholly distinct from a set of absolute traits shared by all positivist works (D, E, and F). The terms do

not define a set of fixed, non-overlapping "classical categories." Rather, they are labels for methodological *family resemblances* shared by pieces of research that may (a) differ from one another in significant ways and (b) share qualities with research in other categories. Second, as a sociological matter, labels such as "interpretivist" and "positivist" often do signal identities that help scholars make sense of their position within their discipline. Just as social identities provide a compass for negotiating political life (Walsh 2004), "methodological identities" help researchers figure out who stands where in relation to themselves. My disagreement is not with Abbott's social-psychological insight; it is with those who would reify such identities. The fact that scholars find it meaningful to say something like "she's a positivist and he's an interpretivist" does not obligate us to view these labels as if they referred to quasi-religious identities grounded in stable, opposed worldviews. For those who value a methodological pluralism, I think it can be counterproductive to do so. Methodological pluralism does not just mean tolerance for diversity across researchers; it also means freedom and flexibility for each researcher—recognition and encouragement of diversity across a given scholar's research projects.

    5. The stereotype questions have been asked in various ANES surveys over the years as follows: "Now I have some questions about different groups in our society. I'm going to show you a seven-point scale on which the characteristics of the people in a group can be rated. In the first statement a score of 1 means that you think almost all of the people in that group tend to be 'hard working.' A score of 7 means that almost all of the people in the group are 'lazy.' A score of 4 means that you think that most people in the group are not closer to one end or the other, and of course you may choose any number in between. . . ." The next set asks if people in each group tend to be unintelligent or tend to be intelligent. "Where would you rate whites [blacks] in general on this scale?" See, e.g., W. Miller, Kinder, and Rosenstone (1993).

    6. Schema theory offers one example. "The primary function of an activated schema is to affect the interpretation of related information. The way ambiguous information is construed and the default values that are assumed for unavailable information are influenced by a schema. Through these interpretive processes, schemas will influence evaluations and other judgments about an object" (R.M. Smith 1998, 403).

    7. As Rubin and Rubin (1995, 11) rightly note, if we assume that the meaning of a term can vary across social contexts and groups, and that such variation may not be transparent to the researcher, then we cannot view uniform question wording or ordering as a precondition for valid and reliable observations. "Asking everyone the same question makes little sense . . . where the goal is to find out what happened and why [or how participants conceive of things], in rich and individualistic terms."

    8. I view this careful division between "emic" (insider) concepts and "etic" (outsider) concepts as a key element of an interpretive approach. It underpins, for example, our hesitation to force participants' conceptions onto analytic dimensions we have constructed in advance (such as a closed-ended survey item). Similarly, in *Unwanted Claims*, I applied the concept of "political action" to the activities that made up welfare participation, and I used clients' conceptions to advance the resulting analysis. But I did not proceed on the assumption that clients would share my political view of their activities. Indeed, the apolitical nature of many clients' understandings proved to be an element of my political analysis.

    9. As noted in the introduction, I do not intend for this chapter to serve as an introduction to the nature and practice of in-depth interviewing. For more detailed discussions of interview *method*, readers should consult Rubin and Rubin 1995; Leech et al. (2002); Spradley (1979); Gubrium and Holstein (2002); Holstein and Gubrium (1995); Berg (1998, 57–99); Dexter (1970); Seidman (1991); Kvale (1996); Douglas (1985); McCracken (1988); and Gluck and Patai (1991).

    10. The deep/shallow distinction refers, of course, to the interview process itself, not to the quality or nuance of the resulting research product. In-depth interview data can be deployed in a manner that is pallid and obtuse, while a study based on data from fixed-format interviews may offer far richer insights into the phenomenon of interest. Such outcomes depend on the knowledge, skill, and creativity of researchers.

    11. On the other hand, I would hardly be the first to note that the working-class men Lane interviewed might have felt less than relaxed in a professor's office at Yale University.

    12. Here, I touch on only a few key points drawn from longer discussions in Spradley (1979); Rubin and Rubin 1995; and Berg (1998).

    13. In a "grounded theory" approach, for example, the entwining of many different data collection, coding, and analysis activities is referred to collectively as "the constant comparative method" (Glaser and Strauss 1967; Strauss and Corbin 1998).

    14. On analytic memos, see Strauss 1987; Emerson et al. (1995). Some of my memos were process oriented: Why am I getting X response? What does this suggest I should do next? Others addressed the major theoretical and empirical questions driving my project. In some cases, I would write multiple memos on the

same topic, trying out different conceptual lenses on the same set of observations to see how each played out. Such memos were useful as starting points for the more systematic analyses I conducted after I completed and transcribed my interviews. Equally important, they were a casual, private activity and, as such, did not carry the same emotional pressures as writing *official dissertation text*. In the months after my fieldwork, I was happy to find that the analytic memos frequently supplied "starter text" for my chapters—often helping me to jump-start a section that had brought on a serious case of self-doubt and writer's block.

15. On balance, my research yielded more positive than negative readings of my interview efforts. People who felt like no one cared about their problems were often grateful for the opportunity to tell their stories to an attentive listener. I attributed this partly to the length of interviews, their setting in clients' homes (or an alternative site chosen by the client), and their focus on clients' experiences, emotions, and understandings. On the other hand, some of my most vivid memories of the field focus on the occasions when I encountered negative responses. At the start of my fieldwork, I spent four months in the community before conducting my first formal interview. During that time I tried to build social networks, get comfortable with new languages and ideas, develop my interview protocol, and make myself and my research into familiar entities for community members. On one occasion, I went to a community meeting in a low-income neighborhood to introduce myself. When I said I had come with the hope of interviewing people in SSDI and AFDC about their experiences in welfare programs, I received a chilly response. An in-depth interview with a welfare recipient was, for this audience, primarily a tool for taking advantage of the vulnerable and producing sensationalist, stigmatizing accounts of poor families. (It was 1994 and, in the lead-up to federal welfare reform in 1996, scornful talk of welfare dependency ran thick in the public discourse.) Standing alone at the front of the room, I was asked to answer for a multitude of sins news reporters and social scientists had committed against people who live in poverty. Could I guarantee that my interviews would produce something different? Wasn't I just passing through on my way to a nice university job, while the people who participated in my study would remain behind long after I was gone? My stumbling answers were nowhere near as good, or as forceful, as the questions I was asked. Miraculously, the conversation seemed to end more positively than it began. A number of people at the meeting that day welcomed me and later provided invaluable assistance. But the initial reaction was an emotionally difficult lesson in the complex politics and ethics of field research—and a powerful demonstration of what interviewing can mean to participants.

16. And here as elsewhere, we cannot assume we know the relevant understandings in advance. I list "white" and "Jewish" together in this sentence, but one person in my study (a black woman) ended a commentary on white privilege by saying, "You probably know what I mean; you're not white either—you're Jewish, right?"

17. My uses of the term "partial" are meant to extend Anne Norton's (2004a) playful invocations of this concept. The last assertion in this list—that all methods are "prone to some bias or another"—is meant to convey that the use of any particular method, relative to some other method, will systematically raise our chances of observing and understanding X while lowering our chances of observing and understanding Z. In addition, I would say that our use of *any* method will reflect our historical, social, and political standpoints—biases that we will tend to see as natural and commonsensical perspectives, if we perceive them as perspectives at all.

18. In some interview projects, however, there are good reasons to forego the verbatim records produced by audio or video recording in favor of partial handwritten notes or jottings made after the interview. For discussion, see Rubin and Rubin (1995, 125–28).

19. By contrast, Nina Eliasoph (1998, 18–19) suggests that fixed-format survey interviews are actually geared toward, and serve to construct, "the kind of person who will cooperatively answer a stranger's questions and not demand dialogue." Reminiscing on her days as a survey interviewer, she recalls individuals trying to resist, alter, or subvert her questions in some way. "My job, however, was simply to repeat the questions exactly as written in the question booklet until the respondent succumbed to the interview format."

20. The trick, in a sense, is how to balance our accounts of coherence and contradiction. On one side, the researcher who uses interviews to doggedly pursue coherent understandings risks creating an individual-level "just-so" story that encompasses and explains everything. On the other side, the researcher who uses interviews to single-mindedly pursue ambivalence and disjunction risks a conceptual world so chaotic that it offers no basis for interpretive explanation.

21. Among scholars who read interpretive research, this point is most familiar in its epistemological form—as an assertion that science is a "gutsy human activity" (Gould 1981) pursued by people who occupy specific cultural, historical, and social vantage points (Harding 1991). By contrast, I raise the point here in

its interpersonal (and ethical) sense of how we relate to the people we encounter in our research projects. Here as elsewhere, my concern is research practice rather than epistemology per se.

22. I find it implausible to treat researcher emotion per se as inimical to good social science. Presumably, we all feel *something* for the people and issues we spend our lives studying. And presumably, one does not need to feel neutral about genocidal killing in order to study the Rwandan genocide in a manner that merits esteem from social scientists. When we try to police the boundaries of social science by dismissing any study in which the researcher's emotions are evident, we risk equating the good social scientist with an automaton or sociopath.

CHAPTER 7

ORDINARY LANGUAGE INTERVIEWING

Frederic Charles Schaffer

I have been interested in culture and language since young adulthood at least. After graduating high school I worked for a year on a fruit farm in Norway and in a children's home in Swedish-speaking southern Finland. I already knew French and a little German from my high school studies, and during my stay in Scandinavia, I learned some Norwegian and Swedish too.

In college I started out studying psychology and psycholinguistics, but soon shifted to international relations (IR), which I thought better spoke to the pressing problems of the world. I discovered quickly, however, that much IR theory rested upon assumptions about human nature that it was ill equipped to assess. In search of answers, I designed my own major, which I called "social theory." I oriented my reading toward those who had something to say about why people do what they do. That project led me eventually to the philosophy of the social sciences, which addressed the deeper question of how we know what we know. At about this time I also spent my junior year in Senegal, where I learned to speak Wolof.

When I returned to the United States, I started exploring the epistemological and ontological assumptions underlying various theories of international conflict, drawing on the work of phenomenologists Edmund Husserl and Maurice Merleau-Ponty. This exercise led to a thesis on "the metaphysics of war." By the end of it, I had become aware of language as a tool for clearing up ambiguities of motive. Merleau-Ponty and other phenomenologists teach us that there is no Archimedean point outside the world upon which to stand. One is always inside the world, and the world is messy. We cannot find answers to all the questions we want to address, I learned, but an attentiveness to language can help with some of them. This realization sparked my interest in ordinary language philosophy, which allowed me to do phenomenological work without the burden of phenomenology's heavy jargon.

In graduate school at Berkeley I had a foreign language area studies fellowship to study Wolof, which made available to me, among other things, a native-speaking tutor. My tutor's mother was active in Senegalese politics, and she would send him cassette tapes of political rallies that she recorded. During my lessons, we often listened to these tapes, and it became clear to me that Wolof words such as "demokaraasi" and "politig" were only roughly equivalent to what I knew as "democracy" and "politics." There was born the idea for my dissertation: to study the (Wolof) vocabulary of politics as a way to understand (Senegalese) political culture. The project became, literally, the study of "democracy in translation."

> You are weaving a thatched roof for your hut. Here you can do it all out in the field.
> You place the frame on the ground, you put it together, you plait the straw. You do
> everything. But you can't lift it yourself. It is too heavy to pick up. You have to call
> someone to help you. You call one person, you call another. Together you all lift it up.
> That is our demokaraasi.
> —*Peanut farmer, village of Ngabu, Senegal; translated from Wolof* (Schaffer 1998, 60)

> When your child is of the proper age and wants to enter a life of marriage, he needs to
> ask permission from his parents—this is demokrasya. If there were no demokrasya, he
> would do anything he wants. He could even go to another country.
> —*Rag maker, Quezon City, Philippines; translated from Tagalog* (Schaffer 2002, 13)

Ordinary language interviewing is a tool for uncovering the meaning of words in everyday talk. It is a tool for uncovering the meaning of *demokaraasi* to the peanut farmer, and of *demokrasya* to the rag maker. By studying the meaning of a word in English—or the meaning of roughly equivalent words in other languages—the promise is to gain insight into the various social realities these words name, evoke, or realize.

This chapter answers some basic questions about ordinary language interviewing: what it is, what can be discovered through it, and how to actually do it. To make its relevance more transparent and its techniques easier to learn, the chapter includes an extended interview excerpt.

WHAT IS ORDINARY LANGUAGE INTERVIEWING?

This interviewing strategy finds its roots in ordinary language philosophy as pioneered by John Austin and Ludwig Wittgenstein. Within the field of philosophy, a fundamental contribution of Austin and Wittgenstein was to recognize that long-standing debates on questions like "do people have free will?" or "is it possible to really know something?" are symptomatic of conceptual puzzlement. To clear up such conceptual confusion, Austin and Wittgenstein teach us, requires looking at the complex and often internally contradictory grammars of words like "will," "freedom," or "knowledge."[1]

"Ordinary language interviewing" is a shorthand label I use for the self-conscious application of interviewing techniques inspired by ordinary language philosophy.[2] It borrows from Austin and Wittgenstein three basic insights. First, *everyday words reflect the accumulated wisdom or shared culture of a community*. As Austin (1979, 182) put it: "Our common stock of words embodies all the distinctions men have found worth drawing, and the connexions they have found worth marking, in the lifetimes of many generations." It follows that we can use a study of words as a window into that shared culture. This point is illustrated well by David Laitin, who, by drawing on Austin's analysis of acceptable and unacceptable excuses, shows how close attention to meaning can shed light on English speakers' shared standards of responsibility:

> Although [Austin] is not explicit on this, one could derive from his discussion a guide to an
> anthropologist or ethnolinguist who came to study the English tribe. The anthropologist
> should notice that it is acceptable to tread on a snail "inadvertently," tip over the salt shaker
> "inadvertently," but *not* to tread on the baby "inadvertently." "Inadvertent" means, according to Austin, "a class of incidental happenings which must occur in the doing of any physical act," and is used when that incidental happening causes some (usually small) distress.

Our foreign anthropologist, in learning English, might capture the sense of "inadvertence" as meaning merely "unintentional" (which, incidentally, is the definition in my dictionary). Suppose he does tread on a baby in one of the native's houses, and offers, "I did it inadvertently." And suppose the native returns with "That wasn't inadvertence! That was pure callousness." What is our anthropologist to think? Is he getting a lesson in the English language (he used "inadvertent" when he should have used "callous"), or was it a lesson in morality (treading on a baby is far more egregious than treading on a snail; and for the former, a simple excuse is not sufficient)? In fact, what the anthropologist is learning is both the English language *and* the standards of misdeeds among English speakers. (Laitin 1977, 154)

To learn the meaning of words like "power," "freedom," or "administration" is to learn not only a part of the English language but also shared standards for calling something an instance of power, freedom, or administration. It is to learn, in other words, what power, freedom, or administration really are.

The second insight borrowed from Austin and Wittgenstein is that *the meaning of a word consists in how the word is used.* As Wittgenstein stated it pithily: "the meaning of a word is its use in the language" (1968, par. 43). To study the meaning of "rights" or "corruption" thus requires more than flipping through a dictionary; it necessitates investigating how people actually use these words in a wide range of (political and nonpolitical) contexts.

The third and last insight is that *complicating a study of meaning in language is the reality that the various uses of a word need not fit together neatly.* Wittgenstein wrote:

Consider . . . the proceedings that we call "games." I mean board-games, card-games, ball-games, Olympic games, and so on. What is common to them all?—Don't say: "There *must* be something common, or they would not be called 'games'"—but *look and see* whether there is anything common to all.—For if you look at them you will not see something in common to *all*, but similarities, relationships, and a whole series of them at that. . . .—Look for example at board-games, with their multifarious relationships. Now pass to card-games; here you find many correspondences with the first group, but many common features drop out, and others appear. When we pass next to ball-games, much that is common is retained, but much is lost.—Are they all "amusing"? Compare chess with noughts and crosses [known as tic-tac-toe in American English—ed.]. Or is there always winning and losing, or competition between players? Think of patience. In ball games there is winning and losing; but when a child throws his ball at the wall and catches it again, this feature has disappeared. Look at the parts played by skill and luck; and at the difference between skill in chess and skill in tennis. Think now of games like ring-a-ring-a-roses; here is the element of amusement, but how many other characteristic features have disappeared! And we can go through the many, many other groups of games in the same way; can see how similarities crop up and disappear.

And the result of this examination is: we see a complicated network of similarities overlapping and criss-crossing—sometimes overall similarities, sometimes similarities in detail.

I can think of no better expression to characterize these similarities than "family resemblances"; for the various resemblances between members of a family: build, features, colour of eyes, gait, temperament, etc. overlap and criss-cross in the same way (1968, par. 66–67; emphasis in original).

The various uses or meanings of a word do not interlock precisely like pieces of a jigsaw puzzle. Consequently, to say that we can identify shared meanings implicit in a word is not to claim that those meanings can be arranged tidily. A word can be used in a variety of different, and sometimes contradictory, ways (even by one person, in one conversation). So when we speak of "the" meaning of a term, we need to include not only points of agreement, but also areas of ambiguity and contestedness.

WHAT CAN BE LEARNED THROUGH ORDINARY LANGUAGE INTERVIEWING?

Careful analysis of the terms people use can be a valuable tool for understanding the social phenomena that political scientists want to investigate. Voting, property, and citizenship are real to political actors themselves. To accurately interpret the intentions of such actors, it is helpful to take seriously their words, and the categories that these words reflect. It would be difficult, for instance, to understand the institution of voting in the United States without learning the meaning of the word "vote." As Charles Taylor explained, "the realities here are social practices; and these cannot be identified in abstraction from the language we use to describe them, or invoke them, or carry them out" (1977, 117).

Of course different tools are appropriate to different research agendas. An ordinary language approach is most helpful when one's analysis rests centrally upon terms that posit a particular set of intentions on the part of political actors. Take for example the study of democracy. Scholars often posit a causal link between free elections and democratic accountability, a link, not incidentally, that today provides one of the theoretical underpinnings for many U.S. and World Bank governance and democracy-building programs around the world. But this link is tenable only if voters do indeed expect elected officials to act in the public interest and in accordance with the rule of law. For this reason, it is important to verify that voters do, in fact, hold such expectations. Looking at how voters use words like "vote," "democracy," or "accountability" might reveal the kinds of expectations they actually hold.

Ordinary language interviewing is all the more helpful when the people under investigation are from a culture different from one's own, when there are significant differences between their intentions (and vocabulary) and one's own. To return to Wittgenstein, we might think of family resemblances as existing between the uses of roughly equivalent words in different languages. That is, there may be a complex pattern of overlapping and crisscrossing similarities shared by a word and its "relatives" in other languages: by English "administration," Dutch *bestuur*, and German *verwaltung*; by English "politics," Arabic *siyasa*, and Hindi *rajniti*; by English "democracy," Chinese *minzhu*, and Wolof "demokaraasi." Differences between the meanings of these words are important because they might reveal, to the outside observer, different repertoires of action and motivation. Interview data from a study I conducted on the meaning of demokaraasi, for instance, showed that to many Senegalese voters, demands for electoral accountability are diluted by concerns about social cohesion and collective security. Voting, like helping to hoist a roof onto a neighbor's hut, is an act of mutual solidarity. When voting, an evaluation of the abilities or achievements of candidates is often less important than keeping village relationships in good repair. The causal link between elections and accountability is thus weak (Schaffer 1998, 86–115).

Ordinary language interviewing, of course, can also be used to investigate fruitfully the intentions of people who speak one's own language. Cultural differences, after all, often exist among speakers of the same language. Consequently, it can be revealing to examine whether the use of particular terms varies across (and within) subcultures of one's own language community. Among the important subcultures of American English speakers are ones defined by class, race, gender, profession, ideology, and sexual orientation.[3] One may even find linguistic particularities (and distinctive repertoires of action and purpose) in groups as restricted as a policy circle, government agency, or local PTA.

HOW DOES ONE CONDUCT AN ORDINARY LANGUAGE INTERVIEW?

The purpose of the ordinary language interview is to look at language in use—to engage the interviewee in a conversation and, within that conversation, to provide the person with occasions to use particular words of interest in ways that reveal their various meanings. Although the ordinary language interview is open ended, it is nevertheless structured to the extent that it is designed to expose the meanings of words through deliberate questioning strategies. Most helpful in this endeavor, I have found, are *judgment questions*. Such questions require the interviewee to express opinions and make discriminations that reveal standards implicit in a term:

- Is there "x" where you live now?
- Is "x" good or bad?
- Is there a place or a country in the world that does not have "x"?

I have also found it useful to employ five other kinds of follow-up questions:

1. *Elaboration prompts* that invite the interviewee to flesh out or amplify what he or she is saying:

   - Can you explain?
   - Can you elaborate?
   - Please say more.
   - Why do you say that?
   - How so?
   - Really?

2. *Example prompts* that can help both you (the interviewer) and the interviewee think more concretely about the question at hand:

   - Can you give an example (from national politics, from your community, from your own personal experience, etc.)?

3. *Internal logic questions* that provide an opportunity for the interviewee to reflect more deeply about what he or she is saying:

   - Earlier you said "x," but now you seem to be saying "not x." Can you explain what you mean by "x" and "not x"?
   - Earlier, you seemed to be saying that "a" has something to do with both "b" and "c." I'm not sure I understand how "b" and "c" are related. Can you explain?

4. *Restatement questions* that confirm that you understand what the interviewee is saying, and also demonstrate to the interviewee that you are listening, that you are taking him or her seriously:
   - If I understand correctly, you are saying that . . .[4]

5. *Direct questions* that ask explicitly what the interviewee understands the meaning of term "x" to be:

- What do you think "x" means?
- To you, what is "x"?[5]

Let us look now at an excerpt from an actual interview. I chose this excerpt because it starts with a seemingly odd, somewhat elliptic statement on the part of the interviewee. But gentle, persistent questioning reveals that the person has something very cogent to say. The interview was conducted in a poor neighborhood of Quezon City, the largest city in the Philippines, by a research assistant I trained in the methods of ordinary language interviewing. I was not present during this interview, which was tape-recorded and later transcribed. The interviewee—Juan de la Cruz (a fictitious name)—is a forty-eight-year-old man. The interview took place in Juan's home, and both the interviewer and Juan were speaking the Tagalog language. We chose Juan, along with the other people we interviewed, at random from the voter registry. One purpose of this study was to explore how urban poor Filipino voters such as Juan understand "demokrasya," the Tagalog rough equivalent of "democracy."

Interviewer: Is demokrasya good or bad? [*scripted judgment question*]
Juan de la Cruz: For me, it's kind of bad. It's a chopping board.
Interviewer: Can you explain please? [*elaboration prompt*]
Juan de la Cruz: Demokrasya is used to take advantage of people.
Interviewer: To take advantage of people, what do you mean? [*elaboration prompt*]
Juan de la Cruz: Well, we have demokrasya, but it's only a pretext.   .
Interviewer: A pretext? A pretext for what? [*elaboration prompt*]
Juan de la Cruz: It's a way to get out of a situation. For me, demokrasya is not right. It doesn't come from good. It comes from bad.
Interviewer: So how is demokrasya used to take advantage of people? [*elaboration prompt*]
Juan de la Cruz: Because of freedom of speech, or freedom of the press. We're in a demokrasya, so you can't stop abusive people from saying whatever they want.
Interviewer: Let's take freedom of speech first. Can you give me an example of what you're talking about? [*prompt for concrete example*]
Juan de la Cruz: When there is freedom of speech in politics, politicians can abuse their opponents.
Interviewer: What kinds of abusive things do they say? [*prompt for concrete example*]
Juan de la Cruz: Rotten things about their opponents' lives. They even dig into the grandchildren, even the family is affected.
Interviewer: What kinds of rotten things? [*elaboration prompt*]
Juan de la Cruz: Badness, corruption, family background.
Interviewer: Family background? [*elaboration prompt*]
Juan de la Cruz: Yes.
Interviewer: For example? [*prompt for concrete example*]
Juan de la Cruz: Even the family, the affairs of the family are dug into, where the family hails from. If they've been immoral, even back to the grandfather of their grandfather. Politicians say that because we're in a demokrasya, they can say that, to inform the people.
Interviewer: You don't condone their use of freedom of speech? [*elaboration prompt*]
Juan de la Cruz: No, it's not acceptable.

Interviewer: Why not? [*judgment question*]

Juan de la Cruz: With freedom of speech, you should be allowed to say good things—you're free to do that; but bad things, you shouldn't be allowed to say those. In Tagalog we say that demokrasya is *kalayaan* [roughly, "freedom"]. But in my opinion, there is no true kalayaan because there are limits that should be respected. You have rights, you can make choices, but there are limits.

Interviewer: Limits? [*elaboration prompt*]

Juan de la Cruz: Yes. That's why you cannot say that you are really free. In essence really, if you consider it, if you look at it, there should be limits to kalayaan.

Interviewer: Let's go back to freedom of the press. How does freedom of the press get used to take advantage of people? [*elaboration prompt*]

Juan de la Cruz: In the press, it's the same. They can say things or report things that will be harmful to a person. That shouldn't be the case. It should be controlled by law. But because they say, "we are free, we have all the rights to inform the people," because we're in a demokrasya, they will write those harmful things.

Interviewer: Do you know of examples here in your neighborhood, so that I can have a clearer idea of what you are talking about with regard to freedom of speech and freedom of the press? [*prompt for concrete example*]

Juan de la Cruz: Yes . . . that . . . the . . . [pause]

Interviewer: For example here in MRB? [MRB stands for "medium rise buildings," the government-built low income housing project in which Juan lives.] [*prompt for concrete example*]

Juan de la Cruz: Here in MRB, there are lots. Because what residents hear doesn't coincide with what's actually happening.

Interviewer: For example? [*prompt for concrete example*]

Juan de la Cruz: They are covering things up at our meetings, even in something as basic as setting the agenda. When you get to the meeting, you see that they've changed the original agenda. When we get to the discussions, things change. When you ask them, they will say, "we have a right to change that, we are free to do that." That's what they'll say to you. Or they will say, "we're not the ones who came out with the agenda you saw."

Interviewer: So if I understand what you're saying: demokrasya isn't really good because there is a tendency to abuse it, to abuse kalayaan? [*restatement question*]

Juan de la Cruz: Yes. That's it. People use it to avoid their responsibilities. Yup, that's my take on demokrasya. During the time of Marcos . . . I am in favor of what happened then.

Interviewer: What about the time of Marcos? [*scripted judgment question, though here brought up by the interviewee*]

Juan de la Cruz: There was a dictatorship, but that was better.

Interviewer: How was it better? [*judgment question*]

Juan de la Cruz: Because the enforcement of law was better.

Interviewer: For example? [*prompt for concrete example*]

Juan de la Cruz: For example in situations of peace and order.

Interviewer: So let me ask you now, do you think there is demokrasya in the Philippines today? [*scripted judgment question*]

Juan de la Cruz: They say we are practicing demokrasya now, but it's like nothing, it's of no use.

Interviewer: Why do you say that it's of no use? [*elaboration prompt*]

Juan de la Cruz: Just look at the differences between the rich and the poor, at the treatment by the government of the rich and poor. . . . [pause] You hear many things. When a candidate doesn't want to be beaten by another he will not concede defeat. He will say he was cheated. Daboy today, what do we hear from Daboy? When the time came and he lost, what did he say?[6]

Interviewer: That he was cheated.

Juan de la Cruz: He was cheated! [laughs]

Interviewer: Is the example of Daboy related to what you were saying about differences in how the rich and poor are treated by the government? [*internal logic question*]

Juan de la Cruz: Yes. Because if there is demokrasya, there shouldn't be discrimination by the government, especially by the government. But the government discriminates against the poor.

Interviewer: How so? [*elaboration prompt*]

Juan de la Cruz: Take government programs that they say are for the poor. In almost all government programs, the aspect of the poor is not absent. Right? You observe that. Their chopping board—their pretext—is the poor. The president, senators—they all justify these programs by saying they will benefit the poor. But look at who benefits.

Interviewer: Who benefits? [*elaboration prompt*]

Juan de la Cruz: The elites, the rich, those who run things. The poor are used as an excuse, as a justification for the programs, but they don't get a thing.

Interviewer: Can you give a specific example? [*prompt for concrete example*]

Juan de la Cruz: I will give you one. Look here in MRB, at this housing project. The beneficiaries of these housing units are not qualified recipients. In the government program, renters—those who don't own their own housing—should have the first priority. But look, almost 70 percent of MRB residents were already homeowners.

Interviewer: Really? [*elaboration prompt*]

Juan de la Cruz: Those who got units here are those who have money, those who can pay. Many people here own property elsewhere already. Their properties in the provinces are very large. They get units here so that while their children are studying in Manila, they have somewhere to live. This is an example of discrimination.

Interviewer: So if I understand correctly: what you're saying is that government programs are publicly promoted as being for the poor, but in reality they do not serve the poor? [*restatement question*]

Juan de la Cruz: Yes, that's it. Those who benefit are rich.

Interviewer: You spoke earlier about elections, about incumbents not willing to concede defeat. [*return to internal logic question*]

Juan de la Cruz: If they lose, they don't want to concede. Where is the demokrasya in that?

Interviewer: Why isn't there demokrasya in that? [*internal logic question*]

Juan de la Cruz: That's not demokrasya because you don't want to recognize defeat. Where is the demokrasya? The people are not free anymore, their votes are ignored. Where is their kalayaan? If there really is demokrasya . . . if you lose, you lose. You don't create problems.

Interviewer: Can you give a concrete example? [*prompt for concrete example*]

Juan de la Cruz: Even here in our place. Here in our association. Our election here is supposedly yearly. But when a person holds a position, he doesn't want to call elections. The person does everything he can to stay in power. This is just small, this association of ours. Things get much worse at the national level.

Interviewer: Let me ask you another question. What does demokrasya mean to you? [*scripted direct question*]

Juan de la Cruz: For me, it's an ideology. If I connect it to religious teachings, it's an ideology of Satan.

Interviewer: Why do you say that? [*elaboration prompt*]

Juan de la Cruz: It's used to ruin the minds of people, to make them go against things that should be obeyed.

Interviewer: Can you explain? [*elaboration prompt*]

Juan de la Cruz: People want to be free, that's what they're after, to be free. But there are laws that should be respected, that's what I was saying earlier. There are laws we should obey.

Interviewer: So how does that make demokrasya a satanic ideology? [*elaboration prompt*]

Juan de la Cruz: It's a satanic ideology because most people don't want to be constrained by laws. They only want to do their own thing.

Interviewer: Why do you think so many people like demokrasya? [*judgment question*]

Juan de la Cruz: Why do they like it? It's money. They can use demokrasya to break the law. That's why I say demokrasya is a satanic ideology because it is being used to justify breaking the law. If not for the anomalies that demokrasya produces, it would be okay.

Interviewer: It would be okay because there would be lawfulness? [*restatement question*]

Juan de la Cruz: Yes, because we would have the rule of law. [chuckles]

We learn that to Juan demokrasya has something to do with unbridled freedom of speech—including the freedom to lie and to say harmful things. It also involves people not only being able to say what they want, but having their voices heard and, more importantly, registered—"not having their votes ignored," as Juan puts it. It also entails fair treatment by the government. "If there is demokrasya, there shouldn't be discrimination by the government," in Juan's words, "especially by the government."

We also learn, and here Juan echoes the sentiments of many people we interviewed, that a major problem with how Philippine demokrasya actually operates is that private citizens and government officials act in ways that are rude, hurtful, and unlawful; that people, especially the poor, are not treated with regard or dignity. A few weeks before this interview was conducted, hundreds of thousands of mostly poor people from Quezon City and other areas of metropolitan Manila rallied in angry protest, calling for a change in government and the establishment of what they called "true demokrasya." True demokrasya, in the eyes of many protesters, seemingly requires the government to treat the poor with consideration—just as, in the rag maker's conception, demokrasya requires children to treat their parents with respect. The words and actions of the demonstrators take on special meaning and intelligibility in light of Juan's, and the rag maker's, remarks.

CONCLUSION

By way of conclusion, let us examine briefly a few methodological issues that attend the use of ordinary language interviewing. To begin with, it is important to recall that language use and meaning can vary with the speaker's class, race, gender, and so on. It is, consequently, essential to get a sample of language use that is representative of different kinds of speakers. A random sample might be used, especially when the community is relatively small. In the Philippines, I studied one urban community with about 14,000 registered voters and randomly selected 2 percent of the people listed on the voter registry. With the help of two interviewers I trained, it took 4 months to conduct 139 interviews, including those with Juan and the rag maker.[7] To study a larger community, a quota sampling strategy might be more feasible.[8] This strategy can be used to ensure that the sample includes speakers of different ages, sexes, classes, education levels, religions, dialects, ethnicities, party affiliations, areas of residence, and the like. When doing fieldwork in Senegal, I used this sampling strategy to interview 100 people from around the country who met various demographic criteria, including the peanut farmer from Ngabu.

It is also helpful to remember that during the interview there are no right or wrong answers. The goal is to elicit meaning, not to correct, instruct, or pass judgment. In this regard, ordinary language interviewing is similar to "elite" interviewing to the extent that the respondent is treated as an expert about the topic at hand. A nonjudgmental demeanor is different, of course, from blankness or impassivity. In conducting any conversational interview, including an ordinary language interview, it is obviously important to put the interviewee at ease. It is thus altogether appropriate to express empathy by smiling, laughing, frowning, or showing surprise at the proper cues. It is also appropriate to be candid and natural when fielding questions posed by the interviewee (as long as the answers do not correct, instruct, pass judgment, or convey information about the words under investigation). Thus when Juan asked, "When the time came and [Daboy] lost, what did he say?" the interviewer, who was familiar with the Daboy affair, was correct to reply, "that he was cheated."[9]

When it comes to the analysis of interview data, to drawing conclusions about how words are actually used, it is useful to recall Wittgenstein's treatment of "games." He prompts us to "look and see whether there is anything common to all." When Wittgenstein himself looks, he sees "a complicated network of similarities overlapping and criss-crossing." One challenge of ordinary language analysis is to sort out this complexity, which is typical of many words and not just "games." I personally find it helpful, as a first step, to organize various usages visually. I draw a Venn diagram to literally map out, roughly, how they relate to one another. Once I build up an understanding from the data, I then try to confirm that it is accurate. In ordinary language analysis, confirmation involves producing examples that sound right or natural to members of the language community.[10] Austin's discussion of "accident" and "mistake" provides a template for constructing a confirmatory example in the form of a question:

> You have a donkey, so have I, and they graze in the same field. The day comes when I conceive a dislike for mine. I go to shoot it, draw a bead on it, fire: the brute falls in its tracks. I inspect the victim, and find to my horror that it is *your* donkey. I appear on the doorstep with the remains and say—what? "I say, old sport, I'm awfully sorry, &c., I've shot your donkey *by accident*"? Or "*by mistake*"? Then again, I go to shoot my donkey as before, draw a bead on it, fire—but as I do so, the beasts move, and to my horror yours falls. Again the scene on the doorstep—what do I say? "By mistake?" Or "by accident?" (Austin 1979, 185 [emphasis in original])

Posing questions of similar form to community members (preferably ones who did not participate in the initial interviews) can help verify that one understands the grammar of a word, or words, more or less correctly.

Another point worth mentioning is that even when studying the terms used by political actors themselves yields important information, political scientists need not limit themselves to the very same terms in making their analyses. That the Nazis never spoke of their actions as "genocide" should not prevent scholars studying the holocaust from describing it as an instance of genocide—

though in arriving at that conclusion they may well need to figure out what the Nazis meant by words such as *endlösung* (final solution), *sonderbehandlung* (special treatment), or *aussiedlung* (evacuation). There may be good and varied reasons for the analyst to construct her own categories. In such cases, an attentiveness to ordinary language can help tether her categories to the experiences of the people she seeks to understand.

Finally, a word about the issue of falsification. Reliance on any kind of interview data poses special problems, for the interview setting itself may affect how people react to your questions. Their answers may reflect what they assume you want to know, or what they take to be in their interest for you to know (Rieder 1994; Schaffer 1998, 19). Ordinary language interviewing, I believe, is less prone to this problem than other forms of interviewing. Certainly in ordinary language interviewing people may shade or misrepresent their true feelings and opinions. People are, however, unlikely to falsify the conventionalized meanings they draw upon when expressing those feelings and opinions. I may lie about whether I think the political system of a country is just, but it would be difficult for me to alter how I use the word "just."

NOTES

An earlier version of this chapter was presented at the Workshop on Interpretive Research Methods in Empirical Political Science held at the 2003 annual meeting of the Western Political Science Association in Denver. I would like to thank Dvora Yanow and Peregrine Schwartz-Shea for organizing the workshop and for inviting me to participate. I am also indebted to Alfredo Metrio Antonio, who skillfully conducted the interview with Juan de la Cruz.

1. An excellent introduction to ordinary language philosophy, and a clear exposition of its significance for social science, can be found in Pitkin (1972).

2. Scholars working from different epistemological starting points have also examined language to gain insight into shared social and political realities. See for instance Hyden (1970), Hymes (1970), Lewis (1988), Geertz (1980), and Johnson (1995).

3. On class see Labov (1966), on race see Labov (1969), on gender see R. Lakoff (1976), on professions see Edelman (1984), on ideology see David Green (1987), and on sexual orientation see Leap (1996).

4. In formulating a restatement question, it is important to mirror carefully what the interviewee has actually said, lest the question become a leading one. Still, in my own experience of interviewing, the most revealing answers have tended to come when I apparently misunderstood what the interviewee was trying to say: "No, that's not what I said. What I really meant was . . ."

5. Direct questions, I have found, are best asked at the end of an interview, where they provide the interviewee an opportunity to make sense of the concrete examples he or she has already brought up. If asked too early, there is a risk that the interviewee might use the particular meaning of "x" he or she articulates to guide all further comments about "x." Saving direct questions until the end permits the conversation to remain open ended.

6. "Daboy" is the nickname of action star Rudy Fernandez, who ran for mayor of Quezon City in 2001. When the vote count showed him losing the race, he accused the winning candidate of committing massive electoral fraud, without furnishing any evidence to back up that claim. This interview took place soon after the 2001 elections.

7. Originally, 278 people were chosen for the sample. In this highly transient area, 107 of them had moved out of the community after registering. Two had died. Of the 171 people who actually still lived there, our response rate was 81 percent, thus the 139 interviews.

8. On quota sampling see Bernard (1988, 96–97).

9. Other useful techniques for putting the interviewee at ease can be found in Leech (2002).

10. On this manner of confirmation see Searle (1969, 12–15), Pitkin (1972, 15), and Cavell (1976, 33–37).

CHAPTER 8

SEEING WITH AN ETHNOGRAPHIC SENSIBILITY

Explorations Beneath the Surface of Public Policies

Ellen Pader

When I was a teenager I was fascinated by how people organized their home spaces. I was even more fascinated that I could tell, with surprising accuracy, much about the ethnic background of my friends simply by entering their homes. This was in the 1960s, before people commonly, and self-consciously, set out to announce their ethnicity on their walls; at that time, people were as likely to try to hide it in order to slip unnoticed into the great melting pot of America. This delight in observing followed me to Kenyon College, where my intellectual endeavors vacillated among studio art, art history, Medieval studies, literature, and psychology. I discovered The Hidden Dimension *by anthropologist E.T. Hall and was struck by his theories of proxemics and his concept that our (culturally specific) attitudes toward space tend to thread through the fabric of society. My senior paper tried to pull all these new ways of thinking together as I explored the implicit cognitive influence of St. Augustine's theories of beauty on the structures of both a Gothic cathedral and Chaucer's* Canterbury Tales. *Here I was, doing a structural analysis, yet it would be another five years, during my doctoral studies at Cambridge University in archaeology and anthropology, before I learned the concept "structuralism."*

Like others of my generation, for me a Ph.D. in the social sciences meant that results were only meaningful if full ≤of numbers, chi squares, and cluster diagrams and had a statistical significance of .05. Although there was something very seductive about artfully uncovering elegant patterns in this manner, the relative trust in a scientific method and distrust of the "art" of studying human behavior never sat well with me. I watched my scientist housemate start an experiment by getting rid of the "noise." Yet I found that the noise, the outliers that blew away my 0.05 level of confidence, was where some of the most interesting information lay. I felt an almost tangible beauty in the patterns, especially ones that outliers helped to foreground; surely they were part of the story.

When I started teaching, to my surprise it was research methods that most inspired me, and, often, the students as well. In whatever class I teach, from The Politics of Material Culture to The Dynamics of Human Habitations, I incorporate an experiential, interpretive approach. For, without seeing the role of their own and others' positionality in how they see and think about the world and their place in it, students might as well be wearing blinders. My greatest pleasure in teaching comes from watching students get excited as they experience the "eurekas" of new insight. The chapter for this book is an attempt to distill twenty years of teaching and a semester's worth of concepts into one chapter. It was both a challenge and my own personal "eureka."

I remember my immigrant grandparents' one-bedroom apartment in the Bronx. It was a long time before I realized the implications of the fact that my father and his two brothers had been brought up in that one-bedroom apartment with the dining room renamed and reconceptualized as a bedroom.

I somehow imagined they had lived like us, one-bedroom-one-child, not putting together what I saw with my eyes—a dining-room-turned-bedroom—and what I knew with my intellect—there simply weren't enough bedrooms for each child to have his own.
—*Ellen Pader, personal reflection*

"I wouldn't have seen it if I didn't believe it."
—*Anonymous*

My first night of fieldwork in Mexico stands out as one of the most enlightening experiences of my life. I arrived in Monterrey late one afternoon with my traveling companions Señor and Señora Padilla, a couple in their sixties who had moved to Los Angeles from La Chaneja, a small village in Mexico, some forty years earlier.[1] I knew them, most of their twelve children, and many grandchildren quite well by this time, as their extended family was the focal point of my ethnographic fieldwork in Los Angeles on the changing relations between domestic space use and social relations (Pader 1993, 1994a, 1994b). We were traveling together to La Chaneja and other parts of Mexico, where they still had strong connections, to do additional, comparative Mexico-U.S. fieldwork.[2] As commonly happens with ethnographic research, as I learned more about the family's sociospatial relations in Los Angeles, new, and sometimes unexpected, questions arose. It quickly became clear that in order to understand the meanings of current sociospatial relationships and be in a position to interpret changes in those relationships, I had to learn more about the people and places the Padillas had left behind.

Before traveling some 1,000 miles to their natal village, where I was to do the bulk of that work, we were visiting with their relatives in Monterrey for a few days. After eating dinner and catching up on family news, it was time for sleep. Where, I wondered, was I to sleep? I hadn't really thought about this in any concrete manner before taking off on the trip, and I'm not sure what I had imagined. But here we were, two bedrooms, six adults, and four children ranging in age from toddler to seventeen. With some panic, I realized that I'd be sharing a room with three other adults (the children's parents and grandmother) and the four children—*and* I'd be sharing the top of a narrow bunk bed with the seventeen-year-old girl, who had been asking her parents if she could be the one to share her sleeping space with the American guest (as is customary for many Mexican hosts). The Padillas, as the senior guests, had the adjoining bedroom, the one the parents usually slept in, to themselves. Although I'd shared sleeping quarters in camp, in college, in youth hostels, and the like, I wasn't prepared for this density and array of generations and genders in a *private* home. It was totally out of my experience. The thought of it made me extremely uncomfortable, but I knew I had no choice, and anyway, if I really believed in the principles underlying participant-observation as a way of learning about and interpreting culture, I needed to accept this arrangement as just one step in putting them into practice. Little did I imagine how important a step it was to be.

I dutifully climbed up the ladder to the top and stiffly lay there wondering if I would spend the rest of the three-week trip with no privacy of body or mind, since the unaccustomed density level so enwrapped me that I could barely think private thoughts lest they somehow be heard by the others. Obviously, no one could hear my thoughts, but you couldn't have convinced me of it at that moment. In no time, all were settled into their shared beds and someone, I no longer remember who, started speaking softly. Then someone else joined in. And soon there was quiet conversation going on all around me. To my amazement, the stiffness left my body, replaced by a feeling of utter comfort and safety as I drifted into sleep, feeling the voices around me.

The morning brought this new experience into focus. With it came questions I don't believe I even could have thought to ask or have been able to comprehend fully had someone brought them up to me only eight hours earlier: Why do we in the United States insist on identifying ourselves with private, individual rooms, even when semi-comatose in sleep? Why do we keep ourselves apart from one another with walls and other physical barriers when the soft chatter and knowledge of other bodies nearby feel so comforting? At this point, I still didn't know about U.S. policies or Dr. Spock-type parental guidance books (e.g., Spock 1976) that told parents it was not healthy for children—even, according to some Western "experts," as infants—to sleep in the same room as their parents and certainly not healthy for children's development as individuals and their future well-being to share a bed. I had not yet started thinking in any systematic manner that there might be an integral relationship between everyday, seemingly mundane activities, such as where and with whom one sleeps, and larger social policies and belief systems.

Participant-observation is the fine art of hanging out—with a difference. The difference is that an ethnographer doing participant-observation attempts to interpret observations and experiences systematically by looking for sociocultural patterns. Each participant-observer goes in with his or her own experiential background, theoretical preferences, research questions, and ideas about how to obtain the appropriate data to answer the initial research questions. As learning develops, these questions are, ideally, continually revisited and revised. A multifaceted research method and theory, participant-observation is the process of living, working, and/or otherwise hanging out with a defined group of people, what might be considered an interpretive community. The goal is to have a more nuanced understanding of the world from their perspectives rather than simply from the researcher's; to have a basis for exploring the multiple ways in which people categorize their worlds; and to understand the significance of those perspectives and categories for the many ways by which people learn their place in society and represent their worldview in policy, art, the built environment, social relations, and other facets of their social and political worlds.

For participant-observers interested in policy and planning, another goal is to extrapolate from these perceived patterns and categories the fundamental structural principles underlying them, as well as their relation to one another, to the development of the observed people's sense of right and proper behavior, and finally to decisions about appropriate policies and planning.

In this chapter I explore how the results of participant-observation, when understood from an interpretive perspective, enable both the original researcher and subsequent readers to make sense of local knowledge, expert knowledge, and the researcher's or reader's own knowledge (among others) in a manner that has potential to accord more equal weighting among the different knowledge bases. I draw examples largely from what has been the central focus of my own research: how people from different backgrounds prefer to use domestic space, how that can lead them to misinterpret another's housing density preferences, and the policy implications of such misinterpretations. I also draw on the work of other participant-observer studies to illustrate the strengths of an *ethnographic sensibility* for producing insights that help ground policy analysis and that could prevent many of the errors of judgment that otherwise can creep into public policies. In focusing on observing, this chapter provides only a partial look at the full range of activities that constitute participant-observation research.

PARTICIPANT-OBSERVATION: WE ALL DO IT, BUT SOME OF US TAKE NOTES AND LOOK FOR PATTERNS

Someone is standing at a crosswalk preparing to walk. She observes the scene around her: How far is it to the other side of the street? How many cars are coming from different directions? How far away are they and are they going fast or slow? We become adept interpreters through sufficient and extensive practice. Putting all this information together, the street-crosser decides: Can I safely make it to the other side? If there's a puddle between here and there, is there sufficient time for me to get to the other side before a car splashes me? Are there so many people crossing from the side I'm heading toward that they'll slow me down too much for me to make it across before the cars start again or I get splashed?

We tend to be categorizers and develop an implicit understanding of how important context, or situational behavior, is for accurate category making and interpretation. These are such mundane acts that we might not be explicitly aware of the multitude of thought processes that go into getting around every day. Some people might find it difficult to articulate the steps they go through in navigating daily life, and most would not conceive of the decisions entailed in daily activities in research terms, that is, as generating basic empirical data. Take, for instance, the traffic on that street. A transportation planner might observe how many people and cars go by at different times of the day to decide whether it is necessary to add a new crosswalk. An environmental psychologist might be watching how people negotiate passage with one another and look for significant patterns based on preselected and emerging variables. Even a parent of a child at the nearby elementary school might be seen as engaging in rudimentary research in ascertaining how safe this crossing is for children and whether a school guard is necessary. There are many more imaginable questions in this scenario, such as whether locals who know this crossing well and newcomers who do not use the same crossing strategy. And within that question, what about visitors from urban New York City, rural Mexico, or suburbs in Massachusetts—would they show differences in their traffic-negotiating strategies and styles? What are considered empirical research data to some are simply the trivia of everyday life to others.

For many in academia, observing is part of teaching. Imagine you're teaching a statistics class for social science students using the U.S. census as your database. You let a student set the research question and he comes up with a question you've not explored yourself: Is there a statistically significant relationship among the number of rooms in a unit, the number and relation of its residents, and their income? You watch how each team of students approaches the problem. You're observing. Using the knowledge you've accumulated during your years of teaching and researching, you "intuitively" reach conclusions about the right way to do the problem, why each team is approaching it in a particular way, why certain choices are selected and others rejected. You can't be sure, however, that your interpretation of a team's rationale is accurate just by observing. So you sit down with one team at a time to listen to their discussions and work with them. Maybe someone says, "In order for this to be meaningful, you have to add geographic location to the equation" or "What about national origin?" Two students debate the relative merits of several statistical methods. Quite possibly, you'll discover that the underlying rationale on which some of the students are depending is one you hadn't considered because it is not part of your life experiences or way of thinking. Now you're participating as well as observing. You are also beginning the process of interpreting.

Taking this analogy a step further, by listening to their discussions, you could learn a lot about the students, their backgrounds, and, perhaps most significantly, how these traits influence what they think is important and worthy of study. You can understand what assumptions implicitly inform what they are doing and assess their validity. Uninformed assumptions can be dangerous to the social researcher. For instance, let's say the student who originally posed the question about the number of rooms, residents, and income was assuming there would be a significant relationship between low income and high density levels. Although not articulated and perhaps not even recognized by the student, the underlying, implicit hypothesis is that given the economic wherewithal, people, as an undifferentiated category, choose homes with sufficient individual rooms to enable each household member to be apart from others at any time. Perhaps such was the ideal in that student's home or he picked it up from the media. The student who wanted to explore geographic location as a potentially relevant variable might have studied architecture or lived in different parts of the United States and realized there is no national norm for house size. She "intuitively" felt that this relationship had to be teased out of the data. The student who wanted to add national origin to the equation might be well traveled or might be from an ethnic background in which it was more highly valued for household members to be together, not apart; he might have noted that his extended family's norms were not the same as those of his Euro-American friends. If the instructor's experiences were similar to the student who posed the question, she might assume that adding the extra variables would be a waste of time, but good pedagogy requires letting students find that out for themselves.

This example begins to demonstrate a particular form of generalization or transferability from one case study or one person's experience to another case or experience. My Mexican example shows that it would *not* be appropriate to make the simplistic assumption that all people who sleep in shared bedrooms do so for reasons of cultural background and choice. Certainly, for many people it is a cultural preference, but it would be naive to deny that for some it is an economic necessity. An appropriate use of these ethnographic data would be to ask the question: In any given interpretive community, is there a relationship between sharing bedrooms and cultural beliefs? What are the clues that enable someone who did not grow up in this interpretive community to learn whether such a relationship exists and to discover the deeper social threads to which the findings relate? These clues come from understanding the life experiences of people who live the situation being studied, not just from the variables that researchers' personal and academic experiences lead them to believe are significant. This is where respecting the insights of participant-observation becomes essential, whether gained through reading others' work or through one's own research.

Granted, sitting in a classroom with your students is a qualitatively different experience than sharing a bunk bed and bedroom with a family you just met in a country with cultural formations alien to yours. But both activities require stepping outside of yourself and giving credence to another's way of approaching a problem—be it a cultural or a statistical problem. They require comprehending others' underlying rationales for approaching the problem as they do and figuring out how that rationale is part of a larger understanding of the world. The researcher needs, in other words, not only to understand *how* someone else interprets "the problem set," but also to acquire the tools necessary for analyzing that person's understanding and interpretation of the issue at hand. Whatever the particular ethnographic situation, understanding and analysis require pattern recognition and an exploration of the logic that creates a particular pattern of thinking and doing.

It is a common experience for outsider observers that, try as they may, their own expectations and experiences, their own logical constructions, fall short of providing them with a way to interpret the situation appropriately because they lack the appropriate cognitive or perceptual "slot" for the situation. A researcher might never quite be able to agree or feel comfortable with someone else's chosen solution to a cultural or statistical problem, yet through participating the researcher gains an *understanding* of and appreciation and respect for the beauty, complexity, and underlying rationale of its patterning. With such an interpretive approach it is harder to make assumptions about higher and lower or more and less proper cultural modes that are different from one's own. In fact, the researcher might start wondering about the primacy of some of his own ways of seeing (J. Berger 1972) when thrown headlong into once-seemingly unpatterned, random experiences.

MAKING THE INVISIBLE VISIBLE

Finding relations and patterns is central to interpretation, but it is not a straightforward endeavor. Conceptually, this is because the commonplaces of our ways of thinking, seeing, and acting seem, to us, normal and natural; and "normal" things typically do not attract analytic attention. Things we do not "see" and do not think to question because of their normalcy are, in effect, invisible. We're less likely to comment on or even notice a house that looks like the other houses around it. It might even seem so mundane and commonplace in its taken-for-grantedness that we implicitly treat it as non-diagnostic (that is, as irrelevant to the research). Alternatively, imagine a 1950s working-class housing tract, such as Levittown, with its limited palette of house styles making all the homes resemble one another. Now imagine an owner in that subdivision renovating that facade by adding two-story-high columns and a large front door with a leaded glass window flanked by long thin windows the height of the door. This house is no longer invisible, due to its strong contrast with its surroundings. It stands out. You notice it. It becomes conceptually visible.

You now have a new way of thinking about what previously were conceptually invisible, look-alike houses. Suddenly, you might notice the simple yet well-proportioned entryway of the original design and determine that its scale makes the old house feel and look welcoming. The renovated front entrance, on the other hand, might make the house feel distant, cold, and unwelcoming. At some level the owners of the redesigned house understood the symbolic significance of the front door as a sign of welcome and status. Yet, unless they were intending to distance themselves from their neighbors, they missed the significance of context and its role in meaning formation—that is, the ways in which not only the specific materials used, but also the placement of other elements—their context—lead to meaning and to particular interpretations.

Along similar lines, you might think about a newly constructed building that you thought was an eyesore. How long was it before it faded into the background and you barely noticed it? At some point the building moved in your consciousness from visible to invisible, as the sight of it became more familiar. The visibility of the redesigned house or the "eyesore" building provides observers with a new set of questions to ask about what features make a house or a building feel in scale or not and how that affects their reading of "home," of neighborhood, or of the people who designed and/or occupy those structures. Some of these elements that carry symbolic meaning might have been outside the observer's realm of knowledge previously, or only tacitly recognized. It is the transition from invisible to visible that enables the glimpse into underlying social patterns.

There is nothing inherent in leaded windows, columns, or large front doors that makes them symbolic of high status and "good" taste. Their meanings are cultural, historical, and contextual. Yet, many often treat these meanings as if they were neutral and natural. In much the same way, we tend to treat our own perspectives on how the world should work as neutral and natural. For example, the social—and policy—concepts "crowding" and "overcrowding" are value judgments based on an unspoken and presumptive norm that is itself derived from experience; the common sense of one interpretive community is, in this example, the discomfort of another. In policy this presumptiveness leads to the creation of occupancy standards, the maximum number of people permitted to live in a unit based on its square footage and/or number of bedrooms (Pader 2002).

Defining the appropriate use and allocation of rooms in a home is no different. Since attitudes tend to thread through the fabric of society (E. Hall 1966), how domestic space is organized becomes a clue to underlying sociocultural patterns and ways of thinking, as are decisions about how to cook a meal, allocate power, plan a ritual, or allocate authority by age, gender, individual attainment, and so forth. The knowledge we draw on calls upon our common sense, "that wonderful, cultural construction of the 'naturally' apparent" (Hummon 1989, 220). The job of a participant-observer is to explore and deconstruct what it is that makes one person's ways of doing, thinking, and saying *feel* so second nature and so goes-without-saying that the person doesn't usually bother to question them, while at the same time making someone else's ways feel wrong.[3]

Accounts from the ethnographic literature provide specific instances of the process whereby the invisible taken-for-granted can be made explicit and visible. Katherine Newman's ethnographic fieldwork (Newman 1999), for one example, took place in New York City public housing projects. She hung around the projects, got to know some of the people better than others, and asked questions about people's behaviors or choices, especially when they did not make sense to her immediately.

A particularly intriguing episode occurred one summer. A low-income woman chose to spend her poverty-level wages on an air conditioner for her apartment and a Nintendo video game for her children. Why would she purchase these luxuries when she was having trouble affording basic food, clothes, and the like? Students in my first-semester graduate urban planning seminar had a range of responses when I asked their reactions to the woman's choices. For some students her choices meshed with their expectations that single mothers in the projects were irresponsible and had to be taught to have more appropriate priorities. Others believed that everyone has a right to pleasure and comfort and that it was, in part, the fault of the media for promoting Nintendo and other such games as "hipness" barometers. Despite a range of responses, no one came close to what Newman reported the mother as saying: In the summer when school is out and child care or camp is too expensive, having a cool apartment and something for her kids to do keeps them safely inside, off the streets and out of trouble while she is at work.

Many of us reading this example will never have had to deal with this mother's quandary: How do you work away from home *and* keep your children safely out of the streets, with their gunshots and gangs, during the hot summer months? Reading this interpretive ethnography provides a new question for policy makers and analysts to ask: What strategies do people develop to keep those they love safe in an unsafe environment? Parents of modest means do not have the same choices my professorial salary allows me. But loving their children as much as I love mine, they have to be more creative and make compromises I could not comprehend without the insights afforded by participant-observation. Thus, new understandings need not derive solely from one's own fieldwork; it is obviously impractical and impossible to do participant-observation research in the multitude of environments for which analysts design policies. Reading another researcher's interpretive analysis of the realities of negotiating daily life as undertaken by people with experiences different from one's own can be an acceptable proxy.

Other examples focus less on visibility than on "hear-ability." Discourse analysis explores the role language plays in how people come to categorize their social world and make the "cultural" seem "natural" in daily use. When two of these seemingly natural, neutral, and invisible discourse strategies are brought together in a policy-relevant context, the participants often are unaware that they are approaching the same situation using fundamentally different *styles* of decision making. How might this disparity affect their ability to collaborate? And perhaps more significantly, how does it affect the ability of the less-dominant discourse style to even be heard? The anthropological subfield of sociolinguistics (e.g., Briggs 1986) examines such questions.

Caroline Tauxe emerged from her ethnographic fieldwork in Mercer County, North Dakota, with some interesting observations—and lessons—about the effect of different discourse styles in the transformation of a farming community into a more industrialized, less rural area (Tauxe 1995). In the 1980s, the energy industry boom brought new development demands to the county. A professional planner from the East Coast was hired. Small business owners tended to be in favor of the new industries, while farmers tended to be against them. The business leaders and planners spoke the same decision-making and land-use language, that of the bureaucrat, with a rational, economic, and technocratic approach that institutionalizes comprehensive plans, treats all people alike, and enacts a monolithic land-use rule by which all must abide.

Through her participant-observation Tauxe came to see this bureaucratic discourse style as a "legalistic ethics" position. She also came to see that the farmers typically used another, competing style, one she dubbed a "moralist ethics" position. The latter ethic derived not from the rationalist, bureaucratic perspective, but rather from the style of the early-twentieth-century farmers who had settled the area. This style emphasized nonconfrontational negotiation, paternal authority (i.e., elders held sway by virtue of their age), a populist stance against big business, individual sovereignty over land, and individual and case-by-case mediation of disputes among the affected parties. The farmers expected a more personal, less formal, less contract-bound verbal and business style. This approach was disempowering them in their dealings with the professional planners, because the latter's rational planning beliefs were more widely accepted than the farmers' discourse style, and they joined these accepted beliefs with the money to back them up. The business leaders and their allies in the "legalistic ethics" camp had more experience in this large-scale development battle than the farmers with their "moralist ethics" approach.

Fundamentally different approaches and beliefs such as these are so deeply embedded as to be almost invisible. Without the insights of the ethnographer, the reasons for the farmers' losing the battle might have been put down to less money, disinterest, being "backward" and less educated, or some other surface explanation of why they were marginalized in the decision-making process and thereby constrained from changing the situation. The role played by differing discourse styles might have been missed. Even though most outsiders would likely see the Mercer County businesspeople and farmers as belonging to the same "ethnic" group, their disparate ways of communicating are similar to inter-ethnic (mis)communication. The analysis of discourse styles in such a case would provide data for policy analysts and planners that no amount of survey data could produce. In this light, it is hard to imagine a conscientious policy analyst not asking a fundamental question that requires observation to answer: Do stakeholders approach decision making in the same way using the same discourse strategies or are they inadvertently talking at cross purposes?

It is not uncommon for groups to negatively stereotype others based on their own emic, socially constructed concepts and experiences, without even recognizing that exploratory questions might be asked. Through their more intimate, and integrative, participant-observation perspective, Scollon and Scollon (1981) were able to realize that Athabaskans, a native people of Alaska and northern Canada, were not receiving the governmental assistance to which they were legally entitled. The Scollons' project concerned the relationship between a nondominant population's culturally created discourse style—roughly defined as what people say, how they say it, and the listener's interpretation—and the dominant group's culturally created perception of the nondominant speakers. Many of the Athabaskans speak English, as do the "American" government workers with whom the Alaskan Athabaskans were trying, often unsuccessfully, to sign up for benefits.[4] Participant-observation showed that the major obstacle was not vocabulary and grammar. Instead, it was more subtle, less visible, facets of language use that caused problems—the cues that each group read differently.

One example of this miscommunication clearly shows how social relations of dominance are enacted differently in the speech patterns of the American social workers and the Athabaskans and how this could lead to problems. The predominant American discourse style requires persons asking for help, the supplicants, to "strut their stuff," to "put their best foot forward," to impress the interviewer with either their knowledge or their need, depending on the context. The Athabaskans expect the opposite: The dominant person does most of the talking and sets the parameters of the discussion for the subordinate.[5] The result is that

> Athabaskans often feel that their clear rights as dependents of the American bureaucratic system have not been granted, even though they have taken the proper subordinate, petitioning position by not speaking and carefully observing the English speaker. English speakers, on the other hand, feel that Athabaskans being interviewed do not display enough of themselves for the interviewer to evaluate their need, that they have become sullen and withdrawn or perhaps even acted superior, as if they needed no help. (Scollon and Scollon 1981, 19)

Both groups end up feeling frustrated. The problem was identified only through intense participant-observation and interpretation of the daily lives of the Athabaskans, including the manifestations of what is meaningful to them in their speaking patterns, integrated with their official and formal interactions with a culturally alien bureaucracy.

It is not just visual and aural data that observation can make visible through deconstructing and reinterpreting "normal," accepted meanings. The same analytic process can work to elucidate the patterns of numerical data as well, as the teaching story and the following case examples show (see also McHenry's discussion in chapter 10). One central tool for U.S. policy analysis and formation is demographic data such as the decennial census, the American Housing Survey, and various other large databases. Participant-observation can play a role in interpreting the meanings of their numbers.

No matter how carefully surveys are designed, they cannot capture practices that only closer, informed observation can reveal. Some of the most interesting, and enlightening, illustrations of this point come from *The Ethnographic Evaluation of the 1990 U.S. Decennial Census Reports*, also known as the Alternative Ethnographic Evaluation.[6] One issue that comes up often in the evaluation reports and in Skerry's (2000) analysis of them is the deceptively complex concept of what constitutes a family or a household. Despite the Census Bureau's insistence that anyone living in the dwelling on April 1 of the census year be counted as part of the household, what it means to be "living" in a place has culturally variable meaning. One study, for instance, conducted by Stepick and Stepick (1992), built upon their longitudinal ethnographic work with Haitians in Miami in a study of several blocks in the Little Haiti section of the city. They found several reasons why the official census had undercounted that population. When Haitians bought houses, they often converted them internally into several apartments, although this might not be visible from the outside, and so what appeared as a single "household" to the census taker was, in actuality, several. Many garages were likewise converted to housing (often illegally), resulting in the same misperception. And the common practice in that community of informal and often impermanent adoption of a relative's child meant that the child might not be listed on the official census record.

Participant-observation, with its emphasis on fewer cases but far greater depth, enables the researcher to identify data-gathering methods appropriate for different populations and, one hopes, to identify these methods' weaknesses as well. One sociocultural misperception, for instance, is that people's attitudes toward self-disclosure are universal and identical to those of U.S. survey makers. Only a close knowledge of respondents would make apparent that this is not always the case. McNabb's (1990) research, for example, found that large-scale preference surveys in several native Alaskan communities were highly problematic. The native Alaskan respondents were loath to give strong answers and tended to cluster them toward the middle numbers of the Likert scale. Restraint, McNabb found, was viewed as a sign of maturity and rationality. Also, the very structure of the survey was alien; data collection in the form of storytelling, while providing far fewer responses, would have been far more nuanced, and those responses could have set the stage for some type of larger-scale questioning using native conceptual categories rather than the etic ones used by the U.S. government workers. Unlike many social scientists who believe that large-scale surveys are valid because of their sample size and replicability, McNabb argues that verification and validity are questionable because there are too many sociolinguistic and cultural factors in survey responses affecting researchers' interpretations of respondents' replies.

Other ethnographic studies provide similar cautionary tales and useful lessons about assuming a monolithic stance cross culturally (in the broadest sense, including across traits such as rural/urban divides, regional urban differences among different cities within a single country, differences across ethnic groups, and other types of difference demarcating interpretive communities). Often, just reading an ethnographic case study provides unanticipated insights that even the ethnographer might not have noticed, but that make sense to readers from different perspectives who might be asking different questions than the ethnographer. In a sense, every ethnography is a living, moving animal with tentacles drawing in many questions and answers from places previously unknown, or known as part of a different context with a different meaning than the researcher's previous expectations would lead her to expect.

ETHNOGRAPHIC SENSIBILITY AND POLICY ANALYSIS

Participatory, experiential, and interpretive approaches to daily behaviors provide a good starting point for understanding various rationales underlying past and present social policies. These approaches start with the assumption that a more profound understanding of the relation between everyday behavior and the success of policies can have significant social and policy implications. Many research stories illustrate ways in which participant-observation makes the difference between accurate interpretations with strong explanatory powers and inaccurate analyses. The latter often perpetuate, even exasperate, ineffectual programs because they start from misconstrued, and often negative, externally derived stereotypes rather than from familiarity. Analyses that start from inaccurate premises or from an ill-informed base are less likely to arrive at truly useful and appropriate programmatic solutions. Too many social policies start from policy analysts' own, emic expectation that others will respond to given situations as they themselves would. Too many analyses start from a commonly unspoken, well-intentioned, but culturally constrained platform of "I want others to have what I want for my own family."[7] As a result, many decision makers end up working from an implicit, individualistic, and inaccurately stereotyped perspective (assuming, for example, that people can succeed if they try hard enough or if they can be taught to respect work over baby making and drug dealing).

The studies related here present only a small selection of cases in which participant-observation demonstrated its efficacy for analyzing and designing policy. In each, had policy analysts or policy makers asked questions from the beginning, rather than making assumptions that all of the stakeholders were, or should have been, more like the politically and economically dominant players, things might have turned out differently—for the better. As these studies show, participant-observation can be a powerful tool for going beyond superficial explanations that see the less powerful losing due to decision makers' misinterpretations of their lifeways based on the decision makers' own ill-placed, and sometimes ignorant, expectations. Instead, analysts grounded in an ethnographic sensibility are more likely to look for the structural impediments to policy success, to ask what in the policy itself or in the larger structures of society might be holding people back (Royce 2003).

This deeper analytic orientation is particularly apparent in one of the central issues in contemporary policy analysis. More and more, planners and policy analysts are looking for ways to incorporate multiple and varied stakeholders in the decision-making process. Yet, as we've seen from the examples in this chapter, including a variety of stakeholders does not ensure that each perspective is accorded equal weight or value by the other participants. This exclusion need not be, and often is not, purposeful, intentional, or explicit. Rather, it comes about due to fundamentally different ways of seeing that are both literally and figuratively invisible to one another. Innes and Booher (2003) make the seemingly obvious, but in practice very difficult, point that collaborative policy making requires finding common ground among the participants/stakeholders in the decision-making process. Yet, as seen in the examples here,

> parties must begin with their interests rather than their positions and . . . they must neither give in nor insist on their own way. *They must learn about each other*. They must seek mutual-gain solutions that as far as possible satisfy all interests and enlarge the pie for all. They must persist in both competing and cooperating to make the negotiation produce durable results. The tension between cooperation and competition and between advocacy and inquiry is the essence of public policy collaboration. (Innes and Booher 2003, 36–37, emphasis added)

In other words, the parties must allow themselves to get to know one another at more than a superficial level. Without knowing the questions to ask, without being able to understand *why* the parties approach problem solving and daily practical living in disparate manners, how can they possibly expect to understand one another sufficiently well to respect difference and communicate across it in a constructive manner? Without such depth of understanding, there is a greater chance that policy makers will pay mere lip service to the concept of participation in lieu of practicing participation. Success entails *listening* and *looking* at a profoundly close and detailed level. It might even mean reading and learning about the "whys" underlying the attitudes and rationale of the other stakeholders. It might entail a facilitator practiced in participant-observation, or at the least participants' willingness to read relevant interpretive ethnographies in order to experience living an alternative reality vicariously, to get those involved to start seeing through different eyes.

Innes and Booher (2003) relate an example of an environmentalist and a businessperson who eventually found themselves bringing each other's perspective to a meeting when their counterpart was not there to do it himself. The environmentalist started understanding the businessperson's concerns, and the businessperson started understanding what drove the environmentalist. Each was able to reflexively consider the basis for his own reactions to the other's point of view, as well as the social and political bases of their respective attitudes, both pro and con. Interestingly, neither interpreted this new relationship as a compromise, a diminishing of their own positions or a letting down of their side of the argument. Rather, Innes and Booher argue, the parties learned to recognize their areas of overlap and dissonance, personal comfort and discomfort, and, above all, mutual respect as they came to appreciate their different discourse and cultural styles, as well as differences in substance.

But how can policy analysts and stakeholders—and researchers, as well—do this if they are unaware of and/or devalue views at odds with their own simply because those views do not fit into their conceptual framework? Recognizing the existence of multiple sources of knowledge (for instance, local knowledges or competing professional knowledges) and holding respect for them, both of which are central to an ethnographic sensibility, are far more likely to lead to mutually beneficial solutions than simply denigrating alternative views. For instance, returning to occupancy standards policies, the goal is *not* to come to a consensus on what should constitute maximum density levels based on the number or relation of individuals to one another or based on what is considered healthy or not. Such a goal sets up a cultural determinism that makes it unlikely that the various stakeholders would agree on matters of content. Rather, a potentially more productive approach would be to attempt to identify the concerns underlying the content issues about which the various stakeholders must come to some consensus if they are to move forward. Is a property owner worried that more than a certain number of occupants will jeopardize profit? Instead of using a predetermined and potentially discriminatory occupancy standard as proxy for that concern, policy makers can research that issue with an eye toward adopting policies that ensure a mutually agreed-upon profit margin. Is a council member concerned that "liberal" occupancy standards might overwhelm the schools? Then policy debates should address the question of classroom size and school staffing. Are civil rights advocates concerned that a two-person-per-bedroom limit will make affordable housing unavailable for their constituents? Are housing reformers concerned for the moral wherewithal of tenants who are living in quarters more dense than they believe appropriate?

Each of these concerns should be addressed directly, without using occupancy rates or health codes as surrogates.[8] But this constructive process requires collaboration among the property owner, the city councilor, the housing reformer, prospective tenants, and other stakeholders, and this is likely to come about only when each of them feels that his or her "culture" is respected (and, ideally, understood at a deeper than superficial level). The closer, deeper attention afforded by observation will also disclose if the concerns are proxies for racism or other issues, which can then be engaged directly. A willingness to engage underlying issues and their internal structures of meaning, rather than focusing on and possibly bogging down in the detailed minutiae of the contents, requires intense respect for differences of opinion and of belief systems as well as a profound ability to listen, to really listen hard to someone else's common sense and logical structure, and to trust the other. It takes an ethnographic sensibility: a feeling, an excitement, and a deep appreciation, maybe even a bit of awe, that human groups create the intricate, rich, and dynamic structures of living we call culture.

CULTIVATING AN ETHNOGRAPHIC SENSIBILITY

Remembering that first night in Mexico can still evoke warm feelings of security in me. Climbing into bed with my recently introduced seventeen-year-old host that night in Monterrey began what has become the foundation of my research interests for nearly two decades: Why are what are deemed comfortable, healthy, and appropriate sociospatial relations in one cultural context deemed significantly uncomfortable; physically, emotionally, and psychologically unhealthy; and even morally inappropriate in another? Why should such seemingly mundane, everyday, and private domestic arrangements become such a contentious public issue? Without the type of experience related in the opening story, it is unlikely that I would have spent nearly two decades coming to grips with policies regulating "appropriate" comfort levels—physical, as well as emotional, moral, and cultural—in domestic settings. A fundamental question for understanding current attitudes and practices concerning occupancy standard preferences is: What is the origin of these ever-changing measures of health, safety, comfort, convenience, and morality that justify such people-to-space ratios? Perhaps more significantly, what is their legacy? The answer requires historical, sociocultural, and political analyses that explore such questions as how domestic space use and other daily practices reflect cultural patterns that themselves encourage or discourage certain ways of perceiving the world and one's place in it.

Although participant-observation led me to the housing density research question with which I started, reading historical sources with an ethnographic eye enabled me to sort out the processes by which certain household densities came to be construed as physically, emotionally, and/or morally unhealthful crowding in policy, law, and popular attitudes. It granted me the privilege of seeing through new eyes to ask new questions. I learned that although the specific ways in which people A or B tend to organize space, set up power relations, or cook and eat their food cannot be transferred wholesale to some other people with whom they share those practices, each insight leads to new questions that are transferable.

One of many lessons I took away from this experience was that the ways I get my data and the types of data I seek critically influence the questions I ask and the subsequent answers I receive, and vice versa. Policies and priorities can only be as good as the questions asked and the assumptions underlying those questions. It is essential that a researcher (whether academic or policy analyst) not assume that etic, predefined categories provide an adequate explanation from which to pursue future research or policy. Census categories such as gender, ethnicity, income, and so forth might hide as much as they elucidate in some research contexts, while survey questions derived from the researcher's own experience and reading with no emic content might tell more about the researcher than the population being researched.

A researcher need not go to Mexico or another country to develop an ethnographic observational sensibility. It is quite possible to hone one's own senses by reflecting upon life in one's own locale. For me, these reflections focus on my parents' working hard, as did many first- and second-generation Americans in the post–World War II years (and since), to ensure that my sibling and I each had our own bedroom while we were both still in elementary school—and certainly our own beds, unlike their own childhood circumstances. It wasn't until after my participant-observation fieldwork in Mexico and Los Angeles that I even thought to ask my mother about sleeping arrangements in her growing-up years in Manhattan; somehow, I had implicitly, and mistakenly, assumed that when my mother and her brother were children, as with my father and his siblings, my grandparents must have had an apartment with more than the one bedroom I had always known them to have. There simply wasn't a cognitive slot in my brain to imagine that any way of organizing sleeping and living spaces other than the one with which I grew up could be normal or even preferred. I had not yet acquired the appropriate knowledge to think these thoughts. I didn't even know there was a question here to ponder.

When I shared a cabin in sleep-away camp with ten other girls or a dorm room in college with a roommate, I implicitly felt that these were situationally appropriate living arrangements, but not arrangements that would feel right in a home. Of course, I knew families in which the children shared bedrooms when I was growing up. I remember one friend with five siblings. They were middle class and lived in my neighborhood; the four girls slept in one bedroom, the two boys in another. But their mother had an accent and was a refugee from Nazi Germany, so that seemed to make sense somehow; they were different. Other friends shared bedrooms too, but I always found an "excuse": They had too little money or too many children for the size of the local houses and apartments. But one thing did somehow move its way to my conscious mind: The homes somehow *felt* different from one another. I can't tell you why, but I became quite adept at differentiating the religious-ethnic-class backgrounds of their residents by how my friends' home spaces were designed and organized, without having religious symbols visible—a hobby that was to become an academic endeavor. The power of experience in framing a question or opening oneself up to trying to see through different eyes cannot be underestimated. I often think about how this reflexivity informs my research, teaching, writing, social activism, and policy work, as well as how I designed my own house (A. Dean 2003).

Participant-observation is not at heart an alien practice, as it is so much a part of what we do in negotiating our daily lives. What is particular to researchers is making explicit, or visible, the patterns that we tend to take for granted as second-nature common sense. This is what differentiates ethnographic observation from daily life. To make explicit the meaning, the significance, of everyday practices in any kind of truly explanatory manner requires going beneath the surface to those messy spaces of our lives where we commonly don't explain why we do what we do. In the commonplaces of everyday life, we just accept these patterns as right. The careful observation and self- and cultural discovery of research, however, turn this acceptance into explicitly stated, empirical data. What makes this so hard is the difficulty of recognizing something that is so close that it is blurred in one's vision. Fortunately, the desire and intention to see and to interpret that sight in multiple ways is what can bring clarity.

Not everyone who has lived with people different than themselves uses the experience as a base to go beyond their own imaginations. Many have lived with people with less money or different goals than their own without realizing that the others, like themselves, probably dream about a safe home, beauty, and contentment—however differently those attributes are defined. For some, this type of experiential learning is pushed aside as irrelevant or interpreted as mere "cultural relativism" and a "backwardness" holding people down. The labeling becomes a medium for derision or patronization. There is no doubt that cultural differences can be threatening to someone who can't, or won't, imagine any other worldview as right. It can be difficult to accommodate competing logic systems simultaneously. Accepting another's perspective may seem to negate or devalue one's own.

Participant-observation is not a panacea. Nor is it always practical to do an in-depth, multiyear, ethnographic study before embarking on a planning, policy design, implementation, or policy analysis project. But this does not diminish the efficacy or flexibility of such a study. Having experienced being part of another way of living, interacting, thinking, and relating using different value structures and having learned to read written and verbal case studies with an ethnographic sensibility, it is hard to ever respond in the old way again. For such experience develops cognitive slots in the brain ready to accept new questions about unknown situations and to see beyond where one could have ever conceived of looking before. Once acquired, this ethnographic sensibility carries over into other settings, other policies, and other research questions. Although it is not reasonable to expect to thoroughly think and respond as the people with whom one is living do, enmeshing oneself in another's world is a teacher unsurpassed by any other I have known.

After several days in Monterrey and time to think about the sociocultural meanings of sleeping arrangements and how I had been enculturated to accept them unthinkingly, I moved on with my traveling companions to their natal village in western Mexico, where I shared a bedroom with their cousin's two teenage girls. There was a double bed and a single bed in the room. On our first night there, one of the girls asked me which bed I would prefer to sleep in, fully expecting that I would prefer to sleep with someone else, rather than to be alone, since I was in a new place. That we were complete strangers was not a relevant factor for her in her role as host. Before I gave my answer, I did think about what would be expected. Nonetheless, I chose to sleep alone in the single bed. I can respect another's culturally constructed preferences and comfortably incorporate them into my policy work knowing they are situationally appropriate, but that doesn't mean I have to make the same choices for myself. That's the beauty of immersing oneself in an interpretive ethnographic sensibility.

NOTES

First and foremost I thank Dvora Yanow and Peri Schwartz-Shea for requesting this chapter and for their careful and patient editing. Angela Harris literally walked with me through the early stages of thinking about this project, and Dvora Pader was instrumental in helping me understand developmental facets of cognitive processes. I am grateful for a National Endowment for the Humanities fellowship and a grant from the Graham Foundation for Advancement in the Arts for supporting the work that led to this chapter. As always, I thank the many households who so warmly welcomed me in Mexico and Los Angeles.

1. As is common in ethnographic fieldwork (unlike journalism), I have changed the names of all people and places to protect their privacy (with the exception of large city names).

2. I received funding for this portion of the fieldwork from the UCLA Program on Mexico and Chicano Studies.

3. I differentiate between a cultural relativity—which is what I am discussing here—and a moral relativity. The latter is far more problematic and complex, and beyond the range of this chapter.

4. Scollon and Scollon (1981) chose to use the umbrella term "English" or "American" to differentiate the dominant American modality from the Athabaskans', although all speak the English language. Although not perfect, the label works analytically to make the point.

5. All analysis of this type relies on generalities; not everyone follows the unspoken, learned rules exactly. However, the patterns are sufficiently well founded, and the people are often not easily able to articulate the rules because they seem so natural, that it is valid to talk in this general manner.

6. "*The Ethnographic Evaluation of the 1990 Decennial Census Reports* discuss behavioral causes and correlates of undercount in the decennial census among Blacks, Hispanics, American Indians, recent immigrants from Asia, and undocumented immigrants primarily from Latin America and Haiti" (www.census.gov/srd/www/byyear.html; accessed March 2, 2005). The reports on the 1990 census may be found at that site under "1992."

7. I discuss such unintended consequences more fully in Pader (2002).

8. For example, in 1997 congressional Republicans authored a bill that, in essence, would have established a national two-person-per-bedroom occupancy standard (H.R. 2 §702). Supported by the National Multi-Housing Association, the major lobbying group for large apartment owners, congressional Republicans rationalized this standard with arguments of increased health and "livability" as well as minimizing wear and tear. It became clear that the latter argument was really the crux of the issue, that is, maximizing profit for apartment owners while minimizing the number of property management and maintenance personnel. I worked with the Democratic staff to provide talking points for the members of the House Banking Committee to defeat this bill. In addition I published an op-ed piece in the *New York Times* on the day it was scheduled to go to the floor for debate (Pader 1997). The combination of this information with the impressive work of the Democratic staff (in particular, Angie Garcia, with whom I worked) and committee members (especially Representative Mel Watts, D-NC) helped defeat the bill before it even got to the floor.

CHAPTER 9

HIGH POLITICS AND LOW DATA

Globalization Discourses and Popular Culture

Jutta Weldes

At the core of my research interests is the question of ideology. My fascination started, I think, when I was about eight. A nun at Sunday school insisted that even people who could not have heard of Jesus—Buddhists and Hindus outside the West, for instance—were of course condemned to hell. This made no sense to me—there could be no "of course" about it—and I didn't believe it. Nor could I understand why others did.

So I study things—the "of course" that Gramsci called "common sense" and Stuart Hall called "the moment of extreme ideological closure"—that I fundamentally do not comprehend: how U.S. national security of course requires the collateral slaughter of innocents abroad; how a structural theory like Marxism of course requires individual-level micro-foundations; how September 11 of course led Americans to wonder, uncomprehendingly, "why do they hate us?"; how neoliberal globalization, despite its catastrophic effects on life chances around the world, is of course both beneficent and inevitable.

In graduate school I avidly explored social theory, from historical materialism, through structuralism, to post-structuralism and feminisms. I initially tackled my questions about ideology through conceptual analysis, challenging, for instance, analytical Marxism's attempt to reconstruct, and depoliticize, Marxism on rational choice's individualist terms. With time, however, I reconceptualized my concerns in terms of a broadly Foucauldian notion of discourse— a more useful tool, for me, than the overly meaning-laden concept of ideology, with its connotations, on the right, of formal systems of thought or, on the left, of false consciousness. In Stuart Hall's post-Marxist cultural studies I found productive analytical tools for dissecting the discourse of U.S. national interests, notably the concepts of articulation and interpellation. More recently, in examining popular culture, I have found the notion of intertextuality both compelling and fruitful.

Although my march through social theory followed a traditional and thus predictable intellectual trajectory, generous lashings of serendipity have intervened as well. My interest in popular culture and its role in the production of common sense resulted from the coincidence that my immersion in cold war U.S. foreign policy discourse was paralleled by a Star Trek *addiction [The* Original Series *and* The Next Generation*]. Through often hilarious discussions with family and friends, I came to see pervasive parallels between the two. Similarly, in making up, under the tutelage of my partner, for a shocking adolescent deficiency in science fiction (SF), I discovered striking parallels between Isaac Asimov's 1950s techno-utopian SF and the discourse of neoliberal* *globalization. These serendipitous juxtapositions led to several publications, to a course on popular culture and international relations, and to an increasing attraction to the theories, concepts, and methods of cultural studies, with its deep appreciation of the indispensability of "low data" and its inextricable interrelations with "high data."*

> Globalization is science fiction. Put slightly differently, globalization discourse, which underpins and makes possible capital's hegemonic project of global neo-liberalization, is a self-fulfilling fantasy that derives its meaning, in part, from a broader globalization/science fiction (SF) intertext. Seeing globalization thus, as SF, renders suspect the neo-liberal project.
> —*Jutta Weldes* (2001, 647–49, passim, and paraphrased)

HIGH POLITICS VERSUS LOW DATA

In the research referred to above, I was interested in critically examining and challenging the predominant meanings attached to the neoliberal notion of "globalization"—and especially its claim to inevitability—espoused, among others, by the United States, the United Kingdom, and international financial institutions (IFIs) such as the International Monetary Fund (IMF), the World Bank, and the World Trade Organization (WTO). I was particularly keen to investigate the common-sense status assigned to the central claims of neoliberal globalization discourse. Why is it widely taken for granted, for instance, that globalization means progress, that globalized markets and technology are beneficial, and that a globalized world brings a liberal, pacific politics? And why is TINA—the assertion that "there is no alternative" to this neoliberal project—so readily accepted by many politicians and publics?

The answer I proposed was that "globalization is science fiction." That is, I argued that the taken-for-granted claims assigned to "globalization" gained both their meaning and their common-sense status (at least in part) from a larger intertext—the networks, conventions and expectations through which a text is read and made meaningful—of which both the neoliberal globalization discourse and techno-utopian American science fiction (SF), along with many other aspects of popular culture, are a part. But how does one get to such a claim? What kinds of evidence might allow us to reach this conclusion? What sorts of documents and other forms of data can and should be explored?

"Mainstream" approaches to international relations (IR)[1] typically take a rather narrow view of the kinds of evidence appropriate to determining the meaning of something like globalization. In fact, the mainstream status of "the mainstream" is sustained precisely by establishing the boundaries of acceptable theory, methods, and data.[2] For many analysts, of course, the question of meaning does not arise at all: We simply assume that we know what "globalization" means and go on to ask questions about its extent, its consequences, and appropriate policy responses to it. When the issue of meaning does arise, mainstream analyses tend to hunt it down in the policy documents of government agencies, of international organizations, and sometimes even of non-governmental organizations (NGOs), asking "What does the U.K. Department of Trade and Industry, for instance, make of globalization?" "How is globalization defined by the WTO?" or "Does the World Economic Forum offer a useful definition of globalization?"

This emphasis on official policy documents stems, at least in part, from mainstream IR's self-imposed state-centrism and its focus on "high politics"—once only the arena of diplomacy and security, war and peace (e.g., Viner 1949), but increasingly also the arena of international economics, of competitiveness and marketization (e.g., Keohane and Nye 1977). High politics—understood as the "domain of hard truths, material realities, and irrepressible natural facts" (Ó Tuathail and Agnew 1992, 192)—is real, serious politics, and vice versa. The canonical (if also shifting) distinction between high and low politics has a methodological manifestation—what one might call the distinction between "high" and "low" data.[3] Appropriate, serious—that is, "high"—data are those that circulate among elite institutions, be they states, international organizations, multinational corporations (MNCs), NGOs, or the media. Eschewed as irrelevant or, worse, as inappropriately frivolous are "low data," particularly from popular or mass culture.[4] Serious analyses of IR do not busy themselves with novels, films, television programs, computer games, advertising, and the like.

But the connections between popular culture and world politics are intimate, complex, and diverse, if also generally obscure, at least to many IR scholars. If we want to know how discourses such as the neoliberal discourse of globalization are constituted, how publics understand these discourses, how dominant discourses become common sense, and how such discourses might be contested, it becomes apparent that "low data" are appropriate, fruitful, and indeed, as I argue below, indispensable. Before discussing varieties of evidence, however, a brief theoretical detour is in order to explain just why low data are a fertile domain for IR or other social research.

A THEORETICAL FRAMEWORK

What justifies looking at low data? To understand how "globalization," for instance,[5] has come to invoke one set of connotations rather than another[6] and to account for its commonsense status, we need to understand how it is represented; why, if at all, those representations are accepted; and how, if at all, they are or might be contested. The reason is simple:[7] State policy and international politics have a fundamentally cultural basis and state and other international actions are made commonsensical through everyday cultural meanings, including those circulating in popular culture. What this means is, first, that decisions and actions of policy elites (state or otherwise) cannot be understood without a corresponding grasp of the field of discourses—the broader cultural repertoire of available meanings—through which those elites apprehend world politics and their own place in it. Second, just as official representations depend upon the cultural resources of a society, so too do the ways in which those elites' representations of world politics are understood. The plausibility of these representations depends upon the ways in which publics understand both world politics and the location of their own and others' states within it, and so how they take up, or not, the representations of policy elites. Both the understandings and the "uptake"[8] are produced not only in and through elite rhetoric, but also and more pervasively in and through the mundane cultures of people's everyday experiences. This, then, directly implicates popular culture in providing a background of meanings that help to constitute public images of world politics and foreign policy. Popular culture thus helps to construct the social reality of world politics for elites and publics alike. I elaborate a bit on this argument before turning to a more practical discussion of varieties of evidence.

The "interpretive turn" in the social sciences, which highlighted questions of meaning and representation, recognized that language does not mirror the world but instead constitutes the world as we know it and function in it. The notion of discourse is one useful way to get at this process of constitution. A discourse is a set of capabilities—a set of "socio-cultural resources used by people in the construction of meaning about their world and their activities" (Ó Tuathail and Agnew 1992, 192–93)—and a structure of meaning-in-use—"a language or system of representation that has developed socially in order to make and circulate a coherent set of meanings" (Fiske 1987, 14). Discourses—like that of neoliberal globalization—are sets of rules for ordering and relating discursive elements (subjects, objects, their characteristics, tropes, narratives, and so on) in such a way that some meanings rather than others are constituted. Conversely, we have reached the boundaries of a discourse when representations fail to be meaningful, when they seem "unintelligible" or "irrational" (Muppidi 1999, 124–25). Discourses, then, are sources of power because ruling some meanings in and others out is already and fundamentally an exercise in power. Moreover, some dominant discourses become common sense—what Gramsci called the "diffuse, unco-ordinated features of a generic mode of thought" (1971, 330, note) that provide our "categories of practical consciousness" (S. Hall 1986, 30). Constructions like "globalization," that is, become common sense when they "are treated as if they neutrally or transparently represent the real" (Weldes 1999a, 226). Alternative discourses, in contrast, can provide a resistant form of power that allows dominant representations to be contested. Discourses are capital in the ubiquitous battle over meaning.

Discourses—whether dominant or not—manifest themselves in assorted representations. "Because the real is never wholly present to us—how it is real for us is always mediated through some representational practice" (M. Shapiro 1988, xii), and these representations are necessarily cultural. Although the term "culture" is contested (R. Williams 1983, 160), we can usefully define it as "the context within which people give meaning to their actions and experiences and make sense of their lives" (Tomlinson 1991, 7). Culture, in this sense, is less a set of artifacts—novels, television programs, paintings, comics, for instance (although it is these things as well)—than a set of practices "concerned with the production and the exchange of meanings—the 'giving and taking of meaning'—between members of a society or group" (S. Hall 1997a, 2). Understood in this way, culture encompasses the multiplicity of discourses or "codes of intelligibility" (S. Hall 1985, 105) through which meanings are constructed and practices produced. This multiplicity, in turn, implies that meanings can be contested. Culture is thus composed of potentially contested codes and representations; it designates a field on which battles over meaning are fought. *Popular* culture constitutes one substantial element in this field of contestable meanings. As a result, "low data" are essential to questions of meaning, its constitution, and its reception.

The links between popular culture and world politics, as noted above, are intimate and complex. On the one hand, popular culture helps to create and sustain the conditions for contemporary world politics. "With the exception of some resistant forms," Michael Shapiro has argued, "music, theater, TV weather forecasts, and even cereal box scripts tend to endorse prevailing power structures by helping to reproduce the beliefs and allegiances necessary for their uncontested functioning" (1992, 1). U.S. popular culture in the mid-1980s, for instance, helped to "redeem Vietnam and Teheran" with such films as *Rambo: First Blood, Part II* (1985) and the "techno-twit novels" of Tom Clancy, such as *The Hunt for Red October* (1984) and *Red Storm Rising* (1986) (Lipschutz 2001, 146). To the extent that popular culture reproduces the structure and content of dominant discourses, it helps to generate approval for, or at least acquiescence to, familiar policies and prevailing world orders. Popular culture is thus implicated in the "production of consent" (S. Hall 1982, 64).

But resistance is not futile. Because dominant readings are not determinate, it is always possible for popular culture to defy the boundaries of common sense, to contest the taken-for-granted.[9] While cultural practices constrain and oppress people, they simultaneously provide resources to challenge those constraints. We can, then, examine popular culture for representations that resist dominant constructions of world politics, that provide alternative visions of the world, and that offer possibilities for transformation. The film *Dr. Strangelove* (1964) is a classic example, ridiculing, among other things, U.S. anticommunist paranoia and the convolutions of nuclear deterrence; *Canadian Bacon* (1995) is another, hilariously deriding jingoism and warmongering. Feminist SF utopias also offer themes critical of, and alternative to, dominant representations of the social and political order, including societies without formal, central government; the rejection of private ownership; concern for sustainable relations with nature; and the peripheral nature of war and violence (e.g., Crawford 2003). They allow us to imagine how we might better organize and structure local and global politics.

Often, popular culture both supports and undermines the common sense of both IR and world politics. The film *Starship Troopers* (1997), for instance, subverts conventional narratives of security by showing how knowledge of the enemy and the self is created and secured while also reproducing the very self/other distinction on which contemporary world politics is based (Whitehall 2003). Whether a particular popular cultural text supports or subverts existing relations of power, or both at once, examining such texts helps us to unravel the workings of power, even in the "high politics" of IR. Popular culture, in expressing, enacting, and producing competing and contesting discourses and their various ideological effects[10] and implicit power relations, is expressly and essentially political.

The concept of intertextuality[11] is useful here. This notion draws our attention to the fact that texts, whether official or popular, high or low, are never read in isolation. Instead, "any one text is necessarily read in relationship to others and . . . a range of textual knowledges is brought to bear upon it" (Fiske 1987, 108). In Bakhtin's more poetic phrasing, each text "tastes of the . . . contexts in which it has lived its socially charged life" (1981, 293).[12] Intertextuality allows us to illustrate and explain the often striking similarities in the way world politics are officially narrated, the way academics represent world politics, and the way stories are told in popular media. Intertextual knowledges—a culture's popular "image bank"—"pre-orient" readers, guiding them to make meanings in some ways rather than others (Fiske 1987, 108). High data and low data, that is, are linked through multifaceted intertextual relations. Both the WTO's and *The Economist*'s discourses of globalization, for instance, read in light of techno-utopian SF, might look not only plausible—we are entering a glorious high-tech future—but benign or downright praiseworthy— this future promises benefits for everyone; it is only by embracing globalization that the poor can benefit. But like all signs, "globalization" is multi-accentual (Vološinov 1986 [1929], 23). The same pro-globalization texts, read in light of techno-dystopian SF, might yield an oppositional reading, one in which globalization brings with it undemocratic rule by transnational corporations, along with organized crime, rampant violence, shocking squalor, and vast inequalities in wealth and life chances. In either case, "studying a text's intertextual relations can provide us with valuable clues to the readings that a particular culture or subculture is likely to produce from it" (Fiske 1987, 108), which readings are likely to be considered plausible, and even which political contestations are likely to arise. By examining the relations between popular and official texts, we can thus unravel some of the conventions—such as images of "spaceship Earth" or the trope of the "global village"—through which world politics are made meaningful.

It is important methodologically to highlight here the (sometimes) serendipitous nature of the discovery of intertextual relations. I have been asked many times why I chose Isaac Asimov's series of *Foundation* novels as my "sample" for the argument that globalization is SF. But this question mistakes what was a matter of the "logic of discovery" for the "logic of justification" (Popper 1959). I did not search for SF or any other popular cultural artifact paralleling neoliberal globalization discourse. Rather, I happened to be reading the Asimov series and was struck by numerous similarities to neoliberal arguments about globalization with which I was already familiar. This led me to investigate the discursive and structural parallels between the two discourses and to ask what they might mean. The answer, most simply, was that these similarities mean that we cannot, or should not, take "globalization" at face value.[13] What if globalization really *is* science fiction?

So, how do we investigate an intertext? What sources of data—high and low—might we examine?

VARIETIES OF TEXTUAL EVIDENCE

"High Data": Accessing the Neoliberal Discourse of Globalization

I began with a range of "high data"—official or semiofficial sources circulating among elites and from elites to various publics—to establish the contours and content of—the leading tropes and narratives defining—the neoliberal discourse of globalization.

- Official sources, including **policy documents and other policy statements**, can be central to such an analysis. In the case of globalization, one might, for instance, investigate official policy documents of the United States, such as the *National Security Strategy of the United States of America* (White House 2002, chapter 6); of the World Bank, such as *Globalization, Growth and Poverty: Building an Inclusive World Economy* (2001); and of the IMF, such as *Globalization: Threat or Opportunity?* (2000). Such high data can provide access to the central representations offered by elites. From such representations, in turn, we can generate a portrait of globalization discourse that illuminates a well-rehearsed set of narratives and tropes, including an Enlightenment commitment to progress, the wholesome role of global markets, a rampant technophilia, the tropes of the "global village" and "spaceship Earth," and the interrelated narratives of an increasingly global culture and an expanding liberal, pacific politics.
- **Speeches** by prominent officials and politicians are an especially good source, as they are precisely intended to sell a particular representation, in this case a persuasive vision of globalization. My own analysis made extensive use of the speeches of Renato Ruggiero (e.g., 1996) and Mike Moore (e.g., 2000, 2001a, 2001b, 2001c), former directors general of the WTO, who are leading proponents of neoliberal globalization. Unsurprisingly, the speeches of both were rife with the dominant pro-globalization tropes and narratives.
- **Congressional or parliamentary hearings** can be fruitful sources as well. For instance, testimony by Charlene Barshefsky (1997), U.S. trade representative, before the Subcommittee on Trade of the U.S. House Committee on Ways and Means provided me with additional evidence of the neoliberal discourse's link between markets and growth.
- In the case of the discourse of globalization, **popular business writings** were exceptionally useful as these also tend to be saturated with neoliberal tropes and narratives. I buttressed my analysis of official state and IFI sources with the writings of business gurus such as Unilever PLC chairman Niall Fitzgerald (1997), management consultant and prolific author Kenichi Ohmae (his work on the end of the nation state [1995] and the borderless world [1999]), and Peter D. Sutherland, chairman of both Goldman Sachs International and BP PLC (1998).
- Globalization is also constructed in **current affairs magazines** like *The Economist, Time,* and *Newsweek,* which typically articulate the dominant globalization discourse. *The Economist,*

for instance, supports the official neoliberal vision of globalization, interestingly using significant SF references. In particular, as Charlotte Hooper has shown, the magazine is awash with images of "spaceship Earth." This ubiquitous trope constructs the increasingly globalized world as, on the one hand, "a single totality, 'the global village,' making it appear easily accessible" while, on the other, positioning it "out there" on "the final frontier" of space (2000, 68). *The Economist*, says Hooper, renders globalization sensible "through imagery which integrates science, technology, business and images of globalisation into a kind of entrepreneurial frontier masculinity, in which capitalism meets science fiction" (65).

- **Newspapers** are important sites for the reproduction, and occasionally the contestation, of official discourses, and especially those dominant discourses that circulate among elites.[14] Although newspaper sources were less important for my account of globalization discourse, they were central to my analysis elsewhere of the cold war U.S. security imaginary and its hegemonic representation of the Cuban missile crisis (e.g., Weldes 1999a). The *New York Times*, for instance, provided many vivid examples of dominant constructions of the Monroe Doctrine ("Monroe Doctrine Guards West" 1960), of Bolshevik despotism (in M. Hunt 1987, 115), and of Castro as Khrushchev's "chief puppet in the Caribbean" ("Summary of Editorial Content" 1961).

- One can of course proliferate such high data sources: **White Papers; reports** from government ministries, departments, and agencies; and **official histories**, such as those of the International Monetary Fund (e.g., Broughton 2001; de Vries 1979, 1985, 1986), are additional examples. And these can be supplemented with the vast and constantly expanding **academic literature** on the discourses and practices of globalization.

"Low Data": Accounting for Neoliberal Globalization Discourse

Although the analysis of "high data" allowed me to develop a portrait of neoliberal globalization discourse, accounting both for the discourse itself and for its common-sense status required additional forms of evidence. If we are asking why this neoliberal discourse makes sense—what renders this vision of globalization seemingly self-evident—we need to look at the broader cultural resources, the cultural image bank, that provide the tropes and narratives out of which it is constructed. This, in turn, required "low data"—the everyday, mundane representations that make meaningful and commonsensical, and sometimes challenge, dominant representations.

- My account of globalization as SF focused almost exclusively on a series of techno-utopian SF **novels**. Asimov's *Foundation* series (initially written between 1951 and 1953 and expanded between 1982 and 1993) provides images strikingly similar to those of neoliberal globalization discourse.[15] For example, in the *Foundation* universe, all planetary worlds—on the model of "the global village"—are singular political and economic units. Central to this universe are images of trade-driven, evolutionary progress and the beneficial effects—indeed, the essential necessity—of technological development. Moreover, in this universe, trade brings peace. These and other similarities help to render neoliberal globalization familiar, sensible, and seemingly "inexorable" (Gray 1998, 206).

    Surprisingly—or perhaps not—underlying the *Foundation* universe lies a barely concealed authoritarian politics, which helps to expose the ideological problematic of neoliberal globalization.[16] Asimov's utopia rests on an obsession with order, stability, and an accompanying authoritarianism: Empire is hailed as the only viable political form; democracy, as neither practical nor long lasting. Contemporary global governance has also been shown to suffer pervasive "democratic deficits" (Scholte 2001, 28), so again there is a parallel with neoliberal globalization discourse, in which democracy is increasingly attenuated and in which, as with its modernization predecessor, stability and order are valued over democratic participation (e.g., Huntington 1965; Kirkpatrick 1979). Low data, then, can illustrate not only the construction of common sense—how and why some images seem familiar and thus sensible—but also the constitutive problematic of dominant discourses.[17]

- **Novels revisited:** With different intertextual relations, globalization could be rendered differently meaningful. Dystopic "futures" such as William Gibson's *Sprawl* series,[18] for example, might well leave us with a different vision of globalization. Rooted in the image, common beginning in the 1980s, of the state as declining at the expense of multi- or transnational corporations (MNCs), the Sprawl series portrays a globalized future in which states have been eclipsed by cyberspace, global corporations, and global organized crime. The global market is dominated by the Yakuza and MNCs: "Power . . . meant corporate power. The zaibatsus, the multinationals that shaped the course of human history, had transcended old barriers. Viewed as organisms, they had attained a kind of immortality" (Gibson 1984, 242). Both Yakuza and MNCs are "hives with cybernetic memories, vast single organisms, their DNA coded in silicon" (1984, 242). Technology has run amok: This is a world of body and mind "invasion" (Sterling 1986, xii); a world of prosthetic limbs (Gibson 1984, 9) and eyes—"sea-green Nikon transplants"—that are "vatgrown" (33). But SF is never just about the future: "It is about us and the world in which we live" (Lipschutz 2003, 96). Gibson agrees: "What's most important to me," he has explained, "is that it's about the present" (quoted in Kitchin and Kneale 2001, 31). Through such dystopic "futures," then, the neoliberal vision of globalization can be challenged.

- **Film** is increasingly a source of data, at least for discourse analysts. One might, as Michael Shapiro does (1999, 82–86), read the Hollywood feature film *Father of the Bride II* (1995) as a "domestic allegory" for the "identity anxieties" produced by globalization. In his analysis, Shapiro contends that "global space" is "explored obliquely" through the juxtaposition of various characters, including Mr. Habib, a wealthy Arab businessman and shrewd "economic predator"—the cultural Other   who threatens "the West," represented by Mr. Banks, an insecure middle-aged family man who just wants his home back. As Shapiro notes, a "remarkable repression" underlies this representation, one that fails utterly to problematize the wealthy lifestyle of Mr. Banks himself and its complicity in global inequalities. This ostensibly "domestic comedy" can be read as allegory to "an increasingly complex set of relations between local and global dynamics."

- **Television fiction** (as well as **nonfiction**) can also provide substantial evidence of meaning construction and the constitution of world politics. For instance, the *Star Trek* universe[19] depicts a utopian global future, one redolent with themes of neoliberal globalization. It is a bright future of intergalactic trade and exploration, in which, within the United Federation of Planets (housed in San Francisco), liberal multicultural values have triumphed, tolerance has overcome discrimination, and poverty has been eradicated. Space has become the "final frontier" in an individualistic and innovative era of "exploration and discovery" (Whitfield and Roddenberry 1968, 203). Development is inevitable, but best accomplished on the model of liberal individualism. Again, a critical analysis of *Star Trek*'s liberal future reveals an unsavory problematic reminiscent of neoliberal globalization, one of rampant militarized intervention, based on a hierarchy of societies. As James Kirk, Captain of the first starship *Enterprise*, infamously asserted: "We owe it to them to interfere" (e.g., Lagon 1993).

- **Advertisements**—among "the most pervasive forms of global communication and a significant site of cultural production" (Tinic 1997, 4)—can also provide useful evidence of meaning (e.g., Hooper 2001, 141–43, 202–3). One might look, for instance, at the Italian clothing firm's "United Colors of Benetton" advertising campaign.[20] This campaign, begun in 1985, could be read as a powerful image of cultural globalization, of the production of a single global culture irrespective of race or national identity. It offered images of world peace and harmony, showing youth of diverse races and ethnicities cavorting happily while wearing the same Benetton clothing (Tinic 1997, 5). As the WTO's Ruggiero triumphantly announced in 1996, globalization was creating a "global audience" and a "global village" in which "From Buenos Aires to Boston to Beijing, ordinary people are watching MTV, they're wearing Levi's jeans, and they're listening to Sony Walkmans" (1996, 2). Interestingly, the Benetton ad campaigns have been quite controversial. Put differently, they have become the site of ferocious battles over meaning: "Benetton's portrayals of racial unity have fueled accusations of racism. Images implying religious tolerance have been called blasphemous" (Tinic 1997, 4).

- Even **e-mail** can provide us with evidence of discursive constructions and meaning production. In a recent article (Laffey and Weldes 2004), my coauthor and I drew on a poem entitled *The Binch*[21] that had been widely circulated by e-mail in the United States and elsewhere in the days after September 11. *The Binch*, which parodied Dr. Seuss's *The Grinch Who Stole Christmas*, was intended to explain the terrorist attacks to young (American) children. The first two verses explained that

> Every U down in Uville liked U.S. a lot,
> But the Binch, who lived Far East of Uville, did not.
> The Binch hated U.S.! the whole U.S. way!
> Now don't ask me why, for nobody can say.
> It could be his turban was screwed on too tight.
> Or the sun from the desert had beaten too bright.
> But I think that the most likely reason of all
> May have been that his heart was two sizes too small.
>
> But, whatever the reason, his heart or his turban,
> He stood facing Uville, the part that was urban.
> "They're doing their business," he snarled from his perch.
> "They're raising their families! They're going to church!
> They're leading the world, and their empire is thriving,
> I MUST keep the S's and U's from surviving!"

We drew on this bit of racist doggerel to illustrate popular explanations—"they hate our values"—offered in response to the then ubiquitous, and uncomprehending, American question "Why do they hate us?"

- As with high data, sources of low data are bountiful. The **Internet** (e.g., Miller and Slater 2000; Saco 1999, 2002), **photography** (e.g., Kennedy 2003; Morrison 2004), **jokes and humor** (e.g., Nevo 1984), **travelogues** (e.g., Clark 1999), and **comics** (e.g., Barker 1989; Mangan 2000), to mention but a few possibilities, can all provide additional forms of textual evidence. Each can tell us something about different constructions of globalization, of politics, of the social order. Other, strictly non-textual sources of low data, but sources that can and should be read as if they were texts, can fruitfully be explored as well. Here examples might include **architecture** or **built spaces** (e.g., Yacobi 2004; Yanow 1996); **music** (e.g., M. Shapiro 2001; Sheeran 2001); **war memorials** (e.g., Moriarty 1997; Pease 1993); **museums** (e.g., Noakes 1997) and **exhibitions** (e.g., Bird and Lifschultz 1998); **sport** (e.g., Arnaud and Riordan 1998; Silk 2002); **Disney World** (e.g., Giroux 1995; Project on Disney 1995); or even **ufology** (e.g., J. Dean 1998; Vaughn 2002). Varieties of low data are virtually infinite.

CONCLUSION: LOW DATA AND HIGH POLITICS REVISITED

I want to conclude by emphasizing a single, vital point: "High politics" cannot be comprehended through an exclusive focus on "high data." What I have been calling "low data" are essential to our understanding of globalization, of politics, and of the social world more broadly. And this, in turn, means that the spatial metaphor of "high" and "low" is as flawed in relation to data as it is in relation to politics or culture: The choice between "high" and "low" data as constructed through this metaphor is ultimately unsustainable because high data and low data do not form discrete, mutually exclusive categories. Each is rendered intelligible, intertextually, in relation to the other. Designating some forms of data (or politics or culture) "low" is thus fundamentally an exercise of power, albeit one that tends to obscure its own functioning, to appear to be sensible, because of the pervasiveness of the binary oppositions—high/good/serious, low/bad/frivolous—structuring most social scientific discourse. As Cynthia Enloe has forcefully argued, we must look for power in unconventional and unexpected places, in the bedroom as well as the boardroom (1996, 193), and in popular culture, if we really want to account for the power it takes to create and maintain the contemporary order. This means taking popular culture, and thus "low data," as seriously as we are typically enjoined to take "high politics."

NOTES

Huge thanks are due to Mark Laffey for his help, and patience, in the writing of this chapter. I am grateful also to Penny Griffin and Laura Shepherd for their insightful comments and helpful suggestions. Many thanks to Dvora Yanow and Peri Schwartz-Shea for their careful editing.

1. The caveat "mainstream" is necessary here. From nonmainstream, non-positivist perspectives, and in numerous other disciplines, using diverse evidentiary bases is old hat. For just the tip of an iceberg, see Rogin's (1987) and C. Weber's (2001) uses of film, Lutz and Collins's (1993) analysis of *National Geographic*, Sharp's (2000) investigation of *Reader's Digest*, Dorfman and Mattelart's (1991 [1971]) critique of Disney comics, Hooper's (2001) exploration of advertising, and my own (1999b) examination of *Star Trek*.

2. See for example, Robert Keohane's various attempts to legislate the boundaries of IR (e.g., 1988, 1989) and, indeed, of all social science (e.g., King, Keohane, and Verba 1994).

3. A similar distinction, in part mediating this pair of distinctions, is the common, if problematic, one between high and low culture (e.g., Storey 2001, 6–7).

4. In common usage, the terms "popular" culture and "mass" culture are used interchangeably, which I do here, although they should perhaps be distinguished. Popular culture is sometimes reserved for those texts and practices actually produced by "the people," and specifically by subordinated classes. In contrast, mass culture designates those texts and practices that, although consumed by the people, are not produced by them (Bennett 1986).

5. One could, of course, examine how anything else has come to take on a particular meaning—be it assimilation policy (Yanow 1996), national interests (Weldes 1999a), counterinsurgency (Doty 1993), "the West" (Milliken 2001), "welfare" (Schram 1995b), or "development" (Escobar 1995).

6. On alternative globalization discourses, from right and left, with correspondingly different connotations, see Rupert (2000).

7. The following is from Weldes (1999b, 119).

8. "Uptake" refers to what Althusser (1971, 174) called "interpellation," the "hailing" of individuals into discursively constituted subject positions such that they speak the discourse "naturally" (e.g., Weldes 1999a, 103–7). One might easily understand—that is, comprehend—a discourse without taking it up as natural, as common sense, as one's own position.

9. A useful approach to different reading positions can be found in Stuart Hall's (1994) conceptions of encoding and decoding, and of three contrasting reading positions, the dominant/hegemonic, the negotiated, and the oppositional.

10. The relationship between discourse and ideology is neither simple nor settled, but it is useful to see discourse as enabling processes of meaning making and ideology as an effect of that process (Purvis and Hunt 1993, 496). A discourse thus has ideological effects in that it, for instance, privileges certain groups and interests over others.

11. This discussion draws on Weldes (2003a, 13–16). On intertextuality see Kristeva (1980); N. Fox (1995); and S. Hall (1997b, 233–34).

12. Thanks to Iver Neumann for this lovely quotation.

13. Investigating the meaning of parallels between two discourses is, of course, a different enterprise than explaining the reasons for the similarities. This latter project would open up a host of questions—such as the extent of changes and continuities in American culture between the 1950s and the 1990s, for instance, or the influence of the U.S. state on popular culture in these periods.

14. For one explanation of the media's tendency to reproduce state discourses, even in societies where it is privately rather than state owned, see Herman and Chomsky (1988).

15. This discussion draws on Weldes (2001, 658–62).

16. This discussion draws on Weldes (2001, 662–66).

17. This is not to say that Asimov's SF writings do not tell us a lot about 1950s America. But it is precisely to say that once such images and narratives have entered the "cultural image bank," other texts are read in relation to them.

18. The *Sprawl* series—which refers to "BAMA, the Sprawl, the Boston-Atlanta metropolitan axis" (Gibson, 1984, 57)—includes the novels *Neuromancer* (1984), *Count Zero* (1986b), and *Mona Lisa Overdrive* (1988), as well as related stories such as "Johnny Mnemonic," "New Rose Hotel," and "Burning Chrome" (in *Burning Chrome and Other Stories*, 1986a).

19. This discussion draws on Weldes (1999b). For a fascinating analysis of the NASA/Trek intertext, see Penley (1997).

20. This particular advertising campaign has spawned an intellectual cottage industry (e.g., Back and Quaade 1993; Giroux 1994; Kraidy and Goeddertz 2003; M. Shapiro 1994).

21. In the email received by the authors, this poem, dated September 13, 2001, was attributed to one Rob Suggs.

CHAPTER 10

THE NUMERATION OF EVENTS

Studying Political Protest in India

Dean E. McHenry, Jr.

My graduate training reinforced my sense that knowledge in political science ought to be grounded upon a science-based epistemology. The foundation should be empirical reality, that is, that which can be seen or detected. Concepts should be used to create generalizations; sets of generalizations constituted theory; and, from theory, generalizations might be taken to use in explanation and/or prediction. The most precise manipulation of concepts to produce generalizations should be done using quantitative techniques. That was my belief forty years ago.

As soon as I took this mindset into the field, problems arose. I remember the first interview I did as part of a survey of cotton farmers in a part of western Tanzania. Helped by a young man who translated for me, I asked the person to step outside for the questionnaire because I did not want to "taint" the responses by the presence of other members of the family. It did not take much time to realize my stupidity. People in that community acted in consultation with others. If I wanted the attitudes that "predicted" behavior, I would have to get the family together. A few years later I did a large survey of Ujamaa villagers in several regions of Tanzania and was left with great doubt about its accuracy, given problems with sampling, language, memory, power relations, and many other factors. Numbers looked neat and could be analyzed easily, yet I had doubts about whether they were accurately representing empirical reality. Those doubts grew over many years.

Today most of my colleagues are very skilled statisticians and they are training our students to be skilled statisticians. We have never required any methods course except quantitative methods. The foundation of such work is the data set. Indeed, there is immense satisfaction and excitement among our students and faculty when a new data set is found. It reminded me of my joy when, as a student of geology, I found a perfectly preserved fossil. And, the numbers in the data sets are now referred to as "empirical." When I went to look at these data sets and compared them with my knowledge and experiences, I often found a significant discrepancy. A couple of examples: When I looked at the Polity III democracy scores for South Africa in the 1980s, I discovered that the regime in that country was very democratic. What nonsense! When I looked at Arthur Banks's Cross-National Time-Series Data Archive data for riots, strikes, and demonstrations in India, I found there were no riots, no strikes, and only four demonstrations in the whole country between 1997 and 2001. Again, what nonsense! Yet, data sets are the foundation of all quantitative "knowledge."

When I would point to such nonsense, my colleagues' response was to challenge me to perfect the data sets, that is, to make them so they accorded with empirical reality. The more closely I looked at the protest events, the more I realized the impossibility of the task. Even if I got the counts right, the numbers would be meaningless. So much that was different among the events had to be ignored in order to categorize them as riots, strikes, or demonstrations that these concepts no longer meaningfully reflected an empirical reality. The chapter that follows describes what is left out when protest events are numerated and suggests that the way forward may be through an "interpretive turn."

It appeared that the word "strike" at times meant something different than a strike as defined by Western scholars. And a vast array of other terms were commonly used to refer to different types of protest action. To put all of these protest actions into "riot," "strike," or "demonstration" deprived the actions of their meaning. That meaning is not only culturally determined, but situationally determined, too.

—*Dean McHenry, personal reflection*

THE PROBLEM

A number representing a summary of the frequency of forms of domestic protest for a year in a country of over a billion people, like India, must substantially simplify reality. The advantage of numeration is that it allows the application of highly sophisticated statistical techniques for processing information. The disadvantage lies in the loss of information. In this chapter, I will argue that the numeration of riots, strikes, and demonstrations leads to such a significant loss of meaning that the use of these broad categories is unlikely to lead to the development of knowledge. Such a numeration may, in fact, misinform and mislead.

The challenge is to find an alternative methodology that will facilitate the creation of knowledge. A logical alternative is an interpretive approach. It builds not from phenomena simplified to virtual meaninglessness, but from phenomena portrayed in their complexities. It uses reason and logic both to provide for missing information and to draw more informed categories from the complex body of information assembled.

I will examine this issue by focusing upon the conceptualization used in the quantitative index of domestic protest in India developed by Arthur S. Banks and placed in the Cross-National Time-Series Data Archive (CNTS).[1] The CNTS contains a vast array of data sets covering most countries of the world over a period of many years developed from a variety of sources. My concern is with three of his measures of domestic conflict: general strikes, riots, and antigovernment demonstrations. The source of the numbers Banks reports is the *New York Times*. The justification for the selection of this index is that it is widely cited in the political science literature, that it embodies the basic characteristics of other numerical indices, and that it deals with a matter of particular importance to India. Furthermore, the size and complexity of India is likely to make more obvious the problems associated with numerating and interpreting the three concepts than would a smaller or more homogeneous country. In the concluding section an assessment will be made of whether interpretivist approaches "put back in" what numeration "leaves out."

THE CONCEPT OF DOMESTIC PROTEST AND ITS
NUMERICAL CHARACTERIZATION

Banks's CNTS includes a simple compilation of the frequencies of demonstrations, strikes, and riots. Although scholars focusing upon events analysis in other parts of the world have sought to gather data on some of the dimensions that seem to be missing in Banks's summary frequencies for these three forms of protest, many of the problems relevant to the Banks data are also relevant to them—the simplifications necessary for the creation of indices gut the concepts of critical information.[2] Banks, basing his definitions on earlier ones of the American scholar Rudolph Rummel, defines the three concepts as follows (all quotes from Rummel 1972, 132):

> *General strike:* "Any strike of 1,000 or more industrial or service workers that involves more than one employer and that is aimed at national government policies or authority."[3]
> *Antigovernment demonstration:* "Any peaceful public gathering of at least 100 people for the primary purpose of displaying or voicing their opposition to government policies or authority, excluding demonstrations of a distinctly anti-foreign nature."[4]
> *Riot:* "Any violent demonstration or clash of more than 100 citizens involving the use of physical force."[5]

In India, there are many forms of protest that do not fit neatly into these categories. Their character is lost or distorted by defining them as strikes, demonstrations, and riots. Among these are:

> *Bandh*: a protest that shuts down normal activity. It may be peaceful or violent; it may or may not involve industrial and service organizations; it tends to be antigovernment, but may be in support of the government.[6]
> *Dharna*: a generic term for protest, often involving a sit-in.
> *Gherao*: a protest in which an official is surrounded by protestors and not allowed to leave.
> *Hartal*: a temporary closing of businesses and transport. It is normally by voluntary appeal, but it may take on some of the characteristics of a bandh.
> *Jail bharo*: a form of protest where many people court arrest.
> *Roko*: a blockage of traffic, for example, a rail roko is where trains are not allowed to pass and a rasta or road roko is where a highway is blocked.
> *Satyagraha*: a fairly generic term referring to some form of nonviolent resistance.
> *Stir*: a general term for a protest demonstration.
> *Yatra*: a journey, procession, or pilgrimage that may be used for political purposes with stops along the way, speeches, and people joining it for portions of the trip. A padayatra is a "foot" yatra, though much of it may be by other means.[7]

Even with those forms that fall most closely within Banks's broad category of demonstrations, there is a problem. To equate a protest against the state's policy of allowing the mining of sand, in which thousands of people extended themselves for forty-two kilometers along the coast of the state of Kerala, calling themselves a "human fort,"[8] with a gherao, in which an official is surrounded by protestors, results in considerable loss of information.

There are forms of protest that are significant in India but that may not meet the minimum number of participants stipulated by Banks to be counted as protests. Perhaps the most significant is the fast. The significance of the fast is exemplified by the oft-cited case of Potti Sriramulu, who in 1952 fasted until he died for the purpose of getting the national government to create the state of Andhra. Almost immediately following his death, the national government conceded his request. His protest, though, would not be included in Banks's data. A large number of other examples might be cited.[9] In 2003 local government leaders in a part of the state of Andhra Pradesh sought to pressure the state to release Krishna River waters to their villages. In response to their fast, Congress Party leaders launched relay fasts and staged a rasta roko, leaders of all parties came to visit the fasting leaders, prayers were organized in churches and mosques, and religious leaders came out to join the protests.[10] The potential power of the fast of one or a few people is recognized by the concern of authorities. Fasts today are watched closely, and if the health of the fasting person is threatened, the police will forcibly take him/her to the hospital. The activities associated with the fast may or may not reach the threshold warranting its inclusion as a protest action. Yet, the fasts themselves rarely reach the 100-participant threshold for inclusion as a demonstration.

The same is true for other forms of individual protest like suicides by farmers or self-immolation. There is a tradition in Indian culture that gives such acts a significance they would not have in American or most other Western cultures. Their exclusion from the Banks index eliminates what may be an important form of protest in India. Banks's measures may cover major forms of protest in the United States, but they ignore many of the forms protests take in Indian cultures.

Aside from the taxonomic problems, Banks's categories leave out so much critical information that quite different events are treated as though they were similar and quite similar events as though they were different. Missing information kinds of categories:

The Magnitude of Protest Events

Banks's definitions set minimum levels of participation, but make no differentiation among protest events once the minimum levels are met. The "or more" stated in, or implied by, the definitions means that Banks's index equates a strike of several million with a strike of a thousand. The same failure to differentiate magnitudes is an equally applicable criticism of the data on riots and demonstrations. Thus, the riots in the state of Gujarat in 2002, where over 2,000 people lost their lives, would be equated with the 2003 Marad riots in the state of Kerala, where nine people lost their lives. The impact of the former on Hindu-Muslim relations throughout the country was much greater than that of the latter. Similarly, there is no differentiation among events on other measures of the magnitude of protest, such as the cost to the economy as a whole or to individual participants in it—all are treated as though they are of equal magnitude.

Information on the Legal Environment of Protest Events

Likewise, the legal environment within which protests take place is treated as irrelevant to Banks's counts of frequencies. Court decisions, expectations of enforcement, and other legal factors may affect both the likelihood of a protest occurring and the numbers who turn out. A protest that takes place in a state where no penalties exist for taking part in it is equated by Banks's taxonomy with one where participants face severe sanctions. Thus, a lower frequency of protest may not mean less opposition but rather a harsher legal environment.

An example is the 2003 public employee strike in the state of Tamil Nadu. Although its primary target was the state government, it had an impact on national policy. It was spurred by the state government's suspension of a variety of benefits to employees. On July 2, 2003, over a million employees struck. In preparation for such strikes, the government, under Chief Minister Jayalalithaa, had passed the Tamil Nadu Essential Services Maintenance Act 2002 (TESMA) the previous year, and two days after the start of the strike the government passed amendments to the act making it even more draconian. In the first four days of the strike the government dismissed over 200,000 employees.

When the workers took the issue to the High Court, the highest court in the state, it ruled on July 11 that the dismissals did not infringe on any fundamental right, though it urged the state to reinstate most of the dismissed employees. The leaders of the strike, many of whom had been arrested before the strike began, were released the next day and the strike essentially ended, though the reinstatement of workers dragged out for some time.[11] The court did not rule on TESMA, but based its ruling on Rule 22 of the Tamil Nadu Government Servant's Conduct Rules, 1973, which denied public employees the right to strike. Clearly, the strikers had assumed the rule would not be employed. In order to get their jobs back, employees had to unconditionally apologize and promise to abide by that rule.

On August 6 the Supreme Court, the highest court in India, reaffirmed the High Court's position that government employees had no legal right to strike.[12] The decision was immediately attacked, especially by political groups on the left throughout the country.[13] As one observer put it: "Leaders of the Left parties are of the view that the judgment must be seen as part of an increasingly unsympathetic and negative attitude to the rights of workers, which, in their opinion, is but a natural corollary of the World Bank-driven neo-liberal regime, to which the governments at the Centre and several States are committed."[14]

Soon afterward, the government of the state of Tamil Nadu filed charges under TESMA against party leaders who supported the strike, including the leader of the Dravida Munnettra Kazhagam (DMK), the main opposition party at the time, the Tamil Nadu Congress Party Committee working president, the state secretary of the Communist Party of India (Marxist) (CPM), and the state secretary of the Communist Party of India (CPI).[15] The likely outcome, not only in the state of Tamil Nadu, will be a diminution in the frequency of strikes—the cause of which is not an increasingly satisfied workforce.

The legal environment is affected not only by court directives, but also by the determination of governments and the police to enforce existing law. As noted above, the state of Tamil Nadu government used a new law, rather than an existing rule, as the basis for its action against its striking employees and those who supported them—though the courts acted on the basis of an old rule. There are many other cases where laws have been invoked to make protests more costly to protesters. None of the impact of this legal environment is embodied in the count of protests.

Actors and Motives

Frequencies do not distinguish among objectives of protest actions, yet the objectives are significant aspects of such actions. Those involved in protest actions may have different purposes or different priorities among the purposes they share, and they may change their objectives, or the priority among objectives, during a protest action. None of this is reflected in the counts of protest actions.

The significance of objectives to the meaning of protest events can be illustrated by three examples. An August 2003 Mumbai bandh brought both the Shiv Sena, a Hindu nationalist party in the state of Maharashtra, and Muslim organizations together in the protest, though for quite different reasons. Shiv Sena's formal reason for participating was to protest a series of bomb blasts in the city that were blamed on Pakistan-inspired terrorists. On the other hand, Muslim participation was attributed to their desire to differentiate themselves from Pakistani Muslims, to promote better relations with Hindus, and to show themselves to be loyal Indians.[16] This "cooperation" differentiates the bandh from other Shiv Sena bandhs, but Banks's data make no such distinction.

A second example illustrating both the complexities and the significance of purposes to an understanding of protest is that of the demonstrations against the Paragodu dam in June of 2003. Both the state of Andhra Pradesh (AP) branch of the Congress Party and the Telugu Desam Party

(TDP) planned protests against the construction of the dam on the Chitravati River, claiming it violated an agreement AP had with the state of Karnataka concerning riparian rights and would adversely impact the supply of water to AP farmers. The protests took place near the border and involved dharnas that blocked the main interstate highway, rasta rokos that delayed trains, and a near-total bandh in the Anantapur district of AP where the protests occurred.[17] Yet, as the demonstrations developed, the TDP and the chief minister, N. Chandrababu Naidu, made the Congress Party a target of the protests. They turned an AP versus Karnataka issue into an attack on the Congress Party government in the state of Karnataka—and, by implication, the Congress Party in AP.[18] None of the subtle impacts of the protest on within-state politics is conveyed by simply numerating this event.

A third example is that of a statewide bandh called by the Samajwadi Party (SP) and the Bahujan Samaj Party (BSP) in the state of Uttar Pradesh (UP) in 1994, when they constituted the ruling alliance. The purpose was to protest threats to their own reservation policy and the possible imposition of President's Rule in the state. An observer contended, "Both parties apparently have an eye on consolidating their votebank by pitting the anti-reservationists against their own party workers. In case of dismissal of the Government, the Scheduled Castes and Backward Classes would rally behind the SP-BSP combine for they have projected themselves as 'true champions' of these classes."[19] In Banks's data set no distinction would have been made that this protest was *by* those governing UP; it would instead have been equated with a protest *against* those governing UP. As this case shows, a high frequency of protest does not necessarily mean great opposition to the state government.

A fourth example is where the instigators may have objectives other than those they articulate, as illustrated by a twenty-four-hour bandh called by the Congress Party three years ago in the state of West Bengal to demand an end to killings of members of the Trinamul Congress Party in Keshpur in Midnapore district. An observer claimed that "While the bandh is against the Communist Party (Marxist) (CPM) and the state government for its inability to maintain law and order, the preemptive strike . . . is a bid to upstage the Trinamul Congress Party and grab the political initiative."[20] In the end the Trinamul Congress Party did not support the bandh, claiming that it opposed the violence often associated with such actions. All this information would be left out when the events were numerated. Yet, it would be essential to an understanding of the political impact of the protest.

Besides the loss of information on objectives, Banks's protest frequencies do not provide any information about who instigated the protest or who protested. The meaning and significance of a protest event often are closely tied to the instigators. For example, there are high-profile people like Medha Patkar of the Narmada Bachao Andolan, a significant environmental NGO, whose involvement lends a protest greater significance than would be the case where no such person was involved. Such people attract both domestic and international attention from the media and from governments. A further example of the variety of instigators is the case of the state of Andhra Pradesh Chief Minister N. Chandrababu Naidu, who early in 2003 urged people to stage dharnas against their representatives and "picket them at their houses every morning" if they failed to resolve people's problems.[21]

Besides the instigators, the meaning and significance of protests, at least in part, depend upon who participates, yet such information is lost, too, in frequency counts of events. Who does and who does not participate is critical to understanding the twenty-four-hour state of West Bengal bandh to which we have just referred. Both citizens and government officials sought either to keep Cauvery river water in the state of Karnataka or to get it released to the state of Tamil Nadu in a series of protest actions during the last half of 2002; and, as noted previously, government participated in the

Andhra Pradesh–Karnataka protests over the Paragodu dam. Yet, government-sponsored protests are not distinguished from non-government-sponsored protests in the Banks data set.

In some protests the police have joined with the government or protested on their own. An example of the former is the UP bandh, noted previously. There, the Allahabad High Court, the highest court in UP, was attacked by leaders of the ruling Samajwadi Party–Bahujan Samaj Party alliance aided by the police. The High Court chief justice's office was trashed; he called the chief justice of India; and the chief justice of India approached the Defence Ministry for protection of the UP High Court justice. According to an observer, "When lawyers protested against the hooliganism of the pro-bandh activists, they were assaulted by the policemen with lathis [long sticks]. . . . There were many reports of forcible closure of shops by the police who were reported to have accompanied the bandh supporters on Tuesday. Those defying the bandh were beaten up by the police." The next day traders in about ten districts of UP observed a hartal in protest against the police excesses.[22] An example of the latter is a case in early 2003 where the state of Jharkhand Men's Police Association called a stir over a variety of work-related issues. It was reported to have involved 20,000 to 30,000 officers who took five days of leave to join the agitation.[23] Following Banks's definitions, it is unclear whether this action and the UP action would be categorized as strikes, demonstrations, or riots—or a combination of two or more of these. Yet, their potential impacts are likely to be quite different than would those of strikes or demonstrations composed of individuals not involved in law enforcement.

Opposition and the Power to Overcome It

Whether or not a protest action occurs depends in part upon the sanctions likely to be faced by those who protest. A measure of the frequency of protest ignores such a contextual factor. For example, in early 2003 when the state of Kerala teachers and government employees proposed a strike, the government responded by making clear to those contemplating the strike that (1) if they were regular employees, they would not be paid for the days they did not work; (2) if they were temporary workers, they would be fired; and (3) if they decided to "report for duty," they would be promised protection.[24] The impact of the Tamil Nadu government's use of TESMA against public employees and the consequent Supreme Court decision against strikes by public employees is very likely to radically change the frequency of strikes.

Earlier in 2003, the Tamil Nadu government faced a variety of other protest actions, one of which was by government medical and dental students starting in late April. The purpose of the action was to seek recognition of a variety of medical courses not recognized, a ban on the opening of private medical colleges, and an increase in the stipend paid, among other things.[25] They went on "strike," though they continued to care for patients in need; they held dharnas, rasta rokos, and fasts; and they courted arrest. The Tamil Nadu Government Doctors Association supported the students' demand for a ban on the opening of private medical colleges by threatening a series of protests starting with a cessation of selective surgeries, then a one day token strike, then a "needle and knife down" protest where all but emergency surgeries would be stopped, and finally an indefinite strike.[26] The Tamil Nadu government argued that it was the national, not the state, government that had the authority to allow or disallow private medical colleges. The government suspended 5,000 striking medical students, yet the threatened dismissals that accompanied the strike by government employees a month and a half later were not imposed. The medical and dental student strike may not have occurred had the participants known of the government's response to the public employees' strike in July. Furthermore, it may not have been counted as a strike at all if, in fact, it was directed at the state rather than the national government.

Finally, most numerated protest data exclude those cases where action is merely threatened. Yet, the threat of a protest action may have as significant an impact as an action itself. Low frequencies of protest may mean that the threat of protest action has taken the place of actual protest in affecting policy and/or authority. Whether or not this is the case depends on an array of factors including previous experiences with protest actions. Protest frequencies provide no information on most of these factors.

Impact and Success

There are many factors related to the context of a protest that can affect its impact and that are lost in summary counts. Two examples are illustrative.

First, in some Indian states there is a long tradition of strikes and demonstrations and in others that tradition is not as well established—yet, frequency counts would ignore the differences. For example, to strike in the state of Kerala is a common occurrence and no "big deal." To strike in the state of Orissa, though, would be a more unusual event for cultural and historical reasons. In other words, protest is more ordinary in Kerala than in Orissa. As a consequence, one might expect similar types of protests of similar magnitudes to have different impacts. None of this information is included in the numerical representation of a protest.

Second, if one were to envision the impact of certain protest actions in India and the same protest actions in the United States today, the impacts of identical protests would be quite different. An example is a form of yatra, called a padayatra in Andhra Pradesh (AP), initiated by the Congress Legislative Party leader Y.S. Rajasekhara Reddy (YSR), covering 1,500 kilometers over a sixty-day period in April to June 2003. The objectives of this long march were several, including to "expose the lackadaisical attitude of the government in tackling the drought conditions in the state."[27] Others saw it as an "'empathy tour' and aimed at infusing confidence among people in facing adverse conditions."[28] The aim was certainly to elicit political support for the Congress Party, too. The Congress Forum for Telangana (CFT), a group of Congress Party members of the state legislature from the Telangana area, viewed the padayatra as a means to further its efforts to create a separate state in the AP region of Telangana.[29] The padayatra was considered a means of getting all factions of the party together. Accompanying the padayatra was a van fitted with a public address system, a doctor and paramedics, security guards, and others who were a part of the entourage.[30] The padayatra began in Hyderabad, where YSR prayed at a temple and a dargah (a tomb of a revered Muslim); moved to the Congress Party headquarters at Gandhi Bhavan; and continued forty kilometers to Chevella in Ranga Reddy district, while thousands of supporters wished him well along the way.[31] As a good omen, "the skies started clouding up and the day cooled somewhat for the Congress [Party] leader to start his pre-election padayatra."[32] There were problems along the way: Congress Party activists in some areas fought each other and at one point YSR was affected by heat stroke, but the padayatra's effectiveness was shown by the flowering of copycat padayatras by other groups. As one commentator said, "Competitive padayatras is the latest political funda [fad] in Andhra Pradesh."[33] Fundamentally, it was a kind of antigovernment protest that Banks might represent as a number, yet the number deprives it of much of its meaning, and that meaning depends to a considerable extent upon the history and character of the areas in which it took place.

The degree of success among protest events differs considerably, though none of this information is available in the frequency accounts. The determination of whether an event is successful or not is a complex task in itself. An example that illustrates this complexity, but one that would be excluded in Banks's index because it was directed at a state rather than the "national" government, was a strike by nearly 100,000 "auto" drivers in the city of Hyderabad in early 2003 over a number of issues involving the effect of government policy on them. It was called off after four days "following a categorical assurance by the Home Minister . . . to resolve several of their demands."[34] Such an outcome may or may not be indicative of success, for "categorical assurances" cannot be equated automatically with appropriate action. According to Shiv Sena and the Bharatiya Janata Party (BJP), the July 2003 Mumbai bandh, protesting the bomb explosion blamed on agents of Pakistan, was a success. Yet, as one observer noted, its "success" was "to bring India's commercial capital to a standstill,"[35] and, as another contended, its "success" was more self-serving because its real objective was simply to attract attention in order to facilitate victory in the forthcoming election.[36]

Another case is the April 2003 ten-day nationwide strike by the All India Motor Transport Congress (AIMTC), a group of transport owners, with a ten-point charter of demands that included stable fuel prices, exemption from the Value Added Tax, and a variety of other goals. By the second day, the AIMTC claimed that the strike had taken 2.7 million commercial vehicles off the road.[37] When no progress was made in talks with the national government, the AIMTC president flew to the city of Hyderabad and met with the chief minister of the state of Andhra Pradesh, N. Chandrababu Naidu. Naidu promised to serve as an intermediary and speak with the prime minister about the AIMTC issues.[38] His party, the Telugu Desam Party (TDP), was an important part of the governing coalition in India at the time. By the eighth day, some groups of truck owners in the states of Andhra Pradesh, West Bengal, and Orissa called off the strike, though the AIMTC claimed it was still on.[39] In Andhra Pradesh, what was called the Joint Action Committee said the strike was over, though major groups such as the AP Lorry Owners Association, the AP Mini Transport Association, and the Hyderabad Lorry Association said they would continue with the strike.[40] There was also a split between AIMTC, representing transport companies, and the All India Confederation of Goods Vehicle Owners Association (ACOGOA), which represents truckers: The former had ten demands and the latter, three.[41] Eventually, the AIMTC said it had gotten agreement to nine of ten demands.[42] Yet, the government maintained that it had not accepted the AIMTC demands and senior members of the AIMTC called the agreement a "sellout" to the government.[43] An editorial in *The Hindu* questioned whether the truckers had gained anything, expressed disappointment with most of the state governments for their indifference while people suffered, and agreed with a comment attributed to the president of the AIMTC that the AIMTC should never strike again.[44]

The success of virtually all protests is ambiguous, not simply because there are so many different ways it may be measured. Some years ago the *Indian Express* reported from the city of Thiruvananthapuram in the state of Kerala on the protests against the state government's education policy: "Destruction of public property, police firing resulting in loss of precious human lives, lathicharge [when police chase citizens with long sticks], blocking ministers, indefinite hunger strike by student leaders and class boycott. . . . Are there any winners in this battle? Certainly, the government has not won it. But can the pro-LDF [Left Democratic Front, a coalition of parties led by the Communist Party of India (Marxist)] students confidentially say that they had scored a decisive point over the government?"[45] Even this report is based on only a few of the possible repercussions that might affect success—directly, indirectly, long-term, short-term. All of this informational ambiguity is lost in an events tally.

Problems in Characterizing "Events"

A major problem with country-level data, such as protest frequencies, is that they contain no information about what is happening in the constituent parts of the country. Even if an accurate compilation of the number of protests were able to be attained, interpreting its meaning is not straightforward: a high (or a low) frequency of protests in a country may be due to a high (or low) level of protest everywhere or a very high (or a very low) level in only one part of the country. The summary number, also, says nothing about the territorial problem of counting protests in various parts of the country. Thus, if there is not accurate information on the territorial distribution of protest, the data set will be of little use for predicting internal conflict.

If an event is counted as a protest only when it is deemed "successful," meaning that a significant proportion of the target population participates or the protest remains peaceful, then how are territorial differences in participation to be combined to determine whether a protest event can be said to have occurred? Again a myriad of examples might be cited. The impact of a twelve-hour bandh in the state of Manipur called by the All Manipur Students Union (AMSU) was described in *The Hindu* as follows: "The strike had a total impact in the Sadar hill and Saikul sub-divisions of Senapati district. However, there was no impact at Ukhrul and Tamenglong districts. In Chandel district, there was partial impact."[46] If "having an impact" is required for the event to count as having occurred, then one is faced with the problem of deciding how to combine "no impact" in some areas with "total impact" in other areas to determine whether the event should be counted. Such a report would require a guess about whether the level of participation met Banks's definitional requirements and whether the target was the national government's policies or authority. As noted, Banks's source of information is the *New York Times,* which is unlikely to report the kind of detail contained in *The Hindu* noted above. So, neither would this problem occur nor would any of this information be obtainable from Banks's frequencies of protest.

A similar problem arises in assessing whether to count as a protest what happened when the People's War Group, a radical guerilla group found in the rural districts of several states, called a statewide bandh in the state of Andhra Pradesh in April of 2003 to protest the killing of one of its senior leaders. "Normal life" was affected in rural areas, but there was little impact in urban areas.[47] This territorial problem is compounded when information is incomplete or in disagreement and when organizational and territorial support are combined. *The Hindu* reported on a July 2001 action against mining in the Western-Ghats mountain area, saying that it "evoked an encouraging response if the overwhelming voluntary support being expressed to it by various organizations and institutions is an indication,"[48] while the *Deccan Herald* said it "failed to evoke even a dismal response in Bellary, Raichur and Koppal, but seems to have in Shimoga and Chikkamagalur districts."[49]

Information on territorial variation in protest, both within India and within parts of India, is not provided by the summary frequencies, yet such information is critical to an attempt to understand the nature and impact of various forms of protest. A frequent answer to the challenge presented by territorial variation in the response to calls for protest is to say the call "evoked a mixed response." If the "mixed response" is counted as a protest event, information on important territorial variation is excluded—as may be other important information as well. The UP bandh, referred previously, was reported to have met with "a mixed response." More specifically, a report on it in the *Indian Express* stated that the home secretary, A.P. Singh, said that "80 per cent of the shops remained closed and life was affected in the plains but conceded that the situation was 'just the reverse' in the hills, where a student-sponsored anti-reservation stir had gained momentum prompting the ruling Samajwadi Party-Bahujan Samj Party combine [combination-ed.] to call Tuesday's bandh as a counter."[50]

In addition to their absence of information about the uneven territorial distribution of protest events, Banks's frequencies provide no clue to the impacts of protest across multiple levels of analysis. Only for strikes does Banks explicitly state that the protest must be aimed at "national government policies or authority" for it to be counted. Many strike actions that are directed at other levels of analysis impact the national government's policies and/or authority or have multilevel impacts, yet they may be excluded. Even if they were included, important information would be lost.

An example is the strike in the state of Andhra Pradesh against the state government–owned Singareni Collieries Company Limited (SCCL) in January and February 2003. The mines employed about 96,000 workers at sixty-four mines.[51] The explicit purpose was to block privatization, though government officials argued that the strike was "a ploy by unions to be in the limelight and woo the workers in view of the elections due in February for identifying the majority union."[52] The unions immediately claimed that the strike was total, while the management said it was partial.[53] Five days after the strike began, a bandh was called in several towns in the coal-mining areas and it was widely observed. In support of the strikers, opposition parties in AP, including the Congress Party, the Left parties, the Telangana Rashtra Samiti party, and the Majlis-e-Ittahadul Muslimeen party, tried to hold a satyagraha near the Secretariat in the city of Hyderabad, but it was broken up by the police.[54] The president of the AP Congress Party Committee, M. Satyanarayana Rao, verbally attacked the chief minister for his "abject surrender to the World Bank and other international lending agencies" and for his support of privatization.[55] At this point, the Union Coal Ministry formed a Crisis Resolution Group to arrange the transportation of coal from other areas to provide several power-generating plants deprived of Singareni coal.[56] After a seventeen-day strike, the state government agreed to the miners' major demands and the strike was called off.[57] Although directed at the AP government controlled by the Telugu Desam Party (TDP), this protest action targeted the National Democratic Alliance (NDA), which controlled the national government of India, and its policy of privatization because the TDP was an important part of that alliance. Banks's definition of a strike requires that it be against more than one employer, regardless of whether the employer is the state. Despite the political significance of the strike, it might have been ignored for both reasons.

Further information is lost because protests against government or its policies at any level may involve a series of events, all of which have a common purpose, that are contemporaneous or sequential. Frequency counts may be capturing merely a difference in strategy of protest, although it may appear as a difference in intensity of protest. That is, the frequency counts may treat as separate protests several parts of a single protest. For example, early in 2003 the central trade unions launched a "peaceful agitation" against the national government's "anti-labor" and "anti-people" economic policies. The action involved nearly two million workers and entailed rasta rokos, jail bharos, and an array of other forms of "sub-protests."[58] Shortly afterward, the employees of "aided" degree and junior colleges in Andhra Pradesh initiated an agitation "to protest against the Government's alleged negligent attitude toward their problems."[59] The protest involved a protest day, followed by a mass dharna, followed by a mass rally, and culminated in an indefinite strike. A third example would be a strike in Karnatika involving 40,000 officers affiliated with the All India Bank Officers' Confederation. The strike was accompanied by "processions, rallies and demonstrations."[60] Banks's frequency counts may include each of these events as separate demonstrations, provided they meet his 100-participants standard. Mere counts deprive us of information about the extent to which the protests are linked to each other.

Finally, it is often argued that protest actions "naturally" increase in the year prior to an election. Such protest actions have a subtle, or not-so-subtle, objective of placing the state or national government of the day on the defensive or of rallying support for a party or an issue. The formal reason for the protest may be nonpolitical, but the informal reason may be political. The numerical frequency of protest, therefore, may be a result of factors unrelated to increased or decreased discontent with the policies or authority of the government.

THE CONCEPT OF PROTEST AND THE
INTERPRETIVE ALTERNATIVE

In early efforts to numerate political protest events, such as that for the 1972 edition of the *World Handbook of Political and Social Indicators*, the authors showed an awareness of many of these problems (C.L. Taylor and Hudson 1972, 62–67). Nevertheless, their numbers are widely used today as "brute data" without reference to the qualms the coders may have had about the simplifications they were making. C. Taylor (1979, 40) refers to "brute data" as "actions which can be identified beyond fear of interpretive dispute." It is quite clear from the many examples of information "left out" that the same problem affects Banks's data. Information on the instigators, participants, objectives, legal environment, magnitude, impact, territorial distribution, and many other aspects are not reflected in the numbers. Furthermore, the categories used fail to encompass major forms of political protest used in India. Indeed, to identify what Banks calls riots, strikes, and demonstrations as "brute data" is inaccurate—or meaningless.

Part of the reason for the simplification of political protest to numbers is the ease with which they may be related to other numerical representations of phenomena to develop generalizations. In positivist social science, developing generalizations is the goal. They are what gold is to the prospector. Theory is simply a set of interrelated and confirmed generalizations; explanation requires generalizations in the form of covering laws, and prediction requires them as well. Yet, the illustrations above suggest that the simplification is a mistake: Banks's numeration of concepts of protest equates very different events and deprives the observer of information essential for the building of knowledge. Indeed, when a protest event in India is reduced to a "1," it is made virtually meaningless.

Those who defend the utility of data sets argue that the missing data are not intrinsic to the concepts. Rather, they are pieces of information that may be treated as external to, or separate from, these concepts. For example, the success of a demonstration may be numerated apart from the occurrence of a demonstration, or the objective of a strike may be numerated apart from the occurrence of a strike. Since the "success" or the "objectives" may be detached from the occurrence of a protest event, their absence does not detract from the empirical value of the concept. In other words, the "missing" information may be treated as variables whose relationship with protest may be empirically tested—or it may be treated as residual variables assumed to have no impact on protest.

Furthermore, much more sophisticated protest data sets have been developed that include the "missing information," that is, the criticisms of the Banks data are not generally applicable. An example would be the protest event data collected on Eastern Europe by Ronald Francisco.[61] He has gathered a wide variety of information on each event—much of which, as I have argued, is missing from the Cross-National Time-Series Data Archive. He collected information on where the protest events took place, when they took place, what the issue was, how many protesters were present, the damage done, the size of the state forces dispatched to deal with them, and many other dimensions. Thus, much of the "missing information" might be obtained.

The core contention of both challenges is that the information cited here as "missing" is not a part of the meaning of the protest concepts, that is, that its absence poses no problem for those who wish to understand the nature and impact of political protest in India. Such a contention is contradicted by the data presented here. First, the categories exclude important protest actions: Major forms of expression of political protest, such as individual fasts or suicides, are excluded. Second, the categories do not correspond unambiguously with major forms of political protest, such as the bandh or a jail bharo. Third, and most importantly, to treat all these pieces of information as external or detachable from forms of protest would give rise to the problem of "too many variables and too few cases." That is, a researcher using numerical tools would be unable to determine the impacts of these many pieces of information on each other and on the protest. The complexity of the events makes their detachment and treatment as independent variables infeasible. All that is achieved is the deletion of information that gives meaning to the protest events.

The simplification of such events to virtual meaninglessness through numeration is only part of the problem faced by a researcher seeking to build knowledge. The information used to describe the cases cited is documentary, that is, it is based on written records. Although those records supply a much more complete description of events than do Banks's indices, they are imperfect representations of protest events. In addition to reports of observations, there is conjecture on the part of reporters, contradictions among sources, missing information, and many other imperfections. Given these severe problems, is interpretivism a possible solution?

The contradictory meanings given to interpretivism by various writers are well summarized by Gerring (2003a, 2–6) in his introduction to the symposium on interpretivism found in the second issue of *Qualitative Methods*. Yet, there are some commonly accepted advantages: It does not require "leaving out" significant information to arrive at conclusions; it implicitly values humility in the development of knowledge, for it recognizes the immense complexity of the subjective, objective, and intersubjective worlds that it seeks to fit together; and it facilitates studies of different cultures by its concern with intersubjective meanings, avoiding the interpretation of "other societies in the categories of our own" (C. Taylor 1979, 55).

Interpretivism's application to building knowledge might involve a set of studies exploring the dimensions found missing in this critique of Banks's numeration of political protest events. That is, one might seek knowledge of events' magnitude, legal environment, objectives, forms, instigators, participants, opposition, success, territorial distribution, and impact, as well as interconnection of events at various levels of analysis, chains and multiform events, threatened events, and the time context in which they take place. The task would be similar to providing thick description, though the set of issues addressed would not be unique to each case. Where information was missing, it would be provided by scholars' "guesses" or interpretations from available data. Events could be compared, similarities noted, and clusters of characteristics related to outcomes—many of the questions addressed with other methodologies might be addressed here. The key differences are that judgment and reason would be the basis for interconnecting parts of the multidimensional description. And, in addition, each interpretation would invite challenges by other scholars, in contrast to the widespread and unquestioning acceptance of the accuracy of numerically represented events.

NOTES

1. The data set is described at www.databanks.sitehosting.net/www/main.htm, accessed April 4, 2006. See also Banks (2002).

2. Ronald Francisco, for example, is employing machine-assisted coding of domestic conflict in most European countries, for which he is getting information on more than twenty variables. A similar codebook was used to collect data on Korea, Burma, and Latin America. See http://lark.cc.ukans.edu/~ronfran/data/index.html.

3. The term "national government" is used throughout this chapter to refer to the central government, i.e., the government for the whole country, as distinct from the governments of India's constituent states or parts thereof.

4. The expression "anti-foreign" refers to those demonstrations that are directed at governments or policies of countries other than India.

5. The CNTS definitions of domestic protest can be found at www.databanks.sitehosting.net/www/var_group.htm. Accessed April 4, 2006. See also Banks (2002).

6. Bandhs come in many forms, such as a "motor bandh," which is limited to keeping motorized vehicles off the road; they may exempt certain groups such as students taking exams; they may be limited to a city or state. None of these variations is captured in counts of bandhs or demonstrations.

7. My awareness that the terms we use in the West to refer to protest do not adequately reflect Indian reality came while I was teaching at the University of Kerala as a Fulbright scholar in the early 1990s. There were several incidents. One day I was in class teaching and a group of students came to my door and politely asked that I stop because there was a "strike." I complied. Subsequently, I asked if any faculty group had called a strike and discovered that none had done so. A group of politically active students acting for a political party had simply enforced a "strike." Some weeks later there was a group of students surrounding one of the buildings on campus for some reason. On inquiry I found that the group was engaged in a "gherao" against an administrator. They were determined not to let the administrator leave until he agreed to their demands. We lived several kilometers from the campus in Thiruvananthapuram, the state capital. Our accommodation was only about a block from the Secretariat, that is, the building that housed the state's parliament and bureaucracy. Just outside the "fence" around the Secretariat there were constant protests with semipermanent signs of various sorts demanding action on a variety of issues. Indeed, there were makeshift beds associated with the signs, and people milled around night and day. The forms of active protest seemed to be in constant flux. Every now and then a mass of people would come to support one group or another. Occasionally, bandhs were called and much of Thiruvananthapuram was closed down.

8. "Thousands Form Human Fort," *The Hindu*, June 17, 2003, www.thehindu.com/2003/06/17/stories/2003061704590400.htm. The English phrase "human fort" is a translation of a Malayalam word, *kota*, which means blockage.

9. For example, Anna Hazare has used the tool successfully in Maharashtra. See "Anna Hazare Starts Silent Protest," *The Hindu*, August 10, 2001, www.hinduonnet.com/2001/08/10/stories/0210000w.htm, accessed April 6, 2006. See also "Anna Hazare Ends Fast," *The Times of India*, August 17, 2003, http://timesofindia.indiatimes.com/cms.dll/html/uncomp/articleshow?msid=134746. Accessed August 18, 2003.

10. "Nalgonda MLA's Fast Enters Third Day," *Deccan Chronicle on the Web*, March 10, 2003, www.deccan.com/regional/default.shtml#MLA%E2%80%99s%20fast%20enter%20third%20day%20draws%20good%20response. Accessed March 9, 2003. Unless otherwise noted, all articles cited from the *Deccan Chronicle on the Web* were accessed on the date they appeared. Because of time differences between India and California, the access date can be one day earlier than the publication date. As this e-journal does not appear to archive its materials, the URLs only work for a while after publication date, and those given here, while providing access at the time, may no longer be functional.

11. S. Viswanathan, "A Strike Suppressed," *Frontline*, Vol. 20, Issue 15 (July 19–August 1, 2003), www.frontlineonnet.com/fl2015/stories/20030801004201500.htm. Accessed July 19, 2003.

12. S. Viswanathan, "A Right Under Attack," *Frontline*, Vol. 20, Issue 17 (August 16–29, 2003), www.flonnet.com/fl2017/stories/20030829005102100.htm. Accessed August 15, 2003.

13. Among the most forceful objections came from the attorney general, Soli Sorabjee. See his "Right to Strike," *The Sunday Express*, August 17, 2003, www.indianexpress.com/print.php?content_id=29768. Also see "'The Working Class Will Oppose the Judgment,' Interview with M.K. Pandhe, General-Secretary, CITU," *Frontline*, Vol. 20, Issue 17 (August 16–29, 2003), www.flonnet.com/fl2017/stories/20030829005402400.htm. Accessed August 15, 2003.

14. S. Viswanathan, "A Right Under Attack."

15. "Strike Shifts Focus to Union, Opposition Rights," *The Hindu*, August 18, 2003, www.thehindu.com/2003/08/18/stories/2003081804120400.htm. Accessed August 18, 2003.

16. "Sena Bandh Gets Muslim Support," *The Times of India*, August 3, 2003, http://timesofindia.indiatimes.com/cms.dll/html/uncomp/articleshow?msid=109969. Accessed August 3, 2003.

17. "TDP Shuts Down Anantapur," *The Times of India*, June 8, 2003, http://timesofindia.indiatimes.com/cms.dll/html/uncomp/articleshow?msid=12114. Accessed June 8, 2003.

18. T. Lakshmipathi, "Protest and Politics," *Frontline*, Vol. 20, Issue 14 (July 5–18, 2003), www.frontlineonnet.com/fl2014/stories/20030718002303300.htm. Accessed July 7, 2003. Also T. Sunil Reddy, "TDP Reins in Paragodu Stir," *The Times of India*, June 3, 2003, http://timesofindia.indiatimes.com/cms.dll/html/uncomp/articleshow?msid=2634. Accessed June 2, 2003.

19. "SP, BSP Call Bandh on September 13," *Indian Express (Kochi)*, September 7, 1994, p. 13.

20. "Congress Calls Bandh Over Keshpur Killings," *The Times of India*, May 23, 2000, www .timesofindia.com./today/23mcal1.htm. Accessed May 23, 2000.

21. "A CM Who Wants Dharnas," *Deccan Chronicle on the Web*, February 5, 2003, www.deccan.com/ headlines/lead4.shtml. Accessed February 4, 2003.

22. Sharad Gupta, "Govt Machinery Misused During UP Bandh," *Indian Express*, September 16, 1994, p. 11.

23. "Second Day of Cops Stir," *The Hindu*, February 25, 2003, www.thehindu.com/2003/02/25/stories/ 2003022503380300.htm. Accessed February 24, 2003.

24. "'No Work No Pay' for Thursday's Strike," *The Hindu*, February 25, 2003, www.thehindu.com/ 2003/02/25/stories/2003022506670400.htm. Accessed February 24, 2003.

25. "Minister's Plea to Striking Medicos," *News Today*, April 25, 2003, http://newstodaynet.com/25apr/ ld2.htm. Accessed April 25, 2003.

26. "TN Doctors Threaten Indefinite Stir," *Deccan Herald*, May 10, 2003, www.deccanherald.com/ deccanherald/may10/n4.asp. Accessed May 9, 2003.

27. "TDP Jittery over YSR's 60-Day Padayatra: CLP," *The Times of India*, April 3, 2003, http:// timesofindia.indiatimes.com/cms.dll/html/uncomp/articleshow?msid=42205892. Accessed April 2, 2003.

28. "YSR Padayatra from Today," *The Hindu*, April 9, 2003, www.thehindu.com/2003/04/09/stories/ 2003040904990400.htm. Accessed April 8, 2003.

29. "CFT to Support YSR's Padayatra," *The Times of India*, April 9, 2003, http:// timesofindia.indiatimes.com/cms.dll/html/uncomp/articleshow?msid=42803801. Accessed April 8, 2003.

30. "PCC Hitches On to YSR's Yatra," *The Times of India*, April 9, 2003, http://timesofindia.indiatimes.com/ cms.dll/html/uncomp/articleshow?msid=42803953. Accessed April 8, 2003.

31. "MSR Leads YSR Brigade at Padayatra," *Deccan Chronicle on the Web*, April 10, 2003, www.deccan.com/city/default.shtml#MSR%20leads%20YSR%20brigade. Accessed April 10, 2003.

32. "YSR Walks Poll Path a Year Early," *Deccan Chronicle on the Web*, April 10, 2003, www.deccan.com/ headlines/lead2.shtml. Accessed April 9, 2003.

33. "A War of Padayatras in AP," *Deccan Herald*, June 2, 2003, www.deccanherald.com/deccanherald/ jun03/n3.asp. Accessed June 2, 2003.

34. "Automen Call Off Strike," *The Hindu*, February 22, 2003, www.thehindu.com/2003/02/22/stories/ 2003022209670300.htm. Accessed February 21, 2003. Also, "Auto Strike Begins from Today." *Deccan Chronicle on the Web*, February 18, 2003, www.deccan.com/headlines/lead5.shtml. Accessed February 17, 2003.

35. "Whom Does the Bandh Benefit?" *The Hindu*, July 31, 2003, www.thehindu.com/2003/07/31/stories/ 2003073102731300.htm. Accessed July 30, 2003.

36. "Thackeray Writ Grinds Mumbai to a Halt," *The Times of India*, July 30, 2003, http:// timesofindia.indiatimes.com/cms.dll/html/uncomp/articleshow?msid=103561. Accessed July 30, 2003.

37. "Truckers' Stir: Delhi Hold the Priceline," *The Times of India*, April 16, 2003, http:// timesofindia.indiatimes.com:80/cms.dll/html/uncomp/articleshow?msid=43507487. Accessed April 15, 2003.

38. "Naidu to Take up Truckers' Issue with PM," *The Hindu*, April 19, 2003, www.thehindu.com/2003/ 04/19/stories/2003041902710600.htm. Accessed April 18, 2003.

39. "Truckers in AP, Bengal, Orissa Call Off Stir," *Indiainfo.com*, April 21, 2003, http://news.indiainfo.com/ 2003/04/21/21stir1.html. Accessed April 21, 2003.

40. "CM Talks Faction Out of Truck Stir," *Deccan Chronicle on the Web*, April 21, 2003, www.deccan.com/ headlines/lead3.shtml. Accessed April 20, 2003.

41. P. K. Bhardwaj, "Split Among Striking Truckers," *The Hindu*, April 23, 2003, www.hinduonnet.com/ 2003/04/23/stories/2003042305820100.htm. Accessed April 24, 2003. Also, "Truckers' Stir Off; 9 Demands Met," *Deccan Herald*, April 24, 2003, www.deccanherald.com/deccanherald/apr24/i1.asp. Accessed April 23, 2003.

42. Ibid.

43. "Load of Promises Ends Truck Strike," *The Indian Express*, April 24, 2003, www.indianexpress.com/ print.php?content_id=22645. Accessed April 24, 2003.

44. "An Unnecessary Strike," *The Hindu*, April 25, 2003, www.thehindu.com/2003/04/25/stories/ 2003042500271000.htm. Accessed April 24, 2003.

45. "No Winners, Only Losers," *Indian Express*, December 4, 1994, p. 5.

46. "Bandh Affects Life in Manipur," *The Hindu*, August 6, 2001, www.hinduonnet.com/thehindu/2001/ 08/06/stories/14062144.htm. Accessed August 5, 2003.

47. "Partial Response to PW Bandh," *The Times of India*, April 9, 2003, http://timesofindia.indiatimes.com/cms.dll/html/uncomp/articleshow?msid=42803745. Accessed April 8, 2003.

48. "Good Response to Bandh Call to Save Western Ghats," *The Hindu*, July 24, 2001, www.hinduonnet.com/stories/0424210n.htm. Accessed July 23, 2001.

49. "Save Tugabbhadra Struggle Forum, Bundh Fails in Bllary, Raichur, Koppal," *Deccan Herald*, July 28, 2001, www.deccanherald.com/deccanherald/july28/s2.htm. Accessed July 21, 2001.

50. "UP Bandh Violence Claims Three Lives," *Indian Express*, September 14, 1994, p. 1.

51. "Strike in Singareni Collieries Total," *Deccan Chronicle on the Web*, January 23, 2003, www.deccan.com/regional/default.shtml#SingareniCollieriesComestoahalt. Accessed January 23, 2003.

52. "Conflicting Claims over Singareni Strike," *The Hindu*, January 23, 2003, www.thehindu.com/2003/01/23/stories/2003012302560400.htm. Accessed January 22, 2003.

53. Ibid.

54. "Miners' Stir: Political Leaders Held," *The Hindu*, February 4, 2003, www.thehindu.com/2003/02/04/stories/2003020403610600.htm. Accessed March 2, 2003.

55. "Opposition Gives Bandh Call," *The Hindu*, February 5, 2003, www.thehindu.com/2003/02/05/stories/2003020504410400.htm. Accessed February 4, 2003.

56. "Centre Steps into Miners Strike, Rushes Coal to Stir-Hit Power Plants," *Deccan Chronicle on the Web*, February 6, 2003, www.deccan.com/headlines/lead3.shtml. Accessed February 5, 2003.

57. "AP Miners Call off Stir," *Deccan Herald*, February 9, 2003, www.deccanherald.com/deccanherald/feb9/n1.asp. Accessed February 5, 2003.

58. "Nationwide Trade Stir Today," *The Hindu*, January 8, 2003, www.thehindu.com/2003/01/08/stories/2003010805511300.htm. Accessed January 7, 2003.

59. "JAC Stir to Protest Against Govt. 'Neglect'," *The Hindu*, February 20, 2003 www.thehindu.com/2003/02/20/stories/2003022003140400.htm. Accessed February 19, 2003.

60. "Strike Cripples Bank Operations in State," *Deccan Herald*, May 3, 2003, www.deccanherald.com/deccanherald/may03/i5.asp. Accessed May 2, 2003.

61. See his site at http://lark.cc.ukans.edu/~ronfran/data/index.html. Accessed July 21, 2002.

PART III

ANALYZING DATA

In traditional presentations of research methods, the next phase of research is formulated as "data analysis." This formulation fits with a methodologically positivist perspective emphasizing the successive "stages" of research, wherein propositions are deductively induced from prior theory, concepts are operationalized and measured, quantitative data are "collected" with respect to those measures, and *then* data analysis commences. This consists typically of analyses drawing on statistics or, in the case of methodologically positivist qualitative research, using, for example, necessary and sufficient logic (Ragin 2000a)—with all such procedures ultimately focused on demonstrating statistically significant relationships (or the lack thereof) or causal mechanisms and/or testing causal models. Conceived in this way, "data analysis" has excluded the kinds of interpretive analytical processes presented here. "Analyzing data" is consistent with the hermeneutic and phenomenological presuppositions of methodologically interpretive approaches—that is, approaches that emphasize the iterative nature of knowledge and knowledge making—more verb than noun—and their ties to the experiences of both researchers and researched.

Interpretive methods of analyzing data, as illustrated by the list in the book introduction (see Table I-1, p. xx) are diverse, and their particular origins and developmental histories can be most fully understood in terms of the reading habits and practices that structure fields of study as epistemic-disciplinary communities. Given this diversity and historical complexity, we have not endeavored to present the full array of analytic possibilities nor to give particularized histories for each (although chapter 1 provides an overview of their philosophical commonalities). Still, the chapters included in this section do give a sense of the wide range of topics and settings in which phenomenological and hermeneutic ideas may be manifested and expressed.[1]

As discussed in the introduction to part II, the demarcation between accessing-generating data and analyzing them is useful for heuristic purposes as a way to discuss what are, in practice, entwined processes. There *are* conceptually clear moments in which analysis is the main task confronting the researcher: when, for example, she has left the field or the archives and is confronted with a body of evidence—data in hand—generated through previous research decisions. Such is the case, for example, in Steven Maynard-Moody and Michael Musheno's chapter 18, which recounts the strategies they used to access and generate stories but then focuses on the analytical exchanges among the research team and the analytical processes they used to make sense of the transcribed stories, informed by their field experiences as participant-observers. Clare Ginger's chapter 19 shares a similar structure, describing steps taken to access and generate data but focusing primarily on steps in their analysis.

In other chapters in this section, the demarcation between access-genesis and analysis is less prominent. Instead, chapter narratives enact the iterative, intertwining processes of access, generation, and analysis, revealing the methodological and theoretical concerns that drive researchers toward one decision or another, ultimately yielding logically coherent research products. For example, in chapter 13, Samer Shehata's recognition that social class, organizational, and cultural expectations precluded his wearing sandals is simultaneously an evidence-generative and data-analytic moment. Such intertwining is perhaps most evident in Dvora Yanow's recounting in chapter 20 of her experiences with and understandings of architectural space, in which the bodily experience and its interpretation are of a piece—almost impossible to demarcate into access, generation, and analysis stages.

Although such procedural complexity might seem daunting, the chapters draw readers in with their specificity. Instead of treating the processes involved in any given method in general, abstract terms, chapter authors draw on their own published research to illuminate the expectations, concerns, and substantive puzzles that framed their research questions, along with detailing the analytic steps they took and the procedures they used. One criterion for the essays included here was that they be sufficiently jargon free that someone coming to an analytic method for the first time would find the ideas accessible without much "foreign language acquisition" struggle. Another criterion was that the essays be reasonably transparent to topic-matter and epistemic "outsiders" so that the methodologies and methods would be accessible without knowledge of, say, the particularities of public law (Pamela Brandwein's chapter 12) or the intricacies of the democratic peace literature (Ido Oren's chapter 11) or the debates within international studies (Cecelia Lynch's chapter 16).

Given the variety of subject matter and the richness of explication, the ten chapters in this section might be grouped in a number of ways. We draw out four themes, according to which they are sequenced. Oren's, Brandwein's, and Shehata's chapters (11, 12, and 13 respectively) focus attention on knowledge claims and knowledge production, highlighting the varied ways in which context (historical, institutional, organizational, and cultural) structures what scholars claim to know and how others react to those claims. Jackson's, Bevir's, and Lynch's chapters (14, 15, and 16) investigate human conduct and action as seen through "texts," whether verbatim transcripts from Bundestag floor debates, evidence of consensus and conflict in local governance traditions and conventions, or archival materials of diplomats' reports and scholars' historical treatises. Schmidt's, Maynard-Moody and Musheno's, and Ginger's chapters (17, 18, and 19) also treat text-based meanings, although they focus less on the historical records of the previous three chapters and more on acts rendered in textual form—from activists debating language policy to workplace stories told by public servants about their decision making—or documents that could themselves be considered actors in the situation, such as reports written by government planners for evaluative purposes. Finally, Yanow's chapter (20) "reads" human meaning in the ordinary landscapes and built spaces of social and political life.

PRODUCING AND MAKING CLAIMS TO KNOWLEDGE

In part I, Robert Adcock (chapter 3), sounding a note that might also be found in science studies,[2] reminds us not to take "methods" as if they themselves were ahistorical, acontextual, and thereby "neutral" in any sense. Like Brandwein (1999) in her analysis of the Supreme Court's construction of historical truth, Adcock shows how it is that one understanding of "comparative historical analysis" has become dominant and widely accepted, although it is not, historically, the only way "history" and "comparative" analyses have been understood and practiced. In this sense, a reflective historical analysis can illuminate the ways in which both disciplinary and professional practices produce knowledge claims.

One might challenge, for instance, our decision to include history as an empirical social science in this volume. In a sense, we are contending with the same taxonomic distinctions and categorical inclusions/exclusions as university and college administrative units: Is history an empirical social science, or is it part of the humanities? There is no bright line here, any more than there is in designing other sorts of taxonomies with their categories; and, in fact, interpretive social science—given its awareness of the crafting of language as itself both a way of world making and a method of analyzing—comes close in most, if not all, of its manifestations to blurring the imputed boundary between the two domains. At the very least, interpretive methods bring elements of "the humanities"—historical analysis, linguistics, storytelling, and narrative— to the study of social science "problems." Given our orientation toward the political dimensions of human life, historical analyses of this sort belong in this volume.[3]

The methodological implications of conceptions of history are made wonderfully clear in Ido Oren's chapter 11. One conception of history dovetails with methodological positivism— history as a repository of "facts" available for the testing of theoretical propositions in the pursuit of universal laws of human conduct. Here, the researcher is characteristically "outside" or "above" history—what feminist theorists have termed the "god trick" or the "God's eye view" (Haraway 1988; Harding 1993). But once the researcher is understood as inevitably "in" history, a different methodological understanding follows—what Oren terms a "reflexive history" in which researchers contextualize and historicize their own research efforts. Oren's chapter tells his own research story, the steps he took to uncover the "intellectual unconscious" of past researchers embedded in the contemporary political science operational definitions of the concept of "democracy." Read in tandem with Dean McHenry's chapter 10 (part II) on the Banks data set, Oren's analysis offers yet another reason to be skeptical of the value of decontextualized and de-historicized databanks.

Pamela Brandwein's (chapter 12) approach to the production of knowledge brings together two analytic methods, frame analysis and science studies, for the purpose of studying the construction and reception of legal scholars' truth claims. Frame analysis builds on the fundamental interpretive insight that "meaning" is not self-evident but, instead, a complex interaction of sensory stimuli and meaning making by human actors. In Brandwein's application of this method in public law, legal scholars' baseline assumptions are seen as shaping "where they looked for evidence of framers' intent, when in history they began looking, and how they knew when they had found it" (p. 236). Science studies open the door to seeing academic, including legal, research as "work"—a social activity characterized by habits of thought, professional networks, and individual and institutional competition. Combining these two approaches allows Brandwein to demonstrate the ways in which particular interpretations made by legal scholars do not depend on the merit of the argument alone, but rely also on connections to scholarly communities and their associated resources.

Placing Samer Shehata's (chapter 13) discussion of his ethnographic research in Egyptian factories in this section highlights the ways in which ethnography is as much an analytic method as it is a method for accessing sources and generating data. His chapter could equally as well have been included in part II, showcasing as it does the evident "facts" (once ignored in the classic anthropological literature) that researchers bring their identities to the field and that those multiple, complex identities affect what data possibilities can and cannot be accessed. His chapter has affinities, as well, to Soss's discussion there (chapter 6) of the emotional entanglements characterizing conversational interviewing.

What he demonstrates so clearly in this chapter is the intertwining of accessing, generating, and analyzing data in the production of academic claims to knowledge. It was by moving *through* the bus stops, organizational offices, factory floors, and cafés that Shehata became able to analyze the obvious and not-so-obvious aspects of social class in Egyptian society—allowing him to dig deeply in the habitus of class, thereby demonstrating its generative and re-generative capacities, in contrast to a more distanced view of class as a "thing" or as a fixed position in a societal structure. What this chapter communicates is how Weber's *verstehen*, empathic understanding, can become a possibility—not through a thought experiment behind the safety of one's desk but in the midst of experiencing aspects of working-class life on the shop floor and in other settings. The reader vicariously experiences a panoply of sensations as well—panic as Shehata's bus driver ignores the road; sympathy with his fellow worker and friend living in poverty; frustration when those in power confidently tell him to change his research method to something more appropriate to his societal status.

As Shehata convincingly demonstrates, researcher identities simultaneously generate dynamics of situational inclusion and exclusion. Some individuals embraced him as a fellow Muslim and man, which, in turn, meant comparatively less, and different, access to Christian Egyptians and women. Ethnographic research is not for those who seek to avoid conflict and risk. It is an approach that brings the researcher into direct contact with his fellow human beings, as Shehata observes, a most "concrete" of methods, which only from the perspective of methodologically positivist presuppositions would be dismissed, rather than embraced, for its subjectivity.

MAKING SENSE OF ACTIONS AS REFLECTED IN TEXTS AND OTHER ARTIFACTS

Patrick Jackson's analytic method (chapter 14) is concerned with preserving the agency of both the researcher and societal actors. It is imaginative in its efforts to delineate how this can be done when working with historical documents, in which projection of scholarly meanings onto the past is especially tempting since actors cannot "talk back" in the ways that are possible, at least conceptually, in contemporaneous ethnographic research. Not coincidentally, we believe, Jackson describes his method as "textual ethnography"—a sort of immersion in the textual data, complete with "field notes" later systematized and marshaled as part of a specific argument. What results is a highly contextualized understanding of what legitimation strategies were, and were not, available to German politicians debating Germany's post–World War II relation to the occupying forces.

Mark Bevir's explanation of narrative (chapter 15) unpacks collective patterns of activity—in this case, governance—as well as individuals' actions in terms of historically grounded beliefs. From this perspective, any method of generating data of any genre type is acceptable so long as the data *analysis* provides interpretations of actors' own meaning making. This analytic method is holistic; that is, individual human action needs to be understood by connecting individual beliefs to societal beliefs and traditions, to what Bevir terms a "wider web of beliefs." Bevir's method assumes a situated agency for human actors rather than a voluntaristic or deterministic extreme. Human beings construct their own beliefs in the context of the traditions of the societies they inherit and inhabit, such that individual autonomy is, if not a myth, highly conditioned. Societal traditions, however, should not be reified in the analysis because individuals recreate and/or reconstruct them on a daily basis as they seek to solve their personal and collective problems, what Bevir calls "dilemmas." These dilemmas create tensions in individual or institutional belief systems, forcing a reconsideration of existing beliefs.

The Jackson and Bevir chapters provide overlapping yet distinctive takes on the interpretive analytic project. Both emphasize the interpretive, meaning making activities of individuals. Both emphasize that researchers, too, are meaning makers and, thus, that the human sciences perforce involve scholars' "interpreting [historical actors'] interpretations" (Jackson, p. 266, this volume) or, as Bevir expresses it, echoing Geertz (1973a) and others, "interpretations of interpretations" (p. 283, this volume). And both offer specific methods that attempt to take into account the contingent nature of social and political outcomes.

The analytic methods presented in these two chapters differ, however, in their discussion of evidence. Bevir is agnostic with respect to evidence, arguing—in effect—that beliefs can be inferred from any type of data, be it models, surveys, documents, statistical tests, and so on, just so long as the scholar's analytic method explicitly involves interpretations of interpretations. In contrast, Jackson focuses on language usage, specifically the deployment of a public rhetoric of legitimation, as especially suited to preserving a double hermeneutic that respects the agency of those studied and, simultaneously, that of the researcher. In our view, interpretive (and other) scholars have emphasized word-based language (written and spoken) on the grounds that it plays a significant role in *constituting* meaning and, thereby, beliefs, often to the exclusion or diminishment of other artifacts that embody and communicate meaning, such as acts, including nonverbal communication, and objects, such as monuments (Lasswell 1979), city council meeting chambers (Goodsell 1988), and other physical artifacts (see, e.g., Rafaeli and Pratt 2005).

Although she does not use the phrase "interpretations of interpretations," like Jackson and Bevir, Cecilia Lynch (chapter 16) focuses on the ways in which scholars' interpretations about the world play a role in making sense of that very world. Her analytic method emphasizes a "critical interpretive" role for scholars who seek to use "re-interpretation" to open up new political spaces both in academia and on the world stage. For example, when interwar peace movements are re-understood as usefully questioning the legitimacy of state action rather than dismissively characterized as "naive and dangerous," contemporary activists are refigured as significant social actors. Lynch's analytic method, as befits the label "critical," is highly reflexive, inquiring not only about the power behind "dominant narratives" but also about what those proposing "alternative narratives" hope to gain. This reflexive criticality is combined with an attention to empirical sources consistent with the best sleuthing: finding logical contradictions and evidentiary gaps in the dominant narrative; figuring out what to look for among the many documentary possibilities, both primary and secondary; critically assessing the credibility of sources as a function of the perspective and power positions of their producers; and understanding that constructing a cumulative case will more likely convince readers than a single proverbial smoking gun.

STUDYING ACTORS' NARRATIVES

Stories about lived experience do not merely describe that experience; they also participate in the creation of their subject. As John Law (2002, 6) noted, "telling stories about the world also helps to perform that world." Even when one considers it to be a subset of "just talk," "conversational interviewing," discussed in part II, suggests a formality that "telling stories" escapes.

Ronald Schmidt, Sr.'s, chapter 17 explores the ways in which conflicting parties to a public policy issue—the drive to force English as the official language in the United States—frame their positions through various narrative devices. His analysis points to the iterative character of interpretive inquiry. As he notes there, descriptions of core policy issues and lists of protagonists may be refined as one learns more about the issue context and the positions actors take. Initial—and provisional—analytic steps take place while one is immersing oneself in learning about the issue, as well as afterward when one is engaged in more directed analysis.

Schmidt's approach is also an excellent example of the ways in which interpretive analyses that begin with an examination of the minutiae of daily life often end up seeing these as elements in a drama, or a narrative, of identity issues on a much broader scale. He initially thought of his study of U.S. language policy debates as being contestations over facts, but soon came to see them as disputes about issues of national and group identity. Similarly, Kristin Luker, in her study of abortion policy conflicts (1984), found the contestation to be less about childbearing itself and more about "lifestyle" questions of the two camps and their visions of adult female identity; and Joseph Gusfield, analyzing the temperance movement (1963), found it a symbolic battle between members of the then-ascendant socioeconomic class and the values and lifestyle they imputed to groups of immigrants who were, they felt, challenging that power and status.[4] It is not yet clear whether seeing the broader scope of human activity enacted in case specifics is an attribute of all interpretive policy studies, of interpretive political analyses more broadly, or of all interpretive work, and not only of those studies that treat the fact-value dichotomy, as Martin Rein's (1976) value-critical approach was intended to do. It is a point of methodological investigation worth asking in reading across a variety of subfields and disciplines.

In conceptualizing interview talk as an opportunity to elicit and hear "stories," Steven Maynard-Moody and Michael Musheno (chapter 18) argue that storytellers experience a partial reliving of their experiences, resulting in less self-monitoring than is normally the case with face-to-face interviews. Such an approach is essential for understanding the views of frontline workers—the cops, teachers, and counselors of their study—because these individuals' views are often subjugated to those of elites at the top of hierarchical, organizational, and policy worlds.

To make sure that they were not projecting their own theoretical preconceptions and categories onto the workers, Maynard-Moody and Musheno took great pains to elicit the day-to-day language and experiences of these government workers in the form of workers' *own* stories; and they went back to storytellers with their transcriptions at least once to make sure that they (the researchers) were not, so to speak, putting words in the workers' mouths. Their analytic method can be usefully summarized as a "close reading" or even a "close listening" of how these workers understand their worlds. And, indeed, workers did *not* understand themselves and their workplace decisions in terms of the categories accepted by policy leaders and academic researchers. Analytical recognition of these silences, a common concern of much interpretive research, is explicated in the chapter.

At the other end of the spectrum of data sources and genres, one hardly expects planning documents to share any of the narrative or rhetorical characteristics that are part of our image of "stories." In chapter 19, Clare Ginger's analysis of Environmental Impact Statements (EISs) shows us otherwise. Using the literary conventions of plot, subplot, and main and supporting characters, she demonstrates how framing and reframing of the reports' arguments were accomplished in a shift from draft EISs to the final versions. In some draft EISs the effects of designating an area a "wilderness" highlighted impacts on agency operations, whereas the final EISs attended to anticipated impacts on communities, a seemingly subtle shift but one with significant political implications for local interest group struggles over federal policy. As significant, Ginger ferrets out the unstated normative assumptions embedded in supposedly apolitical documents and analyses, demonstrating the contrast with "official prescriptions and attitudes [that] emphasize the neutrality and pure calculativeness of the planning texts" (Summa 1992, 144). In sum, she provides analytic means for taking on the presumed "objectivity" of expert analyses—a topic of growing relevance given the increasing reach of rationalizing state power (see, e.g., the argument in J.C. Scott 1998).

"READING" PHYSICAL ARTIFACTS

The final chapter in this section reiterates many of the themes discussed above as well as some from part II. Like Pader (chapter 8) in her discussion of learning observational skills, Dvora Yanow argues that researchers' own knowledge of spatial relations is tacit and must be made more explicit for research purposes. And this learning involves, as Shehata (chapter 13) also argues about ethnographic analysis, recognition that "the self" is the primary instrument of data access and generation, something that may be even more difficult for spatial analysis because of the scholarly valuing of mind over body. Along with Maynard-Moody and Musheno (chapter 18) and Ginger (chapter 19), Yanow emphasizes how power, particularly state power but also corporate power, is manifest in built space, and yet, consistent with Jackson (chapter 14) and Bevir (chapter 15)—as well as Soss (chapter 6) in part II—there still remains the possibility of agency as humans interact with built spaces, sometimes accepting and sometimes rejecting architectural visions.

Yanow's analytic method involves "translating" bodily experience into words, many of them from architectural and design languages but some also from theater and research on nonverbal behavior. As with the labeling of sensory perceptions of color (Roberson 2005), she shows, with numerous examples, that translation of spatial experience is culturally mediated. For example, "up" (as in building height or office location) means higher social status in some cultures and lower social status in others. And even in the same culture, the researcher cannot assume that his or her individual experiences of space will be the same as those of others because those experiences are constituted by the same complex of factors—gender, class, ethnicity, and so on—as are operative in other arenas.

ADDITIONAL THEMES IN ANALYZING DATA INTERPRETIVELY

These chapters clearly demonstrate that "data analysis" need not be equated with or restricted to quantitative techniques or equated with qualitative coding practices. Some of the chapters are more hermeneutic—more concerned with texts and text analogues: Patrick Jackson's analysis of speech on the floor of the Bundestag, Mark Bevir's narrative analysis of governance, Ronald Schmidt's of arguments made by proponents of "English only" in the United States, Clare Ginger's of the language usage in Environmental Impact Statement reports, and Dvora Yanow's reading of design elements in an agency's buildings. Others are more phenomenological, focused instead on lived experiences: Samer Shehata's account of life on the shop floor in Alexandria is the central example in this section of this focus on human life, with Ellen Pader's discussion of the experience of housing densities in part II serving as another example. Steven Maynard-Moody and Michael Musheno's account is an interesting combination of hermeneutic and phenomenological approaches: They use the stories told by cops, teachers, and vocational counselors concerning their work with clients, students, and others as proxies for their actual lived experiences, drawing on observational data to inform their understanding of these narratives.

The distinctions between these two categories are not exact. In treating texts as the physical or material remainders of interpretive communities' acts and their cognitive maps of these acts, interpretive researchers combine text-oriented and act-oriented methods. In addition, the criticism levied by critical theorists against phenomenology in particular—that it is overly blind to questions of power—is not in evidence here. The one chapter that comes closest to an explicitly critical theoretical position—Cecelia Lynch's analysis of peace movements' narratives—shares with the others an orientation toward the indeterminacy of meaning, the need for reflexive analysis of the ideas brought by the "knower" to the crafting of the research, and other elements. But it also shares with other chapters an orientation we remarked on earlier in the book—that when interpretive philosophical ideas are brought into the contexts of empirical research in communities, organizations, governments, and other aspects of human life, they must, and do, perforce engage questions of power. At the very least, the critical reflexivity of these scholars into their own location as researchers and writers—whether from an explicitly feminist standpoint perspective or from a more diffuse critical ethnographic one—engages the relationship between knowledge and power that lies at the heart of critical theoretical work (see, e.g., Foucault 1970).

Pamela Brandwein's and Ronald Schmidt, Sr.'s, chapters (12 and 17) illustrate a central feature of interpretive analyses in policy contexts. From the point of view that the social sciences yield an interpretation of their subject matter rather than an exact replica of it, there is no single, correct solution to a policy problem any more than there is a single correct perception of what that problem is. Interpretive approaches, with their focus on the multiplicity of meaning, shift policy-relevant analysis rather strongly to the framing of problem statements, rather than treating these as given. This point has been touched on in the social problems literature in sociology (see, e.g., Best 1995) and, to some extent, in the constructionist literature in political science (e.g., Schneider and Ingram 2005). These two chapters are suggestive of other directions in which these approaches might develop, both substantively and methodologically.

In identifying authors working in these several modes, we encountered the communities of practice problem described in the book introduction (note 13, pp. xxv–xxvi) with respect to the use of "constructivism" in various epistemic communities. In the international relations community within political science, for example, some constructivist scholars are more realist in their ontological approaches, others are more interpretive, and there is contestation over the use of constructivist versus constructionist along these lines. Similarly, within both the social problems community in sociology and the public policy community in political science, some treatments of "social constructions" objectify them in a realist fashion, dislodging them from the context of processes that phenomenologists saw as central. Psychology also has its own versions of this debate (see Hacking 1999 on the construction of ideas about things, rather than the things themselves; and note 13 on pages xxv–xxvi). Given that our understanding of social constructionism/constructivism is informed by Schütz's writings and those of his students (e.g., Berger and Luckmann 1966), we call on scholars in the interpretive research community—as Milliken (1999) calls on the international relations community—to engage in "more serious reflection" not only on how to do discourse studies (her charge), but also on what they mean when they do constructionist or constructivist research and how their interpretations of this work are similar to or divergent from what Schütz, Husserl, and others meant when they described social constructionist processes. The difficulty we all face in doing such work lies in the fact that analysis treats the observable half-lives of processes that are most difficult to catch while they are unfolding. Yet it can be done, and we urge our colleagues to continue to engage the struggle to do so.

WHAT IS NOT HERE

There is such a wide variety of interpretive methods in use across the social sciences that we could not possibly include examples of all of them here and still retain a book of manageable size and cost. We have tried to include examples of approaches that are not readily available in other methodological collections. The analytic processes of semiotics, ethnomethodology, symbolic interaction, dramaturgy (the application of Kenneth Burke's theories [1969 (1945), 1989]), metaphor analysis, category analysis, and myth analysis, for example, all interesting topics, are available elsewhere (see, e.g., Feldman 1995; Yanow 2000; the latter also includes the analysis of built space, which has been developed further in this volume).

One of the areas not included here is feminist methods, although there are many areas of overlap between arguments for the existence of a distinctively feminist mode of doing research and the interpretive approaches and philosophies represented here. Part of the reason for this omission is that we felt we could not include them without reproducing, rather fully, the debate internal to feminist theorizing as to whether, in fact, there *are* such things as "feminist" methods distinct from other forms of method (see, e.g., Reinharz 1992). The overlaps, to us, appear in an orientation toward interviewing that is conversational, in which the researcher is revealing of herself; in writing, in which, similarly, the author is present and reflective; and in the refusal to treat the knowing "subject" and the knowledge he generates as somehow objective and universal. As Kelly (2003, 179, n. 5) notes, the implication of the insight that "all knowledge is constructed from a particular standpoint" is that observation is theory laden. There are, in other words, no "facts" without a theory that organizes them, renders them relevant, and labels them as such.

This point links to the methodological pluralist's insistence that methods do not stand alone: One needs to know the character of one's evidence and in what ways one wants to marshal it before one picks up one's tools—lest, wielding a hammer always and only, one renders the world the proverbial nail; and one's presuppositions, known tacitly or explicitly, and theoretical framing incline one toward evidentiary sources of a certain character. In other words, what will constitute acceptable and persuasive "proof" is rendered by the type of evidence and its manipulation with appropriate tools.

A standpoint presupposition links, as well, to the requirement not only to reflect on one's standpoint and to make it explicit—hence, the presence of the researcher in her writing—but also to recognize the limitations of claims to universal knowledge and the partial character of all knowledge. This entails an awareness of the politics of knowledge and has led many feminist theorists and empirical researchers alike to focus on making the silences speak: deconstructing texts, events, and official presentations to show what is left out and what parties are silent or have been silenced (see, e.g., Devault 1990; DiPalma and Ferguson 2003; Yanow 2003b). The perceived humanity of both researchers and researched—the possibility of their fallibility—leads to a humility, whether of claims or of conduct, something that William James celebrated a century ago (Connolly 2005, chapter 3; see also Yanow 1997). Furthermore, it leads feminist researchers to leave open the possibility of untidiness and ambiguity, without glossing them over, and to foster methods that share control over interviewing and other processes, that recognize those being studied as collaborators in the construction of "findings" (see, e.g., Behar 1993; Stanley 1990), and that leave the research process open to change and even to "disruption" on the part of research subjects.[5]

Other topics that are not represented here include action research, actor network theory, conversation analysis, critical content analysis (although there are other examples of close readings of texts), discourse analysis explicitly building on Foucault's linking of knowledge to power, deconstruction building on Derrida's analysis of language, an explicitly Foucauldian genealogical analysis, grounded theory, poststructuralist analysis, and pragmatics, to name but a few of the wide range of analytic methods informed by interpretive methodologies.[6] At the same time, we note that many of these approaches overlap. One might construct a taxonomy of "discourse analyses" that includes predicate analysis (Milliken 1999), metaphor analysis (Yanow 1992a, 2000), deconstruction, genealogy, narrative analysis (see, e.g., Feldman et al. 2004 for one version), and so on—any method that problematizes the knowledge/power relationship. Many of these methods have their own philosophical sources—the reading practices issue, again—and separate citation traditions; others are used in various overlapping ways.

None of the chapters here reflect recent developments in the use of computers to analyze word data—Computer Assisted Qualitative Data Analysis Software (CAQDAS). We anticipate, as do most others who have thought critically about this trend (see Atkinson, Coffey, and Delamont 2003 for a discussion and citations), that the use of such software will continue to increase and expand as the software becomes more powerful and flexible and as the scholarly ranks begin to be filled with those generations who have "grown up" online. The advantages of computer-aided analysis—speed, comprehensive searching, the ability to construct complex searches using Boolean logic, and so on—will be powerful attractants. And yet, some of the potential hazards of such computer assistance in interpretive research are quite similar to those raised by other prepackaged, computer-based data-analysis programs: unreflective use of programs, failure to understand the assumptions built into particular programs, naive equation of the use of a program with substantive analysis, and so on. Other hazards are distinctive to interpretive research. As the chapters in this section attest, analysis is rarely a separate and final "stage," and to the extent that software contributes to such thinking, it does damage to the holistic research processes characteristic of interpretive studies. As important, the idea or image of interpretive data analysis should not be restricted to the kinds of "coding processes" enabled by such software. "Interpretive data analysis" includes much more than "coding," as, again, the chapters in this section vividly demonstrate. If software can aid particular projects or be useful for particular research questions, how much the better for interpretive researchers. But interpretive researchers do not need software programs for all the different kinds of questions they ask, nor do they need software programs to legitimize what they do. We have not included data-analysis software here because, in our experience, it does not replace the analytic thinking required of interpretive researchers.

That analytic thinking is amply evident in these "tales of analysis." We hope you find them as fascinating as we have.

NOTES

1. The particular epistemic communities in which authors operate may be inferred not only from chapter topics but also from citations referenced.

2. Science studies, also known as the sociology of scientific knowledge or as cultural studies of scientific knowledge, is a cross- or interdisciplinary approach comprising history, philosophy, and sociology-anthropology (see, e.g., Knorr Cetina 1999; Latour 1990, 1999; Traweek 1988). These divisions are reflected in several disciplinary associations, including SHOT (Society for the History of Technology), SPT (Society for the Philosophy of Technology), and SSSS (the Society for the Social Studies of Science), among others. Feminist theory also has a stream of work in this vein, including work exploring feminist methods. See, e.g., Harding 1986; Longino 1990; Schiebinger 1989; Tuana 1989. See also Pamela Brandwein (1999) and chapter 12 (this volume).

3. Which is not to say that we did not encounter differences of reading and writing practices here. From the perspective that sees writing itself as a method not only of world making but of argumentation, it was interesting to read historical writings against social science. In the writing practices of the latter, parenthetical (author-date) citations are wielded, rhetorically, as an integral part of the writing. Beyond proclaiming "Look whom I'm reading," they are invocations of authority used, often self-consciously and intentionally, to bolster an argument, if not to make it outright. The more humanities-inclined chapter authors in this collection, accustomed to placing citations in notes and notes at the foot of each page, where they become an integral part of one's reading but in a different way, found our editorial requirements strange, at the least.

4. Other policy-related analyses that see such conflicts as concerning broader national and/or group identity definitions and attendant power and status issues include Gusfield 1981; Stein 2004; Stevens 1999; and Yanow 1996, 2003a.

5. Mary Hawkesworth made many of these same points in her comments on the panel "Feminist Research Methods: What We Do and How We Do It" at the 2003 Western Political Science Association conference (March 27–29, Denver, Colorado). "Disruption" is her term.

6. Many of these have been treated by scholars in Europe (see, e.g., *Millennium: Journal of International Studies,* published by the London School of Economics and Political Science) and other non-U.S. locations. Web sites and pages change rapidly; it is hard to keep current. As of the time of this writing, we would mention the *International Journal of Qualitative Methods* based at the University of Alberta, Canada, and focused largely on health-related issues; the Critical Management Studies Workshop based at Lancaster University, UK (as well as the Critical Management Studies Division of the U.S.-based Academy of Management); and the European Group on Organization Studies and its journal *Organization Studies.*

CHAPTER 11

POLITICAL SCIENCE AS HISTORY: A REFLEXIVE APPROACH

Ido Oren

My dissertation, which I defended in 1992, was a mathematical and statistical study of arms races that fell well within the substantive and epistemological bounds of mainstream political science. A decade later, though, I published a book—Our Enemies and US: America's Rivalries and the Making of Political Science—*that questioned the very presuppositions of the science of politics into which I had been socialized. How did this intellectual shift come about?*

After the end of the Cold War, scholarly interest in the previously popular subject of the arms race waned. With the collapse of communism and the apparent spread of democracy, many scholars were intrigued by the prospect of a "democratic peace." By the mid-1990s, the proposition that democracies do not fight one another was gaining widespread acceptance. I was skeptical of the idea that peace between states was enhanced by the shared democratic character of their regimes, but had to admit that the statistical studies of the relationship seemed technically sound. To be effective, a critique of these studies would have to rest on a foundation other than their own scientific grounding.

In this context, a question crossed my mind: How did Woodrow Wilson perceive Imperial Germany—not in 1917, when he declared war "to make the world safe for democracy," but twenty to thirty years earlier? Wilson's legacy was embraced by proponents of the democratic peace thesis, and I thought that the thesis might be undermined if it turned out that Wilson's characterization of Germany as "autocratic" followed, rather than preceded, the German-American conflict. I vaguely knew that Wilson was a political scientist before he entered politics, but I knew little else about the history of political science. At that point, I was fortunate to have a colleague who offered me indispensable tutoring in disciplinary history and who suggested that my investigation might be profitably expanded to include John Burgess, founder of the first graduate school of political science in the United States.

In my research on arms races, I had come to appreciate the power of mathematical models to generate insights that might not have been apparent otherwise. As I immersed myself in the academic writings of Wilson and Burgess, I realized that historical investigation, different though it was from mathematical deduction, gave me a similarly exciting sense of discovery. To my fascination, I discovered that some of the concepts and categories habitually used by Wilson and Burgess had since become virtual taboos (e.g., "Aryan" and other racial categories) and that the present meaning of concepts such as "democracy" differs from the connotations they had a century ago.

Steeped as I was in the present-minded culture of political science, this conceptual elasticity was a revelation that offered a fresh vantage point from which to develop the critique of the democratic peace recapitulated in this chapter. That critique whetted my appetite for exploring the connection between U.S. political science and U.S. foreign relations in greater depth. It was in the course of that exploration—which resulted in Our Enemies and US—*that I realized that my earlier work was reflexive in orientation and that it constituted a radical challenge to political science epistemology as much as a substantive critique of the democratic peace proposition.*

America's identity has historically evolved in ways that made political enemies appear subjectively further and friends subjectively closer to it. . . . Current American social science is not insulated from this process. Polities have numerous objective dimensions by which they can be measured. The dimensions captured by the current empirical measures of democracy came to be selected through a subtle historical process whereby objective dimensions on which America resembled its enemies were eliminated, whereas those on which America differed the most from its enemies became privileged. Thus, the coding rules defining democracy are better understood as a time-bound product of America's historical international circumstances than as the timeless exogenous force that they are presumed to be.
—*Ido Oren* (1995, 268–69)

When American political science emerged as an academic discipline in the nineteenth century, it was institutionally and intellectually bound with the study of history. Francis Lieber, the Prussian-born political scientist who was picked by Columbia College in 1857 to inaugurate the chair in "History and Political Science," the first of its kind in the United States, took his title seriously. As Dorothy Ross observed, he "increasingly saw his task in political science as a historical one," and his "historico-politics defined a broad field on which scholars interested in history and politics could converge" (Ross 1991, 41; see also Farr 1993). The founders of the discipline's two leading graduate programs in the late nineteenth century—John W. Burgess, who succeeded Lieber at Columbia, and Herbert Baxter Adams at the Johns Hopkins University—remained firmly committed to a "practical union of History and Politics" (Adams, quoted in Ross 1991, 69). When the American Historical Association was founded in 1884, its ranks included Burgess, Adams, and other self-declared political scientists. Only in 1903 did the political scientists form their own professional association.

The historico-political scientists of the nineteenth century had two major analytical uses for history. First, they regarded history as a vast repository of facts and events that could be analyzed systematically to discover/verify political principles and generalizations. Lieber sought "to discern the laws of human society" in the historical record (Ross 1991, 40). In a *Memorial for Statistics* he submitted to Congress, he called for "careful collection of detailed [historical] facts, and the endeavor to arrive at general results [generalizations, in current parlance] by a comprehensive view of and judicious combination of them" (quoted in Farr 1993, 71). History, Lieber declared, was "continuous Statistik; Statistik, History arrested at a given period" (1993 [1858], 23).

Second, nineteenth-century political scientists commonly theorized history as a process of continuous change culminating in modern political institutions. In his inaugural address at Columbia, Lieber argued that:

Political science treats of man in his most important earthly phase; the state is the institution which has to protect or to check all his endeavors, and, in turn, reflects them. It is natural, therefore, that a thorough course of this branch should become, in a great measure, a delineation of the history of civilization, with all the undulations of humanity, from that loose condition of men in which Barth found many of our fellow beings in Central Africa, to our own accumulated civilization, which is like a rich tapestry, the main threads of which are Grecian intellectuality, Christian morality and trans-mundane thought, Roman law and institutionality, and Teutonic individual independence, especially developed in Anglican liberty and self-government. (1993 [1858], 32)

Similar historical accounts of the origins of American self-government were integral to the political theories of Burgess, Adams, Woodrow Wilson, and many of their peers.

Inasmuch as they theorized modern political institutions as part of a changing history, the students of historico-politics have assimilated the new "historicist" consciousness that crystallized in the West in the early nineteenth century, namely, the understanding of history as a "realm of human construction, propelled ever forward in time by the cumulative effects of human action, and taking new qualitative forms" (Ross 1991, 3). But, as Ross noted, the students of historico-politics "failed to reach a *reflexive* historicism" (1991, 262; emphasis added). In other words, they stopped short of reflecting on how the discourse of their own emerging discipline may have been embedded in the changing history they were theorizing. Although they were sensitive to the need to interpret political institutions and ideas in contextual historical terms, they failed to contextualize and historicize their own theoretical concepts.

After the establishment of the American Political Science Association in 1903, political scientists and historians gradually grew apart from each other. Departments of "History and Political Science" became rarer over time; political scientists increasingly published in separate journals and attended separate professional conferences. The estrangement was hastened by the growing acceptance within political science, from the 1920s onward, of the idea that the study of politics should be modeled after the natural sciences. The increased reliance on quantitative methods of political research, brought about by the "behavioral revolution" of the 1950s, further deepened the division between political science and history.

But the estrangement of political science from history should not be overstated. For even as political science was severing its institutional ties to the historical profession, and even as the discipline was becoming increasingly quantitative in orientation, political scientists often continued to find history analytically useful in the same two ways that their nineteenth-century predecessors had. First, political scientists never ceased viewing history as a vast repository of events that could be analyzed to verify generalizations. In fact, the advent of statistical methods and computer technology had only made the realization of Lieber's plan—"careful collection of [historical] facts, and the endeavor to arrive at general results"—more feasible than it had been during his lifetime. In the subfields of comparative politics and international relations (IR) in particular, massive efforts have been made to convert history into precisely the "continuous statistik" envisioned by Lieber. Scholars of comparative politics have developed systematic data sets of regime type, most notably the Polity data set, which stretches back to the turn of the nineteenth century.[1] These data sets have in turn been employed in numerous quantitative analyses of the causes and consequences of democracy. Similarly, IR scholars have published scores of statistical analyses employing the data gathered by the Correlates of War (COW) project; the COW data were created by gleaning from historical sources a multitude of facts related to international conflicts since 1815 and systematically quantifying these facts.[2]

Contemporary political science also contains significant traces of the second, historicist way in which nineteenth-century political scientists used history—explaining modern institutions as products of a continuous process of qualitative historical change. Historicist research programs have (re)emerged in the past half century in all the discipline's major subfields. In comparative politics, the predominant theory of the 1950s and 1960s, modernization theory, envisioned a trajectory of "development" from backwardness to modernity analogous in form, if not in substance, to nineteenth-century accounts of the origins of modern American institutions. In political theory, republican theorists have challenged the view that the U.S. Constitution reflected liberal-individualist values, arguing instead that "an important republican or communitarian tradition descended from the Greeks and Machiavelli through seventeenth-century England to the American Founders" (R. Putnam 1993, 87, describing the work of Pocock 1975, among others). Partly inspired by this republican-communitarian theory, Robert Putnam, in his famous *Making Democracy Work*, explained the thriving associational life of contemporary Northern Italy by tracing its origins to "a momentous time of transition on the Italian peninsula, nearly a thousand years ago, as Italians were emerging from the obscure era justly termed the Dark Ages" (R. Putnam 1993, 121). In IR, historically minded scholars produced rich accounts of the origins and evolution of the modern sovereign state (Barkin and Cronin 1994; Bartelson 1995; Kratochwil 1986; Reus-Smith 1999; Spruyt 1994). And in the field of American politics, institutional analysis has made a grand comeback in recent decades; although some proponents of the "new institutionalism" approached the subject from the ahistorical perspective of game theory, other scholars turned to history either in search of "master programs of order and regularity" in institutional development or in search of more "contingent temporal alignments and simultaneous movements of relatively independent institutional orderings" (Orren and Skowronek 1995, 306–7). The new historical institutionalism does not display the strong teleological character of the old historico-politics, but it does share with it the historicist understanding of history as a continuous process of qualitative change shaped largely by human actions.

Alas, Ross's criticism of historico-politics at the turn of the twentieth century—that it failed to reach a *reflexive* historicism—is equally applicable to political science at the turn of the twenty-first. Even though in the twentieth century a number of prominent social theorists developed reflexive modes of thinking (for example, Adorno 2000, esp. 145–49; Bourdieu and Wacquant 1992; Gouldner 1970; Horkheimer 1995), their theories had little resonance in the mainstream of American political science. Political scientists today are hardly more open than the founders of the profession to contextualizing and historicizing the concepts that constitute their disciplinary discourse. They scarcely reflect upon the possibility that the history of the study of politics may be intertwined with the history of the politics being studied.

A reflexive political science is a science that takes into account the historical position of its own scholarship. It is a science that theorizes historical political processes in ways that illuminate the relationship of these processes to the theoretical discourse of the discipline itself. The form that such a political science would take is difficult to imagine because, as I noted earlier, it has scarcely been tried. Still, we do have a few examples of reflexive analysis in the extant political science literature that may be used to give the reader an idea of how to approach such research and why it may be valuable (see Doty 1996, esp. chapter 7; Grunberg 1990; Long and Schmidt 2004; Oren 1995).

In what follows, I draw on one of these examples—my critique of the "democratic peace" proposition (Oren 1995; see also Oren 2003)—to sketch the contours of a reflexive historical approach to political research. I begin with an exposition of the democratic peace literature, focusing on the ways in which proponents of that thesis have analyzed history. I then contrast their analysis with my more reflexive mode of historical research. I will try to explain how I reoriented the research question, what historical sources I investigated to answer the question, what I looked for in these sources, and how my findings shed new light on the subject.

Before proceeding, I should confess that my graduate training in political science was rather conventional, and it did not introduce me to the idea of reflexivity. In fact, my critique of the democratic peace was not consciously conceived as an exercise in reflexive analysis; only after its publication did I discover the concept of reflexivity and come to see that my critique was reflexive in orientation. Thus, the reader should not regard my step-by-step presentation of the reflexive research process as a description of how my own research actually unfolded so much as a stylized, post hoc reconstruction of it. Nor should the reader regard my presentation as a recipe that could readily be applied across cases, issue areas, or time. A commitment to reflexive histori-cal analysis is more akin to an orientation of mind than a rigid program of research. It behooves the analyst to design, within the broad parameters of this orientation, a research strategy appropri-ate to the particularities of the question and the case(s) she seeks to investigate.

THE USES OF HISTORY IN DEMOCRATIC PEACE RESEARCH

In the past two decades, IR scholars have come to claim with growing frequency that democratic states rarely if ever go to war against each other. This claim—known as the "democratic peace proposition"—has become so widely accepted in the discipline (as well as in policy making circles) that IR scholars have repeatedly quoted, approvingly in most cases, a colleague who stated that "the absence of war among democracies comes as close as anything we have to an empirical law in international relations" (Levy 1989, 88). Dozens of quantitative studies have been devoted to analyzing this "empirical law" (prominent examples include Ray 1995; Russett 1993; Russett and Oneal 2001; Ward and Gleditsch 1998).

Quantitative analyses of the democratic peace generally involve three stylized steps. First, the analyst defines and operationalizes the dependent and independent variables stipulated by the proposition—peace (or war) and democracy (regime type), respectively. Second, based on such operational definitions, the analyst develops a quantitative database describing the incidence of conflict between states, their regime type, and other factors that putatively affect the likelihood of conflict between them (their relative military capabilities, for example). Each "dyad" of states receives numerical scores for each calendar year and, thus, this data-making procedure produces a very "large" 'n.' Third, analysts employ advanced statistical techniques to compare the incidence of conflict between democratic countries and its incidence between non-democracies, or between democracies and non-democracies. Overwhelmingly, they find that the data support the democratic peace proposition; that is, they find that—after controlling for the effects of putative confounding factors such as relative military capabilities—the likelihood of war between democracies is close to zero and that it is substantially smaller than its likelihood in non-democratic and mixed dyads.

Because systematic data collection requires an "immense effort" (Russett and Oneal 2001, 11), quantitative democratic peace researchers were fortunate to benefit from earlier efforts to convert historical facts into "continuous statistik," especially the COW and Polity projects. Bruce Russett and John Oneal, for example, acknowledged that "much of the data on militarized dis-putes, alliances, national capabilities, and international organizations originated with the Corre-lates of War project, founded by J. David Singer; we, like so many social scientists of international relations, owe a great debt to those who have labored in that project. We owe a similar debt to the Polity III project of Ted Robert Gurr and Keith Jaggers for information on types of national political systems" (2001, 11).

In the quantitative democratic peace literature, then, history functions primarily as a repository of raw facts that, having been laboriously harvested and processed into neatly packaged "data sets," serve to "test" the proposition. Regrettably, democratic peace researchers pay almost no attention to the possibility that the data against which the proposition is tested do not constitute neutral facts so much as artifacts shaped by the analytical concepts and "coding rules" that governed their collection and classification. Nor is any attention paid to the possibility that these analytical concepts and coding rules are themselves historical subjects more than objective instruments without a history.

Although most empirical analyses of the democratic peace employed quantitative techniques, several scholars sought to assess the proposition qualitatively, through an in-depth study of a small number of historical cases (Elman 1997; Owen 1994, 1997; Weart 1998). These scholars point out that quantitative analyses, though they effectively demonstrate a "correlation" between democracy and peace, "can neither explain the causal process that drives this correlation nor assess whether decision makers speak, write, and otherwise behave in a manner consistent with the theory's predictions" (Elman 1997, 474). Qualitative analysts thus set out to construct a "causal story linking the alleged cause, liberalism, to the effect, liberal peace" (Owen 1997, 11) and to "put the general theory to the test of detailed historical analysis: have leaders tended to act and think in ways consistent with the theory?" (Elman 1997, 33).

The case studies of the democratic peace are richer and more self-consciously historical than their quantitative counterparts. They approach history without the mediation of prepackaged data sets, and they attempt to reconstruct the world as it was seen through the eyes of past actors. Nevertheless, the logic of inference employed by case study scholars and the use they make of history are not radically different from those of the quantitative analysts. All qualitative scholars use the "controlled comparison" method, which, according to its chief proponent in IR, "resembles the statistical method in all respects," save for the small number of cases that do not "permit systematic control by way of partial correlations" (A. George 1979, 49). Indeed, virtually all case study scholarship of the democratic peace involves the formulation of hypotheses and their "testing" against the historical evidence (Ellman 1997, 1; Owen 1997, 57). Ultimately, then, history remains a storehouse of facts usable for the purpose of verifying generalizations. Qualitative analysts are hardly more reflective than quantitative researchers about the historical embeddedness of their own disciplinary discourse. They admirably attempt to historicize the analytical categories and perceptions held by foreign-policy decision makers but stop short of historicizing the categories and perceptions held by political scientists.

Contemporary political science, as I observed earlier, not only carries on Francis Lieber's "endeavor to arrive at general results" based on "careful collection of detailed facts" (quoted in Farr 1993, 71); it also exhibits traces of Lieber's twin endeavor to explain modern institutions as products of a process of historical change. The democratic peace literature illustrates the latter endeavor as much as the first. Implicit in this literature is a narrative of historical progress culminating in the realization of a modern zone of liberal peace. Michael Doyle originated this narrative in an influential article, published in 1983, in which he argued that Immanuel Kant's 1795 treatise *Perpetual Peace* provided the "best guidance" for grasping the liberal peace (Doyle 1996 [1983], 21). According to Doyle:

> Kant argued that the natural evolution of world politics and economics would drive mankind inexorably toward peace by means of a widening of the pacific union of liberal republican states. In 1795 this was a startling prediction. In 1981, almost two hundred years later, we can see that he appears to have been correct. The pacific union of liberal

states has progressively widened. Liberal states have yet to become involved in a war with one another. International peace is not a utopian ideal to be reached, if at all, in the far future; it is a condition that liberal states have already experienced with each other. (1996 [1983], 55)

Doyle proceeded to cautiously predict, by extrapolating from past rates of liberal-democratic expansion, that "global peace should be anticipated, at the earliest, in 2113" (1996 [1983], 57). His evolutionary narrative has become so widely accepted in the literature that IR scholars now commonly refer to "Kantian peace" (Oneal and Russett 1999), a "Kantian system" (T. Mitchell 2002), or "Kantian process" (Modelsky 1990, 1), interchangeably with liberal/democratic peace.

Some scholars delved even deeper into history than Doyle in search of the origins of the modern democratic peace. Russett (1993) attempted to discover its seeds in ancient Greece and in premodern societies, while Weart (1998) traced the evolution of the democratic peace from ancient Greece through medieval Italy and early modern Switzerland to the present international system.

Alas, none of these historical narratives reached reflexive historicism. Although they endowed the democratic peace with a history, they—much like the quantitative and qualitative analyses of history qua data—stopped short of historicizing *the science of* the democratic peace.

A REFLEXIVE CRITICAL ANALYSIS OF THE DEMOCRATIC PEACE

The term "reflexivity" derives from the Latin word *reflexus*—"bent backward"—and in social theory it generally refers to the turning of science back upon itself. For some of its proponents, the practice of reflexive social science pivots on the individual scholar. Alvin Gouldner (1970, 489), for example, argues that the social scientist must consciously seek "knowledge of himself and his position in the social world."

I, however, adhere to the view of Pierre Bourdieu—whose commitment to reflexivity stands out in the landscape of contemporary social theory—that the "primary target [of reflexive analysis] is not the individual analyst but the *social and intellectual unconscious* embedded in analytic tools and categories" (Bourdieu and Wacquant 1992, 36; emphasis in original). For Bourdieu, "reflexivity means, not intellectual introspection, but ongoing analysis and control of the categories used in the practice of social science" (Swartz 1997, 273). He urges social scientists to subject to systematic critique the "presuppositions . . . built into concepts, instruments of analysis (genealogy, questionnaires, statistical techniques etc.), and practical operations of research (such as coding routines, 'data cleaning' procedures, or rules of thumb in fieldwork)." This critique, Bourdieu insists, must include a historical dimension: "the history of sociology, understood as an exploration of the *scientific unconscious of the sociologist* through the explication of the genesis of the problem, categories of thought, and instruments of analysis, constitutes an absolute prerequisite for scientific practice" (Bourdieu and Wacquant 1992, 40, 213; emphasis in original).

Bourdieu's call for a critical, historical exploration of social scientific concepts and categories should not be confused with the agenda of political methodologists such as David Collier, who had repeatedly reminded political scientists that "discussions of research design . . . must pay central attention to conceptual issues" (Collier and Adcock 1999, 538). Collier thoughtfully analyzed methodological issues of concept formation, conceptual validity, conceptual "stretching," and the like (1993, 1997, 1999). But his analyses—critical and illuminating though they might be—do not involve the turning of social science back upon itself, as advocated by Bourdieu. The focus of Collier's work is on how to develop or choose the most appropriate analytical constructs

for grasping political processes, not on analyzing how these constructs themselves may be products of political processes. In other words, Collier's work stops short of investigating how past
politics may have left their marks upon the ostensibly neutral concepts employed by political
researchers. These marks constitute, in Bourdieu's language, an "intellectual unconscious embedded in [the] analytical categories and tools" of political science, and exposing them is the task
of a reflexive political science.

A reflexive critique of the democratic peace, then, would aim to uncover the "intellectual
unconscious" embedded in the operational definitions of democracy and/or peace and in the
coding rules employed by the collectors of the Polity and COW data. Rather than pose the conventional research questions—does the historical record support the democratic peace proposition, and does history contain the "seeds" of the modern democratic peace?—the first step in a
reflexive inquiry is to reorient the question toward the history of "democracy," or "peace." How
have past generations of political scientists understood and defined these analytical concepts,
how have their definitions of these concepts changed in time, and what was the politics of their
change? To what extent has historical change in the academic meaning of these political concepts
been shaped by historical change in international politics?

My critique (Oren 1995) focused on the concept of democracy. In the democratic peace literature, democracy is typically defined in terms of electoral process. For example, Russett and Oneal
define it as "a country where (1) most citizens can vote, (2) the government comes to power in a
free and fair election contested by two or more parties, and (3) the executive is either popularly
elected . . . or is held responsible to an elected legislature" (2001, 44). This definition is consistent
with, and builds upon, the analytic categories and coding rules employed by data-gathering projects
such as Polity. In the Polity data set, polities are coded on a scale that takes competitiveness and
fairness of electoral processes, as well as constraints on the freedom of executive action, as the
defining empirical features of democracy. A reflexive approach directs us to inquire whether the
understanding of democracy implicit in these coding rules is consistent with the ways in which
past generations of political scientists grasped this concept. And it directs us to wonder whether
these coding rules, and hence the data they order and classify, may have been shaped by the very
same history of international conflict that constitutes the empirical testing ground for the democratic peace proposition.

If the first step in a reflexive political analysis involves redirecting the investigation toward
disciplinary history, the second step is to select a set of past political scientists and texts to analyze. There is no general formula for making the selection—it rather depends on the research
question. Some substantive questions may call for a focus on nineteenth-century texts, whereas
other questions may be more effectively explored in the writings of more recent authors; some
questions may call for selecting past scholars who specialized in American institutions, while for
other questions it may be more appropriate to select past "area studies" specialists. For example,
if we seek to expose the "scientific unconscious" of contemporary research in African politics,
we should probably unearth the writings of past specialists in African colonial administration
and/or in issues of race. As a rule of thumb, it is often appropriate to select authors who, though
they may be forgotten today, enjoyed high professional standing in their lifetime, as attested by
indicators such as the honors their peers conferred upon them (presidency of the American Political Science Association, for example), the professional institutions they directed, or favorable
reviews of their books in professional journals. But even this rule of thumb is just that, not an iron
rule, for some questions may be tackled more effectively by recovering voices from the margins
of the profession. For example, a critical reflexive analysis of current theorizing of gender may be
enriched by exploring the careers of the handful of women who earned doctorates in political

science during the Progressive era and who "were steered to social work and reform activities or to the women's colleges, precincts the men were defining as outside the scientific and academic mainstream" (D. Ross 1991, 158). In sum, there is no universal procedure for deciding which texts to analyze; ultimately, it is incumbent upon the analyst to justify her selection in terms of its relevance to the substantive problem at hand and its potential for producing fresh insights into the problem.

In my critique of the democratic peace, I chose to focus on pre–World War I political science. That war looms large in the literature in two ways. First, current proponents of the democratic peace consciously draw inspiration from Woodrow Wilson's vision of a world made "safe for democracy," which he articulated when he declared war on "autocratic" Germany. For example, the motto of Russett's important book *Grasping the Democratic Peace* (1993, 3) is excerpted from Wilson's 1917 war message to Congress, in which Wilson contrasted American "self-government" to Germany's undemocratic system. Second, the "coding" of the case of World War I had generated controversy in the literature. Some early critics of the democratic peace thesis suggested that the regime of Imperial Germany exhibited democratic features and that the case of World War I may therefore constitute an important refutation of the claim that democracies do not fight each other. But proponents of the democratic peace, though they concede that Imperial Germany was a "difficult case" (Doyle 1996 [1983], 13), insist—much like Wilson did in 1917— that the German polity fell critically short of satisfying the criteria for liberal democracy. I wanted to compare this current understanding of Imperial Germany—which counterposes its regime to Anglo-American "democracy"—with the perceptions of Imperial Germany harbored by its contemporaries, for I thought that if I could show that the view of Germany as "autocratic" followed, rather than preceded, the onset of German-American rivalry, it would suggest that patterns of international conflict shape perceptions of "democracy" as much as the other way around. Because the German Imperial regime collapsed as a result of its defeat in the war, exploring how it was viewed by contemporaneous scholars required that I turn to texts written in the prewar years, especially in the years before the turn of the twentieth century, when a war between the United States and Germany was still unthinkable.

Of the political scientists who gained prominence in the profession in the late-nineteenth century, I chose to explore the careers of two important scholars: Woodrow Wilson and John W. Burgess. The rationale for studying Wilson had as much to do with his place in the democratic peace literature as with his stature as a political scientist. Because his legacy is firmly embraced by democratic peace scholars, it would have seriously undermined the credibility of their thesis if I were able to demonstrate that Wilson's portrayal of Imperial Germany in, say, 1890, was substantially more positive than the view he articulated when he declared war on it in 1917. Examining the political theory of John Burgess in addition to that of Wilson made the selection more representative of early American political science. Wilson and Burgess represent two distinct, if immediately successive, professional generations. Burgess was the most prominent member of the German-trained generation that founded professional political science in America whereas Wilson belonged to the first Ph.D. cohort "minted in America." Burgess taught at Columbia University whereas Wilson was trained at Johns Hopkins University, then Columbia's rival for the discipline's leadership. I made the case that Burgess and Wilson epitomized different shades of the theoretical concerns, political views, and professional experiences of mainstream American political scientists in the late nineteenth century.

The third step in a reflexive historical investigation constitutes its "meat and potatoes": a close, careful reading of past texts, primarily the books and journal articles produced by the selected authors. These materials can be found in any major research library and thus they are easily accessible. To the extent that the selected authors' private papers are available for inspection, and to the extent that traveling to the archive in which they are deposited is logistically and financially feasible, I would recommend exploring these papers in addition to the published materials. In my experience, consulting a scholar's private letters, lecture notes, or unpublished drafts is often helpful in clarifying his views and in interpreting his published texts.[3]

Wandering through the thousands of printed pages produced by prolific scholars such as Burgess and Wilson can be a tedious exercise unless it is disciplined and guided by our research questions. What specific questions we might pose to the texts would depend, of course, on our substantive research agenda. In my research into the "democratic" peace, I read the major theoretical texts written by Wilson and Burgess (and, in the case of Wilson, his personal papers) with the following questions in mind: (1) What were the criteria and norms relative to which Burgess and Wilson classified and compared political systems? (2) To the extent that they compared political systems relative to the norm of "democracy," how did they understand it, and how does their understanding differ from that which is implicit in the coding rules and definitions employed by democratic peace researchers? (3) How did Imperial Germany compare with England, France, and the United States based on the criteria employed by Burgess and Wilson? Did Germany appear to be more similar to the other polities relative to these contemporaneous criteria than it appears to have been relative to the norms implicit in the Polity data set?

The endeavor to answer research questions based on a close reading of texts is essentially an exercise in hermeneutic interpretation. According to Charles Taylor, interpretation is "an attempt to make clear, to make sense of an object of study. This object must, therefore, be a text, or a text-analogue, which in some way is confused, incomplete, cloudy . . . —in some way or another, unclear" (1977, 101). The texts written by Wilson and Burgess are "cloudy" in the sense that neither one of these scholars produced a concise essay that provides clear, exact answers to all my questions—after all, they had their own research questions to address, rooted in the historical and political context of their time. My job, thus, was tantamount to collating such an essay for them from the materials they *did* produce, that is, finding in these materials clues relevant to the questions at hand and piecing them together into a clear, coherent picture of the authors' views of Germany in a comparative perspective, their understanding of democracy, and so on.

In the preface to *The Order of Things*, Michel Foucault explained that the book arose out of a passage in Borges, in which the Argentinean author quoted from a Chinese encyclopedia that divided animals into the following categories: "(a) belonging to the Emperor, (b) embalmed, (c) tame, (d) sucking pigs . . . (n) that from a long way off look like flies." It is when we come across such strange categories of thought, Foucault argued, that we apprehend "the limitation of our own, the stark impossibility of thinking *that*" (1994, xv). Indeed, the most rewarding, even exciting, moments in analyzing old texts involve precisely such encounters with ideas and categories that prompt the analyst to wonder: "Did they really think *that*?" To me, realizing the centrality of racial categories of analysis in the political theories of Wilson and Burgess constituted such a revelatory moment. Did Burgess really believe that the "the United States also must be regarded as a Teutonic national state" or that "Teutonic political genius stamps the Teutonic nations as political nations *par excellence*, and authorizes them . . . to assume the leadership in the establishment and administration of states" (Burgess 1994, 39–40)?[4] Did Wilson really think that to understand the origins of modern government, one need not study the "savage" traditions of "defeated" primitive groups but rather the contributions of the "survived fittest," primarily the groups making up the Aryan race? Did he really admire the municipal "self-government" of Berlin, declaring that the German capital was not a foreign example but "a Pan-Teutonic example of processes that seemed to inhere in the ancient policy of the people to which we belong" (see Oren 1995, 286,

293)? It is precisely upon encountering such presently "impossible" thinking that one begins to see the limitations, the ahistoricity, of current democratic peace research. For if a century ago categories of political thought and classification were different than "democracy," as it is defined in the current democratic peace literature, in what way can a presumably timeless "empirical law" of a democratic peace apply to that era? By the same token, will this empirical law remain valid, and will anybody care or know about it, if, a hundred years into the future, Americans will have adopted new categories of thought that are hardly imaginable today?

As I indicated above, John Burgess classified nations based on their racial makeup as much as their regime type. He commonly portrayed the United States as a republic more than a democracy, and to the extent that he used the latter term, it denoted a constitutional republican polity, not an electoral process. Wilson, too, though he was more favorably disposed toward "democracy" than Burgess, did not conceptualize the term in a way that corresponds to the definition presently used in democratic peace research. Wilson was a Burkean conservative who, long before he pledged to make the world safe for democracy, strove to make democracy safe for the world by entrusting it to a professional managerial class. In his eyes, the civil service examination was an "eminently democratic" method of leadership selection. He defined democracy more in terms of its outcome—rule by "the men of the schools, the trained, instructed, fitted men"—than in terms of the procedure yielding that outcome (see Oren 2003, 174). Relative to Wilson's conception of "democracy" circa 1890, let alone relative to Burgess's ideal polity—a Teutonic, "democratic [read: constitutional] state with an aristocratic government" (Burgess 1994, 75)—Germany appeared then to be far more similar to the United States than it appears to have been in hindsight, when measured against the norms implicit in the Polity coding rules. Whereas in the Polity data set Imperial Germany is ranked significantly behind the United States, Britain, and France on the democracy scale, in the 1890s Wilson clearly regarded the German political system as superior to France's immature democracy, while for Burgess, "there [was] no state, large or small, in which the plane of civilization [was] so high" as in "the United States of Germany" (1915, 94).

The fourth and final step in a reflexive-historical research program, perhaps the most challenging one, is to develop an argument embedding the history of the analytical concepts we investigated in the politics they commonly serve to analyze. In other words, we need to explain how past political processes have shaped—in ways that present-day political scientists are "intellectual[ly] unconscious" of (Bourdieu and Wacquant 1992, 36)—the ostensibly objective concepts, categories, and coding rules current political researchers use to analyze these processes. Applied to democratic peace research, the challenge is to elaborate an argument explaining how the concept of "democracy" employed by the researchers is the product of the very same history of international conflict that serves as the empirical testing ground for the proposition.

My argument was that "democracy" should be interpreted as meaning "America," and that political scientists' claim of a democratic peace should hence be understood as a special case of a more general claim about peace among nations that are "America-like." The definition of democracy (that is, of the United States) manifest in the data sets employed by IR scholars is the product of a subtle historical process in which those aspects of the concept that made America resemble its enemies have been discarded, while those dimensions that magnified the distance between America and its enemies have become privileged. Thus, Burgess's vision of democracy qua constitutionalism became a casualty of World War I because, measured against its standards, constitutionless England appeared less democratic than Germany. Wilson's elitist, managerial vision of democracy survived the Great War and folded into technocratic visions of "democratic social control" elaborated by leading political scientists in the interwar years, only to be dealt a massive blow by the struggle against Nazism, which provided a vivid lesson in the perils of managerial efficiency. Visions of "industrial democracy" and "democratic planning" that enjoyed substantial resonance in the discipline during the Great Depression gave way during the cold war to the procedural view of democracy, not least because these visions affirmed ideals to which "people's democracies" laid claim too. The conception of democracy implicit in the Polity coding rules and, by extension, in democratic peace research reflects the procedural vision of democracy that triumphed during the cold war.

When the "regime type" data created by these coding rules are unreflexively projected upon the international history that gave rise to them, it should not be surprising that the proposition that "America-like countries do not fight each other" assumes the appearance of an "empirical law." After all, the concept of a democratic peace was shaped by the very same historical patterns of war and peace that, transformed into "data" or "cases," are being used to validate the concept. My argument consequently reveals that the democratic peace proposition has a tautological quality. Political scientists' classification of countries as "democracies" is as much a product of the (past) peacefulness of these countries in relation to one another as the peacefulness of these countries is a product of their shared democratic character.

CONCLUDING THOUGHTS

My analysis of the "democratic" peace proposition illustrates how a reflexive approach can yield insights that are counterintuitive and nonconventional from the standpoint of the discipline's mainstream approach. More fundamentally, it illustrates how a reflexive approach to theories and concepts in social science can expose the limits—indeed, demonstrate the futility—of aspirations to uncover objective truth claims that are valid across time and space. In the case of the democratic peace, a proposition that the discipline's mainstream views as a timeless "empirical law" is shown by my reflexive analysis to be but a timebound thesis rooted in particular historical and political circumstances peculiar to the late-twentieth-century United States. It is not implausible to expect that by the late twenty-first century, political science, if it still exists as an academic discipline, may be different than it is today—its geographical center of gravity may shift away from the United States, its practitioners may develop new understandings of "democracy," or they may discard the concept altogether. To them, the notion of a "democratic peace" may appear as strange as Wilson's claim that "not universal suffrage constitutes democracy" or Burgess's portrayal of the United States as a "Teutonic national state" appear to us today.

But what if the reader of our reflexive analysis—say, a person committed to the idea of political or social science *qua* science—does not "buy" our argument? What if the reader "does not 'see' the adequacy of our interpretation" (Taylor 1977, 103)? As Taylor pointed out, "we can only convince an interlocutor if at some point he shares our understanding of the language concerned." If he remains firmly committed to the positivist, empiricist conception of social science, if he does not come to share our reflexive orientation, then "there is no further step to take in rational argument; we can try to awaken these intuitions in him, or we can simply give up" (Taylor 1977, 103–4). Ultimately, there is no neutral, value-free way of adjudicating between textual readings or judgments.

To the empirical mainstream of political and social science, of course, such subjectivity is intolerable. Mainstream political and other social scientists firmly believe that they can get beyond subjectivity by turning historical events and facts into "brute data"—the Polity data, for example—and using these data to verify "empirical laws," such as the democratic peace. Alas, my reflexive analysis suggests that the attempt to escape from subjectivity is bound to fail, for the data, rather than being the brute units of information devoid of judgment that their users presuppose them to be, in fact bear the marks of value judgments and interpretations rooted in the politics of days past. A reflexive examination of empiricist political science reveals it to be as subjective and value laden as the interpretive approaches it rejects, if not as honest about its character.

NOTES

1. The Polity data collection project was founded in the late 1960s by Ted Robert Gurr, who sought to "provide coded information on political institutions for all independent states from 1800 to the present" (Gurr biographical sketch, at www.cidcm.umd.edu/bio.asp?id=10 [accessed October 21, 2005]). The project is currently in its fourth phase (Polity IV). It is housed at the University of Maryland's Center for International Development and Conflict Management, where researchers continue to update the data series. Information on the procedures Polity researchers use to code political regime characteristics, as well as the resulting data, can be accessed at the Polity IV Web site, www.cidcm.umd.edu/inscr/polity/ (accessed October 21, 2005). The Polity project is not related to the journal bearing the same name.

2. The COW project was founded in the 1960s by J. David Singer of the University of Michigan, who directed it for many years. It is now housed at Pennsylvania State University. The COW data, coding procedures, information about the project's history, and a bibliography of the numerous quantitative studies that employed the COW data can be accessed at www.correlatesofwar.org.

3. Fortunately for me, the fact that Woodrow Wilson's papers have been edited and published in a multivolume series lessened my need to travel to Princeton University, where the papers are archived. Due to financial constraints, I was unable to consult Burgess's personal papers, archived at Columbia University Libraries.

4. Burgess's major theoretical book, *Political Science and Comparative Constitutional Law,* was published in 1890. This quotation is taken from an abridged version of that book, published posthumously in 1933 and reissued in 1994. Burgess prepared the abridged version before World War I, but a contract to publish it was rescinded during the war because of the author's pro-German sympathies.

CHAPTER 12

STUDYING THE CAREERS OF KNOWLEDGE CLAIMS

Applying Science Studies to Legal Studies

PAMELA BRANDWEIN

Constitutional law has traditionally been the turf of political scientists and law professors, and so, given that interest, I majored in political science and initially planned to go to law school. I ended up with a Ph.D. in sociology because I decided to follow the advice of my undergraduate advisor, Kim Scheppele, a sociology–political science hybrid, and pursue graduate studies under one of her mentors, the sociologist Arthur Stinchcombe. Art later told me I was an "odd" sociologist, and I suspect the label still holds.

I arrived in graduate school deeply interested in civil rights law and already sold by the argument that the meaning of the Fourteenth Amendment was constructed and not "found." My early interest in gender studies, which revealed the socially constructed nature of gender categories, made this seem obvious to me. So did Berger and Luckmann's The Social Construction of Reality, *which I had also read as an undergraduate. But although legal scholars were routinely emphasizing the constructed nature of legal discourse, I found myself drawn to the "how" questions. Yes, legal discourse was constructed, but how? How were legal meanings constructed? How were they contested? How did aspects of society get "into" law? The sociology of law, which focused mainly on the work of lawyering, did not take up these questions. Neither did the law and society literature, which at that time did not focus on constitutional law. The judicial politics literature in political science was least helpful, as it remained dominated by the behavioral tradition that swept the discipline in the 1950s. Legal historians, at least, situated legal decision making in its historical context, and I gleaned as much as I could from their work.*

As I was in a sociology department, I turned to the sociology of knowledge to find research tools. I got lucky when Susan Leigh Star, a scholar in a field I had never heard of, the sociology of scientific knowledge, interviewed for a position in the department. Following the footnotes in her work, I found my way to various corners of the science studies literature. I have been lucky, though, not once but twice. A university colleague and political theorist, Douglas Dow, introduced me to the Cambridge School methods of Pocock and Skinner, two historians of political discourse. Because I was not formally trained in either science studies or Cambridge School methods, I did not want to be vulnerable to the criticism that I was using these methods in a dilettante-ish way. I did my homework and sought out a set of readers whose areas of expertise combined to cover all the areas in my work. I am still cobbling together a set of research tools that feels right to me; it is a tool kit that clearly did not come prepackaged.

> What is it in competing knowledge claims that renders them more or less
> institutionally "credible" at any particular historical juncture? By drawing
> from science studies, we can map trajectories of credibility that attach to
> knowledge claims in the world of academic law. We can see how institutional
> pressures and forces work to privilege certain knowledge claims over others.
> —*Pamela Brandwein* (2000, 11)

It is comforting to think that the success or failure of a knowledge claim in the academic world is a result of its intrinsic merit or lack thereof. Contestable, if not dubious, knowledge claims, however, have gained institutional victories and maintained their dominance for extended periods. Consider, for example, a famous scholarly dispute between two law professors, Charles Fairman (1949) and William Crosskey (1954). Fairman and Crosskey debated the history of the Fourteenth Amendment, specifically whether its privileges or immunities clause[1] originally applied the Bill of Rights to the states. Law professors often refer to this debate as the incorporation debate, as in: Did the Fourteenth Amendment (1868) originally incorporate the Bill of Rights, that is, apply it to the states? The Bill of Rights was part of the original Constitution, and the Supreme Court had said in 1833 that it applied only to the federal government.[2]

Fairman argued that the Fourteenth Amendment did not originally apply the Bill of Rights to the states, and his nonincorporation thesis buttressed the view of the Supreme Court, which had taken a nonincorporation position in the 1870s.[3] Crosskey argued against Fairman, asserting that the Amendment did in fact incorporate the Bill of Rights. At the time, Fairman won this debate easily and his account enjoyed wide success. His article became an instant source of authority on the Fourteenth Amendment for those who followed, including legal scholar Alexander Bickel. Bickel was clerk and protégé to Justice Felix Frankfurter, who himself had asserted a nonincorporation position in *Adamson v. California* (1947). In a well-known article, Bickel (1955, 5) cited Fairman's article and gave this simple comment: "Fairman demonstrated that the argument [for incorporation] was based on a misreading." For Bickel, this was enough. The matter was closed (for now).

Fairman's institutional "win" was not a product of the intrinsic merit of his account. The documentary evidence did not demand Fairman's victory. In fact, there was a closer fit between Crosskey's history and the historical evidence. Fairman's account contained significant anachronisms, which Crosskey had escaped. Only recently, though, has Crosskey's history begun to gain acceptance (Amar 1992; Aynes 1993; Curtis 1986).

How can we explain the initial success of Fairman's account? What explains the recent upswing in the trajectory of credibility that attaches to Crosskey's account? In short, how can we investigate the "careers" of these competing knowledge claims?

This chapter outlines a set of techniques for investigating the careers of competing knowledge claims—that is, the processes by which some knowledge claims come to "win" institutionally, while others fail to do so. The problem of meaning is central here, for we are dealing with dueling interpretations of word-based data, for example, the Reconstruction debates,[4] political speeches,[5] judicial correspondence,[6] and Supreme Court decisions themselves.[7] Since there is no neutral standpoint for determining the meanings of these historical texts, they become contested ground. Scholarly constructions of meaning and the careers of these meanings become open to sociohistorical analysis. It is one of the more difficult tasks of social science to connect the study of meaning construction to the analysis of institutions. The methods outlined here supply tools for this job.[8]

In order to investigate how contestable knowledge claims gain institutional credibility, the first order of business is to study how competing meanings of documentary data are first built. For this task, the metaphor of a "frame" is exceptionally useful. A frame refers to a collection of taken-for-granted assumptions and beliefs. As described in more detail below, these cognitive elements shape the way documentary data are ordered and organized, that is, made meaningful.

Studying the reception of knowledge claims is the second order of business, and this requires linking the study of frames to the study of institutions. Particular knowledge claims must be connected to particular interpretive communities (a concept discussed below), as well as various institutional forces and pressures. In order to study the reception of dueling knowledge claims, this chapter draws from a literature called the sociology of scientific knowledge, or simply science studies, as this literature has developed techniques for studying the production and accreditation of knowledge. In adapting the methods of science studies to the study of constitutional law, I show how we might study the social and institutional settings in which knowledge claims in the legal academy meet and compete for credibility. With this second set of methods in hand, the careers of knowledge claims—that is, their trajectories of credibility—become amenable to investigation. The concept of a career implies action over time, and science studies methods permit us to relate changing assessments of credibility to changing institutional environments.

These techniques, it should be noted, position researchers to investigate the complex feedback loops that exist between the legal academy and the Supreme Court. Critically, cross-institutional dynamics between the legal academy and the Court help give rise to prevailing legal orthodoxies. Historical and doctrinal orthodoxies hold enormous symbolic power when it comes to the justification of Fourteenth Amendment decisions due to the unique institutional "grammar" of legitimacy that pertains to the Court. According to this grammar, only certain forms of constitutional argument are considered legitimate: historical, doctrinal, textual, structural, and prudential (Bobbitt 1982). The methods outlined here position researchers to study how "winning" claims in the legal academy influence the Court and help give rise to legal orthodoxies about history and doctrine. We are ultimately dealing, then, with the worlds of both academic law and Supreme Court decision making.

Indeed, there are connections between the techniques outlined here and the interpretive-historical approach to Supreme Court decision making that within the public law community is increasingly being called "New Historical Institutionalism" (NHI).[9] In brief, NHI explores how institutional contexts shape judicial decisions. Moving beyond a view of institutions as either facilitating or impeding the exogenously formed policy preferences of justices (Epstein and Knight 1998), NHI scholars have developed a conceptualization of legal institutions as "constitutive" in nature (Brigham 1987; McCann 1994). In one of the founding essays of NHI, Rogers Smith (1988) argues that legal institutions are independent influences in Court decision making, creating distinctively "legal" values, perspectives, and rhetorics of justification. The deliberate behavior of Court justices, Smith explains, becomes understandable only in the context of institutionally constituted purposes and perspectives.

The methods of science studies and frame analysis provide a systematic and empirical way of investigating this constitutive process "in action." Indeed, these methods are enormously useful to the study of constitutional development and cross-institutional impacts on the Court, major concerns of NHI (Epp 1999; Graber 1991; Kahn and Kersch 2006; Lovell 2003; Novkov 2001). As NHI seeks to explain constitutional change with reference to shifts in institutionally constituted purposes and perspectives,[10] a methodological focus on the careers of knowledge claims is especially suitable toward this end. Convergence between NHI and the methods outlined here—a convergence rooted in the shared treatment of legal institutions as constitutive, porous, and dynamic—is thus one of the notable features of this essay.

At this point, a more extended introduction to frame analysis and science studies is in order. Following these introductions are two applications that demonstrate the use (and usefulness) of these interpretive-historical methods.

FRAME ANALYSIS

The concept of an interpretive framework or "frame" has been used by scholars across a variety of disciplines to illuminate the problem of meaning (see e.g., Bateson 1972; Burke 1965 [1935]; Fish 1980; Goffman 1974; Rein 1983; Schon and Rein 1994). This work holds in common the idea that individuals hold frameworks of interpretation, which select and organize among raw experiential data, thereby making it meaningful. Frames are sets of taken-for-granted assumptions. These sets of assumptions shape understandings of reality or "definitions of the situation" (W.I. Thomas 1923).[11]

This constructivist idea that understandings of reality are prefigured by interpretive frameworks can be traced back to Mannheim's sociology of knowledge (1985 [1936]) and the work of William James (1950 [1869]). For sociologists, this constructivism has found well-known expression in the phenomenology of Schütz (1962) and Berger and Luckmann (1966). In political science, the idea of a frame has been utilized in policy studies. Drawing on the work of Yanow (1995a) and others, Swaffield (1998, 205) has used the concept of framing to analyze the "points of view" that attach to competing policy prescriptions in a comparative context. In a U.S. policy context, Linder (1995) has isolated the discursive elements that underlie competing problem definitions. Linder's attention to underlying discursive elements is significant, for in order to study interpretation as a process, we must maintain an important analytic distinction.

This analytic distinction is between baseline categories of thought (taken-for-granted beliefs and assumptions) and the interpretive products of these categories (definitions of the situation). When an individual confronts and construes a situation, baseline categories shape the way this situation is made meaningful. For example, a baseline belief in essential sex differences produces the view that sex segregation in the workplace is natural and inevitable. Alternatively, a baseline belief that gender roles are socially constructed produces the view that sex segregation is an expression of social hierarchy and not inevitable. In both cases, beliefs about gender (baseline categories) shape a view of the origins and fairness of sex segregation (a definition of the situation).[12]

In using the term "frame," some political scientists have blurred this analytic distinction between baseline assumptions and their interpretive products. Schon and Rein (1994, 23), for example, define frames as "underlying structures of belief, perception, and appreciation."[13] Because they use one concept, a frame, to encompass both baseline categories of thought and their products, the process of interpretation is hidden.[14]

There are other reasons the analytic distinction between baseline categories of thought and their products should be maintained. By analytically isolating these baseline categories, it becomes possible to show how authors use a single set of assumptions to produce knowledge claims in a variety of contexts. Scholars, after all, tend to make claims about a variety of things. A discursive relationship between these knowledge claims can then be identified through their parent assumptions.

Thus, frame analysis, as defined here, requires the analytic isolation of taken-for-granted assumptions and beliefs, that is, categories of thought. This can be done by logical inference. Analyzing the structure of the logic of an author's argument, which includes the author's interpretation of evidence, can yield an understanding of the conceptually prior assumptions and beliefs that shaped that interpretation and argument. Indeed, the exercise of deducing an author's assumptions from a variety of their published works and finding similarities across them increases confidence that these categories of thought are really there and not the figment of the researcher's imagination. These deductions are, nonetheless, certainly up for question, and so scrutiny by other researchers serves to increase the sense of their validity.

Frame analysis also requires an explanation of how categories of thought work together to shape perception and define a situation. It must be illustrated how cognitive categories operate to organize, shape, and classify raw experiential material, that is, make it meaningful. In detailing this process of meaning construction, it must be shown how the process of constructing meaning is, simultaneously, a process of constraining meaning. As Burke stated, "[E]very way of seeing is also a way of not seeing" (1965 [1935], 49). Fish (1980, 356) has made the same point: "[W]ithin a set of interpretive assumptions, to know what you can do is, ipso facto, to know what you can't do; indeed, you can't know one without the other; they come together in a diacritical package, indissolubly wed."

Yet another part of frame analysis is the specification of overlap between competing frames. Though divergence in frames is more easily spotted than overlap, it remains important to mark out this overlap. The overlap is what permits people with divergent definitions of a situation to interact within one "conversation" (e.g., an academic dispute or policy dispute). Divergence in frames may lead participants in a dispute to "talk past" each other, but the overlap is what permits participants to engage in the conversation in the first place, even if they come to see themselves as engaging in a dispute. Agreement that certain rules apply to the dispute—for example, no ad hominem attacks—may also be a feature of overlap. In general, overlap marks out the boundaries of dispute. In a legal dispute, for example, all participants might hew to the institutional "grammar" of legitimacy, making arguments based on original intent, legal precedent, and so on, even if their interpretations of original intent or precedent are divergent.

A frame analysis, finally, might integrate a dimension of action and purpose. Although Schon and Rein's concept of framing (1994) is problematic because it blurs the analytic distinction between baseline categories of thought and their products, they have usefully introduced the dimension of action into a theory of framing. In earlier work, Rein (1983) has insisted on the importance of including purpose and action as essential parts of the knowing, naming, and thinking process. "A frame is a way of describing how people think about reality *and* linking this description to human purposes" (1983, 101, emphasis added). A frame denotes "the perspective by which we see reality and act on it. . . . A frame is broader than a theory because it contains the normative action implications of a theory and the interests served by it" (1983, 97). Yanow (1995a), too, integrates a dimension of action into her frame analysis, conceptualizing frames as both models of prior thought and models for subsequent action. This integration of action and purpose into frame analysis makes eminent sense because, in real life, purposes attach to the use of cognitive categories. We must remember, though, that many different actions and purposes can attach to a single set of baseline categories. Again, an analytic distinction must be preserved, this time between the use of cognitive categories and actions/purposes.

By following Schon, Rein, and Yanow, and integrating perspective and purpose into a concept of framing, we may expand the scope of problems in public law that frame analysis might reach. Judicial purpose is primary among them, for, as Gillman (1999) has emphasized, judicial purposes are institutionally constituted no less than perspectives. The purposes of legal actors, in construct-ing or invoking particular knowledge claims, become subject to investigation as well.

SCIENCE STUDIES

The metaphor of a frame is useful for studying the construction of knowledge claims, but we need additional tools to study the institutional reception of knowledge claims. For this, we can look to science studies, which treats the production of scientific knowledge as a social activity. Challeng-ing the standard view of science—that scientific knowledge is determined by the actual nature of the physical world and is therefore not amenable to social analysis—science studies takes the character of scientific knowledge as its province of inquiry.[15] The focus of attention is the way in which scientific knowledge comes to be produced and accredited.

A mainstay in science studies is the study of fact making and the investigation of successful scientific theories (see, e.g., Latour and Woolgar 1988; Star 1988; Woolgar 1988). Although traditional interpreters of the history of science have explained facts and successful theories by their intrinsic merits, science studies researchers have taken a different approach. They refute the possibility of a distinction between "internalist" explanations of scientific knowledge, which point to the natural unfolding of ideas, and "externalist" explanations of knowledge, which point exclu-sively to societal and political factors. Emphasizing that the success of a knowledge claim is partially but not exclusively dependent on the logical tenets of the claim itself, science studies researchers conceptualize successful knowledge claims as institutional artifacts.

The concept of work permits science studies researchers to refuse the internal/external distinc-tion. We do not usually think of knowledge production as work, but science studies researchers fruitfully treat scientific fact making and theorizing as forms of work. Like all forms of work, the work of science involves habits of thought, routines, and encounters with uncertainties. And, like other forms of work, scientific work is situated within institutional contexts characterized by networks, status hierarchies, and resource competitions. The concept of work, then, is uniquely configured to interface with both the dynamics of meaning construction and the dynamics of institutions. The concept of work has been developed by sociologists, and so it is likely to be a new thing to many political scientists.

To investigate the work of knowledge production, Susan Leigh Star sums up the methodologi-cal directives for researchers: "Try to understand the processes of construction and persuasion entailed in producing any narrative, text, or artifact. Try to understand these processes over a long period of time. . . . Understand the language and meanings of your respondents, link them with institutional patterns and commitments and, as Everett Hughes said, remember that 'it could have been otherwise'" (1988, 198). Hughes's point is central as it helps ward off the tendency to treat current arrangements as inevitable.

Law professors, like scientists, are involved in claims making, and so Star's directives are applicable to the study of knowledge production in academe. The refusal of an internal/external distinction in science studies is especially applicable to the study of legal knowledge given the constitutive and porous nature of legal institutions.[16]

Star's directive to understand the language and meanings of respondents is especially worth noting because it opens the door to a marriage of science studies and frame analysis. Such a marriage, however, requires an additional concept: an interpretive community. A shared interpre-tive framework identifies or defines individuals as members of an interpretive community (Fish 1980, 320, 331–35). The operations (thinking, seeing, and reading) of the extending agents who make up these interpretive communities are similarly enabled and constrained.[17] Interpretive communities are the institutional sponsors of specific frames, and identifying the amount of resources that accompany sponsorship is central to studying the careers of knowledge claims. I will return to this point shortly.

We should first, however, bring in the notion of commitment or "interest." Swaffield (1998, 206), for example, uses the metaphor of a frame to link individual language use to broader groupings of attitudes and interests, described by Sabatier (1988) as advocacy coalitions. In showing that contests over the meaning of particular terms in the policy arena express different advocacy positions and that policy advocacy is linked to broader patterns of interest, Swaffield (1998, 200) explains that "the challenge for policy analysis is to develop methods of interpretation which reveal the significance of [plural meanings]."

The same challenge applies in legal studies. In examining the significance of competing knowledge claims in the legal academy, we must first link frames with interpretive communities. How can researchers identify members of interpretive communities? One way is to identify shared assumptions embedded in research products (papers, articles, and books). Another way is to examine citation patterns and acknowledgments. It also pays to track down the institutional affiliations of major contributors to the discourses with which one is concerned. If one is studying an interpretive community that is tied to an academic center of unusual influence (say, a particular law school, a center for survey research methods, or a center noted for a particular diagnostic approach), others are likely to have studied these academic centers (Kalman 1986; Seligman 1978). These studies are good resources for identifying interpretive communities, as are intellectual histories of academic disciplines (e.g., D. Ross 1991).

Once frames are linked to interpretive communities, the next step is to attend to institutional resources held by interpretive communities. The institutional power of interpretive communities is a key variable here, for this power can privilege even weak knowledge claims. Indicators of power—that is, control of institutional resources such as faculty positions and symposia funds, placement of students as law clerks, prestige of university affiliations, and individual reputation—must be identified. Prestige and reputation are a significant though intangible resource, and they are hard to measure. Publications in "top" law journals are also an important resource and more easily identified (though of course the definition of "top" may be contested). For legal academics, as for academics generally, networks among members of interpretive communities nourish the knowledge claims of their members. Networks are of enormous help in the accumulation of academic currency (e.g., citations, jobs, officer standing in professional organizations, editorships, contributions to edited volumes, etc.), and this currency can support knowledge claims in both direct and indirect ways.

Of course, "losing" claims are also attached to particular interpretive communities. By focusing on the networks among the losers, we can study the accessibility and transmission of perspectives that may, one day, gain in credibility. Indeed, one might do a comparative analysis between winning and losing sides on an issue at one point in time, in terms of their relative "assets." A key point to remember is that conventional knowledge and dominant perspectives often inspire resistance, and it is important to identify the ways heterodox perspectives survive and circulate.

A key question remains to be discussed. This chapter has referred to Fairman's win in the 1950s. But what is the evidentiary basis for such a claim? For researchers interested in studying competition among knowledge claims, there are several things to look for in determining who "wins." One major indicator is that subsequent adherents to the winner's position will offer a reduced defense of that position. As we saw previously, a simple citation to Fairman's article was sufficient for Alexander Bickel. When mention of the losing claim disappears, this signals that the contest is no longer even recognized. Ratcheted up defenses of viewpoints are also important signals. If adherents to a viewpoint defend it more zealously than did previous adherents, this may be a signal that the viewpoint has been destabilized. Of course, it is wise to think of credibility along a continuum and not in dichotomous terms. In general, citation patterns hold major clues about the balance of credibility that attaches to specific knowledge claims.

The significance of a win is the final thing that researchers must address, for researchers must explain why it matters that one claim wins and not another. How, then, can the significance of a win be assessed? By looking at what later legal actors *do* with this now-established knowledge claim. What legal results are justified by legal academics and by the Court with citations to this knowledge claim? What social groups benefit from these results? Answering these questions is another way of connecting contests over meaning to social arrangements and the distribution of resources.

In sum, the major steps to take when investigating the career of a knowledge claim include:

- isolate the underlying interpretive framework;
- explain how it enables and constrains meaning;
- identify the balance of credibility that attaches to the knowledge claim;
- link the underlying framework to its sponsoring interpretive community;
- identify the resources and commitments of this sponsoring interpretive community;
- follow the balance of credibility over time and connect it to shifting institutional arrangements; and
- explain the significance of a win or loss at each stage in its career.

Lastly, before moving on to applications of these methods, it is worthwhile to briefly address questions about the validity and trustworthiness of interpretive research on framing and the careers of knowledge claims. In their study of framing, Schon and Rein (1994, 41) worry that there is "no reasonable basis for deciding among . . . frames, all of which may be internally consistent and compelling in their own terms and, hence, equally worthy of choice." They refer to these concerns as the "relativist trap."[18]

Other theorists, however, provide ways out of this trap. In a more general context, Stanley Fish (1989a, 1989b) has argued that there are limits on reflexivity and that these limits explain why a researcher can confidently make knowledge claims while advancing a theory of knowledge in which all meaning is contingent and provisional.[19] In the context of competing knowledge claims about historical texts, the subject of this chapter, Cambridge School historians of political discourse (Ball and Pocock 1988; Ball, Farr, and Hanson 1988; Pocock 1985, 1987; Skinner 2002) are perhaps more helpful. Their methods provide a way of refereeing among competing legal-historical knowledge claims. They supply a set of criteria for establishing the trustworthiness of certain historical readings over others.[20] The use of such methods can reveal anachronisms in the winning knowledge claims of legal academics, and these anachronisms can serve as a valid basis for rejecting these claims.[21]

TWO APPLICATIONS

The following two applications apply, if only in skeletal fashion, the methods of frame analysis and science studies. The legal academy is at the center of the first application, whereas the Supreme Court is more visible in the second application. The applications work as a pair for an additional reason. There is an impulse to regard the recognition of a previously rejected and historically worthy claim, such as Crosskey's, in the first example, through a lens of justice and fairness. The second application is offered, in part, as an antidote to this impulse.

Legal Orthodoxy and the History of the Fourteenth Amendment

The first application of these interpretive methods involves the debate with which this chapter began. This debate was between Charles Fairman and William Crosskey over whether the Fourteenth Amendment originally applied the Bill of Rights to the states. For both Fairman and Crosskey, the process of making the documentary evidence meaningful was ordered, though by different mechanisms. Space constraints prevent me from detailing the content of Fairman's and Crosskey's frames and the way their frames structured their interpretation of the documentary evidence.[22] It will have to be enough to note that their frameworks structured their sense of relevant evidence. Their frameworks shaped where they looked for evidence of framers' intent, when in history they began looking,[23] and how they knew when they had found it. In short, the play of symbolic structures that made up each of their frames organized different definitions of appropriate investigative techniques and faithful readings of the evidence.

How do we know that Fairman's account was dubious? By applying the methods of historians of political discourse. Pocock and Skinner focus attention on the use of language in institutional settings, and by language, they do not mean ideologies or arguments. Rather, languages are vocabularies and concepts that develop over time, shaped by institutional actors. Pocock and Skinner focus on what historical actors do with language, in order to arrive at the historical meaning of texts.[24]

In the present case, Fairman, writing in the mid-twentieth century, did not understand the nineteenth-century vocabulary of the Republican framers of the Fourteenth Amendment. Among other things, he judged Republican references to the Civil War as an "inapt way" to express intent to incorporate the Bill of Rights (Brandwein 1996, 307–9). Although such references may have been inapt in 1949, they were not in 1866. Indeed, we can understand the historical meaning of these Civil War references by studying the way Republicans used them in conjunction with criticism of Southern suppression of civil liberties and criticism of *Barron v. Baltimore* (1833), the Court decision ruling that states need not guarantee the civil liberties listed in the Bill of Rights. Debate over the Southern suppression of civil liberties was a central element of slavery politics, and Fairman's account was weaker due to anachronisms that led him to "miss" references to this civil liberties debate.

Despite Fairman's historical errors, various institutional arrangements and forces worked to privilege his account. Situated institutional players made up the audience for the Fairman/Crosskey dispute, and these actors brought a range of institutional pressures to bear. Most significantly, Fairman belonged to a Harvard-based interpretive community, which carried enormous prestige at the time. This interpretive community was the institutional sponsor of Fairman's frame. This Harvard network included Justice Felix Frankfurter, who condemned an earlier presentation of the incorporation thesis by Justice Hugo Black in *Adamson v. California*.[25] Frankfurter was mentor to Henry Hart, who also had ties to Harvard. Hart (1954) was the author of an influential negative review of Crosskey's 1953 book, *Politics and the Constitution*, which damaged Crosskey's reputation as a legal historian. Other reviews of this book (Brant 1954; Goebel 1954) were also damaging. Indeed, it is highly likely that institutional audiences were predisposed to think negatively of Crosskey's work. Still, even if Crosskey's reputation had emerged intact from these book reviews, it is unlikely that he would have won his debate with Fairman. Justice Black was also attacked for his incorporation thesis in *Adamson*, and he was not burdened by reputation problems as Crosskey was.

In explaining Fairman's initial success, we can see how definitions of "good" research are constituted by complex interactions among cognitive factors, personal networks, institutional pressures, and citation patterns. Crosskey's account, by arguing that the Court had been wrong for seventy years, raised fundamental questions about Court legitimacy. Crosskey and the recent scholarly movement legal realism had stirred up insecurities about the nature of legal reasoning that Fairman's history assuaged. Fairman's history also affirmed the tradition of state authority over personal rights, a tradition that was coming under threat from a New Deal Court that was expanding federal control over rights.

In his 1949 article, then, Fairman was able to "act at a distance," a phrase used by Woolgar (1988, 78–79) to capture the dynamic whereby researchers can successfully claim that their representations of their data have not been affected by the relocation of that data from their point of origin (i.e., in this case, that their representations are not anachronistic). If a researcher can claim successfully that he has not distorted the character of his data from what existed prior to his research crafting, that researcher can be said to have "acted at a distance." Fairman's ability to act at a distance was linked to his ability to mobilize fears and beliefs that were deeply institutionalized. He became the trusted teller of the tale, perceived as standing apart from the character of the documentary evidence.

What is the significance of Fairman's victory? For one thing, it meant that credible Fourteenth Amendment history became linked to political distributions that disadvantaged blacks. Fairman's victory did not prevent the emergence of the Warren Court majority, whose antisubordination decisions alleviated the second-class citizenship of blacks. However, Fairman's victory enabled critics of the Warren Court to gain credibility for their charge that the Court's decisions were the product of "politics, not law" (Bork 1990). Fairman's victory gave critics of the Warren Court a weapon that they would wield once the Court membership had turned over.[26]

Crosskey's history, although superior to Fairman's in its faithfulness to the historical evidence, must still be understood as an institutional product. Crosskey accepted the structure of originalist inquiry, which limited his ways of seeing. More specifically, Crosskey accepted the normative position that departing from original intent was improper. He therefore maligned the Court for its nonincorporation position in the *Slaughter-House Cases* (1873; see note 3, this chapter). In doing this, Crosskey obscured alternative normative evaluations of the Court's nonincorporation thesis.

A full investigation of the competition between Fairman and Crosskey requires that this alternative evaluation be laid out, for it highlights the boundaries of interpretation established by Crosskey's frame. This alternative view considers whether it would have been foolish for the Court to be "true" to the Republican intent to incorporate the Bill of Rights. In 1873, economically conservative justices were gaining strength and searching for a way to defeat state regulations of business. If the Court acknowledged incorporation and broadly expanded national power, this might have given the conservatives the weapon they sought. This would have been a perverse result. The dichotomous categories of originalism (fidelity: good/betrayal: bad) cannot capture this predicament. In fact, the normative structure of originalist inquiry obscures it. By laying out a picture of these rapidly changing politics, an alternative view of the Court comes into focus. Although Crosskey's originalist framework led him to represent the Court as embracing conservatism, laying out a picture of these politics leads us to see the Court as thwarting conservatism.[27] The key point, then, is that although Crosskey escaped certain anachronisms, his account remained structured by a legal problematic (originalism) that limited his ways of seeing. This problematic led him away from considerations of the rapidly changing politics of the early 1870s, which blinded him to a more sympathetic appraisal of the Court. Thus, Crosskey's account, too, can be understood as institutionally constituted.

In sum, the initial success of Fairman's nonincorporation history can be explained by his institutional positioning. In the world of academic law at the time, Harvard ties carried enormous prestige, and Fairman was embedded in a Harvard network. The interpretive framework of that community structured Fairman's reconstructive practices. This community also validated Fairman's conclusions.

In recent times, the status of Fairman's history has declined in the legal academy. This, too, can be linked to institutional developments. Crosskey's damaged reputation is less salient to contemporary readers, enabling his incorporation thesis to be assessed independently from responses to his 1953 book. More important, Crosskey's incorporation thesis has gained credibility thanks to a major development in law schools since the Second Reconstruction: the establishment of a revised history of Reconstruction, which recovers "old" Republican political and constitutional theory (Graham 1968; Wiecek 1977). When Crosskey first pointed to this "old" theory in 1949, there was no literature to support his contention. William Dunning (1907) and his followers (Bowers 1929; Fleming 1919) supplied the dominant Reconstruction history at that time, a history that portrayed the Republicans in highly distorted and negative terms. Dunning School history provided legitimacy to Fairman's account, which invoked the dominant negative image of the Republicans.

Dunning School history is now rejected by historians. Eric Foner's (1986) history of Reconstruction is widely accepted, and this has provided a foundation for Crosskey's newfound credibility. Indeed, a network of scholars in the interpretive community that accepts Foner is currently nourishing Crosskey's incorporation thesis. Mapping the recent upturn in the trajectory of credibility that attaches to Crosskey's account requires mapping citations not only to Foner, but also to the legal scholar Michael Kent Curtis (1986), whose work has done the most to resuscitate Crosskey's incorporation thesis. The credibility of Curtis's work is supported not only by Foner but by the work of legal historians since the Second Reconstruction. Large-scale developments in both history and legal history have thus provided a foundation for the increasing acceptance of Crosskey's account.

Scholarly Orthodoxy and the Civil Rights Cases

The same scholarly movement in the legal academy that has supported the resuscitation of Crosskey supports the marginalization of a different knowledge claim—that of Frantz in 1964—that also has a significant degree of historical merit. The careers of Crosskey's claim and Frantz's claim intersect, and this intersection brings cautionary lessons for researchers who view the resuscitation of Crosskey as an unqualified "good" and as a triumph of justice and fairness.

Laurent B. Frantz is part of a new debate emerging in the legal academy. This debate concerns the proper interpretation of a crucial Fourteenth Amendment decision, the *Civil Rights Cases* (1883).[28] This decision is conventionally viewed as the foundation of "state action" doctrine, the rule that Fourteenth Amendment rights are protected against infringement by the government but not by private persons.[29] An important corollary, presumed to follow logically, is the rule that Congress may not regulate private action under its Section 5 power to enforce the Amendment.[30] This corollary was Frantz's target.

In 1964, Frantz challenged this corollary, which scholars viewed as established in the *Civil Rights Cases* and other decisions of the time.[31] He argued that these decisions had been misread and that they in fact supported congressional power to regulate private, racially motivated crimes under the Fourteenth Amendment when states failed to redress those wrongs. According to Frantz's reading, state failure to punish crime equally was "state action" within the meaning of the Fourteenth Amendment, and Congress could remedy this violation by punishing the crimes the state left unremedied. Frantz's reading of these cases was a "competing possible"

(Bourdieu 1977, 169). Indeed, there was textual support for much of his argument. Frantz's claim, however, was ignored.

The distinction between Frantz's "state failure" reading and the conventional "state action" reading should be highlighted. As scholars understand "state action," for example, if state authorities systematically fail to punish the race-based violence of the Ku Klux Klan, there is no violation of the Fourteenth Amendment and the federal government may not prosecute the Klansmen. Under the state-failure reading advanced by Frantz, the neglect of state authorities does count as a violation, and the federal government may bring prosecutions. Thus, Frantz's state failure reading offers a less restrictive interpretation of Congressional power to enforce the Fourteenth Amendment.

The validity of Frantz's claim that the *Civil Rights Cases* has been misread can be demonstrated (again) using the Cambridge School methods of Pocock and Skinner, though it is impossible here to summarize the intricacies of this analysis (see Brandwein 2006). In brief, Cambridge School methods permit recovery of the nineteenth-century legal categories used by the Waite Court to articulate the concept I call "state neglect." With the recovery of the old, nineteenth-century legal paradigm, it becomes clear that the conventional view of Congress's Section 5 power is a product of an anachronistic reading of the *Civil Rights Cases*.

Frantz's claim is no less heterodox than Crosskey's, so how can we explain why Frantz was initially ignored while Crosskey was initially condemned? To answer this question, we need to ask a series of questions: What practical impact would Frantz's claims have had? What were the institutional commitments of powerful communities of law professors? Was Frantz part of any interpretive community that would have cited his work? Which social groups had an interest in Frantz's claims and were they powerful enough to be heard?

In order to identify the practical stakes attached to Frantz's claims, we must examine Supreme Court decisions at the time. What we find are Court decisions that dramatically lowered the practical stakes attached to Frantz's claims. Frantz's argument that the Waite Court's Fourteenth Amendment decisions permitted Congress to regulate private action carried little practical significance after the Warren Court approved congressional regulation of private action under the Commerce Clause and the Thirteenth Amendment.[32] Social groups that were interested in protecting black rights got the outcomes they wanted from the Court. They no longer needed to search out legal arguments (like Frantz's) that could help them.

The practical stakes for Frantz's claim were low, then, while the practical stakes for Crosskey's claim were much higher.[33] Something else helps explain why Frantz was ignored: reputation. It was not that Frantz's reputation was tarnished by poor reviews of prior work. It was that Frantz was not even a law professor. He was an editor at Bancroft-Whitney Law Publishers in San Francisco, and his acknowledgments mentioned only one person, the late Professor Douglas B. Maggs of Duke University Law School (Frantz 1964, 1353). Frantz was not a part of a vibrant scholarly network, which prevented his article from gaining currency (through citations, for example).

Although reputation is significant, we must also look to the institutional commitments among law professors to complete an explanation of why Frantz was ignored. Frantz wrote at a time when a new wave of scholarship was sweeping the legal academy. This new literature, written during the 1950s and 1960s, condemned the Court of the 1870s and 1880s for dismantling Reconstruction and abandoning blacks to their former masters (Gressman 1952; Harris 1960; Woodward 1966 [1951]). State action doctrine was identified in this literature as a central vehicle of the Court's subversion of Reconstruction. This scholarship, in short, demonized the Court of the 1870s and 1880s. In Frantz's article, the Court looked far less demonic.

This new wave of legal scholarship was strengthened by the work of academic historians. A major revision of Reconstruction history was going on in history departments,[34] and citations to the work of academic historians by law professors became easily observable at this time.[35] Other developments in law schools reinforced this cross-fertilization, for example, a new law-and-history movement in the legal academy (Kalman 1996). Understanding how the commitments of law professors contributed to the marginalization of Frantz requires mapping these cross-institutional dynamics.

We must be careful investigating the effects of this legal historiography, however, for they are complex. The legal historiography that helped marginalize Frantz—the one that recovered the old political and constitutional theory of the Republican framers of the Reconstruction Amendments, along with condemning the Waite Court for the supposed abandonment of this vision—also provided the foundation for the resuscitation of Crosskey. The careers of Frantz's knowledge claim and Crosskey's knowledge claim thus intersect. Although it might be tempting to regard the institutional developments that supported the resuscitation of Crosskey in purely positive terms, studying the career of Frantz's knowledge claim brings a more nuanced view. The movement that brought Crosskey due recognition also worked to deny due recognition to Frantz. We must be careful, then, about characterizing the institutional trends that bring accreditation to knowledge claims that we take to be superior.

In the past several years, Frantz's article has been increasingly noticed and praised (Post and Siegel 2000; Brief of Petitioner Christy Brzonkala, *United States v. Morrison* [Nos. 99–5, 99–29] 1999). The trajectory of credibility that attaches to Frantz's article has clearly turned in a more positive direction, though not to the extent of Crosskey's. How can we explain this? We should ask the same questions as before: What is the practical impact, today, of Frantz's claims? Are there powerful interpretive communities that now share Frantz's assumptions? Are there social groups that now have an interest in his claims and are they powerful enough to be heard?

In recent years, the practical stakes have soared in the dispute over the interpretation of Waite Court cases due to the federalism and separation-of-powers decisions of the Rehnquist Court.[36] In restricting congressional use of the Commerce Clause to authorize civil rights measures, the Rehnquist Court has returned state action doctrine to legal prominence, relying upon it to justify decisions striking down federal civil rights statutes. With the return of state action doctrine to practical significance, challenges to conventional readings of Waite Court cases, built quietly in preceding decades (e.g., Benedict 1978), are gaining a higher profile. Social groups with an interest in the Violence Against Women Act of 1994 now look to Frantz (Brief for Brzonkala). Today, a highly reputable group of law professors supports Frantz-like readings of the *Civil Rights Cases* (McConnell 1995; Post and Siegel 2000; G. Stone et al. 1996). This adds reputational weight to Frantz's knowledge claims, something that was absent in 1964. Today, there are also new challenges to the conventional legal historiography of Reconstruction (Labbé and Lurie 2003; M.A. Ross 2003). The critical accomplishment of these recent challenges is to suggest that the Court's settlement of Reconstruction has not yet been understood. This permits Frantz's claim, which suggests the same thing, to appear more credible. The current generation of legal scholars, who did not author the legal historiography of the Second Reconstruction, also has greater distance from this legal historiography and so may increasingly see it with fresh eyes.

The story of Frantz's knowledge claim, of course, is still in its early chapters, and it is too soon to tell if or when it will gain wide acceptance. What is clear is that its career is inextricably tied to the reassessment of the conventional legal history of Reconstruction. Many legal academics remain deeply vested in this conventional historiography, an investment that is visible in their work, and so institutional sources of resistance to Frantz's claim remain strong.

CONCLUSION

We return, then, to the basic idea that legal academics are institutionally "embedded" (Powell and DiMaggio 1991) in a variety of ways. Legal scholars share certain assumptions with academics and with Court justices. Legal scholars, working in academic institutions, and justices, working in legal institutions, also share assumptions and beliefs about, say, race and gender (R.M. Smith 1993). The methods of frame analysis and science studies permit highly specific investigations of these sorts of characteristics that are shared across such disparate institutional contexts. In general, these methods provide a way of generating data about the assumptions that underlie knowledge claims and about the institutional contexts that shape the reception of rival knowledge claims. These methods also provide a way of analyzing data. We become able to link various levels of the social totality: the individual, the collective, and the institutional. We become able to understand the careers of knowledge claims in terms of institutional arrangements and resource distributions. Without the tools of science studies, especially, these sorts of investigation would be impossible.

NOTES

1. U.S. Const., amend. XIV, sec. 1, clause 2, "No state shall make or enforce any law which shall abridge the privileges or immunities of citizens of the United States" (1868).

2. *Barron v. Baltimore*, 32 U.S. (2 Pet.) 243 (1833).

3. *Slaughter-House Cases*, 83 U.S. (16 Wall.) 36 (1873); *United States v. Cruikshank*, 92 U.S. 542 (1876).

4. The Reconstruction debates span the thirty-ninth to forty-third congresses (1866–75).

5. See, e.g., Fehrenbacher (1962) and Simpson (1998).

6. See, e.g., Ross (2003).

7. E.g., *United States v. Reese*, 92 U.S. 214 (1876); *United States v. Cruikshank*, 92 U.S. 542 (1876); *United States v. Harris*, 106 U.S. 629 (1883); *Civil Rights Cases*, 109 U.S. 3 (1883).

8. Fraser (1995, 160) discusses this challenge as it pertains to feminist scholarship. The goal is to "connect the discursive analyses of gender significations with structural analyses of institutions and political economy."

9. For overviews of New Historical Institutionalism that situate it relative to behavioral and strategic–rational choice approaches to the study of public law, see Kahn and Kersch (2006), Gillman (1999), and Clayton and Gillman (1999). The interpretive-historical approach of NHI, as one might guess, is not entirely new. There are convergences between NHI and both the pre-behavioralist institutionalism of Corwin (1934) and Haines (1922), and the "political systems" institutionalism of Dahl (1957) and R. McCloskey (1960). For a discussion of these convergences, see Clayton and Gillman (1999).

10. Legal historians have shown that conceptions of judicial roles and purposes can be reconstituted over time (Siegel 1990; Grossman 2002; and Horwitz 1993). These legal historians have not associated themselves with NHI, though their work is clearly relevant for NHI research agendas.

11. Gusfield (1989, 42) asks an important question: "If frameworks of thought limit and constrain how experience is conceived, from where do we develop" these frameworks of thought? Tracking the creation and institutional establishment of frames is a project in and of itself and likely beyond the scope of any frame analysis.

12. See Schultz (1990). For other examples, see Eagly and Karau (2002), who explain how beliefs about women's character shape the evaluation of women's leadership potential and the evaluation of women's actual leadership behavior. See also Krieger (1995, 1186–211).

13. The term "appreciation" is taken from Vickers (1983, 187): "a set of readinesses to distinguish some aspect of the situation rather than others and to classify and value these in this way rather than that." The term "appreciation," all by itself, blurs the distinction between assumptions and the classifications to which they give rise.

14. See, e.g., Schon and Rein's discussion of the "contrasting frames of discretion and entitlement" in policy debates over homelessness (1994, 141): "The official frame, sponsored by the public agencies, saw housing as a scarce resource whose distribution was properly a matter for governmental discretion. The

advocates, on the other hand, saw housing as a legal entitlement enforceable in a court of law." There is no analytic way here to isolate the divergent sets of baseline assumptions that led to these divergent definitions of the situation.

15. Woolgar (1988) offers a good introduction to the science studies literature, situating science studies in relationship to both the classical sociology of knowledge and the classical sociology of science.

16. In NHI studies of the Supreme Court, Kahn and Kersch (2006) put the terms "internal" and "external" in brackets in an attempt to signal the mutually constitutive nature of legal reasoning and social and political factors.

17. The term "extending agents" is meant to recognize agency in individuals, that is, their capacity to achieve modification and change in concepts they have received. For a discussion relating interpretive frameworks and agency, see Sewell (1992).

18. Schon and Rein (1994, 41–44) offer several ways out of this trap: appeals to a shared larger reality, appeals to shared criteria for evaluating frames, and frame translations, which involve attempts to understand conflicting viewpoints.

19. Fish is responding to the perceived crisis in truth triggered by anti-foundationalist epistemology, that is, a general account of knowing in which all meanings are contingent and provisional. Speaking to those who worry that there is a contradiction between making knowledge claims and supporting an anti-foundationalist epistemology, Fish explains that there is no contradiction because none of us, positivist and anti-foundationalist alike, can escape our local truths. It is these local truths (taken-for-granted assumptions and beliefs) that shape a researcher's perception of a legitimate research goal and perception of relevant and weighty evidence. It is these assumptions and beliefs, too, that give the researcher confidence in her research product. The whole of these assumptions and beliefs, however, is not subject to self-examination because some set of assumptions are necessary in order to "see," i.e., in order to construe meaning, and these are not subject to reflexivity. There is no contradiction, then, between advancing knowledge claims and supporting an anti-foundationalist epistemology because it is impossible for any researcher to enact a stance of *general* openness and *general* indeterminacy.

Fish's work is important here because it points to the limits to reflexivity. Reflexivity may take a variety of forms, and we may speak of levels or degrees (personal, institutional, etc.) of reflexivity. A scholar may reflect on her own personal experience and consider how that experience shapes her research questions or her response to research subjects. A scholar might also identify hegemonic assumptions in his discipline that shape the production of institutional knowledge. For example, Ido Oren can explain how hegemonic assumptions in political science generated the "democratic peace" axiom (see chapter 11, this volume). However, Oren cannot identify the taken-for-granted assumptions and beliefs that underwrite his own sense of relevant and weighty evidence in support of his critique. This is not a criticism of Oren, for it is impossible for any researcher to be fully cognizant of the sources of his own practice.

Consider, too, my study of the career of Fairman's knowledge claim. I can identify the hegemonic assumptions and standard concepts among legal actors that made Fairman's claim persuasive in the 1950s. Indeed, like Oren, I historicize institutional discourse, which is one form of reflexivity. But the set of assumptions that make me deeply confident that Fairman was wrong remain outside my view. Of course, my assumptions do remain subject to evaluation by others, just as all scholarly assumptions do. The point, then, is that a researcher reaches the limits of reflexivity when it comes to identifying the sources of her own confidence in her research product.

20. Pocock (1985, 10) explains that confidence that an idiom existed for actors in history increases to the extent "(a) that diverse authors employed the same idiom and performed diverse and even contrary utterances in it, (b) that the idiom recurs in texts and contexts varying from those in which it was at first detected, and (c) that authors expressed in words their consciousness that they were employing such an idiom and developed critical and second-order languages to comment on and regulate their employment of it." See, generally, Skinner (2002).

21. The *New Shorter Oxford English Dictionary* defines anachronism as "the relating of an event, custom, or circumstance to a wrong period of time" (New York: Oxford University Press, 1993). Fairman, for example, assumed that the vocabulary for debating incorporation in the post–Civil War era was the same as the contemporary vocabulary of the 1940s and 1950s, and this led him to misunderstand the meaning of many speeches. Crosskey did a better job at recovering the historical idiom in use during the Reconstruction debates. For a complete discussion of the variety of anachronisms in Fairman's account, see Brandwein (1996, 304–24). For a discussion of anachronisms in conventional legal and historical accounts of the Fourteenth Amendment doctrine of state action, see Brandwein (2006).

22. For this discussion, see Brandwein (1999, 96–131).

23. Socio-legal scholar Kim Scheppele (1989, 2094–97) has taken up the question, when does a story begin? She discusses how the boundaries of legal narratives are shaped by "legal habits." The traditional legal habit is to look (narrowly) to when "the trouble" began, i.e., the set of events that gave rise to the legal question at hand. A wider angle of vision, however, is possible.

24. To understand the meaning of the Reconstruction debates, for example, we must understand the speeches "intertextually." This means tracing the use of terms that appear in the speeches. Terms gain their meaning from their place within an extensive network, and in order to understand these terms, we must fully trace the entire network. Thus, by tracing wider patterns in the use of Civil War references, the meaning of these references can be inferred. The goal, it should be emphasized, is not "to perform the impossible task of getting inside the heads of long-dead thinkers." Rather, the goal is "to grasp their concepts, to follow their distinctions, to recover their beliefs and, so far as possible, to see things their way" (Skinner 2002, 3). This methodological emphasis on tracing the use of terms flows from the basic recognition that texts belonging to the history of legal discourse were public acts of communication and argumentation. Usage had to be conventional for communication to take place.

25. *Adamson v. California*, 332 U.S. 46 (1947).

26. See the discussion of Fairman's history as an institutional resource for Warren Court dissenters in Brandwein (1999, 97, 155–84).

27. For an extended discussion of how originalist debate over the *Slaughter-House Cases* obscures certain questions and normative visions, see Brandwein (2004 [reviewing Ross's (2003) argument that the Court's non-incorporationist view was meant to block the new and rising power of economic conservatism]). For a discussion of overlapping frames in another context, see Brandwein (1996, 293, 328–30).

28. *Civil Rights Cases*, 109 U.S. 3 (1883).

29. See *Shelley v. Kraemer*, 334 U.S. 1 (1948); *Burton v. Wilmington Parking Authority*, 365 U.S. 715, 721 (1961).

30. U.S. Const., amend. XIV sec. 5, "The Congress shall have power to enforce, by appropriate legislation, the provisions of this article."

31. *United States v. Reese*, 92 U.S. 214 (1876); *United States v. Cruikshank*, 92 U.S. 542 (1876); *United States v. Harris*, 106 U.S. 629 (1883); *Civil Rights Cases*, 109 U.S. 3 (1883).

32. The Warren Court minimized the practical impact of state action doctrine, permitting Congress to reach private conduct under the Commerce Clause. See *Heart of Atlanta Motel*, 379 U.S. 241 (1964) and *Katzenbach v. McClung*, 379 U.S. 294 (1964). The Court soon added the Thirteenth Amendment as an additional source of federal power to regulate private action. See *Jones v. Alfred H. Mayer Co.*, 392 U.S. 409 (1968).

33. Today, it is accepted by jurists and scholars that the Bill of Rights is applied to the states through the due process clause of the Fourteenth Amendment (not the privileges or immunities clause). When Crosskey wrote, the application of the Bill of Rights to the states, through any means, was still disputed.

34. During the Second Reconstruction, historians delegitimated Dunning School histories of Reconstruction, which cast Reconstruction as a mistake and presented the white redeemers of the South as heroes. Progressive histories of Reconstruction, which presented Republicans as corrupt rulers interested only in economic hegemony, were also delegitimated. For a summary of the history of Reconstruction historiography, see Foner (1986).

35. Indeed, this cross-institutional dynamic between the legal academy and academic history is most easily observable in citation patterns. It can also be observed in conference participation, the number of law professors trained in both law and history, and law school subscriptions to academic history journals.

36. *City of Boerne v. Flores*, 521 U.S. 507 (1997); *Kimel v. Florida Board of Regents*, 528 U.S. 62 (2000); *United States v. Morrison*, 529 U.S. 598 (2000); *Board of Regents v. Garrett*, 528 U.S. 62 (2000). Cf. *Nevada Dep't of Human Resources v. Hibbs*, 123 S. Ct. 1972 (2003) and *Tennessee v. Lane*, No. 02-1667 (2004), which show that the Court is willing to support certain civil rights legislation on narrow grounds.

CHAPTER 13

ETHNOGRAPHY, IDENTITY, AND THE PRODUCTION OF KNOWLEDGE

Samer Shehata

I never intended to become an advocate of participant-observation and ethnographic methods. The research methods we employ, after all, should be determined by the questions we ask and the subjects we seek to explore. I became a proponent of participant-observation and ethnography through practice, *only after conducting research using various methods—including participant-observation/ethnography—and comparing the character and types of knowledge different research methods produce.*

My initial research project was to investigate working-class politics and culture in Egypt, and, more specifically, shop floor politics, working-class culture, and class formation at the point of production, inside the factory. Although a significant literature existed on the Egyptian working class in both Arabic and English, surprisingly, few if any of these authors had ever spent any significant time in Egyptian factories or with Egyptian workers, either because they thought it unnecessary or because they simply could not gain access. The literature that existed, therefore, dealt with questions of class and class formation almost exclusively, through instances of strikes, labor organization, and collective action. The analysis was mostly limited to discussions of textual sources; analysis of print media, newspaper accounts, pamphlets, institutional histories of unions, and instances of strikes; and a few interviews with union leaders. What was sorely lacking was an analysis of ordinary workers and working life. Not only did we know very little about what went on inside Egyptian factories, we also knew remarkably little about working-class culture and shop-floor politics.

Ethnography rather than questionnaires, interviews, or archival research was best suited for studying workers' lived experiences and the social world of the factory. What better way, after all, was there to penetrate what Marx called "the hidden abode of production. On whose threshold there hangs the notice—'No Admittance Except on Business'" (Marx 1967, 172).

There are of course other reasons that drew me to ethnography and participant-observation. It always made intuitive sense to me that if one really wanted to learn about something, there was no better way than to see things for oneself, speak with those involved, and experience the phenomenon as much as one could—in short, to get to know something well by being there, as Clifford Geertz suggests (1988, 4–5).

Moreover, it has always seemed to me that the most important questions in the social sciences are not about macro structures, large processes, or social institutions—but about people: living, breathing, flesh and blood, real people who, it turns out, whether intentionally or not, produce structures, set processes in motion, and establish institutions. And because the human sciences must remain primarily about humans, any science about the social world must provide the perspectives of those responsible for establishing institutions, setting processes in motion, and producing structures: that is, the perspectives of the participants (whether we end up accepting these perspectives or not is irrelevant—they remain important and part of what must be explained). And by the "perspectives of the participants" I do not mean the generic rational "choices" that actors make. I mean how real people understand their situations and social world. There is no better method for providing these perspectives (and ground-level analysis more generally) than participant-observation.

For many of the people I worked with, I was the only person they knew who lived in the United States. As *Amrika* has a definite place in the Egyptian imagination (as in many other countries), my presence provided them an opportunity to learn about *ard al-ahlam* (the land of dreams) directly. It provided me an opportunity to learn about Egyptian social structure.

Workers weren't the only people shocked and amazed at the method I had chosen for my research. Middle- and upper-class friends and relatives could not believe what I was up to, and the Chairman of the Board of Directors who interviewed me before allowing me to undertake the research had a specific question in mind: Why would someone who was *ibn naas* (the son of respectable people), with a Master's degree and doing a Ph.D. at Princeton, want to work in a factory, on a machine? It made no sense to him either.
—*Samer Shehata* (2004, 248, 256)

When I decided to study working-class politics and culture in Egypt as a participant-observer in two textile factories in Alexandria, the last thing I imagined was writing about myself or my personal experiences. Preparing a conference paper about identity and research, I realized that the questions people had been asking about "what the natives thought of me" were themselves quite serious and scholarly. People wanted to know how I was received in the factory. How did workers react? How was I treated and what did people make of my research? Was my presence on the shop floor disruptive or unusual? What everyone seemed most curious about was how "the natives" perceived me. Indeed, these were crucial epistemological questions about my research and the character of ethnographic knowledge. Although personal, they were also about method and had to be taken seriously.

Questions about ethnographic text are especially important to me because I am not an anthropologist. What some anthropologists take for granted—ethnography as method—I must consciously defend, day in and day out. As a political scientist I find that my colleagues are generally quite wary of ethnography. If taken seriously, it is viewed with suspicion—not as competing method but as pseudoscience.[1]

In the classical ethnography of anthropology (see, e.g., Malinowski 1922), the ethnographer is nowhere to be found; identity and the subjective experience of fieldwork are erased.[2] The traditional monograph, in fact, looks as if it were produced by an "objective machine." It is a purely scholarly production and the conditions of its birth are noticeably absent. Occasionally, and only occasionally, the ethnographer emerges from the text, usually in the introduction and "arrival story," only to convince the reader that "what they say is a result of their having . . . 'been there.'"[3] This approach to ethnography began to be questioned by the end of the 1960s. For example, Peggy Golde (1970, 2) wrote that one of the primary issues that her edited volume *Women in the*

Field: Anthropological Experiences was meant to address was "how the characteristics of the ethnographer may indirectly and inadvertently affect the process of research." More recently, some of these issues have resurfaced under the guise of reflexivity and postmodernism. In the work of James Clifford, George Marcus (1986), and Clifford Geertz (1988), three highly influential anthropologists, reflexivity has meant an analysis of, in Geertz's phrase, "the anthropologist as author." Rather than examining "the problematics of fieldwork" (Geertz 1988), these anthropologists concentrate on writing, discourse, and authorship; in short, how ethnographic *texts* function and how they convince. The analysis is literary and discursive, focusing on narrative structure, trope, metaphor, language, and rhetorical style.[4] Textual reflexivity seems to be the dominant mode these days.

Reflexivity, however, has also meant the examination of fieldwork as a personal and epistemological activity. In this mode, the field encounter is analyzed as a method of knowledge production, and the ethnographer is placed at the center of the drama. Consciously autobiographical and explicitly personal, these works abandon many of the traditional conventions of academic writing. Self-reflexivity is, at times, highly entertaining, revealing aspects of fieldwork that normally would not make it to the printed page. The ethnographer appears not as scientist but as human. Here, reflexivity means being self-conscious about fieldwork and the role of the ethnographer in the production of knowledge; it is a reflexivity not about writing and textuality (although these concerns are legitimate), but about fieldwork as method and the ethnographer as "positioned subject."[5]

It has become more acceptable to view ethnographers not as "objective machines" but as "positioned subjects"—human, constructed, "natives" somewhere, with emotions, ideas, and agendas.[6] They bring their identities as well as their theories to the field. Ethnographic fieldwork is, in this sense, a thoroughly "subjective" experience, based, as it is, on the personal interactions of the ethnographer in "the field."[7] *Thus, in ethnography, the ethnographer's self becomes a conduit of research and a primary vehicle of knowledge production.* How does this affect the production of knowledge? How does the ethnographer's identity affect the ethnographic encounter? The answers I propose to these difficult questions are tentative and come from a critical examination of my own fieldwork. Reformulated, the questions become: How did my identity affect my fieldwork? What did "the natives" think of me? Which categories did they employ to make sense of me and my research? And ultimately, how does the essentially "personal and subjective" ethnographic encounter affect the ostensibly "scientific" production of "objective" knowledge?

Reflecting critically on my own identity in relation to my fieldwork—how I was perceived and what "the natives" thought of me—has proven especially useful in illuminating the subject of my research: the social world of the factory and the class structure of Egyptian society. I set out to study workers in two textile factories in Egypt, and my fieldwork experiences reflect, in part, my problematic place within the Egyptian class system. I learned about the significance and meaning of social class in Egypt firsthand, in a way I never intended or expected. As an Egyptian-American, a semi-indigenous researcher, and someone who was definitely not a worker, I *experienced* social class. I was thrown into (or, more aptly, thrown up against) a rigid class structure, and I experienced the reactions of those within it to my research and identity. How people reacted to what I was doing and their expectations of me were revealing of their attitudes and understandings of what social class in the factory and society is all about. Examining these interactions and reflecting upon them has proven useful for understanding the social world of the factory and the class structure of Egyptian society.

In order to address questions about how my identity—my ethnographic self—worked to generate insights into the Egyptian class structure, I must be somewhat autobiographical. This causes great anxiety for most social scientists, and I am certainly no exception. As a political scientist I feel especially uneasy, guilty, and unprofessional. After all, we are taught as researchers that the personal is trivial, uninteresting, and certainly not the serious business of science. However, since my identity proved crucial in shaping my findings, I will briefly outline those features of my identity that my workmates took to be most salient. Each of these facets of my identity colored my presence and affected my research. (It is important to note that these characteristics, as will become apparent later, are certainly not unproblematic or stable themselves.) Then I will discuss how these characteristics impacted my fieldwork and affected my findings.

Although born in Alexandria, I have lived most of my life outside Egypt, in England and the United States, and fit neatly into the category of the "hyphenated American." Put differently, I am an Egyptian-American fluent in Arabic. At the time of the research, I was not married. As a social scientist and researcher, I had significantly more formal education than the workers I studied. And, except for a few engineers in the highest ranks of the administration, I had more formal education than most in the company. Although I am not terribly connected in Egyptian society, especially compared with others of similar family and class backgrounds living in Egypt, compared with the workers I was *wasil* (connected)—connected enough to gain access to the factory and the shop floor. I also came from a significantly different class background than my coworkers, as well as most of the administrative and engineering staff for that matter. Moreover, I am male, Muslim, and originally from the region where the research was undertaken. My identity is obviously more complicated than this simple combination of features. These characteristics, however, turned out to be most important to those I worked with and studied.

In the sections that follow, I recount the specifics of a variety of research events, encounters, and stories from my twelve months of field research. These stories might be organized in a variety of ways as they reflect different combinations of the features of my identity. To simplify the explication, I have organized them according to the approximate importance (in my view) workers, management, and engineers accorded different features of my identity. Some stories reveal ways in which "the natives" were able to make sense of me in terms of fairly common categories of region, gender, religion, and organizational membership. As I was thus "pegged" by the people with whom I was working, facets of the setting were either revealed to me (e.g., as a Muslim) or concealed (as a male). In other stories, my identity and my research purposes proved much more disruptive, as "natives" struggled to understand why an educated, connected Egyptian-American would study working-class people, much less work alongside them. It was these situations—provoked by my failure to fit standard expectations—that proved most revelatory about the functioning of the Egyptian class system. By analyzing all of these interactions and presenting the knowledge I gained from them, I demonstrate how I learned about the social world of the factory and the class structure of Egyptian society, in part, *through* my identity.

EGYPTIAN-AMERICAN

It seemed like I spent the first month of my twelve-month sojourn in the factories answering questions. Most Egyptians are both friendly and curious, and it felt like the limits of the personal and private were significantly different from what I was accustomed to. Questions came not only from workmates but also from almost everyone with whom I came into contact, including people I had never met, inside the factory and elsewhere. Everything about me was fair game and open for investigation, from my father's occupation, to the exact amount of my research stipend, to the extent of my religious observance.[8]

Of all the questions, however, the two that seemed most frequent and especially important to my questioners were: "Which is better—America or Egypt?" and "Are you going to marry an Egyptian or a foreigner?" Obviously, my identity as an Egyptian-American was at the root of both questions. Despite the difficulty of answering potentially sensitive questions like these, not to mention the problematic nature of the questions themselves, I soon established comfortable answers that, as well as being true, seemed to satisfy my questioners. I told my questioners that both Egypt and the United States had advantages and drawbacks and "which was better" depended on how one prioritized these qualities. As far as marriage was concerned, I mimicked the classic Egyptian and superficially fatalistic response of *isma wa nasib* (meaning, basically, whatever fate had in store for me).[9]

Being Egyptian-American produced a set of responses that smoothed my entrance into the factory. It produced warmth and kindness. My being American produced interest and curiosity. Interest in the United States (*Amrika*, as it was called) generated questions that are fascinating in and of themselves for what they reveal in terms of background knowledge, perspective, and orientation. These questions also provided an opportunity for me to ask similar questions and explore related issues. For instance, I was bombarded with inquiries about life in Amrika, which included everything from the particulars of household consumption (i.e., how much milk people drink daily, especially children) and gender relations to union activity and perspectives on society and politics more generally.[10] Explicit comparison was made easy and much information was gathered in this manner.

Mohamed, an illiterate coworker in my department who dropped out of fourth grade and attended an anti-illiteracy program in the evenings, was particularly fascinated with my notebook and what I wrote in it. Once, after watching me scribble something by the side of a machine, he approached and asked, "Do all people who know English write from left to right or is it just you?" Our conversation covered a number of topics including life in the United States. After a long, rambling monologue about how great Amrika must be in terms of standard of living, personal and political freedom, and so on, Mohamed ended, without pause and in the same tone of voice, by stating (about Americans), "Lakin ma aendahumsh din . . . min al-dar ila al-nar" ("but they have no religion . . . from home to hell").[11]

Other workers' impressions of the United States (and the West more generally) were no less interesting or complex. Many described the United States and Europe as having "Islam without Muslims," while Egypt had "Muslims without Islam" (*Islam bala Muslimeen* and *Muslimeen bala Islam*).[12] This was a short but sophisticated, double-edged ethical and religious critique of both the "West" and Egypt (in the same breath!). While praising the "West" for having "Islam"—referring to fair and just systems of government, the absence of significant corruption, the seriousness of work, economic development, equality, and high standards of living—they criticized the "West" for not believing in Islam, for not being Muslim. At the very same time, in this short phrase, workers criticized Egyptians for not living by Islamic principles of justice, fairness, order, charity, and so forth, and, thus, of being Muslims in name only—"Muslims without Islam," as it were.

RESEARCHER

As a social scientist studying working-class culture and the social organization of production, I experienced reactions of bewilderment, confusion, and respect. Despite my determined efforts to explain exactly what I was doing, for the longest time many workers believed that I was studying the machines on the shop floor and not the social relations of production. Workers' only previous experiences of research were engineers who occasionally marched onto the shop floor, oblivious to the workers, to study some aspect of the machines or a technical matter relating to production.[13] Six weeks into the research, for example, Fathy, a winding machine operator with whom I worked closely, asked whether I would become an English teacher after I finished at the factory. Although I had previously explained to everyone in the department, on a number of different occasions, exactly what I was studying and for what purpose, people were quite genuinely confused. I was the only "social scientist" most had ever met.

As a university graduate with an advanced degree, I experienced reactions of respect and deference that varied from opinions concerning what work I could and could not do to where I should sit on the company bus. One of the most memorable incidents regarding my status as a social scientist (with formal education) occurred on my first day of work at my second research site. This, too, was a textile firm: a large company that employed 11,000 people and occupied over 500 *feddans*.*

Equipped with its own power and water stations, it was located some distance outside the city. All employees were transported to work each day on a fleet of company buses. The previous week, while visiting the factory, I was told to wait for one of the company's buses at a certain location, the closest scheduled stop to where I was living. The company official responsible for my research introduced me to the driver, told me exactly which bus to get on, described the other employee who boarded at this particular stop, and explained when and where to wait.

On my first day I did exactly as I was told, arriving ten minutes early, at 6:00 A.M., on a chilly summer morning. When the bus finally arrived several minutes late, the driver turned out not to be the same person I had previously met and the passenger I was told would board was nowhere to be found. Nervous and unsure of myself, I boarded and walked toward the middle of the bus, where I spotted many empty seats. All of a sudden I heard several different voices, including the bus driver's, all speaking loudly and at the same time. It didn't occur to me that they could be speaking to me. After all, I did not know anyone on the bus and had never seen these people before. For a brief moment there was a tremendous ruckus, seeming chaos, and commotion. Attempting to make sense of the different sounds and voices I heard, I began to think that everyone on the bus was yelling at me.

In fact, they *were* yelling at me! All the passengers were trying to get my attention. People were asking me, in a flurry of raised and overlapping voices incomprehensible together, where I was going and insisting that I sit in a particular seat—"my seat." This included the driver, who was now turning around, watching me in the aisle (and not looking at the road) while steering the bus at fifty kilometers an hour! Everyone on board, although only half awake at 6:10 A.M. on the first day of a new workweek, looked on, fixated. I hurriedly made my way to the seat toward the front of the bus where I was ordered to sit. Nervous but in "my seat," sweating and with my heart pounding, I thought, What had I done? Had I boarded the wrong bus? Had I committed some grievous crime relating to the peculiar culture of the bus? Had I violated a sacred code relating to bus etiquette of which I was unaware? Doing ethnographic fieldwork, I thought, was not all the fun and games it was purported to be. A few stops later, a middle-aged man boarded and without saying a word sat down beside me. There was hardly a sound or word uttered during the entire ride, and certainly nothing approaching the commotion that I had caused earlier. For the next forty-five minutes on the way to the factory, I recounted the incident in my mind over and over again, trying to figure out what had happened and why.[14]

---

*One *feddan* is approximately 1.038 acres.

Toward the end of the shift, the production director called me into his office. It was my first day of work, and he wanted to make sure there were no problems and that things were going well with respect to my research. I related what had happened during the morning bus ride, and after a short outburst of laughter, he explained the company's complicated system of "assigning" seating on all buses. I hadn't boarded the wrong bus. It turned out that as well as providing three different types of buses for different grades of workers and employees (not to mention minibuses and private cars for the very important people in the company like the production director), seating on all buses was "assigned" based on a combination of seniority and educational attainment. This usually corresponded closely with one's position in the company. Not only were there three different sets of buses for shift workers, daytime workers and white-collar employees, and higher-level management; the more senior and better educated in each bus had the privilege of sitting closer to the front, in the "first class" section, as it were.[15]

What had happened on the morning bus ride was that I, innocently and unknowingly, attempted to sit somewhere other than my "assigned" seat. Once assignments are made, a person's "place" on the bus is known by all. Not sitting in my assigned seat caused chaos as the driver and others intervened to set the situation right. My designated seat, behind the driver, was the third best on the bus and fitting for someone who had received a master's degree![16] Thus, despite the fact that the bus was never full and there were plenty of empty seats in the middle and back, I had to share a relatively small seat (an undivided padded bench with a back) with someone else. For the rest of my time at the company, I wished, every morning and afternoon, that I could sit on one of the empty seats in the middle of the bus, where I would have had an entire seat to myself. But no, my status and *brestige* (the Arabic rendering of "prestige") would not allow it!

The bus incident revealed the importance of education in determining social status and the extent of practices that reflected such hierarchy (e.g., the seating system on company buses). The incident also revealed that these hierarchical systems had become accepted and internalized as legitimate by employees (e.g., everyone trying to get me to sit in my proper seat).

My status reflected itself in another, more immediate, form—how I should be addressed. How one is addressed is relatively important in Egypt, as it reflects status and respect. The use of titles and honorifics is quite common. One often notices close friends who are doctors, for instance, address each other as "Doctor So-and-So." Even within families, one often hears siblings refer to their brothers and sisters who have received medical degrees or Ph.D.s as "Doctor So-and-So."

Although I was never asked, different people came up with various ways of addressing me. Some insisted on calling me "Doktor" or "Ya doktor Samer," in line with the Egyptian custom of labeling someone a doctor from the moment they finish a master's degree and begin pursuing a doctorate. Needless to say, having come from an academic subculture where titles and formality are looked at disparagingly, I was embarrassed and uncomfortable with this particular title.[17] Other workers chose to call me by the more familiar and common factory title of *Ya bash muhandis* (engineer), although I wasn't an engineer and knew nothing about engineering. Addressing engineers as "Engineer So-and-So" is important in the factory. So important that several petty conflicts occurred among white-collar staff between those who had engineering degrees and deserved to be addressed as such and those who were not engineers (and had other types of degrees) but were mistakenly referred to by that title by others.[18]

Another, very colloquial and quite *shaabi* (popular) word for engineer is *handasi*, and several workers referred to me this way ("Ya handasi"). Other titles sometimes placed before my name included *Ustaz* (Mr.), *Bey,* and *Basha*.[19] Although many people, after a few months on the job, simply called me by name, several refused and insisted on using some kind of honorific title (Doktor, Ustaz, etc.). This group, incidentally, included Fathy, the coworker whose sense of honor figures in the next story.

When I finally made it onto the shop floor, I received a rather unexpected welcome. After having struggled for months to get the necessary approvals to do fieldwork, dealt with various government agencies, interviewed with the relevant authorities, explained time and again what I wanted to study (and what I would not study)—in short, after having gotten access to my field site—both shift supervisors and workers did not want me to work.

I was introduced to my shift supervisor by one of the company's head engineers. The engineer explained that I was a *doktor* coming from the United States and would be conducting research in this particular shop floor for the coming months. The shift supervisor was asked to be as cooperative as possible.

When I showed up for work the next morning he was indeed extremely cooperative. His cooperation, however, extended only to a point. He insisted that I not do any work! I literally had to argue and fight for the first week in order to actually work. Out of politeness, courtesy, and respect, feigned or otherwise, or simply people's understanding of the way the Egyptian class system functioned, workers and shift supervisors did not think that performing manual labor was appropriate for me. The first day the shift supervisor stated this in terms of my being a "guest" and it not being appropriate for guests to work. The next day he said that I should not work "so that I would have fond memories of them and the shop floor." After all, to them I was an educated, upper-class doktor coming from the United States, and although it was well and good that I study whatever I liked, especially since this was approved by the "people upstairs," working on a machine, getting my hands dirty, and being ordered around by a shift supervisor simply made no sense.

After struggling to work my first week, the following week a new shift supervisor appeared with a different group of workers who were just as adamant that I neither work nor "tire myself" in any way. This shift supervisor went so far as to order one of "his" workers to bring me his own chair, the only chair on the shop floor, to sit on. After making it clear to everyone that I wanted to work, that performing manual labor was part of the research, and that I would work despite any and all protestations, things changed and working became less of an issue. Up until the very end of my research, however, Fathy, a coworker, would not allow me to sweep around my machine with the broom, part of the job assignment for the winding machine I operated. He accepted the fact that I could work, eat, joke, and laugh with him, but I could not be allowed to clean—that wouldn't be right. And on several occasions he literally fought me for the broom, saying, "May sah hish ya doktor" ("doctor, it's not right") while wrestling it out of my hands. The reactions of white-collar employees and engineers to this aspect of my research were just as interesting. Word spread among some of the younger bureaucrats, administrators, and engineers that I was actually working on a machine, and this seemed to amuse them no end. Some made silly jokes or references, and a few even came down to the shop floor, something most white-collar employees never did, to see for themselves what the doktor was up to.

All of these examples of workers and shift supervisors not wanting me to work, my coworker not allowing me to sweep around my machine, and the disbelief of many in management that I was actually working on the shop floor revealed what people in the factory took for granted about appropriate and inappropriate behavior by someone who had received higher education (e.g., a researcher with a master's degree who was pursuing a Ph.D.). These encounters exposed the assumptions and "commonsense" understandings of those in the factory—from workers to management—about the proper relationship between educational attainment, status, and appropriate and inappropriate labor.

UNKNOWN, POTENTIALLY DANGEROUS OUTSIDER

One of the reasons for using participant-observation as a research method, aside from the possibility of directly observing the social relations of production, was the hope that actual work alongside other workers would bridge, to some degree, the social distance between myself and my coworkers. This, in fact, happened to a considerable extent. We worked, ate, and joked together, used the same facilities, got searched the same way when we exited the factory, and socialized outside of work. Nevertheless, caution and calculation did mark some of my interactions, especially with people with whom I did not work directly.

The idea of the state or the company administration placing spies among workers is by no means far fetched. This has happened and continues to occur in Egypt today. Even more common, however, are certain workers who inform on workmates in exchange for favors, easy work routines, and favorable relations with superiors. It was said, in fact, that the public relations department was nothing other than the company's own intelligence gathering agency. Although I had no relationship to the company administration other than simply asking and being allowed to conduct fieldwork, it took some time before most people felt comfortable enough to talk openly about certain subjects in front of me. On several occasions workers and employees asked directly about my relationship to the top people in the company. Others asked who would be reading my notes. After some time, after I became friendly with many workers and a high degree of trust was established, we joked about what I did and did not write. Some reminded me they had "families to care for and kids to feed" and that I should be careful in terms of what I wrote. "Ihna eandani awlad" ("We've got kids") or "Shaklina han khush al-sign" ("Looks like we're going to jail") were often repeated and always produced a great deal of laughter on everyone's part.

On several occasions, particularly at the beginning, certain people were hesitant to speak openly in my presence. Once, while in the cafeteria with a group of young, white-collar employees, conversation turned to a recent scandal in which an administrator was caught embezzling money and was transferred to another department. While the events were being described, an older woman turned to her younger colleague narrating the story and said, "Limi nafsik" ("Watch your words" or "Take care"), since, I assume, I was sitting at their table.

I cannot forget feeling outraged that the older, female employee whom I saw in the cafeteria almost every day, exchanging polite greetings, would feel this way about me. I, after all, had absolutely no relationship to the administration and would never inform on anyone in any circumstance. I considered confronting her the next day but stopped myself, thinking that this might only make the situation more unpleasant. Moreover, although I would never have informed on anyone, she did not know exactly who I was or what I was doing. If you add to this the almost complete lack of trust between top management and employees (both workers and white-collar staff) and the fact that she was in the firm for life whereas I would be there for less than a year, her reaction becomes quite understandable.

On another occasion, I approached two workers, only one of whom I knew well, who happened to be discussing privatization and how this might affect them. The person I didn't know suddenly became silent as I got close and only resumed speaking when the other worker (the one I knew) said, "Huwwa maeana" ("He's with us"). Similar incidents also took place during my interactions with higher-level administration and engineers. Several days after a mechanic on my shop floor showed me what he considered to be substandard work produced by the company's machine shop, explaining how this negatively affected production, I heard that someone had recounted the incident to a worried engineer in charge of the machine shop.

Fear and distrust were the cost of admission ("entrée") to my research site, a cost I had no choice but to pay. But it was through my interactions and as a result of my perceived relationship to the administration that I witnessed workers' distrust of the company. These interactions also revealed that fear and distrust were not the monopoly of workers or lower-level white-collar employees, but extended to higher level employees and engineers as well.

CLASS

My status as a researcher, presence in the factory (and what this entailed), and class background are intimately related and only analytically distinct in terms of how they affected my research experience. From the very beginning there was tension, struggle, and negotiation concerning my identity in the factory. Many people, mostly "respectable" upper- and middle-class types, both inside and outside the company, had a difficult time understanding or accepting what I was doing or why I was doing it. They were amused and fascinated by my accounts of life on the shop floor and my knowledge of the working-class masses. Even top-level company administration did not, at first, understand what I was up to. In fact, before being allowed to undertake research, I was interviewed, the purpose of which was not to understand my research project or the effect I would have on production. Neither was the interview intended to determine whether I was potentially a security risk. It was, as I was told directly, so they could try to understand why someone who was ibn naas (the son of respectable people) wanted to work in a factory *as a worker*—even if it was research.[20]

In a very significant way, the reactions of high-level company administrators and upper- and middle-class Egyptians paralleled those of workers on the shop floor. To all concerned, my presence in the factory as a "worker" toiling away on a machine was disruptive, in a fundamental sense, of their understanding of the way the Egyptian class system worked. The idea that an upper-class doktor who was ibn naas would actually work, eat, joke, and socialize with shop floor workers was bizarre. The idea that I would become friends with many workers, show them respect, and get to know them as human beings, even as a consequence of research, defied their expectations, as it went directly against what everyone knew and took for granted about the Egyptian class system and the way it functioned.

In fact, I believe that this is one reason why more research of an ethnographic sort has not been done in Egypt and elsewhere in the Middle East by local academics. When most Egyptian academics and intellectuals study workers (or peasants), it is usually through interviews, questionnaires, or surveys. For academics also occupy a particular position in the rigid Egyptian system of social hierarchy. The idea that after achieving the status and social distinction that comes with a higher degree, they would willingly—even for research work in a factory on a machine or as an agricultural laborer (for a significant period of time) is almost unimaginable.

The tension and conflict my presence caused extended to the reactions I received from the middle-class white-collar administrators and engineers I interacted with daily. After the research was approved, I was sent to a senior engineer who was made responsible for me from that time onward. After hearing what I intended to do, his reaction was no different from what I described above. Without my having asked for his advice, he immediately suggested, with great seriousness and conviction, that I simply change my research method. During our next meeting he proposed that I work in the quality control department as a supervisor (*muraqib*) instead of working on a machine as a production worker. This way, he explained, I would have all the daily interaction with workers I wanted, but would not have to work or be with "them" constantly. As a supervisor, he explained, I wouldn't get my hands dirty or be exposed to the constant noise of the shop floor.

He thought he was doing me a favor, helping me out. I cannot describe how I felt at that moment. After I had spent months thinking about the project, reading the academic literature on the subject, writing a research proposal for my department, getting it approved, applying for grants, and finally making it through the ridiculously inept and ossified Egyptian bureaucracy (not to mention the paranoid and hypersensitive security apparatuses), this man was telling me, after meeting me for less than five minutes, to change my research method! It was, in one sense, quite absurd.

Because I was processed in the company bureaucracy as a "new worker," all of my paper work went through the training department (*qism al-tadreeb*). Naturally, I got to know the secretaries and director quite well. My first weeks, I spent many hours in the department completing forms, filing papers, and asking questions. The staff proved to be just as interested in me as I was in my new research setting. When it came time for my company identification card to be issued and my working hours to be finalized, the training department staff tried, quite hard, to persuade me to keep management and not factory hours. Management, including all bureaucrats, administrators, and most, although not all, engineers, arrived at work at 8:00 A.M. each morning and left at 2:00 P.M. Workers, by contrast, arrived earlier, at 7:00 A.M., and left later, at 3:00 P.M. For no logical reason other than their feeling that I should come and go with the rest of the administration and white-collar staff, they tried to convince me to keep their hours and not "the difficult factory hours." "Why come and go with the workers?" one of the secretaries asked. "You should come and go with us." What I experienced in the training department was a struggle over who I would identify with (the administration or the workers)—a struggle over my allegiance and identity.[21]

Aside from the difficulties I encountered simply trying to work once I reached the shop floor, the reactions of both workers and supervisors to my presence, and the issue of how I was to be addressed by my workmates, the moment that caused the most upheaval for administrators, engineers, and white-collar staff occurred when I casually mentioned to my young friends in the administration, on a very hot and humid Egyptian summer day, that I was thinking about bringing sandals to work and wearing them on the shop floor—like most workers in the factory. After all, sandals made much sense with the temperature outside over 100 degrees and the humidity unbearable.

The reaction I received was quite fascinating. Each and every one of them was shocked that I could even consider doing such a thing. I had reached, it seemed, the absolute limits of what I could and could not do, and wearing plastic sandals like the other workers was definitely out of the question and impermissible. I was *told*, in no uncertain terms, that it would not be appropriate. Sandals, it turned out, are one of the most important signifiers of one's status in the factory. They are a sign that says unmistakably, "I am a worker," and for me to even propose wearing anything other than shoes shook the entire semiotic system of class in the company.[22]

GENDER

One of the goals of the research was to explore working-class culture outside the factory, away from production, in the realms of consumption and reproduction. Being an unmarried man, however, was one of the primary reasons I was unable to access the working-class home. Although I socialized with many of my workmates, some of whom became genuine friends, this never occurred in their dwellings. Although a week would not pass without someone on my shop floor inviting me to have lunch at his home, for reasons one can barely describe in words, I felt these were formal invitations and not genuine ones. These were the types of invitations one is supposed to politely turn down. Although I was able to enter the homes of young, middle-class, white-collar employees, the presence of their wives and/or unmarried girls and the general gender ideology were some of the reasons why I never managed to make it into working-class homes. Cost and convenience were other reasons. Inviting someone into one's home, especially in Egypt, requires a suitable home and suitable things to offer. Embarrassment regarding workers' apartments and living conditions more generally could have been other reasons why I was not invited into workers' homes. If you live in an old, sixty-square-meter apartment in a poor district of town with your wife, nine kids, and your unmarried sister, as Darwish, my closest friend in the factory, did, there is hardly space for yourself, let alone guests.[23] We did our socializing in public places—coffee shops, downtown, the occasional outdoor wedding, and Alexandria's *corniche* (the wide coastal road).

Similarly, being male limited my access to and shaped my interaction with women workers and employees. Many factory shop floors are segregated by sex, and I worked on a floor where there were no women workers. But just as my identity closed certain doors, it opened others. Being male provided access to discourses on women, sex, manliness, and gender relations more generally. I was often told stories, and overheard others, that depicted women, and particularly wives, as only suitable for housework, constantly stirring up trouble, and having limited mental capacities compared to men (*naqsan aqlan wa dinan*—"lacking in reason and religion")[24]—qualities, incidentally, that were said to be found in all women. In short, although being male constrained my access to and interaction with women in their roles as employees and wives, it also exposed me to sexism and an ideology of patriarchy, subjects I might otherwise not have encountered.

RELIGION

Like my being male, my identity on the shop floor as a Muslim was not something I actively sought or cultivated. I was cajoled into praying with a shift supervisor and a workmate my second week on the shop floor. Although this was the only time I ever prayed at work, from that moment onward my status as a Muslim was defined for me.[25] Being Muslim exposed me to discourses on religion and politics and was, without any intention on my part, a source of bonding and membership between me and others in the factory, both workers and non-workers. Just as membership has its privileges, however, it also has disadvantages. As well as engendering solidarity, warmth, trust, and unlimited conversation about things religious, membership was also troubling, as it exposed me to what I found to be offensive discourses about *other* people, specifically, Egyptian Copts and Coptic Christianity. In other words, bigotry turned out to be the ugly side of identity, the seemingly inevitable result of the differentiation of oneself from the *other*.

I cannot overemphasize the importance of religion, and more specifically my religion, during fieldwork. Some workers went to great lengths to determine my faith. At my second research site, on my second day on the job, Gamal, a pulling machine operator whose machine was adjacent to mine, started chatting. Barely a minute had passed before his conversation quickly turned into a series of poorly disguised questions. It was clear. Gamal was trying to figure out whether I was Christian or Muslim.

The previous day the shift supervisor had introduced me by my first name. Gamal soon asked about my last name. His was more than a simple question, however. He was doing something quite common in Egypt: trying to make out my religion from my name. Some names clearly indicate one's religion. Someone named Mohamed, Ahmed, Ali or Mustapha, for example, is obviously Muslim, while someone named Boutros, Gerges, George or Michael, for example, is clearly Christian.

Unfortunately for Gamal, some names have no religious meaning or connotation (such as Gamal or Samer for instance) and therefore reveal nothing about their bearer's religion. After being unable to determine anything from my family name, he inquired, undeterred, about my father's name. My full name, however, also reveals nothing about my religion.[26] Thus, poor Gamal was particularly unlucky. After asking about both my last name and my father's name, he was no closer to his goal than when he began.

A different approach was needed and Gamal proceeded without hesitation. Once again, he attempted to conceal his questions, quite unsuccessfully, as stemming from a general interest in the United States and life there. Gamal asked which day of the week "we" (or I) prayed on in the United States. At this point I became genuinely annoyed at his persistent questioning and insistence on determining my religion, something, I believed, that was neither relevant nor any of his business. Without deliberately attempting to confuse him, I answered the question as accurately as possible. I told him that unlike in Egypt, Friday is a workday in the United States and that although Friday prayers exist, they are not well attended. Sunday, I proclaimed, is when the largest communal prayers take place. This confused him no end and he asked me to explain further. For as far as Gamal was concerned, things were quite simple. Muslims prayed on Friday and Christians prayed on Sunday. The idea that Muslims abroad could pray together on Sunday, because of a different work schedule, was not a possibility as far as he was concerned. He soon left, more confused and unsure of my religion than when he first began.

Immediately afterward, Ayman, another worker in the department and Gamal's close friend, came over and set the record straight. He stated, politely but nevertheless quite bluntly, that Gamal had been trying to determine my religion and my answers had only confused him. I told Ayman I was Muslim, and in less than twenty minutes, it seemed as if the entire shop floor, or at least the Muslims, had been informed of the "good news." At the end of the workday a group of workers gathered by my machine to celebrate the fact that I was Muslim, to welcome me into the club. They spoke generally about religion, praising Islam and comparing it to other religions, and advised me to beware of a certain Christian coworker who was known to cause trouble. One of the men gathered recounted a story about a conflict that had occurred between this particular Christian worker and a *sheikh** who also worked in the hall. From that moment on, it seemed I had won the lottery in terms of friends: friends who wanted to talk, socialize, and ask and be asked questions.

My Christian workmates also tried to determine my religion. After hearing my three-part name and learning that I was living in the United States, one Coptic coworker assumed that I was Christian. This led to a series of comments about the way former President Sadat was greeted when he traveled to Washington, D.C., to visit President Carter. The reference, which seemed out of place and cryptic at the time, concerns a well-known story about Coptic Egyptian-Americans protesting outside the White House during one of Sadat's visits to the United States. They were protesting the condition of Copts in Egypt, the restrictions on building and refurbishing churches, and the generally tense relations between Copts and Muslims at the time. The incident passed into the popular treasure chest of folklore and knowledge about Egyptian politics, and this particular worker was trying to bond with me by recounting it.

Not everyone on the shop floor was bigoted or hateful toward workers who did not share their religion. Unfortunately, it seems that all ethnic, national, and religious groups (and maybe all groups for that matter) have tales they tell about "the other." As Edward Said (1978) so power-

---

*In the factory, *sheikh* was a religious title of distinction. "Sheikh" literally means an older man in Arabic, but here, and more commonly, it refers to a religiously learned individual.

fully described in *Orientalism*, racist tales were standard fare in the history of "European scholarship" about the "East" and continued in the form of imperialism and foreign policy. If my religious identity had been different, I would have heard similar things said about "the other," whoever "the other" happened to be. And since the purpose of this essay is not to vilify any particular religion, idea system, or group, it is important to state this explicitly in the hope that exposing bigoted views and ideology does not, in turn, reproduce other racist and bigoted views.

REGIONAL BACKGROUND

Being from the same city as some of my workmates was not only a source of bonding; it was also one of the ways I gained the trust of coworkers. Many asked where exactly in the city my family had lived before we emigrated. Sharing this information and recounting the particular urban geography of my origin made me somehow less different and more familiar. Thus, where I was from turned out to be an unexpected source of identity and solidarity.[27] My identity was made less abstract. As with religion and gender, my regional background established a similarity between myself and others based on our common difference from workers from other parts of Egypt. But even for those who were originally from other parts of the country, either Upper Egypt or the Delta, knowing where I was from, I sensed, was reassuring as they now could associate me with a particular place, a place, it turned out, many of them knew firsthand. My familiarity with the city provided another common experience—a concrete experience—that we could share and that made me more familiar.

Regional identity, I determined, remained a distinctive sociogeographic marker for many in the factory, differentiating workers from urban areas from those originally from the rural provinces. And among workers originally from rural areas, regional identity functioned as a source of solidarity and bonding based on the particular province of origin.

Although regional identity was a distinctive sociogeographic marker, it was less divisive than religion, which, as recounted above, sometimes produced troubling, even bigoted, conduct. Regional differences were important but were taken much less seriously than religious differences, as indicated by the fact that we could joke about regional differences in a way that would never occur with religion. The fact that people were from many different parts of Egypt also meant that the divide was not binary, unlike the religious divide between Muslims and Christians.

CONCLUSION: PRACTICAL KNOWLEDGE AND
THEORETICAL INSIGHT

My multiple identities produced a variety of reactions in the field. My gender, religion, and regional background produced both common membership and solidarity (*inclusion*) as well as *exclusion* from certain groups and interactions. My relationship to the company administration produced *fear* and *distrust*. My identity as an Egyptian-American provoked *curiosity* and *interest*. My social position and class background produced, at least outwardly, *deference*. As a formally educated social scientist studying the working class, I elicited reactions of *bewilderment, confusion,* and *respect*.

Reflecting critically on identity in relation to my fieldwork—and more specifically, how I was perceived and what "the natives" thought of me—shaped my understanding of both identity and class, specifically, class identity and structure. In the most general terms, I learned that identity is never singular; like culture, it is forever in the plural. Fieldwork made me acutely aware of the complexities of both my identity *and* the identities of the people I was studying. For just as I am male, Muslim, Egyptian-American, a researcher with a certain class background, from a particular region in the country, and so on, they too had multiple and overlapping identities. They were Christians and Muslims of varying degrees of religiosity; workers, administrators, and engineers, with differing levels of education and skill; male and female; young and old; from different geographic regions within Egypt; and so forth. At different times and in various contexts, each of these characteristics, as well as others, proved important.

To say that identity is not singular, permanently fixed, or static, however, is not to say that it is completely up for grabs, constructed out of thin air, as some would have us believe, dependent only on what I choose to consume today, for example. I came to my fieldwork with certain, relatively specific features and characteristics, which themselves were partially of my own making and which I then chose to, in part, emphasize or de-emphasize. The individuals with whom I came into contact then gave me other characteristics and markers. They proceeded to interpret and then react to my identity for themselves. All of this, of course, took place within specific contexts and particular situations.

I cannot overemphasize the importance of *context* for identity. Context, as the philosophers of language (e.g., Saussure 1996), have taught us, is, in large part, where meaning comes from. This is certainly the case for language as well as other symbolic systems of meaning. Context is so important and so obvious, in fact, that it often appears invisible. It is the background against which all social action takes place. Although I participated in the shaping of my identity, through my actions and practices (my "presentation of self," in Erving Goffman's [1959] sense), my identity was more the outcome of negotiation between myself and others in particular contexts and specific situations than the result of conscious manipulation on my part. Thus, identities are neither completely given nor completely constructed, neither fixed and unchanging nor arbitrary and up for grabs. Identities are *negotiated*: negotiated within limits—limits that themselves are socially produced, contingent structures (e.g., gender and class), and these structures in turn are themselves the outcomes of human agency.

My most important insights on class identity and structure were products of those aspects of my identity that were most disruptive. Anthropologists have often claimed that one of the primary ways they learn about other cultures and societies is by *unknowingly* breaking social rules and unspoken conventions. By violating implicit and unacknowledged codes, anthropologists make these codes explicit.[28] My presence on the shop floor as "a worker" did precisely this: It broke the rules and conventions governing social class in Egyptian society. It was thoroughly disruptive of everyone's understanding of the Egyptian class system and the way it functioned, from the production workers to the chief executive officer, as well as those outside the factory gates. As a result, there was a significant amount of tension, struggle, and negotiation about who I was, what social role I would occupy, and with whom I would identify (the workers or the administration). For some people in the company this was genuinely threatening, as their very definition of self is predicated on their daily differentiation from others. Thus, my entry into the social world of the factory and my partial disruption of its operating principles was one of the primary ways I explored and experienced the phenomenon of social class in Egypt.

It was in part through my interactions—and how people reacted to me and my identities—that I learned about the extent of hierarchy (e.g., where I sat on the bus) and the meaning of social class in the factory (e.g., the significance of wearing plastic sandals). Although I did not experience class as a worker at a very deep level—what it means to struggle simply to survive and provide for one's children in a world of unbelievable scarcity and subsistence wages, where everyone works two jobs and when illness or an unforeseen expense can ruin one financially (and otherwise)—this was not the intention of the fieldwork. I did not and could never have become an

Egyptian worker in the way that a few early anthropologists mistakenly thought they could understand the natives by *becoming* native. My not fitting easily into already established categories and my unwillingness to play by the rules of the game made these categories, and the class structure of which they are a part, more apparent.

Class and class structure, after all, are not simply about "one's relationship to the means of production," in Karl Marx's words, where one fits into the division of labor, or a set of quantitative data about income and education—languages that are unfortunately often used but are essentially misleading. Class structure is also not simply the occupational geography of a place. Nor is it about the different positions people occupy within a division of labor. Following Anthony Giddens (1979), I take structures to be both constituted through and the outcome of human agency. Conceptualized as such, class structure should no longer be understood as a fixed, definite, rigid set of primarily "economic" relations (i.e., division of labor, level of technology, etc.) independent of the individuals who make up these relations and radically separate from human action. Rather, like all structures, the class structure of society has a virtual nonexistence in time and place: Because structures (in the realm of human action) are produced and reproduced through the practices and ideas of individuals, they have an ephemeral/fleeting quality to them. This is what renders class structure virtually nonexistent; it is not a "thing" (especially as compared with the more commonsense understanding of "structures" as buildings, which are solid, concrete, unmovable, and so on).

Moreover, agency necessarily includes within it the ideas agents give to their actions. It is in this sense that the actions and idea systems (implicit and explicit understandings, dispositions, habits, taken-for-granted knowledge, "common sense" in Gramsci's [1992] usage, and so on) that individuals in a given society practice and hold—and that refer to social class—make up an important part of a society's class structure. It is precisely through these practices and idea systems that the class structure is, in part, reproduced. Thus, the ideas and practices concerning class that I encountered in the factory are one very important part of the class structure of Egyptian society. My very experiences enacted what it was that I had come to study.

How would my understanding of the Egyptian class structure be different if my identity had been different? Obviously, I can only speculate about this. I probably would still have noticed that seating on the bus reflected patterns of social hierarchy within the company and society, for example. Through observation and questioning, I could have come to understand the basis on which certain people sit in particular seats. Implicit, unstated, almost instinctive understandings of social class, hierarchy, appropriate and inappropriate behavior, and the ideology relating to this (who wears plastic sandals and the struggle over my identity), however, might not have been as easily encountered and explored. Unlike which bus you get on or where you sit, the attitudes, expectations, dispositions, "commonsense" understandings, and implicit knowledge involving social class—the habitus (Bourdieu 1977, esp. chapter 2) of class, as it were—cannot be directly observed. But it is the class habitus that structures social practice and produces the seating assignment.

It was this that my various interactions made visible to me. Even if my identity did not affect my research in the most radical way—that is, did not directly determine my findings—it was partially through my identity, how I was perceived, and the attempt to incorporate me, somewhat clumsily, into systems of hierarchy, power, and prestige, that I came to understand the social world of the factory. For instance, the system of seating on the bus was not a result of my presence. It existed independently of me. But it was through my presence—and more particularly, the way this system attempted to incorporate me—that I learned about the seating system and what was behind it. My "findings"—my understanding of class, religion, power, hierarchy, and so on—were articulated through my identity and fieldwork encounter.[29]

Finally, through my fieldwork and my reflections on the productive nature of identity in the field, I have come to believe that the strengths of ethnography are underestimated at best and misunderstood at worst. Ethnography is best suited to exploring things that cannot be observed directly because they do not have a physical presence in the world, and yet these "things" shape it in very real ways: the implicit assumptions, operating principles, relations among concepts, and categories of thought and understanding that people take for granted and do not make explicit— in short, the "structuring structures" (Bourdieu 1977) of daily life. Other methods of research either cannot accomplish such analysis or accomplish it less well. Ethnography is, after all, the most empirical of methods, the most concrete—dependent upon actual observation, with the re-searcher physically present, taking nothing for granted, using less mediated knowledge than other methods. It is ironic that it is considered the most "subjective," where that term is commonly used to deny its empirical grounding. And despite being the most concrete, ethnography is best suited to explore what cannot be seen (or easily measured or counted): culture (meaning, ideas, catego-ries, concepts, narratives, discourse, and so forth). And I mean here "thick culture," not the "thin culture" of values, attitudes, and opinions that much survey research measures.

Reflexivity further strengthens ethnography. Ethnographers need to scrutinize and analyze their interactions with "the natives" for what these interactions—additional "data points" if you will—can reveal about the "natives" and their social world. Through my "subjective experi-ence," I learned about other people's worlds. I found these interactions incredibly revealing and informative; they generated the knowledge I claim to have about my research questions. They left me not just with a set of specific personal experiences but also with knowledge be-yond my interactions with workers—knowledge about their social world, priorities, values, understandings, and so on.

Recognizing ethnographer-"native" interactions as significant turns some of the traditional thinking about participant-observation and ethnography on its head. For example, one often hears the charge that the presence of a researcher/outside observer itself somehow changes, alters, distorts, or corrupts the research environment. And although one response to this charge is that this is true of all research, this "problem" is particularly acute and unavoidable with ethnography because the presence of the researcher is often obvious and obtrusive, and it changes the very character of the social dynamics. But the opposite is also true—those moments when you are not in the background (observing) but instead are at the center of the action can also be informative (e.g., unintentionally breaking conventions and learning about the social world of the factory in the process). Rather than bemoaning the idea that the ethnographer's presence somehow "cor-rupts" or "distorts" the research environment (language that invokes a natural science model, even an experimental model positing a sterile environment), I argue that ethnographers can, and should, reflect on and learn from their "personal, subjective" interactions and encounters with the people they are studying because of what these interactions say about "the natives" and their values, ideas, and social world.

This is what I mean by these interactions being additional "data points" (in the language of positivist social science). Rather than being a drawback, the presence of the ethnographer is a way to actively produce knowledge: He or she both participates and observes that participation itself, and learns from it. This is quite different from the older idea that participation was prima-rily a means to an end, the end being observation; it was believed that by being in "the field" for months and eventually melting into the background of social life, the ethnographer could come to accurately observe the social setting being investigated (without "contaminating" it through one's temporary, short term, disruptive presence). Participation was instrumental—to gain people's trust so that they let you observe them in their "natural" condition. What I have demonstrated, I hope, is that one should also observe the participation—the interaction itself—and see how people react to you, and that this can also be revealing about their social world, values, and so on.

It was a classic ethnographer, Malinowski, who argued that ethnography's "peculiar character is the production of ostensibly 'scientific' and 'objective' knowledge based on personal interaction and 'subjective' experience" (quoted in Stocking 1992, 51). For some, this has been, and continues to be, quite troubling. Rather than being a cause for concern, a potential problem, or a danger, however, I believe this is ethnography's fundamental strength. The problem lies not with ethnography but with the dominant paradigm of knowledge and the conceptualization of the human sciences. By accepting the natural sciences as *the* model for the human sciences, and more specifically the idea of the strict separation of the "personal" and "subjective" from the "objective," ethnography as method appears inherently problematic—at least as "science." The complete separation of subject and object, researcher and object of research, however, is illusory and particularly inappropriate for the human sciences (Reed-Danahy 1997). Thus, the problem is not with ethnography or anthropology but with the natural science model and its relevance for the human sciences.[30] The ethnographer, after all, is not an objective machine but a positioned subject, never outside the field of research and always radically implicated in the production of knowledge. All researchers are implicated in the knowledge they produce. In ethnography, however, this becomes particularly difficult to disguise, in light of the central role of the ethnographic self in the production of claims to knowledge.

NOTES

1. See Bayard de Volo and Schatz (2004). The fact that Bayard de Volo and Schatz need to write an article arguing for the potential utility of ethnography as a method for students of politics, something that should be quite obvious, reflects the current state of the discipline, dominated as it is by quantitative methods, formal modeling, and other non-fieldwork, non-qualitative approaches to the study of politics. Moreover, the authors temper their enthusiasm for ethnography as method with statements such as, "[E]thnography has shortcomings, but if used judiciously, its contribution is noteworthy" (2004, 267). Although their hearts are in the right place, the authors display an incredible defensiveness about ethnography, as if somehow it is inherently problematic in a way that other research methods are not. Bayard de Volo and Schatz do not address the more complex issues about the role of the ethnographer in the production of knowledge discussed in this essay.

2. Some have called these "author-evacuated texts." See Okely and Callaway (1992).

3. For an excellent analysis of the arrival trope see Pratt (1986).

4. In fact, Geertz claims that epistemological questions about "the problematics of field work" (and the status of ethnographic knowledge) have actually obscured the real question. He expresses the problem this way: "The difficulty is that the oddity of constructing texts ostensibly scientific out of experiences broadly biographical, which is after all what ethnographers do, is thoroughly obscured" (1988, 10). For Geertz, this is a "narratological issue," not an "epistemological one."

5. See Judith Okely's prescient "The Self and Scientism" (1975). See also Okely (1992) and Hastrup (1992, esp. page 119).

6. See Okely (1992, 14) and Caplan (1988, 15).

7. For an interesting analysis of the place of "the field" in anthropology, see Gupta and Ferguson (1997).

8. Some of those I worked with most closely occasionally asked even more personal and, at times, embarrassing questions, which would be considered completely off limits in other social contexts and possibly other class contexts.

9. In some ways, my loyalty to Egypt was at stake in my answers. It also seemed that people wanted contradictory, or at least complicated, answers to the first question. "Of course, Egypt is better than anywhere else including the United States. It is, after all, where we are from!" At the same time, however, one can only deceive oneself so far, and if I did not begin with complaints and criticism about the political, economic, and social problems in the country, they did. Although most people were fierce and unthinking nationalists, they were also filled with unending criticism of the state of affairs in the country.

10. After Fathy asked about milk consumption in the United States, he said, "I would be lying to you if I told you my kids drink milk every day."

11. This phrase, *min al-dar ila al-nar* ("from home to hell"), rhymes in Arabic.

12. Interestingly enough, this sentence was first uttered by Mohamed Abdou while characterizing the differences between Europe and the Middle East. Abdou (1849–1905) was one of the leading Egyptian thinkers of the nineteenth century. Exiled for three years, he traveled to Paris and London, eventually returning to become the Mufti of Egypt in 1899. These workers, however, did not know the origin of the phrase.

13. When engineers did arrive to scrutinize the machines or production, they never acknowledged the workers on the shop floor.

14. Few spoke while riding the bus to work. Although some conversed during the ride home (in the afternoon), they were a minority. This made the outburst, noise, and confusion even more worrying—and puzzling.

15. I later noticed that the buses used for shift workers were in significantly worse condition than the other two types of buses. The buses reserved for top management also had higher, more comfortable seat backs. Except for the nice buses reserved for senior employees, seats were similar to those found on school buses in the United States: not individual seats separated from one another, but padded benches with back rests. Thus, not only was hierarchy reflected in which bus you rode (and with whom), but it was also reflected in the quality of the buses, the comfort of the seats, and where specifically you sat inside the bus.

16. At the firm I worked at the longest, my company issued me an identification card that stated, quite unnecessarily, that I had received a master's degree and listed my field of specialization.

17. Not to mention the fact that I had not finished my Ph.D.

18. In one case, a young female engineer was assigned to work in a lab in which the director, although older and more senior, did not have an engineering degree. It was frequently said, including by the young engineer herself, that the lab director resented the fact that one of her employees was referred to by the prestigious title of *bash muhandisa* (engineer), which she herself, not being an engineer, did not receive. A minor dispute resulted between the two women because of this issue.

19. Both *Bek* and *Basha* were official titles of status conferred on distinguished members of Egyptian society (usually large landowners) by the monarchy before the 1952 revolution. Beks and Bashas were two different degrees of lordship, and both titles are used colloquially today in an informal manner.

20. *Ibn naas* literally means "the son of people," referring to not just any people but people of character, standing, and respectability. The meaning seems to have evolved over the last few decades. At first, ibn naas primarily referred to respectability and morals. Today, however, wealth and economic status seem to be just as essential for qualification for this category. In the context of the interview, ibn naas referred to my similarities with the interviewers: sharing the same class background, mixing in similar social circles, membership in the same sporting clubs, and so on.

21. The possibility of management's wanting to keep an eye on me as the reason for the training department staff's reacting this way to my work hours is highly unlikely. First, it was the secretarial core that primarily reacted, not the security people. Second, I am certain management did keep an eye on me, but they did not need to be physically present to do so. Finally, I got my way in the end and showed up at 7:00 every morning and left at 3:00 every afternoon.

22. Another reason wearing sandals entered my mind is that I noticed that the director of the training department kept a pair of quite nice leather sandals under his desk, which he would wear on his way to the administration bathroom to wash before praying. He was ridiculed behind his back by the young administrators for doing so. It was simply not right that a director ("of all people") should wear sandals at work, whatever the reason.

23. Darwish was usually the first one on the shop floor each morning, arriving well before the beginning of the shift. This was somewhat unusual as many tried their hardest to arrive at the very last minute. Darwish was also in no rush to leave when the bell rang. This could have been because his apartment was simply too small and uncomfortable for him and his family.

24. It is popularly believed that this is a quotation from the Qur'an. When it is repeated, it is done so as such. To the best of my knowledge, however, it is not.

25. Although I have no proof, I am certain that the news that I prayed was conveyed to other workers who worked different shifts with me on the same shop floor.

26. Egyptians (and the Egyptian state) often speak of *ism al-thulathy*, one's three-part name (first name, father's first name, and last name).

27. Egypt, like much of the Third World, has experienced mind-boggling rural-urban migration in the decades since World War II. Many of those I worked with had migrated to the city where the factory was located. I, quite literally, witnessed both rural-urban migration and a related process, proletarianization—the transition from agricultural to factory labor.

28. See, for example, Stocking's (1992, 36–40) account of William Rivers's "General Account of Method."

29. The term "findings" often suggests a positivist model of the human sciences in which knowledge is assumed to be "out there," existing already, independent of us, pre-research and pre-theory, waiting to be "discovered"—very much like Columbus "discovered"—or shall I say found—America. This is in contrast to a model of the human sciences based on the idea that knowledge is produced.

30. Whether this model is even appropriate for the natural sciences is a legitimate, although thoroughly different, question. As such, it cannot be addressed here.

CHAPTER 14

MAKING SENSE OF MAKING SENSE

Configurational Analysis and the Double Hermeneutic

PATRICK THADDEUS JACKSON

September 1994. I'm in class—Introduction to International Relations, 6801—and the assigned reading for the second week of the course is Designing Social Inquiry *by King, Keohane, and Verba. I have two distinct reactions, stemming from the two parts of my undergraduate background. The math major part of me is deeply concerned with how* primitive *the statistical models in the book are. (Linear equations? If there are equations governing social life, they must be nonlinear at the very least, if not chaotic.) The philosophy and literary theory part of me is struck by the absence of any sustained philosophical reflection in the book, and by the authors' charming naiveté in declaring that they were interested in "causal inference"—as though this cleared anything up. And then there was their rather odd use of counterfactuals. . . .*

As an undergraduate I had been pulled in two directions—directions that didn't seem incompatible to me most of the time, but that was largely because I compartmentalized them and didn't really think about them as somehow informing one another. I was pursuing programs in international relations (IR) and mathematics, since those seemed to capture the two things in which I was most interested: social relations (especially on a global level) and logical computations. I'd been interested in both for as long as I can remember, filling out the classic stereotype of the computer geek who spent more time observing his classmates than interacting with them. In high school I'd gotten very interested in political philosophy, and that was my entrée into the world of social thought, which I read and discussed avidly when I wasn't programming a computer or learning about some puzzle in high-energy physics.

Parallel tracks. The first person who suggested to me that they might go together was my undergraduate IR advisor, and he initially thought that I was interested in modeling international interactions formally when he looked at the courses I was taking. Honestly, I had never thought about it. After he posed this possibility I toyed with the idea, but then rejected it rather quickly because of what seemed to me to be the obviously different philosophical bases on which the two endeavors (mathematics and social theory) rested: Logic was certain in its own terms; social theory was inescapably normative.

What really got me off of the mathematics track and confirmed my path as one involving social theory, however, was a more specific revelation involving the Gödel Undecidability Theorem: the demonstration that no logical system of finite axioms with sufficient power to capture processes like basic arithmetic could ever be both complete and consistent at the same time. It was always possible to find a moment of undecidability that would disrupt the system's purity; but this *meant that the stability of social life simply could not be reduced to* any *system of equations. Certainly not linear ones. This fascinated me: If social stability does not arise from logic, where does it come from and how is it sustained?*

Everything else followed from this: opposition to the dominant, mainstream models of social inquiry presented during graduate school; further independent reading in social and political philosophy as part of a search for better alternatives; decisions to teach research methodology courses in the Weberian mode stressing the incompatibilities between value commitments and the diverse (and irreconcilable) insights generated by the ideal-typical approaches that stem from them. And, eventually, this chapter.

> **Chancellor Konrad Adenauer**, Christian Democratic Union (CDU): The opposition has to take a position on this question—this, and no other, is the relevant question: Are they prepared to send a [German] representative to the Ruhr Authority, or not? And when they say no, then they know because of the clarification that General Robertson gave me that the demolition program will be carried out through to its end.
>
> **Kurt Schumacher**, Chairman of the opposition Social Democratic Party (Sozialdemokratische Partei Deutschlands, SPD): That's not true! (Shouts of "hear, hear!" and counter-calls from the government parties. Further heated shouts from the SPD and the Communist Party [Kommunistische Partei Deutschlands, KPD]. President's bell sounds.)[1]
>
> **Renner**, KPD: What does this mean? (Shouts from the left:[2] Are you still a German? Are you speaking as a German chancellor?)
>
> **Schumacher**: Federal Chancellor of the Allies! (Loud shouts of protest from the middle and right. Great noise from the opening and closing of desk covers. Representatives of the SPD and the CDU/CSU rise from their places and engage in heated disputes. Prolonged tolling of the President's bell. Long-lasting din.)
>
> —*Verhandlungen der Deutschen Bundestags,* Stenographische Bericht, *Bonn,* (November 24–25, 1949, 524–25)

Kurt Schumacher's accusation against Konrad Adenauer in the early morning of November 25, 1949, is an emblematic and significant moment in the history of postwar German reconstruction. Coming near the end of a strident parliamentary debate concerning the proper German response to an initiative by the occupying Allies[3] to internationalize control of the industrial Ruhr region, it neatly exemplifies the basic dilemma of Chancellor Adenauer's position. On one hand, in order to keep the Allies happy, he had to be responsive to their demands and requests, lest they simply dismiss the entire German government and install one more to their liking. On the other hand, in order to keep his position within German political life, he had to avoid appearing as simply a tool for the occupying powers. Coming from the leader of the largest opposition party (the SPD), Schumacher's challenge was particularly significant, as it was also a thinly veiled call to replace Adenauer with someone who would stand up for the German people on issues of territorial sovereignty and the ongoing demolition of industrial facilities—namely, Schumacher himself.

But there is more going on here than might be apparent at first. In a way, Schumacher's outburst fed directly into a more or less deliberate strategy on Adenauer's part to cast Schumacher as a nationalist alternative to his policy of cooperation with the "Western" occupying powers (Schwarz 1995). At the same time, Schumacher's public stand on this occasion paralleled the stance taken by the Communist Party, which implicitly reinforced the argument often advanced by Adenauer and other conservatives that all Marxist parties were the same: materialist, nationalist, old-fashioned, and unfit to govern responsibly. On most occasions, "socialists . . . were the most effective anti-communists," arguing that Marxist thought did not necessarily point in the direction of communism and providing by their own example an alternative path (Mark 1989); Schumacher was no exception. But in this instance he made common cause with the more radical parties of the left, simultaneously undercutting his presentation of social democracy as an alternative to communism *and* displaying a hot-headedness that resulted in a suspension from the floor of the Bundestag (the German parliament).

How are scholars to make sense of this emblematic moment? The configuration of social resources that made it possible for Schumacher to accuse Adenauer of being a servant of the occupying powers is not the only configuration that might have existed; nor was Schumacher's accusation (or Adenauer's subsequent response) somehow inevitably produced by that configuration. Instead, the observed patterns were more contingent, depending simultaneously on the ways that the historical actors interpreted their situations and on the way that subsequent scholars have interpreted their interpretations.

I suggest that scholars turn to a configurational analysis of social action. Adopting such an approach would preserve agency at the level of methodology and empirical practice, and not merely by conceptual or theoretical fiat. Social actors in this conception are like the "cognitive *bricoleur*" described by Roy Bhaskar, "the paradigm being that of a sculptor at work, fashioning a product out of the material and with the tools available to him or her" (Bhaskar 1989, 78).[4] The work of empirical analysis, then, should involve delineating the resources available and tracing the ways that they are deployed in practice, while sticking close enough to the data that statements about available resources have more of an empirical than a conceptual character.

For example, from this perspective, the parliamentary exchange appears as a legitimation struggle. Both Adenauer and Schumacher were faced with problems of legitimation: In order to subsist in their positions and to accomplish policy goals, they needed to provide publicly acceptable justifications for their preferred courses of action.[5] My central analytical claim is that legitimation is constrained by the available configuration of publicly shared "rhetorical commonplaces"—those vague notions that command more or less general assent in the abstract but that stand in need of detailed specification before they can be determinately linked to specific courses of action (Laffey and Weldes 1997; Ringmar 1996; Shotter 1993b). The work of legitimation involves deploying the available commonplaces so as to rule out alternative courses of action and to justify one's own preferred option. And the stakes are high, inasmuch as the process of legitimation exercises a profound causal impact on social and political outcomes (P.T. Jackson 2003).

Scholars engaged in such research are faced with what Anthony Giddens would call a "double hermeneutic" problem (Giddens 1984): They have to interpret what is said by historical actors while keeping firmly in mind the fact that what they are interpreting are interpretations of situations that those actors themselves have made. Both of these interpretations feature creative uses of rhetorical commonplaces. Even if the historical character of the case under investigation prevents these two hermeneutic circles from interacting in a causal or reciprocal sense (Hacking 1999), a thorny methodological problem remains. The challenge is to incorporate the active character of both streams of interpretation simultaneously, and not to reify one for the purpose of clarifying the other. Inasmuch as active interpretation is closely linked to agency, this challenge must be met decisively.

In what follows I will argue that an appropriate way to meet that challenge involves a linked set of three analytical tasks: The cultural resources on which actors draw when engaging in legitimation struggles must be delineated; the specific histories of those resources, from which their practical efficacy stems, must be disclosed; and the specific ways that those resources are deployed in a concrete episode must be traced. All three of these tasks need to be accomplished in such a way that the analyst never loses sight of the fact that she or he is promulgating a theoretically informed account of an episode, and never simply revealing the world "the way that it really is." Doing so requires taking the ideal-typical, or "prosthetic," character of scholarly accounts more seriously than other approaches do. I begin with this philosophical consideration before turning to a more detailed explication of the three analytical tasks and how to carry them out.

AGENCY AND THE DOUBLE HERMENEUTIC

Interpretation, whether it is being performed by the historical actors who are the objects of analysis or by the scholarly researcher carrying out that analysis, "is never a presuppositionless apprehending of something presented" to the interpreter (Heidegger 1962 [1927], 191–92). Instead, interpretation is more of a process of assembling (even if in an unconscious way) extant cultural resources to form specific patterns.[6] This process of interpretation does not take place inside of heads, but instead involves the manipulation of intersubjective resources of signification—resources that we might call "cultural" (Geertz 1973a; Geertz 1980; Wedeen 2002). It is thus "public" in a conceptual sense, even if the act of interpretation in question is performed away from the popular gaze—or even in the privacy of one's own mind, inasmuch as one always uses publicly available resources to think (Wittgenstein 1953). Thinking and interpreting are irreducibly conversational activities, oriented toward a shared social context and arising out of the potentialities afforded by that context (Shotter 1993a).

Agency is implicated in these interpretive activities both to the extent that social outcomes are dependent on particular combinations of cultural resources *and* to the extent that those combinations are not inevitable (and thus epiphenomenal) products of other factors. Agency, in Giddens's formulation, "refers not to the intentions people have in doing things but to their capability of doing those things in the first place. . . . Agency concerns events of which the individual is the perpetrator, in the sense that the individual could, at any phase in a given sequence of conduct, have acted differently" (Giddens 1984, 9). The range of possible options at any point in time is a function of a combination of cultural resources that did not need to be combined in the way that they factually were. Giddens's definition thus highlights the connection between agency and a certain radical indeterminism: Agency means that things could have been different, save for the impact and implications of certain actions. A meaningful concept of agency is thus opposed to notions of determinism and inevitability (Abbott 2001, 201–2), and retaining or preserving agency necessitates a reconceptualization of the explanatory capacity of one's account of some situation.

When it comes to meaningful social action, agency is creativity and contingency: the creativity of actors in assembling particular cultural resources in a specific way, and the contingency of the patterns that are thus produced. This applies equally to the social actors under investigation and to the scholarly researcher conducting the investigation, although the contexts in which their interpretations take place are somewhat different. But both kinds of actors are engaged in similar procedures of assembling extant cultural resources to justify their claims and activities. There is a "prosthetic" character to this process, in that combinations of resources form

an instrumental means *through* which to achieve our ends. As such, they are "transparent"
—blind people do not feel their sticks vibrating in the palms of their hands, they experience
the terrain ahead of them directly as rough, as a result of their stick-assisted "way" of
investigating it in their movement through it. (Shotter 1993b, 21; emphasis in original)

Combinations of resources, then, function as instruments that reveal the world in particular
ways. When applied to scholarship, this insight requires an acknowledgment of the ideal-typical
character of scholarly accounts of the world. Such an acknowledgment, if made in an active and
ongoing manner, helps to prevent scholars from becoming entrapped by their narratives. Such
entrapment would lead to a misrepresentation of the world revealed by scholarly prosthetics as
though it were *real* in the sense of existing outside of all social practices of interpretation (Heidegger
1962 [1927]). As Max Weber argued in his famous (and often misunderstood) essay on "'objectivity,'"[7] ideal types are

formed through a one-sided *accentuation* of *one* or *more* points of view and through bringing together a great many diffuse and discrete, more or less present and occasionally absent
concrete individual events, which are arranged according to these emphatically one-sided
points of view in order to construct a unified *analytical construct* [*Gedanken*]. In its conceptual purity, this analytical construct [*Gedankenbild*] is found nowhere in empirical reality; it is a utopia. (1999a, 191; emphasis in original)

Ideal types are pragmatically useful rather than "true" or "false" (M. Weber 1999a). Inasmuch
as the first criterion of an ideal type is its pragmatic and analytical character, we can begin by
tossing out claims to have accurately apprehended the essence of the situation under investigation. This means, among other things, that no single scholarly account of a situation can be mistaken for a "definitive" or "final" word on that situation (Shotter 1993a). Instead, scholars should
focus on what their particular theoretical specifications actually do in practice and what kind of
world they help to produce. Scholars cannot avoid their responsibility for the values embedded in
particular ideal-typical conceptual prosthetics and must therefore self-consciously exercise responsibility in selecting their analytical tools.

But the prosthetic character of combinations of cultural resources applies just as much to
claims made on the Bundestag floor about the direction of postwar German reconstruction as it
does to claims made by researchers about how and why that reconstruction effort took place in
the way that it did. In both contexts, cultural resources deployed in the course of claims making
reveal the world in a specific way and afford certain courses of action and not others.[8] Both the
social actors under investigation and the scholarly researcher conducting the investigation exercise agency to the extent that the social contexts in which they are situated are not conceptualized
as being fully closed and determinate. "Conceptualization" is central here precisely because terms
like "agency" and "context" are themselves prosthetics, revealing the world in specific ways and
not in others. "Preserving agency" therefore means generating accounts that leave room for the
indeterminacy, creativity, and contingency of social action.

In adopting a broad understanding of methodology as "a concrete practical rationality"
(Flyvbjerg 2001), rather than a narrow understanding that would collapse methodology into mere
"method," the preservation of agency appears as a methodological issue. Methodology is complicit
in the production and reproduction of the world. Focusing on this complicity and conducting
research from within it, as it were, involves a commitment to "reflexivity": an awareness of how
the habits and experiences that one is bringing to bear on a situation shape and construct that

situation (Kondo 1990). Such research has as its primary goal to make explicit and visible the prosthetics at work in a given situation, to "denaturalize" them and make them less transparent (Weldes 1999a, 241–42)—that is, to make them more apparent and less taken for granted. In addition, research of this sort should illustrate how those prosthetics interact and concatenate so as to produce practical outcomes, and it should do so in a way that respects and preserves creativity and contingency both for the social actors under investigation and for the scholarly researcher conducting the investigation.

By deploying appropriate conceptual and theoretical prosthetics, an analytic that takes the double hermeneutic seriously can preserve agency in a way that other approaches to the study of social life cannot. But this is surprisingly difficult to do.

NEOPOSITIVISM

Consider, for instance, the way that a "neopositivist" research methodology would approach the parliamentary exchange between Schumacher and Adenauer. The neopositivist explanatory approach aims "at showing that the event in question was not 'a matter of chance,' but was to be expected in view of certain antecedent or simultaneous conditions," and it seeks to identify systematic connections between factors that hold true across cases (Hempel 1965, 235; see also King, Keohane, and Verba 1994, 55–63, 76–82). Public rhetoric in a neopositivist account is primarily an expression of underlying "ideas," understood as subjectively held "beliefs," which are also variable attributes amenable to comparative hypothesis testing (Goldstein and Keohane 1993; Laffey and Weldes 1997).[9] In order to demonstrate the causal effect of some factor (say, nationalist beliefs that permit an opponent to be characterized as a mere pawn of the occupying powers), it is necessary to figure out in advance what such beliefs imply, so that the actual outcome can be compared with the hypothetical prediction.

In this conception, Schumacher simply matched his underlying preferences with the efficiently predicted effects of accusing Adenauer of betraying the German nation—and any actor with a similar preference structure placed in the same situation would *inevitably* have made the same choice. But this means that the theoretical capacity to do otherwise, along with any creative aspects of Schumacher's action, has been effectively eliminated from the account. The scholar's action in specifying the character of particular social actions in advance (or at least in supposed isolation from the data) ends up depriving the actors under analysis of much of their agency. An actor selecting from among solid, stable "ideas" whose determinate character is specifiable in the abstract is reduced to the role of a supermarket shopper selecting from among competing brands. Individual *agents* may be preserved, but *agency* is sacrificed.

The neopositivist approach to public rhetoric is a kind of "necessity individualism" (see P.T. Jackson 2003) and is not really designed to preserve agency. In effect, it downplays both aspects of the double hermeneutic: The actors under investigation are less active producers of their situation than passive consumers of it, and the scholarly researcher is not a creative interpreter of the situation so much as an accurate reflector of it.

SINGLE HERMENEUTICS

Methodological approaches that are more focused on the question of agency often emphasize one or the other of the two hermeneutic circles implicated in the double hermeneutic. By doing so, they introduce some measure of agency into their accounts, but end up restricting that agency somewhat arbitrarily.

Consider those approaches that minimize the importance of the hermeneutic circle between the social actor and the actor's environment in favor of a focus on the activity of scholarly interpretation. This kind of work tends to disregard the "surface" manifestations of action—the tangible, empirical aspects—in favor of a process by which events are understood exclusively through terminology provided by a particular abstract theoretical perspective. These abstract categories, often involving "class" (O'Connor 2001) or "rationality" (Bates 1998; Hardin 1995) or the "functions" fulfilled by particular courses of action (Habermas 1975), permit the scholar to impose a certain order on the machinations of everyday life, and to reveal a broader significance lurking around or behind actions like legitimation struggles. Puzzling events thus become comprehensible by being brought under the sway of an abstract typology.[10] Such an approach, however, virtually eliminates the agency of the social actors under investigation, in that they are understood to be largely at the mercy of forces of which they may not even be aware.[11]

On the other hand, consider those approaches that minimize the importance of the hermeneutic circle connecting the scholarly researcher to her or his subjects in favor of a precise delineation of the nuances of a system of meaning. The methodological goal of such interpretation is to get an "accurate" picture of the meanings-in-use of the persons under investigation. Such approaches presume that "the interpretation of the object-culture is *definitive* (certain) and the ideal social scientist investigates his or her subject-matter with a *conceptual tabula rasa* (passively)" (Bhaskar 1998, 149; emphasis in original). This is equally true of ethnographic practices that concern themselves with the ways that field notes "ignore, marginalize, and obscure indigenous understandings" and "suggest alternative procedures . . . that avoid such impositions" (Emerson, Fretz, and Shaw 1995), and of textual analyses that aim to elucidate the "unsaid" meanings that surround what is actually said publicly, or to flesh out the more or less determinate "context" within which episodes like the Schumacher/Adenauer exchange take place (Foucault 1972). In all of these cases, the scholarly researcher becomes "entrapped" within her or his narratives, forgetting that scholarly accounts "are instruments, not depictions" (Shotter 1993a). The scholar stops exercising agency, becoming instead a more or less neutral conduit through which supposedly "objective" facts about the situation can flow.[12]

These single hermeneutic accounts have more space for agency than neopositivist accounts do, but they force a choice between the agency of the scholar and the agency of the social actors under investigation. They restrict the domain of agency by utilizing prosthetics that do not preserve both parts of the double hermeneutic.

LEGITIMATION: PRESERVING THE DOUBLE HERMENEUTIC

So how should one go about making sense of a social situation so as to preserve both hermeneutic circles simultaneously? The heart of my solution is to select a prosthetic that permits the social actors under investigation to exercise meaningful agency. For this purpose, a prosthetic that regards public rhetorical deployments as elements in a legitimation struggle is an appropriate choice.[13] Such a prosthetic conceptualizes legitimation as an ongoing process, "a coordinated group of changes in the complexion of reality . . . an integrated series of developments unfolding in conjoint coordination in line with a definite program" (Rescher 1996, 38).

Understood in this way, legitimation—whether that of the researcher or that of the persons involved in the situation under investigation—is conceptually "local" to particular times and places. Any particular legitimation struggle produces only a relatively stable justification for a particular course of action, and not a transcendently or eternally valid one. Instead of more or less parametric "structures" encompassing and enfolding action, we have spaces of practical activity within which the stabilization of social relations takes place (Shotter 1993a; Tilly 2002) and that generate emergent "figurations" (Elias 1991) or "social arrangements" (Onuf 1998). Legitimation is therefore ongoing, never entirely finished, and never exhaustive; even the most apparently solid set of legitimating reasons might lose their public appeal under the right conditions.

At the same time, the local stabilizations highlighted by this prosthetic cannot simply be reduced to the deliberate and instrumental decisions of historical actors. Indeed, actors, too, are endogenized to ongoing social processes, and in particular to the social processes involving the attribution of responsibility and the delimitation of boundaries of acceptable action (P.T. Jackson 2004; Ringmar 1996). Instead of transcendental subjects speaking, or essential individuals exercising full control over the meanings of their words and deeds, the prosthetic of legitimation struggles discloses specific persons as *sites* in a complex cultural network of institutional, organizational, and rhetorical resources (Foucault 1972).

The location of persons in this cultural network affects the agency that they can exercise. To be more precise: In this approach, potentials for action arise from what we might call the double failure of social arrangements to cohere on their own (P.T. Jackson 2003). First, particular constellations of resources and strategies are never inevitable, but represent ongoing accomplishments of practice (Doty 1997). The "fit" of particular legitimating practices with one another has less to do with intrinsic properties of the practices themselves, and more to do with active processes of tying practices together to form relatively coherent wholes (Laffey and Weldes 1997). Second, cultural resources for action are always ambiguous and do not simply present themselves as clearly defined templates for action (Sewell 1992). Instead, cultural resources provide opportunities, but actualizing those opportunities demands practical, political, and discursive work (Neumann 1999; Tilly 1998).[14]

If we keep in mind both the ideal-typical character of this conception of legitimation struggles and the openness of the conception itself to creativity and contingency on the part of the social actors under investigation, it should be possible to preserve both parts of the double hermeneutic simultaneously.[15]

IMPLEMENTING THE PROGRAM: MOMENTS AND MECHANISMS

Legitimation, like any social process, is analytically composed of and sustained by mechanisms that "account for variation in how processes unfold" (P.T. Jackson and Nexon 2002, 105). Concrete historical outcomes are a product of the contingent concatenation of multiple mechanisms and practices; the analytical work suggested by such a stance involves detailing how these concatenations come to pass and what effects they exercise (McAdam, Tarrow, and Tilly 2001, 13; Tilly 1998). In order to explain the impact of particular legitimation practices at some particular point in time, it is necessary to examine the specific historical context out of which they emerge, along with the specific ways in which those cultural practices interact with one another.

But a conventional historical narrative will not suffice here. Scholarly researchers only know that some resource or practice was important in retrospect, which is to say after it has been deployed in a concrete context or legitimation struggle and has thereby taken on a locally specific meaning with practical implications for the issues at hand. Therefore, one has to begin at the point at which a legitimation struggle concretely takes place, then move "backward" in time to sketch out the specific historical context, and finally come back "forward" in time to the resolution of the concrete legitimation struggle itself. This temporal tacking back and forth is crucial to the exercise.

The analysis of a legitimation struggle along these lines therefore involves three analytical tasks:

- First, it is necessary to *delineate the cultural resources*—and in particular the rhetorical commonplaces—drawn upon by the actors under investigation. This delineation is an analytical description rather than a recoding of particular situations according to an abstract schema; the categories used in the delineation come from the situation under investigation, and not from any general account of social life. The method appropriate to fulfilling this task is "textual ethnography"—a careful reading of the written traces of social practices.
- Second, the *specific histories* of these commonplaces—how they came to be available, and what kinds of potential they contain because of that specific history—need to be detailed, particularly for those commonplaces that appear central to the earlier delineation. The method appropriate to fulfilling this task is "genealogical analysis" of a particular sort.
- Third, the *deployment* of those cultural resources needs to be traced through an account of the interactive tactics and strategies that actors utilize to draw on the potentials of the available social resources so as to achieve a specific and unique outcome. Once again, "textual ethnography" is the relevant method here.

These three tasks must be accomplished in this order, since the analyst has no way of knowing which cultural resources need to be subjected to genealogical analysis without having first performed a textual ethnography on the material of the legitimation struggle in question. The result of following this procedure is an account of a situation that respects both parts of the double hermeneutic simultaneously, and thus adequately preserves agency.

Delineating Cultural Resources: Rhetorical Topographies

Delineations of cultural resources available in a specific historical situation must begin by stepping away from the tendency among intellectual historians to speak in terms of general and coherent "positions" or "themes" that attempt to capture whole eras: isolationism versus interventionism, freedom versus slavery, good versus evil (Foucault 1972; Shotter 1993b). These "great debates," upon closer examination, are composed of a number of specifiable rhetorical elements, many of which are shared between the opposing "sides" of a debate. What is important here is not the presence or absence of a particular commonplace among the arguments used by partisans of one or another course of action, but the pattern of commonplaces that is characteristic of those arguments.

Of particular interest are any commonplaces that are (weakly) shared by the opposing sides, over the precise meaning of which the parties continue to struggle throughout the episode. The fact that these commonplaces may be found in arguments devoted to very different ends demonstrates that they are so widely shared throughout the universe of speakers and audience that they actually do form part of the cultural equipment through which people make sense of a variety of situations. The fact that the specific implications of these commonplaces vary so widely demonstrates the practical limits of the agency that speakers can exercise in the situation: Commonplaces are vague, always standing in need of further elaboration before they can unequivocally point toward one or another implication, but they are not completely indeterminate.

For example, "the German nation" as a commonplace does not directly indicate that cooperating with the Allies counts as high treason, but it does make such a charge possible. The commonplace "the German nation" means, at the very least, that the German nation is a concrete entity with interests and desires of its own; events affecting it should at least be discussed by the nation's authorized representatives. This leaves quite a bit of room to maneuver, inasmuch as the specifics are still very much up in the air and subject to discussion. And the fact that the commonplace occurs on both sides of the Schumacher/Adenauer debate helps to elucidate the contours of agency in postwar Germany, in that the notion clearly shapes both sides of the argument.

There is no automatic, formalizable process for the disclosure of commonplaces and their relationships (Ganter and Wille 1996). The frequency of words and phrases, as in quantitative content analysis, is insufficient to establish the commonplace character of a particular locution, since notions relevant to the framing of particular questions may not be repeated all that often during the course of a debate (Hopf 2004). Procedures like "predicate analysis" (Milliken 1999) and the description of "plot units" and narrative "functions" (Alker 1996), while providing enormously subtle readings of linguistic data, have no defensible claim to have exhausted the texts under analysis.[16] Indeed, in principle any piece of textual data—such as, in this case, the stenographic reports of a raucous Bundestag session—can be cut up in multiple ways depending on the categories used in the analysis.

Hence, the construction of analytical mappings of the "topography" of available commonplaces is necessarily ideal-typical in the Weberian sense discussed above. One does not formulate an ideal type out of thin air; it emerges only through an immersion in the empirical data and is principally to be evaluated in terms of its utility in making sense of the empirical situations from which it is abstracted and derived (M. Weber 1999a). Weber is quite clear that there are as many ways to oversimplify a situation for analytical purposes as there are value orientations that analysts bring to their work. A rhetorical topography serves as an interpretive tool, and is produced through an encounter between the theoretical concerns of the analyst and the textual record of debates and discussions relevant to some specific issue.

There are various techniques for generating a rhetorical topography, but the one that I have found most helpful in my own work might be best characterized as a form of "textual ethnography." The practice is a form of disciplined reading in which one engages in a kind of "participant-observation" of the textual records of some legitimation struggle, jotting "field notes" as one reads—much as one would when studying the social practices of some group of people (Emerson, Fretz, and Shaw 1995, 36–37). One does not read the textual record without presuppositions; rather, one comes to the textual record familiar with secondary source material about the episode in question, as well as with a set of theoretical and philosophical commitments that serve as preliminary suppositions about the issues at stake. The textual "field notes"—I type them in the same data file where I record illustrative quotations, usually putting them in bold-faced type to make it easier to find them later—record one's developing sense of the rhetorical commonplaces being deployed in the situation. After reading through the relevant documents, a serious effort to systematize the "field notes" will tend to produce a rhetorical topography:

> As creator of the notes in the first place, the ethnographer has been creating and discovering the meaning of and in the notes all along . . . when an ethnographer thinks he has "a substantial amount of data" on a topic, it is not so much because of something inherent in the data; rather it is because the ethnographer has interpreted, organized, and brought the data to bear on the topic. (Emerson, Fretz, and Shaw 1995, 59)

In addition, because the "field notes" are linked to specific illustrative quotations from the documents, the resulting rhetorical topography can be justified empirically through the mobilization of direct quotations.

Space does not permit a detailed presentation of the evidentiary basis for the commonplaces that I have identified in my previous work on postwar German reconstruction (P.T. Jackson 2002b, 2006). But drawing on this work I would characterize the central difference between Adenauer and Schumacher as involving the position of one commonplace in particular in their public articulations: the commonplace of "Western Civilization." Although Adenauer and Schumacher agreed on the basic proposition that Germany belonged, *culturally*, to the Western world (Artner 1985, 43–44; Herbst 1989, 7, 110), Schumacher drew few of the conclusions for German foreign policy and German identity that Adenauer did. Hence, the relevant historical context within which to situate Schumacher's accusation is a debate about Germany's identity and future: Would a social democratic Germany try to fulfill its democratic mission and pursue reunification without binding ties to any of its occupiers, or would a "Christian-Western" Germany join the emerging "Western" institutions and cooperate with some of its conquerors in an effort to reduce the burdens of the occupation? The relative centrality of the commonplace "Western Civilization" to each position, and the ways that this commonplace was used to help concretize the meaning of other notions, is critical to any explanation of the events in question—and, in fact, to an explanation of their eventual outcome.

Specific Histories: Genealogical Investigation

The second step in analyzing rhetorical commonplaces is to investigate the histories of the commonplaces involved in a given situation. This investigation should be genealogical, seeking "to maintain passing events in their proper dispersion . . . to identify the accidents, the minute deviations—or conversely, the complete reversals—the errors, the false appraisals, and the faulty calculations that gave birth to those things that continue to exist and have value for us" (Foucault 1977, 146). Unlike approaches to the history of thought that seek to read the historically developed categories of mature modes of analysis backward into history and tell a tale about their emergence as a more or less rational process, a genealogical approach remains sensitive to the completely unintended nature of many important discursive shifts.[17]

Rhetorical commonplaces provide potentials for action. These potentials derive from the specific history of the notion: how it has been deployed in the past, which affinities and antipathies it has acquired in a particular context, and what precedents exist for its deployment under present circumstances. This specific history does not provide us with any kind of "essence" of the commonplace, but simply conveys a sense of the historical possibilities—particularly those on which actors drew in the situation under investigation. It is these possibilities that are "tapped" when the commonplace is deployed in subsequent legitimation struggles. For the case at hand, the genealogical question concerns the prominence and specific history of "Western Civilization" as a concept, because my textual ethnography indicated its importance to the debates. To illustrate the approach, I will briefly trace the development of this important concept.

It is not the case that there was *always* something called "the West," which people simply began to think about differently in the late-nineteenth century; rather, "the West" in the form in which we know it today did not exist, and could not have existed before the discursive shifts that took place during this period. In fact, "Western Civilization" in its contemporary form is one of the rhetorical commonplaces tossed up by the general mutation in discourse during the nineteenth century that brought an end to simple progressivist accounts of "civilization" in which all societies would inevitably converge on the series of universal values understood to have been first disclosed in Western Europe.[18] This general mutation owed much to Hegel's (1988) dialectical combination of universal progress with the essential separateness of cultural "worlds," especially as Hegel's followers generally selected either universality or particularism as the principal lessons that they took from his work. Those selecting cultural particularism (the more conservative, anti-Marxist "right-Hegelians") stood on Hegel's assertion that the civilization of the contemporary

("Germanic") world formed, in some way, a unity, and that Germany had a privileged role as a world-historical nation within that unity.

The heart of this world-historical role rested on the widespread idea that the Germans enjoyed a privileged relationship with the Greeks. Philhellenes remained constantly on the lookout for additional ways to demonstrate and strengthen the Greek/German connection, pressing the parallel to ever more extreme lengths, until "in effect, the Germans *were* the Greeks; they represented, as it were, the Greeks to modern Europe" (Gress 1998, 65–66, emphasis in original). Particularly useful in this respect was the conservative Catholic concept of the *Abendland*, literally, the "evening country," or the place where the sun goes down, which gained currency among Catholic intellectuals after the French Revolution. The Abendland was an entity of its own, with a cultural and moral essence distinguishing it from other groupings of human beings; one could not simply "join" the Abendland, nor could one leave it—although one could *betray* it by abandoning one's heritage and embracing revolutionary or decadent ideas. Thus, the contemporary Germans could continue as the spiritual *and civilizational* heirs of the Greeks, united by their common participation in the Abendland—"Western Civilization."

These haphazard, contingent processes resulted in a novel commonplace—the notion of "Western Civilization" as one entity among others—being made available for use in discussions from the late nineteenth century onward.[19] From its specific history the commonplace acquired three basic characteristics that would be tapped in subsequent policy debates. First, "Western Civilization" was a supranational entity, in which other states and nations were "nested" (Ferguson and Mansbach 1996, 47–51). Larger and older than its component states, it was also somewhat superior to them; "civilizational" concerns trumped merely national ones. Second, "Western Civilization" was an exclusive, essential community: Not everyone was "Western" and not everyone could or should be "Western." There was thus a modicum of recognition of other civilizations, and some kind of civilizational coexistence was conceptually possible.[20] Third, "Western Civilization" was already linked to a series of other commonplaces, such as the defense of freedom and an opposition to Russia; hence it was no great trick to draw out those connections in the ensuing debates. These aspects of the commonplace are quite prevalent in the policy debates about postwar German reconstruction.

Deployment: The Singular Causal Analysis of Strategies and Tactics

The final step in analyzing how rhetorical commonplaces shape outcomes involves a focus on the historically unique combinations of and interactions between notions operative in a given historical situation. It is not possible to remain consistently true to the vague and ambiguous character of a commonplace, or to the space for agency (understood here as contingent interpretations by historical actors) to which this ambiguity gives rise, by seeking to subsume situations under one or another covering law describing *inevitable* connections between inputs and outputs. Instead of this neopositivist search for generalizable regularities, the analysis of commonplaces lends itself to "singular causal analysis" of the sort advocated by Max Weber:

> In the given historical constellation certain "conditions" are conceptually isolatable which would have led to that effect in the presence of the preponderantly great majority of further conditions conceivable as *possibly* occurring, while the range of those conceivable causal factors whose presence probably would have led to another result . . . seems very limited. (1999b, 286; emphasis in original)

Singular causation is sharply different from the necessary-and-sufficient kind of causation advocated by neopositivists, in which the aim is the isolation of systematic correlations of factors across cases (King, Keohane, and Verba 1994, 75–82). By contrast, Weber advocates a more speculative procedure, in which a causal configuration—itself an ideal-typical account of a historical situation[21]—is identified and demonstrated by showing how the configuration in question interacts with a range of possible factors, where possible factors emerge from a historically grounded study of the situation itself. In other words, scholars know that some configuration of factors is causally adequate if they cannot plausibly conceive of that configuration *not* producing the outcome in question.

Causality in this conception involves the concatenation of *causal mechanisms*: the contingent coming together of processes and patterns of social action in such a way as to generate outcomes (McAdam, Tarrow, and Tilly 2001, 13). Although each specific combination of mechanisms is historically unique, the mechanisms themselves may occur in other contexts and other combinations (Tilly 1995). Any comparison or generalization that takes place in this sort of research occurs at the level of mechanisms and their concatenation, and not at the level of presumptively whole and stable "cases" subject to assumptions of causal homogeneity (P.T. Jackson and Nexon 2002). The basic analytical bet is that similar patterns of action in different contexts and in different sequences will generate different outcomes, and the empirical task is to parse the situation at hand using a spare and abstract specification of causal mechanisms in order to see what insights can be generated.

For the analysis of legitimation, the component mechanisms are the conventional tactics by which rhetorical commonplaces may be combined or opposed.[22] *Specification*, which involves the attempt to define a commonplace and its implications in a relatively precise way in the course of a debate, is the chief tactical mechanism, since rhetorical commonplaces by definition always stand in need of further elaboration before they can be definitively linked with a particular outcome in a particular context. Specification gives rise to two subordinate mechanisms, *breaking* and *joining*, with the former referring to the use of a specified commonplace to disrupt the bond between commonplaces simultaneously held by an opponent and the latter referring to the use of a specified commonplace to help to "lock down" the meaning of another one.

These mechanisms, in turn, give rise to bargaining tactics like brokering alliances or threatening rejection by a represented constituency if certain demands are not met. For example, Adenauer regularly used the threat of a Schumacher-governed West German state to induce the occupying Allies to be more sympathetic to his demands. This option was enabled by his use of "Western Civilization" to encompass both Germany *and* the occupying Allies in a way that Schumacher simply did not: Adenauer, as a fellow "Westerner," was someone whom the Allies could trust, whereas Schumacher's nationalist-flavored criticism of Allied policies and his insistence that Germany should remain more distant from emerging institutions of Western European cooperation made the prospect of a Schumacher government unappealing. Mechanisms involving rhetorical commonplaces, one might say, are the more basic conditions of possibility for these other bargaining tactics.

How did these mechanisms operate to produce Schumacher's accusation and Adenauer's policy against which it was deployed? Adenauer's policy of cooperation with the occupying Allies was publicly justified with reference to "Western Civilization" as a larger civilizational community in which both Germany and Germany's conquerors participated. At a party rally in 1947, Adenauer declared that present circumstances lay a sacred duty upon us: never to slack off in our work, never to exhaust our patience, and always to remain true to the task which God has given to us. That applies to us, to the CDU and CSU in Germany, above all, because we see ourselves also as the guardians of the Christian-Western spirit. [*christlich-abendländischen Geistes*] (Konrad-Adenauer-Stiftung 1975, 351)

Adenauer suggested that only a certain kind of Europe would do: a Christian-Western one. But Adenauer did not stop merely with Europe:

The West [*Abendland*], the Christian West, is no geographical concept: it is a spiritual and historical concept that also encompasses America. It is this Christian West that we want to try to save. We will do everything in our power, in the hope and with the conviction that God will not abandon the German people. (Konrad-Adenauer-Stiftung 1975, 351)

Several things are notable about this specification tactic: the prominent use of the term "Abendland";[23] the definition of "the West" as something out of the history of the spirit (invoking Hegel and his successors); the explicit inclusion of America as a part of a larger "Abendland" community of which Germany is also a part; and the portrayal of the stakes as the very survival of "the West." From these notions Adenauer drew his policy recommendations: an embrace of the aid offered by the Americans under the auspices of the European Recovery Program, cooperation with the occupying Allies as a way of enhancing what might be called "civilizational defense," and a general tempering of his public criticisms of occupation policy on most occasions.

Adenauer's "Western" strategy also provided the grounds for an impressive critique of Schumacher's more nationalist and oppositional stance—a critique that combined the breaking and joining of connections between commonplaces. Exploiting Schumacher's anticommunism, Adenauer often argued that one could not consistently oppose political and institutional cooperation with the occupying Allies while claiming to be a staunch opponent of Russia and communism. Adenauer thus used his specification of the "Western Civilization" commonplace (and Schumacher's ready assent that Germany belonged *culturally* to "Western Civilization") in an effort to break anticommunism away from the SPD and attract anticommunists to his side by joining anticommunism to Adenauer's own version of "Western Civilization." True to form, Schumacher's rebuttals took the shape of a more and more explicit embrace of nationalist language, as he attempted to use *his* specification of that commonplace as the grounds upon which to oppose both communism and the Allied occupation policy.

The debate on November 24 and 25, 1949, was particularly charged, since Germany's proposed joining of the Ruhr Authority would also be accompanied by the authority's seating of a representative from the Saar—a territory claimed by Germany but treated by the occupying French as an independent country. So joining the Ruhr Authority might be tantamount to recognizing the separation of the Saar from the new Federal Republic as well as consenting to the international administration of Germany's industrial resources. If one maintained that Germany and the occupying Allies were part of a single civilizational community, this turn of events appeared more palatable, but to Schumacher's combination of commonplaces it must have seemed like high treason. Hence his accusing cry against Adenauer, which can be seen as a sharp effort to specify the commonplace of "the German nation" and turn it against Adenauer's actions. Hence also the irony of Schumacher's subsequent suspension from the Bundestag for several days on the grounds that he had impugned the good name of the German government—hardly the sort of action that would be expected of a firm nationalist.

Indeed, by playing this nationalist card, Schumacher continued to lend a measure of support to Adenauer's contention that everyone who was *not* a Christian Democrat was advocating a return to the policies that had gotten Germany into geopolitical trouble under the Nazi regime. Schumacher's critique was perhaps the best one that he could have practically offered, but it was unable to gain purchase because of the tensions within it that Adenauer was able to exploit. Adenauer, in turn, was only able to sustain the claim that he was *not* the "Federal Chancellor of the Allies" by virtue of the rhetorical commonplace of "Western Civilization" on which he and his policies stood. Precisely because he could advance a socially plausible claim to justify courses of action that otherwise might easily have seemed like simple kowtowing to the occupying Allies, he was able to hold together his party and his coalition long enough to institutionalize the commitment of the new German state to "the West." The commonplace of "Western Civilization" and the pattern that Adenauer and his allies constructed around it made that outcome possible.

CONCLUSION

Methodology is enacted philosophy. It is "philosophical" in that it embodies and stands upon ontological and epistemological commitments. It is "enacted" in that it is not satisfied with simply *thinking* these commitments, but endeavors to apply these ontological and epistemological commitments to concrete questions of how research is to be conducted. Methodological reflection, then, is about designing prosthetics appropriate to the commitments that ground the researcher and her or his research community. This is the logical prerequisite to applying such prosthetics in a rigorous manner. That this is necessarily a value-laden enterprise does *not* detract from its "scientific" character, inasmuch as scientific objectivity always involves bringing values and data together. "A fact is a particular ordering of reality in terms of a theoretical interest," as David Easton argued a half century ago (Easton 1971 [1953], 53). M. Weber would agree:

> There is simply no "objective" scientific analysis of cultural life—or, put perhaps somewhat more narrowly but certainly not essentially differently for our purposes—of a "social phenomenon" *independent* of special and "one-sided" points of view, according to which—explicitly or tacitly, consciously or unconsciously—they are selected, analyzed, and representationally organized as an object of research. (1999a, 170; emphasis in original)

Actual empirical situations are generally ambiguous enough to permit and sustain multiple readings, but this general observation sheds little light on specific occurrences. Precisely which aspects of a situation are picked out by a given scholarly analysis is, at least in part, a function of the cultural values surrounding and informing the inquiry—which raises doubts about any categorical declarations that a particular interpretation is somehow universally or transcendentally correct. But this situation is not unique to the *social* sciences; even as "naturalistic" an activity as the study of the rock formation known as "dolomite" displays the contingency and value ladenness flagged by Weber and Easton (Hacking 1999). Methodological questions are methodological questions, regardless of their domain of application; in all cases they involve the effort to systematically reveal the world in one way rather than another.

In this essay I have argued for a methodology that respects both aspects of the double hermeneutic as a way of preserving agency at the most fundamental level of a research project. Such a project is an effort to produce "facts" that flow from a certain set of values, and as such is a contribution to the preservation of those values in the sphere of the social sciences. By demonstrating some of the implications of taking "the preservation of agency" seriously, the empirical work thus produced may contribute to a debate about the importance of this philosophical commitment.

NOTES

For helpful feedback and comments on earlier drafts, I would like to thank the editors, Rebecca DeWinter, Kiran Pervez, and Maia Hallward.

1. In the German Bundestag a bell is used to call the house to order, much like a gavel is used in U.S. parliamentary bodies.

2. Seating in the Bundestag is by parties along a left-to-right scale, so shouts "from the left" are both shouts from the left side of the hall and shouts from the more radical political parties—Social Democrats and Communists, in this case.

3. In this chapter, "occupying Allies" refers to the United States, the United Kingdom, and France. By 1949, the Soviet Union was an "Ally" only in a very tenuous sense.

4. Bhaskar and other critical realists, however, fail to maintain a consistent focus on practical discursive activities. As Patomäki and Wight argue, critical realists instead talk about "underlying structures, powers, and tendencies that exist, whether or not detected or known through experience and/or discourse." This leads them to suspect that "the surface appearance of objectivity, although possessing causal power, is typically distinct from its underlying—and potentially hidden, reified, or mystified—essential relations" (Patomäki and Wight 2000, 223–35). Their empirical work shifts from a detailed tracing of the patterns of social activity to a transcendental explication of the foundational principles putatively governing or underlying those patterns. This metaphysical commitment produces several thorny problems (Shotter 1993a, 75–78), but one need not adopt the whole critical realist package in order to appreciate its emphasis on active processes of social construction.

5. Arguably, every political figure in every type of political regime faces this kind of problem (M. Weber 1976, 122–23). "Legitimation" in this sense has been a concern of philosophers for millennia, forming one of those perennial subjects of interest to political and social analysts. But the problem is perhaps particularly acute (at least in a technical sense) in a modern industrial democracy with a wide range of public media outlets, inasmuch as a plethora of such outlets dramatically expands the arenas and forums within which legitimation can take place. This is true even if the country is under military occupation.

6. This applies regardless of whether the patterns in question are "novel" or not; the reproduction of an established convention or pattern of reasons is just as creative an action as the formulation of a radically different pattern (Wittgenstein 1953, §232; Winch 1990, 57).

7. Weber's argument is, in brief, that "the *specific* objectivity . . . which alone appears to be solely realizable in the social sciences" is "at base a radicalized *subjectivity*" (Hennis 1988, 124; emphasis in original). For whatever reason, many commentators miss this.

8. Social action thus has a "metaphorical" character (Ringmar 1996, 68–69), and specific actions draw on resources that function not unlike the "policy frames" disclosed by other analysts (see Brandwein, chapter 12, this volume, and Schmidt, chapter 17, this volume, for examples and elaborations). My focus on the prosthetic character of action instead of on the disclosive character of resources is a deliberate effort to prevent undue and unnecessary reification of those resources.

9. Note that scholars of the "role of ideas" also tend to shift the question from a "sociological" one about the impact of social actions to an "economic" one about the motivation for those actions (P.T. Jackson 2002a). But this issue is not my central focus here.

10. This differs from neopositivist approaches to the extent that the abstract typology in question need not involve cross-case correlations between independent and dependent variables. "Class" and "rationality" aren't necessarily variable attributes, and their use in a particular account may well involve less correlating and more interpreting according to the decontextualized, abstract template that they provide.

11. The issue here is not whether notions like "class" or "rationality" can produce useful and illuminating analytical insights; if handled ideal-typically, they can certainly do so. The problem is that such insights ordinarily come at the cost of the preservation of agency understood as creativity and contingency. See below.

12. Note that "reflexive" ethnography, which deliberately strives to avoid this kind of flat-footed empiricism, can easily slip off into a kind of single hermeneutic in which the scholar is simply playing with her or

his own categories and conceptual tools. To the extent that ethnographic analysis tries to simultaneously highlight both hermeneutic circles under discussion here, it moves closer to the model that I sketch later in the chapter.

13. "Structural" prosthetics—those that conceptualize events as occupying relatively determinate positions relative to other events and institutions and that seek to delineate a kind of transcendental grammar governing those relations—replicate the problems of the single hermeneutic analyses that emphasize the scholar's active interpretive role. "Agentic" prosthetics either operate with a more or less determinate conception of the interests and preferences of social actors, in a neopositivist manner, or replicate the second set of problems by trying merely to describe what those actors think and do. Both kinds of prosthetic are certainly available for scholarly use, but neither fulfills the imperative of preserving agency as well as the "processual/relational" (P.T. Jackson and Nexon 1999) prosthetic on offer here.

14. "Legitimation" is not the only process that can be conceptualized in this manner, of course; "routinization" and "institutionalization" have been similarly reconfigured by other scholars.

15. Technically, what I am proposing here is a *relational social constructionism*: relational inasmuch as it analytically privileges "bonds" rather than "essences" and dynamic social ties rather than static social and constitutive relations (Tilly 1998, 18–22); constructionist inasmuch as it emphasizes contingency rather than naturalistic inevitability (Hacking 1999, 6–7); and social inasmuch as it focuses on action (behavior plus meaning) rather than behavior conceptually devoid of meaning (Parsons 1954a, 234–35; M. Weber 1976, 11–12; Ringmar 1996, 66). The extent to which this is a form of "interpretivism" broadly understood remains, to my mind, an open question, particularly since many forms of interpretivist analysis eschew or at least minimize causation and causality (Geertz 1973a, 5).

16. Serious practitioners of these techniques make no such claims. But at the same time they are not as clear as they might be about the ideal-typical character of their analyses.

17. Genealogical analysis enjoys a broad and varied history. The procedure was initially pioneered by Friedrich Nietzsche at the end of the nineteenth century (Nietzsche 1967) as a critique of the Enlightenment philosophical project of integrating diverse social phenomena under the banner of Reason centered on the knowing subject. Genealogical analysis involves, among other things, a suspension of the temptation toward functionalism and teleological reasoning characteristic of much of classical social thought, and a focus instead on how the exercise of power affects the subsequent meaning that we assign to some piece of social life. Michel Foucault refined the procedure in his seminal studies of prisons and sexuality (Foucault 1978, 1979) and is perhaps the single most important figure in the development of this analytical technique.

18. In a sense, "Western Civilization" is the mirror image of what Edward Said calls "orientalism" (Said 1978). Where Said focuses on the "sense" that Europeans made of others, I focus more on the "sense" that Europeans (and some Americans) made of themselves.

19. Before it was used in postwar German reconstruction debates, the commonplace was central to the case for militarism made during World War I, as well as an important component of the interwar effort to make sense of Germany's defeat as indicative of a general civilizational crisis (P.T. Jackson 2006, chapter 4).

20. Somewhat unreflectively, Samuel Huntington (1996) replicates this argument. I would suggest that the reason why aspects of his book have at least an intuitive plausibility is precisely the fact that it deploys an existing commonplace—"Western Civilization"—and taps one of its historical potentials.

21. Although Fritz Ringer (1997, 111–6) provides an excellent discussion of Weber's strategy of "singular causal analysis," his presentation does downplay the extent to which Weber's delineation of causal moments is ideal-typical rather than "objective" in a neopositivist sense (Ringer 1997, 70–71) and also misunderstands what Weber's treatment does to the traditional notion of "objectivity" (Ringer 1997, 125–26; cf. Hennis 1988).

22. As with the delineation of rhetorical commonplaces, this specification of causal mechanisms derives from my previous work on the subject. Other specifications are of course possible.

23. "Abendland" is not simply the German word for "West." There are at least two other terms—"West" and "Okzident"—that would also serve, so it is significant that Adenauer uses this term and not one of the available synonyms.

CHAPTER 15

HOW NARRATIVES EXPLAIN

MARK BEVIR

As a political theorist, I have no narrative of hard-won freedom, no story of the personal and social disadvantages I overcame in pursuit of my dream of interpretive work. To the contrary, because my graduate work was on the history of socialist thought in Britain, I almost inevitably set out to study beliefs or meanings expressed in texts. Soon afterward I started thinking and writing about the philosophy of intellectual history. In doing so, I carved out a distinctive interpretive theory, a theory that I soon took to apply across the humanities and social sciences. (Several of my critics have phrased the same point rather less kindly, suggesting that my theory neglects what they take to be specific aspects of the study of the past or, more narrowly, of canonical texts.)

By then, I was employed in a department of politics and, being of a sociable nature, I entered into various discussions with my colleagues, notably Professor Rod Rhodes. Rod found that my theory helped him resolve dilemmas he confronted in thinking about changes in British politics. I wanted to experiment with my theory beyond the history of ideas. Together we began to use that theory to write about British governance. We also worked with others to use it to explore comparative governance.

All this collaborative work has brought me into greater contact, much to my surprise, with subfields of political science in which interpretive approaches do not have the ascendancy they do in the history of political thought. Ironically, I thus find myself part of a broad interpretivist category that neglects the dreadfully important, if sublimely subtle, distinctions with which I had so laboriously carved out my distinctive philosophy of intellectual history.

> Gladstone hoped to trump Cabinet doubts and party unease by the
> production of a great bill.
> —*Henry C.G. Matthew* (1995, 236)

> Family relationships were powerfully affected by the concept that the
> pursuit of individual happiness is one of the basic laws of nature.
> —*Lawrence Stone* (1979b, 178)

Interpretive approaches rest on a philosophical analysis of the human sciences as being concerned to unpack meanings as beliefs. This analysis inspires a distinctive narrative form of explanation in which beliefs are situated in wider webs of beliefs that themselves are situated against traditions and dilemmas.

An interpretive approach has inspired, for example, narrative explanations of governance (Bevir, Rhodes, and Weller 2003c). One popular, positivist-informed explanation for the growth of governance posits that advanced industrial societies develop through a process that involves functional and institutional specialization and fragmentation (Rhodes 1988). By contrast, interpretivists might highlight the ways in which patterns of governance vary depending on inherited traditions.

Interpretivists might distinguish, for example, between an Anglo-Saxon antistate tradition, a Germanic organic state tradition, a French Jacobin tradition, and a Scandinavian tradition that mixes the Anglo-Saxon and the Germanic (Dyson 1980; Loughlin and Peters 1997). In the Germanic tradition, state and civil society are part of an organic whole; the state is *rechtsstaat*—a legal state vested with exceptional authority but constrained by its own laws—and civil servants are personifications of this state, not just public employees. The Anglo-Saxon tradition draws a clearer boundary between state and civil society; there is no legal basis to the state, and civil servants have no constitutional position. The Jacobin tradition regards the French state as the one and indivisible republic, exercising strong central authority to contain the antagonistic relations between state and civil society. The Scandinavian tradition is also "organic"—characterized by rechtsstaat—but it differs from the Germanic tradition in favoring a decentralized unitary state with a strong ethic of participation.

Varied traditions inform the content of governance, conceived as proliferating networks, in different states. The Danish tradition, with its ethic of participation, has confronted governance as an issue of how to retain democratic control of multiplying networks. In the Germanic tradition, the legal framework sets the boundaries of, and also guides, official action, so the direct imposition of control is seen as unnecessary, and there is consequently a comparatively high degree of tolerance for the multilevel networks—*politikverflechtung*—so common in federal systems. The Jacobin tradition with its assumption of conflict between state and civil society suggests that networks are a potential threat to state authority unless they are subject to state control through, for example, strong mayoral leadership.

State traditions operate at a high level of abstraction. Hence, interpretivists also decenter these traditions to show how forms of governance arise as products of actions that embody the multiple beliefs legislators, bureaucrats, and others have come to adopt through a process of modifying diverse traditions to meet specific dilemmas. In Britain, liberal conservatives promoted markets to deal with the dilemmas they associated with the corporate state, including state overload and the capture of policy networks by vested interests. Later, social democrats actively promoted networks, or joined-up governance, as a response to a dilemma of integration they believed had been exasperated by marketization. Perri 6, a key adviser to New Labour, argued that governments confront "wicked problems" that do not fit with functional government based on central departments and their policy networks (Perri 6, 1997). He advocated holistic governance to span departmental cages, with holistic budgets, cross-functional outcome measures, and integrated information systems. British governance arose as a result of successive waves of public sector reform, each of which was informed by a different tradition reacting to different dilemmas (Bevir and Rhodes 2003).

We can explain the practice of governance in different states by means of narratives that unpack them by reference to beliefs that arose against the background of distinct traditions. On what concepts does narrative rely? What makes it a valid form of explanation for human actions and practices? What grammatical structure defines narrative explanations such as those of our two epigraphs?

PHILOSOPHY AND METHOD

Perhaps we might begin by asking what is meant by an interpretive approach. Presumably we could describe the accounts natural science provides of physical stuff as interpretations. Yet whereas accounts of physical stuff are interpretations, accounts of actions can be interpretations of interpretations. Whenever we interpret an action by describing the beliefs of the actor, we interpret the actor's interpretation of the world, for their beliefs are, of course, an interpretation of the world. The distinctive nature of interpretive approaches typically derives from such an analysis of the human sciences as being about interpretations of interpretations. Interpretivists concentrate on elucidating the meanings—the beliefs and traditions—that are embedded in actions and practices.

Interpretivism rests, in this view, on a philosophical analysis of the meaningful nature of human action. Later, I will consider how this analysis inspires a narrative form of explanation. For now, I want to emphasize the gap between a philosophical analysis of this sort and commitment to any particular method. To argue that the human sciences offer interpretations of interpretations is not to imply that particular methods are the only, or best, ones by which so to do. On the contrary, interpretivists can devise their interpretations of interpretations by drawing eclectically on data and heuristics associated with all kinds of methods. They can use participant-observation, questionnaires, interviews, mass surveys, statistical tests, and models, as well as read memoirs, newspapers, and official and unofficial documents. Interpretivism rests on a philosophical analysis of action as meaningful, and this analysis does not prescribe any particular heuristic or any method of creating data; rather, it prescribes a particular way of recounting data and theories that might be generated using any of a variety of methods and heuristics. Interpretivists believe that human scientists should recount data and theories in narratives that accord with a philosophical analysis of the human sciences as being about interpreting interpretations.

Although interpretivism rests on philosophical analysis rather than adherence to a particular methodological tool kit, it does perhaps lend an especial importance to methods traditionally known as qualitative. Interpretivists seek to recover the beliefs or meanings that make actions and practices possible: Although different methods might generate relevant data, the data should be taken as evidence of such beliefs and meanings. Suppose that data and heuristic insights provided by formal constitutions, large-scale surveys, or models lead us to ascribe a web of beliefs to people. Insofar as the creation of such data typically abstracts from individual circumstances to find common patterns, it risks eliding differences between people, even lumping together people who act in broadly similar ways for entirely different reasons. Surely, therefore, we will make the most of any opportunity we might have to undertake more detailed studies of the beliefs of the relevant people by means of textual studies, participant-observation, or in-depth interviews. Much contemporary political science seems, in contrast, to denigrate textual studies and ethnography in favor of abstract models, typologies, and correlations. So, although interpretivism does not require an exclusive use of any one type of data or method, it does help to redress the balance in favor of studies of a kind more often associated with anthropology and history than with political science.

The distinctiveness of interpretive approaches derives from a philosophical analysis of the human sciences. The crux of this analysis is the need to treat data as evidence of beliefs or meanings. Of course, interpretivists are far from being alone in paying such attention to beliefs or meanings. What makes them more distinctive is their widespread belief that the human sciences are about beliefs or meanings, as we might say, all the way down. Interpretivists account for beliefs by locating them in wider webs of beliefs in large part because they think, first, that beliefs are in some way constitutive of actions and, second, that beliefs are necessarily holistic in nature. Consider the constitutive nature of beliefs in relation to actions. When other human scientists study voting behavior in terms of, say, surveys of the attitudes of voters or models of rational action given certain beliefs and preferences, they thereby differentiate beliefs from actions so as to seek a correlation or deductive link between the two. By contrast, interpretivists often suggest that such surveys and models cannot tell us why, say, raising one's hand should amount to voting, or why there would be uproar if someone forced someone else to raise their hand against their will, or why only certain people should be regarded as eligible to vote (C. Taylor 1971). To explain these sorts of things, they continue, we must appeal to the intersubjective beliefs that underpin the practice of concern to us. We need to know, for example, that voting is associated with making a free choice and so with a particular concept of the self. We need to know what counts as an infringement of free choice and who is regarded as being capable of making such a choice. Practices and beliefs are constitutive of one another: Practices could not exist if people did not have appropriate beliefs; and beliefs or meanings would not make sense in the absence of the practices to which they refer.

Now consider the holistic nature of beliefs. Many interpretivists emphasize that people hold beliefs for reasons of their own, so we can make sense of their beliefs only by locating them in the context of the other beliefs that provide reasons for their holding them. Hence, even if human scientists establish a correlation between, say, a positive attitude to social justice and voting for the Democrats, they cannot properly explain people's voting Democrat by reference to this attitude; after all, people who have a positive attitude to social justice might nonetheless vote Republican if they believe still more strongly in conservative values or if they believe the Democrats will not implement the policies they avow. To grasp why someone with a positive attitude toward social justice votes Democrat, we have to unpack the other relevant beliefs and desires that relate that attitude to that vote. To explain an action, we cannot just correlate it with a single isolated attitude; we must interpret it in relation to a whole set of beliefs and desires. A wide range of human scientists typically treat beliefs, meanings, ideas, norms, and the like as if, first, they could be differentiated from actions and, second, they could be related individually to actions. Interpretivists stand out in their insistence that beliefs or meanings form holistic webs that are constitutive of actions and so of practices.

Interpretivists concentrate on unpacking the beliefs or meaning embodied in actions and practices. The concept of meaning does well here in that it has less cognitive a ring than does "belief," thereby reminding us to extend our concern from big ideas and movements to the subconscious beliefs that inform habitual acts. Equally, the concept of belief does well in that it serves the extraordinarily valuable role of challenging the spurious dichotomy between understanding and explanation, for it echoes the micro-level commitment of rational choice theory and folk psychology to explaining actions in terms of beliefs and desires. Interpretivists often imply that the human sciences explain actions and practices by pointing to beliefs and desires that cause them. Models, typologies, and correlations can do explanatory work only if they are unpacked in terms of such a narrative. This analysis of narrative challenges those political scientists who appear to think of ideas as one kind of variable to which we might give more prominence within a constitutive logic that compliments a more general causal logic (Wendt 1998). Our analysis of narrative suggests that non-ideational variables can do explanatory work only if they are unpacked in terms of ideas or beliefs. It implies that correlations between variables never do any explanatory work; they merely point to a conjuncture that might inspire us to adopt a particular narrative to explain something. It leads us to conclude that constitutive logics, far from being useful additions to more mainstream causal logics, are in fact the only type of causal logic that applies to human actions, although, of course, other causal logics might apply to things other than human actions.

NARRATIVE EXPLANATIONS

In everyday life we often explain why someone did something by appealing to the concepts of what philosophers call "folk psychology."[1] When we thus explain actions as products of reasons— beliefs and desires—we suggest that the people concerned could in some sense have reasoned differently, and if they had done so, the objects would not have come into being as they did. If an object depends on the reasoned decision of a person, we must explain it as the product of that decision, so we cannot explain it as a determined outcome of a law-like process; after all, choices would not be choices if they were fixed by causal laws. Hence, folk psychology precludes our explaining meaningful objects using the concept of causation associated with the natural sciences; it requires us instead to deploy narratives.

Many philosophers have distinguished interpretive approaches from positivist ones that mimic natural science. Often they go on to define the latter in terms of the provision of causal explanations and the former in terms of the understanding of beliefs, motives, and actions; they suggest that interpretivists try to understand or reconstruct objects, not to explain them. In contrast, interpretivists often write as if their narratives explain actions by pointing to their causes. When they do so, they typically use the word "cause" to indicate the presence of a significant relationship of the sort they believe to be characteristic of explanation in the human sciences as opposed to the natural sciences; they reject the idea that all causal explanations are of the same type.

Narratives explain actions and practices by reference to the beliefs and desires of actors. The clearest examples apply to particular actions, whether decided upon by individuals or groups. Consider Matthew's explanation of W.E. Gladstone's sensational production in 1886 of the controversial Government of Ireland Bill. Matthew describes how the Liberal Party was excluded from processes of discussion and how even the Cabinet was not given adequate time to examine the proposals. "Gladstone," he explains, "hoped to trump Cabinet doubts and party unease by the production of a great bill" (Matthew 1995, 236). Matthew explains the tactics Gladstone deployed in terms of a desire to win support for his proposals and a belief, albeit surrounded by doubt, that he could do so through the drama of a great bill. He thus provides an example of how a narrative form of explanation might work with respect to particular actions.

Equally, narrative explanations can apply to broad patterns of behavior associated with social movements and to the dynamics of social change. Although the relevant beliefs and desires can become multiple, complex, and hard to disentangle, it is still to them we might turn, at least implicitly, in explaining human life. Consider Lawrence Stone's explanation of the rise of the nuclear family (L. Stone 1979b). Stone explains the decline of kinship and clientage largely by reference to the rise of beliefs that emphasized allegiances other than private and local loyalties to individuals: The Reformation stressed a moral allegiance to God; a grammar school and university education in humanism stressed allegiance to the prince; and an Inns of Court education stressed allegiance to an abstraction, the common law. Stone then explains the rise of a form of family life based on affective individualism largely by reference to the spread of Puritan beliefs. The Puritans bequeathed a legacy, including an ideal of matrimony based on love, and a respect for the individual, that went beyond the religious sphere of life. Puritanism, humanism, and the like then provided the context in which Enlightenment beliefs took root. "Family relationships were powerfully affected by the concept that the pursuit of individual happiness is one of the basic laws of nature, and also by the growing movement to put some check on man's inhumanity to man" (L. Stone 1979b, 178). Stone explains large patterns of social change by showing how new beliefs inspired new patterns of human action.

Every form of explanation works by postulating pertinent connections between entities or events. Narrative explanations relate actions to the beliefs and desires that produce them. Their abstract form is: An action X was done because the agent held beliefs Y according to which doing X would fulfill a desire Z. Narrative explanations postulate two types of connections. The first is that which relates actions, beliefs, and desires in a way that makes them intelligible in the light of one another. Let us call these conditional connections. Conditional connections can relate agents' beliefs to one another, including their beliefs about the likely effects of their actions, so as to make sense of the fact that they thought the actions would fulfill one or more of their desires. For example, Matthew makes Gladstone's actions intelligible by connecting his preference for getting the bill passed to his beliefs that there would be opposition to the bill in his party, that his party would rally around during a great drama, that he could make such a drama out of the bill, and so on. The second type of connection relates desires to the actions they motivate. Let us call these volitional connections. Volitional connections enable us to make sense of the fact that agents moved from having desires, to intending to perform actions, and then to acting as they did. For example, Matthew explains Gladstone's actions by postulating his preference for the bill being passed, so as to assume that this desire, in the context of the beliefs just discussed, gave him certain intentions upon which he acted.

Conditional connections relate agents' beliefs and desires to one another so as to make sense of the fact that they thought an action would fulfill one or more of their desires. Conditional connections exist when the nature of one object draws on the nature of another. The former is conditioned by the latter, so they do not have an arbitrary relationship to one another; but equally, the former does not follow from the latter, so they do not have a necessary relationship to one another. More particularly, conditional connections exist when a belief reflects, develops, or modifies themes that occur in other beliefs. Any belief will give us intimations of associated ideas that might or might not have been picked up by the person involved. When they are picked up, they become themes that link the relevant beliefs. For example, a concern about corruption in the church suggests a distrust of the church and so a greater focus on the direct relationship of the individual to God, which, in turn, hints at a greater emphasis on individual virtue, and so at affective individualism. These religious ideas are not linked indissolubly to one another, but neither are they an arbitrary set; rather, they go together in that they take up, elucidate, and develop intimations found in one another.

Because conditional connections are not arbitrary, themes must be immanent within the objects they bring together. Equally, because conditional connections are not necessary, themes must be given immediately by the content of the beliefs they connect. Interpretivists do not identify a theme as an instance of a general law defining a fixed relationship between the objects they are considering. They describe a theme solely in terms of the content of the particular objects that exhibit that theme. That is to say, when people cannot see the connection between themes, interpretivists can bring them to do so only by describing other beliefs that fill the connection out. Imagine that people can see no connection between a stress on the individual's direct relationship with God and affective individualism. We could not show them the connection by appealing to some general law. All we could do would be to describe various other ideas that act as intermediate stages between the two principal ones. For example, we might say that a stress on the individual's direct relationship with God implies that a person's salvation depends primarily on his virtue, which points to a concern with the emotional and moral life of the individual, which, in its turn, then encourages affective individualism. The interpretive analyst thereby further develops a narrative explanation of the subject under study.

Volitional connections enable us to make sense of the fact that agents moved from having desires for states of affairs to intending to perform actions and then on to acting as they did. Whereas our beliefs and desires give us all sorts of grounds for doing all sorts of things, the individual will selects the particular actions we are to perform from among the alternatives thus presented to us. The will forms an intention to act by deciding which action we should perform out of the many we have grounds for performing. We have to postulate the will here because there is a space separating desires from intentions. This space suggests that we should conceive of the will reaching a decision in an unrestricted process in which previously formed intentions, current preferences, and future possibilities all interact with one another. Although our decisions give us intentions, we can act on such intentions only because of the ability of the will to command us to do so.

Volitional connections come into being when the will operates so as to transform one's stance toward a given proposition, first, from being favorable to it to a decision to act on it, and then from a decision to act on it to a command so to do. No doubt human scientists are unable to say much about the way the will operates—they can say little other than that an individual will did operate with a particular result—but that they are unable to do so is not a failing so much as a necessary consequence of the nature of the will: The will is a creative faculty. Typically, then, human scientists do not unpack volitional connections so much as take them for granted. Folk psychology tells us people are capable of acting on their beliefs and desires, and because they can do so, to elucidate the relevant beliefs and desires is to explain an action or practice. Hence, as we saw earlier, to understand these beliefs and desires is just to explain the relevant action or practice.

TRADITIONS AND DILEMMAS

Narratives explain actions and practices by pointing to the conditional and volitional connections between beliefs and desires embedded in them. They explicate actions in relation to the webs of beliefs of the actors. Once we accept this analysis of narrative, we confront the question: How might we explain why actors hold the webs of belief they do? Explanations of webs of belief revolve around two sets of concepts. The first set includes concepts, such as tradition and paradigm, that explore the social context in which individuals exercise their reason. The second set includes those, such as dilemma and anomaly, which explore how and why agents change their beliefs.

Because interpretivists emphasize the holistic nature of beliefs, they conceive of all reasoning and experience as laden with prior theories, so they reject any strong concept of autonomy. For interpretivists, people cannot have pure reason or pure experience; individuals necessarily construe their experiences using theories they inherit. People's experiences can lead them to beliefs only because they already are embedded in traditions. However, although tradition is thus unavoidable, it is so only as a starting point, not as something that governs later performances. We might be cautious of representing tradition as an unavoidable presence in everything people do in case we leave too slight a role for local reasoning. Tradition is not constitutive of the beliefs people later come to hold or the actions they then perform. It is just a first influence on people who possess a capacity for situated agency.

No doubt some interpretivists appear to leave little, if any, room for agency.[2] They suggest that languages, paradigms, or epistemes determine the beliefs people adopt and so the actions they might attempt. They argue that meanings or beliefs arise from the internal relations of self-sufficient discourses. Clearly though, we do not need to throw out the concept of situated agency along with that of autonomy. Just because individuals start out from an inherited tradition does not imply they cannot adjust it. On the contrary, the ability to develop traditions is an essential part of our being in the world. We are always confronting slightly novel circumstances that require us to apply tradition anew, and a tradition cannot fix the nature of its application. So, traditions are products of individual agency—they develop out of activity individuals undertake for reasons of their own—even as agency only ever occurs in the context of tradition—activity is always situated against the background of tradition. It is the need to allow for situated agency that makes tradition a more satisfactory concept than rivals such as language, paradigm, and episteme. The latter concepts all appear to invoke a social force that determines the beliefs of individuals. By contrast, tradition suggests a social heritage that comes to individuals who can adjust and transform this heritage through their own activity.

A particular relationship must exist between beliefs if they are to make up a tradition. Traditions must be made up of beliefs that were passed from generation to generation. Socialization—the relaying of beliefs and practices from teacher to pupil—may be intentional or unintentional. The continuity lies in the themes developed and passed on over time. As beliefs pass from teacher to pupil, the pupil adapts and extends the themes linking the beliefs. Although we must be able to trace a historical line from the start of a tradition to its current finish, the developments introduced by successive generations might result in beginning and end having nothing in common apart from such temporal links. Traditions also must embody suitable conceptual links. The beliefs a teacher passes to a pupil display a minimal level of consistency. A tradition could not have provided someone with an initial starting point unless its parts formed a minimally coherent set of ideas. Traditions cannot be made up of purely random beliefs and actions that successive individuals happen to have held in common.

Although the beliefs in a tradition must be related to one another both temporally and conceptually, their substantive content is unimportant to their ability to explain. Because tradition is unavoidable, all beliefs and practices must have their roots in tradition; they must do so whether they are aesthetic or practical, sacred or secular, legendary or factual, premodern or scientific, valued because of lineage or reasonableness. The explanatory concept of tradition differs, therefore, from that concept of tradition that some human scientists use to describe customary ways of behaving or the entrenched folklore of premodern societies. At the heart of the explanatory concept of tradition are individuals using local reasoning consciously and subconsciously to modify their contingent heritage.

Concepts such as dilemma, problem, and anomaly help to unpack the role of situated agency in traditions. Our capacity for situated agency implies that change originates in the responses of individuals, albeit these responses are always influenced by traditions. Whenever someone adopts a new belief or action, he has to adjust his existing beliefs to make way for the newcomer. To accept a new belief is thus to pose a dilemma that asks questions of one's existing web of beliefs. A dilemma here arises for an individual or institution when a new idea stands in opposition to existing beliefs or practices and so forces a reconsideration of these existing beliefs. Human scientists can explain change within traditions, therefore, by referring to the relevant dilemmas. Tradition changes as individuals make a series of variations to it in response to any number of specific dilemmas.

Dilemmas often arise from people's experiences. However, we must add immediately that this need not be the case. Dilemmas can arise from theoretical and moral reflection as well as experiences of worldly pressures. The new belief that poses a dilemma can lie anywhere on a spectrum from views with little theoretical content to complex theoretical constructs only remotely linked to views about the real world. What is more, we cannot straightforwardly identify dilemmas with allegedly objective pressures in the world. People vary their beliefs or actions in response to any new idea that they come to hold as true. They do so irrespective of whether the new idea reflects real pressures or, to be precise, irrespective of whether it reflects pressures that human scientists as observers believe to be real. In explaining change, interpretivists do not privilege their academic accounts of the world; rather, they again offer interpretations of interpretations, concentrating on the subjective and intersubjective understandings of the actors who bring about the change.

EPISTEMIC VALIDITY

Interpretive approaches instantiate a narrative form of explanation in which actions are explained by pointing to conditional and volitional connections between beliefs and in which beliefs are explained in terms of traditions and dilemmas. As such, interpretivism deploys the same type of narrative structures found in works of fiction. We can acknowledge this similarity without assimilating interpretive studies to fiction. Human scientists typically offer us narratives that they believe retell the way in which things happened in the past or really are today, whereas writers of fiction do not do so. Human scientists cannot ignore the facts, although we surely should accept that no fact is simply given to them.

Critics of interpretive research still might argue, however, that all narratives are constructed in part by the imagination of the writer, so if interpretivism relies on narrative, it lacks proper epistemic legitimacy. This argument even seems to be made by some advocates of interpretive approaches. Louis Mink, for example, doubted whether one could resolve the problem that although narrative "claims to represent . . . the real complexity of the past," it is an "imaginative construction, which cannot defend its claim to truth" (1978, 45). Similarly, Hayden White argues that human scientists endow the past with meaning by "the projection" of narrative structures on it, where the choice of narrative structures, or "genres of literary figuration," is the result of an a-rational, aesthetic judgment (1987, 47).

In fact, we can easily defend the epistemic legitimacy of narrative provided only that we reject naive positivism. The failings of naive positivism are recognized so widely now that I hope I will be excused for taking for granted the assumption that we cannot have pure perceptions of given facts, but rather must always approach the world with a prior body of theories, concepts, or categories that help to construct the experiences we have. This rejection of naive positivism implies, first, that in all human knowledge—natural science as well as narrative—we imaginatively construct the world of our experience. Thus, we can accept that narratives are in part imaginative constructs and still defend their epistemic legitimacy, for their legitimacy cannot be undermined by the fact that they exhibit a characteristic that is common to all knowledge. Many concerns about the epistemic legitimacy of narrative make sense only if one assumes the possibility of forms of knowledge that do not entail anything akin to what Mink called "imaginative construction." Certainly, White's reference to the way in which we project narrative structures onto the world becomes critical only if one assumes the possibility of a sort of pure data onto which we do not project prior categories.

The second important consequence of rejecting naive positivism is that we must judge the epistemic legitimacy of a form of explanation by reference to the reasonableness of the theories, concepts, or categories it embodies. There are, of course, numerous competing postpositivist analyses of what counts as reasonable in this context. Fortunately, we do not need to decide between these competing analyses to defend the epistemic legitimacy of narrative. Narrative rests on the theories, concepts, and categories central to folk psychology, and these surely must be judged reasonable; indeed, the failings of positivism appear to leave human scientists no viable option but to work with folk psychology. A rejection of naive positivism implies that the past does not present itself to us as a series of isolated facts upon which we impose a narrative so as to bring the facts to order. Rather, experience presents itself as an already structured set of facts. Human scientists cannot grasp facts about the world save in their relation to one another and also to the other theories they hold true. They cannot experience the past apart from the categories given them by folk psychology. We might say, therefore, that the world they experience already has a narrative structure. We are, to circle back, working with interpretations of interpretations.

NOTES

1. Philosophers typically use the term "folk psychology" to describe those concepts that thus govern our prescientific thought and language about the mental; often they do so in contrast to formal psychologies and especially cognitive science.

2. Although Foucault is a leading example, even he appears to have needed a concept of agency at times (Dews 1989).

CHAPTER 16

CRITICAL INTERPRETATION AND INTERWAR PEACE MOVEMENTS

Challenging Dominant Narratives

CECELIA LYNCH

In discussing my way into interpretive theory and methods, I often feel like the proverbial parent who lectures the child about how I walked five miles to school and back in the snow just to grasp a bit of knowledge. I, perhaps like others, am rather proud of the effort and determination involved, but at the same time I know that there must be an easier way for both myself and my students to make the trek. My own path was anything but linear, and I can't say whether or not the allegedly straight methods make one a better scholar in the end.

During my graduate years I had a love-hate relationship with the field of international relations (IR). Living on the Upper West Side of New York City (after Missouri, Iowa, and Paris), I became involved almost immediately in "social justice" activities: helping to start a soup kitchen, helping run a shelter for homeless men, working with law and social work students to get social security and other welfare benefits for our guests, protesting money spent on nuclear weapons and Central American death squads. The disconnect between being involved in this activism and studying nuclear strategy and levels of analysis theory was interesting, to say the least. Yet I was also exposed to bits and pieces of critical theory in IR, especially applications of the work of Antonio Gramsci to U.S. hegemony.

On my return from doing research in Brussels, where I also became involved in European peace movements, I knew I needed time away from graduate school and took jobs in social service and peace groups for several years. When I eventually decided to return and finish my Ph.D., it was with a new dissertation topic on interwar peace movements and with a determination to negotiate, somehow, the disconnect between my previous activist involvement and academic study. I sought out an adviser (Friedrich Kratochwil) who was supportive and able to steer me toward new interpretive literatures and spoke with other faculty, such as Jean Cohen, to learn about theories of "new social movements." Then, when I was in London for archival research in 1989, I attended the International Studies Association annual meeting for the first time and found rapidly growing groups of feminist, postmodern, and critical scholars whose work was theoretically sophisticated and called into question the way in which I was trying to demonstrate peace movement "influence." With the end of the cold war the field imploded, and I felt there could be space for all of us.

Since that point, I have probably gone through too many phases in my understanding of how to relate interpretive theory and methods to concerns in world politics to document clearly. Suffice it to say that the journey is ongoing, fed by numerous friends and colleagues in many fields in and out of academia; students in both graduate and undergraduate classes; my children's all-too-apt questioning of authority; and my own continued reading and questioning. More than anything, the road has taught me to reexamine certainties constantly, my own and others', political and academic, with all the epiphanies and angst that that entails.

> This reinterpretation [of interwar peace movements and the creation of the United Nations] demonstrates that a critical analysis of the interwar period and the role of peace movements in it not only disturbs entrenched categories and ways of theorizing, but also tells us something useful about the role of social forces in international life.
> —*Cecelia Lynch* (1999, 215)

What does this reinterpretation, or construction of an alternative narrative, tell the reader about the role of peace movements?

> Their primary significance lies in their ability to contest, to loosen the boundaries of conventional notions of interest by exposing their contradictions (as in the Coolidge Conference and Kellogg-Briand Pact debates), and to use discursive compromises to open the way toward further contestation.
> —*Cecelia Lynch* (1999, 214)

More specifically, regarding the construction of the United Nations:

> Peace movements helped to foster and to legitimize norms underpinning global international organization. But what is important about global international organization is not so much whether or not it represents a decline in state sovereignty or whether it fulfills state goals. What is important is that it has represented an important site of social struggle over the normative meaning and legitimacy of state practice and an alternative to the state for social groups to enable new practices to take form. The state and international organization are both permeable as well as powerful entities, and both have functions that are constantly reevaluated, reinterpreted, and recreated, in large part because of the claims and demands advanced by social movements.
> —*Cecelia Lynch* (1999, 215)

And finally, what do these findings mean for disturbing "entrenched categories and ways of theorizing" (from the first epigraph)?

> Laying bare the normative positions of interwar movements forces us to look at the reasons why peace groups acted as they did; that is, it forces us to compare the logic of their behavior against that of the "lessons" taught by the dominant narratives and to ask anew whether the former should of necessity be seen as naive and the latter as prudent.
> —*Cecelia Lynch* (1999, 215)

My study of interwar peace movements, the construction of the United Nations, and the construction of international relations (IR) theory comprised nonlinear and multicausal notions of how and why events happened, attempted to draw out points at which illogical and/or incoherent arguments about peace movements had been made by others and investigate them anew, and used evidence for constructing both a new narrative of peace movement influence and a critique of dominant narratives of realpolitik. In this chapter I reexamine, first, my nonlinear path of conducting this research, and, second, the practical lessons I learned in doing so about methods of critical interpretation that, I hope, will be useful to others.

Like many scholars undertaking critical interpretation and narrative (re)construction during the 1990s, I operated methodologically in a vacuum. My book attempted to flesh out a critical interpretation of the "hard case" of peace movements: the interwar period. Peace movements were accused of naivete and of causing appeasement in Britain and isolationism in the United States. I wanted to see if an alternative construction of peace movements' actions and meaning was possible.

To research this topic, I knew I had to (and wanted to) examine a variety of archives, but I had not been trained in archival research. I was contesting mono-causal argumentation, but I still needed to demonstrate influence empirically. I was running headlong into major issues in the philosophy of science, including whether researchers can ever obtain sufficient evidence for our knowledge claims and, if so, what constitutes sufficient evidence, as well as problems of interpretation (addressed below), but it was some time before I related the substantive concerns I had about peace movements and the interwar period to philosophical issues of evidence and interpretation.

One thing I did know was that in undertaking such a project, I was adopting a critical stance toward dominant narratives, or meta-narratives. I knew from being both an activist in peace movements and such "social justice" causes as hunger and homelessness and a graduate student in New York City during the 1980s that there existed a double standard for what types of research and related activities could be considered "objective," and this led me to question the possibility of scholarly neutrality early on and gravitate toward theories that challenged facile claims of objectivity in the social sciences. For example, a number of prominent IR faculty of the time had consulted for the U.S. national security establishment (the CIA, State Department, etc.), which, as long as they continued to publish, appeared to add luster and gravitas to their curriculum vitas. However, my experience appeared to be different, since I would be questioned later about whether my activism in peace movements had compromised my objectivity. Thus, early on in my work, I began to question not only whether and how a more peaceful world could be constructed, but also how it was that the field of IR privileged some paths and denigrated others. Several scholars have now mined this subject more thoroughly than I can in this chapter (see esp. Oren 2003 and Tickner 2001), but it is worth mentioning here in the context of what led me to question the authoritative claims of the field of IR in the 1980s. I (and many others) reacted skeptically to the cold war security theories and nuclear weapons doctrines upon which much of 1980s IR was based. They simply seemed illogical. It was not a huge step to see gaps in the logic of the literature on the interwar period as puzzling and worthy of further inquiry.

I recite my own narrative to make the point that the "critical" part of critical interpretation generally entails a process of questioning, critiquing, and challenging established theories, concepts, and claims of popular and scholarly "truth." It means, in other words, not taking the teachings of scholarly, official, or popular hegemonies at face value. All researchers interpret, but to interpret critically indicates that we question the assumptions underlying material that is already interpreted, especially when such assumptions ground claims by powerful entities that people should engage in some particular actions and beliefs and not in others. In my case, both IR theorists and officials of powerful governments made mutually reinforcing claims about the role of social forces (naive and dangerous) and the means to peace (through dominance, or through diplomatic cunning vis-à-vis irrational others). I wondered how they could be so sure of claims that either stated or implied that (a) governments knew better than citizens how to ensure security, (b) the arms race was a given and could not be reversed, and/or (c) citizen criticisms of government defense strategies were ill-advised at best.

Yet if I was going to challenge the certainties of others, I also needed to take a strongly self-reflective stance toward my own conclusions. For my project, this entailed a certain humility vis-à-vis the evidence. Numerous aspects of the interwar period had been mined already, and extensive documentation existed. More importantly, it required the awareness that I, like others, could not escape the hermeneutic circle: I could not develop a once-and-for-all explanation of peace movement influence that was separate from the late–cold war context and critiques of it, nor could I remove completely the lenses through which I experienced and analyzed this context and these critiques. In other words, because academics cannot get outside of what we might call our individual subjectivity as scholars, I needed to acknowledge why certain questions about peace movements were important to me during the 1980s, and how my concerns fit into knowledge practices that made some topics and types of questions more salient than others during this period of time.

From the above narration of my often-stumbling autodidactic path toward understanding a substantive and theoretical problem in critical as well as historical terms, I now move to what I learned and the specific steps that I hope to pass on to others engaged in critical interpretation. I condense the "lessons learned" into the following aspects of critical interpretation. First, I discuss the dual nature of the project of critical interpretation; then, I move to a series of points on the relationship among interpretation, narrative, and evidence.

IDENTIFY DOMINANT INTERPRETATIONS

Critical interpretation initially requires laying out the specifics of dominant interpretations (in other words, meta-narratives) that are constructed and reproduced most frequently by those in power. Dominant interpretations have enormous influence, because they shape not only the way scholars (as well as those outside the academic community) see a particular set of issues, but also what kinds of questions about these issues are considered legitimate for scholars to ask and what kinds of actions leaders and their publics are supposed to take.

In the interwar case, the dominant interpretations, or meta-narratives, accused peace movements of being naive and dangerous. The lesson was that peace movements led to imprudent or nefarious foreign policies. This lesson has had a strong impact on "real life": Leaders in the United States and Britain, from Anthony Eden in Suez to Ronald Reagan in Central America to George Bush in the Persian Gulf, used the "appeasement bogey" against subsequent peace movements. People were supposed to be quiet, know their place as followers, and not stir up public sentiment against U.S.- and/or British-led wars.

Yet many contradictions existed in the dominant narratives about peace movement influence. First, why was it that the conventional wisdom persisted in calling peace movements naive and dangerous (and could they be both?), while historians who examined particular interwar policies inevitably cited not such movements but strategic or economic reasons as causes? In other words, how could peace movements be dangerous if they were ineffective? Second, if the League of Nations was such a failure, why did anyone bother to construct a United Nations in 1945? Who was pushing for global international organization, how, and why?

In the interwar case (and I suspect in most others), the dominant narratives were full of contradictions that, in my view, cried out for examination and critique.

ADDRESS THE ISSUE OF ALTERNATIVE INTERPRETATIONS

Critical interpretation also requires, however, a decision either to construct an alternative interpretation or set of interpretations or explicitly to forego such construction altogether. One can have a combination of substantive and theoretical reasons for the choice of constructing an alternative versus eschewing alternative interpretations, but scholars should be clear that, either way, it is a methodological and epistemological choice.

In my case, I always wanted to find a "better" construction of the evidence first and foremost, primarily for substantive reasons of historical understanding—I wanted to see if I could understand peace movement activism during the 1920s and 1930s, which had always been considered the "hard case," that is, the case that many scholars and pundits unquestioningly believed was problematic and ill advised. After beginning my project, I encountered a considerable body of work, based on Foucault and others, that eschewed the construction of alternative narratives altogether, because every construction is partial and any new dominant narrative carries with it its own mechanisms of power, permitting some questions but foreclosing others. Although I was sympathetic to this deconstructionist mode of thinking, it did not ground my original motives for undertaking the study. However, this type of critical thinking did influence my understanding of what I could accomplish in any reinterpretation. Hence my claim that I was constructing "an" interpretation, one that I found better, more complete, and more coherent, but that was also inevitably shaped by the available knowledge and mode of inquiry of my own historical time. I appealed to Gadamer (e.g., Warnke 1987), Ricoeur (1993 [1981], 1988), and others to make this claim.

COLLECT PRIMARY EVIDENCE

The process of collecting primary evidence, as a result of the existence of dominant narratives, necessarily entails a tacking back and forth between dominant interpretations and possible alternatives. This means understanding that documents are repositories of interpretations—made by others. When Foreign Office and State Department diplomats wrote dispatches to London and Washington, they expressed their own assessments—interpretations—of particular situations at particular points in time. Such assessments are not, and cannot be, completely "factual." They can report that a meeting occurred at a certain time between certain people on a certain day, but their understanding of what was said and why it was said, and the meaning of participants' different positions, inevitably varies. Some documents may help in constructing a reinterpretation; others may be more useful in deconstructing dominant narratives; still others may do both.

One of my favorite documents was a piece written by a Foreign Office official in 1931. The document reflected on peace movement demands over the course of ten years for disarmament and the passing of the Geneva Protocol (which would have banned aggressive war and required arbitration of international disputes) and noted that the government's intransigence vis-à-vis peace movement demands had been counterproductive:

> A very large part of the Protocol has already been wrung from us since 1924. If, in 1924, we could have offered spontaneously what we have now been forced to give with not too good a grace, we might almost have secured a Disarmament Conference in that year. . . . We have done this before, we have said, "thus far and no further," and only some years after have we discovered that, while asseverating our complete immobility, we have been pushed several miles further along the road. (Alexander Cadogan memo, March 13, 1931)

This memorandum indicates the power of the peace movement to continue its contestation of security policies and norms, and it also attests to the power of dominant narratives, which shaped the government's refusal to move more aggressively on movement demands for disarmament and arbitration.

ASSESS SECONDARY EVIDENCE

The process of assessing secondary evidence is also a process of "historiographic construction." Historiographies review the secondary work that has been done on a particular topic and may also set these works within a broader political context of scholarship. In my work, several extremely helpful historiographies of peace movements and interwar diplomacy had already been published. These enabled me to see, for example, that scholarship on the interwar period moved from an emphasis on charismatic and influential leaders during the 1950s, to structural analyses during the 1960s and 1970s, to a reassessment of multiple causes during the 1980s. The historiographies assisted in the critique of dominant narratives; allowed me to reflect on the practices of the times, which encouraged my own reinterpretation; and made it possible for me to set my interpretation among those of others and argue why a reinterpretation was warranted.

CHOOSE SOURCES FROM DIFFERENT PERSPECTIVES

Especially if one is constructing an alternative narrative, it is critical to examine a wide variety of sources from different perspectives. For the case of interwar peace movements, I was struck that many scholars of the interwar period did not examine peace movement documents yet were content to make judgments about the movements. These judgments, it seemed, were based primarily on conventional wisdom and/or leaders' assertions that the movements were troublesome, naive, or dangerous. In other words, they were based on "dominant narratives" that were not themselves called into question and analyzed. Those who did examine peace movement as well as government documents tended to focus on specific events during the period, such as the World Disarmament Conference of 1932. Peace movement historians sometimes examined official documentation as well as a variety of group archives, but they tended to analyze the former selectively. Was it possible to escape completely the problems inherent in the selective examination of documents? For this particular case (or series of cases, depending on how one looks at the interwar period), there had to be some justifiable method for choosing to examine some documents and not others. In part, my strategy followed from the questions I was asking about peace movement influence. In part, however, it also followed from the process of archival research. I first began to examine British peace group archives at the London School of Economics and Political Science. Later, when I looked at Foreign Office documentation at the Public Record Office (PRO) and the papers of key players at the British Library, I found that I could document interaction between governments and peace groups for some events and not others, or document the impact of previous events on debates about later ones, so these findings and experiences guided my subsequent research. For example, I had little idea arriving in London that the Geneva Protocol would play such a huge role in the minds of peace groups and be such a thorn in the side of Foreign Secretary Austen Chamberlain and his successors. This became evident during the course of my research.

DEVISE A METHOD OF SELECTION WHEN SOURCES ARE TOO NUMEROUS

Despite my argument against the sort of selectivity noted above, scholars had excellent reasons for being selective in those ways. Far too many primary sources (let alone secondary sources) on the interwar period existed for any single scholar to read in a lifetime, let alone for one book. What was I to do about this problem? Here, I think my own naivete played into my determination to look at events from a variety of perspectives. Not being a historian, I simply did not realize the vast number of sources available in any given archive, even after doing initial research in archival reference sources (e.g., *Diplomatic Records* 1986). Yet I found myself interacting quite a bit with historians during my archival research and eventually devised a system whereby I focused on the contours of particular, more or less temporally bounded events, while cross-checking any interesting assertions in the records with other documents and keeping the option open to investigate additional evidence (both supporting and contradictory) as I found it. Now, whenever I read positivist treatises on the "rigor" of the scientific method of "testing," I know that scholars who employ archival methods engage in extremely thorough and systematic analysis of evidence and that the criticism that qualitative and interpretive methods lack such characteristics is simply wrong (on the term "rigor," see C. Lynch 2005; and Yanow, chapter 4, this volume). Because of this, I was extremely pleased after the publication of my book that it received praise from historians.

UNDERSTAND THE PHILOSOPHICAL PROBLEMS OF EVIDENCE ACCUMULATION

In IR we often talk about a theory's or an event's being "overdetermined" or "underdetermined" by the evidence. World War I is a major example of overdetermination according to conventional academic wisdom: There were so many significant causal factors that converged to make it happen that it could not have been avoided. However, it is important to remember that theories about events (even World War I) are actually underdetermined by the available evidence; that is, scholars can never have enough "facts" to prevent value judgments from entering into our explanations for events, and the facts themselves are objects of interpretation. As philosophers of science such as Mary Hesse have pointed out, "Theories are logically constrained by facts," but "they can be neither conclusively refuted nor uniquely derived from statements of fact alone" (1978, 1). Her point is that statements of fact can always be repackaged in different ways, resulting in different theories (for example, about why an event occurred), and scholars must look beyond the realm of "fact" to that of value to understand why some explanations are preferred to others.

So how do researchers in the social sciences decide which theory is the most persuasive? The major criterion for the success of a theory is the "pragmatic criterion," which means that it appears to work better than others to explain more aspects of the (political) environment. But the problem with the pragmatic criterion is that it sometimes runs up against an obstacle that makes crucial aspects of the theory fall apart. So it was with the pre-Galilean assumption about the earth's shape; so it is, I assert, with the realpolitik assessment of the interwar period.

RESEARCH THE PRACTICAL PROBLEMS OF EVIDENCE ACCUMULATION

Using archives requires an understanding of classification systems. These can differ enormously from country to country and among nongovernmental groups, as can the rules for declassification of official archives. For example, in Britain, the PRO declassifies some government documents after thirty years, others after fifty years, and others after an even longer period of time. I conducted dissertation research at the PRO in 1988–89, which meant that a number of documents relating to peace groups from the Czech crisis in 1938 had just been declassified. I eagerly ordered these documents, and though I did find a great deal of useful and interesting information in them, most of it was far from earth shattering. I then found out from talking to archivists that documents may be kept classified for longer than thirty years for a variety of reasons: In many cases this is simply because no one got around to examining them for release.

DO NOT EMPHASIZE FINDING "SMOKING GUNS"

Although many scholars search for smoking guns, in fact they are rarely uncovered, largely as a result of the previous two points. What constitutes a smoking gun is also a matter of interpretation and is subject to how scholars construct the pragmatic criterion of evidence accumulation and analysis. In other words, whether a piece of evidence appears to make one story or explanation fall together (and others fall apart) depends on the way in which that story fits into broader narratives concerning what is known about an event. Thus, I found no single statement by government officials in the United States or Britain that peace movements had nothing at all to do with inter-war policies of appeasement and isolationism, nor did I find any corresponding statement that peace movements were responsible for these policies. Yet, even if I had, such a statement could only be analyzed in conjunction with when and how and by whom it was being made and what else was going on at the time. As a result, building a case for an alternative interpretation through the careful buildup of plausible evidence and constructing a logical and coherent understanding or explanation of events is just as (if not more) useful as finding a smoking gun, since the latter can never be "proven" to the satisfaction of all.

PUT THE EVIDENCE TOGETHER

Given the dual nature of critical interpretation—that is, outlining the "dominant interpretation(s)" at issue and deciding whether to construct an alternative narrative or explicitly forego such a construction—how do scholars go about putting the evidence together? I found that questioning and reexamination—of my own assumptions, of others' assumptions and conclusions, of the evidence, and of the views of the actors involved—are absolutely necessary components of analysis. I believe that this questioning and reexamining is where any move toward distance (if not objectivity) in social scientific analysis occurs. This is the basis of cross-checking, or validity checks, or testing, or other similar methodological terms, which all connote doing one's best to ensure that the evidence used is reliable—meaning that it comes from bona fide sources and is persuasive and logical according to a criterion of coherence. However, not only the evidence must be checked and reevaluated; so must the assumptions the researcher brings to the analysis. If the researcher engages in such questioning and cross-checking of both assumptions and evidence, she can also better evaluate critically how the evidence "fits" into the dominant narratives constructed by others.

A useful rule of thumb for putting the evidence together using critical interpretation is to outline the dominant assumptions about a situation or event, how events are packaged to fit these assumptions, and how the resulting constructions of knowledge embed power relations between political and social actors. If the researcher constructs an alternative narrative, he then needs to document, describe, and analyze the self-understandings of actors and their relevant conditions of action, always cross-checking the evidence against the interpretations and evidence provided by others.

BE SELF-REFLEXIVE ABOUT ETHICAL IMPLICATIONS

Finally, I believe researchers need to be clear about stating up front our position concerning why we think our interpretation is better than others, and we need to understand that this position entails both evidentiary and ethical rationales. Scholars should understand—and work through—how conclusions and recommendations might translate into policy and think about the various meanings that could be assigned to such conclusions, recommendations, and policies. This does not mean that we should avoid conclusions that might be difficult if our evidence leads us to them. Instead, it means that we should acknowledge that unspoken ethical or worldview assumptions can shape our very research questions, the methods we use to examine them, and the conclusions we draw from them. In other words, scholars' research can affect policies and, consequently, people's lives. Therefore, we need to be more cognizant of whether our conclusions feed into, or challenge, meta-narratives about world politics, and why and how they might do so. In undertaking this ethical evaluation, however, scholars must continue to be reflexive and even self-critical. If we avoid this responsibility, our interpretations become more dogmatic than critical, and we forego the opportunity to gain continued insights in the future.

Thus, careful substantive (or "empirical") work, combined with questioning assumptions about events, can help to destabilize dominant interpretations. The task of critical interpretation challenges the belief, so prevalent in much of the social sciences, that arguments are won or lost based on their merits alone. Rather, critical interpretation assumes that we must analyze the situatedness of the arguments themselves, the evidence used to support them, and the ethical lessons drawn from them, to understand the power relations that they support or deny. In evaluating this combination of arguments, evidence, and ethics, the researcher must also be aware of the context that underlies her own questioning stance. Conversely, scholars cannot engage in persuasive critical interpretation without examining a good deal of evidence, if possible from a variety of sources. The promise of critical interpretation is that the interaction between empirical grounding and critical questioning can permit scholars to break through powerful, and possibly stale, paradigms to gain new insights on politics, power, and ethics.

CHAPTER 17

VALUE-CRITICAL POLICY ANALYSIS

The Case of Language Policy in the United States

RONALD SCHMIDT, SR.

My political science career began with an emphasis in political theory as an undergraduate and beginning graduate student during theory's "golden years" at UC Berkeley in the 1960s. There I took political theory courses under such luminaries as Sheldon Wolin, John Schaar, Norman Jacobson, Hanna Pitkin, Michael Rogin, Peter Euben (then a teaching assistant), and Joseph Tussman (from the philosophy department). Smitten by political theory's engagement with "deep" issues of political significance and meaning, and its epic-scale political questions, I couldn't get enough.

With my M.A. degree in hand I set out for a career in community college teaching, but after a year in a temporary position, I found that getting a tenure-track job in a community college was no easy matter. As a result, I spent fifteen months in a new and unanticipated career: as a local administrator in Lyndon Johnson's "War on Poverty," trying to piece together and implement an adult basic education program for migrant farm workers in California's San Joaquin Valley. This was a life-changing event for me, as I came to see the importance, immense complexity, and difficulty of trying to bring people together to make good things happen in the "real world" outside academia.

Returning to graduate school at UC Riverside, I decided to make public policy my emphasis, with political theory as a secondary field. It seemed to me then (and still does today) that the field of public policy offered the perfect opportunity to combine my interests in good ideas for making the world a better place with the difficult questions involved in actually making good things happen. And I had the good fortune at UCR to study under a mentor, Michael Reagan, who had an eclectic appreciation of multiple approaches to political knowledge, as well as a commitment to working toward the public good through political science. I was also fortunate to be part of a cohort of graduate students who shared my interest in approaching public policy both norma-tively and empirically, embracing the literature of political theory as well as political science to engage issues of public policy.

I was also very lucky to land a job at California State University, Long Beach, where I've taught since 1972. During my years at CSULB, I've been allowed by an unusually congenial group of colleagues to pursue my wide-ranging interests, and this has enabled me to teach in several fields: public policy and administration, racial and ethnic politics, and political theory. It was within this supportive setting that I initiated a course on "Public Values and Public Policy" that has enabled me to hone my ideas on value-critical policy analysis by testing them on my students. Their responses to my efforts have been humbling, encouraging, and exhilarating, and always richly rewarding.

> In this context, the central language policy conflict is not about the continued dominance of the English language as such, but over how the country should deal with its other languages in public policy. And here, the primary issue is not language per se, but social identities and their relationship to justice and the common good.
> —*Ronald Schmidt* (2000, 224)

How can systematic policy analysis respond when fundamental value disagreements make it unlikely that analysis of "the facts" will resolve policy conflict? This chapter articulates an interpretive method of policy analysis, a *value-critical* approach, which may be helpful in just such situations. It does so both discursively and by example, with the latter drawn from the author's book *Language Policy and Identity Politics in the United States* (R. Schmidt 2000).

In doing research on the language policy debate in the United States, I gradually came to realize that the most important questions in this conflict are not about matters of "fact," but about differences of interpretation and fundamental value disputes that center on issues of identity. What kind of "nation" is the United States? What are the ties that bind Americans to each other as members of a nation-state? What is the role of language in creating and sustaining those ties? And how does the public role of "language" intersect with questions of "justice" for ethno-linguistic and ethno-racial minorities, and with questions of how to promote the "common good"?

On the one hand, I came to realize that there was little hope that scientifically rigorous "value-neutral" policy analyses, no matter how well done, could lead to a resolution of the language policy debate. On the other hand, I also came to realize that most articulations of the values at stake in this issue by partisans in the debate are of the "value-committed" variety, leading almost always to fruitless "value-smashing" exercises between the protagonists. I found myself repeatedly returning to the concept of value-critical policy analysis, first articulated by Martin Rein (1976), in the hope of shedding light on what is really at stake in the U.S. language policy debate, and how the United States might best resolve this conflict in a way that maximizes both justice for minorities and the common good. My aim below is to share the fruits of my effort to conduct a value-critical analysis in hopes of aiding the work of others in similar situations.

The concept of value-critical policy analysis comes from Martin Rein's book *Social Science and Public Policy* (1976). In that book, Rein distinguished this method from both value-neutral and value-committed approaches to public policy analysis. Guided by the canons of positivist social scientific research, the *value-neutral* approach takes the normative aims or goals of public policies as given and seeks to predict (through modeling and causal analysis) which of several alternative means of achieving a policy's goal is most likely to succeed and at what costs. Similarly, during and after a policy's implementation value-neutral analysts attempt to describe and explain the degree to which the policy succeeded or failed to achieve its goals.

The *value-committed* approach to policy analysis has a long history. Here, the analyst attempts to justify a given policy in terms of values to which he or she is already committed by marshaling arguments and evidence that point in that direction. Typical examples of this form of policy analysis include the testimony of interest group representatives before legislative committees, as well as ideologically grounded policy arguments made by scholars and public commentators.

In contrast, the *value-critical* approach was defined by Rein as one that "subjects goals and values to critical review, that is, values themselves become the object of analysis; they are not merely accepted as a voluntary choice of the will, unamenable to further debate" (Rein 1976, 13). Nor, on the other hand, does the value-critical analyst begin with an unexamined faith in a set of ideological commitments, as in the case of the value-committed approach. Rather, on the assumption that values discourse can be conducted rationally, the analyst approaches public policy aims with a skeptical spirit, seeking to subject them to rigorous, but not cynical, analysis. The aim of value-critical analysis, then, is to contribute to the public discussion of policy conflicts by taking the *goals* of policy seriously as subjects of analysis.

My book *Language Policy and Identity Politics in the United States* is an attempt to employ Rein's concept of value-critical policy analysis and to demonstrate its usefulness in illuminating what is at stake in a hotly contested policy debate. The book aims to get to the root of the country's conflict over the most appropriate public policy responses to the fact that some 18 percent of the U.S. population most frequently speaks a language other than English. The conflict centers on three policy issues that have generated the most controversy: (1) education for non- and limited-English-speaking students in the public schools (and particularly the role of bilingual education for such students); (2) the degree to which non-English languages should be used or promoted by the state to ensure "linguistic access" to civil and political rights (e.g., the right to vote, using non-English ballots and election materials as required by amendments to the Voting Rights Act of 1965); and (3) whether English should be adopted as the sole "official" language of various levels of government in the United States. And, as noted above, the analysis centers on the claim that these debates are fundamentally grounded in a dispute over how to interpret the social identities of U.S. nationals, and the role of language in that interpretation.

VALUE-CRITICAL ANALYSIS: A STEP-BY-STEP ARTICULATION

How can policy analysts work to systematically assess the value conflicts that underlie important public policy issues? Rein has not, to date, presented an explicit, self-reflective account of how to do value-critical analysis. So the following represents this author's approach to a step-by-step articulation that might be seen as fruitful by others. Each step requires the policy analyst to interpret the meaning and significance of an important aspect of the public policy issue under study. Before beginning these steps, of course, the analyst must gather information, the basic data from which descriptions, interpretations, and analyses are drawn.[1] Where are these data found? Public policy debates typically take place in a variety of forums but, among other sources, "raw materials" about the protagonists, their policy positions, and their arguments can be gathered from magazine and journal articles, newspaper accounts of the controversy, books by partisans and by observers of the controversy, op-ed pieces in newspapers and magazines, and government documents (e.g., transcripts of legislative testimony, agency reports, committee investigations), as well as directly from the protagonists themselves (e.g., from personal interviews, published materials, or Web sites). Participant-observation is another very useful way in which to gather data for an analysis of this type.

A second essential preliminary step is for the policy analyst to clarify her own value positions in relation to the policy issue under study. During the process of gathering information about the policy controversy and its primary protagonists, and then repeatedly throughout the analytical process, the policy analyst should maintain and update an explicit and fairly detailed statement regarding her own bent on this issue. Where do your sympathies lie when reading and/or listening to the statements and arguments of the main protagonists in the debate? Can you identify what motivates those sympathies? What are your own core values about the public policy issue at hand? Identifying and articulating these core values will be helpful when the analyst attempts to develop and articulate a "balanced" and "complete" overview of the policy context, the primary arguments of protagonists, and their core values. It will also be helpful when the analyst begins his critical analysis of the protagonists' core value positions, as it will put him on guard against his own biases.[2] I will come back to this issue again near the end of the chapter.

Step One: Identifying the Issue and the Protagonists

Once the data-collection process has produced results, the first step in the analytical process is to *describe the policy issue in focus in the study* and to *identify the primary protagonists* engaged in the policy conflict. This sounds simple, but in fact it is often quite difficult because the terrain of public policy conflict is inherently overlapping and contestable. The aim at this stage is to describe the basic contours of the policy issue and the protagonists engaged with it. For example, what is the problem or situation that protagonists are arguing about? How do the competing camps in the policy struggle identify themselves in relation to each other?

Typically it takes several iterations before this initial part of the process is settled enough for further analysis. In the case of my language policy book, for example, I began with the understanding that the issue was a conflict over the appropriateness of bilingual education in the public schools as a way of improving the schools' effectiveness in educating children whose native language is not English. As I studied bilingual education more closely, however, it became clear that there were other, closely related conflicts that raised the same kinds of questions and generated political involvement from the same set of protagonists, even though the issues did not always land on the agendas of the same policy makers. Although a study focusing only on the bilingual education conflict would be quite legitimate, I decided that—given the underlying value conflicts in this issue—it would be more useful to take a broader view. Accordingly, I broadened my perspective to include other issues that had generated involvement from many of the same set of protagonists that I found involved in the conflict over bilingual education (e.g., the Voting Rights Act amendments requiring voter officials to provide ballots and other election materials in languages other than English under certain circumstances, and "official English" policies making English the sole "official language" of the United States or one of its sub-jurisdictions). In any case, through much reading, discussion, thinking, and writing, I came to believe that the *core issue* in this controversy is how the United States should respond—through public policy—to the fact that an increasing number of the country's people usually speak a language other than English. In short, I came to believe that this is really the core policy question mobilizing the same protagonists in all three debates: bilingual education, non-English ballots and election materials, and "English-only" official language policy.

What the policy analyst needs to do at this early stage, then, is to provide a description of the core issue that drives protagonists to be at odds with each other over a particular policy or set of interrelated policies. And arriving at such a description is a reiterative process because frequently the analyst's understanding of the issue deepens and broadens after moving further into the analysis (i.e., the steps outlined below). When that happens it becomes useful to return to the description of the core policy issue, to rethink and rewrite how it might best be understood and described.

Intertwined with, and in dialectical relationship with, this process of describing the policy's core issue is another: *identifying the main protagonists* in the conflict. That is, value-critical policy analysis presupposes a significant conflict of values between two or more camps that are opposed to each other in relation to the policy issue. In doing this type of policy analysis, therefore, it will be necessary to provide an informative description of just who is involved in the conflict, and why. What is needed here is not a simple list of organizations that have weighed in on the issue, but rather a description of the main camps (each of which may contain many specific organizations) that have staked out opposing claims in the debate over this particular policy issue. Further, the reader will need some sense of what motivates the members of each set of protagonists. What do they want? Why do they care about this issue? In a preliminary way, the goal is to describe the backgrounds, motivations, and key positions of each set of protagonists in the debate. Once again, this is done by sifting through the materials the analyst has gathered through research: newspaper and magazine accounts of policy debates, internet Web sites posted by political organizations, lists of witnesses testifying before legislative committees, and the like.

In writing my book, for example, I quickly found that in the United States, language policy conflict is waged primarily between two opposing camps. On the one hand, a number of groups and individuals want policies promoting English as the sole public language of the United States, so that public policy will motivate speakers of other languages to make English their own public language. This camp believes that public policy certainly should *not* encourage the use of languages other than English in the public spaces of the country.

On the other hand, a competing set of groups and activists sees the United States as historically multilingual and believes that non–English-speaking communities have been treated unjustly for their linguistic "difference." Accordingly, these protagonists want policies that promote bilingualism, so that members of language minority communities will become fluent in English, but also so that their home languages will be treated with respect and dignity by their government. Following terminology used by some partisans in this debate, as well as by some outside observers, I labeled the former group "assimilationists" and the latter "pluralists."

Step Two: Describing the Context and the Protagonists' Policy Proposals

Once the policy analyst has described the core issues in the policy conflict and the protagonists that are fighting over these issues, the next step involves describing more fully the *context* and the *policy proposals of the primary protagonists*. This step involves describing the historical setting and social context from which the conflict has emerged and the conflicting policy proposals being made by the protagonists.

The first part of this step involves *preparing a brief description of the historical context in which the policy conflict has emerged.* Answering questions like the following will help in addressing this important phase of the analysis: What has been going on in the social setting of this policy issue that has generated a demand for a new or revised policy? What sorts of social changes— that is, demographic, economic, technological, cultural, political—have been occurring that might account for the emergence of this policy conflict?

In the case of language policy, for example, there is a major conflict between the partisans over how to understand the historical context of U.S. linguistic diversity, and outlining these competing understandings is itself illuminating in coming to terms with what is at stake in this conflict. Linguistic pluralists see the relevant historical context as one in which the dominant Anglo and English-speaking majority in the United States has consistently, over several centuries, treated members of ethno-linguistic minority groups unjustly by working to marginalize and subordinate their cultures and languages as not really "American." Pluralists also believe that this unjust treatment is integrally related to the fact that many U.S. ethno-linguistic minority groups first became Americans not through voluntary immigration or choice, but through conquest or purchase and annexation (e.g., American Indians, Mexican Americans, Puerto Ricans, etc.), and that these groups were racialized after being forcibly incorporated into the country's population. It is this understanding of the social context of language use and status that shapes the outlook of pluralists and motivates them in the language policy debate.

Assimilationists, on the other hand, have a very different view of the relevant social context: Their attention is fixed on the massive number of new immigrants—most from non–English-speaking countries—who have become part of the U.S. population in recent decades, and whom they see as being encouraged by misguided or self-interested ethnic political activists to resist linguistic (and cultural) assimilation, to the detriment of the immigrants and the whole country. Moreover, assimilationists believe that this contemporary context is very different from that of previous periods of high-level immigration to the United States, arguing that previous immigrants understood that assimilation was the necessary result of migrating to a new country and that this understanding was supported and facilitated by the educational and other public policies of those earlier periods. Understanding the language policy conflict between pluralists and assimilationists, then, begins with an understanding of their very different views of the relevant social context underlying their policy proposals.

Other policy issues, of course, have other relevant social contexts that give rise to political conflict. In the case of transportation policy, to give another example, those who favor expanding governmental support for mass transit systems have a view of the social context that stresses the negative consequences of Americans' overwhelming reliance on the automobile (e.g., environmental damage; waste of economic and natural resources; dependence on foreign oil in an increasingly dangerous world; inequitable access to convenient transportation for the young, old, and impoverished parts of the population; etc.). In contrast, those who favor continued reliance on the automobile as the country's primary means of transportation articulate a very different view of the relevant social context, one that stresses the immense "sunk costs" already invested in automobile usage and that sees continued technological innovation as the key to diminishing both the environmental destructiveness and the global insecurities related to gas-powered vehicles.

In describing the social context, therefore, the policy analyst needs to focus on the larger societal forces shaping the positions of protagonists in the policy debate. The primary aim of the analyst, again, is to clarify what is at stake in a particular public policy conflict. Accomplishing this clarification can be greatly helped by understanding and articulating the protagonists' views on the forces that have shaped social life in directions that have led to the protagonists' calls for a particular kind of public policy response.

Once the policy analyst has arrived at a balanced and accurate description of the protagonists' views of the social context shaping political efforts in relation to a given (actual or proposed) public policy, *it will now be helpful to articulate carefully, accurately, and as succinctly as possible the policy positions of the protagonists*. What, exactly, are the proposals being made by the competing camps about the issue in contention? For example, what kinds of laws or administrative regulations do the protagonists want to see legislators and/or executive officials adopt in order to deal with the situation that has resulted in the policy conflict? The aim here is to be comprehensive and synoptic in getting an overview of the situation, rather than to go into detail on precisely what is being proposed. This is so because most of the time slight variations in policy approach do not involve shifts in underlying values. Incremental shifts sometimes signal important symbolic differences between camps, and they are often the stuff of compromise at the final stages of policy development, but they do not inform us much about the underlying value conflicts.

In the case of language policy conflict, the basic positions of the two sides have remained fairly consistent over a long period of time, despite a multitude of specific policy proposals and counterproposals and a never-ending evolution of new terms and acronyms for the underlying ideas and approaches. Pluralists, for example, want language policies that aim at *both* English-language acquisition by non-English speakers and support and respect for the maintenance of additional languages that they see as fundamentally part of the "American" ethno-linguistic land-scape. They want to see both the country and its peoples as fluent as possible in at least two languages. Thus, pluralists support bilingual education programs in the schools and linguistic access policies that enable all Americans to vote, interact with their governments, and make use of their civil and political rights in languages other than English.

Assimilationists, in contrast, want language policies that channel non-English speakers toward a language "shift" to English, particularly in public places, and they are especially determined that governments and public agencies provide no incentives for people to retain non-English languages in the public domain. For this reason, they oppose bilingual education and non-English ballots and voting materials, and they have sought official English language policies for both symbolic and substantive reasons. In any case, outlining the basic policy positions taken by pro-tagonists in response to their understanding of the context of the issue prepares the way for the next step in the analysis, to which I now turn.

Step Three: Describing the Arguments and the Core Values

The third step in my approach to value-critical policy analysis is to *describe the central arguments* made by the protagonists on behalf of their main policy proposals *and the core values* that underlie those arguments. And this is not just a matter of "recording" what the protagonists are saying; rather, it involves a reiterative process of sifting through a variety of arguments made by a diversity of partisans in overlapping public policy debates. What is needed here is a *distillation* of the primary arguments being made, and this requires the analyst to see past the details to patterns of argumenta-tion that may be found across a variety of specific policy debates. The aim is to accurately and concisely represent the central arguments in the debate and the core values underlying those argu-ments. One helpful approach to making this distillation is to use the "raw materials" gathered through one's research to develop a list of key arguments being made in response to specific issues or ques-tions. Then, organize the distillation around these key issues or questions.

It is also crucial at this stage to explicitly distinguish between conflicts that are articulated as *factual disputes* revolving around issues of *cause and effect,* and those that are articulated as *value disagreements* that involve disputes over *interpretations of meaning and significance* (see Grant 2002 for an excellent discussion contrasting these two frames of reference for understanding social and political realities). This is important because some disputes might be resolvable through meth-ods of cause/effect analysis (and thereby amenable to value-neutral policy analysis), while others—those being highlighted in this chapter—involve issues in which value conflicts lie at the heart of the debate. Distinguishing between these two kinds of argument can be indispensable for determining the kind of analysis needed to clarify what is at stake in the dispute under study.

Returning once again to language policy for purposes of illustration, why do assimilationists want policies that promote language shift to English-only, and why do pluralists want policies described as "English-plus"? What are their central arguments? What are the core values that underlie these arguments? Often the protagonists articulate their arguments using "factual" (e.g., "cause and effect") statements. Assimilationists, for example, have suggested repeatedly that the continued presence of limited-English-speaking children in bilingual classrooms beyond one or two "transitional" years is "proof" that bilingual education has "failed." By the same token, some pluralists have argued that the "fact" that limited-English-speaking students who have been placed in English-only classrooms often score below average on standardized English literacy exams is "proof" that they should be in bilingual classrooms. But both of these arguments, articulated in the form of cause-and-effect "factual" statements, beg a number of underlying questions requiring interpretation and judgments of value. In writing my book, much of my own analytical work involved uncovering and articulating those underlying questions, to subject them to critical analysis.

Thus, after a great deal of such analytical work (reading, discussing, reflecting, thinking, reflecting more, rethinking again), I reached the position that there were three central arguments, revolving around two core values, at the heart of the U.S. language policy debate. The two core values are *justice* and the *common good*. The two arguments about justice involve two different disputes about the implications of disparate understandings of equality in relation to language policy, while the argument about the *common good* centers on the relationship between language policy and *national unity*. And each, I think, can be best understood in relation to a central question that drives the debates. I will briefly summarize the arguments here.

Argument 1 ("justice" issue): What kind of language policy can best help "disadvantaged" language minorities achieve greater social equality in U.S. society?

This first argument has to do with the relationship between language policy and social mobility (i.e., higher levels of educational attainment, better jobs, more income and wealth, more prestige, etc.) for language minorities in the United States. There is not space here to develop more than a cursory overview of the arguments. So, very briefly, assimilationists believe that since the United States is an English-speaking country, it is very obvious that the path to greater social equality for "disadvantaged" non-English speakers is to adopt policies that provide strong incentives for them to master English and provide no incentives for them to avoid mastering English. Pluralists, on the other hand, reject the assumption that the United States is "simply" an "English-speaking country," though they do recognize that access to English is crucial for social mobility. Because of the country's long history of racialized domination, however, pluralists also believe that true social equality cannot be achieved until the languages and cultures of dominated groups are accorded more respect and standing in public policy. Further, they believe that mastering a second language works best when it is "added" to a person's native language, rather than "substituted" for that person's first language.

To summarize, the two sides are in disagreement about whether assimilationist or pluralist policies are more likely to result in greater social mobility for language minorities in the United States. At first glance, accordingly, this argument looks like a dispute about causality, and therefore it should be amenable to settlement through the methods of positivist social science. My analysis, however, claims that there is no way to disentangle "cause" and "effect" through "sticking to the facts," because one's *interpretation* of the relationships among "identity," ethno-linguistic memberships, and the *meaning* of U.S. nationality is completely intertwined with one's understanding of both "cause" and "effect" in this dispute. As such, this seemingly factual dispute must be addressed interpretively if it is going to be analyzed accurately and without distorting the "facts" through the presuppositions of one's analytical framework (see note 2).

Argument 2 ("justice" issue): What kind of language policy is necessary to meet the requirements for "equal rights" in the United States?

This question is more obviously normative in nature, and it is one pressed most fully by pluralists, who argue that the rights of language minorities are trampled or denied by language policies premised on the assumption that the United States is an English-speaking country, and that equal justice requires the protection and even the promotion of multiple languages through public policy. Once again, the question is too complex to be fully summarized here, but assimilationists generally accept "toleration"-oriented language rights (that is, they agree that the government should not be allowed to deny individuals the right to speak in the language of their choice or to teach their children languages other than English). Assimilationists insist, however, that these are "private" rights of individuals, and they are deeply opposed to so-called promotion-oriented rights in which the government is obligated to "promote" the use of non-English languages in American public or civic life. And once again, my analysis argues that this cannot be seen accurately as a simple or straightforward question of what is required for "equal rights." Rather, the answer to this question hinges on one's interpretation of the relationships among "identity," ethno-linguistic memberships, and the meaning of U.S. nationality.

Argument 3 ("common good" issue): What kind of language policy is necessary to promote social harmony and national unity?

It is assimilationists who raise this question most fervently, believing that pluralistic policies in the U.S. foster conflict and division in that society and undermine our national unity to the detriment of the common good. Assimilationists argue that attempting to provide "equal respect" to multiple languages and cultures, especially in a context where they are manifestly not equal in terms of constituting our national identity, can only result in endless rounds of contention and argument, sapping the country of energy and goodwill. Pluralists, in contrast, again make the argument that the assimilationist position is premised on the false assumption that it is the non-English speakers who are trying to create dissonant change by insisting on a pluralist policy. In reality, they continue, the United States has *never* been a monolingual English-speaking country, so it is manifest that insisting that it *become* one is the real source of dissonant change that is generating the political conflict and internal division. After summarizing each of these arguments in greater detail, my analysis claims once again that it is the underlying conflict over U.S. national identity that lies at the heart of the language policy conflict, and this is not an issue that can be resolved through a positivist social scientific method of policy analysis, such as cost-benefit or systems analysis. Rather, a value-critical analysis is needed to illuminate just what is at stake in the conflict over U.S. language policy.

Step Four: Value-Critical Analysis of the Core Arguments and Values

The fourth step in this form of policy analysis is to *explicitly subject the value arguments of the key protagonists to critical analysis.* There are a variety of fruitful ways in which this might be done. My own approach is to begin by reexamining the lines of agreement and disagreement between the protagonists, and to recontextualize their conflicts, before narrowing my focus to a critical analysis of their respective positions. That is, after summarizing the protagonists' core arguments and value commitments as accurately and fairly as possible (step three, above), I think it is useful to review the nature of their disagreements, looking for areas of agreement as well as disagreement, distinguishing between factual and value conflicts, and looking for an illuminating way in which to contextualize the conflicts that remain. Taking that step of review and reorientation helps in determining what needs to be done to critically assess the protagonists' respective arguments. And that is the core of what needs to be done in this fourth step of value-critical policy analysis: critically interrogating each protagonist's value-based arguments, finding and articulating the relative strengths and weaknesses in each case.

This raises the question of the criteria used for evaluation. On what bases is it possible to make critical evaluations of the value positions of protagonists in a policy dispute? Some scholars, of course, have argued that there are no criteria for values that can make any valid truth-claim at all, since statements of value are in themselves meaningless expressions of personal preference, much like one's preference for this taste over that (see, e.g., Ayer 1959). Thus, if my preference is for really creamy vanilla ice cream, while yours is for really crispy potato chips, whose preference is more valid, more true? Other scholars disagree, however, as do most human beings living their lives—almost all human beings have criteria we use for distinguishing the greater or lesser validity of statements of value, and it would be nearly impossible to live without the use of such criteria. Most of the time, nevertheless, our criteria for making these judgments are implicit; quite frequently, as well, they are not the result of careful thought and critical analysis.

As noted at the outset of this chapter, the premise of value-critical policy analysis is that it is fruitful to subject our own, as well as others', value preferences to systematic critical analysis. This is so because—as human beings, as citizens, as policy makers, as policy analysts—we typically (and perhaps necessarily) take a great deal for granted in living our day-to-day lives, including our basic orientation toward, and evaluation of, the social processes, events, and arrangements in which our lives are embedded. In political life this means that we often take positions or policy stances based upon a frame of reference involving loyalty to past allies, judgments made based on information gathered in a cursory fashion under time pressure, animosities based on a limited range of negative experiences from which we have generalized to larger social settings and groupings, and so forth. Some of this information may be outdated; some of it may have been "wrong" even from the beginning based on an incomplete understanding of the situation. Placing our own value positions under critical scrutiny may help us better understand our own situation as well as that of the larger social and political world of which we are a part. Placing the value positions of others, including our fellow members of a political community, under critical scrutiny can help us in the same way. The aim throughout is to develop a narrative framed in terms of a complex and comprehensive understanding of the issues at stake in the conflict, a narrative that seeks to give each relevant policy camp's perspective a "fair hearing" that accurately represents the policy advocates' claims and understandings of the contexts and stakes involved in the policy dispute.

The political role of policy analysts is useful as a frame for discussing these issues. At the outset of this chapter, I distinguished between value-neutral, value-committed, and value-critical policy analysis. What do these three forms of analysis entail regarding policy analysts as persons doing public work, their political roles, and their values? What roles do their values play in the analysis itself? As noted previously, a value-neutral policy analyst attempts to "bracket out" her own values (and takes as "given" the values embedded in policy goals) in order to concentrate the analysis exclusively on "factual" questions.[3] And the presumed political role that accompanies this orientation toward public values is that of the detached, scientific, professional "expert" with no personal stake in the issue. Since her only commitment is to the factual "truth" as revealed by her presumed "scientific" procedures of investigation and analysis, the public and its policy makers are expected to have faith in the analytical product—unless, of course, her deployment of these procedures has been faulted by other, equally detached, scientific and professional experts.

A value-committed analyst, by contrast, uses his policy values as a foundation for organizing and developing rhetorical strategies (typically by weaving together a narrative that includes both factual interpretations and value statements) that maximize the persuasiveness of his own previously adopted policy position for a particular audience. The political role assumed by the value-committed policy analyst is that of the partisan activist or policy advocate. Adopting such a role signals to policy makers and citizens alike that the analysis developed and articulated by the policy analyst is likely to be biased by his commitments. Does this mean that such analysis is so biased that it is not useful to the development of good public policy? Not necessarily. Within the liberal political tradition, at least, so long as the various partisans to policy disputes have a fair opportunity to make their "best case," both citizens and public officials can draw upon their partisan depictions of the situation or context, their proposed policy solutions, and their arguments on behalf of their policy solutions to come to an optimal solution through the well-known process of the "free marketplace of ideas."

What, then, about the values of the value-critical policy analyst? Answering this question, I think, can be illuminated by sketching out the presumed political role of the value-critical policy analyst in this comparison. Who plays such a political role? Is the value-critical analyst an "expert" in *values*, just as the value-neutral analyst is presumed to be in relation to *facts*? Are there organizations or institutions that employ such people? Is there a legitimate role for a value-critical policy analyst in the "real" world? As I conceive the value-critical analyst's role, it is akin to that of the citizen and/or public official who ultimately must take a position and make the decision on adopting public policy. That is, the value-critical analyst presumes to think like a public-spirited citizen or public official whose aim should be to support and adopt public policies that enhance the "public good." This implies, of course, that the value-critical analyst/citizen/public official is motivated by a fundamental commitment to the "public good" and therefore seeks to support and adopt public policies that will make her political community "better off" than it would be in the absence of such policies. In this sense, the assumption is that the policy analyst—like the "good" citizen and public official—seeks to avoid being guided primarily by selfish and narrow interests and genuinely seeks policies that enhance the common good. It further presumes that in trying to discern the shape of such policies, the policy analyst—like the "good" citizen and public official—seeks out the best possible information and is as clear as possible about her own values, interests, biases, and policy-relevant value commitments in order to avoid prejudging the issue under study and analysis.

My own approach to developing this narrative is to try to hear the "voice" of a policy advocate's likely critical response to my representations, then correcting them when I "hear" an inaccuracy or misstatement pointed out. After going through this process, I have tried to check my narrative with as many partisans and/or fellow citizens with some knowledge of the issue as possible. In the end, the aim is to articulate the partisans' positions as judiciously and comprehensively as possible before subjecting these positions to the analyst's critique. The narrative aims to be "balanced," "accurate," and "comprehensive" in the sense that the policy advocates involved in this policy dispute would/do agree that their views have been treated with respect and have been given a "fair hearing" by the policy analyst. Ultimately, the worth of the analyst's efforts at this sort of "balanced" and "comprehensive" analysis must be judged by her readers, including the very advocates whose work has been critiqued, as well as by policy makers, citizens, and other scholars of public policy.

In sum, then, I think that all policy analysts have, or should have, value commitments about the policies they work on. But there is a key difference between value-critical and/or value-committed *policy analysis* (intellectual and moral *processes*) and the *policy analyst* (the thinking/ acting/feeling *subject*). As I understand it, the (valuing) policy analyst should try to approach all the values (those congruent with her own values and those at odds with her own values) in a critical (and self-critical) way. The aim is to be as even-handed and fair as possible in understanding and articulating the strengths and weaknesses of the value aims and goals of all sides in a policy controversy. The assumption is that we can learn from our opponents as well as from our allies.

Although I am aware of few public administrative agencies or policy advocacy organizations employing individuals to conduct this type of analysis (the former would be criticized for usurping the role of elected officials in typical U.S. understandings of democracy; the latter probably do not wish to pay for critiques of their own understandings of their policy commitments), there exists at least one prominent public occupation that can and should play such a role in a complex society. University professors in political science and public affairs are ideally situated to engage in such forms of policy analysis. University professors, after all, are employed to do research with their students on the cutting edge of the "truth" in many fields and to share the fruits of that research both with the public and with other students of the subject. Why not engage in systematic scholarship that might actually help citizens and policy makers improve their understanding of the central values at stake in a highly controversial public policy issue? This does not mean, of course, that professors and their students—like citizens and public officials—do not have their own biases and personal interests that might affect their judgment on the issues under study. But they are in a social and political role that typically provides a greater opportunity for rigorous value-critical analysis than do other roles: that is, relative freedom from the pressures of profit seeking and/or political decision making (partisan ties and loyalties, previous commitments), and a community of other scholars willing and ready to critique their work.

Within this context and throughout the analytical process, the value-critical analyst attempts to understand and keep clear her own preexisting value commitments in relation to the policy issues under study, but also attempts to reexamine her understanding of those values and their policy implications in the light of critical analysis and reflection. This requires a strong commitment and an openness to continued learning on the part of the analyst. That is, the underlying assumption of this stance is that whatever understanding the analyst has of the values at stake in the policy issue under study, her own policy values and their implications for the development and implementation of public policy might be improved through critical (and self-critical) reflection and analysis. The whole point here is to seek ways to help public policy do its work "better" by having a better understanding of the values at stake in public policy conflict. To the extent that the policy analyst's own value interpretations stand in the way by biasing her analysis, or by blinding or distorting her view on some important aspect of the policy issues in contention, the analyst must work toward a better understanding of what is really at stake and why it is important.

How can this important work be done? One of the ways this can be done is through critical self-reflection, subjecting one's own value understandings to the same critical analysis as those of the partisans in the policy conflict under study (see below for several examples). Another important method of doing this is through frequent and ongoing discussions with policy advocates in the field of study (e.g., as participant-observer or simply as an "outside" observer committed to the public good), as well as with other interested parties (e.g., colleagues, friends, public officials, fellow citizens).

Within this role context and intellectual frame of reference, then, the policy analyst turns finally to a critical analysis of the value positions being espoused by policy advocates in the public policy conflict under study. What sorts of criteria for evaluation are valid and/or helpful in doing this sort of critical analysis? How is the analyst to discern between a "weak" and a "strong" understanding of the value stakes involved in a given public policy conflict? It is not possible to adequately summarize the wide range of helpful approaches here. The following, therefore, are given as illustrative examples and are not meant to be exhaustive in any sense.

Examining the Context *of the Argument for* Accuracy *and* Comprehensiveness

Nearly all policy arguments involve an implicit or explicit contextual frame of reference from which they derive part of their rhetorical power of persuasion. As Yanow has shown, policy disputes typically involve conflicts between "communities of meaning" that frame alternative understandings of the policy issue (Yanow 2000, 10–13). An implicit or explicit "picture" of the social context is "drawn" by policy advocates that lends support to their own views of the direction in which public policy should move. How, then, do we respond when others point out that we have "stacked the cards" in our depiction of the situation? How comprehensive are our "pictures" lending support to our policy positions? Can we make our policy frames more "accurate" and/or more comprehensive in this sense, and, if so, does this change our view of the most appropriate policy approach to take? Are there important legitimate group interests or communities of meaning that are being left out of the picture being drawn by one set of protagonists, for example? If so, will their inclusion change our understanding of the most appropriate policy solutions for the situation?

In the case of the U.S. language policy conflict, as noted above, pluralists and assimilationists have very different understandings of the social context relevant to this issue. Pluralists have emphasized the history of ethno-racial domination and exclusion in this country and the injustices visited upon ethno-linguistic minorities, while assimilationists have fixated on contemporary immigrants and the presumed differences between the social context of the "old" and "new" immigration.

In my value-critical policy analysis of the protagonists' arguments, I argued that both "pictures" are incomplete, and therefore inaccurate. Most pluralists seem to have little to say about the reality that the vast majority of non-English speakers in U.S. society today are, in fact, recent immigrants who have voluntarily chosen to migrate to this country and who must feel some obligation to adjust culturally to the country in which they have chosen to live. At the same time, I argued, most assimilationists have a very distorted and romanticized view of the reality of immigrant incorporation in this country, both now and in the past. Their assumption that the "old" immigrants of the late-nineteenth and early-twentieth centuries were eager to assimilate culturally and linguistically in order to become fully "Americanized" is highly distorted, as is their understanding of the racialized context within which contemporary immigrants are being "assimilated" (R. Schmidt 2000, chapter 7). Accordingly, a just language policy requires attending to the depictions of the social reality of our time contained in both accounts in relation to U.S. language diversity.

In this example, as in many similar cases, "the facts" cannot be taken as givens for purposes of resolving the policy dispute. Rather, the meaning and significance of the facts lie in their interpretation, and this is a matter of judgment. The strengths and weaknesses of these judgments cannot be determined through the use of positivist social scientific methods, but this does not mean that they are simply matters of preference or taste. Subjecting our individual and collective judgments to open and systematic critical analysis, rather, can help us determine the extent to which they are inaccurate, incomplete, or shallow (Grant 2002). And this is a public task in which policy analysts can play helpful roles.

Examining the Internal Logic *of* Moral Arguments

Another mode of critical analysis involves the systematic examination of moral arguments for the consistency of their internal logic. Making moral claims persuasive involves not only painting a contextual "picture" that seems compelling, but also making logical claims that are presumed to derive from widely accepted premises. Critical analysis focuses here on subjecting these claims and premises to systematic interrogation. Are the argument's *premises* really unobjectionable? Are they truly reasonable and widely accepted as such? Are the steps in the argument derived from these premises logically consistent? Often we make value judgments on the basis of unexamined first premises and our logic building from these premises is often unexamined as well. Critically assessing these aspects of our policy positions can be both humbling and illuminating, and may even lead to better public policy.

Once again, my value-critical analysis of the U.S. language policy debate offers an illustration. Despite their desire to shape the public use of language toward English as our sole national language, most assimilationists claim to want to protect the individual freedoms of non-English speakers and their equal opportunity to realize their "American dreams." Like most Americans, that is, assimilationists recognize the moral validity of the individual human being's *freedom* to determine her own goals in life, and the *equal* worth of each person's claim to have an opportunity to realize those goals in her life. But how can we reconcile this claim to equal freedom of opportunity with a language policy that aims to erase some languages from the public realm? Assimilationists argue that these two goals can be reconciled easily because the equal freedom to cultivate, use, and reproduce non-English languages is not being restricted at all; this is a "private" right that is open to every family and/or ethnic community. That is, if individuals and families value their culture and non-English language, they have every right to use it and reproduce it in their homes, religious institutions, and so forth, but they have no claim to *public*, governmental support for these minority cultures and languages. Much like our constitutionally protected freedom of religion, then, the state protects the right of everyone to practice their culture and language, but there can be no proper claim that the government is obligated to ensure that minority languages are reproduced from generation to generation.

What is wrong with the logic of this argument?[4] Borrowing from Kymlicka's (1989, 1995) analysis of cultural difference and liberal political philosophy, my critique claims that the assimilationist argument makes several invalid moves. First, assimilationists err in their premise that the government can be neutral in respect to language. Whereas it is possible for us to make our government wholly secular in respect to religion, we cannot have a government that is impartial in respect to language use. Government without language is impossible, since it is through language that government functions at all. Accordingly, if the government uses *your* language and not *my* language, it is giving you a *public* (not private) advantage in realizing your life goals that is not available to me. So the premises about "equal freedom of opportunity" from which we began are being violated by this assimilationist assumption. Second, the assimilationist response to this problem is to interject that English is clearly the country's "real" national language and that's why it is so important to make English the country's *official* language. Every country must have a national culture in which individuals can realize their life goals, assimilationists argue, and that's why it is so important that we ensure that immigrants recognize their obligation to become assimilated into this national culture when they voluntarily migrate to this country.

But once again, my critique argues, this assimilationist position begs the very question that it claims to resolve. English is *not* the sole language of the United States, nor has it ever been. The United States contains multiple ethno-linguistic communities that became part of the country's fabric not through voluntary immigration, but through conquest or purchase and annexation and were subsequently subjected to various forms of racialized subordination. Many recent immigrants, especially from Latin America, the Caribbean, and Asia, are being incorporated into these racialized ethno-linguistic communities in a process described by sociologists as "segmented assimilation" (see, e.g., Portes and Rumbaut 2001). As such the moral equation for "equal freedom of opportunity" must take this reality into account. Doing so, in turn, requires a much more complex understanding than that provided by most assimilationists of the logical steps involved in designing a language policy that facilitates equal respect for each person's opportunity to realize her "American dreams" (see R. Schmidt 2000 for a fuller description of this argument).

As noted, there are many more fruitful and illuminating approaches to critically assessing the value assumptions and claims of advocates involved in public policy disputes, but these should suffice for illustrating what is meant by a "value-critical" analysis. In each case, an effort is made to systematically interrogate the assumptions and value claims made by protagonists in the policy conflict under study. The point I want to stress here is that this form of critical analysis is interpretive and involves making judgments, but this does not mean that the criteria for judgment and interpretation are without standards of validity. So long as the analyst makes explicit her or his reasoning and the standards being used for judgment and interpretation, readers are able to respond critically as well, facilitating the kind of dialogic process that is essential for clarifying—and sometimes resolving—public policy disputes.

Step Five: Drawing Conclusions; Making Recommendations

The final step in this form of value-critical policy analysis involves drawing conclusions from one's analysis and possibly making policy recommendations as well. Drawing conclusions from a value-critical analysis involves making as clear as possible just *what is at stake, for whom,* in a public policy dispute. That is, having critically assessed the strengths and weaknesses of each major protagonist's core arguments and value assumptions, the analyst needs to provide an overview of the larger meanings and significance of the analysis itself. What, finally, does this dispute come down to? How can we summarize, finally, what is at stake, for whom, in this public policy conflict? And this is not just a matter of restating what one has written before; rather, what is needed here is a distillation, a clarifying reformulation of the meaning and significance of the analysis itself.

In my value-critical analysis of the U.S. language policy debate, I concluded with the argument that what is finally at stake in this debate is not principally about language at all, but that rather the stakes are concerned with "identity politics," with what kind of country we are, and, more specifically, with the relationships between multiple levels of human identity: individual, ethno-linguistic group, and nation. Is the United States fundamentally a "monistic" society when it comes to language and culture, or is the country a "pluralistic" society in relation to these forms of human identity? This question ultimately directs us to the fundamental stakes involved in the U.S. language policy debate, and assimilationists and pluralists are in fundamental disagreement in relation to this question. Resolving this disagreement would go a long way toward resolving the language policy debate; it cannot be resolved at the level of language use alone. And though my value-critical analysis faults both sides in the debate, it was on the basis of this analysis that I came to the judgment that pluralists provided a better argument overall than did assimilationists.

In addition to providing a concluding analysis of the public policy dispute, the value-critical analyst might also want to offer recommendations for how the policy argument could best be resolved. That is, in light of the findings of the value-critical analysis, it may be appropriate for the policy analyst to suggest the shape of a preferred public policy on the issue at hand. This, of course, will depend on the role of the analyst. In the event that a city council employed someone (or assigned a staff member) to do a value-critical analysis of an important issue, its members might wish to see only the critical analysis of major value assumptions and arguments made by protagonists in a policy debate, and not care to hear the recommendations of the staff member. It is conceivable though that other policy makers might want the analyst to offer well-reasoned recommendations as well.

As noted above, academics such as the present author are in a social role that enables us to make recommendations that we believe flow directly from our analyses. In the case of my analysis of the language policy debate, I concluded with a recommended policy approach that combines aspects of both the pluralist and assimilationist arguments, as well as my critique of both. My recommendations, then, combine a pluralist language policy with an assertive immigrant settlement policy, as well as measures aimed at reducing the growing disparity between the wealthy and the poor in U.S. society (R. Schmidt 2000, chapter 8).

CONCLUDING THOUGHT

This chapter has aimed at helping the reader better understand what is involved in a value-critical policy analysis—why such an approach might be valuable, to whom it should be valuable, and how it might be done—as well as how this approach differs from both the value-neutral approach and the value-committed approach. The latter distinction is crucial for explicating how the policy analyst is not really one of the protagonists and has not "stacked the deck" in the analytic process. The question is, did the policy analyst represent the arguments, the values, and the interpretive frameworks of the various protagonists in an even-handed and balanced way? Where can his interpretation be criticized? Perhaps he *did* "stack the deck." If so, the analyst should be condemned for doing a poor job, for having slipped into a value-committed analysis that only pretends to be value critical. In the end, it is only the reader who is really in a position to make that judgment.

NOTES

The author thanks the students in his spring 2003 and 2004 courses on "Public Values and Public Policy" for helping him to work through the ideas contained in this chapter. Their course projects were the "laboratory materials" that enabled the author to refine his articulation of the steps involved in doing a value-critical policy analysis. I am also grateful to Dvora Yanow and Peregrine Schwartz-Shea for inviting me to present an earlier version of this chapter at the Workshop in Interpretive Research Methods in Empirical Political Science, held at the annual meeting of the Western Political Science Association in Denver (March 2003).

1. Though the processes of gathering and of interpreting/analyzing data are here presented as two separate steps, in reality they are inextricably intertwined; that is, we have already begun the process of interpretation when we decide what kinds of information to gather, and the process of gathering information really doesn't "end" until the analyst stops writing/interpreting/analyzing.

2. In doing this work, my assumption is that, to a large degree, educated and thoughtful persons share common understandings of "balanced" and "fair" and even "accurate" or "inaccurate" critical thinking skills. That is, we can tell when a person is being one-sided or unfair in articulating and evaluating a public policy argument about the goals or aims of the policy. Being "balanced" means giving "both" or "all" sides their due and making the best case possible for each "side," and also being willing to articulate the weaknesses of each side of the argument with a rough degree of fairness. It means being able to listen to the arguments of others, and, when writing, being able to imagine their criticisms and comments on what you have written, then responding with revisions and enhancements until you can imagine that they will be satisfied that you have given their position a fair articulation. To the degree that that is not done, our analysis should be criticized by others who can point out its weaknesses and lack of "balance" or "fairness." This criticism comes in the form of statements like the following: "Though X said 'this,' he neglected to acknowledge 'that' and this makes his analysis unbalanced or unfair because it doesn't give equal treatment to the needs or aspirations of all parties to the dispute"; or, "Z described the situation as follows, but his description is inaccurate because it neglected to include 'this' and 'that,' thereby distorting his depiction of the situation."

3. The validity and appropriateness of this set of assumptions and procedures, of course, is highly controversial, and a number of other chapters in this volume address these questions. They are not pursued in this chapter.

4. Due to space limitations, this section summarizes my critique of the assimilationist value position on language policy only; see R. Schmidt 2000, 198–209, for my critique of the pluralist position.

CHAPTER 18

STORIES FOR RESEARCH

Steven Maynard-Moody and Michael Musheno

SM-M: *In the late 1970s, when I was a grad student, debates on the competing virtues and sins of quantitative and qualitative research filled doctoral seminars. At that moment, not long after the behavioral revolution but just before the formal theory coup, new ideas about methods and knowledge were explored and argued over. I instinctively recoil from either/or choices and have always been attracted to both qualitative and quantitative research. As a researcher I'm most content in the field talking to "locals" or reading, once again, interview transcripts. But I can get lost for weeks trying to discern meaning from those unbending numbers in a data set. I have long been struck by a dilemma: I have much greater confidence in the insights and generalizability of my more qualitative research, while it is easier to convince others that statistically reported findings have greater explanatory power.*

My interest in stories grew out of my restlessness with standard interview and fieldwork practice. In the early 1990s, discussions of narrative and meaning spread across many disciplines. To learn more, I assigned a doctoral seminar some reading on the epistemology of narrative and sent the students out in the field to collect stories about public managers' relationships to elected officials.

Coauthor Michael Musheno and my long-standing interest in implementation theory and street-level bureaucracy, plus Michael's interest in identity questions, combined with stories to form the research described in the chapter here, which, as the chapter notes, changed our views of all three subjects. Michael and I had collaborated on a study of community corrections in the mid-1980s and were looking for a way to work together again. We decided to try to "think big" and, on the second attempt, received funding from the National Science Foundation for our two-state, multisite field research project. A few lines from the acknowledgments of our book best capture our experience of exploration and discovery, which is discussed in the chapter that follows.

The place was different but the moment was the same: for Michael it occurred in a police patrol car; for Steven it was in the meeting room of a vocational rehabilitation office. The moment was when each of us collected our first story, and we knew we were hearing and, in our mind's eye, seeing governing at the front-lines. We were entering the world of street-level work; a world of tensions, ambiguity, and difficult, often painful, choices and judgments. At these moments we were not sure what these first stories, and the many stories that followed, would tell us or if they would fit into a larger narrative. . . . But, with so much yet to do, we felt it all coming together; we felt we were on to something although at that time we had only the faintest clues what that something was. This research project has been a wondrous intellectual adventure. . . .

—*Maynard-Moody and Musheno* (2003, xi–xii)

316

MM: *I had an interpretive field research moment very early in my academic career, although I did not know it at the time. As a graduate student in the mid-1970s, I was pursuing a dissertation on the impact of decriminalization policy, particularly related to public inebriation and substance abuse, using a quasi-experimental design and interrupted time-series analysis. As I arrived at the door of a detoxification center in Washington, D.C., to pick up "data" for my impact assessment, a "client" of this civil commitment policy burst out the door, causing me to tumble down a set of concrete steps and break my arm. As I tried to get back on my feet, I could see the client running away and program staff deciding he was too fast for hot pursuit. When I asked the staff why their client was on the run, they told me in a matter-of-fact way that most people in their program far preferred jail to the intrusiveness of a detoxification center.*

I never forgot that moment; and yet, I went on my way collecting and analyzing intake data from detoxification centers and local jails. Sometime in the early 1990s, a couple of graduate students asked me to do a readings course and conference with them on meaning making and identity. That led to a seminar on "identity, legality, and justice" and a series of assignments asking students to use intensive field methods in search of meaning making, particularly related to law, policy, and justice. When I read their papers, I remembered the day when I was leveled by the client at the detoxification center, wishing I had pursued him to hear his stories about the streets, the state, and legal reforms. The following chapter is one story about how to chase that topic as field-intensive interpretive inquiry, but while looking the other way—at those state workers who make everyday judgments about whether and how to engage in hot pursuit of clients.

> The work world of cops, teachers, and counselors is a baffling terrain dense with law, rules, and procedures; bounded by overlapping hierarchical and agency relationships; populated with the diverse and hard-to-read faces of citizens, clients, supervisors, and co-workers. It is a world where identity and moral judgments are bound up with the quotidian work of the state. This is the front line of public service.

> [S]treet-level work is as much a process of forming and enforcing identities—of both citizen-clients and street-level workers—as of delivering services and implementing policy. More than bureaucratic politics, identity politics shape the citizen-client.
> —*Steven Maynard-Moody and Michael Musheno* (2003, 8, 153)

The interpretive claims in these two epigraphs are intended as straightforward renderings of how front-line workers make sense of their work and pass judgments on the people they encounter in doing the everyday work of the state. Taken from our book *Cops, Teachers, Counselors: Stories from the Front Lines of Public Service*, they indicate where our research took us, but not where it began. At journey's end, we reached this point of interpretation only after considerable struggle, questioning, conversation, and argumentation, all revolving around repeated close reading of and writing about stories told to us by front-line workers.

Descriptions of social research often tell of an orderly progress from literature review to hypothesis forming, data collection, statistical analysis, and findings. Our research, a combination of intensive fieldwork, story collection, and continuous interpretation, was a different experience. Rather than following a carefully mapped and well-worn path, our research was more like meandering in a forest: There were moments of order and clear vision, but we often felt lost due to the echoes of the many voices we heard and the particularities of our field observations. We did have a carefully designed research plan, but the plan did not preclude the surprises that waited for us in the field.

Our research was funded by the National Science Foundation, which requires a detailed proposal.[1] Our first proposal was not funded in part because the research plan was, for NSF reviewers, inadequately specified, a common problem for interpretive research. The second and funded proposal described in considerable, even tedious, detail each step in our research process, from entering the field to collecting and interpreting the narratives. The more step-by-step research design in the second proposal did not eliminate the surprises and the necessary meanderings and dead ends that waited for us in the field, but it did provide an essential guide for us as we implemented our research. Counterintuitively, our research plan, which gave structure and direction to the entire project, also gave us the confidence to allow ourselves to momentarily feel baffled and lost when in the field. In addition, it provided a common approach as different members of the research team worked in different field settings.

Nonetheless, our encounters and observations in the field and our close reading of the narratives generated during fieldwork continually stretched our capacity to make sense of all we were hearing and seeing. Our process of interpretation was more one of coming to grips with surprises than of confirming expectations, however carefully laid out in our grant proposal. We saw and heard things we did not expect, such as the police officer deliberately ignoring a direct order to prosecute a hard-working, illegal Mexican immigrant. We also did not see and hear things we expected; for example, street-level workers did not reference policy implementation or discretion in making judgments.

The very richness and complexity of field-based research—the reasons we are drawn to the field—was unsettling because we heard unexpected claims about street-level work. Also, being in the field was at times disorienting because the observation of the moment often seemed crucial to making sense of our subjects and yet it was not automatically connected to what we heard or saw immediately before or after. Nor was finding compelling patterns of street-level judgments always made easier in the exchange of ideas between our subjects and us. Giving the subjects of our inquiry a voice in the interpretive process, a crucial part of our pedagogy of inquiry as described below, was sometimes humbling, as one is reminded continuously about the inadequacies of one's explanations. Perhaps the most humbling of all is telling someone in the field—in our case, police officers, teachers, and counselors—of some hard-earned insight and being met with a polite "that's obvious" stare.

Moreover, in our desire to forge compelling interpretations, there is a continual risk of asserting more clarity and pattern than actually exist in social life. John Gilliom makes the essential points: "If we are truly listening to lots of different people, we get lots of different stories, and it is often impossible—and certainly inappropriate—to assert a universalizing meta-narrative over their tales. Too much sense-making can be a real problem" (personal communication, August 17, 2001). These cautionary tales notwithstanding, we experienced interpretive, field-based research as having a pungency and reality—dare we say a "validity"—that is hard to match in more traditional forms of social research. Close, intense encounters with research subjects in their workplaces provide a solid basis for forming and questioning field-based interpretations.

The research that forms the basis of the interpretive claims rendered in our book and other writings from this project involved fieldwork at five sites in two states with three different types of front-line or street-level workers: police officers, teachers, and vocational rehabilitation counselors.[2] The research team was composed of the two authors of this chapter plus our two research assistants, Trish Oberweis and Suzanne Leland, who made essential contributions to all aspects of this research. The work resulted in two books, two dissertations, and several articles (Maynard-

Moody and Leland 1999; Maynard-Moody and Musheno 2000, 2003; Oberweis and Musheno 1999, 2001).

The research process included direct observation, in-depth entry and exit interviews, and a questionnaire, but stories told to us by the street-level workers formed our primary source of data. In many ways our three years of fieldwork, story collection, and story analysis followed by two years of book drafting were a process of continual discovery, as we tried to listen ever more closely to the words of street-level workers. In interpretive research, writing cannot be separated from analysis. Putting accounts of what is heard and learned in the field into words and subjecting narratives to critical reflection, including taking your words back to those whose stories you are telling, is as much a part of interpretation as close readings of the narratives collected in the field. Through these two, interactive phases of narrative analysis, we gained an interpretive perspective that is close to that of the workers, a perspective that is distinct from the dominant perspective represented in the extant literature on street-level decision making.

That perspective will be rendered in the ending of this chapter, but the story line of this essay is a retrospective pedagogy of choices and constraints that constitute our mode of conducting intensive field-based, narrative analysis. It is coupled with a practicum of taking this mode of interpretive inquiry into the field. It concludes with thoughts on the role of discovery, collaboration, and inconclusiveness that interpretive story analysis enables, particularly in the context of team-based research.

NARRATIVE FIELD RESEARCH AND DISCOVERY

One great advantage of narrative field research is that its rich, variegated, nuanced, and often conflicting textual information—what Geertz (2000; see also 1995) famously called "thick descriptions"—simultaneously presents challenges to preconceived ideas and grist for insight. Narratives retain more of the social world's complexity than do quantitative renderings of social life. Our observations and theories are always simplifications; necessary simplifications, but simplifications nonetheless. In narratives the contradictions and tensions of everyday social life remain less filtered than is common in quantitative social research. The required discipline for narrative field researchers is to put aside, at least for the moment, their "expertise" and literature-based knowledge and to engage in perspective taking and listening to and learning from those we study (see Fergusen and Musheno 2000). We are not the experts on their worlds; they are.

Like many scholars going into the field, we presumed to know much about our subject matter: how street-level workers make sense of their everyday work and how their judgments fit into the work of the state. And, like others doing research on street-level workers, we owed (and owe) our greatest intellectual debt to Michael Lipsky's *Street-Level Bureaucracy* (1980; see also 1978). In particular we had a mind-set about street-level workers as the "ultimate policy makers" who remake policy as they deliver services and interact with citizens. Like Lipsky and others, we saw street-level work in the context of policy implementation and considered the fundamental question of street-level work to be the application and abuse of discretion. We came to define this perspective as the "State-Agent Narrative" (Maynard-Moody and Musheno 2003, chapter 2).

The State-Agent Narrative is told by elites in and scholars of the state; it is embedded in our formal understanding of our governmental institutions. This narrative portrays our democratic state as an edifice built on law and predictable procedures that ensure that like cases will be treated alike. Deviations from law and policy are allowable only if workers adapt law to the circumstance of cases in a manner that is consistent with policy and hierarchical authority. Such deviations are defined as "discretionary decision making." Discretion, accountability, and control are the prominent themes of the State-Agent Narrative and are understood within the context of structure and authority. The State-Agent Narrative focuses on how democratic theory accommodates to the presence of administration and hierarchy in the modern state.

After three years of fieldwork, story collection, and interpretive engagement, we learned, as suggested in the prefacing quotes, that street-level workers did not define their work in relation to policy makers, policy, laws, or rules. Discretion and accountability were nearly absent from street-level narratives, in contrast to more widely present issues of identity and moral judgment. Based on the dominant themes in the existing literature and the related expectations we took into the field, we were initially startled, but the more closely we listened to the street-level workers, the more audible an alternative narrative became. Before we examine this counter-narrative, the one we have called the Citizen-Agent Narrative, we locate our mode of narrative inquiry as "story based" and identify key choices we made in collecting and analyzing stories, revealing the interpretive framing of our method of inquiry. This pedagogy, although rich with choices, is also constituted by the demands, some might say the constraints, of scholarly inquiry.

A PEDAGOGY OF STORY-BASED RESEARCH

Storytelling is an act of "world-building" and "world-populating" (L. Polanyi 1985). On hearing a story we enter, if only for a moment, this created world and interact with its invented characters. Storytellers recreate their world as they see it and as they want to present it to others. These recreations are not photographically accurate accounts of events and people. Researchers cannot separate the storytellers' interpretations and their decisions regarding what to present and how to present the story from the events recounted (or invented) and the characters described (or imagined). Stories are not facts or evidence waiting for interpretation; they are, from the moment they are conceived through their many tellings and retellings, the embodiment of the storytellers' interpretations.

The process of interpretation in story-based research begins with the task of ascertaining the storytellers' interpretations that form the story text, whether spoken or written. Stories are told deliberately to communicate meaning and points of view. Our interpretations began by seeking to understand what the storyteller was trying to say through the inclusion of certain details, the choice of words and phrases, the sequencing of events, and the use of storytelling techniques, such as repetition. Hearing, transcribing, reading, and rereading stories is not standard social research practice, even among intensive field-based researchers who traditionally rely on direct observation, in-depth interviews, and documents. Nevertheless, if the root question is not "how much" or "how many," but rather "how do" people—in our research, street-level workers—comprehend their own experiences, then stories provide a powerful and revealing research instrument. "Storytelling and understanding are functionally the same thing," Roger Schank (1990, 24) reminds us.[3] To understand a story is to understand the storyteller.

STORIES AND OTHER TEXTS

The various textual forms of interpretive and qualitative social science, such as historical accounts, ethnographic field notes, in-depth interview transcripts, and observational reports, are forms of narratives. They describe events and exist within a historical moment. No clear line separates these narrative forms from stories. Often, a person being interviewed makes a point by telling a story, and storytellers often punctuate their narration with asides of commentary that are indistinguishable in form and content from interview responses.

That said, our working definition of "stories" is close to the everyday use of the term. Stories in our research have plot lines, however simple or tenuous. They have a beginning, which could be nothing more than an arbitrary opening—"Let me tell you a story about . . ."—or which could concern a specific initiating event—"A few years ago this guy walked into my office. . . ." Stories have a middle, which may include one or more digressions, and an end, which brings events to their logical or surprising conclusion. The conclusion may resolve the dilemmas or issues raised in the story, but some stories end with the main issues unsettled; they just stop. Our specific working definition of stories and our procedure for story collection are described later in this chapter.

The in-depth interview that is oriented toward identifying, locating, ascertaining, and describing facts, events, and observations remains an essential tool for accessing and generating data in qualitative and interpretive research, but stories offer several important advantages over this more standard method. Storytelling occurs naturally in any social setting. Hayden White comments, "To raise the question of the nature of narrative is to invite reflection on the very nature of culture and, possibly, even on the nature of humanity itself. So natural is the impulse to narrate, so inevitable is the form of narrative for any report of the way things really happen, that narrativity could appear problematic only in a culture in which it was absent" (1980, 1). Interviews are always an artifact of the research process, whereas storytelling and stories exist outside the research project. They are told in social settings when the researcher is absent; unlike interviews, stories have a "life" of their own.

Because of this, perhaps the ideal method of story collection would be for the researcher to become a "participant-listener," recording stories as they are naturally, and inevitably, told in social settings. The participant-listener could record the responses of other listeners as well as aspects of setting and context. One drawback to this strategy is that it can be prohibitively time consuming and inefficient. The challenge for a social scientist with a limited amount of time to spend in the field is, therefore, to develop a research protocol that solicits "naturally occurring" stories, rather than waiting for ones that come along or that are invented just for the researcher. Without "participant-listening," we cannot be certain that stories told to researchers are similar to those told in the natural setting, but William Labov, a linguist, suggests that stories told to researchers will correspond to stories told to insiders. He observes that in retelling stories, storytellers do not monitor and censor their own speech to the extent common in face-to-face interviews. Storytelling can become so engaging that the teller may say more than he or she consciously knows. As Labov writes:

> The most effective of these techniques produces narratives of personal experience, in which the speaker becomes deeply involved in rehearsing or even reliving events of his past. . . . Because [these narratives] occur in response to a specific stimulus in the interview situation, they are not free of the interactive effect of the outside observer. The form they take is in fact typical of discourse directed to someone outside of the immediate peer group of the speaker. But because the experience and emotions involved here form an important part of the speaker's biography, he seems to undergo a partial reliving of that experience and he is no longer free to monitor his own speech as he normally does in face-to-face interviews. (1972, 354–55)

STORIES FOR RESEARCH

Selecting Storytellers. Telling and hearing stories are central to the construction and maintenance of social groups from friendships to nations, underscoring their potential as subjects for interpretive research. Nevertheless, we were compelled to ask how we could get others to tell their stories in a form that is useful for interpretive social researchers. In making these decisions, how do we honor the people whose stories we acquire and the words they render?

For starters, we decided not to impose aesthetic demands on our storytellers. Only some storytellers are gifted writers or raconteurs; others whose stories are equally as important to tell are less-gifted storytellers. With the focus of our research on questions of meaning, judgments, and decision making in everyday life, we selected storytellers who would enable us to capture a diversity of perspectives on whether and how notions of justice and injustice give meaning to street-level work and decision making, keying on differences in seniority and experience, gender, race and ethnicity, and generations of workers. In embracing a diversity of perspectives, we dedicated ourselves to analyzing many stories over few, as well as those told by gifted and less gifted storytellers. Still, not all the stories we collected shaped equally our developing interpretations. Stories are not cases in a data set, each contributing proportionately to our findings. Some stories, fully rendered and well told, were particularly valuable for revealing the voices of the workers and summarizing key interpretive findings. We illustrate the value of such stories in the conclusion of this chapter.

In addition, we anchored our interpretations in the comparative analysis of stories collected in five different organizational settings or "work sites." We looked for points of shared meaning and discursive tension within work sites. For example, the counselors we studied worked together in local vocational rehabilitation field offices, police officers were members of squads who shared shifts and beats, and teachers worked as members of the eighth-grade team of an urban middle school. This approach provided us the opportunity to see what patterns of meaning making among workers were unique to specific work sites and types of street-level workers and to judge whether some patterns carried across site and type of worker.

Problem of Gists. Whereas in picking storytellers we emphasized diversity of the tellers over aesthetic criteria of the telling or the tale, we wanted stories that were fully rendered. Some stories that are well known to insiders, and are therefore culturally potent, are often told to other insiders with only a brief reference or gist. For example, a faculty member in an academic department discussing a current tenure case may say, "Remember Professor Smith." This brief reference may signal an elaborate narrative to colleagues: "Professor Smith was denied tenure because she never finished her book. When finished, the book was acclaimed, and Professor Smith became a star." Or, "Professor Smith was well liked but marginal, and, after we tenured her, she became a disgruntled and unproductive colleague."

Clearly, gists carry meaning to insiders, but they offer little interpretive guidance to the outsider: An outsider would not necessarily know what the gist of "Remember Professor Smith" is. Although we engaged in intensive participant-observation with our storytellers, we never presumed to be in the position of insiders. Thus, one essential criterion of a good research story for our purposes was that it was told in a fully rendered version, one that was intelligible to both insiders and outsiders. Full rendering of stories—fleshing out the gists in the stories narrated by insiders—can require deliberate effort by the researcher.

Accurate Accounts or Fiction? Another issue that is troubling to social researchers, especially those who think of social science as a means of discovering replicable facts, is that stories often blend elements of nonfiction and fiction. Many stories have a foundation in actual events and individuals, but the telling and retelling of stories allows considerable adaptation of those social realities. Some stories conflate events and characters, while others embellish or invent them. Accounts and inventions can be so intermingled as to become indistinguishable. When studying norms and beliefs, the distinctions between fact and fiction are meaningless: Inventions and embellishments may be more revealing about beliefs and judgments than responses to carefully written questionnaires. Though we advise narrative researchers not to worry about the distinction, we must be clear that we are not collecting, presenting, and interpreting narratives as if they were accurate accounts of events. We treat them, rather, as revealing accounts of norms and beliefs.

Analyzable and Reanalyzable Stories. If the purpose of the research is to present and publish observations that are compelling to others, then good stories for research are in a form that can be examined, analyzed, and archived for reexamination by other research teams. Stories for research, in contrast to stories collected for other reasons, need to contribute to interpretive arguments that can withstand the rough-and-tumble of scholarly debate. Interpretive researchers must acknowledge that there are no definitive interpretations.

To contribute to scientific discourse, we must demonstrate how our views are grounded in data and encourage others to challenge our views based on the same data. This requires the careful, time-consuming, and often costly reproduction of transcripts, notes, and other field data and, with proper safeguards for confidentiality, the open sharing of field data. It is not possible to reproduce and share every note and impression, but the credibility of our interpretations are only strengthened by allowing others to examine our sources.[4]

Many stories relevant for social research are oral, rather than written, and are told and heard, rather than read. Such storytelling is a performance, with each performance varying depending on the setting and listeners. In contrast to written storytelling, oral storytelling is elusive and evanescent, making analysis all the more difficult. (Advances in storing and examining digital audio and video, however, may facilitate the reproduction and analysis of oral storytelling events.) At present and.in part because social researchers communicate findings through publication, oral renditions are most often translated into written texts prior to analysis. As with all translations, some things are lost, but written stories have the advantages of providing fixed, readily available texts that can provide the foundation for evidence-based interpretations. Written texts can be reproduced and included in publications to document and justify interpretations to enhance the credibility of the research.

It is crucial that the written text produced by the researcher reflect the story that the storyteller wants to render. To make sure that we captured their stories, we took the transcriptions back to the storytellers at least once and sometimes several times. For our research purposes, a story was not treated as a final text until the storyteller was fully satisfied that the written story was the account he or she wanted to convey.

Adequate Numbers. Although much can be learned from the careful reading of a single story, interpretations and analyses of the sort we were engaged in are strengthened and broadened when based on an adequate number of diverse stories. Themes and patterns are rarely developed in a single story, nor can we be confident that the insights contained in a handful of stories will enable the rendering of interpretations of significant breadth to have meaning beyond the single setting or individual experience. Selecting units of analysis remains a central question in research design. Interpretive researchers who closely examine one or a few life histories or cases are unlikely to rely on a single story from each individual, drawing, instead, on the collage of narratives that constitute an individual life or a case. We designed our research to look for patterns of meaning across organizational setting and form of street-level work.

Although there is no formula for what constitutes an "adequate" number of stories, the guidelines are similar to those for intensive field interviews. Researchers should collect and examine enough stories such that one is hearing similar accounts coming from different storytellers, suggestive that wider patterns of beliefs and judgments are being revealed. In addition, enough stories should be examined to assure that variations in accounts and views reflect the diversity of people and places under study. As more and more stories are collected and heard and as the first iteration of the interpretive-analytic process proceeds, the researcher will recognize the initial signs of patterns and variation.

In sum, "good" research stories provide details about events, settings, and the interaction, relationships, and feelings of the characters. Details about events, settings, and characters often present conflicting, ambiguous portraits, but each nuance helps guide interpretation. Although narrated as empirical observations, the details included in a story represent the storytellers' interpretations, not necessarily replicable observations. By probing the meaning in story details, researchers frame their interpretations based on the storytellers' interpretations, yielding a variegated analysis derived from the interweaving of insider and outsider interpretations.

A PRACTICUM FOR DOING FIELD-BASED STORY RESEARCH

There are many ways to engage in story-based research.[5] In our research, in addition to imagining a pedagogy of story-based research, we engaged in a series of pragmatic steps to put our ideas about field-intensive story collection and analysis into practice. This practicum is the subject of attention here.[6] We note, however, that telling a story about our story-based research makes the process appear more orderly than it was. Field-based story research is always improvisational.

Engaging in street-level inquiry required a chain of permissions that followed agency hierarchies down to the street level. Organizational advocates for our project, often current or former students holding positions in these agencies, provided initial contacts with key administrators and later served to provide us legitimacy as we approached key personnel in street-level work sites to carry out our project. We based our fieldwork in work units: police patrol units working shared shifts or geographically bounded areas, often called beats; classroom and specialized teachers who composed the eighth-grade team of an urban middle school; and vocational rehabilitation counselors in branch offices. At the street level, we first asked the work units for collective permission to do fieldwork in their workplaces, but group acceptance could not stipulate or require that all members of the group would be willing to be interviewed and provide stories. Once we were assured at the collective level that we would be welcome in the work setting, we asked individuals if they would willingly agree to participate in the interviews and story collections. In all settings, all or nearly all workers agreed to participate.

STORY COLLECTION

Once all the permissions were secured, we engaged in intensive participant-observation, seeking to establish trust among front-line workers and learn the nuances of the work, their discursive practices, and the organizational environments of their work sites. This early phase of field immersion allowed us to calibrate how to word interview questions that would flesh out our background knowledge. For example, after some trial and error, we discovered that the word "justice" is loaded, especially for police officers, and its use in any protocols prompted workers to repeat official agency positions rather than firsthand, personal accounts about their decision making. We found that "fairness" and "unfairness" captured the meaning we were after in asking about "justice," but those terms fit the everyday world of patrol officers, teachers, and vocational rehabilitation workers much more closely and were more likely to trigger their more personal reflections about relations with fellow workers and clients alike.

After this initial reconnaissance phase, we set up an initial, entry interview with each participating storyteller. During the entry interview, we asked a series of open-ended questions about the worker and his or her work. We discussed in greater detail the story collection process and gave each worker a story sketchbook that included instructions and blank pages for taking notes and outlining stories. We advised the street-level workers to take notes about the stories but not to write them out. Writing imposes demands of clarity and formality that, we felt, would inhibit many of our storytellers. We did not want our street-level workers worried about professor-researchers correcting their grammar and spelling! The goal of the sketchbook was to help them recall and retell stories that they told or heard during their workday. The sketchbook served as a means to prompt their thinking about the stories between the initial interview and the first story collection. Our purpose was to encourage the street-level workers to tell us stories that were part of their work setting, not just those that might be manufactured in response to the research. The storytellers themselves would become our "participant-listeners." The instructions were restated in the sketchbook:

> Over the next several weeks, we would like you to use this sketch book to write down a rough outline of 2 to 3 different stories. These stories should describe situations that take place within your agency during this time, or that you might recall from the past. The rough outlines will help you remember the story when you tell it to us later; you will not be required to share these notes with us.
>
> We are interested in stories about how or when your own beliefs about fairness or unfairness help you make decisions. At times your beliefs may have conflicted with the department's formal and informal policies; at other times, policies may have facilitated your reliance on your own beliefs.
>
> Stories can involve an encounter between you and clients, be about encounters between you and your agency, or among you and other members of your agency. You may also retell a story that happened to someone else, even if you are not a character in the story.
>
> The stories should, as much as possible: (1) have a plot or storyline with a beginning, middle, and end; (2) tell us who the characters are; (3) explain the relationships among the characters; (4) describe the feelings of the characters toward each other and the events; and (5) include a description of the setting and circumstances in which the event(s) occurred. (Maynard-Moody and Musheno 2003, 169–70)

We then set up a subsequent appointment to collect our first stories two to four weeks after the entry interview. We deliberately postponed the first story collection to further encourage the likelihood of collecting stories that would be told within the work unit, not just to researchers. Research team members arrived for our appointments early to allow time to sit in waiting rooms, the teachers' lounge, or the principal's office. Research team members often rode with police officers, observing the work routines and collecting stories while on patrol. In this way, the story collection appointments became opportunities for ongoing field observation.

Story collection began with a simple request to tell the story, which was tape-recorded. Some, but not all, storytellers referred to their story sketchbooks. After the storyteller finished, we used standard probing techniques to encourage storytellers to provide greater detail about events, setting, and characters. Probes encouraged the full rendering of the story. We recorded as many stories in each session as the street-level worker was willing to tell, usually two or three. For teachers and vocational rehabilitation counselors these story-collecting interactions were usually limited to approximately one hour between classes or appointments. Many of our police stories were told while on patrol during down times between calls. After each session, we would schedule the next story collection for two to four weeks later. We would remind the storyteller of the instructions, emphasizing our interest in stories told and heard within the work setting. We limited the number of story collections to a maximum three for each storyteller to keep within the six to eight months of time for fieldwork in each setting.

The workers' stories, our probes, and additional details added in response to our probes were then transcribed verbatim and in the sequence of the interaction. Transcription began after each story collection encounter. We then revised the stories, incorporating the added details from the responses to probes into the story text to create the fully rendered story. Although transformed from oral to written texts, revisions minimized the changes in the spoken structure of the stories. After all the stories were collected for each setting, we shared edited, written versions of their own stories with individual street-level workers, who were allowed to revise and further edit their stories. We did not share the stories with the group, just with those who told them. No storyteller made significant changes, but some did embellish their stories further or qualify them in the direction of greater caution. A few, especially the teachers, eliminated verbalisms, such as "you know." We wanted to be assured by and to assure the storytellers that these were their stories, so that to the extent possible, our interpretations would be based on their narratives. These edited versions were the texts we used for analysis.

STORY ANALYSIS

Our analysis of the stories was not as orderly as it may appear in this rendering of our interpretive engagement with the material, but the research team did follow a set of procedures. We developed a "Story Cover Page" for each story. This identified the site and storyteller as well as several common characteristics of each story.[7] We also developed a set of codes to classify text elements based on our evolving interpretive frames. Text elements could be a word or phrase or as much as a paragraph. We used two types of codes. "Story Codes" referenced different narrative storytelling elements, such as repetition and causal statements. "Thematic Codes" referred to theoretically relevant constructs, such as decision norms or workplace relational dynamics.[8] Each story was coded by one member of the research team and then check-coded by another.

This process encouraged a close reading of the texts as the coders had to think about the thematic relevance of each story element. By forcing us to compare our analytic summaries, the codes enabled us to ascertain that our interpretations of the meanings of the texts were shared: They facilitated conversation and highlighted differences of interpretation. We were less concerned with producing precise inter-rater reliability measures than with developing intersubjective consensus; disagreements were discussed until consensus emerged. Comparing the two codings provided an opportunity to negotiate shared meanings of texts among the four members of the research team. When research team members independently coded the same word, phrase, or passage in the same manner, we could see common interpretations emerging. Disagreements among coders provided opportunities to challenge each other's readings and to encourage continual interpretation.

The codes also provided a form of indexing that enabled us to locate the individual stories and the places in the stories where specific themes were discussed. We created a database identifying each theme present in each story. So, for example, when drafting the book chapter entitled "Street-Level Worker Knows Best" (Maynard-Moody and Musheno 2003, chapter 10), we could identify all of the stories that spoke to this theme.

As we discussed individual codes and text elements, we quickly learned that in story interpretation, one cannot meaningfully take statements out of their narrative context; doing so obscures their meaning. Words, phrases, and other text elements were meaningful only within the context of the story; they lost most of their meaning when isolated from the descriptions of events and characters and the plot sequence that were so essential to a story's integrity. For example, the statement in the "Happy Ending" story reproduced below that they "got creative" means little out of the context of the narrative. In the end, there were no shortcuts to carefully reading the texts and then discussing interpretations with research team members.

ONE STORY OF MANY

In our research, patterns and themes emerged because we examined a range of narratives—we would not have heard the Citizen-Agent Narrative theme and identified its patterns and elements from a single story—but interpretation proceeds one story at a time. Stories have an intactness, a wholeness, that should not be fractured during analysis. In our research we collected 157 stories, and most of our insights came as we discovered patterns of judgment and sense making about street-level work across numerous stories. But some stories stood out, either at first reading or after having analyzed many, for their ability to contain and express what we heard across an array of story texts and contexts. One such exemplar is depicted below. It, like other exemplars, conveys key elements of the Citizen-Agent Narrative and has a richness that enables readers to gain a feel for how workers confront the dilemmas inherent in street-level work. Before we describe the various dimensions of the Citizen-Agent Narrative, let us first listen to the voice of a street-level worker as he describes encounters with one client, as it was from these voices that this alternative narrative emerged. This story was told by a vocational rehabilitation counselor. We emphasize that the words of this story are the storyteller's, not ours.

Midwestern Vocational Rehabilitation, "A Happy Ending"

This is a happy-ending story. This is one of those that poor [supervisor] would probably just faint away dead. This is one she [the supervisor] does not want to know about. . . .

This is about a lady with severe chronic mental illness. She came through the mental health center through the support of an employment grant.

This is somebody who had been Miss Texas or Miss Oklahoma or something. You know, a real high achiever and then bang. I don't remember if it was depression or what happened. Well, anyway, she ended up in a series of mental hospitals. Somewhere along there she was married and had a little boy and was divorced. So now she is in [Midwestern City], she is a single mom living with zero money practically in a real bad part of town with this little guy.

And she worked so hard to put herself back together. She was doing so well. She had picked up an associates degree in electronics something, computer something, but had never actually worked with the degree or anything because of her mental illness.

Meanwhile back at home in the neighborhood, her little boy was probably the only white guy in the neighborhood and the neighborhood bullies were just beating the crap out of this little guy. The parents were like, "So what?" . . . So all these other stresses were coming back on her. She couldn't move until she got a job and she can't get a job.

Somehow she caught a ride to [nearby town] and interviewed. And they were hiring bachelor's degree people to do these jobs . . . and somehow she waltzed in there and convinced them that she could do the job . . . and they hired her, which was amazing in itself. And plus she had done it on her own which was even more wonderful except she didn't have a car.

And now she found somebody that had a good dependable older little Toyota for like $1,500. Well, if you have no money $1,500 might as well be $15 million. Somehow the mental health center could come up with $400, just kind of seed money. So I came up with $340 for maintenance, but that still left a bunch.

So we got creative. I wrote up enough money to cover insurance, car tags, and fees, and, you know, called them interview clothing and gas knowing good and well that these are things she is going to need but the money is really for the car. So she went and bought her car.

So she finally moved . . . and lived happily ever after. Her little boy is still in school and is doing great. She has advanced into a better position. They love her.

Everything worked out beautiful, but if we had gone by the rule book she would not have gotten the car, she would not have gotten the job. She would have ended up back in the hospital. (Story 1.1 in Maynard-Moody and Musheno 2003, 6)

CITIZEN-AGENT NARRATIVE

"A Happy Ending" places the construction of the client's identity, not policy implementation, at the center of the narrative.[9] The client is a single mother with limited education and severe chronic mental illness, not a promising start as the label "severe chronic mental illness" usually signals the worker's judgment that this is a troublesome client with little hope of success. Workers often provide only what the law requires for clients with such limited prospects; they do not invest much time, emotion, and effort into what they perceive as hopeless cases.

But the storyteller's construction of client identity does not end with these easy labels. The client was in the past a high achiever—"somebody who had been Miss Texas or Miss Oklahoma or something"—who had fallen on hard times. The worker focused on her positive character traits: She was a responsible single mom with a "little boy" coping with hard living conditions. She is not presented as a fallen and demanding prima donna, as were other characters in other stories we were told, but someone who, on her own, is trying to put her life back together. She is someone who calls out for help and, as importantly, is someone who can be helped.

As the story unfolds the described character of the client is entwined with the decision making of the worker. In story analysis it is essential to remember that the storyteller selects and presents the descriptive details about the clients to explain (or justify) to the listener the reasons for the judgments made and actions taken. In "A Happy Ending" the single mom had, on her own, obtained a good job. She did not wait for the counselor to find her work, but now she needed a car to get to work. She even found herself a reliable car, nothing flashy as would have befitted her previous status as a beauty pageant queen; the contrasting characterization is embedded in the storyteller's description of "a good dependable older little Toyota."

But here is where policy and worker judgment collided. Policy allowed for some "seed money" and money for car maintenance but did not allow for vehicle purchase. Policy did not meet the client's needs, so, for this worthy client, the worker "got creative." He "wrote up enough money to cover insurance, car tags, and fees, and, you know, called them interview clothing and gas knowing good and well that these are things she is going to need but the money is really for the car." In the story, the worker admits to fraud, albeit without labeling it as such explicitly, yet it is this deliberate breaking of the rules—of sabotage or shirking so denounced in the common State-Agent Narrative—that, in the end, leads to policy success. It was a happy ending for the client: She bought the car and kept the job. But it was also, and importantly, a happy ending for the state, which through the fraudulent act of this street-level worker was able to help a deserving citizen and, in the end, save taxpayer dollars. And it was a happy ending for the worker, who was able to use his position as an agent of the state to help this one client. A deep irony of the Citizen-Agent Narrative is that by rejecting their assigned role as faithful policy implementers, street-level workers can make the formal apparatus of the state work for clients, citizens, and themselves.

THE REVELATIONS OF SILENCE

This story illustrates one of the central features of storytelling analysis. Interpretation requires attention to what is not said, but this silence is often only "audible" in contrast to the researcher's expectations. We expected to hear stories that placed street-level judgment in the context of the State-Agent Narrative, and the near absence of these themes opened our ears to what we came to call the Citizen-Agent Narrative. It is important to note that what appear to the researchers as themes left out of the stories may not be recognizable as important elements to either the storytellers or others in the research setting. The worker-storytellers did not have the expectations of hearing the State-Agent Narrative that we carried into the field and did not recognize its absence. This marks an important difference between stories and some interviews. Interview questions are typically framed from the perspective of the researcher and, depending on how they are asked, may guide the respondent to frame an answer in the context of the researcher's expectations. Stories more fully retain the storyteller's point of view.

In "A Happy Ending," hierarchy and accountability are mentioned but have no influence on the story's events or outcomes. The storyteller suggests that the supervisor is deliberately kept in the dark: "This is one she [the supervisor] does not want to know." From our field observations and interviews with the supervisor, we suspect that she most likely not only "knew" about but also supported the worker's judgment. This suggests the deliberate and delicate interaction between worker and supervisor in which the worker carefully protects the supervisor from having to enforce proper procedure.

Policies are present in the narrative but only to underscore their inadequacies in meeting the client's needs. The $740 that could legitimately be provided to help the client purchase the essential and modest used car underscores the futility of following the rules: "Well, if you have no money $1,500 might as well be $15 million." The vocational rehabilitation counselor does use state resources to meet the client's needs, but this requires going well beyond what the rules and policies allow. The story underscores Robert Merton's (1957) classic point that following rules and procedures can result in failure for the client and ultimately for the policy. Hierarchy and policy, although present in the stories, remain part of the setting or context that creates dramatic tension with the street-level worker's own judgments. The reference point in this and other narratives is the client, not the policy, and this insight allowed us to hear the Citizen-Agent Narrative.

THOUGHTS ON DISCOVERY, COLLABORATION, AND INCONCLUSIVENESS

Interpretive and other forms of qualitative research are often dismissed as "exploratory," the first and lesser step preparing the way for the more significant work of quantification and hypothesis testing. But exploration is a most demanding conceptual journey. It requires discipline and rigor but also an open and inventive mind and the willingness to learn from those we study. The driving force in interpretive research is not how well our data support our theoretical presuppositions but how well our interpretations can capture and elucidate social life.

Toward this end, collecting and examining stories provides a powerful means for offering interpretations grounded in people's understandings of their own contexts. Though distilled by the storyteller, stories retain much of the ambiguity, contradictions, and complexity of social life. Although not factual in the narrow, positivist sense of the word, these texts have an evidentiary status of their own: They can be read, reread, shared, and argued over. Although there may be no definitive interpretations, story texts allow us to base our interpretations on the interpretations of others—in our case, street-level workers—and, as important, these texts allow us to demonstrate to others the bases for our insights.

Collaboration among the research team proved essential to our discovery process. We operated on the simple rule that our individual observations, interpretations, and counterarguments must be based on the story texts. As we developed, challenged, and reconsidered our interpretations, we forced each other to listen ever more closely to the storytellers. It is essential to note that the process of reading, interpreting, rereading, and reinterpreting stories takes time; impatience is the enemy of insight. The many draftings of the publications based on this research were essential parts of the analytic process. The themes, arguments, and interpretive findings grew out of our close reading of the stories in the context of our fieldwork, but our findings were further refined by the writing process. In narrative research, writing is itself a method of interpretation.

Story texts make our interpretations contestable, an essential characteristic of good social research. For example, in the story "A Happy Ending," the worker does reference the significance of race and ethnicity in making a judgment when saying that the client's "little boy was probably the only white guy in the neighborhood and the neighborhood bullies were just beating the crap out of this little guy." Others examining this story may make more of this point and probe additional stories among those we present to critically engage our treatment of race and ethnicity. Such critical confrontations with story texts are crucial to the interpretive process, making clear that general explanations, like the one we offer about street-level judgments, are never sufficient for understanding fully the social and cultural dynamics of state power.

NOTES

1. This research was supported by the National Science Foundation grant number SBR-9511169.
2. We worked with teachers in a single school site, but with both police officers and counselors we worked in two sites in two different states.
3. See also Dienstag (1997).
4. Our book included complete or near complete transcriptions of approximately a third of the stories used in the analysis. All of our stories, as well as entry and exit interviews, and questionnaire data are archived at the Inter-University Consortium for Political and Social Research at the University of Michigan.
5. For a recent discussion and an alternative approach, see Feldman et al. (2004).
6. For a detailed discussion, see Maynard-Moody and Musheno (2003, chapter 3 and appendix A).
7. For a copy of the cover page, see Maynard-Moody and Musheno (2003, appendix D).
8. For a list of codes, see Maynard-Moody and Musheno (2003, appendix E).
9. A full discussion of the Citizen-Agent Narrative is in Maynard-Moody and Musheno (2003, chapter 2).

CHAPTER 19

INTERPRETIVE CONTENT ANALYSIS

Stories and Arguments in Analytical Documents

Clare Ginger

I am most interested in questions about how people make sense of ambiguous situations and concepts as they develop and implement public policy. My interest in these kinds of questions, and my use of interpretive methods, reflect my experience in both applied policy settings and academia. This experience has occurred in contexts where people piece together various ways of analyzing, interpreting, and synthesizing what is "known" about environmental issues and possible responses to them.

Working in agencies at the state level in Massachusetts and at the federal level in the Bureau of Land Management, I found myself in situations where people came from varied positions and had distinct stories to tell about the issue at hand. We synthesized these stories, often across disciplines (e.g., ecology, engineering, public health, law), into plans of action. These experiences emphasized the value and challenges of drawing on multiple approaches to make sense of an issue and argue for action in government.

As a student in a master's program in environmental law, I learned how to identify arguments embedded in judicial opinions through legal case analysis. At the same time, we considered the nature of scientific knowledge and how it is used in law. Analyzing majority, concurring, and dissenting opinions in any given case emphasizes the importance of making connections through arguments, between general principles of law and the facts of the case. It also highlights how connections can be made in varied ways, leading to divergent conclusions.

As a Ph.D. student in an interdisciplinary program at the University of Michigan, I took methods classes that included statistics, policy analysis tools, and research paradigms. One class provided me with experience in gathering and interpreting qualitative data. It opened up a dialogue that continued beyond the semester. This dialogue informed my use of interpretive approaches in my research. I also taught technical communications in the engineering school. Through this experience, I formalized my understanding of structure and argument in technical documents.

I take a pragmatist's view about the choices these experiences suggest, finding value in whatever methods seem most helpful in responding to the question at hand. Interpretive methods often provide a very useful way to respond to the kinds of research questions I ask. At the same time, I see a critical need in the field of environmental policy to work across disciplinary boundaries. As a result, I spend a fair amount of time thinking about how to create connections between disciplines that draw on quite different methodological traditions. Key to creating such connections are open minds and a capacity to articulate the grounds for choosing a method and to describe how it is applied to gather, analyze, and interpret data.

In the 1980s the Bureau of Land Management (BLM) produced wilderness environmental impact statements (EISs) that evaluated 855 areas, comprising 24 million acres of public land, and recommended for or against wilderness designation of these areas. . . . An examination of arguments in the BLM wilderness EISs reveals the structure of stories about wilderness designation. It shows how BLM personnel joined technical analyses to recommendations through conflicting arguments about wilderness designation. . . . Analyzing how arguments connect technical information with political recommendations provides a useful way to examine how agencies bring together technical analyses and political positions to frame issues.
—*Clare Ginger* (2000, 292–93; 307–8)

In 1988, I began my dissertation research focusing on the implementation of wilderness policy in the Bureau of Land Management (BLM). I used ethnographic methods and became a participant-observer in agency offices in Washington, D.C., Utah, and Arizona for sixteen months, distributed over five summers, in the role of student intern. As a part of this project, I analyzed a set of wilderness environmental impact statements (EISs) using interpretive methods to assess their structure and content for stories and arguments. I drew on an understanding of writing as an activity through which we convey meaning by choosing, organizing, and describing content at various levels: in report structure, paragraph and sentence construction, and word choices. My approach provided an avenue for understanding how the EISs served as an arena for agency personnel to tell stories and make arguments about wilderness policy through technical analysis. In describing my analytical approach in this chapter, I illustrate one avenue for assessing technical documents to understand how they frame policy issues. I begin with background information about the policy context of the wilderness EISs, define some terms, and, finally, describe some of the methods I used to analyze these documents.

This assessment reveals some of the ways that politics enter technical analyses. I show how implementing structural uniformity in documents can affect the information contained in EISs, and how this uniformity brought coherence to the agency's story about wilderness despite variation across field offices and local politics. The analysis provides a way to assess a change in public lands policy: the incorporation of wilderness policy, which is meant to protect land from commodity development, into an agency that historically has promoted commodity development. I also detail how to analyze arguments to understand how it is possible for people to use the *same* scenarios to draw *opposite* conclusions.

POLICY CONTEXT FOR THE BLM WILDERNESS EISS

The BLM manages over 260 million acres of public land in Alaska, Arizona, California, Colorado, Idaho, Montana, Nevada, New Mexico, Oregon, Utah, Washington, and Wyoming for resources that include minerals, oil and gas, range (livestock grazing), timber, recreation, cultural elements, wildlife, and wilderness. The agency is organized as a geographically nested hierarchy with offices at four levels: Washington, D.C.; states; districts; and resource areas. Within each of these levels, personnel are hired into programs organized by resource and are known as resource specialists (e.g., minerals specialist, recreation specialist, or wildlife specialist). These specialists wrote the wilderness EISs during the 1980s.

The wilderness EISs represent a response to two pieces of legislation, the National Environmental Policy Act of 1969 (NEPA) and the Federal Land Policy and Management Act of 1976 (FLPMA), and draw on a third, the Wilderness Act of 1964. Through NEPA, Congress required federal agencies to generate EISs to assess the impacts of "major Federal actions significantly affecting the quality of the human environment" (National Environmental Policy Act 1969, 4332). EISs provide a mechanism for participants in policy debates to frame arguments and make decisions about future federal actions through analysis of environmental impacts. The federal action that the wilderness EISs analyze is the potential designation of public land as wilderness areas. This action arises from FLPMA, which directed the BLM to review land in its jurisdiction (excluding land the agency manages in Alaska) by 1991 to recommend areas for wilderness designation (Federal Land Policy and Management Act 1976, 1782). The agency produced the wilderness EISs as a part of its response to this mandate.

The EISs assess 855 wilderness study areas, comprising 24 million acres of public land, and make recommendations for or against wilderness designation of the areas. They describe wilderness characteristics of each area based on attributes defined in the Wilderness Act of 1964. Such an area:

> (1) generally appears to have been affected primarily by the forces of nature, with the imprint of man's work substantially unnoticeable; (2) has outstanding opportunities for solitude or a primitive and unconfined type of recreation; (3) has at least five thousand acres of land or is of sufficient size as to make practicable its preservation and use in an unimpaired condition; and (4) may also contain ecological, geological, or other features of scientific, educational, scenic, or historical value. (Wilderness Act 1964, 1131[c])

The EISs I examined were generated during the second phase of a three-phase wilderness review (Bureau of Land Management 1978). In the first phase, the BLM inventoried public lands to identify areas with wilderness attributes. Land that passed on to the second phase, the study phase, was assessed in parcels known as wilderness study areas, which were evaluated in the wilderness EISs. In the third phase, the BLM produced reports to document agency recommendations. The EISs produced in the second phase also identified other resources in the study areas, development potential for the resources, and impacts of wilderness designation and non-designation alternatives.

Production of the EISs themselves occurred in four steps: (1) BLM personnel in field offices wrote draft EISs; (2) staff in Washington, D.C., in the Department of the Interior, Office of Environmental Project Review (OEPR), and in the BLM Branch of Wilderness Resources (Washington Office), as well as members of the public, commented on the drafts; (3) reviewers from Washington, D.C., and field personnel negotiated over changes to be made; and (4) field personnel wrote final EISs. In generating the EISs, field personnel worked in teams of resource specialists. Together, they characterized connections among their resource programs, the wilderness program, and the study areas. They defined tradeoffs between wilderness designation and other resource uses. Their initial efforts appeared in draft EISs. Comments from the OEPR and the BLM Washington office often asked the field personnel to restructure their analyses. According to the OEPR, many of the draft EISs contained vague, improperly focused analyses, irrelevant issues, and inconsistent arguments about the impacts of wilderness designation. In contrast, and as a result of changes made in response to OEPR comments, the final EISs consistently focus on study areas, evaluate specific scenarios of future development, and clarify the logic of arguing for or against wilderness designation.

The wilderness review occurred amidst polarized debate about wilderness designation of public lands. The debate reflected the fact that the wilderness mandate challenged the BLM's historical focus on resource development.[1] Within the agency, this highly contentious debate about tradeoffs among policy goals was channeled, in part, into debate about technical analyses in the EISs. Agency staff used technical analyses to generate scenarios, or stories, about future activities in wilderness study areas and about the impacts of wilderness designation. Through these stories, they made sense of and framed the issue of wilderness designation. Their analyses reflected normative positions about what the future ought to bring in terms of resource development and protection. As a result, technical information in the documents cannot be separated from political debate about whether public lands should be designated as wilderness. To assess the stories and arguments in these EISs about designating wilderness areas on public lands, I conducted an interpretive content analysis of them.

DEFINING TERMS: CONTENT ANALYSIS, STORIES, AND ARGUMENTS

Researchers from varied traditions with quite different research questions look to the content of written documents as a source of data. As a result, there exist many approaches for analyzing the content of documents. In political and other social sciences, some researchers have developed methods for coding documents at the paragraph, sentence, and word levels to characterize content. Political scientists have used such coding systems to generate numeric data and conduct statistical analyses to relate political positions to a range of variables, including voting behavior, post-election policy implementation, and government coalition building (Budge, Robertson, and Hearl 1987; Gabel and Huber 2000; Ginsberg 1976; Klingemann, Hofferbert, and Budge 1994; Laver and Budge 1992; Laver, Benoit, and Garry 2003). In contrast, coming from the fields of discourse studies and communications, Killingsworth and Palmer (1992) used rhetorical methods to analyze the content of BLM EISs. Retaining data in word form, they characterized and compared style, voice, and language in texts written by agency experts and in the texts of comments written by citizens in response to draft EISs. Through their analysis, Killingsworth and Palmer addressed questions about communications between experts and the general public. In all of these examples, the methodological approach focuses on selected content of documents as data, with an expectation that systematic analysis of that content-data will provide evidence to answer the research question at hand.

Early in my research, I posed the question: How did the BLM personnel interpret "wilderness policy" as they implemented it? In making connections to the academic literature in policy, I used concepts of narrative and argument articulated by Roe (1994) and Majone (1989). The overall policy context involved high levels of ambiguity and polarization (arising from multiple and conflicting interpretations of the value of public lands and wilderness), uncertainty (related to incomplete information about future conditions for commodity development such as minerals), and complexity (due to the interconnectedness of issues associated with the multiple uses of public lands). Roe (1994) argues that narrative policy analysis is useful for understanding and developing alternative policy approaches in such circumstances. In analyzing the content of the wilderness EISs, I used definitions of stories and arguments informed by his work. He suggests that the researcher start with "the conventional definition of stories," and he defines stories as having "beginnings, middles, and ends, as in scenarios" (Roe 1994, 3). As noted above, one of the main tasks that agency analysts pursued in producing the wilderness EISs was to develop future scenarios about the public lands and resource use and protection. Analyzing the documents to identify their story lines reveals how the EISs contributed to the framing of wilderness policy inside the agency.

Roe (1994, 3) indicates further that "if the stories are in the form of arguments, they have premises and conclusions." Majone (1989, 23) asserts that "practicing policy analysts often engage in argumentative discourse [as they] debate values, question objectives, agree or disagree about assumptions, and advocate or justify courses of action on the basis of less-than-conclusive evidence." In his estimation, "argument is the link that connects data and information with the conclusions of an analytic study" (Majone 1989, 10). In examining the wilderness EISs, I considered the form of arguments they contain in terms of premises and conclusions, how evidence (e.g., data and information) is linked to conclusions in them, and how the arguments they contain draw on normative positions about wilderness designation of public lands. Analysis of arguments in these terms provides a systematic means to show how the EISs contribute to framing the policy issue of wilderness designation.

In summary, I examined how agency analysts interpreted and framed the issue of wilderness in the EISs through stories and arguments that link technical information to policy recommendations. Because the documents exist in both draft and final form, I also considered whether there existed evidence of changes in the framing of the wilderness issue between earlier and later versions of these documents. Changes in the framing of the wilderness issue provide evidence about policy change for public lands management more generally.

Before describing components of the analysis, I comment on how I arrived at the point of conducting an interpretive analysis via a project that involved statistical analysis of data and recommendations in the EISs. The interpretive analysis was, in part, a response to that project.

FROM STATISTICAL TO INTERPRETIVE ANALYSES

At the same time that I began my ethnographic study, I was hired as a research assistant for a project at the University of Michigan to help analyze a set of wilderness EISs produced by the BLM. The objective of the analysis was to determine whether there existed statistically significant relationships between technical information in the documents and agency recommendations for designations of wilderness areas. This project led to a disjuncture that helped to motivate and inform my interpretive analysis of the EISs.

In conducting the statistical analysis of the wilderness EISs, I coordinated the efforts of a group of students to code information and policy recommendations from the documents. I worked with the principal investigator on the project to conduct statistical analyses. The academic literature on EISs included questions about whether and how technical information in them is linked to decision making. We tested for such relationships using regression analysis. We reported that this analysis indicated that very little of the technical information was related, with any degree of statistical significance, to BLM policy recommendations. We concluded that this lent support to the idea that the BLM had produced these EIS documents primarily to fulfill a legal mandate rather than to inform substantive policy decisions (Ginger and Mohai 1993).

This conclusion generated a small crisis for me. On the one hand, I was gaining valuable research experience and helping to produce outputs valued in academia. On the other hand, our conclusion did not reflect the complexity that I was experiencing as a participant-observer in the agency. Furthermore, I felt I had to share our analysis with BLM personnel who had provided me with access to the agency.[2] I wondered whether the study results would have a negative impact on my relationships with them. I provided copies of our findings to several key people at BLM. Their responses were mixed. Although one person thought there was some validity to our findings, others were polite but lukewarm. One person expressed confusion. This was not what he thought I was working on in my research. He felt that the nature of the study did not match the content of interviews I was conducting or the nature of my other activities in the agency. More important, the findings did not reflect his experience with the EISs. With some awkwardness, we moved past the breach as I explained that the statistical study was distinct from my dissertation research. Three years passed before I confronted this discrepancy and undertook to analyze the EISs using interpretive methods.

In assessing the relevance of the EISs to implementing wilderness policy in the BLM, I had to address the fact that the statistical analyses did not convey much about the processes through which the documents were generated. They also did not offer insight into how the EISs were connected to efforts that had been occurring inside the agency since 1976 to make sense of wilderness policy. As I faced down these missing pieces, three things occurred to me: (1) in coding information from the documents for the statistical analyses, the team of students had had more difficulty with some documents than others because they were organized differently; (2) from my experiences teaching technical writing, I knew that a different organization meant a different story line; and (3) if any patterns existed in changes in the organization of EIS documents from draft to final report, these might provide evidence of a change in the story about wilderness presented in the documents and about shifts in public lands policy. The interpretive content analysis that followed took shape quickly.

EISS, SENSE MAKING, AND INTERPRETIVE ANALYSIS

To understand the range of options available for conducting content analysis, it is useful to recognize that when we write, edit, and read written material, we are working with multiple layers of documentary organization; that is, words are organized into sentences, paragraphs, sections, and full documents. We can assess word choices and sentence-level grammar. We might ask whether the sentences in a paragraph provide a flow from one idea to the next, linked by a main point. We can consider whether the text is organized into a well-structured outline and what messages that overall outline sends. Relative to the substantive content of a document, we can evaluate the information included from the perspective of logic and whether evidence is provided to support premises and conclusions. We might examine a paper to see whether it conveys contradictory ideas that are not resolved. We can identify technical language and rhetorical devices, such as analogies and metaphors. We also can extend our evaluation to consider the context by inquiring about who produced a document, how, and why, as well as about the intended audiences and whether and how the text is adapted to communicate with them. It is possible to address these and other questions in the writing, reading, and analysis of a text.

In my analysis, I focused on the outline or overall structure of the EISs to identify their story line. I assessed the types of technical information included in them as these related to the story line, and assessed the structure and normative positions of arguments that linked the technical information to wilderness recommendations. This evidence became a part of my effort to understand how agency personnel interpret and make sense of wilderness policy. I drew data from 48 pairs of draft and final documents, 1 unpaired draft, and 4 unpaired final EISs for a total of 101 documents. They covered 670 study areas (78 percent of the total) and were chosen based on their availability from the BLM and university libraries. I also reviewed 3 marked-up draft EISs and 3 memos, all conveying comments from reviewers in Washington, D.C. I already had data about the study process from interviews with 3 staff members from the BLM Washington Office, a staff member from the OEPR, and 3 BLM field personnel.[3] In addition, I observed a review meeting and participated in efforts in one state to revise a draft EIS into final form.

The following four subsections describe components of my analysis of these data. They include a description of the creation of the "future scenarios" that form the core of the technical analyses in the documents, as well as assessments of document structure, information content, and arguments.

Constructing Future Scenarios—Storytelling in EISs

To understand the EISs as a forum for telling stories, I considered how field personnel in the BLM constructed future scenarios. Understanding future scenarios is important for three reasons. One, I learned from internal memos from reviewers (Bureau of Land Management 1983; Office of Environmental Project Review 1983, 1986) and in interviews with field personnel and reviewers (field notes, Interviews 103, 404, and 406) that developing scenarios of what would happen in the wilderness study areas with and without their designation as wilderness became an important analytical task for resource specialists in the field offices. Two, Roe (1994) suggests that scenarios are a form of stories. Three, the way in which field personnel constructed scenarios illustrates that agency analysts play a role as advocates in promoting the use of particular resource values on the public lands.

Comment memos from Washington, D.C., reviewers emphasized the need to make future scenarios detailed and specific to each study area, including predictions about development and its impacts. An excerpt from one memo illustrates this point:

> The descriptions of alternatives, especially for minerals, contain some information, but stop short of providing estimates of major actions that will occur in the wilderness study areas. A projection of the type, amount, and location of development is needed before an analysis can be completed. Projections should describe what development would involve, including roads, drill pads, open pit mines, underground mines and ancillary facilities, and how disturbance would be distributed in the wilderness study area. (Office of Environmental Project Review 1986, 4)

One of the people I interviewed, a wilderness specialist, commented on changes between the draft and final EISs relative to future scenarios and the request for specific analyses:

> In this state we had lengthy scenarios [in the finals] because they [the OEPR] were not happy with the drafts, with the mineral guy just saying, a hundred thousand acres of high-value mineral land and twenty thousand acres of low-value mineral land would be withdrawn *forever* from useful exploitation by mining interests. Those were the analyses in the draft. In the final it was, they have that same fact about potential *zones* of high, medium, low mineral values but, in addition, we project that sixteen medium mines, four large mines, sixteen prospecting operations would be denied under the all wilderness alternative. [We] got very specific and put numbers, people, and, in large mines, even dollar impacts. (Interview 404)

This interviewee described the pressure to increase the level of specificity in the documents with respect to future scenarios. To assess the effects of this pressure across field offices, I compared the relative specificity of this information between draft and final EISs. Of the forty-eight paired draft and final documents, thirty increased in specificity of scenarios from draft to final form, ten pairs were equally specific in both draft and final form, four pairs were equally general in both draft and final form, and four pairs decreased in specificity from draft to final form. Overall, most field offices followed the direction from reviewers to make future scenarios specific.

To make sense of this pattern of local compliance, I considered who participated in writing these EISs and their roles in the organization more generally. I learned about the role of resource program specialists in producing EISs through the EIS texts themselves, in interviews, and through participant-observation. In brief, teams of resource specialists representing the various programs in the agency produced these documents, as reflected in each EIS's list of preparers. In addition, interviewees talked about working in teams on this task (Interviews 406 and 505). Finally, in my own work in the agency I participated in various activities to generate environmental assessments, which enabled me to observe how people contributed and put together information reflecting various program interests. I also produced some documents myself and went to the various resource specialists to gather information and analyses. From such evidence I learned that one important role of these specialists is to advocate for the interests of their particular programs. Here is how one wilderness program specialist described the process of developing specific scenarios, including the desire to be heard in EISs and interactions based on program interests:

> If the geologist said, "I'm not doing anything," the rancher said, "I'm not doing anything," and the wildlife guy said, "No aprons or catchments," you say, "Under 'no wilderness,' conditions would remain pretty much unchanged." . . . But they tended to have a lot of action under "no wilderness." I think they felt they had to put a lot of stuff in to make sure that they were heard, that wilderness should be impacted. . . . Like on [place name], they had a pretty extensive scenario. So, not only was minerals going to town there, but I could go to town, saying, "I'll *protect* this from the copper pit. We're saving three miles of riparian, and all these critters and saguaros." So, it was done that way. (Interview 404)

This description shows how developing specific future scenarios was a process of telling stories based, in part, on program interests.

For some BLM personnel, program interests were related to normative positions about wilderness designation as compared to resource development. For example, if designation would, in their judgment, have a negative impact on their capacity to promote their program's interest in developing resources, they might oppose designation. Conversely, if they believed that designation would positively affect the interests of their program, they might favor designation. Overall, the content of the wilderness EISs reflected the goals and ambiguity of the agency's multiple-use mandate, which indicates that land in its jurisdiction is managed for recreation, range, timber, minerals, watershed, wildlife and fish, and natural scenic, scientific, and historical values (Federal Land Policy and Management Act 1976, 1702, 1712, 1732). The documents contain information about these many uses of public lands; the scenarios became a mechanism for program specialists to gain a voice in the EISs and make a case for particular future uses of the land in the study areas. As agency personnel made potential development activity more specific, the idea of wilderness designation took on more specific meaning as well. Thus, developing specific future scenarios contributed to making the concept of wilderness more operational and tangible for public lands.

Concerns about resource program interests inside the BLM were reflected in the structure of

EISs, decisions about the inclusion and exclusion of information, and the normative premises of policy recommendations.

Assessing Structure and Story Line—Framing the Issue of Wilderness Designation

The outline or structure of a technical document is linked to its communication purpose or message.[4] This message is a key element of the narrative or story line of the document. The underlying structure and story line of the EISs is twofold: (1) cause and effect, that is, federal decisions as a cause and impacts of such decisions as effects, and (2) comparisons of different decisions' impacts on components of the environment. In the BLM wilderness EISs, the federal decisions consisted of recommendations for or against wilderness designation of parcels of public land called wilderness study areas. To tell the cause-effect story of EISs, agency personnel had to define the components of the environment that would be affected by such decisions.

To assess the story line of the documents, I examined the structure of the 101 wilderness EISs and the substantive content of the specific headings they employed. What I mean by structure is the order in which the headings were sequenced; things like "resource programs" or "wilderness study areas" are the content meaning of the headings. To do this, I examined the first, second, and third levels of documentary organization in the texts of the forty-eight pairs of draft and final EISs, one unpaired draft, and four unpaired final reports. The analysis showed that the dominant structure of some of the EISs changed as they went from draft to final form. All but one of the final documents I reviewed used wilderness study areas as the first order of organization. Thus, the structure in the final EISs was nearly uniform in telling a story about how various options for wilderness designation would affect wilderness study areas. In contrast, some drafts used resource programs in the agency (minerals, range [i.e., livestock grazing], wildlife, recreation, cultural resources) as the first order of organization. The message in these EISs changed from a draft story line about how wilderness designation might affect agency programs to a final story line about how wilderness designation might affect study areas. This change reframed the issue of wilderness designation.

The reframing can be understood in terms of plot, subplot, and main and supporting characters. The main plot in the *final* EISs concerns places (specific wilderness study areas), with names and human activities (wilderness designation, resource use) that may affect the character of those places in the future. The subplot is about how resource programs might be affected by such wilderness designation (in the main plot). The main "characters" are study areas, and programs play supporting roles. In contrast, some draft EISs tell a story in which programs are main characters in a plot about how designating certain areas as wildernesses might affect them. Study areas serve as "scenery" in the background of this plot and, in a few cases, do not appear at all. Thus, the structural change from draft to final EISs shifted attention away from programs and toward study areas in stories about how future wilderness designation of those areas might affect their existence. Through this change, wilderness designation was reframed in a way that deemphasized its potential impact on agency operations. The reframing provided a positive basis for designating public lands as wilderness by redirecting the focus of analysis to areas where the presence of wilderness values had already been established.

In commenting on my interpretation of these data in a journal submission, one reviewer suggested an alternative interpretation of the reframing of EIS structures: "The change might arguably have resulted from an objective of providing a more uniform structure to these planning documents, rather than efforts by BLM and OEPR staff to frame the wilderness arguments." The idea that people wanted to provide a uniform structure for the EISs is not invalid, but it does not address the direction or focus of the structural changes. This direction had the effect of raising the status of wilderness values over and above the status of agency programs in the EISs. Internal memos commenting on draft EISs addressed the question of the intent of the D.C. staff reviewers. These comments indicated that the reviewers did, in fact, intend for the changes to go in a particular direction. For example, one comment stated: "We are evaluating the impacts of management actions on environmental subjects such as wilderness values . . ." (Office of Environmental Project Review 1986, 2). Wilderness values are located in and recognized through the delineation of land as a wilderness study area. The comment indicates that the focus of the analysis should be on wilderness values and study areas first and foremost. One might consider that FLPMA directed the agency to review areas with wilderness characteristics and make recommendations about their suitability for preservation as wilderness. This mandate directs attention to the study areas and not to agency programs; it indicates a statutory basis for the direction of the change, which was substantive in character more than it was format related for the sake of report conformity.

Irrespective of intentions and statutory justifications, the organizational structure of the documents exists as a part of their content and frames their subject matter. The change in some of the EISs highlights a general principle: The structure of technical documents like EISs frames policy issues. Potential sources of policy content for such framing include laws, agency guidance, and individuals who generate the documents. Whether changes occur or not, we can examine the structure of technical documents as narratives or story lines to identify how they frame policy issues.[5] In this case, the structure of these documents frames the wilderness issue as a story about causes and effects across various configurations of wilderness designations. The structure of the final EISs, along with changes in some drafts, provide evidence of movement in how the agency as a whole framed the wilderness issue: The evidence is found in the shift in the story line about what would be affected by designation decisions. This demand from the reviewers in the D.C. offices generated a structure for the EISs that could serve the political purpose of highlighting how wilderness designation protects wilderness values in the study areas from development impacts. The changes in framing may have provided a way to accomplish political objectives in seemingly nonpolitical ways, that is, by asking for uniformity of structure in technical documents.

This change in frame had direct consequences for the BLM's technical analyses because it brings greater attention to some things (e.g., wilderness values) and reduces attention to others (e.g., impacts on agency programs). As detailed in the next section, it had the potential to affect the type of information that was included in and excluded from the EISs.

Assessing Information Content and Issue Framing—Inclusion and Exclusion of Information

In my analysis, I considered what information was included in the documents and how these inclusions and exclusions might be related to the story lines and framing of the issue. Internal reviewers asked field personnel to remove irrelevant information from the documents (Interview 103). The basis for judging relevance, from their perspective, was whether the information was related to the impacts of wilderness designation recommendations. If something would be affected by the recommendations, then it was relevant; otherwise, it was to be omitted. Judgments about relevance of information are tied to the cause-effect story line of the EISs: A shift in attention from resource programs to study areas would render some things relevant that had not been so before, because the definition of what is being affected would change.

Table 19.1

Inclusion and Exclusion of Information Based on Structure

EIS content	Resource program structure	Study area structure
Starting point	All BLM resource programs.	All wilderness study areas.
Assumptions about affected environment	All resource programs potentially affected by designation	All study areas potentially affected by designation
Resulting rationale for including and excluding information in findings	EISs as vehicle for reporting findings for resource programs. BLM personnel decide whether to include study areas	EISs as vehicle for reporting findings for study areas. BLM personnel decide whether to include resources and programs
Logical basis for including resources	If resource present in organizational chart, then include resource	If resource exists in study area and is potentially affected by designation, then include resource
Logical basis for including study areas	If resource exists in study area, then include study area	If study area identified in inventory, then include study area

Source: Ginger 2000, 300.

To understand the link between story line and the relevance of information, I considered document structure as the starting point for analysis, including what it indicates about the affected environment. Starting from the two different possible points of departure, resource programs and wilderness study areas, I identified the logics of each for including particular kinds of information. Table 19.1 shows how each of these starting points creates a different focus and logic for making decisions about what information to include in an EIS.

The resource program and study area structures differ in their starting points, assumptions about the affected environment, and basis for including and excluding information in the EISs. The logical basis for decisions about including resource programs and study areas in the analyses differs, then, based on the structure of the document. The resource program structure creates the potential to exclude study areas in the context of programs. The study area structure creates the potential to exclude resource programs in the context of study areas. Where the analysis starts with resource programs, any resource that has a place in the organizational chart is included in the analysis, and study areas are included based on whether a particular resource is present in that area. Where the analysis starts with study areas, all study areas are included, and field offices include only those resources present in the areas and potentially affected by wilderness designation.

To understand the implications of this analysis for practice, I examined the EISs to assess the inclusion and exclusion of information about various resource programs. Resources were to be removed from the field analyses when impacts were not anticipated in either direction (development affecting wilderness values; wilderness designation affecting development). In many cases, the number of resources identified for analysis decreased, and specific information about some resources was eliminated from final documents based on assessments of "no impacts." The BLM included a statement at the beginning of each EIS identifying the resources that did not involve

Table 19.2

Inclusion of Resources as Issues in Draft and Final Documents (n = 48 pairs)

Resource	Included in draft and final analysis based on projected impacts	Deleted from final analysis based on finding of "no impacts"	Included in draft and final analysis despite finding of "no impacts"
Range	10	25	13
Minerals	6	14	28

Source: Ginger 2000, 301.

impacts and so were not analyzed in the document. However, this did not occur uniformly across all programs. Two programs in particular were not handled consistently in terms of assessments of their impacts, range (livestock grazing) and mineral resources. These resources are of interest because they are (1) historically associated with the BLM, and (2) linked to development and so have potential to be affected by wilderness designations. In short, these are resources in which the stakes of a wilderness designation are highest. This may particularly be the case for some field offices in particular states or sections of the country.

Data from the forty-eight pairs of EISs indicated an overall decrease in the detailed analysis of the presence of range and mineral resources between draft and final versions. In some of the final documents the deleted analysis reflected an assessment in those reports of "no impacts." However, this pattern was uneven. Table 19.2 shows a greater reduction associated with range resources and a lesser reduction associated with minerals resources. In ten pairs of draft and final EISs, range resources were included in both reports based on analysis of the presence of impacts. In twenty-five pairs, range resources had been included in the draft analyses with a finding of "no impacts" and were deleted from the final analyses because impacts were not expected. In thirteen cases, they were included in both draft and final analyses despite a finding of "no impacts." Mineral resources were included in both reports based on analysis of the presence of impacts in six pairs of draft and final documents. In fourteen pairs, mineral resources had been included in the draft analyses with a finding of "no impacts" and were deleted from the final analysis because impacts were not expected. However, in twenty-eight pairs they were included in draft and final analyses despite a finding of "no impacts."

In interpreting these data, I considered the agency's historical focus on commodity uses (established in the literature, e.g., Culhane 1981; Foss 1960) and assessed the significance of a message that conveyed an assessment of "no impacts." The history of the BLM suggests that range and mineral resources are of central importance to understanding the agency's public lands and management activities. I took account of the possibility that this history influenced the selection of information to include in the EISs. I drew on my observations of a meeting in which reviewers from the OEPR and field staff discussed and negotiated changes to a draft EIS. Participants acknowledged that the two groups, reviewers and field staff, had different goals for the EIS and different grounds for judging the relevance of information contained in it. The Washington-based reviewers were most interested in meeting NEPA requirements for analyzing impacts, while the field staff indicated that they were also interested in providing the public with information more generally. Participants in the meeting noted that this difference became a problem where the EIS raised issues that were unnecessary for NEPA analysis but that were important for public relations locally. From a local perspective, conflicts between wilderness designation and land use for livestock grazing and minerals development purposes were a concern, and field office person- nel wanted to include consideration of these issues throughout the documents, while OEPR re- viewers said that addressing these resources was only important where impacts were expected. Inclusions and omissions, then, were a central issue with organizational and political significance far beyond the conformity of reports to a uniform structural outline.

This meeting suggests that it is important to consider the message conveyed about range and mineral resources by an assessment of "no impacts." A message of "no impacts" suggests that commodity production will not be disturbed by wilderness designation; it downplays conflict. As noted above, this message may appear as a statement at the beginning of a document that identi- fies which resources will not be affected by wilderness designation and so are not included in the analysis and report. Where an EIS repeats this point for each study area, the repetition itself emphasizes that wilderness designation will not disturb commodity development. Furthermore, given that Congress allows grazing in wilderness areas (U.S. Congress, H.R. 96-1126 [1980]), the EISs that repeat the assessment of "no impacts" throughout the analysis do so with the as- sumption that wilderness values and grazing use will coexist in the areas after their designation as wilderness. I concluded that a repeated message of "no impacts" might be best understood as an effort to defuse conflict between historical and emerging goals for public lands. Why this mes- sage was repeated more often for minerals resources than range resources is not clear. It may reflect the fact that Congress has established general allowances for grazing, but not for minerals development, in wilderness areas.

The wilderness EISs illustrate how the organizational structure of analytical documents, to- gether with decisions about what information to include in them, affects the framing of policy issues. The evidence provided in the documents is linked to the cause-effect story they tell. In the case of the wilderness EISs, as people made decisions about what information to include, Washington- based reviewers established a general principle of including only the information deemed rel- evant based on the presence of wilderness-designation impacts on study areas and resources. Some field office personnel wanted to communicate information beyond such impacts in order to recognize and address local commodity interests, such as grazing and minerals development, which have the potential to conflict with wilderness designation. Although structural changes in the draft reports produced more uniformity and potentially drew greater relative attention to wil- derness values as compared to commodity values, some field offices responded to local concerns by assessing commodity values whether or not they thought these values would be affected by wilderness designation.

To understand how the structure of the EISs and decisions about what information to include are related to policy decisions, it is necessary to examine the role of arguments in the documents.

Understanding Arguments as a Link Between Information and Recommendations—Identifying Unstated Normative Premises

In proceeding with my analysis, I took account of an additional demand from the reviewers in Washington, D.C., that the field staff treat assumptions associated with the future scenarios con- sistently. I related the implications of this demand to general patterns of argument associated with making wilderness designation recommendations. In taking this step, I also drew on data from interviews and comment memos in order to assess the logical connections between premises and conclusions within EIS arguments.

A reviewer from the OEPR said that a key problem with the draft EISs was a lack of consis- tency in the use of assumptions in the analyses (Interview 103). This concern also appears in one of the comment memos, which notes that some drafts shifted from one set of assumptions to another between and within analyses of specific study areas, resulting in a confused analytical process (Office of Environmental Project Review 1986). The reviewers asked field personnel to use a consistent set of assumptions in their study area analyses. An example illustrates how this sort of inconsistency in analysis is related to more general arguments about wilderness designation.

The reviewer indicated that an EIS should not shift assumptions by stating that wilderness designation would preclude mineral development in a study area while at the same time declaring that no mineral development would occur in that area in the absence of wilderness designation (Office of Environmental Project Review 1986, 2–3). The comment memo describes the problem in general terms and requests elimination of "unbalanced arguments" applied to the same area:

> The estimate that the effects are unlikely or that impacts "could" occur is both a waffle on the point involved and an inconsistent estimate. Developments that will be foregone or precluded by wilderness designation have to be equally treated as occurring and therefore, having impact when no-wilderness designation is involved. This analysis . . . should be examined throughout the chapter to eliminate these *unbalanced arguments*. (Office of Environmental Project Review 1986, 3; emphasis added)

Recalling that all study areas contain wilderness values by definition, this inconsistency suggests two arguments against wilderness designation based on the presence or absence of commodity resources (e.g., minerals, range [grazing]). They can be set out analytically, shown in Table 19.3 as Arguments A and B. To make the analysis clearer, I specified the reverse set of arguments that one might make to support a recommendation for wilderness designation, shown in Table 19.3 as Arguments C and D. In specifying this reversal, the two sets of arguments show the presence of double, indeterminate arguments against and in favor of recommendations for wilderness designation. They are indeterminate not only because of unstated normative premises, but also because they fail to weigh wilderness values *against* development values.

For analytical purposes, these arguments can be examined in four pairs to understand how they can be used in policy debates about wilderness designation. Arguments A and B can be paired to oppose wilderness designation irrespective of the presence of commodity resources, and arguments C and D can be paired to support wilderness designation, also irrespective of the presence of commodity resources. Although these arguments were not laid out explicitly in the EISs, it is these pairings that the OEPR highlighted in their comments about the need to use consistent assumptions within analyses for each wilderness study area.

In addition, arguments A and C can be paired where both commodity resources and wilderness values are present, and arguments B and D can be paired where only wilderness values are present. These latter two pairings are indeterminate on the question of wilderness designation. In the presence or absence of commodity resources, one can argue in favor of or against wilderness designation. The pairing of arguments A and C highlights the argument that where commodity resources and wilderness values coexist in an area, a normative position about commodity development and/or wilderness protection is *required* to arrive at a recommendation. These normative positions appear as unstated premises in Table 19.3 and were not articulated in the EISs. Where only wilderness values exist (pairing of arguments B and D), a normative position is not required on the relative value of commodity development and wilderness. However, some assessment of the purposes of wilderness designation *is* required. These normative positions also appear as unstated premises in Table 19.3 and were also not articulated in the EISs.

Taken together, these four arguments reflect the polarized context of the wilderness issue.

Table 19.3

Arguments Against and In Favor of Wilderness Designation

A. *Against* wilderness designation

Premise 1. Wilderness values are present in the area.

Premise 2: Commodity resources are present in the area.

Premise 3: Wilderness designation would prevent development of commodity resources.

(*Unstated premise: Promoting commodity development is good.*)

Conclusion: Therefore, we should not designate the area as wilderness.

B. *Against* wilderness designation

Premise 1. Wilderness values are present in the area.

Premise 2. Commodity resources are not present in the area.

Premise 3: Development impacts are unlikely.

(*Unstated premise: The purpose of wilderness designation is to protect wilderness values from development impacts.*)

Conclusion: Therefore, we should not designate the area as wilderness.

C. *In favor of* wilderness designation

Premise 1. Wilderness values are present in the area.

Premise 2: Commodity resources are present in the area.

Premise 3. Developing commodity resources would have a negative impact on wilderness values.

Premise 4: Wilderness designation would prevent development of commodity resources.

(*Unstated Premise: Protecting wilderness values from impacts of development is good.*)

Conclusion: Therefore, we should designate the the area as wilderness.

D. *In favor of* wilderness designation

Premise 1. Wilderness values are present in the area.

(*Unstated Premise: The purpose of wilderness designation is to recognize wilderness values.*)

Conclusion: Therefore, we should designate the area as wilderness.

There exist two arguments on each side of the issue, each addressing the possible scenarios with respect to the presence of commodity resources in an area. In directing field personnel to use consistent assumptions in the development of scenarios, OEPR demanded that the documents show consistent fact claims about the areas vis-à-vis the resources they contained. These fact claims were generated through technical assessments to create future scenarios. In turn, the fact claims are connected to recommendations through normative positions, not articulated in these EISs, about commodity development, wilderness protection, and the purposes of wilderness designation.

This analysis shows how normative positions are required to interpret these technical documents. It also illustrates that the technical information is related to policy recommendations in politically important ways, even if not in relationships that are statistically significant. The EISs do not explicitly articulate the value premises that underlie the conclusions of policy recommendations. The documents do draw conclusions, however, and readers are left to connect the information to the conclusions through arguments unstated in the EISs. Readers also can make different arguments and arrive at different conclusions because the technical analyses alone are insufficient to support a single conclusion.

Analysis of the EISs in terms of structure, content, and arguments demonstrates the limits of defining and treating technical analysis as separate from normative positions and politics. Examining the EISs using interpretive content analysis provides a way to describe how the technical reports serve as a mechanism for debating and, possibly, contributing to a change in the agenda for public lands policy, through technical assessments. The content analysis makes clear the value differences that lie at the core of policy debates over wilderness designation and how these value differences are reflected in the technical assessments in the EISs. It emphasizes the critical importance of examining arguments to understand how policy-relevant publics use the same scenarios to draw opposite conclusions. Such an examination shows precisely and clearly how protagonists in contentious policy debates can talk past each other because of the failure to acknowledge value differences directly.[6]

CHECKING IN WITH THE BLM

I constructed the core components of this analysis after I completed my research activities as a participant-observer in the BLM. It became one piece of my dissertation. I described how implementation of wilderness policy in the agency evolved through the phases of the wilderness review and analyzed how agency personnel made sense of this policy as they implemented it. At the same time that I was writing the dissertation to meet requirements for an academic degree, I also felt a responsibility to report my findings to BLM personnel. With respect to the EISs more specifically, I wanted to check back in with people who had read and responded to the statistical analysis. I had personal motives in doing so: I wanted closure on this topic, given my earlier experience with the reception of the statistical analysis.

This time, a positive response from informants who reviewed the findings of my interpretive analysis of the EISs indicated that I had gotten the story "right" from their perspective as agency members and actors in the setting of my study. The affirmation was important because I hoped to describe and interpret the experience of these informants as a topic of my research. My interactions in seeking this review of my analysis emphasized the recursive nature of my research. I gathered a range of perspectives from inside the agency, analyzed them using interpretive methods, and then returned to the research setting to gain input on my analysis. Because I was interpreting the ways in which people inside the setting make sense of policy, this approach provided an appropriate check on the trustworthiness of my analysis.[7]

SUMMARIZING QUESTIONS IN AN INTERPRETIVE APPROACH TO TECHNICAL DOCUMENTS

In analyzing the EISs, I examined the documents themselves and the context in which they were produced. To transfer this approach to other documents and settings that involve multiple goals and interpretations of a policy issue, it is useful to summarize some key questions that a researcher or policy analyst conducting such an analysis might ask. Although in practice analysis of documents and analysis of process intertwine, they are separated here for the sake of clarity:

Analyzing documents

- What story line(s) is (are) evident in the structure of a document? Who are the subjects and what are the objects, and what relationships between or among them does the story line convey? What dominant and subordinate themes appear?

- What information is present in and, as important, absent from the documents? What are the grounds for establishing the relevance of information? How might selected information be related to the story line and to normative positions reflecting program (or other) interests?
- What arguments and normative positions serve to connect technical information to policy decisions? What patterns exist in argumentation?
- In what ways does the framing of the issue in the documents' technical analyses highlight or deemphasize particular normative, political positions?
- How are stories and arguments in the document related to broader policy contexts?

Analyzing process

- Who made decisions about the documents (e.g., to include certain information and exclude other elements)?
- Do participants draw on similar or different logical premises, normative assessments, and policy purposes relative to the issue?
- Who produced the document, and what is the nature of their roles and relationships in the context of the document and the more general policy context?
- How was the document produced, and how does this process fit into the stream of activities in which people are engaged?

In approaching this kind of analysis, my experience suggests other things to keep in mind:

- It is important to listen to the people who are the "subject" of the research. That the statistical analysis was not fully relevant to agency experience with the EISs was readily apparent to me in light of my firsthand familiarity with the agency. In pursuing an interpretive approach, I had multiple people from whom I could hear policy- and agency-relevant stories. I also could draw on the structure of the process they used to produce the EIS documents and of the organization more generally (i.e., resource programs; field and Washington, D.C., offices) to categorize agency perspectives on these documents.
- The structure of the research question has an important influence in directing analysis. Because the research focus strongly affects what one sees in documents, it is important to consider alternative ways to interpret them. It is possible to ask oneself directly about alternatives. However, it can be difficult to step outside of one's own framing of the research. Therefore, it is important to ask others to review one's analysis. Such review can come from those who are members of the context under study, as well as from those who are outside of it. I submitted portions of this research project for review in an academic journal context, but, as important, I returned to BLM personnel with my analysis of the EISs for their review.

My experience in using an interpretive approach to analyze the wilderness EISs shows some ways to take account of multiple and potentially shifting stories that people tell to frame policy issues. The changes between the draft and final EISs can be "read" in terms of the politics and negotiations of a shifting policy agenda. This approach to analyzing technical documents illustrates how seemingly "apolitical" documents are very political, in that seemingly subtle shifts in frame can fundamentally affect the story line and information reported in the documents. It emphasizes that escape from value judgments through technical analyses is not possible.

This approach also suggests that, as researchers, our purposes and audiences may vary and that this will influence how we synthesize our analyses and place them in context. Using interpretive methods can be an iterative process that includes interactions with people in both practitioner and academic settings. These interactions can be both challenging and enriching. They can also generate dilemmas. They provide opportunities to develop deeper understandings of the questions we ask, the data we gather, the analytical approaches we use, and the interpretations we craft about policy processes.

NOTES

1. Culhane (1981) and Foss (1960) have documented the BLM's historical focus.

2. I believed it was important to share the findings of the statistical study because, as I gained access for my dissertation study, I indicated that I would share my findings. Although the statistical study was not a direct part of my dissertation work, it seemed to me that any findings I presented publicly about the agency fell into the category of information I should share.

3. These interviews were a subset of a larger group of fifty interviews from my dissertation. Interviews quoted below were part of that same set: the interview numbers refer to the numbering system that I used for the whole set of interviews for the research project.

4. Mathes and Stevenson (1991) outline eight patterns, or structures, commonly used in technical documents. These include what they term four persuasive patterns (persuasion, problem/solution, cause/effect, and comparison and contrast) and four informational patterns (analysis, description, process or instructions, and investigation).

5. It is also important to recognize that some narratives may take forms other than stories in a traditional sense. Roe (1994) notes that some narratives occur as non-stories (for example, a circular argument without a beginning, middle, and ending) and counter-stories (an alternative story to the dominant narrative).

6. I extended my analysis to consider the role of arguments in EISs where the focus of analysis is development projects and not wilderness designation (the arguments do not take the same form; Ginger 2000). This consideration of the form of arguments in EISs more generally led to insights into the role that EISs serve in framing issues in the context of multiple statutory mandates: "Where mandates conflict, the conflict is likely to appear in EISs. Where mandates coincide, EISs provide a process through which the environmental protection mandate of another statute can be promoted. This happens as political agendas are connected to the analytical reform associated with NEPA, through projection and analysis of the future" (Ginger 2000, 307).

7. Miles and Huberman (1994, 275–77) describe reasons to seek advice from informants and provide advice on how to do so.

CHAPTER 20

HOW BUILT SPACES MEAN

A Semiotics of Space

Dvora Yanow

I'm not sure what led me to focus on built spaces: No one in my family is either an architect or an engineer, although I remember paying a lot of attention to wallpaper colors and designs as an adolescent imagining redesigning my bedroom. But I have long been interested in settlement patterns and their spatial organization—my first undergrad major was Middle Eastern archaeology, and for the first course I wrote a paper on house-shaped burial urns and their relationship to cemeteries, which were located outside of residential areas.

I began my professional life (post-B.A., pre–grad school) as a community organizer in an Israeli "development town." My first assignment was to "map" the town, not only in terms of the traditional planning divisions of residential-commercial-industrial-governmental land use, but, more importantly for our purposes, in terms of which "race-ethnic" groups and socioeconomic classes lived where, where their respective synagogues and clubhouses and other gathering places were, where the competing and complementary social service agencies were, who talked to whom, and which groups and leaders were not on speaking terms. I did this by walking around—a lot. To this day, I can usually get back to someplace I've been once, without consulting a map, as long as I navigated there the first time—but I can't always tell you the street names.

I ended up doing my doctorate in the Department of Urban Studies and Planning at MIT, located in the School of Architecture and Planning. I had earlier taken a seminar in national urban development policy taught by Paul Ylvisaker (then dean of the Harvard Graduate School of Education and creator of the Ford Foundation's "grey areas" programs, which eventually became the War on Poverty programs), after making two aborted attempts at master's degrees in urban studies in Israel. There, I had been captivated by land-use planning in Israel and its history under successive Ottoman, British, and Jewish legal regimes. So somewhere in my makeup is an orientation toward spaces.

I have learned that I have an acute sense of pattern, texture, and light—more those than building materials. While in the Ph.D. program, I had a handful of close friends who attended to architecture, landscape, and interior design; interactions with them enhanced my own latent sensibilities, including my sense of color. I always go to sit in the back of a lecture hall, where I can see what's going on, and I commonly attend to who is sitting, or standing, where, whether I'm teaching, running a meeting, or observing. I pay similar attention to how space is arranged in a conference room when I'm presenting.

Whatever experiences or predilections predisposed me to be sensitive to spaces, at some point it just became "self-evident" to me that built spaces convey policy and/or organizational meanings. I just have to figure out how they do that.

[T]he dimensions of place, such as above and below, right and left,
come to be in relation to our position,
according as we turn ourselves about.
—*Aristotle* (quoted in Casey 1993, 45; italics in original)

We shape our buildings, and afterwards our buildings shape us.
—*Winston Churchill, speaking to the House of Commons* (October 28, 1943)

The typical Community Center was to be "a large building, spacious and comfortable," centrally located and easily accessible. . . . By virtue of [their] size, scale, materials, and surrounding exterior space . . . Center [buildings were] also markedly different from the town's . . . other public and residential buildings. . . . The architecture, landscaping, interior design, and furnishings of the Community Center buildings represent[ed] concepts of Western, middle-class Israeli life. . . . [In the words of their founders, they were intended to provide local residents with] "a pleasant atmosphere of social and cultural well-being which is often absent from their impoverished dwellings. . . ."
—*Dvora Yanow* (1996, chapter 6, passim)

Solvitur ambulando!
[Solve it by walking!]
—*Edward S. Casey, quoting unnamed ancient Romans* (1997, 224)

Political philosophers, policy makers, and politicians from Aristotle to Churchill have been attuned to the role of built space and its uses in communicating and shaping meaning; but with rare exception, this has not been the subject of contemporary empirical analysis or methods textbooks outside of those place-oriented social sciences such as anthropology, human (social) geography, environmental design, planning, and community organization.[1] The reasons for this omission are speculative. Spaces are so much around us that they seem to recede into the taken-for-granted backdrop of cognizance, except for those people, such as architects, designers, planners, and dancers, who are, in some innate or educated way, attuned to moving in and through space and who command space-oriented vocabularies. In addition, so much of our comprehension of and response to built space and other artifacts is tacit knowledge (in M. Polanyi's sense, 1966) that is made explicit only with great difficulty. Finally, its omission from academic analyses also has to do, at least in part, with the heritage of the mind-body distinction and separation and with ideas about science and knowledge. The taboo placed in Western society on bodies (linked to the mind-body separation) likely extends to studying spaces or making their role explicit[2]—if, indeed, built spaces are spatialized, projected bodies whose study requires researchers' attention to their own bodies as they move through space, as argued here.

Conceptions of what constitutes science also likely contribute to the disinclination to engage spatial issues. The universality with respect to person, time, and place that methodological positivism embeds in scientific laws or principle scatches researchers in its sway, rendering them conceptually interchangeable: This is what makes it possible for them, by definition, to generate valid data. That universality is likely to turn a blind eye as well toward place as a contextualizing element, including what David Livingstone (2003, 1) has called the "geographies of science." He describes the invention of the scientific laboratory as "a conscious effort to create a 'placeless' place" for the conduct of science (Livingstone 2003, 3).[3] Furthermore, Fyfe and Law (1988, 6) link the mind-body distinction to "visual marginalisation" in social science: "[W]hen the body was deleted from social theory, so, too, was the eye," leading most social scientists to be "blinded to the visual" and, hence, to the "social character of perception and reproduction" (i.e., representation). The absence of reflective methodological attention to space, too (outside of place-oriented sciences), is understandable in this light.

In this chapter, I explore how an analysis of built space might proceed, focusing on some of the conceptual aspects of such analysis. I speak of built space, rather than buildings or space, in order to emphasize both the human role in shaping the spaces we traverse and the diversity of the kinds of spaces that communicate social-political-cultural meanings. "Built" space encompasses landscapes, including those that surround and "contain" governmental, educational, corporate, domestic, and other types of buildings. It also includes wildernesses or "ordinary landscapes" (Meinig 1979), which are neither empty nor "virgin" (H.N. Smith 1957; see also Nash 1967). In analyzing built space I assume a hermeneutic relationship (as described in chapter 1) between elements of spatial design and the meaning making of their designers and users. In detailing a method for the analysis of spatial meanings, I am seeking to articulate that semiotic relationship and explore its attributes.[4]

My appreciation for and analysis of built space is also informed by a critical phenomenology. Phenomenology's orientation toward the "lifeworld" (as discussed in chapter 1) is hospitable toward the idea that "place grounds our subjective, embodied experience" (R. Malone 2003, 2318; see also Casey 1993, 1997). The critical dimension adds the understanding that in shaping behavior and acts, spaces may enact power relationships existing between some users and others (e.g., designers, policy makers, organizational executives). As R. Malone notes, "All human relationships have spatial aspects . . ., [both] because we are material beings with bodies that move and have volume, [and] because our proximity to or distance from others and from places [has] meaning for us" (2003, 2317). Studying space makes clear that it does more than just "contain" bodies and their activities. Space is not neutral. As Churchill so well understood, their physical setting also "orders and manages human activities; it distributes bodies in a certain space" (Kornberger and Clegg 2004), and so perforce entails power relations.[5] In this vein, Hajer notes, for example, with respect to difficulties in participatory politics, "[I]t is not so much participation itself that is the problem, but the very [physical] conditions under which the exchange of ideas has *to take place*" (2005, 625, emphasis added). At the same time, humans moving through and using built spaces are not without agency. A phenomenological orientation adds an iterative cyclicality missing from Churchill's couplet: We, the actors in his statement, are not only subject to our spatial designs once we have created them; we maintain agency, and we can, and do, act on our spaces. "Afterward" has no finality.

The study of space in social, political, organizational, and cultural contexts is, then, a unique research site from a methodological perspective in that it combines both phenomenological and hermeneutic elements. I shall not argue further for the importance of space in shaping and understanding human action. For those in need of additional persuasion, the works cited in note 1 provide ample evidence. In what follows, I discuss the centrality of the researcher's body to the study of built spaces, both in the way that spatial meaning making entails the kinesthetic movement of bodies in space and in the ways in which spatial design recapitulates bodily design. Analytic taxonomies drawing on theatrical metaphors that see settings for human action as stages suggest where to look for space data and what to look for. The role of the researcher's body in discovery suggests the potential utility of nonverbal communication categories for analyzing data in both the kinesthetic stage of fieldwork and the more sedentary stage of deskwork.

STUDYING BUILT SPACES

In contexts of "doing," such as policy implementation, court hearings, or parliamentary debates, language rarely works alone to communicate meaning. Research in nonverbal communication suggests that words convey as little as 7 percent of the meaning in an interpersonal exchange (Mehrabian 1972). The rest is conveyed through two other categories of artifacts: acts—such as gestures, facial expressions, posture—and objects—the physical artifacts we create and vest with meaning and through which we communicate collective values, beliefs, and feelings. Among physical artifacts are the spaces in which words are spoken and read and in which people act and interact, as well as the things that populate those spaces, to which words refer and that acts engage. Studying built spaces as settings for action may also include analyzing their furnishings, decor, landscaping, and other space-related artifacts, as well as the uses people put them to and how "users" negotiate spatial meanings.

Studying spaces and other physical artifacts with a focus on their role in meaning and its communication typically rests on several methodological presuppositions. One is the representational relationship posited by hermeneutics between meaning—values, beliefs, and/or feelings—and the artifacts people create that embody them. As chapter 1 notes, meaning and artifact stand in a symbolic relationship to one another: The artifact is understood to be the more concrete representation of the more abstract, underlying meaning(s). This semiotic approach looks to investigate the meanings that built spaces represent (see, e.g., Gottdiener and Lagopoulos 1986). Analysis might investigate such things as function- or purpose-oriented design (such as the way an interior cavity is broken up and areas are designated for specific usages), materials, appurtenances, and "climate" or "ambient environment" (Baldry 1999). In studying policy, organizational, communal, occupational, and/or other collective meanings, the researcher is typically interested less in meanings that artifacts hold for separate individuals than in meanings shared among members of interpretive communities, such as social and/or economic classes, "race-ethnic" groups, organizations (or divisions or departments), neighborhoods, or some other community of meaning and practice. To access such meanings, the researcher seeks to identify the character, the "feel," of the space and artifacts commonly used in that situation, event, or practice, inquiring into their significance in context-specific terms to situational members and/or other situation- or setting-relevant audiences or stakeholders.

Such inquiry entails interpretation (as also discussed in chapter 1)—a second central presupposition: Meaning cannot merely be perceived and grasped. Inquiry constitutes an intentional "reaching" for the other's meaning. This has a particular aspect in space analysis: Because of its three-dimensional character and because space is experienced bodily, the intentional effort to understand what it means to another entails a projective imagining that draws on the researcher's own experience of the space. I return to this below.

Interpretive researchers, then, are dealing with both "primary" and "secondary" interpretations: Their knowledge claims come from reflective sense making of *their own experiences* of being in others' spatial worlds, as well as from interpreting others' firsthand spatial experiences (themselves "primary" interpretations) as these are narrated to or observed by them (including reading accounts of such experiences as a form of observation). (This is the double hermeneutic noted by Giddens and discussed by Mark Bevir and Patrick Jackson in their respective chapters, this volume.) Both researcher and researched are situated entities: The meaning making of and meanings made by both are contextualized by prior knowledge, including of history and surrounding elements (other events, other experiences)—a third central presupposition.[6] This situatedness has several implications for the character of interpretive research and its practices.

Presupposing the context specificity of meaning implies that spatial "realities" may be construed differently by different people, because of the different "a priori's" they bring to present-day events and circumstances. Meaning is culturally and/or situationally specific, whether at national, regional or local, or departmental, organizational or industry levels.[7] Living in a social world of potentially multiple "realities" and multiple interpretations means that a researcher needs to be aware of the wide variety of "users" of a research-relevant space, both near and far (for example, readers of an annual report containing photographs of organizational headquarters). Moreover, researchers must be very cautious about assuming that a spatial design carries the same meaning for all of these audiences and users. As with other interpretive methods, although the researcher uses himself as an "instrument" of research, interpretations are always provisional, held up for confirmation or disconfirmation against evidence from other observations, documents, and/or conversations, and subject to corroboration, or refutation, by members of the situation under study.[8]

ACCESSING SPACE DATA

In beginning to think about a research question involving space, researchers need to identify both the settings and/or the situations that are potential sources of space data and the processes for accessing them.

Inquiry processes: Where to look, what to look for? Various categories that were developed initially for dramaturgical and literary analyses, along with theatrical metaphors used in social science, highlight the performative dimensions of space design and its use. They are helpful in space analysis in directing researchers' attention beyond the scaffolding and sheathing that is readily present for viewing.

Burke's analogy to drama (1969 [1945]; see also Feldman 1995; Gusfield 1989) yields a useful set of categories for provoking reflection about where to locate meaning-focused data in an action context. He proposed analyzing human action in terms of the "scene" or setting, as well as the agent, act, agency, and purpose (corresponding to the where, the who, the what, the how, and the why of the episode or event; I return to acts below).

Implicated in Burke's five-part category set is a sixth that emerged later in literary theory concerning the locus of meaning. Earlier theories had debated whether textual meaning resides in the texts themselves (see, e.g., Ciardi 1959—in this case, the analogy is to building design and attendant objects—or in the author's intent (here, designers and/or those commissioning the space). Reader-response theories (e.g., Iser 1989) render this binary relationship problematic by introducing the idea that readers bring their own interpretive lenses to their readings of texts. This is the missing sixth element in Burke's schema: the audience (or reader) beyond the so-called fourth wall of the stage. Moving beyond intended authorial or designers' meanings and the materials themselves to include users' interpretations is a central third dimension of spatial analysis.

One of the central presuppositions of interpretive analysis emerges in such an approach: In according agency also to "audiences" of a communicative act, interpretations of meaning-in-action extend analysis beyond what was intended by the initiator of the communication—in the case of built spaces, their designers and/or the clients commissioning the design. This expanded view of meaning making parallels the critique of earlier sender-receiver-noise models of communication as overly simplistic (see, e.g., Neuman, Just, and Crigler 1992; L. Putnam and Pacanowsky 1983). According agency to readers–audience members of intended, "authored" meanings—such as the users of an architect-designed parliamentary building—moves them from the more passive-reactive role in which they or their behaviors are seen only as being shaped by the space, to a more active one, in which they, too, are perceived as acting on built spaces, modifying them, rejecting their intended uses, and so forth.[9] In light of the inherent possibilities for multiple interpretations (given divergent prior experience, background, education, and so on), such an approach focuses attention on the possibility of tensions among situational members' interpretations, including those between designers and users, between authored meaning and constructed meaning. This potential multiplicity of meaning needs to be explored in any interpretive analysis.

The dramatistic metaphor as invoked by Goffman (1959) is more psychological. In distinguishing between front and back stages in individual self-presentation, he attends to the ways in which individuals highlight some aspects of self while relegating others to a less publicly available arena (or at least intending to do so, with varying degrees of success). The four-cell "Johari window" of Joseph Luft and Harry Ingham (Luft 1963) provides a more nuanced elaboration of this distinction. They point out that individuals know some things about themselves and some are known to others; but in addition, people at times seek to hide things from others that they know about themselves, and there are other aspects of identity that may not be known even to the individual. In other words, individuals are aware of the "public self" that they are presenting on the "front stage," but observers may also see elements of which the person being observed is unaware (the "blind self" in the Johari window). Similarly, individuals are aware of the "private self" of elements they seek to keep "backstage."[10]

The front stage–back stage distinction is less a comment on architectural design—architects, after all, intentionally build in spaces for storage and support activities (usually); this is typically an explicit part of the client conversation. Rather, it is a comment on the usage of space: governmental buildings that house activities intended to be kept out of sight or "below the radar" (figuratively, if not literally) or areas within a built space that an organization determines are not part of the public "face" that they want to put on their activities. At the same time, it can be a comment on space users' readings of intended design meanings: Users may in fact be aware, even if only tacitly (until asked to reflect on them), of organizational executives' intentions for spatial design even when the latter think they are hidden from public view. The siting and extent of difference between back and front stage spaces can be critical elements of an analysis, as can the variety of front and back stages in any study—their types, the degrees of differentiation between them, their relationships to each other, the "assignment" of certain types or degrees of stage to certain groups of people, and so on.[11]

What this discussion points to is the fact that the various "inhabitants" of a built space may find themselves negotiating among disparate, if not discordantly divergent, meanings of those spaces. Ellen Pader's analyses (e.g., 1993, 1994b) of the conflict between culturally based norms embedded in U.S. residential occupancy codes and the norms of some occupants, or Sandra Stein's analysis (2004) of teachers' and children's at times conflicting uses of school spaces—for example, in "lining up for integration" for ESEA Title I implementation purposes—provide examples of the intricacies of the negotiation of spatial meanings.

These several categories can help a researcher think about where to look to access data in a spatial study, and what to look for.

Inquiry processes: How to look? The primary research mode for accessing spatial data is to walk in front of, around, and through the built spaces that are the settings for one's study. This statement may appear so self-evident as to go without saying. From a phenomenological point of view, that would be the case; and yet this can be a novel idea for researchers who have not given much thought to the fact that spaces and other physical artifacts may play a role in their subject of study.[12] In his discussion of Kant, Whitehead, Husserl, and Merleau-Ponty, Casey establishes the solid grounding in their work for the view that "the lived body is the origin of 'spatializing' as well as 'spatialized' space" (1997, 230). For both Husserl and Merleau-Ponty, kinesthesia—bodily movement through space—produces that space (Casey 1997, 229; see also Weisman 1992, 11–15).[13] The precise meanings that spaces have, however, vary across cultures, as discussed below.

Researchers often access space data, then, initially, through observing and engaging or using the spaces and their props themselves and observing others' uses, with follow-up conversational interviewing and/or reading to check the researcher's provisional inferences. Although moving through space is the primary mode of study, it is not necessarily always the first mode, chronologically. In some cases a point made in an interview or a comment written in an organizational memo can draw the researcher's attention to the significance of a built-space element to a research question. An extended example from my own field research in the Israel Corporation of Community Centers (ICCC) (Yanow 1996) illustrates this process. That research drew on all three modes of accessing data (observing, conversational interviewing, and the close reading of documents); data generated through one process suggested inquiry to pursue through the others.

A second phase of research followed five years after the initial, extended participant-observer stage. During that phase, at the same time that I was reading memos, correspondence, annual reports, and other written materials in ICCC archives to see how founders and others talked about organizational purposes, I was engaged in extensive conversational interviewing with founders and staff and observation of local center (*matnas*) programs. During the first phase, I had, among other research activities, used the matnas building where I was located in various ways: walking through and past it between the town center and the marketplace; entering, ordering a coffee, and sitting in the lounge area to drink it; visiting the library, offices, classrooms, and other areas; talking to or folk dancing with or partying with other staff and visitors (client-customers, professional counterparts from other agencies, volunteers, etc.) in these spaces, and so forth. All the while I was watching and listening to others—staff, residents, and visitors of all ages, occupations, "race-ethnicities," and other "classes"—who entered and engaged the space, talking with them about what they were doing there and what they thought and felt about that—in short, "indwelling" with them in everyday sorts of ways following the dictates of my participant role as community organizer. "Engaging" with the built spaces also entailed engaging with other physical artifacts in them, such as the furnishings, paintings, books, matnas programs, and so on (as well as with two other categories of data, acts and language; Yanow 1992a, 1996).

As I embarked on the second phase of the research, then, I felt I was intimately familiar with the building in terms of the purposes (activities, classes, programs, meetings, and other activities) its design was intended to accommodate, but I had not thought much about it as an artifact communicating meaning. Reading in the archives one day, I came upon copies of a few letters written by the then chairman of the board, which referred to the design of the matnas buildings overall. These letters made reference to the buildings' central location, scale, building materials, specific design elements (kinds of rooms, for example), and the fact that useful models for community center construction—they were a relatively new concept in Israel—existed in the United States. Not long after that, I set out to interview the director of a community center in a city I'd never been to. As I entered the city, I thought to head toward the area of the city hall and the open-air market and to look for a "matnas kind of building"—although in that moment I could not have spelled out what that meant. I found the center in moments.

This observational experience—in particular, my diffuse sense that there indeed was such a thing as a "matnas kind of building"—led me to the reflection, some days later, that the design was, in fact, both distinctive and common to the *matnassim* (plural) I had seen in different locales. Trying to make explicit to myself what that distinctiveness entailed led me to review the chairman's letters and to consider that his comments were not solely articulations of his personal aesthetic sensibility and values, but rather that he was expressing the collective intent of the ICCC founders to convey, through the design of the matnas spaces, certain collectively held values, beliefs, and feelings. These "organizational" meanings, held by both board members and agency staff, comprised the agency's internal identity and the image it desired to project externally; and they were being expressed, in speech and writing as well as in built materials, to several different, very specific publics, among them clients, other organizations (local, national, and international), and potential donors (also local, national, and international). I learned subsequently through other sources that these intended meanings were by and large being "read" (not always uncritically) by agency-relevant publics near and far, including many would-be clients. Here, as I came much later to see, were enacted both hermeneutic and phenomenological principles concerning the artifact-meaning relationship in the context of the organization's life-world and its collective "Self."

Some time after this site visit, I found articulated in letters written by other board members the same relationship among specific design elements, underlying meanings, and intentional communication to a broad spectrum of "readers" of these built spaces, confirming my provisional interpretation. Two of these letters, in particular, linked these meanings to intended changes in client behavior. Subsequent conversations (including formal interviews) with founding and later board members, ICCC staff, staff of other agencies, local residents, more distant publics, and others confirmed this desire and intent (as suggested by the epigraph taken from that analysis) and indicated how these intended meanings were perceived and understood by others (Yanow 1996). All of this generated field notes for subsequent deskwork, when I began to make sense of the observations, conversations, interactions, correspondence, and so forth in a more explicitly analytic mode. It also corroborated my provisional sense making that organizational meanings were being communicated through the buildings themselves. But how was this happening?

ANALYZING SPACE DATA: SPACE AS NONVERBAL COMMUNICATION

Space data (and other physical artifacts) may be elements in an ethnomethodological, symbolic-interactionist, or some other interpretive analysis (see, e.g., Feldman 1995), or they may be the exclusive concern of research seeking to establish the ways in which spatial elements communicate contextually specific meaning (see, e.g., Goodsell 1988; Pader 1993, 1994b; Yanow 1993, 1998). I take the latter as my focus here.

Built spaces, as with other objects, may be literally mute, but they have their own vocabulary or "language" (of building materials, size, scale, mass, color, shape, proximity to surroundings, appurtenances, and other design elements) through which they articulate properties, identities, values, and so on without recourse to words. Much in the way that humans communicate through nonverbal means, built spaces (and other objects) communicate their artifactual meanings nonverbally, through these design vocabularies. As experience and meaning making of built space initially invoke bodily and affective responses rather than cognitive and linguistic ones, insights and categories from research in nonverbal communication (such as those discussed below) are useful analytically in suggesting how this takes place. And much as some people are more adept than others at "reading" nonverbal human behavior, some are more attuned to "reading" built spaces and other physical artifacts (although enhancing such abilities is possible in both instances).[14]

Moreover, it is not just that we experience built spaces and other physical artifacts initially through nonverbal, physical-kinesthetic means: feeling on and through our bodies the mass and scale and ambient environment—the "airiness" and lighting characteristics—of the oversized, glass-paned entryway into the new parliament building; seeing the award plaque hanging on the wall and perceiving its shape, color, size, and so forth before reading the text. In many respects, human design of built spaces appears to recapitulate human bodily experience, as noted by phenomenologists, social geographers, and linguists. Tuan (1977, chapter 4), G. Lakoff and Johnson (1980), Weisman (1992), and others have remarked on the orientational aspects of language and their connoted meanings: high-low, up-down, front-back, central-peripheral, and so forth.[15] "These spatial orientations," wrote Lakoff and Johnson, "arise from the fact that we have bodies of the sort we have and that they function as they do in our physical environment" (1980, 14). To the extent that acts and language are interrelated, built spaces may "embody" meaning in a quasi-literal as well as a figurative sense.

Drawing on their work, Casey (1993) notes that the binary character of our bodily structure establishes a set of dyadic relationships—up-down, right-left, above-below, near-far—in ways that both arrange and constrain our choices, directions, and movements: "Even as it acts to project a field of possible actions, my body closes down the prospect of unlimited choice. Hence, it poses to itself constantly (even if often only implicitly) determinate choices between, say, going forward and re-treating. Being in the center of things, my body can always move here *or* there, up *or* down, this way *or* that" (1993, 48; emphasis in original). Reflecting on the observations of key phenomenologists,[16] he concludes that "the directionality inherent in the lived body in place precedes the dimensionality of inert matter in space" (1993, 50). From a phenomenological perspective, "I am here in/as my body. *You* are here, too, in and with your body. . . . Thus it is by my body—my lived body—that I am here" (1993, 50–1; emphasis in original). Seeing built spaces as recapitulating our experiences of our bodies opens paths for analysis, as illustrated in the next section.

Researchers' understandings of built space draw on human bodily experience in another way. Because of the nonverbal character of spatial communication (including furnishings and other attendant physical artifacts), in particular, and because of the highly tacit nature (in M. Polanyi's, 1966, sense) of members' knowledge of the meaning(s) being communicated, researchers commonly use their own responses—affective, behavioral, and especially kinesthetic—as proxy for others' interpretations in formulating provisional inferences about how buildings mean (Yanow 2000, chapter 4). As Casey puts it, we "have reliable orientational knowledge . . . thanks to our 'knowing body'" (1993, 52). Van Maanen extends the point further, noting, with respect to eth-nography, "[T]he self is the instrument of research" (1996, 380).[17] It is the orientational character of the human body, along with its perceptual elements, that lies at the center of the claim that we come to appreciate built spaces, both as ordinary users and as researchers, through our bodies' moving in and through those spaces.

Aside from the fact that spatial meanings are communicated nonverbally, several other ana-lytic categories used in the study of nonverbal communication (e.g., Mehrabian 1972; Weitz 1974) lend themselves to analyzing physical settings. These direct our focus toward:

1. the "vocabulary" of design elements and construction materials and the ambient environ-ment these create (corresponding to the nonverbal categories of physical characteristics, such as height or body type, and personal decoration, such as clothing, jewelry, etc.);[18]

2. design "gestures" that use design vocabularies to communicate relationships, such as affect and status displays (corresponding to the nonverbal category of kinesics, facial expressions and hand gestures that do the same);
3. proxemics, the uses of spatial proximity and distance;
4. "decor" itself.[19]

The categories focus analytic attention on different ways in which built spaces may communicate meaning(s), suggesting the kinds of spatial elements (symbols or signs) the researcher might analyze. Symbols, processes, and the meanings themselves are highly culturally and contextually specific.

Design Vocabularies

Design vocabularies include such things as shape, height, width, and mass; materials (glass, wood, cement, stone, shingle, etc.) and their color, tone, and texture; landscaping; the quality of light and dark, airiness and coziness; and so on. The historical or aesthetic reference points of architectural design (e.g., classical Greco-Roman columns, modernist styling), the "labeling" of rooms and spaces and their designation as "appropriate" to certain activities,[20] and the values, beliefs, or feelings they represent and evoke are also included here.

Analysis of design vocabulary is often comparative, sometimes explicitly so: Whether a building, a courtyard, or a reception area, a usage designation is analyzed in light of the concern, explicit or implicit, "As opposed to what?" It is a situationally specific comparison of similarities and differences. For example, in trying to understand the significance of the community center design to clients and potential clients at various socioeconomic levels living in different parts of town, I compared the design elements used in those buildings with the elements used in other buildings affiliated with other organizations, public and private, intended to serve similar purposes in the same locale (so, the same geographic and socioeconomic context, but varying the organizational type); with other public buildings serving various purposes (i.e., varying the program type); and with surrounding residences of various types. The contrasts highlighted the features that were unique to the center buildings, both externally—size, scale, mass, materials (glass, stone), and siting—and internally—ceiling heights, furnishings (upholstered armchairs), and decorative elements (reproductions of Impressionist paintings).

Design vocabularies are usefully analyzed in terms of their meanings in a broader societal or cultural context. These meanings may be attributed to the occupants of the spaces marked by these elements. So, for example, in cultures in which quantity is an indicator of status, designs entailing great expense may be read with similar meaning. In the United States, the greater the number or the costlier the quality of furnishings, or the better the quality of construction materials, or the larger the space, the higher the rank or other status (typically) of the occupant relative to others in a similar grouping (e.g., town residents or an occupational grouping). (In organizations, equivalent rank or status is also attributed to the occupant's secretary relative to other secretaries.) And vice versa: Lesser quality space and less-costly design elements are typically assigned to occupants of lower rank and status. As rank is commonly correlated with power, this spatial association is what makes for the seeming anomaly and ensuing surprise at the discovery that persons with lesser rank and its spatial and other artifactual associations—in an organizational setting, for example, the ground-floor receptionist, the mail sorter in the basement, tech support on the lower floor, or the janitor whose "office" is a closet—may be centers of power (in these cases, due to their respective commands of information, in some cases correlated with physical location).

Interpretations of such meanings echo those of physical bodies and the cultural values attached to their various parts. In many cultures height, broad shoulders, and an erect posture, in a man, are read as signs of physical power and financial or social stature.[21] How much space a building or other built space—an office, for instance—takes up is often read similarly as a statement of power through taking up space. Building height is a common vocabulary element in this; breadth—square footage—works in a similar way.

It is common in the United States and in other Western countries, for instance, to "read" the top floor office as a symbol of its occupant's high status within the organization. Humans "embody" vertical, erect bodies; Western society values reason and the rational, which are seen as brain activities; brains reside at the topmost position of our bodies; and so we position quarters for the *heads* of our *corpor*ations and *organi*zations—those at the heights of hierarchy (itself part of this conceptual configuration), control, income, and therefore economic, social, and organizational power—at the tops of our buildings. Such correlations play out in community and residential planning as well. In class discussions,[22] students familiar with Oakland, California, topography and socioeconomic conditions will note the local distinction between the wealthier "hill dwellers" and the poorer or working class "flatlanders." Some correlate this privileging of "up" or "top"-ness with God's "residence" in the heavens.

People from cultural backgrounds other than the United States or Western Europe often interpret spatial meanings in other ways.[23] An Indian colleague noted that executive offices in Indian organizations are more typically located on the ground or second through the sixth floors (or were in the 1980s when these particular observations were made). With little, no, or inconsistent electricity and nonexistent or unpredictable elevators, office space on floors easily accessible by foot is more desirable than a grand view (Mazumdar 1988, III-145). Here, too, however, there may be a body-centered, cultural, or meaning-focused explanation for such a design choice, one that draws on Hindu traditions. The Upanishads relate that the center of human consciousness lies just below a hand's span from where the lowest ribs converge. Also, according to the legend, the world (in the form of a lotus blossom) sprang from the god Vishnu's navel while he slept. For a culture that locates the soul in the center of the body and values it (rather than the head) as the source of humanness, it makes less sense for corporate headquarters to be at the heights of buildings (Yanow 1993).

A Ghanaian student seconded Mazumdar's analysis, indicating that there, also, having one's office on the highest floor would signal that the occupant was of relatively low status. She further noted that only poorer Ghanaians lived in the hills because hill residents had to walk longer distances from the downtown markets, carrying heavy bundles on their heads. Moreover, in Ashanti culture, she said, gods are in the earth as well, and libations are poured to them on the ground. Her American classmates' association of height with the heavens and God and human social status perplexed her.

Design "Gestures"

Whereas the analysis of design vocabularies treats their meanings in the context of the society or culture in which they are situated, analysis of design gestures examines vocabularies in the context of the immediate surroundings of the built space in question. Invoking the language of gesture might appear to suggest that buildings or parts of them actively undertake to move, quite aside from a more reactive swaying in strong winds or in earthquakes. In design terms, however, buildings are treated as being in relationship to their surrounding spaces, built and otherwise. Such relationships, whether affirming or negating, are suggested through the use of design vocabularies: recapitulating the roofline, materials, or colors of a nearby building is seen as giving the nod, metaphorically, to spatial predecessors (whether historical or present) and, through the use of complementary design elements, seeking to take a place among them; ignoring those elements and using contrasting ones that bear no relationship to them "turns the back" on the surrounding neighborhood. These inferred meanings are often attributed to the organization that owns, built, and/or occupies the space.

Contrasts of height, mass, quality of materials, and the like may be read as status and/or authority gestures, and such inferences are typically attributed by spatial users and other research-relevant publics to the organization that arranged for the design and construction or the retrofit. An organization that designs and constructs a new building that "towers" over its immediate surroundings or, at a geographic remove, over others in its industry may be read as intending to signal its higher status relative to those of neighboring organizations or competitors. Such a marked difference in height is especially visible when a built area leaves large amounts of surrounding property unbuilt and open to view. In this and other circumstances, the contrast might be seen as intending to convey a "hands-off" unapproachability.

Proxemics

A third analytic approach draws on E. Hall's (1966) notion of proxemics—the social and personal spaces between people, and perceptions of those spaces, that implicitly and tacitly shape human behavior and interaction. Hall determined that there were different, culturally specific zones of distance within which different types of relationship were enacted: intimate, personal, business, and public, in an ever-widening use of space, and each potentially with internal variations. Whereas analysis of design gestures looks at what is conveyed through the elements of design vocabularies of individual spaces, proxemic analysis looks specifically at the spatial relationship or orientation of a built space (or part of one) to others in the immediate area.

As with spatial gestures, this is a relational view that sees built spaces not as stand-alone entities, but within a broader setting, as parts of a "neighborhood," so to speak. Whereas gestures involve material design elements, proxemic analysis considers the vocabularies of proximity, siting, and interval: setbacks (from the street, from the sides, at the back, as relevant), spatial surrounds used (open, inviting spaces; walls or other barriers), approaches and activities encouraged or prohibited by these (a broad, open expanse with glass doors might encourage passers-by to enter, whereas other design elements might signal that only those who have business inside should enter)—all in the context of culturally specific meanings.

Much as Hall found that people feel uncomfortable with strangers encroaching on their "personal" space (eighteen inches to four feet, in the North American norm), a sense of discomfort may arise for the person who has to traverse a passage between buildings that are experienced as being too close to each other, maneuver in office spaces that are too constraining of movement, and so forth. The discomfort may be experienced by onlookers as well as participants. Conversely, a room that is felt as being too large for the activity it contains may also be experienced as uncomfortable by those gathered in it (e.g., depending on the cultural norm, a hall designed to accommodate 120 people being used for a meeting of 15).

As noted above, a building's command of space is associated with power much in the same way that the amount of space human bodies command is. In proxemic terms, this observation might extend to a built area that leaves large amounts of surrounding property unbuilt and open to view. Religious or governmental buildings in Europe and in North America that stand alone on expansive boulevards without encroaching buildings are widely perceived as displaying status and power. Mosse's (1975) analysis of the architecture of Third Reich buildings or Lasswell's (1979) study of U.S. governmental buildings are two examples of such analyses.

Decor

Lastly, built spaces may be analyzed with respect to their "decor" or furnishings, using that term broadly to encompass not only desks, chairs, and other furniture proper, but also displays of artwork, family photographs, jokes and cartoons, signage, and the like. Even uniforms could be considered an element of decor (such as at Disneyland; Van Maanen 1991): One might argue that the general dress code, including hairstyles and facial hair, rather than being an aspect of personal, individual choice, was externalized, objectified, and collectivized as part of the organizational decor communicating organizational meanings (see, e.g., M.G. Pratt and Rafaeli 1997; Rafaeli et al. 1997).

As with other analytic categories, these four elements are usefully distinct for analytic purposes: Each highlights different features of built spaces used in the communication of meaning, and the analytic separation imparts some conceptual and procedural systematicity to such studies. In practice they may overlap, as when analysis of the meanings communicated to and read by various publics explores the interplay of design vocabularies, gestures, and proxemics. In the community center case, analysis of the meanings conveyed through design gestures, proxemics, and decor supported the assessment of the meanings communicated through materials and other design vocabularies, as well as, in the larger study, through organizational and societal acts and language. In short, there is an "intertextuality" operative in spatial meanings: Much as words get their meanings from other words, sentences from other sentences, passages and entire texts from other passages and texts, spatial elements develop meaning from other spatial elements.[24]

MAKING SENSE OF SPACES

Settings for human action are, then, neither empty nor neutral. Through various ways, they communicate meaning(s). Moreover, although built spaces act on people in shaping behavior and action, they are not necessarily determinative of them: According agency to their users means recognizing that users can "act back" on others' designs. Attention to all of this is part of the researcher's sense making in spatial analysis; and the sense making has to be sensitive to the situational, contextual, and cultural specificity of meaning.

Although the distinction between methods of accessing data and methods for analyzing them is analytically neat, in practice, analytic categories inform the ways one looks at built spaces, including the kinds of data one looks for. In accessing, generating, and analyzing data, a context-specific comparative analysis of similarity and difference is central. What made the centers' design distinctiveness stand out was the sharp contrast of their design vocabulary with other buildings serving similar purposes, other public buildings, and local residences. The clearest answer to the question "How do built spaces mean?" may be: through relationships of similarity and difference to their surroundings. These comparative elements become occasions for inquiry; the central analytic question is, "The same or different with respect to what?" The appropriate analytic comparison may not become evident until one has dwelled with one's data for some time—in the community center case, drawing on metaphor analysis in combination with space analysis and finding appropriate comparisons in corner grocery stores and public libraries from the perspective of their purposes and uses (Yanow 2000)—and the comparative case(s) may then suggest new ways of seeing, new data to access, and new questions to explore.

In the community center example, when local residents engaged the centers' design elements and/or interior spaces (e.g., in moving through them), this engagement staged a nonverbal interaction between the values embedded in those spaces—values of a particular socioeconomic class and its cultural practices, and hence societal status—and their own. As suggested by the epigraph, although local residents were, by and large, of a different (lower) class and status, they nonetheless read ICCC founders' intended meanings in the center buildings and responded to them. Data from other, nonspatial areas of the organization (written documents and conversational interviews) supported this argument (Yanow 1996). Such interaction takes place regardless of whether the engagement is passive, reactive, or proactive (that is, whether people note the spaces while passing by en route to another destination, through physical entry, or through actual use of the space).

Presupposing that we do live in a world of potentially multiple meanings, and possibly conflicting ones at that, underscores the necessity of exploring design elements from the perspective of each research-relevant audience or group of "readers." It is crucial not to assume uniformity of meaning, that founders' or designers' (architects', CEOs') intended meanings are those that are read in the built spaces by other members of the organization, or that researchers' own personal responses to the space or its appurtenances are shared by organizational members. Different stakeholder groups—different "interpretive communities," "discourse communities," "communities of meaning"—may interpret artifacts differently. These groups may fall along occupational or professional lines, in "communities" of practitioners (Orr 1992); they may develop along geographic or consociational lines or axes of spatial proximity (an executive and her secretary, for instance), such that their locational viewpoint creates a community of shared meaning, despite the fact that members conduct disparate practices; or some other setting- or extra-situational element may occasion shared interpretive perspectives.

This caveat is especially critical when there are differences of power and/or authority between designers and those for whom they design, on the one hand, and intended users of the intended design, on the other. As Edelman (1964, 96) noted, a space that seeks to convey or reinforce such status distinctions "focuses constant attention upon the difference . . .," creating in the participant a "heightened sensitivity" to "connotations . . . [and] authority." The directed design and use of space in this way is often found in government agencies, such as social welfare, automobile licensing, and "justice" offices (jails, courthouses, police departments), as well as in some manufacturing plants or other settings that bring management and labor together in a single space. In addition, in assessing users' experiences of built spaces with respect to the intended meanings of designers and/or their clients, the researcher needs to know whether a building or space was designed for the organization using it or for some other occupant and purpose and retrofitted or taken over for "re-use" by that organization. The research question and setting might also call for attending to the distinction between those who use the built space and those who observe it from a distance, whether near (as passersby) or far. The relative familiarity and comfort of some users with particular spaces may be another analytic element.

The most difficult part of studying space, especially for a researcher without an orientation toward spatial design, is acquiring the habit of moving spatial elements front and center in the analysis, out of the backdrop for actors and activities, agency and purpose. In studying built spaces—where the data are the bricks and mortar, so to speak—analysis proceeds by "translating" the visual vocabularies and sensate experiences that are space data into words and verbal categories (e.g., size and scale, stone and glass, blue and green, light and airy). Even photographs, maps, sketches or other forms of representation that are used to portray the spaces do not stand alone: Analysis is mediated by a descriptive narrative that turns visual data into words, rendering the artifact a particular form of "text analogue" (Taylor 1971; see also Casey 2002; Fyfe and Law 1988; Latour 1999; M. Lynch and Woolgar 1990a; and T. Mitchell 1991 on maps and other representations).

Analysis, then, is already one step removed from immediate experience: The experience of space and its meanings is initially one of bodily sensations evoked by visual and spatial elements; initial firsthand, nonverbal sense making and interpretation are responses to these, rather than to the words that come later. Analytic trustworthiness relies on descriptions of a sufficient level of detail to support inferences and enable the researcher to reproduce the reasoning process by which she derived those inferences. What Scheflen writes with respect to another research context obtains here:

> It should be noted that I did not count these behaviors or measure them. For I am interested in their meaning, and . . . the meaning of an event is in its relationship to the larger picture, not in the qualities of the event itself. . . . I must know, to derive meaning, exactly how each behavioral unit fits in relation to the others in the larger system. So I shall not present charts and statistics, but only simple descriptions, and later abstractions not unlike those that every [analyst] makes. The advantage is that *I can retrace my steps and tell exactly how each is derived.* (1974 [1966], 184; emphasis added)

The systematic character of space analysis lies in sustained inquiry over time, which produces myriad "observations" (in the sense in which that term is used in large 'n' studies); in the careful choice of sites to observe, individuals to talk to, and documents to read; and in the procedural systematicity brought about through the various categories for accessing and analyzing data.

The extent to which analysis of spatial meaning draws on bodily experience should not be underestimated. Casey captures this well when he writes:

> My body continually *takes me into place*. It is at once agent and vehicle, articulator and witness of being-in-place. . . . Without the good graces and excellent services of our bodies, not only would we be lost in place—acutely disoriented and confused—we would have no coherent sense of place itself. Nor could there be any such thing as *lived* places, i.e., places in which we live and move and have our being. Our living-moving bodies serve to structure and to configurate entire scenarios of place. (1993, 48; emphasis in original)

This only adds to the puzzle of academic analysis in such fields as organizational or political studies (i.e., those that are not primarily space oriented) that lack an orientation to the play of spatial elements in a "sheer herelessness" (Casey 1993, 52): How can researchers be so tuned out of space, yet not experience themselves as "dis-oriented"?[25] As the philosopher Ernst Cassirer noted, the human "body and its parts are the system of references to which all other spatial distinctions are indirectly transferred" (quoted in Casey 1993, 82). And yet T. Mitchell provides a clue that links experiential and methodological herelessness: in the mid-nineteenth-century development of personhood conceived of "as something set apart from a physical world," as one who by nature controls "his own physical body and will" (1991, 19), body was subordinated to mind, and this detached observational attention was deemed "objective." To the extent that built spaces have been seen as body analogues, they have been relegated to the same observational and analytic blind spot: Bodies, and built spaces, were to be controlled, not engaged, and social science, in order to render objective, detached, external observation, would perforce have to focus elsewhere.

The language I have used here may seem, at times, either to suggest that buildings speak for themselves or to attribute to them the meanings intended by their "authors" (founders, executives, architects) alone. I have written, for example, "buildings convey," when what I mean is, "the buildings comprise elements that their designers intended to use to convey" or "users and passersby interpret these spatial elements to mean. . . ." I have shorthanded my language to avoid a certain cumbersomeness, but I do not intend to suggest that meaning resides in the artifact. Meanings are what we read in design elements, whether "we" are architects, critics, researchers with a more schooled awareness of such processes, or research-relevant publics with more tacitly known understanding. Settings address a wider audience than that immediately present to observe the acts therein contained, as Edelman (1964, 100) pointed out, and spatial meanings are communicated differently to those who pass through and engage the artifacts and to those who only look upon them. In the end, the interpretation is important not only for its own sake, but, as others have also noted (e.g., Schon and Rein 1994 and the Brandwein and Schmidt chapters in this volume), for the fact that interpretive schemas typically lead to action in conformity with their organizing categories.

Lastly, we commonly think of interpersonal interactions as the occasions in, and through, which social realities and their meanings are created. Yet, at times, spaces and their appurtenances stand in for at least one party in this exchange. This is eminently visible—even to those not possessed of a natural spatial "intelligence"—in considering prisons, where the power of the state is made manifest in all manner of physical design elements. Pondering such "extreme" designs may help researchers become more attuned to the role of space in communicating other sorts of meanings. It may also sensitize them—us—to the role of space in less- or non-extreme settings.

NOTES

My thanks to Anat Rafaeli and Michael Pratt for comments on an earlier version of this chapter. Four subsequent readers kept me from getting "lost" in space. Ellen Pader and Clare Ginger kept me honest with their close, informed readings of the draft of this chapter; and Jo Hatch and Peri Schwartz-Shea provided the cheerleading that worked out the final knots and moved it to its present form.

1. Some of the exceptions attending to political and policy meanings are Edelman (1978, 1995); Goodsell (1988, 1993); Lasswell (1979); Mosse (1975); and Pader (1988, 1993, 1994b, 1998); see also Law and Whittaker (1988). Works focusing on archaeology and on cartography and on other forms of representation are also space- and/or place-oriented (e.g., Abu El-Haj 2001; Casey 2002; T. Mitchell 1991; Orlove 1991; Zerubavel 1995), albeit in different ways. In human (social) geography, urban design, semiotics, cultural studies, and organizational studies, see, e.g., F. Becker and Steele (1995); C. Cooper (1976); Gottdiener and Lagopoulos (1986); Hatch (1990); J.B. Jackson (1980, 1984); Kirshenblatt-Gimblett (1998); K. Lynch (1960, 1972); Meinig (1979); Noschis (1987); Preziosi (1979); Rapoport (1976, 1982); and Zeisel (1981); cf. Goodman and Elgin (1988) and Casey (1993) for philosophical treatments. Other organizational studies that discuss spatial elements include Doxtater (1990); Feldman (1989); Ingersoll and Adams (1992); Kanter (1977a); Kunda (1992); Orr (1996); Rosen (2000); Rosen, Orlikowski, and Schmahmann (1990); Steele (1973, 1981); and Van Maanen (1978, 1991). Anthropology has also had a long-standing interest in space and place, some of which addresses spatial meanings in a sociopolitical context (see, e.g., Levinson 1996; Low 2000; Low and Lawrence-Zúñiga 2003). Goodsell (1988, chapter 1), Rapoport (1982, chapter 1), and Lawrence and Low (1990) provide good overviews of what is an enormous field of inter- and cross-disciplinary research. My own work in this area has been both substantive (Yanow 1993; 1996, chapter 6; 1998) and methodological (2000, chapter 4).

2. Casey appears to be making a similar argument: "Place rediscovered by means of body? . . . If we are surprised at this clue, it is only because one of the main agendas of philosophical modernity is the subordination of all discrete phenomena to *mind*" (1997, 203; emphasis in original). Although his central concern is the distinction between place and space, his discussion there of Descartes and others' "subsumption of every

sensible appearance . . . under a representation whose status is unremittingly mental" finds parallel in T. Mitchell's (1991) arguments about representation and objectivity; see discussion below.

3. Edward Soja similarly notes the void of space, so to speak, in social theorizing, especially of a critical theoretical sort. He locates this spacelessness in an "essentially historical epistemology" (1989, 10) that emerged in the second half of the nineteenth century with the universalizing impulse of Marx's and later Marxist arguments for the internationale, which subordinated space to time, "occlud[ing] a comparable critical sensibility to the spatiality of social life" (1989, 11).

4. I am eliding here a philosophical distinction made by some, although not always unambiguously, between space and place (see, e.g., Casey 1993). The "place" literature appears, on the whole, to focus on the phenomenological experience of "being somewhere" that space-contexts can create (see, e.g., Hiss 1990). This literature appears to treat "space" as an amorphous, generic, neutral entity. As my discussion makes clear, I treat spaces as having, creating, and/or fostering place-specific feelings and meanings. My use of "built space" is closer to the sense of place than it is to a possibly more diffuse notion of space; but I choose that language over "place" because it allows me to emphasize the human creative dimension and to avoid reifying the notion that a "placeless space" is possible (although I do not deny that built space elements may be better or worse at creating that sense of place).

I might also seem to be equating hermeneutics with semiotics. In some ways, they are quite distinct. Hermeneutic philosophy has a long-standing and much broader tradition of ferreting out the often largely implicit rules developed and used by an interpretive community in analyzing texts—and, hence, by application, to other artifacts, from paintings to acts. Semiotics ranges from a narrower focus on signs, structures, and codes and their meanings (e.g., as outlined by de Saussure) to a broader analysis of semiotic systems as social practices that situates them in their social and political context (more along the lines of Peirce's work; see, e.g., Gottdiener and Lagopoulos 1986; Hodge and Kress 1988). In some applications, however—and I think built space is at times one of these—hermeneutics and social semiotics overlap significantly in their concerns for language and other artifacts as mediating elements in self-expression and mutual understanding and interpretation within a sociopolitical domain. It is in that sense that I use them here, in keeping also with Barthes's (1986) shift from "sign" to "symbol" as the central analytic device. For a similar orientation, albeit with a vastly different focus, see Kerby (1997).

5. Churchill (1943) said these words in the context of an October 28, 1943, address on the subject of rebuilding the House of Commons. The members were meeting in the House of Lords as their house had been destroyed during the war. Churchill supported rebuilding it in its old form, despite the fact that the space was inadequate for their numbers, arguing that on the occasion that a debate attracted members in large numbers, the sight of them spilling out into the aisles would create a "sense of crowd and urgency."

6. This position is shared by critical theorists and echoed in feminist "standpoint theory" (e.g., Hartsock 1987; Hawkesworth 1989; cf. Jacobson and Jacques 1990). It is in this sense that research writing, itself, constitutes a way of "world making" (the phrase is Nelson Goodman's, 1978; see Yanow 2000, chapter 6, on this point).

7. P. Berger and Luckmann's (1966, part II) discussion of intersubjectivity explains how this comes about.

8. An interesting issue arises when the interpretations of situational members and those of the researcher collide. I do not mean to imply that the researcher would always relinquish his interpretation in favor of theirs. Instead, as discussed in chapter 4, I would argue that the interpretation presented has to be faithful both to the lived experience of the situation and to the researcher's analytic "experience." Negotiating a research report that is doubly faithful in this way is not always easy. See also chapter 5, this volume, on establishing research trustworthiness.

9. There is yet another parallel in public policy studies, where interpretive policy analysis contests the designation of those for whom policy programs are designed as policy "targets"—as if they were entirely lacking in agency and completely passive in waiting for programs to "hit" them.

10. And there is also, at least conjecturally, an area of self known neither to the self nor to others.

11. Ellen Pader (personal communication, August 17, 2004) suggests that front and back stages may exist more on a continuum than as entirely discrete points. She also reminds me that some spaces are liminal (see, e.g., Turner 1974). Analyses of border spaces (e.g., Anzaldúa 1987), one example of potentially liminal space, suggest that they have their own character.

12. I say this based on the responses I have received in presenting built-space analysis to a variety of academic audiences. For those attuned to the role of spaces and other physical artifacts, it can be quite difficult to comprehend how unnatural this is for others.

13. Casey notes that "Husserl singles out the experience of walking as illuminating the mystery of how I

build up a coherent core-world out of the fragmentary appearances that, taken in isolated groupings, would be merely kaleidoscopic" (1997, 224). Sense making from such physical activity may be related to the researcher's sense making based on the physical activity of taking notes, transcribing interviews, and so on noted in chapter 4.

14. Howard Gardner (1993, chapter 8) makes the argument for spatial skills as one form of intelligence, distinct from the cognitive intelligence that is assessed through IQ tests. He distinguishes between spatial intelligence and bodily-kinesthetic intelligence (chapter 9), although in my view, as I try to show here, they are intimately, and perhaps even necessarily, related, at least in some applications, as in analyzing the meanings of built spaces. J. Berger (1972); Dondis (1973); Rapoport (1982); Tufte (1990); and Weisman (1992) are useful sources for developing visual-spatial reading skills.

15. For example, G. Lakoff and Johnson (1980) write that in American English, "up" is associated with control ("He's at the *height* of his power," [15]); more of something is "up," as the pile gets taller ("My income *rose* last year," [16]); and "status is correlated with (social) power and (physical) power is up" ("He has a *lofty* position," [16]). It is important to emphasize that although this is the case for American English, it may not be so for all cultures, as Levinson notes: "Many languages do not use the planes through the body to derive spatial coordinates, i.e. they have no left/right/front/back spatial terms" (1996, 356). See also Weisman (1992, 11–15) on both points. The implication of such cultural specificity for design and the meanings of built spaces is illustrated in the discussion below.

16. He cites the theories of Merleau-Ponty (that spatializing space precedes spatialized space), Heidegger (that spatiality precedes space), and Husserl (that bodily kinesthesias precede the idealizations of space). Husserl, he notes, "designates the here to which the body brings me as the 'absolute here'" (Casey 1993, 51). For a supporting argument on the link between cognition and bodily experience, see G. Lakoff and Johnson (1999).

17. See also Samer Shehata's discussion (chapter 13, this volume) of this point, although he does not treat the physical (bodily) aspect of this process.

18. This is analogous to Rafaeli and Pratt's (1993) "attributes of dress" category.

19. The other two analytic categories commonly used in studying nonverbal communication (in addition to physical characteristics, personal decoration, kinesics, and proxemics) are paralanguage (the sound of the voice) and tactile behavior, or rules for touching, which, as Weitz (1974, 203) implies, is one end of the proxemics continuum. Rapoport (1982) also takes a nonverbal communication approach to the study of built space. As I read him, he appears to be arguing primarily for the centrality of built space as one way in which human meaning(s) is (are) communicated nonverbally—that is, he seems to be bringing space to the nonverbal research community—whereas I am arguing for the utility of observational categories developed within that community for the analysis of *how* spaces communicate meaning. Our approaches overlap where he brings examples of how spaces mean by way of illustrating their nonverbal character.

Many of the elements subsumed under nonverbal communication categories have also been treated as nonreactive (or unobtrusive) "measures" (Webb et al. 1981 [1966]). One should proceed with caution, however, in drawing too heavily on the notion of nonreactivity in accessing meaning. Webb and his coauthors were heavily invested in controlling research processes that would "contaminate" the data being accessed, including the impact of the researcher's person—hence, "nonreactivity." From an interpretive perspective, however, so-called interviewer effects or response biases are accepted as given, following from the third presupposition, that knowledge and knowing are situated.

Influenced by phenomenological humanism, many interpretive interviewers would argue that it would be unethical *not* to bring themselves into the engagement, quite aside from the impossibility of not doing so, in their view (see, e.g., Holstein and Gubrium 1995 for an argument in favor of interviewer "reactivity").

20. My thanks to Ellen Pader for reminding me of the role of designation here.

21. I cannot demonstrate that built space is correlated with masculinity, only that building design, especially in the corporate and governmental organizational worlds, invokes status symbols associated with culture-specific masculinity. But see Kemper (1990) on the association of testosterone, an erect spine, and mastery in men, and Weisman (1992, esp. 15ff.) for a discussion of the gendered bases of the built environment.

22. As related in Yanow (1996, chapter 6).

23. Indeed, the research cited by Levinson (1996) would support this. See also note 15.

24. My thanks to Jo Hatch for helping me bring out this point.

25. Even the etymology of this word "dis-oriented" is place related: we "orient" ourselves toward the "Orient," the East, the place of the rising sun (from a certain "orientation").

PART IV

RE-RECOGNIZING INTERPRETIVE METHODOLOGIES IN THE HUMAN SCIENCES

From an overarching meta-perspective, the debates about methodologies and methods within the social sciences are an expression of a much broader set of issues—those concerning what might be called the "work practices" of sociology, political science, anthropology, even economics, and the various fields of their application, such as planning, public administration, public policy, communication studies, social work, the health care fields, and management. It is not just that understanding interpretive methods as a scientific undertaking requires situating the debate within definitions of "science." What is at stake are questions of disciplinary identity and practitioner identity, including the establishment and regulation of membership criteria and boundaries. These are the concerns of two other fields of inquiry: the sociology of the professions, and social studies of science (or science studies).

The former, often engaged in the professional schools, asks such questions as, How does a professional in X field know how to do what she does? In what contexts and settings and through what processes does such learning take place? How does one craft a professional identity? Many of the early Chicago School field studies documented professional practices (e.g., H. Becker et al. 1977 [1961]), and these have an affinity with studies of work in general (e.g., Bittner 1990; Blau 1963 [1953]; Crozier 1964; R. Kaufman 1960; Manning 1977; Van Maanen 1978) and with other studies of workplace socialization and management (e.g., Bailyn 1980; Schein 1978). Social studies of science have, to date, focused largely on practices in the natural and physical sciences (see, e.g., Keller 1985; Kuhn 1970; Latour 1987; Latour and Woolgar 1990; Traweek 1988), with analytic approaches organized along philosophical, historical, and sociological-anthropological lines.[1]

What becomes clear in taking a step back from the minutiae of methods-as-tools argumentations is that in these debates, the social sciences are reflecting on their own practices, including their own knowledge-production processes. The "Perestroika" debates in the context of the American Political Science Association are an example of this enactment, focusing as they have not only on methodological issues but also on journal editorial practices; associational governance; departmental hiring, retention, and promotion; and curricular issues (see the essays in Monroe 2005). What becomes clear in this context is the extent to which methods currently serve as identity markers for various fields, including as gatekeepers for doctoral students embarking on comprehensive exams and dissertation research, graduating Ph.D.s seeking jobs, junior faculty

Table IV.1

Types and Dimensions of Disciplinary Knowledge

		Knowledge for whom?	
		Academic setting, audience	Extra-academic setting, audience
Knowledge for what?	Normal science	DISCIPLINE	APPLIED (policy, consulting, government, military)
	Change	CRITICAL	ENGAGED/PUBLIC

Source: Adapted from Burawoy (2005).

seeking promotion and tenure, and all seeking research funding, opportunities to present work in conferences, and publication outlets for research. And the issues arise as well in teaching, curricular design, and textbook contents.

The final chapters offer two different perspectives on such matters. Timothy Pachirat, in chapter 21, reminds us, in a most poetic fashion, of the human dimension of our research enterprise. We *are* in search of meaning, he notes, and we would do well, also, to remember that this is such a central facet of human endeavor that we remark on those who are incapable, whether from age or illness, to engage in such meaning making. Meaning making is the unmarked, taken-for-granted norm—we tend, that is, to note it in its absence, as he observes, as in health-related conditions— yet the capacity for doing so is central to our lives. Interpretive social science is "merely" an enactment of this social fact.

In the final chapter, the editors seek to contextualize the methods debates in the context of scientific identities and practices. As a framework for the observations in that chapter, we build here on some ideas recently articulated by Michael Burawoy, 2003–4 president of the American Sociological Association (Burawoy 2005). In response to questions in sociology about disciplinary identity, he has articulated an argument for "public sociology." He describes the disciplinary issues in ways that resonate with the current debates in political science and possibly in other social sciences as well.

Burawoy frames the argument in terms of the questions "Knowledge for whom?" and "Knowledge for what?" thereby generating, in good sociological fashion, a "2 x 2" table. Four modes of doing social science or being a social scientist then become apparent. In light of the methods debates engaged in this book, it seems useful to adapt his table somewhat, as a way of casting these arguments more broadly (see Table IV.1).

Burawoy sees the left-hand question, "Knowledge for what?" in means/ends terms, which leads him to see knowledge as either instrumental (serving means primarily) or reflexive (asking what ends are being served). We turn the question slightly, rendering it as, "What purposes are being served by the knowledge generated by social science?" In sociology of knowledge terms, then, the question, in a Kuhnian vein, is asking, "Are we in a period of normal science or are we in a period of change?" Normal science requires little reflexivity, little awareness of one's own knowledge-production roles and processes. Its purposes are to further clarify accepted research procedures and to embed them in established practices. This procedural normalization intertwines with a methodological positivism in which the generation of knowledge is not problematized. The dominant scientific identity resides in the upper-left cell of the table: the disciplinary professional generating knowledge (in the form of papers and articles) for consumption by disciplinary colleagues (at conferences and in journals and books) and replicating disciplinary norms through socializing students (through curricular practices) and through hiring, retention, and promotion of junior faculty.

In several social sciences, the present period of questioning is being driven by, and is itself driving, a reflexivity—this enacts the science studies concerns for the production of knowledge—and a set of career-related issues such as socialization through curricula, editorial practices, hiring, and so on—these are the sociology of the professions concerns. This is the "critical" cell in the table, populated today by Post-Autistic Economics and D. McCloskey's writings (1985), Perestroika (in U.S. political science), critical sociologists, cultural anthropologists of the 1970s to 1990s, culture studies, critical legal studies, critical race theory, feminist theories, queer studies, and so on. Burawoy's call for a "public sociology" parallels the call within the U.S. Perestroika for an "engaged" political science—and both would fill the vacuum created by the deaths or (self-) silencings of the "public intellectuals" of the 1960s to 1970s and earlier (see, e.g., Posner 2001). The thrust of this book lies in that lower-left, critical cell, with the potential to move into the lower-right one to the extent that chapter authors are also engaged in substantive changes (e.g., policy related) outside the academy (the thrust of the evaluative criteria of "criticality," "pragmatic use," or "community purpose," as noted in chapter 5).

The critical, engaged, and applied cells in this table take scholars out of what are considered normal disciplinary practices, with varying effects. Whether those effects aid or are detrimental to scholars' careers seems to depend on the "Knowledge for whom?" dimension, whether knowledge is applied and serves its "clients"—those who commission studies—or whether that knowledge asks of its audience, whether scholarly or more broadly societal, a change in conceptual thinking and values.[2] On the whole, those researchers who practice their science to serve external audiences—particularly politically powerful audiences such as government or corporations—are generally rewarded, not only by these audiences but within the academy as well. In contrast, those scholars who criticize scholarly, governmental, and corporate activities (e.g., Piven and Cloward's 1977 challenge to the welfare system) may be either actively "punished" or simply "not valued" (for example, by depriving them of institutional supports of various kinds, such as funding, office space, etc.).

Cecilia Lynch (chapter 16) briefly describes her own realization of this key distinction. She observes how the "objectivity" of faculty who consulted for the U.S. national security establishment was not questioned, whereas her own involvement in peace movements was said to compromise her research. Contesting the possibility of value-free definitions of politics, Mary Hawkesworth (chapter 2) provides further grounds for questioning the claimed neutrality of "experts" and "consultants" advising foreign governments on modernization, democratic institutions, and market economies. Those scholars who serve power, or who domesticate their critiques, seem to be routinely rewarded both inside and outside of the academy.

There seems to be comparatively less evidence about the outcomes for scholars in the bottom two "change" cells, probably because fewer scholars venture there, given the lack of rewards and the possible dangers, compared to the more familiar ground of standard disciplinary activity. Given the espoused ideals of scholarly inquiry, one might think that the scientific attitude of doubt would mean that those advocating change *within* the academy would be welcomed. That this is not necessarily so is the theme of both science studies and the sociology of the professions literatures that examine the relationships among knowledge production, its reception, and power. As Brandwein's chapter 12 on the "careers" of knowledge claims documents, reason and evidence alone do not suffice to win arguments. More anecdotally, the perceived need for anonymity on the part of the founder(s) of the Perestroika e-mail list (and subsequent anonymous posts from that person or persons and from others) also speaks to the risks of asking for disciplinary change.

Challenging the analyses and ideals of the wider society, including power holders, would also seem an appropriate role for institutions of higher education. Yet many recent events speak to the risks of such action, from the reception of University of Colorado professor Ward Churchill's challenge to received views of the September 11 attacks (Brennan 2005), to legislative efforts to curtail tenure (Finkin 2000; Healy 1997), to efforts by student groups to monitor the "objectivity" of professors' lectures (Hebel 2004). Underlying much of the debate over the propriety of scholarly research and analyses are conceptions of "objectivity" tied to conceptualizations of "science," a topic examined in chapter 4 of this volume.

No 2 x 2 table can do justice to the complexity of the issues briefly reviewed here. The purpose of this broad framework, as we discuss in our final chapter, is to acknowledge, and to enable analysis of, the connections between the varied receptions of scholars' work and the themes of this book—conceptions of science tied to method.

There is a sense in which social scientists' relationship with their methods parallels that of natural and physical scientists with their tools as it evolved from the sixteenth century to the twentieth. As described by philosophers of technology, early scientists crafted their own tools and maintained an intimate connection—of knowledge, of practice: a hands-on intimacy—with them. Think, for example, of Von Leeuwenhoek with his lenses and microscopes, having to grind and assemble them in order to conduct his observations. Gradually, technology—understood as the "tools" used in a practice—became increasingly separated from science and its practices, from investigation.

So it is, today, with social scientists and our "tools," at a conceptual level if not at a physical one. The physical relationship used, in fact, to be more palpable: Even with the old mainframe computers, Fortran, and data punched on cards, analytic technologies and research substance were much more closely related. One had the hands-on experience of transforming words into numbers and engaging with machines that processed them. Research seems to be increasingly more distanced from technology in this day of microprocessors, packaged statistical programs such as SPSS, and massive databases online.

This is part of what makes methodological debates appear (to some) to be methods fetishism, as if we were squabbling over hammers versus hoes, diverting energy from studying substantive matters of greater consequence. This is a misperception both of the importance of the debate and of the character of methods. To take the latter point first: As argued and demonstrated throughout this book, methods rest on philosophical presuppositions. These remain embedded in them, even if they are not taught or discussed or attended to explicitly. Treating methods as "tools" alone denigrates their significance and denies them their character.

This attitude carries into and supports the wider debate. As noted above, this is one way of policing professional boundaries. Labeling the debate "fetishism" only serves to dismiss it as inconsequential, rather than seeing the role that methods and their attendant professional-disciplinary concerns play in the construction of individuals' personal and professional identities (which, for academics, are often closely intertwined). But even more than this, the debate may well constitute a "myth" of academic practice, serving to deflect collective attention away from an area of incommensurable values about which there is no consensus—that "knowledge" is always and deeply "political," tied to the humanity of its producers (the interpretive position), rather than able, somehow, to escape the bounds of the physical, social, and historical embeddedness of its human producers (the methodologically positivist position). Where researchers stand on this metaphysical issue is often indicative of the gestalt with which they approach their research and their lives. Focusing on methods as tools alone and dismissing the more philosophically grounded debates serves to defer confronting these deeper, more personal questions. The final two chapters of the book dwell on these matters.

NOTES

1. These include, among others, the Society for the Social Studies of Science, the European Association for the Study of Science and Technology, the Society for the History of Technology, and the Society for the Philosophy of Technology. See note 2 in the introduction to part III.

2. To be clear, clients may request change-oriented research, but those providing funding resources often have certain types of change in mind or parameters of critique within which scholars are expected to remain.

CHAPTER 21

WE CALL IT A GRAIN OF SAND

The Interpretive Orientation and a Human Social Science

TIMOTHY PACHIRAT

Growing up in Thailand with a Thai father of Chinese descent and an American mother of English-Norwegian descent, I devoted a lot of explicit attention to meaning making from a very early age. Being caught between Thai and American identities meant that I never felt completely a part of either, and yet I had an exhilarating freedom to travel between the two and selectively appropriate from them as I pleased. Although I didn't think of it in these terms at the time, this in-between quality of my childhood made me something of a perpetual stranger and shaped my understanding of the world as a complex and multilayered place where meanings are continually negotiated and renegotiated. When in my late adolescence the Thai military brutally repressed a pro-democracy demonstration in the streets of Bangkok in the name of traditional Thai values, my love affair with the study of politics through the lens of contested meanings was born.

Eventually, this love led me to graduate school at Yale University, where I took the standard offerings in statistical and advanced quantitative methods. Although I excelled in and recognized the potential of these approaches, they left me feeling strangely empty and disengaged from the problems I cared so much about. What I loved about the study of politics was its potential to carry me closer to the lived experiences and understandings of people, its potential to transform me as well as the world around me. Framing research problems in terms of hypotheses that specified independent and dependent variables seemed to prematurely foreclose on so much of the stuff of politics by asking and answering through researcher fiat the very questions that perhaps should be asked and answered in large part through sustained interaction between a researcher and those she seeks to understand. I also began to chafe against the constraints of disciplinary lines of sight, and reaching out to literature and fellow students in anthropology, sociology, and the humanities helped me to envision the very definition and study of politics as a profoundly inter-disciplinary endeavor.

Talking to my fellow graduate students and picking up on the just-burgeoning perestroika movement within political science, I saw how a desire for grant money, departmental resources, and success on the "job market" can lead many students to accede to the dominant ways of seeing in the discipline before they've really examined the going alternatives. This can result in a disciplinary methodological orthodoxy that reproduces itself primarily through funding and training pressures, rather than because of a genuine intellectual attractiveness and persuasiveness. As someone still engaged in my own dissertation research, I'm keenly interested in opening up a more expansive universe of possibilities for defining and approaching the study of politics.

Humans making meaning out of the meaning-making of other humans: Translated plainly from the philosophical tongue of ontology and epistemology, this is the heart of what it means to be an interpretivist. And in this very basic sense, we are all interpretivists, from our beginning in the world as newborn infants turning toward the familiar voice and the well-known smell to the attempt in our dying days to make sense of our lives, to tell a story about what it has meant that we too once walked the earth. Perhaps nothing so starkly reveals the centrality of meaning making to the human condition than those tragic instances in which projects of meaning making appear to break down: the toddler diagnosed with autism, unable to decipher the profound mystery of another's laughter, of an embrace, of a kiss. Or the bewilderment in the eyes of someone with Alzheimer's as once familiar landmarks and toeholds of the mind crumble and yield one by one to a terrifying deconstruction that knows no reconstruction.

Indeed, shared meaning making is so central to our lives in common that we purge as "the mad" those who too energetically rebel, whether by choice or otherwise, against those meanings that we have come to call facts. Nor is the sphere of meaning making constricted only to humans' relationships with other humans. As Wislawa Szymborska reminds us in "View with a Grain of Sand":[1]

> We call it a grain of sand,
> but it calls itself neither grain nor sand.
> It does just fine without a name,
> whether general, particular,
> permanent, passing,
> incorrect, or apt.
>
> Our glance, our touch mean nothing to it.
> It doesn't feel itself seen and touched.
> And that it fell on the windowsill
> is only our experience, not its.
> For it, it is no different from falling on anything else
> with no assurance that it has finished falling
> or that it is falling still.
>
> The window has a wonderful view of a lake,
> but the view doesn't view itself.
> It exists in this world
> colorless, shapeless,
> soundless, odorless, and painless.
>
> The lake's floor exists floorlessly,
> and its shore exists shorelessly.
> Its water feels itself neither wet nor dry
> and its waves to themselves are neither singular nor plural.
> They splash deaf to their own noise
> on pebbles neither large nor small.

And all this beneath a sky by nature skyless
in which the sun sets without setting at all
and hides without hiding behind an unminding cloud.
The wind ruffles it, its only reason being
that it blows.

A second passes.
A second second.
A third.
But they're three seconds only for us.

Time has passed like a courier with urgent news.
But that's just our simile.
The character is invented, his haste is make-believe,
his news inhuman.

If a world emptied of meaning making is the inhuman one that Szymborska evokes, if meaning making is so intimately bound with the human condition, then why, it makes sense to ask, are approaches to the study of politics that seek out and underscore the interpretation of meaning currently waging a guerrilla war with mainstream social sciences from a position of "invisibility or marginalization in the face of hegemony" (Schwartz-Shea, chapter 5, p. 110, this volume)?

Indeed, dear reader, be not deceived. However their professor-like demeanor and academic style may have led you to interpret them, what we actually have in some of the contributors to this book are guerrilla fighters intent on resisting a political and social science that would ignore, crowd out, or actively repudiate the unavoidably interpretive nature of all inquiry into humans and their various common and contested projects of meaning making.

As with all guerrilla wars, however, questions of identity and tactics inevitably push themselves to the fore. Taken collectively as a group, many of the chapters seem to be saying, "We know what we are united against." But, I ask, are we as certain about who we are? About what we are united for? About who will be permitted to join our movement and who will fall beyond its boundaries? About what our practices and repertoires of resistance should be?

First, I turn to the question of identity. The differences separating interpretive and positivist approaches are distinctively mapped in these chapters, and much attention is justifiably given to disarming critiques lobbed at interpretive approaches from across this particular divide. But I think it is also important to ask about interpretivists' relationships with others, such as poststructuralists, who also share a profound skepticism toward a positivist approach to the study of social life. Perhaps these relationships also harbor important distinctions that lurk underneath the surface of a shared opposition to a momentarily larger and more powerful opponent.

Interpretive work, at least as understood by Mark Bevir (chapter 15), is or ought to be united by an insistence that all humans, everywhere, possess a situated agency that expresses itself through actions that are in turn constituted by beliefs. This emphasis on beliefs carries implications for the relationship between interpretivists and poststructuralists in particular.[2] Discussions of the place of situated agency and belief within an interpretive orientation might aptly be subtitled, "Is Michel Foucault an interpretivist?"[3] Certainly, the Foucault of *The Order of Things* would appear to fall outside of an interpretive boundary marked by an emphasis on belief. As Foucault writes in the "Foreword to the English Edition" of that volume:

I tried to explore scientific discourse not from the point of view of the individuals who are speaking, nor from the point of view of the formal structures of what are they saying, but from the point of view of the rules that come into play in the very existence of such discourse. . . . If there is one approach that I do reject, it is that which gives absolute priority to the observing subject, which attributes a constituent role to an act. (1994, xiv)

To the extent that poststructuralists retain and extend structuralism's dismissal of the conscious subject as the primary frame of reference, seeking instead to excavate the formal elements that create even the very possibilities and conditions of consciousness, the potential for a major divide between interpretivists and poststructuralists is strengthened. Conversely, to the extent that poststructuralists seek to undermine structuralism's reliance on rigid formal systems with precisely defined binaries, seeking instead to show the deeply contingent, even constructed, nature of all systems of thought, the potential bridges between poststructuralism and the interpretive orientation are strengthened. Another way of stating this with reference to Foucault's work is to say that the Foucault of *The Order of Things* underscores some of the key potential differences between the interpretivist and poststructuralist approaches while the Foucault of *Discipline and Punish* underscores some of their potential commonalities.

From the interpretive standpoint, the important question, of course, is not whether this or that particular thinker should be called interpretivist, but whether an emphasis on the animating, explanatory role played by belief unnecessarily drives a wedge between interpretive and poststructuralist orientations. Even if interpretivists define belief broadly to include tacit knowledge, know-how, and even perhaps what Pierre Bourdieu calls *habitus*, the constitutive, explanatory role attributed to belief might potentially exclude work that seeks to highlight, for example, the ways in which action is capable of generating belief rather than vice versa. Might it not be possible to say that interpretivists hold that actions and beliefs are co-constitutive, and that it restricts the possibilities for inquiry too much to claim a priori that in every case it is one that explains the other? Depending on how these issues are negotiated, it is possible that interpretive and poststructuralist approaches have a potentially major fault line running through the question of human agency. But perhaps it is a fault line that produces occasional earthquakes that are worth living with, rather than one that results in two completely separate continents.

I turn next to the question of tactics and repertoires of resistance. Some of the chapters in this book are explicitly devoted to either developing or reclaiming a vocabulary of resistance capable of enlarging the space for interpretive work within the social sciences. Implicit or explicit in each of these is the recognition that a common criticism leveled against interpretive work is that it lacks standards, or that the standards that it does have are somehow insufficient to qualify it as "true" social science.

There are at least two important dilemmas facing an interpretivist who seeks to counter these criticisms. The first and most basic is whether or not interpretivists should indeed aspire to some common set of standards or criteria, some shared template by which work can be judged. Confronted with continual criticism that one lacks standards, the immediate temptation is to devise a neat, self-contained list of criteria that rivals the list toted by the other side. Yet to do this may be to win the battle and lose the war. The danger posed by parallelism here is not simply that an interpretive list of criteria might end up replacing positivist criteria with their own synonyms (as Schwartz-Shea, chapter 5, this volume, shows that Lincoln and Guba [1985] do), but rather that interpretivists attempt to devise any such definitive list at all. The impulse to "KKV-ize"[4] the interpretive orientation—that is, to force the wild, messy intercropping of criteria and practices that is the interpretive orientation into tamed, mono-cropped rows—might very well prove fatal to what it is that makes interpretive approaches so fertile to begin with.

Some of the chapters in this book are sensitive to this threat and strive to avoid the sterility that often accompanies a deductive approach to criteria. Their authors draw on actual practices employed by interpretivists and speak from a bottom-up and experiential, rather than top-down and deductive, perspective. The potential advantage of this practice-centered approach lies, I think, in its acceptance of fluidity and change, in its openness to new criteria and techniques for understanding how humans make meaning. It resists and subverts the calcification of any one list of criteria into what Yanow (chapter 4, this volume) describes as "an external authority [that] distances us from these problems [of human judgment] and eliminates the messiness that is part of being human; [an external authority that] maintains the illusion of human perfectibility and scientific 'progress'" (p. 83, this volume). The challenge, then, is to discuss interpretive criteria in ways that enable human judgment, rather than in ways that disable it by erecting yet another inhuman external authority to which an epistemic community can blindly appeal. Beginning from a practice-centered point of view is a solid beginning, but I wonder if it, too, might not be capable of inadvertently generating that external authority that it seeks to avoid.

The second dilemma facing those who seek to answer the charge that interpretive approaches lack criteria is what Schwartz-Shea (2004) calls the reclaim or invent quandary. Should interpretivists counter their critics by reclaiming terms like "rigor" and "objectivity," or should they seek instead to free themselves from these terms and invent a new vocabulary more appropriate to their endeavor? Each tactic has its own potential strengths. In reclaiming rigor for interpretive approaches, for example, Yanow (chapter 4, this volume) demonstrates how improvisational theater can serve as a metaphor for ethnographic field work, opening up understandings and practices of rigor in ways that liberate researchers from its stepwise, inflexible connotations.

And at the same time that several chapters show how interpretive practices carry potential to reclaim existing terms like "rigor" and "objectivity," others suggest that the interpretive orientation might also fruitfully develop its own unique vocabulary of judgment. One example of this involves including the use(s) of research as relevant to how it is judged. Indeed, as an approach that gives unapologetic priority to the meaning making of its subjects, the interpretive orientation does appear to be uniquely situated to strengthen the voices and visibility of those who often go unheard and unseen, raising the provocative question of whether particular research approaches lend themselves more readily to particular kinds of political and moral concerns. Also by way of developing alternative vocabularies for judgment, some interpretive approaches seek to substitute for management techniques the telling and listening-to of stories. This emphasis on storytelling over and against management also seems potentially subversive, for if every story must have a teller, then interpretive approaches have the capacity not only to bring new voices to the policy-making table, but also to transform entirely the terms of the conversation.

The reclaim or invent quandary, then, is not a binary one. In seeking to find their own voice, to tell their own story, interpretive approaches in the social sciences must both reclaim and invent, and must do so in ways that open up rather than close down possibilities for inquiry.

Ultimately, if interpretive approaches are to flourish, they must do so not only by the cogency of their rebuttals to critiques leveled against them by other approaches, but also by the attractiveness and persuasiveness of what they contribute. A serious omission in much graduate education is a sustained conversation about that black box that every researcher at one time or another must confront: How do I get/find/have a good idea? Our training as social scientists is increasingly preoccupied with techniques useful for analyzing ideas once they come into existence; the birth of creative, new, and risk-taking ideas is seldom addressed. Like young children who have yet to learn how babies are really made, we tend to treat ideas as if they are dropped in cloth diapers from the sky by wobbly-legged storks who fly high overhead and bless some while withholding from others. Yet this failure to educate, ignite, and release the imagination has the potential of leading to graduate programs—and ultimately entire disciplines of inquiry—that reproduce technicians rather than create thinkers. And the reproduction of technicians to the detriment of thinkers can, in turn, clot the arteries that carry those fresh and sometimes subversive lines of sight so essential to the health and vitality of any field of study. As C. Wright Mills writes in *The Sociological Imagination*:

> Adequate technicians can be trained in a few years. The sociological imagination can also be cultivated; certainly it seldom occurs without a great deal of often routine work. Yet there is an unexpected quality about it, perhaps because its essence is the combination of ideas that no one expected were combinable—say, a mess of ideas from German philosophy and British economics. There is a playfulness of mind back of such combining as well as a truly fierce drive to make sense of the world, which the technician as such usually lacks. Perhaps he is too well trained, too precisely trained. Since one can be trained only in what is already known, training sometimes incapacitates one from learning new ways; it makes one rebel against what is bound to be at first loose and even sloppy. But you must cling to such vague images and notions, if they are yours, and you must work them out. For it is in such form that original ideas, if any, almost always first appear. (1959, 212)

One of the interpretive orientation's most attractive contributions, I believe, is an environment especially hospitable to the work of imaginative theorizing, of crafting genuinely new and exciting ideas, of nourishing the "playfulness of mind" so necessary to the goodness of social science. An openness to messiness; a high tolerance of ambiguity; the intentional cultivation of new lines of sight through an expansion of literary and experiential resources; the disciplined practice of maintaining a state of childlike wonder and awe over what one encounters; an intentional reflexive attention to the internal reactions, including the emotional reactions, experienced by the researcher; an appreciation for the way in which a situation always already interacts with the presence of the researcher and is never revisited in the same way twice; a commitment to keep the research question in flux and to avoid premature evidentiary closure: These are all trademarks of an interpretive orientation to the human sciences. Which is to say: They are all trademarks of an approach to the study of social and political life that unapologetically celebrates the human character of the scientific endeavor.

What does it mean to do interpretive work? The most satisfying answer, I suggest, lies not in some list or cluster of criteria and techniques, but rather in a recognition and celebration of the unavoidably human character of inquiry into human meaning making. To do interpretive work is to be walking on a beach and, stooping with one's face just inches from the ground, to look and say not, "It is a grain of sand," but rather, with Wislawa Szymborska, "*We call it* a grain of sand." And then, to take that grain of sand between one's fingers, hold it up against the salty spray of the sea, against the open blue sky, and continue with William Blake:

"To see a world in a grain of sand."

NOTES

An earlier version of this essay was presented as comments at the "What Does it Mean to Do Interpretive Work? Evaluative Criteria and Other Issues" session of the American Political Science Association annual meeting, Chicago, IL, September 2–5, 2004. I thank the presenters at that session—Mark Bevir, Martha Feldman, Peregrine Schwartz-Shea, and Dvora Yanow—for stimulating papers that provided the ingredients for this essay. I especially thank Dvora Yanow, session chair, for inviting me to comment at the panel and for her guidance and encouragement throughout the writing of the essay. And my deepest gratitude goes to Julie Jay, without whom this would not have been possible.

1. "View with a Grain of Sand" from *View with a Grain of Sand: Selected Poems,* transl. Stanislaw Baranczak and Clare Cavanagh (New York: Harcourt Brace, 1995). Copyright © 1993 by Wisława Szymborska. English translation copyright © 1995 by Harcourt, Inc. Reprinted by permission of the publisher.

2. By poststructuralist I mean the broad philosophical orientation that is at once a critique and an extension of the structuralism typified by Claude Lévi-Strauss, Jacques Lacan, and Roland Barthes. This broad orientation is characterized primarily by the work of Michel Foucault, Jacques Derrida, Jean-François Lyotard, and, to some extent, Richard Rorty. As a *critique* of structuralism, poststructuralism seeks to destabilize structuralism's reliance on precisely defined binaries and to highlight the deeply contingent nature of all systems of thought. As an *extension* of structuralism, poststructuralism often retains structuralism's dismissal of the conscious subject as the primary frame of reference, seeking instead to explicate how elements of formal systems shape and create even the very conditions and possibilities for consciousness. For a helpful synopsis of the ways in which poststructuralism both critiques and extends structuralism, see Gutting (1998).

3. In what follows, I discuss Michel Foucault as an exemplar of the poststructuralist approach because his work is often the most immediately relevant to the concerns of social scientists.

4. "KKV" refers to King, Keohave, and Verba (1994). The work has taken on such a central role in methods argumentation (they advocate grounding qualitative research on positivist methodological procedures) that rendering the book a verb is sensical [eds].

CHAPTER 22

DOING SOCIAL SCIENCE
IN A HUMANISTIC MANNER

DVORA YANOW AND PEREGRINE SCHWARTZ-SHEA

> These latter studies used observational methods to obtain data on self-identification, but the data are mainly subjected to a narrowly conceived quantitative analysis. . . . Such methodological melding usually eliminates the richness of the field observational data and fails to capture the vitality of the interactive processes undergirding the development of children's identities. . . . The process is simply too complex and multilayered to capture adequately with conventional survey and psychometric methods.
> —*Debra Van Ausdale and Joe Feagin* (2001, 91–92)

> The ideal study in political science today would be the comparative study of health regulation of noodles in one hundred and fifty countries. In this way you have a sufficiently large mass of material to reach generalizations, and you don't ever have to have eaten a noodle— all you need is that data.
> —*Stanley Hoffmann* (quoted in Cohn 1999)

Although word-based, meaning-focused methods such as those presented and discussed in this book have long had a place in the social sciences, their legitimacy as tools of scientific inquiry has been increasingly challenged since the post–World War II behaviorist revolution, which generated significant emphasis on the research use of, and doctoral training in, quantitative methods. This challenge has produced uneven consequences across the social sciences in the United States, with some disciplines, such as anthropology and sociology, retaining an emphasis on field research and ethnographic or participant-observer methods and others, such as political science, becoming predominantly quantitative in their research practices. Within the last decades, however, there has been a resurgence of interest in qualitative methods, as indicated by the success of the Sage handbooks on qualitative research,[1] the creation of the journal *Qualitative Inquiry,* the establishment of an Inter-University Faculty Consortium on Qualitative Research Methods,[2] the prominent place of qualitative methods in the 2004 *Sage Encyclopedia of Social Science Research Methods* (Lewis-Beck, Bryman, and Liao 2004),[3] a 2003 workshop on "Scientific Foundations of Qualitative Research" funded by the National Science Foundation (NSF),[4] the 2003 establishment of the Organized Section in Qualitative Methods within the American Political Science Association, and the First International Congress of Qualitative Inquiry (May 2005), among others.

We are simultaneously heartened by this recognition of qualitative methods and qualitative methodology and concerned that the ways in which they are being conceptualized and treated will once again marginalize and devalue interpretive methods and methodology. The danger, as Van Ausdale and Feagin (2001) (quoted in the first epigraph) recognize, is that "methodological melding" typically means giving precedence to positivist purposes and evaluative criteria, such that what is distinctive about interpretivism—its emphasis on meaning making anchored in specific ontological and epistemological presuppositions—is subjugated, if not "disappeared" altogether.

Consider, as one example, the mixed signals contained in the executive summary and parts I and II of the 2004 NSF *Report of the Workshop on Scientific Foundations of Qualitative Research* (Ragin, Nagel, and White 2004).[5] Although there is much that is laudatory in these sections—notably the recognition of the "centrality of meaning systems" and the "researcher's positionality" (i.e., that the "investigator is the primary data collection instrument"; 2004, 14)—there is no mention, much less discussion, of epistemological matters. In this way, the report reinscribes the fallacious quantitative/qualitative dichotomy, which continues to cloud communication among scholars, at the same time that it denies interpretive methodologies their full due. For example, the criterion of "replicability," described in the report as being "ways in which others might reproduce this research" (2004, 18), may be appropriate for the evaluation of positivist qualitative research but, as discussed in chapter 5 (this volume), it is inappropriate for the evaluation of interpretive research, which contests the possibility of universal causal laws.

Equally worrisome is the NSF report's general endorsement of "attempts to combine qualitative and quantitative methods in social research" (Ragin, Nagel, and White 2004, 15). In the one-page summary, it is evident that positivist understandings of research inform the discussion. From a methodological perspective, combining quantitative and qualitative methods is a coherent strategy *only if and when* they are understood as sharing similar ontological and epistemological presuppositions. Interpretive views, for example, of triangulation (discussed in chapter 5) or of numerical analysis as a way of "world making" (the implication of McHenry's chapter 10; see also Yanow forthcoming), however, are not suitable as partner research strategies for methodologically positivist methods because of their *different* epistemological underpinnings, and this understanding is eclipsed by the report's treatment of "qualitative" methods. To be recognized as a genuinely scientific undertaking, to be judged on its own terms with apt evaluative criteria, and, hence, to be treated as a legitimate alternative to research informed by methodological positivism, research that endorses interpretive ontological and epistemological presuppositions needs explicit recognition *as interpretive research.*[6]

How might this subjugation of interpretive research be understood? We find some answers to this question in perspectives offered by science studies and the sociology of the professions, as well as in the debates about the meaning of "science" *within* interpretive epistemic communities. Situating methodological debates within these contexts highlights the extent to which the issues are central to practices enacting professional identities, that is, in the establishment and maintenance of communities of practice that share epistemic orientations and in the discourses that accompany and define them. We argue that the subjugation of interpretive research must be vigorously contested not only because of its inherent methodological differences, but also because a fully articulated interpretive methodology offers a historical opportunity to reclaim the "human" sciences.

PERSPECTIVES FROM THE SOCIOLOGY OF THE PROFESSIONS AND SCIENCE STUDIES

The methods conversation (some might say debate) that this book engages is taking place in a context far greater than "just" methods of accessing, generating, and analyzing data. It is taking place within the broader context of the sociology of the professions, and this conversation's implications for the conduct of research impinge upon disciplinary practices, including questions of the continuity of professional communities and their practices through new and coming generations of scientists.

To begin with, these spheres of research activity—the accessing, generating, and analysis of evidence—have been conceptually curtailed and directed by the research and analytic methods *available* in training programs and *accepted* by practitioner communities. If, for example, cost-benefit analysis or rational choice theory or participant-observation is the available and accepted tool, that is what sociologists or planners or policy analysts are trained to do. By "accepted" we mean that the method is the basis of papers delivered at associational meetings and published in mainstream journals, thereby developing expectations for professional training and, hence, becoming the subject of textbooks and the focus of graduate school and other curricula, not to mention faculty positions defined and applications evaluated by search committees. Science studies scholars, such as Latour (1987) and Traweek (1988), describe this process in the context of bench science, physics, and other natural and physical sciences; the larger framework of their arguments holds for a wide variety of academy-based practices, including the social sciences.

Interpretive communities within an academic context are not just groups that follow similar reading habits. Reading is a practice; reading, research, and other practices unite epistemic communities and distinguish them from others; and methods, which constitute rules of evidence and of interpretation, are central elements in these communities of practice. They need to be codified and specified at times when community norms are not clear or are being challenged.

What concerns interpretive researchers (and others reflecting on this situation) is the danger that methods-driven research narrows the range of questions that the social sciences can usefully entertain and explore. In short, if the research question calls for sensitivity to contextually specific meanings, it is likely to be addressed more usefully by some form of interpretive method than by a quantitative method. If it is important to the research question to know what the eating of noodles means to the lives, national identities, or self-constructions of residents of each of Stanley Hoffmann's 150 countries (in the second epigraph) for their cultural or administrative practices, and if this meaning making is to be allowed to emerge from the data themselves (i.e., through conversational interviews and/or participant-observation, supported by documentary evidence, intended to elicit an insider's understanding of the cultures involved), then statistical analysis of data gathered through a survey is unlikely to be helpful.[7]

The methods "project" that the chapters in this book address has multiple trajectories. Some of us are engaged in critique: identifying the limits of quantitative methods for helping us say something about what we want to know (as in Mary Hawkesworth's chapter 2). Others of us are engaged in the articulation of interpretive methodological options: what it is that researchers actually do when we do interpretive (and qualitative) methods—the explicit delineations of research procedures (the chapters in parts II and III).[8] Still others are devoting their energies to a "sociology of the profession" analysis, examining the gatekeeping role of researchers' choices of methods tools in regulating admittance to professional circles and other concerns central to the field of science studies. This third trajectory analyzes methods issues relative to the generation and perpetuation of disciplinary practices: the graduate curriculum; graduate training through theses and dissertations, and committees' approvals or denials of research proposals; hiring practices, and subsequent promotion and tenure decisions; writing practices; and publishing and conference section domains and scopes (e.g., Büger and Gadinger 2005; Burawoy 2005; Schwartz-Shea 2003, 2005). Practices in all of these areas contribute to the perception of a discipline either as a monolithic, methodologically unified entity or as a more methodologically pluralistic one. They also contribute to its perpetuation over time, as the methods of accessing, generating, and analyz-ing data are passed on to students, who learn them through studying exemplars of well-regarded studies in coursework and through subsequent learning-by-doing on-site, both aspects of which become their own touchstones for teaching the next generation of students.

A generational analysis of academic practices highlights the fact that individuals' professional choices are not made in a vacuum. The *range of options* from which undergraduate and graduate students choose is not equally available, being, instead, historically and institutionally situated; interpretive, postmodern, and other turns notwithstanding, positivist ideas still permeate society and societal understandings of "science." As Bentz and Shapiro write, "[M]ost of us, before we knew that there were even such things as epistemology and the philosophy of science, were indoctrinated into positivism in high school [if not before that—eds.], when we were told there was something called the 'scientific method' based on observation, hypothesis, and verification, and when we were given the general idea that the march of science and technology is the key to human progress" (1998, 26). Such understandings of "science" (which, by implication, position the "humanities" as the "other") at the high school level have yet other effects. As a parent, one of us (Schwartz-Shea) has observed that high school students are introduced to crude versions of the fact/value dichotomy, taught to devalue their own "opinions" and, instead, to value "authorities" (as measured in grading by the *number* of citations they use in their papers), and instructed that the third person is the only legitimate voice in expository writing (an understanding Yanow's graduate students continue to enact). High school students seem not to be taught to take them-selves seriously as people capable of critiquing others' arguments, much less constructing (or deconstructing) their own arguments.

Most important, high school students with hermeneutic and aesthetic sensibilities are steered toward the humanities, because "science" is conceived of in narrow, even stereotypically posi-tivist terms as an undertaking in which there is no room for those who would play with words rather than numbers. Such steering further influences selections of majors at colleges and uni-versities, although, potentially, there is considerable room for readjustments of the meaning of "social science" at that stage. Such readjustment, however, rarely occurs, because "methods" classes at the undergraduate level continue to reinforce the same conceptions of science taught at the high school level, if methods texts are any indication. So steering and self-selection processes are replicated in college: Behaviorist-influenced, computer-based social science is unlikely to attract those with hermeneutic or observational talents, at least to the extent that course work and curricular requirements communicate that abstract, mathematical theorizing is the most prized and status-rewarding trait. Given those understandings of "science" and asso-ciated steering and selection processes at the high school and undergraduate levels, those stu-dents most likely to excel in interpretive methodologies may never enter the social sciences, and those who do enter them may not find their way to such methods—at least not quickly—whereas students who "click" with positivist methodologies will be recruited for the social sciences and will find them without difficulty.

What this sort of analysis makes clear is why the project engaged in this book, the delineation of interpretive methods, is so necessary. Explicit methods discussions among interpretive re-searchers have tended to consist of "off-line," private conversations among peers, focusing on the trials and tribulations of being "in the field" or "in the archives." The dearth (until fairly recently) of explicit, fine-grained delineations of interpretive methodological procedures has created a void in the education of social scientists to the detriment of the development of interpretive scholarly communities. We have lost, and continue to lose, the rhetorical battle with quantitative research in no small part because of the lack of explicit, written delineations of the entailments of interpretive methods, and because quantitative methods lend themselves to delineation in a stepwise fashion much more readily than interpretive ones: The "rigor" of the latter is enacted in the very narrative format of textbooks and journal article methods' sections. Many of the social sciences are marked by a generation gap: Senior scholars, many of them now retiring, even if they chose to pursue non-interpretive research, were educated in ontological and epistemological questions underpinning methods choices; subsequent generations have been schooled only in computer-based quantitative tools, without this methodological base, and have themselves trained newer scholars similarly. There is a "missing generation" with respect to methodological education. For these reasons, at least, interpretive researchers need to do a far better job of making our tacit how-to knowledge in interpretive methods as explicit as possible. We repeat: This is not a call to make interpretive methods rule driven. We need writings that are more reflexively explicit and transparent about how it is that we do what we do, whether in fieldwork mode or in "deskwork" or "textwork" modes (Yanow 2000), and we need to continue to develop *and make public* an articulated set of criteria based in interpretive presuppositions for judging the "goodness" of interpretive research, as argued in chapter 5.

For some methodologists, the problem of contesting approaches is resolved by the use of both positivist-informed and interpretive methods in a single research context, each one informing the other.[9] We hope that we have shown through these several chapters that the ontological and epistemological groundings of interpretive methods are so different from and contradictory to those of methodologically positivist methods that the two approaches are incompatible, resulting, all too often, in the kind of subjugation apparent in the NSF report and elsewhere. Indeed, in such combinations, it is *not* the same research question that is being engaged: When shifting from one approach to another, the research question is itself reformulated, although the two formulations may both be exploring the same topic. In that sense, then, both approaches can be useful in informing knowledge on the topic of concern, but the research itself proceeds differently in each case, starting from conceptualizing the character of the knowledge that the researcher is interested in accessing and that she proceeds to generate. (Such a shift is actually illustrated, by implication, in the tongue-in-cheek reformulation, above, of Hoffmann's noodle study from a survey project to an interpretive one.)

Tools and techniques do not exist in an epistemological or ontological void. Methods are linked to methodologies, which themselves are understandings of or stances concerning the reality status of what those methods allow us to study and the knowability that we presume about that world. From a sociology of knowledge and sociology of the professions perspective, demarcating "qualitative methods" from "interpretive" ones begins to move toward regrounding methods in methodologies and methodologies in the philosophies of science and social science. Deconstructing the qualitative-quantitative taxonomy and raising the visibility of interpretive methods within social scientific research practices takes us further toward the conceptual complexity that marks the human sciences.

ARE THERE, INDEED, INTERPRETIVE "METHODS"? DEBATES WITHIN INTERPRETIVE EPISTEMIC COMMUNITIES

Methodology, then, we understand to be concerned with a set of deliberations within the realm of the philosophy of (here) social science: epistemological presuppositions, their ontological entailments, and the implications for processes of learning and knowing and claims making. But what of "method" in discussions among interpretive epistemic communities? Is "interpretive *method*" an oxymoron?

Addressing this question requires definitional delineations. Many interpretive researchers for whom "method" means "technique" answer in the affirmative. For them, interpretive work has no techniques, and proudly so, like ethnography, which (according to many of its practitioners) "insists that it lacks a cut-and-dried technique" (Gellner and Hirsch 2001, 2). In their shared commitment to flexibility, to being able to respond and adapt to the needs of the circumstance, which makes them (at times seemingly endlessly) iterative, interpretive research processes bear not the slightest resemblance to the so-called scientific method, which lays out its procedural steps in a most linear, non-recursive, "rigorous" fashion. If "method" means "first this, then that" at a level of specificity that can be established before one begins the research, interpretive work decidedly has no method.

For others, and we count ourselves among them, a research method is a way of treating data such that others can understand where the data—which are generated, not "given"—came from and what sort of character they have as evidence for claims making. This is what distinguishes research from fiction writing: Interpretive researchers, unlike novelists, undertake an explicit and conscious effort to produce an understanding that is a faithful rendering of lived experience. Interpreting words or acts or objects in a scientific fashion may be an act of creating meaning, but it is not an act of imagination *ex nihilo*. In this sense, interpretive work is as method-ical as any other.

Procedural delineation also makes claims-making rationales transparent. Conversational interviewing has identifiable steps and procedures and attitudes, as Soss (chapter 6) and Schaffer (chapter 7) show, and these are recognized as accepted practices by members of the interpretive research community. Participant-observation similarly has recognized and accepted procedures and sensibilities. Indeed, the heart of McHenry's (chapter 10) critique of the Banks dataset is that its categories are insufficiently grounded in lived experience, generated as they were without benefit of an ethnographic sensibility and its practices (discussed by Pader in chapter 8); McHenry does not go so far as to claim that the Banks data are acts of imagination. The wealth of procedures available for analyzing word and other genres of data in an interpretive way, illustrated in part III of this book, similarly reveal their grounds for claims making.

Some within interpretive epistemic communities may argue that procedural delineation stifles scholarly creativity. We see no evidence for such concerns in the contributions here. Rather than shutting down researchers' imaginative processes, as some fear it would, more explicit delineation of procedural entailments, in our view, invites those searching for new ways of addressing research questions to consider interpretive methods, precisely because of the greater understanding of their range and scope that results. Methods delineations offer novices guidance and welcome newcomers into communities of practice that may otherwise appear inaccessible; they need not limit experienced practitioners' imaginative innovativeness.

We have yet another reason to argue for interpretive *methods*, and it is an explicitly and consciously rhetorical, and hence political, move—and one that joins our science studies perspective and motivates us to argue, as well, for the scientific character of interpretive work. To yield the language of "methods" is to yield the terrain of science. Given the social standing that attaches to science in contemporary society, we are loath to abandon that domain—not because of status loss to ourselves or our colleagues, or our work, but because doing "science" still supports truth claims in a way that doing humanities does not. The claim to scientific status in Western societies still carries significant societal weight, commanding respect and, at times, funding that supports research as well. Interpretive research adheres to what we see as the two central characteristics of science overall, systematicity and an attitude of doubt or testability.[10] In maintaining that interpretive science *is* a science, we seek to expand the terms of engagement—to encourage dialogue rather than to walk away from methodologically positivist challenges to its scientific claims. Along with other interpretive methodologists and researchers, we yield much of the desire to predict and control upon which positivist science rests its claims; but we still contend that interpretive perspectives offer a path to understanding in a systematic, methodical way.

This line of thought addresses another aspect of the argument against interpretive "methods": The language of "methods" positions the work in the realm of social science, whereas (according to proponents of this view) the tenets of interpretive philosophy place its applications outside science entirely, better situated within the realm of the humanities. Although we agree with the tenor of this claim—understanding it as an argument that interpretive research can never meet the standards of methodologically positivist research and its normative scientific method—we maintain that interpretive work can be, and is, scientific, if "science" is understood as a systematic mode of observing and explaining within an attitude of doubt. At the same time, although we are among those who recognize that interpretive empirical research and theorizing in the humanities have affinities, even to the point of overlapping at times (especially when dealing with close readings of texts, and, by extension, of acts and objects rendered as texts), we still see quite clearly distinctions between the two when it comes to writing and reading practices (aside from the data access, generation, and analytic processes to which this book is devoted).

Those boundaries emerged rather strongly in the course of assembling chapters for this book. The writing practices of scholars in empirical fields—urban planning, legal studies, international relations, comparative government, public policy, public administration, environmental studies, etc.—who are engaged in interpretive analyses resemble each other much more closely than they do the writing practices of those doing feminist, social, or political theory, even when both camps are concerned with close readings of texts. It is not just a matter of different vocabularies: The "high theory" of feminist theoretical analyses of, say, Hannah Arendt or Jürgen Habermas has become more familiar and increasingly more accessible to those doing empirical research; so terminology is not the dividing line.

Rather, the distinction seems to concern different orientations toward making and supporting different sorts of truth claims. "Empiricals" typically write for empirically oriented readers; even when marshalling abstruse theories, they maintain an orientation toward grounded social realities and practices, and this produces a much more "grounded" text: The organizational structure is more stepwise and report-like, and the writing may appear (especially to a "theorist") to be more direct, less nuanced, less "sophisticated." "Theorists" reason and write in a different cultural style; their work tends to be more concerned with conceptual meanings and less with workaday practices of lived experience. Interpretive empirical research, then, must negotiate the somewhat fungible boundary between the social sciences and the humanities, reading and talking across it while situating the work on the science side. We still are, in a way, two cultures, although perhaps no longer quite in the sense meant by Snow.[11]

Interpretive studies are increasingly found at major social science conferences, in the pages of mainstream journals, and in textbooks and curricula. The depth and breadth of the philosophical underpinnings of interpretive approaches are becoming more widely known, and scholars increasingly understand that interpretive work is supported on its own merits, rather than merely in relation to methodological positivism. As a consequence, interpretive research methods for accessing, generating, and analyzing data such as those discussed in parts II and III of this book are themselves becoming better understood and judged according to their own presuppositions, rather than against positivist scientific criteria for validity and reliability that they cannot meet. Reclaiming "science" for interpretive methods is, then, both substantively and politically an important project.

WHAT IS AT STAKE? KNOWLEDGE MAKING AND POLITICS

Most researchers in an interpretive vein do not argue for replacing quantitative-positivist methods wholesale. Such a universalizing move would contradict a central interpretive philosophical tenet: Good contextualists that we are, we mostly argue in favor of letting the research question drive the choice of methods, itself an implicit argument (and sometimes made explicitly) that positivist-informed methods are good for some questions, interpretive-informed methods, for others.[12]

Although interpretive philosophies contest its claims for universal generalizability, positivism itself is not the enemy. Personally, we are happier living in a world run according to positivist presuppositions than we imagine ourselves being in one ruled by metaphysical explanations: happier to live under the concept of social and political "equality" borrowed from positivism's notion of universal laws and its implications for class, race-ethnic, gender, religious, and other equalities, in a world run by "the laws of men" (and women) and bureaucratized decision making rather than by the whims of monarchs and popes, and in a post-metaphysics world of biological science rather than one of witchcraft, cupping, and superstition. The late sociologist Richard Harvey Brown made the point quite forcefully:

> Thus, however brilliantly positivism and foundationalism have been criticized by academics, they remain powerful supports for institutions and practices that few of us are willing to abandon: academic freedom, professional judgment, civil liberties, and due process of law. . . . As a child of liberalism and the Enlightenment, [methodologically positivist] social science has been a major ideological force in the victory of civility over violence, reason and evidence over passion and prejudice, clear communication over cloudy commitment. Thus, we should not dismiss positivist social science too blithely, nor imagine with Richard Rorty that all one needs is a more congenial vocabulary. Instead, if we are to make critical social theory consequential in the public and political arenas, we must consider its ramifications outside the halls of academe. Social inquiry has been more than a conversation in a philosopher's salon; it also helps turn the wheels of state. (1992, 220–21, citing Peters 1990)

However, although we are sympathetic to Brown's argument that positivism-informed methods have, historically, been a force used to emancipate humankind in the various ways he discusses, it is also clear to us that this is not always the case. Indeed, the historical scale may have tipped: No researcher of the twenty-first century can afford to be sanguine about the uses to which social science may be put or to ignore the very real ways in which one understanding among the social sciences of what it means to do science has drowned out all others over the last several decades; and this has had a very real cost. The "scientization" of social knowledge has largely meant its mathematization (on this process, see Foucault 1971; Luke 2004). Together with its routinization in institutions of higher education, this scientizing has established quantitative, "objective," humanly neutralized forms of knowledge as "authoritative knowledge" (Jordan 1992; Suchman and Jordan 1988), at the expense of most forms of local knowledge (Yanow 2004).

A passage from Galileo suggests one way to understand this mathematization:

> Philosophy is written in this grand book the universe, which stands continually open to our gaze. But the book cannot be understood unless one first learns to comprehend the language and to read the alphabet in which it is composed. It is written in the language of mathematics, and its characters are triangles, circles, and other geometric figures, without which it is humanly *impossible* to understand a single word of it; without these, one wanders about in a dark labyrinth. (quoted in Sobel 1999, 16; emphasis added)

Galileo's view simultaneously evokes hope and fear: hope in mathematics as a means of understanding; fear of the labyrinth of human meaning making. It is our hunch that many in the social sciences still share Galileo's hopes and fears: Mathematics is, indeed, a powerful language—one that has proven its use in the natural sciences and produced some impressive applications in the social sciences as well (e.g., Kanter 1977b; Martine, Das Gupta, and Lincoln 1999; Riley and McCarthy 2003). There is an attractive purity to mathematical logic,[13] but the rub, as Galileo's own words attest, is that it is still *a language*. As such, the meaning and significance of its symbols, models, and proofs still require interpretation and "translation" if their implications are to be communicated beyond the few who "speak" mathematics. That interpretive act brings forth the sorts of ambiguities, the "dark labyrinth" of ordinary language, that Galileo appeared to fear and that still frustrate many in contemporary social science who understand it solely in terms of "variables" research and the latter's attendant focus on precise measurement and statistical analysis.[14]

Considerable time has passed since Galileo's investigations. In the interim, interpretive researchers of the twentieth and twenty-first centuries have assembled means of, and rationales for, navigating the labyrinth of language in ways that claim a scientific character. That these accomplishments continue to be ignored or discounted speaks to the allure of mathematical tools, including their promise of incontestability in the form of universal laws. Interpretive researchers have a historical understanding of the harms done by mathematical approaches built on positivist presuppositions (discussed, e.g., by Hawkesworth in chapter 2, this volume) and so are leery of their dominance. An exclusively methodologically positivist, quantitative knowledge base is unnecessarily narrow and thin. M. Douglas and Ney (1999), for example, argue that the overemphasis on positivism and quantitative research negatively affects public policies by legitimizing only the thinnest knowledge of human circumstances, to the neglect of richer pictures of "problems" and "problem people."[15] They charge that the human dimension is missing altogether in the social sciences, which may be an exaggeration for some disciplines, such as anthropology, but it captures much of the character of methodological graduate training in sociology, political science, and economics, heavily focused as they are on context-free, universalizing quantitative reasoning and modeling.[16] It may not be surprising, then, that two of these three disciplines have been the sites of recent scholarly "movements" seeking diversity in methodology—"Perestroika" in U.S. political science and "Post-Autistic Economics" in European economics.

Characterizing the motives of these movements' diverse participants is difficult, but one concern voiced by many in both movements is the alienating effect of much contemporary research practice, which emphasizes precise measurement and technical competence and neglects or marginalizes normative concerns. Members of these movements have been asking: "Is this the way I want to spend my life?" "Is this the *only* way to do social science?"[17] Interpretive researchers, as evident in this book, offer as an alternative a *human* science that embraces, theorizes, and struggles with the humanity of both researchers and those they study. As we have argued above, interpretive researchers need not cede "science" to methodological positivism. But beyond just claiming "science," we seek also to join that label with "human," because a "social" science emphasizing "prediction" and "control" can too easily use the veil of "objectivity" to hide a dehumanizing impulse.[18] We are not arguing that natural and social scientists of necessity follow such impulses, only that methodological positivism entails principles that at a conceptual level encourage the distancing of scientists from the issue of "the use" of their findings, whereas interpretivism expressly engages this question.

RECLAIMING HUMAN SCIENCE

As ideas about knowledge and the sciences were developing, two terms emerged in the German literature to denote the separation of the study of the human world from the study of the rest of creation. *Naturwissenschaften* designated the latter, usually translated as "natural sciences." *Geisteswissenschaften* designated the former, and it is often translated as "human sciences" as a closer rendering of the German than "social sciences."

One test of whether a science qualifies as "human" is whether its scientists willingly apply their own theories and research findings to themselves, seeing themselves as a part of humanity rather than being "above" or "superior to" (or simply "the exception to") those they study. For example, discussing a study of scholars "utterly committed to highly deterministic models of social causation," H. Becker reports that it "was *only in discussing their own lives* that the deterministic theories were not adequate explanations; when they talked about other people, more conventional social science talk worked just fine" (1998, 30; emphasis added). In contrast, the interpretive practice of reflexivity would encourage researchers to attend to and analyze their possible personal power vis-à-vis those they study, to ask, in effect, whether they, too, are "determined" by external factors. Indeed, it might be argued that interpretive research philosophy and practice work against scholarly hubris in ways that other philosophies and methodologies do not. Besides reflexivity, interpretive research traditions emphasize getting out of one's office into the field to talk with people—in Hoffmann's scenario, to eat noodles instead of downloading data sets about noodles—a tradition supporting human connection. Similarly, interpretivism admits the possibility of local knowledge, potentially humbling and decentering scholarly expertise.

Alford and Hibbing provide an example of the kind of social science that we would seek to avoid. They warn the reader not to dismiss an evolutionary theory of political behavior "because of unscientific aversion to its implications" (2004, 707), a comment that implicitly invokes the mantle of methodologically positivist "science" to inoculate their theory against criticism. But one of their admonitions to reformers shows the dangers of this approach:

> People do not wish to be in control of the political system; they only want those who *are* in control to be unable to take advantage of their position. . . . Current American foreign policy might be improved, for example, if decision makers realized that, like Americans, people in Afghanistan and Iraq do not crave democratic procedures. Kurds simply do not want to be dominated by Sunnis; Sunnis do not want to be dominated by Shiites; Uzbekis by Tajiks; and Tajiks by Pashtuns. (2004, 713; emphasis in original)

The authors do not cite empirical work to support these representations of the named peoples' political desires. Their advice implies that American foreign policy makers need not consult directly with Sunnis, Shiites, Uzbeks, Tajiks, or Pashtuns. A deductively developed, a priori, supposedly universal theory—the evolutionary theory of political behavior—is presented as sufficient evidence for understanding what people generally desire of politics.

In contrast, it is their focus on context—geological, chronological, or cultural—that makes many interpretive researchers especially concerned about the connections between the academy and politically powerful elites.[19] "Knowledge for whom?" is a legitimate and pressing concern for interpretive researchers as they consider research topics. And this concern, in turn, connects to the interpretive emphasis on local, tacit knowledge and the ways in which its existence is threatened by the juggernaut of globalization. Interpretive social science is not only marginalized; it is actively threatened by proponents of "one best way" of conducting scientific research who seek to spread those models of higher education (including graduate training) from the United States to Europe and the rest of the world (e.g., Dowding 2001). A loss of diversity among approaches to knowledge and the devaluation of local knowledge threaten our collective capacity to understand and encourage the myriad ways in which human beings can flourish.[20]

In the halls of higher education it is common to hear the claim that the politics of academia are so trivial because the stakes are so low. We argue, instead, that the politics of academia—understood as the politics of knowledge making—are not trivial by any means. On the contrary, how we conceive of scientific knowledge and who gets to claim its authoritative mantle matters a great deal. If knowledge is power, then methodological pluralism disperses that power, whereas "one best way" concentrates it. Re-embracing interpretive approaches as a legitimately scientific undertaking, then, strengthens both the human sciences and democracy.

Lest these themes seem utopian, we note that interpretive scholars recognize that engaging the politics of knowledge is neither easy nor without pitfalls. Researchers' positionality, the cognitive-emotional dimensions of research identity, the human need to make a living, the impact of interests on research judgments (as treated in the sociology of knowledge literature)—all the factors *ignored* under positivist understandings of objectivity[21]—mean that interpretive research, like the human condition, is complex. The "labyrinth," however, is not as dark as it once was because, as evident from many chapters in this book, interpretive scholars are innovative in their pursuit of new paths. Schaffer's use of ordinary language philosophy (chapter 7), Brandwein's combining of science studies with frame analysis (chapter 12), Oren's deeply historical analysis of social scientific concepts (chapter 11), Jackson's valuing of both sides of the double hermeneutic (chapter 14)—all these and more demonstrate the creativity of interpretively theorizing about sense making, knowledge claims, and research trustworthiness. Interpretive methodologies promise to engage the complex societies of the twenty-first century with a variegated and creative human sciences agenda.

A RE-TURN TO HUMANISM

The painting by René Magritte that graces the cover of this book illustrates the way in which representations of the world construct our knowledge of it. The title of the canvas, *La condition humaine*, draws our attention to the innate, and inescapable humanism of interpretation. That includes interpretive methods—the researcher meets people as people; he can't hide behind abstractions or numbers or surveys. Dorinne Kondo, for example, a Japanese-American doing field research in Japan on "the Japanese identity," is met with responses ranging from amazement to anger when she misuses the language or stumbles over everyday knowledge: "How could someone who *looked* Japanese not *be* Japanese?" (1990, 12).[22] Surveys instantiate the privilege of distance: They seek to protect us from all of the very human responses that may arise in being studied by others and in studying them. Meaning-focused interpretive research does not allow such antiseptic distance.

Our contention in this book has been that interpretive methods are useful precisely for the sorts of research questions that center on meanings underlying social, political, and other actions, and especially in circumstances where there is likely to be a discrepancy between word (attitudes, or espoused theories) and deed (acts). Such an approach requires, among other things, challenging the presumption that useful, legitimate knowledge is held only by those with the technical-rational expertise of university-based training. It is not uncommon, for example, to find textbook descriptions of analytic processes that identify the first steps as: establish the context, formulate/define the problem, specify objectives/determine evaluation criteria, and explore/evaluate alternatives (see, e.g., Bonser, McGregor, and Oster 1996; Patton and Sawicki 1993). Such a formulation implies that researchers generate issue-relevant knowledge in a void, from their heads. Nowhere does it ask which or whose knowledge should be included in these steps or how to access or generate such knowledge.

But suppose we could get out of this cycle of expectations and back to the kinds of acts that communal, organizational, policy, governmental, and other processes actually entail, drawing on an ethnographic sensibility. Such an approach legitimates the role of local knowledge in social life—whether that "locale" is the grass roots of a neighborhood in Cairo (Singerman 1995) or in Ellen Pader's (chapter 8) housing density studies in New York, the shop floor of a Japanese industry (Kondo 1990) or of Samer Shehata's factory in Alexandria (chapter 13).

Increasingly complex modeling along with computational methods, themselves increasingly abstracted from human social realities, enable social scientists using them to distance themselves from that human, semiotic world, replacing "explanation[s] in terms of meaning . . . with explanation[s] in terms of mechanism" (Turkle 2004, B26). To paraphrase Sherry Turkle's comments on the effects of computerization, our methods are doing things not just *for* us, but also *to* us, "changing the way we see ourselves, our sense of human identity" (2004, 1326); presentation has fetishized form at the expense of content.

The challenge is to enact our theories (a point made also by Kondo 1990, 43). Theories of knowledge have implications for researcher conduct, but also for writing practices. For example, are questions of the origins of research topics admitted as useful, as in the narratives that precede the book chapters here, or treated as purely theory driven or as irrelevant? Does the knowing "I" get buried in the passive voice in order to create objectivity-by-rhetoric?

To some extent, and perhaps a great one, the battle over methods and methodologies is not so much one about the ontological or epistemological character of evidence, but, not to be overly melodramatic, a battle for the soul of social science and its practitioners. Seen from the perspective of the "disciplines" of social science, the battle is a reactionary war against the forces of depersonalizing technicism and depersonalized rationalism, manifested in the "person" of the ever-encroaching late-twentieth-century machine, the computer, and its computational abilities. If they are nothing else—and we hardly maintain that—interpretive methodologies and methods are efforts to hold out for a central humanism in the practices of the human sciences. They reject the dehumanizing move of positivist-influenced scientific procedures that seek to control for researchers' humanity, rendering survey researchers as close to emotionless automatons as is humanly possible (which, in our view, is not possible at all), ridding statistical analyses of any vestiges of human presence, turning models into mechanical portraits.

The challenge posed by interpretive methods goes far beyond a question of mere tools. Insisting on the primacy of context resists a flattening out of detail and difference, a globalizing homogenization of spatial particularities. Schatzman and Strauss recognized this with respect to field research, describing its practice as "pragmatist, humanist, and naturalist" (1973, vi). We believe that this impulse holds for all those methods that are conjoined within the interpretive category. For some who hold to other schools of thought, proponents of interpretive work may appear to be a group of Luddites fighting a rearguard action. We hope not—we do not see ourselves in this light—but we also see that the point of contention has less to do with whether social scientists are practicing an "engaged" research—after all, many (if not all) practitioners of rational choice, modeling, and regression analyses would claim to be doing work that will have some impact on improving "the world"—than with the character of that engagement: a researcher bringing a very human, skeptical systematicity to the study of a problem, versus a researcher intending to be detached from that essential humanity. Therein lies the source of our concern, and our hope.

NOTES

1. The first *Handbook of Qualitative Research* was published in 1994 and the second edition in 2000. To update the massive second edition (1,143 pages), it was broken up into three separate tomes: *Landscape of Qualitative Research*, 2003, 696 pages; *Strategies of Qualitative Inquiry*, 2003, 480 pages; and *Collecting and Interpreting Qualitative Materials*, 2003, 704 pages. Sage markets these as the "definitive source for qualitative researchers."

2. The Inter-University Faculty Consortium on Qualitative Research Methods (CQRM) was formed in 2000. The Web site, hosted by the Arizona State University Department of Political Science, is www.asu.edu/clas/polisci/cqrm/.

3. The encyclopedia lists the following general categories for qualitative research: basic qualitative research, discourse/conversation analysis, ethnography, interviewing in qualitative research, life history/biography, qualitative data analysis, and sampling in qualitative research.

4. The workshop was conducted in 2003 and the NSF report was issued in 2004; see Ragin, Nagel and White (2004).

5. Part I is entitled "General guidance for developing qualitative research projects" and part II is entitled "Recommendations for designing, evaluating, and strengthening qualitative research in the social sciences." Appendix 3 of the report contains the twenty-four papers presented at the workshop, wherein substantive issues are discussed in considerably more depth than in the sections focused on here. Nevertheless, it is these sections that have the imprimatur of the National Science Foundation in the sense that they represent the "guidance" and "recommendations" of the agency based on the workshop as a whole.

6. Tashakkori and Teddlie's (1998) *Mixed Methodology: Combining Qualitative and Quantitative Approaches* is another example of the subjugation of interpretive concerns to positivist assumptions and purposes. This case is more puzzling: Despite explicit discussion of epistemological issues, the interpretive purpose of understanding meaning and meaning making is absent and the language of variables and causality, preeminent. See also Tashakkori and Teddlie (2003).

7. But such a meaning-focused study is unlikely to tackle 150 disparate cultural sites!

8. For an extensive discussion of the origins and the confusing contemporary usage of the term "qualitative," see the section entitled "So What's Wrong with 'Qualitative'?" pages xv–xix in the introduction to this book. Suffice it to say here, some research using the "qualitative" label *is* interpretive and our discussion hereafter applies to that research.

9. Joe Soss (chapter 6, this volume) argues that a question-driven research project can lead the researcher to use some methods some times and others at other times. Other researchers are more firmly embedded in ontological-epistemological positions (or the positions are embedded in their way of being in the world), such that they are more likely to frame all or most of their research questions from one perspective rather than another. We have no intention of essentializing or reifying researchers' methodological identities, and we have tried to refrain from labeling chapter authors in ways that are not in keeping with their own self-definitions. Indeed, it would be curious if such ontological-epistemological positions were correlated with psychometric test scores or personality-career inventories or some other developmental psychology scheme. Anecdotal evidence suggests that methodological stances, in fact, behave as a stage theory (as in the work of Jean Piaget, Abraham Maslow, or Lawrence Kohlberg) would suggest (i.e., with each stage prerequisite to succeeding ones): Given present educational systems, with schooling predominantly in positivist images of science, it may be difficult, if not impossible, to conceive of interpretive science as a science; but it is only from the vantage point of interpretive science that this point makes any sense.

10. Dvora Yanow thanks Tim Pachirat (personal communication, 2003) for drawing her attention to the fact that positivist and interpretive researchers most likely understand "testability" in different ways. As he notes, the difference reflects, at least, the distinction between seeing findings as reflections of objective reality—as reflected in the statement "I was wrong about my findings"—and seeing them as constructions of that reality. The latter invokes the researcher's willingness to subject his findings to scrutiny in an attitude of

humility in the face of the possibility that he might be wrong, coupled with the passionate conviction that he is right (Yanow 1997).

11. C.P. Snow (1959) attributed the decline of Western civilization to what he saw as the inability of people versed in either side of an absolute split between two cultures, science (especially physics) and the humanities, to comprehend elements on the other side (he was particularly concerned with the lack of what today would be called "scientific literacy" among people who considered themselves educated intellectuals).

12. Geertz (quoted in Gerring 2003b, 27–28) expressed this point about research questions' driving the choice of methods in an interview: "[I]f you want to figure out traffic patterns in New York . . . I don't think you should spend a lot of time asking each individual driver what they were doing. It might help to give some understanding but, in general, I would agree that the way to do it is to pick a place and measure the number of cars that go by and correlate it with the time of day and find out how the traffic flow works." He clarified, however, that an "interpretivist tends not to ask that sort of question [about correlation] first. One is trying to get a story, a meaning frame to provide an understanding of what's going on" (Gerring 2003b, 27). Methodologically positivist research, such as that of McGwin, Metzger, and Rue (2004), is appropriate and valuable for these reasons.

13. Modelers laud the "transparency" of their approach and contrast it with the ambiguities of other language-based approaches. This characteristic has been offered as an explanation for why there may be greater agreement among article reviewers examining mathematical models as compared to, say, among reviewers examining comparative case studies.

14. *How to Lie with Statistics* (Huff 1993), *Damned Lies and Statistics* (Best 2001), and other such titles play, of course, on such fears. See also Gusfield (1981) for an analysis of the policy-related power of numerical analyses.

15. The "evidence-based" movement in various areas of public policy (medicine, psychotherapy, welfare, and education, among others) similarly treats "evidence" in a narrow way, restricting its meaning to the controlled experimentation of laboratory research (Yanow "Evidence-Based Policy," forthcoming).

16. Anthropologists venturing into medical and health-related realms contend with such situations as well, for example when working with epidemiologists. Schwartz-Shea (2003) documents the dominance of quantitative methods in political science doctoral curricula.

17. Such poignant self-disclosure typically, although not exclusively, comes from anonymous graduate students. One may subscribe to Perestroika at perestroika_glasnost_warmhouse-owner@yahoogroups.com; see also Monroe (2005). The Post-Autistic Economics newsletter is available at www.paecon.net.

18. The relationship among scientists, power, and political regimes is complex historical and theoretical terrain. Doctors and anthropologists in the Third Reich (see, e.g., Lifton 1986; Schafft 2004) and U.S. birth control researchers (Franks 2005) are examples of scientists and research put to use by politicians in ways that arc, we hope, perceived as nefarious and unacceptable by contemporary readers. The Tuskegee experiments (e.g., Jones 1981) and the ex post facto deliberations concerning exploding the atomic bomb over Hiroshima illustrate other aspects of the concern.

19. For a fascinating, quite different commentary on the relations among political science, methodology, and power, see "American Democracy in an Age of Rising Inequality," specifically pages 661–62 (American Political Science Association Task Force on Inequality and American Democracy 2004). Although the report authors' "inspirational" take on disciplinary history might be read with some sympathy, they ignore contemporary emphases on careerism (Luke 1999) as well as the early racism of the profession (R. Smith 1993).

20. Indirect but no less significant threats to interpretive research include the policies of some institutional review boards (see note 2, p. 126, introduction to part II, for a brief discussion and citations), as well as increasing corporatism in institutions of higher education in the United States. The corporate university's emphasis on productivity for productivity's sake devalues time-intensive methodologies such as participant-observation and ethnography, putting at risk the U.S. social sciences' capacity to understand communities, organizations, and governments in a richly textured, insider-perspective way.

21. See, for instance, Harding (1993), who argues for "strong objectivity," which means taking positionality into account so that the relationship of knowledge to power can be understood. She argues that the standard, methodologically positivist assumption that scholarly position can be ignored produces "weak objectivity," in which power, such as class- or gender-based power, still operates but without accountability.

22. She continues: "In my cultural ineptitude, I represented for the people who met me the chaos of meaninglessness." This is an example of the reflexivity in writing characteristic of ethnographic, participant-observer, and some other interpretive approaches and writers.

REFERENCES

Abbagnano, Nicola. 1967. "Positivism." In *Encyclopedia of Philosophy*, ed. Paul Edwards, vol. 6, 414–19. New York: Macmillan.

Abbott, Andrew. 2001. *Chaos of Disciplines*. Chicago: University of Chicago Press.

Abu El-Haj, Nadia. 2001. *Facts on the Ground: Archaeological Practice and Territorial Self-Fashioning in Israeli Society*. Chicago: University of Chicago Press.

Adcock, Robert. 2003a. "The Emergence of Political Science as a Discipline: History and the Study of Politics in America, 1875–1910." *History of Political Thought* 24: 459–86.

———. 2003b. "What Might It Mean to Be an 'Interpretivist'?" *Qualitative Methods: Newsletter of the American Political Science Association Organized Section on Qualitative Methods* 1 (2): 16–18.

Adcock, Robert, and David Collier. 2001. "Measurement Validity: A Shared Standard for Qualitative and Quantitative Research." *American Political Science Review* 95: 529–46.

Adorno, Theodor W. 2000. *Introduction to Sociology*. Stanford, CA: Stanford University Press.

Agar, Michael H. 1986. *Speaking of Ethnography*. Newbury Park, CA: Sage.

Alford, John R., and John R. Hibbing. 2004. "The Origin of Politics: An Evolutionary Theory of Political Behavior." *Perspectives on Politics* 2: 707–23.

Alker, Hayward. 1996. *Rediscoveries and Reformulations: Humanistic Methodologies for International Studies*. Cambridge: Cambridge University Press.

Almond, Gabriel A., and James S. Coleman, eds. 1960. *The Politics of the Developing Areas*. Princeton, NJ: Princeton University Press.

Alston, William P. 1989. *Epistemic Justification: Essays in the Theory of Knowledge*. Ithaca, NY: Cornell University Press.

Altheide, David L., and John M. Johnson. 1994. "Criteria for Assessing Interpretive Validity in Qualitative Research." In *Handbook of Qualitative Research*, ed. Norman K. Denzin and Yvonna S. Lincoln, 485–99. Thousand Oaks, CA: Sage.

Althusser, Louis. 1971. "Ideology and the Ideological State Apparatuses." In *Lenin and Philosophy and Other Essays*, trans. B. Brewster. London: New Left Books.

Amann, Klaus, and Karin Knorr Cetina. 1990. "The Fixation of (Visual) Evidence." In *Representation in Scientific Practice*, ed. Michael Lynch and Steve Woolgar, 83–121. Cambridge: MIT Press.

Amar, Akhil Reed. 1992. "The Bill of Rights and the Fourteenth Amendment." *Yale Law Journal* 101: 1193–284.

American Political Science Association Task Force on Inequality and American Democracy. 2004. "American Democracy in an Age of Rising Inequality." *Perspectives on Politics* 2: 651–66.

American Psychological Association. 2001. *Publication Manual of the American Psychological Association*, 5th ed. Washington, DC: American Psychological Association.

Anderson, Benedict. 1991. *Imagined Communities: Reflections on the Origins and Spread of Nationalism*, rev. ed. London: Verso.

Anderson, Elizabeth. 1995. "Feminist Epistemology: An Interpretation and a Defense." *Hypatia* 10: 50–84.

Anderson, Terry L., and Randy T. Simmons, eds. 1993. *The Political Economy of Customs and Culture: Informal Solutions to the Commons Problem*. Lanham, MD: Rowman and Littlefield.

Anzaldúa, Gloria. 1987. *Borderlands*. San Francisco: Spinsters/Aunt Lute Press.

Argyris, Chris, and Donald A. Schon. 1974. *Theory in Practice*. San Francisco: Jossey-Bass.

Arnaud, Pierre, and James Riordan, eds. 1998. *Sport and International Politics*. New York: E&FN Spon.

Artner, Stephen J. 1985. *A Change of Course: The West German Social Democrats and NATO, 1957–1961*. Westport, CT: Greenwood Press.

Asimov, Isaac. 1951. *Foundation*. New York: Del Rey.
———. 1952. *Foundation and Empire*. New York: Del Rey.
———. 1953. *Second Foundation*. New York: Del Rey.
———. 1982. *Foundation's Edge*. New York: Del Rey.
———. 1986. *Foundation and Earth*. New York: Del Rey.
———. 1988. *Prelude to Foundation*. New York: Bantam Books.
———. 1993. *Forward the Foundation*. New York: Bantam Books.
Atkinson, Paul, Amanda Coffey, and Sara Delamont. 2003. *Key Themes in Qualitative Research: Continuities and Change*. Walnut Creek, CA: AltaMira Press.
Atkinson, Tony, Bea Cantillon, Eric Marlier, and Brian Nolan. 2002. *Social Indicators: The EU and Social Inclusion*. Oxford: Oxford University Press.
Atwood, George E., and Robert D. Stolorow. 1984. *Structures of Subjectivity: Explorations in Psychoanalytic Phenomenology*. Hillsdale, NJ: Analytic Press.
Austin, John L. 1979. "A Plea for Excuses." In *Philosophical Papers*, ed. J.O. Urmson and Geoffrey J. Warnock, 3rd ed., 175–204. Oxford: Oxford University Press.
Ayer, A.J. 1959. *Logical Positivism*. New York: Free Press.
Aynes, Richard L. 1993. "On Misreading John Bingham and the Fourteenth Amendment." *Yale Law Journal* 103: 57–104.
Back, Les, and Vibeke Quaade. 1993. "Dream Utopias, Nightmare Realities: Imagining Race and Culture within the World of Benetton Advertising." *Third Text* 22: 65–80.
Bailyn, Lotte, in collaboration with Edgar H. Schein. 1980. *Living with Technology: Issues at Mid-Career*. Cambridge: MIT Press.
Bakhtin, Mikhail. 1981. *The Dialogic Imagination*. Austin: University of Texas Press.
Baldry, Chris. 1999. "Space–The Final Frontier." *Sociology* 33: 535–53.
Ball, Terence, and J.G.A. Pocock. 1988. *Conceptual Change and the Constitution*. Lawrence: University Press of Kansas.
Ball, Terence, James Farr, and Russell L. Hanson, eds. 1988. *Political Innovation and Conceptual Change*. Cambridge: Cambridge University Press.
Banks, Arthur S. 2002. *Cross-National Time-Series Data Archive*. Binghamton, NY: Center for Social Analysis, State University of New York.
Banks, Arthur S., and Robert B. Textor. 1963. *A Cross-Polity Survey*. Cambridge: MIT Press.
Bannister, Robert C. 1987. *Sociology and Scientism: The American Quest for Objectivity, 1880–1940*. Chapel Hill: University of North Carolina Press.
Barker, Martin. 1989. *Comics: Ideology, Power, and the Critics*. Manchester: Manchester University Press.
Barkin, J. Samuel, and Bruce Cronin. 1994. "The State and the Nation: Changing Norms and the Rules of Sovereignty in International Relations." *International Organization* 48: 107–30.
Barley, Nigel. 1983. *The Innocent Anthropologist*. New York: Penguin.
Barshefsky, Charlene. 1997. "Testimony Before the Subcommittee on Trade for the House Committee on Ways and Means, Hearing on US Trade with Sub-Saharan Africa" (29 April). Available at http://waysandmeans.house.gov/trade/105cong/4-29-97/4-29bars.htm (accessed July 3, 2001).
Bartelson, Jens. 1995. *A Genealogy of Sovereignty*. New York: Cambridge University Press.
Barthes, Roland. 1986. "Semiology and the Urban." In *The City and the Sign*, ed. Mark Gottdiener and Alexandros Ph. Lagopoulos, 87–98. New York: Columbia University Press.
Bartlett, Steven J., ed. 1992. *Reflexivity*. Amsterdam: Elsevier.
Bates, Robert H. 1998. "The International Coffee Organization." In *Analytic Narratives*, ed. Robert H. Bates, Avner Greif, Margaret Levi, Jean-Laurent Rosenthal, and Barry R. Weingast, 194–230. Princeton, NJ: Princeton University Press.
Bateson, Gregory. 1972. *Steps to an Ecology of Mind*. New York: Ballantine Books.
Bauer, Martin W., and George D. Gaskell, eds. 2002. *Qualitative Researching with Text, Image and Sound*. London: Sage.
Bayard de Volo, Lorraine, and Edward Schatz. 2004. "From the Inside Out: Ethnographic Methods in Political Research." *PS: Political Science and Politics* 37: 267–71.
Beam, George, and Dick Simpson. 1984. *Political Action*. Chicago: Swallow Press.
Becker, Franklin, and Fritz Steele. 1995. *Workplace by Design*. San Francisco: Jossey-Bass.
Becker, Gary S. 1981. *A Treatise on the Family*. Cambridge: Harvard University Press.

Becker, Howard S. 1998. *Tricks of the Trade: How to Think About Your Research While You're Doing It.* Chicago: University of Chicago Press.

Becker, Howard S., and Blanche Geer. 1957. "Participant Observation and Interviewing: A Comparison." *Human Organization* 16 (3): 28–32.

Becker, Howard S., Blanche Geer, Everett C. Hughes, and Anselm L. Strauss. 1977 [1961]. *Boys in White: Student Culture in Medical School.* New Brunswick, NJ: Transaction.

Beer, Samuel H. 2005. "Letter to a Graduate Student." In *Perestroika! The Raucous Rebellion in Political Science,* ed. Kristen Renwick Monroe, 53–60. New Haven, CT: Yale University Press.

Behar, Ruth. 1993. *Translated Woman.* Boston: Beacon Press.

Bellah, Robert, Richard Madsen, William Sullivan, Ann Swidler, and Steven Tipton. 1985. *Habits of the Heart: Individualism and Commitments in American Life.* New York: Harper and Row.

Bendix, Reinhard. 1968. "Concepts in Comparative Historical Analysis." In *Comparative Research Across Cultures and Nations,* ed. Stein Rokkan, 67–81. The Hague: Mouton.

———. 1978. *Kings or People: Power and the Mandate to Rule.* Berkeley: University of California Press.

Benedict, Michael Les. 1978. "Preserving Federalism: Reconstruction and the Waite Court." *Supreme Court Review* 1978: 39–73.

Bennett, Tony. 1986. "The Politics of 'the Popular' and Popular Culture." In *Popular Culture and Social Relations,* ed. Tony Bennett, Colin Mercer, and Janet Woollacott, 1–21. Milton Keynes, UK: Open University Press.

Bensel, Richard. 2003. "The Tension Between American Political Development as a Research Community and as a Disciplinary Subfield." *Studies in American Political Development* 17: 103–6.

Bentz, Valerie Malhotra, and Jeremy J. Shapiro. 1998. *Mindful Inquiry in Social Research.* Thousand Oaks, CA: Sage.

Berg, Bruce L. 1998. *Qualitative Research Methods for the Social Sciences,* 3rd ed. Boston: Allyn and Bacon.

———. 2001. *Qualitative Research Methods for the Social Sciences,* 4th ed. Boston: Allyn and Bacon.

Berger, John. 1972. *Ways of Seeing.* London: British Broadcasting Corporation and Penguin.

Berger, Peter L., and Thomas Luckmann. 1966. *The Social Construction of Reality.* New York: Anchor Books.

Bernard, H. Russell. 1988. *Research Methods in Cultural Anthropology.* Newbury Park, CA: Sage.

Bernstein, Richard J. 1978. *The Restructuring of Social and Political Theory.* Philadelphia: University of Pennsylvania Press.

———. 1983. *Beyond Objectivism and Relativism.* Philadelphia: University of Pennsylvania Press.

Best, Joel. 1995. *Images of Issues: Typifying Contemporary Social Problems.* New York: Aldine de Gruyter.

———. 2001. *Damned Lies and Statistics.* Berkeley: University of California Press.

Bevir, Mark. 1999. *The Logic of the History of Ideas.* Cambridge: Cambridge University Press.

———. 2003. Comments during discussion at the roundtable "Constructivist and Interpretive Methods," American Political Science Association Annual Meeting, Philadelphia, PA (August 28–31).

Bevir, Mark, and Rod Rhodes. 2003. *Interpreting British Governance.* London: Routledge.

Bevir, Mark, R.A.W. Rhodes, and Patrick Weller. 2003a. "Traditions of Governance: Interpreting the Changing Role of the Public Sector." *Public Administration* 81: 1–17.

———. 2003b. "Comparative Governance: Prospects and Lessons." *Public Administration* 81: 191–210.

———. 2003c. "Traditions of Governance: History and Diversity." Special issue, *Public Administration* 81: 1–210.

Bhaskar, Roy. 1989. *Reclaiming Reality.* London: Verso.

———. 1998. *The Possibility of Naturalism,* 3rd ed. London: Routledge.

Bickel, Alexander. 1955. "The Original Understanding and the Segregation Decisions." *Harvard Law Review* 69: 1–65.

Bird, Kai, and Lawrence Lifschultz, eds. 1998. *Hiroshima's Shadow: Writings on the Denial of History and the Smithsonian Controversy.* Stony Creek, CT: Pamphleteer's Press.

Bittner, Egon. 1990. *Aspects of Police Work.* Boston: Northeastern University Press.

Blau, Peter. 1963 [1953]. *The Dynamics of Bureaucracy.* Chicago: University of Chicago Press.

Blee, Kathleen M., and Verta Taylor. 2002. "Semi-Structured Interviewing in Social Movement Research." In *Methods of Social Movement Research,* ed. Bert Klandermans and Suzanne Staggenborg, 92–117. Minneapolis: University of Minnesota Press.

Blumer, Herbert. 1956. "Sociological Analysis and the 'Variable.'" *American Sociological Review* 21: 683–90.

Blyth, Mark, and Robin Barghese. 1999. "The State of the Discipline in American Political Science: Be Careful What You Wish For." *British Journal of Politics and International Relations* 1: 345–65.

Boas, Franz. 1973 [1896]. "The Limitations of the Comparative Method in Anthropology." In *High Points in Anthropology*, ed. Paul Bohannan and Mark Glazer, 84–92. New York: Alfred A. Knopf.

Bobbitt, Philip. 1982. *Constitutional Fate: Theory of the Constitution.* New York: Oxford University Press.

Bock, Kenneth E. 1956. *The Acceptance of Histories.* Berkeley: University of California Press.

———. 1974. "Comparison of Histories: The Contribution of Henry Maine." *Comparative Studies in Society and History* 16: 232–62.

Bonnell, Victoria E., and Lynn Hunt, eds. 1999. *Beyond the Cultural Turn.* Berkeley: University of California Press.

Bonser, Charles F., Eugene B. McGregor, and Clinton V. Oster. 1996. *American Public Policy Problems: An Introductory Guide.* Upper Saddle River, NJ: Prentice Hall.

Bork, Robert. 1990. *The Tempting of America: The Political Seduction of the Law.* New York: Free Press.

Bourdieu, Pierre. 1977. *Outline of a Theory of Practice.* Cambridge: Cambridge University Press.

Bourdieu, Pierre, and Loïc Wacquant. 1992. *An Invitation to Reflexive Sociology.* Chicago: University of Chicago Press.

Bowers, Claude. 1929. *The Tragic Era.* Cambridge: Harvard University Press.

Brady, Henry E., and David Collier, eds. 2004. *Rethinking Social Inquiry: Diverse Tools, Shared Standards.* Lanham, MD: Rowman and Littlefield.

Brandwein, Pamela. 1996. "Dueling Histories: Charles Fairman and William Crosskey Reconstruct 'Original Understanding.'" *Law & Society Review* 30: 298–334.

———. 1999. *Reconstructing Reconstruction: The Supreme Court and the Production of Historical Truth.* Durham, NC: Duke University Press.

———. 2000. "Disciplinary Structures and 'Winning' Arguments in Law and Courts Scholarship." *Law and Courts: Newsletter of the Law and Courts Section of the American Political Science Association* 10 (3): 11–19.

———. 2004. "Can the Slaughter-House Cases Be Saved from Its Critics?" Review of Michael A. Ross, *Justice of Shattered Dreams* (2003) and Ronald Labbe and Jonathan Lurie, *The Slaughterhouse Cases* (2003). Available at www.h-net.org/~law/reviews/labberm.htm (accessed November 8, 2005).

———. 2006. "The Civil Rights Cases and the Lost Language of State Neglect." In *The Supreme Court and American Political Development,* ed. Ronald Kahn and Ken Kersch. Lawrence: University Press of Kansas.

Brant, Irving. 1954. "Mr. Crosskey and Mr. Madison." *Columbia Law Review* 54: 443–50.

Brennan, Charlie. 2005. "Churchill Defiant in Face of Outcry." *Rocky Mountain News* (Denver, CO; February 5). Available at www.rockymountainnews.com (accessed June 8, 2005).

Brief of Petitioner Christy Brzonkala, *United States v. Morrison* (Nos. 99-5, 99-29). 1999.

Briggs, Charles L. 1986. *Learning How to Ask: A Sociolinguistic Appraisal of the Role of the Interview in Social Science Research.* New York: Cambridge University Press.

Brigham, John. 1987. "Rights, Rage, and Remedy: Forms of Law in Political Discourse." *Studies in American Political Development* 2: 303–17.

Broughton, James M. 2001. *Silent Revolution: The International Monetary Fund, 1979–1989.* Washington, DC: International Monetary Fund.

Brower, Ralph S., Mitchel Y. Abolafia, and Jered B. Carr. 2000. "On Improving Qualitative Methods in Public Administration Research." *Administration and Society* 32: 363–97.

Brown, Harold. 1977. *Perception, Theory and Commitment: The New Philosophy of Science.* Chicago: Precedent.

Brown, Richard Harvey. 1976. "Social Theory as Metaphor." *Theory and Society* 3: 169–97.

———. 1992. "From Suspicion to Affirmation: Postmodernism and the Challenges of Rhetorical Analysis." In *Writing the Social Text,* 219–27. New York: Aldine de Gruyter.

———. 1998. "Modern Science and Its Critics: Toward a Post-Positivist Legitimization of Science." *New Literary History* 29: 521–50.

Brown, Wendy. 1988. *Manhood and Politics: A Feminist Reading in Political Theory.* Totowa, NJ: Rowman and Littlefield.

Bruner, Jerome S. 1990. *Acts of Meaning.* Cambridge: Harvard University Press.

Budge, Ian, David Robertson, and Derek Hearl, eds. 1987. *Ideology, Strategy, and Party Change: Spatial Analyses of Post-War Election Programmes in 19 Democracies*. New York: Cambridge University Press.

Büger, Christian, and Frank Gadinger. 2005. "Circulating Knowledge." Presented at the International Studies Association Annual Conference, Honolulu, Hawai'i (March 1–5).

Burawoy, Michael. 2005. "Provincializing the Social Sciences." In *The Politics of Method in the Human Sciences*, ed. George Steinmetz, 508–25. Durham, NC: Duke University Press.

Bureau of Land Management. 1978. *Wilderness Inventory Handbook*. Washington, DC: U.S. Department of the Interior (September 27).

Bureau of Land Management, Washington Office, Division of Recreation, Cultural, and Wilderness Resources. 1983. "Internal Memorandum" (September 13).

Burgess, John W. 1915. *The European War of 1914: Its Causes, Purposes, and Probable Results*. New York: McClury.

———. 1994. *The Foundations of Political Science*. New Brunswick, NJ: Transaction.

Burke, Kenneth. 1945. *A Grammar of Motives*. New York: Prentice Hall.

———. 1965 [1935]. *Permanence and Change*. Indianapolis, IN: Bobbs-Merrill.

———. 1969 [1945]. *A Grammar of Motives*. Berkeley: University of California Press.

———. 1989. *On Symbols and Society*. Chicago: University of Chicago Press.

Burns, Thomas F. 1980. "Getting Rowdy with the Boys." *Journal of Drug Issues* 80: 273–86.

Burrell, Gibson, and Gareth Morgan. 1979. *Sociological Paradigms and Organisational Analysis*. London: Heinemann.

Burrow, John W. 1966. *Evolution and Society: A Study in Victorian Social Theory*. Cambridge: Cambridge University Press.

Cadogan, Alexander. 1931. "Disarmament: Historical Review of the Obligations of Great Britain in the Matter of 'Security.'" FO371/15704. Kew, UK: Public Record Office.

Campbell, Donald T., and Julian C. Stanley. 1963. *Experimental and Quasi-Experimental Designs for Research*. Boston: Houghton Mifflin.

Cannella, Gaile S., and Yvonna S. Lincoln. 2004. "Dangerous Discourses II." Special issue, *Qualitative Inquiry* 10: 165–309.

Caplan, Pat. 1988. "Engendering Knowledge: The Politics of Ethnography (Part 2)." *Anthropology Today* 4 (6): 14–17.

Carter, Keith, and Sara Delamont, eds. 1996. *Qualitative Research: The Emotional Dimension*. Aldershot, UK: Avebury.

Casey, Edward S. 1993. *Getting Back into Place*. Bloomington: Indiana University Press.

———. 1997. "By Way of Body." In *The Fate of Place*, 202–42. Berkeley: University of California Press.

———. 2002. *Representing Place*. Minneapolis: University of Minnesota Press.

Cassell, Joan. 1980. "Ethical Principles for Conducting Fieldwork." *American Anthropologist* 82: 28–41.

Catlin, George. 1964. *The Science and Method of Politics*. New York: Archon Press.

Cavell, Stanley. 1976. *Must We Mean What We Say?* Cambridge: Cambridge University Press.

Chapman, Malcolm. 2001. "Social Anthropology and Business Studies: Some Considerations of Method." In *Inside Organizations: Anthropologists at Work*, ed. David N. Gellner and Eric Hirsch, 19–33. Oxford: Berg.

Charon, Joel M. 1985. *Symbolic Interactionism*, 2nd ed. Englewood Cliffs, NJ: Prentice Hall.

Charusheela, S., and Eiman Zein-Elabdin. 2003. "Feminism, Postcolonial Thought, and Economics." In *Feminist Economics Today: Beyond Economic Man*, ed. Marianne A. Ferber and Julie A. Nelson, 175–92. Chicago: University of Chicago Press

Chock, Phyllis Pease. 1995. "Ambiguity in Policy Discourse: Congressional Talk About Immigration." *Policy Sciences* 28: 165–84.

Churchill, Winston. 1943. "Speeches and Quotes." Washington, DC: The Churchill Centre. Available at www.winstonchurchill.org/i4a/pages/index.cfm?pageid=388 (accessed August 17, 2004).

Churchland, Paul M., and Clifford Hooker. 1985. *Images of Science*. Chicago: University of Chicago Press.

Ciardi, John. 1959. *How Does a Poem Mean?* Boston: Houghton Mifflin.

Clair, Robin P. 1993. "The Bureaucratization, Commodification, and the Privatization of Sexual Harassment through Institutional Discourse: A Study of the 'Big Ten' Universities." *Management Communication Quarterly* 7: 123–57.

Clark, Steve, ed. 1999. *Travel Writing and Empire: Postcolonial Theory in Transit*. New York: Zed Books.

Clayton, Cornell W., and Howard Gillman. 1999. *Supreme Court Decision-Making*. Chicago: University of Chicago Press.

Clifford, James. 1986. "Introduction: Partial Truths." In *Writing Culture*, ed. James Clifford and George E. Marcus, 1–26. Berkeley: University of California Press.

Clifford, James, and George E. Marcus, eds. 1986. *Writing Culture: The Poetics and Politics of Ethnography*. Berkeley: University of California Press.

Cohn, Jonathan. 1999. "When Did Political Science Forget About Politics?" *The New Republic* (October 25).

Cole, Stephen. 1976. *The Sociological Method*. Chicago: Rand McNally.

Colebatch, Hal, and Pieter Degeling. 1986. "Talking and Doing in the Work of Administration." *Public Administration and Development* 6: 339–56.

Collier, David. 1993. "Conceptual 'Stretching' Revisited: Adapting Categories in Comparative Analysis." *American Political Science Review* 87: 845–55.

———. 1998. "Comparative-Historical Analysis: Where Do We Stand?" *APSA-CP* (newsletter of the Comparative Politics Section of the American Political Science Association) 9 (2): 1–5.

Collier, David, and Robert Adcock. 1999. "Democracy and Dichotomies: A Pragmatic Approach to Choices About Concepts." *Annual Review of Political Science* 2: 537–65.

Collier, David, and Steven Levitsky. 1997. "Democracy with Adjectives: Conceptual Innovation in Comparative Research." *World Politics* 49: 430–51.

Collier, Ruth Berins, and David Collier. 1991. *Shaping the Political Arena: Critical Junctures, the Labor Movement, and Regime Dynamics in Latin America*. Princeton, NJ: Princeton University Press.

Collini, Stefan, Donald Winch, and John Burrow. 1983. *That Noble Science of Politics: A Study in Nineteenth-Century Intellectual History*. Cambridge: Cambridge University Press.

Collins, H.M. 2001. "What Is Tacit Knowledge?" In *The Practice Turn in Contemporary Theory*, ed. Theodore R. Schatzki, Karin Knorr Cetina, and Eike von Savigny, 107–19. New York: Routledge.

"Community Centers in Israel." 1971. Jerusalem: Israel Corporation of Community Centers [Hebrew and English].

Comte, Auguste. 1853. *Course in Positive Philosophy*. London: Trubner.

———. 1854. *System of Positive Policy*. New York: B. Franklin.

Connolly, William E. 1981. *Appearance and Reality in Politics*. Cambridge: Cambridge University Press.

———. 2005. *Pluralism*. Durham, NC: Duke University Press.

Cook, Thomas. 1985. "Postpositivist Critical Multiplism." In *Social Science and Social Policy*, ed. R. Lance Shotland and Melvin Marks, 21–62. Beverly Hills, CA: Sage.

Cooper, Clare. 1976. "The House as Symbol of the Self." In *Designing for Human Behavior*, ed. Jon Lang et al., 130–146. Stroudsberg, PA: Dowden Hutchinson and Ross.

Cooper, Lane, ed. 1945. *Louis Agassiz as a Teacher*. Ithaca, NY: Comstock. Available at www.gutenberg.org/dirs/etext04/agasz10.txt (accessed November 11, 2004).

Corwin, Edward S. 1934. *The Twilight of the Supreme Court*. New Haven, CT: Yale University Press.

Crawford, Neta. 2003. "Feminist Futures: Science Fiction, Utopia, and the Art of Possibilities in World Politics." In *To Seek Out New Worlds: Exploring Links Between Science Fiction and World Politics*, ed. Jutta Weldes, 195–220. New York: Palgrave.

Creswell, John W. 1998a. *Qualitative Inquiry and Research Design*. Thousand Oaks, CA: Sage.

———. 1998b. "Standards of Quality and Verification." In *Qualitative Inquiry and Research Design*, 193–218. Thousand Oaks, CA: Sage.

Crick, Bernard. 1962. *In Defense of Politics*. London: Weidenfeld & Nicolson.

Crosskey, William W. 1954. "Charles Fairman, 'Legislative History,' and the Constitutional Limitations on State Authority." *University of Chicago Law Review* 22: 1–143.

Crozier, Michel. 1964. *The Bureaucratic Phenomenon*. Chicago: University of Chicago Press.

Culhane, Paul J. 1981. *Public Lands Politics*. Baltimore, MD: Johns Hopkins University Press.

Curtis, Michael Kent. 1986. *No State Shall Abridge*. Durham, NC: Duke University Press.

Czarniawska-Joerges, Barbara. 1992. "Budgets as Texts." *Accounting, Management & Information Technology* 2: 221–39.

Dahl, Robert. 1957. "Decision-Making in a Democracy: The Supreme Court as a National Policy-Maker." *Journal of Public Law* 6: 279–95.

———. 1961. *Who Governs? Democracy and Power in an American City*. New Haven, CT: Yale University Press.

———. 1971. *Polyarchy: Participation and Opposition*. New Haven, CT: Yale University Press.

Dallmayr, Fred. 1981. *Beyond Dogma and Despair*. Notre Dame, IN: University of Notre Dame Press.

Dallmayr, Fred R., and Thomas A. McCarthy, eds. 1977. *Understanding and Social Inquiry*. Notre Dame, IN: University of Notre Dame Press.

Dalton, Melville. 1959. *Men Who Manage*. New York: Wiley.

Damasio, Antonio R. 2001. "Emotion and the Human Brain." *Annals of the New York Academy of Sciences* 935: 101–6.

Darnton, Robert. 1984. *The Great Cat Massacre and Other Episodes in French Cultural History*. New York: Basic Books.

———. 2003. *George Washington's False Teeth: An Unconventional Guide to the Eighteenth Century*. New York: W.W. Norton.

de Vries, Margaret Garritsen. 1979. *The International Monetary Fund, 1966–1971: The System Under Stress*. Washington, DC: International Monetary Fund.

———. 1985. *The International Monetary Fund, 1972–1978: Cooperation on Trial*. Washington, DC: International Monetary Fund.

———. 1986. *The IMF in a Changing World, 1945–1985*. Washington, DC: International Monetary Fund.

Dean, Angela. 2003. *Green by Design*. Layton, UT: Gibbs Smith.

Dean, Jodi. 1998. *Aliens in America: Conspiracy Cultures from Outerspace to Cyberspace*. Ithaca, NY: Cornell University Press.

Dean, Mitchell. 1994. *Critical and Effective Histories: Foucault's Methods and Historical Sociology*. New York: Routledge.

DeHaven-Smith, Lance. 1988. *Philosophical Critiques of Policy Analysis*. Gainesville: University of Florida Press.

Denzin, Norman K., and Yvonna Lincoln, eds. 1994. *Handbook of Qualitative Research*. Thousand Oaks, CA: Sage.

———. 2000. *Handbook of Qualitative Research*, 2nd ed. Thousand Oaks, CA: Sage.

———. 2003a. *Collecting and Interpreting Qualitative Materials*, 2nd ed. Thousand Oaks, CA: Sage.

———. 2003b. *The Landscape of Qualitative Research: Theories and Issues*, 2nd ed. Thousand Oaks, CA: Sage.

———. 2003c. *Strategies of Qualitative Inquiry*, 2nd ed. Thousand Oaks, CA: Sage.

Devault, Marjorie. 1990. "Talking and Listening from Women's Standpoint: Feminist Strategies for Interviewing and Analysis." *Social Problems* 37: 96–116.

Dews, Peter. 1989. "The Return of the Subject in Late Foucault." *Radical Philosophy* 51: 37–41.

Dexter, Lewis Anthony. 1970. *Elite and Specialized Interviewing*. Evanston, IL: Northwestern University Press.

Dictionary of the History of Ideas. 2003 [1973–74]. An online version of the original. Philip P. Wiener, orig. ed. New York: Charles Scribner's Sons. Available at http://etext.lib.virginia.edu/DicHist/dict.html (accessed May 22, 2005).

Dienstag, Joshua Foa. 1997. *"Dancing in Chains": Narrative and Memory in Political Theory*. Stanford, CA: Stanford University Press.

Dilthey, Wilhelm. 1976. *Selected Writings*, trans. and ed. H.P. Rickman. Cambridge: Cambridge University Press.

DiPalma, Carolyn, and Kathy Ferguson. 2003. "What Are We Doing When We Do Feminist Scholarship? Some Thoughts on Method." Presented at the Western Political Science Association Annual Meeting, Denver, CO (March 27–29)

Diplomatic Records: A Select Catalog of National Archives Microfilm Publications. 1986. Washington, DC: National Archives and Records Administration.

Dondis, Donis A. 1973. *A Primer of Visual Literacy*. Cambridge: MIT Press.

Dorfman, Ariel, and Armand Mattelart. 1991 [1971]. *How to Read Donald Duck: Imperialist Ideology in the Disney Comic*. New York: International General.

Dosse, Francois. 1999. *Empire of Meaning: The Humanization of the Social Sciences*, trans. Hassan Melehy. Minneapolis: University of Minnesota Press.

Doty, Roxanne. 1993. "Foreign Policy as Social Construction: A Post-Positivist Analysis of U.S. Counterinsurgency in the Philippines." *International Studies Quarterly* 37: 297–320.

———. 1996. *Imperial Encounters: The Politics of Representation in North–South Relations*. Minneapolis: University of Minnesota Press.

———. 1997. "Aporia: A Critical Exploration of the Agent-Structure Problematique in International Relations Theory." *European Journal of International Relations* 3: 365–92.

Douglas, Jack. 1985. *Creative Interviewing*. Beverly Hills, CA: Sage.

Douglas, Mary, and Steven Ney. 1999. *Missing Persons: A Critique of the Social Sciences*. Berkeley: University of California Press.

Dowding, Keith. 2001. "There Must Be an End to the Confusion: Policy Networks, Intellectual Fatigue, and the Need for Political Science Methods Courses in British Universities." *Political Studies* 49: 89–105.

Dowse, Robert. 1966. "A Functionalist's Logic." *World Politics* 18: 607–22.

Doxtater, Dennis. 1990. "Meaning of the Workplace." In *Symbols and Artifacts*, ed. Pasquale Gagliardi, 107–27. New York: Aldine de Gruyter.

Doyle, Michael. 1996 [1983]. "Kant, Liberal Legacies, and Foreign Affairs." In *Debating the Democratic Peace*, ed. Michael Brown, Sean Lynn-Jones, and Steven Miller, 3–57. Cambridge: Cambridge University Press.

Dreyfus, Hubert, and Paul Rabinow. 1983. *Michel Foucault: Beyond Structuralism and Hermeneutics*, 2nd ed. Chicago: University of Chicago Press.

Dryzek, John S. 1986. "The Progress of Political Science." *Journal of Politics* 48: 301–20.

———. 1990. *Discursive Democracy*. Cambridge: Cambridge University Press.

Dunning, William. 1907. *Reconstruction: Political and Economic, 1865–1877*. New York: Harper and Row.

Durkheim, Emile. 1938 [1895]. *The Rules of Sociological Method*, trans. Sarah A. Solovay and John H. Mueller. Chicago: University of Chicago Press.

Dyson, Kenneth. 1980. *The State Tradition in Western Europe*. Oxford: Martin Robertson.

Eagly, Alice H., and Steven J. Karau. 2002. "Role Congruity Theory of Prejudice Toward Female Leaders." *Psychology Review* 109 (3): 573–98.

Easton, David. 1971 [1953]. *The Political System: An Inquiry into the State of Political Science*, 2nd ed. New York: Alfred A. Knopf.

Edelman, Murray. 1964. *The Symbolic Uses of Politics*. Urbana: University of Illinois Press.

———. 1977. *Political Language*. New York: Academic Press.

———. 1978. "Space and the Social Order." *Journal of Architectural Education* 32 (2): 2, 2–7.

———. 1984. "The Political Language of the Helping Professions." In *Language and Politics*, ed. Michael J. Shapiro, 84–60. Oxford: Basil Blackwell.

———. 1988. *Constructing the Political Spectacle*. Chicago: University of Chicago Press.

———. 1995. *Art and Politics*. Chicago: University of Chicago Press.

Eisner, Elliot W. 1991. *The Enlightened Eye: Qualitative Inquiry and the Enhancement of Educational Practice*. New York: Macmillan.

Elias, Norbert. 1991. *The Society of Individuals*. Oxford: Basil Blackwell.

Eliasoph, Nina. 1998. *Avoiding Politics: How Americans Produce Apathy in Everyday Life*. New York: Cambridge University Press.

Ellis, Carolyn, and Arthur P. Bochner. 2003. "Autoethnography, Personal Narrative, Reflexivity: Researcher as Subject." In *Collecting and Interpreting Qualitative Materials*, ed. Norman K. Denzin and Yvonna S. Lincoln, 2nd ed., 199–258. Thousand Oaks, CA: Sage.

Elman, Miriam Fendius, ed. 1997. *Paths to Peace: Is Democracy the Answer?* Cambridge: MIT Press.

Emerson, Robert M., and Melvin Pollner. 2002. "Difference and Dialogue: Members' Readings of Ethnographic Texts." In *Qualitative Research Methods*, ed. Darin Weinberg, 154–70. Malden, MA: Blackwell.

Emerson, Robert M., Rachel I. Fretz, and Linda L. Shaw. 1995. *Writing Ethnographic Fieldnotes*. Chicago: University of Chicago Press.

Engeström, Yrjö, Anne Puonti, and Laura Seppänen. 2003. "Spatial and Temporal Expansion of the Object as a Challenge for Reorganizing Work." In *Knowing in Organizations*, ed. Davide Nicolini, Silvia Gherardi, and Dvora Yanow, 151–86. Armonk, NY: M.E. Sharpe.

Enloe, Cynthia. 1996. "Margins, Silences and Bottom Rungs: How to Overcome the Underestimation of Power in the Study of International Relations." In *International Theory: Positivism and Beyond*, ed. Steve Smith, Ken Booth, and Marysia Zalewski, 186–202. Cambridge: Cambridge University Press.

Epp, Charles R. 1999. "External Pressure and the Supreme Court's Agenda." In *Supreme Court Decision-Making*, ed. Cornell Clayton and Howard Gillman, 255–79. Chicago: University of Chicago Press.

Epstein, Lee, and Jack Knight. 1998. *The Choices Justices Make*. Washington, DC: Congressional Quarterly Press.

Erlandson, David A., Edward L. Harris, Barbara L. Skipper, and Steve D. Allen. 1993. "Quality Criteria for a Naturalistic Study." In *Doing Naturalistic Inquiry*, 131–62. Newbury Park, CA: Sage.

Escobar, Arturo. 1995. *Encountering Development: The Making and Unmaking of the Third World*. Princeton, NJ: Princeton University Press.

Eulau, Heinz. 1963. *The Behavioral Persuasion in Politics*. New York: Random House.

Eulau, Heinz, and James March. 1969. *Political Science*. Englewood Cliffs, NJ: Prentice-Hall.

Everdell, William R. 1997. *The First Moderns: Profiles in the Origins of Twentieth Century Thought*. Chicago: University of Chicago Press.

Fairman, Charles. 1949. "Does the Fourteenth Amendment Incorporate the Bill of Rights?" *Stanford Law Review* 2: 5–139.

Falco, Maria J., ed. 1987. *Feminism and Epistemology*. New York: Haworth.

Farr, James. 1993. "Political Science and the State." In *Discipline and History: Political Science in the United States*, ed. James Farr and Raymond Seidelman, 63–79. Ann Arbor: University of Michigan Press.

———. 2002. "The Historical Science(s) of Politics: The Principles, Association, and Fate of an American Discipline." Paper presented at the "Historicizing the Political" Conference, University of California, Berkeley (September 27–28).

Fay, Brian. 1975. *Social Theory and Political Practice*. Boston: George Allen and Unwin.

Fearon, James. 1991. "Counterfactuals and Hypothesis Testing in Political Science." *World Politics* 43: 169–95.

Federal Land Policy and Management Act. 1976. 43 U.S.C. § 1701 *et seq.*

Fehrenbacher, Don. 1962. *Prelude to Greatness: Lincoln in the 1850s*. Stanford, CA: Stanford University Press.

Feldman, Martha S. 1989. *Order Without Design*. Stanford, CA: Stanford University Press.

———. 1995. *Strategies for Interpreting Qualitative Data*. Thousand Oaks, CA: Sage.

Feldman, Martha S., Jeannine Bell, and Michele Tracy Berger, eds. 2003. *Gaining Access*. Walnut Creek, CA: Altamira.

Feldman, Martha S., Kaj Sköldberg, Ruth Nichole Brown, and Debra Horner. 2004. "Making Sense of Stories: A Rhetorical Approach to Narrative Analysis." *Journal of Public Administration Research and Theory* 14: 147–70.

Fergusen, Jennifer, and Michael Musheno. 2000. "Teaching with Stories: Engaging Students in Critical Self Reflection About Policing and In/Justice." *Journal of Criminal Justice Education* 10: 329–58.

Ferguson, Yale, and Richard Mansbach. 1996. *Polities: Authority, Identities, and Change*. Columbia: University of South Carolina Press.

Fernandes, Sujatha. 2003. "Fear of a Black Nation: Local Rappers, Transnational Crossings, and State Power in Contemporary Cuba." *Anthropological Quarterly* 76: 575–608.

Filmer, Paul, Michael Phillipson, David Silverman, and David Walsh. 1972. *New Directions in Sociological Theory*. London: Collier-Macmillan.

Finifter, Ada W., ed. 1983. *Political Science: The State of the Discipline*. Washington, DC: American Political Science Association.

Finkin, Matthew W. 2000. "The Campaign Against Tenure." *Academe* 86: 21–23.

Finlay, Linda, and Brendan Gough, eds. 2003. *Reflexivity: A Practical Guide for Researchers in Health and Social Sciences*. Oxford: Blackwell.

Fischer, Frank, and John Forester, eds. 1993. *The Argumentative Turn in Policy Analysis and Planning*. Durham, NC: Duke University Press.

Fish, Stanley. 1980. *Is There a Text in This Class? The Authority of Interpretive Communities*. Cambridge: Harvard University Press.

———. 1989a. "Commentary: The Young and the Restless." In *The New Historicism*, ed. H. Aram Veeser, 303–16. New York: Routledge.

———. 1989b. *Doing What Comes Naturally*. Durham, NC: Duke University Press.

Fiske, John. 1987. *Television Culture*. London: Routledge.

Fitzgerald, Niall. 1997. "Harnessing the Potential of Globalization for the Consumer and Citizen." *International Affairs* 73: 739–46.

Flanigan, William, and Edwin Fogelman. 1971. "Patterns of Democratic Development: An Historical Comparative Analysis." In *Macro-Quantitative Analysis*, ed. John Gillespie and Betty Nesvold, 475–97. Beverly Hills, CA: Sage.

Fleming, Walter. 1919. *The Sequel to Appomattox*. New Haven, CT: Yale University Press.

Flyvbjerg, Bent. 2001. *Making Social Science Matter*. Cambridge: Cambridge University Press.

Foner, Eric. 1986. *Reconstruction: America's Unfinished Revolution, 1863–1877*. New York: Harper and Row.

Foss, Phillip O. 1960. *Politics and Grass: The Administration of Grazing on the Public Domain*. New York: Greenwood Press.

Foucault, Michel. 1970. *The Order of Things: An Archaeology of the Human Sciences*. New York: Random House.

———. 1971. *The Order of Things*. New York: Pantheon.

———. 1972. *The Archaeology of Knowledge*, trans. A.M.S. Smith. New York: Pantheon.

———. 1973. *The Order of Things: An Archaeology of the Human Sciences*. New York: Vintage.

———. 1977. "Nietzsche, Genealogy, History." In *Language, Counter-Memory, Practice*, ed. D.F. Bouchard, 139–64. Ithaca, NY: Cornell University Press.

———. 1978. *The History of Sexuality*, trans. R. Hurley, vol. 1. New York: Vintage.

———. 1979. *Discipline and Punish: The Birth of the Prison*. New York: Vintage.

———. 1984. "Nietzsche, Genealogy, History." In *The Foucault Reader*, ed. Paul Rabinow, 76–100. New York: Pantheon.

———. 1994. *The Order of Things: An Archaeology of the Human Sciences*. New York: Vintage.

Fox, Charles J. 1990. "Implementation Research." In *Implementation and the Policy Process*, ed. Dennis J. Palumbo and Donald J. Calista, 199–212. New York: Greenwood Press.

Fox, Nicolas. 1995. "Intertextuality and the Writing of Social Research." *Electronic Journal of Sociology* 1 (2). Available at www.sociology.org/content/vol001.002/fox.html (accessed July 20, 2005).

Franks, Angela. 2005. *Margaret Sanger's Eugenic Legacy: The Control of Female Fertility*. Jefferson, NC: McFarland.

Frantz, Laurent B. 1964. "Congressional Power to Enforce the Fourteenth Amendment Against Private Acts." *Yale Law Journal* 73: 1353–84.

Fraser, Nancy. 1995. "Pragmatism, Feminism, and the Linguistic Turn." In *Feminist Contentions*, ed. Seyla Benhabib, Judith Butler, Drucilla Cornell, and Nancy Fraser, 157–72. New York: Routledge.

Frayn, Michael. 1998. *Copenhagen*. London: Methuen Drama.

Freeman, Edward. 1873. *Comparative Politics*. London: Macmillan.

Freire, Paulo. 1972. *Pedagogy of the Oppressed*, trans. Myra Bergman Ramos. New York: Herder and Herder.

———. 1973. *Education for Critical Consciousness*. New York: Seabury Press.

Fuglesang, Andreas, 1982. *About Understanding*. Uppsala, Sweden: Dag Hammarskjöld Foundation.

Furner, Mary O. 1975. *Advocacy and Objectivity*. Lexington: University Press of Kentucky.

Fyfe, Gordon, and John Law. 1988. *Picturing Power: Visual Depiction and Social Relations*. New York: Routledge.

Gabel, Matthew J., and John D. Huber. 2000. "Putting Parties in Their Place: Inferring Party Left-Right Positions from Party Manifestos Data." *American Journal of Political Science* 44: 94–103.

Gadamer, Hans-Georg. 1976. *Philosophical Hermeneutics*, trans. and ed. David E. Linge. Berkeley: University of California Press.

Gagliardi, Pasquale. 1990. *Symbols and Artifacts*. New York: Aldine de Gruyter.

Gamson, William. 1992. *Talking Politics*. Cambridge: Cambridge University Press.

Gamson, William, and Kathryn Lasch. 1983. "The Political Culture of Social Welfare Policy." In *Evaluating the Welfare State: Social and Political Perspectives*, ed. Shimon E. Spiro and Ephraim Yuchtman-Yaar, 397–415. New York: Academic Press.

Gans, Herbert. 1976. "Personal Journal: B. On the Methods Used in This Study." In *The Research Experience*, ed. M. Patricia Golden, 49–59. Itasca, IL: F.E. Peacock.

Ganter, Bernhard, and Rudolf Wille. 1996. *Formal Concept Analysis*. Berlin: Springer.

Gardner, Howard. 1993. *Frames of Mind: The Theory of Multiple Intelligences*. New York: Basic Books.

Garfinkel, Harold. 1977. "What is Ethnomethodology?" In *Understanding and Social Inquiry*, ed. Fred R. Dallmayr and Thomas A. McCarthy, 240–61. Notre Dame, IN: University of Notre Dame Press.

Geertz, Clifford. 1968. *Islam Observed*. Chicago: University of Chicago Press.

———. 1973a. *The Interpretation of Cultures*. New York: Basic Books.

———. 1973b. "Thick Description: Toward an Interpretive Theory of Culture." In *The Interpretation of Cultures*, 3–32. New York: Basic Books.

———. 1980. *Negara: The Theatre State in Nineteenth-Century Bali*. Princeton, NJ: Princeton University Press.

———. 1983. *Local Knowledge*. New York: Basic Books.

———. 1988. *Works and Lives: The Anthropologist as Author*. Stanford, CA: Stanford University Press.

———. 1995. *After the Fact: Two Countries, Four Decades, One Anthropologist*. Cambridge: Harvard University Press.

———. 2000. *The Interpretation of Cultures: Selected Essays*. New York: Basic Books.

Gellner, David N., and Eric Hirsch, eds. 2001. *Inside Organizations: Anthropologists at Work*. Oxford: Berg.

George, Alexander. 1979. "Case Studies and Theory Development: The Method of Structured, Focused Comparison." In *Diplomacy: New Approaches in History, Theory and Policy*, ed. Paul Lauren, 43–68. New York: Free Press.

George, Sara. 2002. *The Beekeeper's Pupil*. London: Review.

Gergen, Kenneth J. 1999. *An Invitation to Social Construction*. London: Sage.

Gerring, John. 2000. "Causation." In *Social Science Methodology: A Criterial Framework*, 128–51. Cambridge: Cambridge University Press.

———. 2003a. "Interpretations of Interpretivism." *Qualitative Methods: Newsletter of the American Political Science Association Organized Section on Qualitative Methods* 1 (2): 2–6.

———. 2003b. "Interview with Clifford Geertz." *Qualitative Methods: Newsletter of the American Political Science Association Organized Section on Qualitative Methods* 1 (2): 24–28.

Gibson, William. 1984. *Neuromancer*. New York: HarperCollins.

———. 1986a. *Burning Chrome and Other Stories*. New York: HarperCollins.

———. 1986b. *Count Zero*. New York: HarperCollins.

———. 1988. *Mona Lisa Overdrive*. New York: Bantam Books.

Giddens, Anthony. 1976. *New Rules of Sociological Method: A Positive Critique of Interpretative Sociologies*. London: Hutchinson.

———. 1979. *Central Problems in Social Theory: Action, Structure and Contradiction in Social Analysis*. Houndmills, UK: Macmillan.

———. 1984. *The Constitution of Society*. Berkeley: University of California Press.

Giddings, Franklin. 1896. *The Principles of Sociology*. New York: Macmillan.

———. 1904. "Concepts and Methods of Sociology." *American Journal of Sociology* 10 (2): 161–76.

Gillman, Howard. 1999. "The Court as an Idea, Not a Building (or a Game): Interpretive Institutionalism and the Analysis of Supreme Court Decision-Making." In *Supreme Court Decision-Making*, ed. Cornell Clayton and Howard Gillman, 65–87. Chicago: University of Chicago Press.

Ginger, Clare. 2000. "Discourse and Argument in Bureau of Land Management Wilderness EISs." *Policy Studies Journal* 28: 292–312.

Ginger, Clare, and Paul Mohai. 1993. "The Role of Data in the EIS: Evidence from the BLM Wilderness Review." *Environmental Impact Assessment Review* 2: 109–39.

Ginsberg, Benjamin. 1976. "Elections and Public Policy." *American Political Science Review* 70: 41–9.

Giroux, Henry A. 1994. "Consuming Social Change: The 'United Colors of Benetton.'" *Cultural Critique* 26: 5–32.

———. 1995. "Memory and Pedagogy in the 'Wonderful World of Disney.'" In *From Mouse to Mermaid: The Politics of Film, Gender, and Culture*, ed. Elizabeth Bell, Lynda Haas, and Laura Sells, 43–61. Bloomington: Indiana University Press.

Glaser, Barney G., and Anselm L. Strauss. 1967. *Discovery of Grounded Theory*. Chicago: Aldine.

Gluck, Sherna Berger, and Daphne Patai. 1991. *Women's Words: The Feminist Practice of Oral History*. New York: Routledge.

Glymour, Clark. 1980. *Theory and Evidence*. Princeton, NJ: Princeton University Press.

Goebel, Julius. 1954. "Ex Parte Clio." *Columbia Law Review* 54: 450–83.

Goffman, Erving. 1959. *The Presentation of Self in Everyday Life*. New York: Doubleday.

———. 1974. *Frame Analysis*. New York: Harper and Row.

Golde, Peggy, ed. 1970. *Women in the Field: Anthropological Experiences*. Chicago: Aldine.

Golden-Biddle, Karen, and Karen Locke. 1993. "Appealing Work: An Investigation in How Ethnographic Texts Convince." *Organization Science* 4: 595–616.

———. 1997. *Composing Qualitative Research*. Thousand Oaks, CA: Sage.

Goldstein, Judith, and Robert O. Keohane. 1993. "Ideas and Foreign Policy: An Analytical Framework." In *Ideas and Foreign Policy*, 3–30. Ithaca, NY: Cornell University Press.

Goodman, Nelson. 1978. *Ways of World-Making*. Indianapolis, IN: Hackett.

Goodman, Nelson, and Catherine Z. Elgin. 1988. "How Buildings Mean." In *Reconceptions in Philosophy*, 31–48. Indianapolis, IN: Hackett.

Goodnow, Frank. 1904. "The Work of the American Political Science Association." *Proceedings of the American Political Science Association* 1: 37.

Goodsell, Charles T. 1988. *The Social Meaning of Civic Space*. Lawrence: University Press of Kansas.

———. ed. 1993. "Architecture as a Setting for Governance." Special issue, *Journal of Architectural and Planning Research* 10: 271–356.

Gordon, Peter. 2004. "Numerical Cognition Without Words: Evidence from Amazonia." *Science*. Available at www.sciencemag.org (accessed August 19, 2004).

Gottdiener, Mark, and Alexandros Ph. Lagopoulos, eds. 1986. *The City and the Sign*. New York: Columbia University Press.

Gould, Stephen Jay. 1981. *The Mismeasure of Man*. New York: W.W. Norton.

Gouldner, Alvin. 1970. *The Coming Crisis of Western Sociology*. New York: Basic Books.

Graber, Mark A. 1991. *Transforming Free Speech: The Ambiguous Legacy of Civil Libertarianism*. Berkeley: University of California Press.

Graham, Howard Jay. 1968. *Everyman's Constitution: Historical Essays on the Fourteenth Amendment*. Madison: State Historical Society of Wisconsin.

Gramsci, Antonio. 1971. *Selections from the Prison Notebooks*, trans. and ed. Quintin Hoare and Geoffrey Nowell Smith. New York: International.

———. 1992. *Prison Notebooks*. New York: Columbia University Press.

Grant, Ruth. 2002. "Political Theory, Political Science, and Politics." *Political Theory* 30: 577–95.

Gray, John. 1998. *False Dawn: The Delusions of Global Capitalism*. London: New Press.

Green, Daniel M. 2002. *Constructivism and Comparative Politics*. Armonk, NY: M.E. Sharpe.

Green, David. 1987. *The Language of Politics in America*. Ithaca, NY: Cornell University Press.

Green, Donald P., and Ian Shapiro. 1994. *Pathologies of Rational Choice Theory*. New Haven, CT: Yale University Press.

Greenhalgh, Susan. 2001. *Under the Medical Gaze: Facts and Fictions of Chronic Pain*. Berkeley: University of California Press.

Greenstein, Fred, and Nelson Polsby. 1975. *Handbook of Political Science*, vols. 1–7. Reading, MA: Addison-Wesley.

Gregor, A. James. 1968. "Political Science and the Use of Functionalist Analysis." *American Political Science Review* 62: 425–39.

Gress, David. 1998. *From Plato to NATO: The Idea of the West and Its Opponents*. New York: Free Press.

Gressman, Eugene. 1952. "The Unhappy History of Civil Rights Legislation." *Michigan Law Review* 50: 1323–58.

Groenewald, Thomas. 2004. "A Phenomenological Research Design Illustrated." *International Journal of Qualitative Methods* 3 (1), Article 4. Available at www.ualberta.ca/~iiqm/backissues/3_1/pdf/groenewald.pdf (accessed May 14, 2004).

Grossman, Lewis. 2002. "James Carter Coolidge and Mugwump Justice." *Law & History Review* 20: 541–629.

Groth, Alexander J. 1970. "Structural Functionalism and Political Development: Three Problems." *Western Political Quarterly* 23: 485–99.

Grunberg, Isabelle. 1990. "Exploring the 'Myth' of Hegemonic Stability Theory." *International Organization* 44: 431–77.

Guba, Egon G., and Yvonne S. Lincoln. 1989. *Fourth Generation Evaluation*. Newbury Park, CA: Sage.

———. 1994. "Competing Paradigms in Qualitative Research." In *Handbook of Qualitative Research*, ed. Norman Denzin and Yvonna Lincoln, 105–17. Thousand Oaks, CA: Sage.

Gubrium, Jaber F., and James A. Holstein. 2002. *Handbook of Interview Research*. Thousand Oaks, CA: Sage.

Gunnell, John. 1986. *Between Philosophy and Politics*. Amherst: University of Massachusetts Press.

———. 1993. *The Descent of Political Theory: The Genealogy of an American Vocation*. Chicago: University of Chicago Press.

———. 1995. "Realizing Theory: The Philosophy of Science Revisited." *Journal of Politics* 57: 923–40.

———. 1998. *The Orders of Discourse: Philosophy, Social Science and Politics*. Lanham, MD: Rowman and Littlefield.

Gupta, Akhil, and James Ferguson, eds. 1997. *Anthropological Locations: Boundaries and Grounds of a Field Science*. Berkeley: University of California Press.

Gusfield, Joseph R. 1963. *Symbolic Crusade*. Chicago: University of Illinois Press.

————. 1981. *The Culture of Public Problems: Drinking-Driving and the Symbolic Order*. Chicago: University of Chicago Press.

————. 1989. "Introduction." In *On Symbols and Society*, by Kenneth Burke, 1–49. Chicago: University of Chicago Press.

Gutting, Gary. 1998. "Poststructuralism in the Social Sciences." In *Routledge Encyclopedia of Philosophy*, gen. ed. Edward Craig, vol. 7, 600–604. New York: Routledge.

Habermas, Jürgen. 1975. *Legitimation Crisis*, trans. T. McCarthy. Boston: Beacon Press.

Hacking, Ian. 1999. *The Social Construction of What?* Cambridge: Harvard University Press.

Haines, Charles G. 1964. "General Observations on the Effects of Person, Political, and Economic Influences in the Decisions of Judges." In *Judicial Behavior: A Reader in Theory and Research*, ed. Glendon Schubert, 40–49. Chicago: Rand McNally.

Hajer, Maarten. 2005. "Setting the Stage: A Dramaturgy of Policy Deliberation." *Administration and Society* 36: 624–47.

Hall, Edward T. 1966. *The Hidden Dimension*. Garden City, NY: Doubleday.

Hall, Stuart. 1982. "The Rediscovery of 'Ideology': Return of the Repressed in Media Studies." In *Culture, Society and the Media*, ed. Michael Gurevitch, Tony Bennett, James Curran, and Janet Woollacott, 56–90. London: Methuen.

————. 1985. "Signification, Representation, Ideology: Althusser and the Post-Structuralist Debates." *Critical Studies in Mass Communication* 2 (2): 91–114.

————. 1986. "The Problem of Ideology—Marxism Without Guarantees." *Journal of Communication Inquiry* 10 (2): 28–44.

————. 1994. "Encoding/Decoding." In *Media Texts: Authors and Readers*, ed. David Graddol and Oliver Boyd-Barrett, 200–211. Clevedon, UK: Multilingual Matters.

————. 1997a. "Introduction." In *Representation: Cultural Representation and Signifying Practices*, 1–11. London: Sage.

————. 1997b. "The Spectacle of the Other." In *Representation: Cultural Representation and Signifying Practices*, 223–90. London: Sage.

Halpern, Edward S. 1983. "Auditing Naturalistic Inquiries: The Development and Application of a Model." Unpublished doctoral dissertation, Indiana University.

Hammersley, Martyn, and Paul Atkinson. 1983. *Ethnography: Principles in Practice*. London: Tavistock.

Haraway, Donna. 1988. "Situated Knowledges: The Science Question in Feminism and the Privilege of the Partial Perspective." *Feminist Studies* 14: 575–99.

Hardin, Russell. 1995. *One for All: The Logic of Group Conflict*. Princeton, NJ: Princeton University Press.

Harding, Sandra. 1986. *The Science Question in Feminism*. Ithaca, NY: Cornell University Press.

————. 1989. "Feminist Justificatory Strategies." In *Women, Knowledge, and Reality*, ed. Ann Garry and Marilyn Pearsall, 189–201. Boston: Unwin, Hyman.

————. 1990. "Feminism, Science, and the Anti-Enlightenment Critiques." In *Feminism/Postmodernism*, ed. Linda J. Nicholson, 83–106. New York: Routledge.

————. 1991. *Whose Science? Whose Knowledge?* Ithaca, NY: Cornell University Press.

————. 1993. "Rethinking Standpoint Epistemology: What Is 'Strong Objectivity'?" In *Feminist Epistemologies*, ed. Linda Alcoff and Elizabeth Potter, 49–82. New York: Routledge.

Harkess, S., and C.A. Warren. 1993. "The Social Relations of Intensive Interviewing: Constellations of Strangeness and Science." *Sociological Methods & Research* 21: 317–39.

Harper, Douglas. 2003. "Reimagining Visual Methods: Galileo to Neuromancer." In *Collecting and Interpreting Qualitative Materials*, ed. Norman K. Denzin and Yvonna S. Lincoln, 2nd ed., 176–98. Thousand Oaks, CA: Sage.

Harré, Rom. 1986. *Varieties of Realism*. Oxford: Basil Blackwell.

Harris, Robert. 1960. *The Quest for Equality: The Constitution, Congress, and the Supreme Court*. Baton Rouge: Louisiana State University Press.

Hart, Henry M. 1954. "Book Review, Politics and the Constitution." *Harvard Law Review* 67: 1439–44.

Hartsock, Nancy C.M. 1987. "The Feminist Standpoint." In *Feminism & Methodology*, ed. Sandra Harding, 157–80. Bloomington: Indiana University Press.

Hastrup, Kirsten. 1992. "Writing Ethnography: State of the Art." In *Anthropology and Autobiography*, ed. Judith Okely and Helen Callaway, 116–33. London: Routledge.

Hatch, Mary Jo. 1990. "The Symbolics of Office Design." In *Symbols and Artifacts*, ed. Pasquale Gagliardi, 129–46. New York: Aldine de Gruyter.

Hatch, Mary Jo, and Dvora Yanow. 2003. "Organizational Studies as an Interpretive Science." In *The Oxford Handbook of Organization Theory: Meta-Theoretical Perspectives*, ed. Christian Knudsen and Haridimos Tsoukas, 63–87. New York: Oxford University Press.

Hawkesworth, M.E. 1988. *Theoretical Issues in Policy Analysis*. Albany: Southern University of New York Press.

———. 1989. "Knowers, Knowing, Known." In *Feminist Theory in Practice and Process*, ed. Micheline Malson, Jean O'Barr, Sarah Westphal-Wihl, and Mary Wyer, 327–51. Chicago: University of Chicago Press.

Hawkesworth, Mary, and Maurice Kogan, eds. 1992. *Encyclopedia of Government and Politics*. London: Routledge.

———. 2003. *Encyclopedia of Government and Politics*, 2nd rev. ed. London: Routledge.

Healy, Patrick. 1997. "Mass Higher Education Leaders to Seek Abolition of Tenure." *Chronicle of Higher Education* (November 14), A36.

Hebel, Sarah. 2004. "Patrolling Professors' Politics: Conservative Activists and Students Press Campaigns Against Perceived Bias on Campuses." *Chronicle of Higher Education* (February 13), A18.

Hegel, G.W.F. 1988. *Introduction to the Philosophy of History, with selections from the Philosophy of Right*, Trans. L. Rauch. Indianapolis, IN: Hackett.

Heidegger, Martin. 1962 [1927]. *Being and Time*, trans. J. Macquarrie and E. Robinson. San Francisco: HarperCollins.

Heldke, Lisa. 1989. "John Dewey and Evelyn Fox Keller: A Shared Epistemological Tradition." In *Feminism & Science*, ed. Nancy Tuana, 104–15. Bloomington: Indiana University Press.

Hempel, Carl. 1965. "The Function of General Laws in History." In *Aspects of Scientific Explanation and Other Essays*, 231–44. New York: Free Press.

Hennis, Wilhelm. 1988. *Max Weber: Essays in Reconstruction*. London: Allen and Unwin.

Herbst, Ludolf. 1989. *Option für den Westen*. Munich: Deutscher Taschenbuch.

Herman, Edward S., and Noam Chomsky. 1988. *Manufacturing Consent: The Political Economy of the Mass Media*. New York: Pantheon.

Hesse, Mary. 1978. "Theory and Value in the Social Sciences." In *Action and Interpretation: Studies in the Philosophy of the Social Sciences*, ed. Christopher Hookway and Philip Pettit, 1–16. Cambridge: Cambridge University Press.

———. 1980. *Revolutions and Reconstructions in the Philosophy of Science*. Brighton: Harvester Press.

Hiley, David R., James F. Bohman, and Richard Shusterman, eds. 1991. *The Interpretive Turn*. Ithaca, NY: Cornell University Press.

Hinchman, Lewis, and Sandra Hinchman. 1997. *Memory, Identity, Community: The Idea of Narrative in the Human Sciences*. Albany: Southern University of New York Press.

Hiss, Tony. 1990. *The Experience of Place*. New York: Random House.

Hochschild, Jennifer L. 1981. *What's Fair? American Beliefs About Distributive Justice*. Cambridge: Harvard University Press.

Hodge, Robert, and Gunther Kress. 1988. *Social Semiotics*. Cambridge, UK: Polity Press.

Hofmann, Jeanette. 1995. "Implicit Theories in Policy Discourse: An Inquiry into the Interpretations of Reality in German Technology Policy." *Policy Sciences* 28: 127–48.

Hollis, Martin, and Steve Smith. 1990. *Explaining and Understanding International Relations*. Oxford: Clarendon Press.

Hollway, Wendy, and Tony Jefferson. 2000. *Doing Qualitative Research Differently: Free Association, Narrative and the Interview Method*. Thousand Oaks, CA: Sage.

Holstein, James A., and Jaber F. Gubrium. 1995. *The Active Interview*. Thousand Oaks, CA: Sage.

Hooper, Charlotte. 2000. "Masculinities in Transition: The Case of Globalization." In *Gender and Global Restructuring*, ed. Marianne H. Marchand and Anne Sisson Runyan, 59–73. New York: Routledge.

———. 2001. *Manly States: Masculinities, International Relations, and Gender Politics*. New York: Columbia University Press.

Hopf, Ted. 2002. *Social Construction of International Politics: Identities and Foreign Policies, Moscow, 1955 and 1999*. Ithaca, NY: Cornell University Press.

———. 2004. "Discourse and Content Analysis: Some Fundamental Ambiguities." *Qualitative Methods: Newsletter of the American Political Science Association Organized Section on Qualitative Methods* 2 (1): 31–3.

Hopper, Kim. 2003. *Reckoning with Homelessness*. Ithaca, NY: Cornell University Press.

Horkheimer, Max. 1995. "Traditional and Critical Theory." In *Critical Theory: Selected Essays*, 188–243. New York: Continuum.

Horwitz, Morton J. 1993. "Foreword: The Constitution of Legal Change: Legal Fundamentalism Without Fundamentalism." *Harvard Law Review* 107: 32–117.

Hoy, David, ed. 1986. *Foucault: A Critical Reader*. New York: Blackwell.

Huberman, A. Michael, and Matthew B. Miles. 1983. "Drawing Valid Meaning from Qualitative Data: Some Techniques of Data Reduction and Display." *Quality and Quantity* 17: 281–339.

Hudson, William Donald. 1970. *Modern Moral Philosophy.* New York: Anchor Books.

Huff, Darrell. 1993. *How To Lie with Statistics*. New York: W.W. Norton.

Hume, David. 1975 [1748]. *An Enquiry Concerning Human Understanding*, ed. Lewis Amhurst Selby-Bigge. 3rd ed., with text revised and notes by P. H. Nidditch. London: Oxford University Press.

———. 1978 [1739]. *A Treatise of Human Nature*, ed. Lewis Amhurst Selby-Bigge, 2nd ed., rev. by P.H. Nidditch. London: Oxford University Press.

Hummon, David. 1989. "House, Home, and Identity in Contemporary American Culture." In *Housing, Culture and Design: A Comparative Perspective*, ed. Setha M. Low and Erve Chambers, 207–28. Philadelphia: University of Pennsylvania Press.

Humphreys, Willard. 1969. *Perception and Discovery*. San Francisco: Freeman, Cooper.

Hunt, Darnell M. 1997. *Screening the Los Angeles "Riots": Race, Seeing, and Resistance*. New York: Cambridge University Press.

Hunt, Michael H. 1987. *Ideology and U.S. Foreign Policy*. New Haven, CT: Yale University Press.

Huntington, Samuel. 1965. "Political Development and Political Decay." *World Politics* 17: 386–430.

———. 1996. *The Clash of Civilizations and the Remaking of World Order*. New York: Simon and Schuster.

Hyden, Goran. 1970. "Language and Administration." In *Development Administration: The Kenyan Experience*, ed. Goran Hyden, Robert Jackson, and John Okumu, 112–25. Nairobi: Oxford University Press.

Hymes, Dell. 1970. "Linguistic Aspects of Comparative Political Research." In *The Methodology of Comparative Research*, ed. Robert T. Holt and John E. Turner, 295–341. New York: Free Press.

Hyneman, Charles. 1959. *The Study of Politics*. Urbana, IL: University of Illinois Press.

Ingersoll, Virginia Hill, and Guy Adams. 1992. *The Tacit Organization*. Greenwich, CT: JAI Press.

Innes, Judith, and David Booher. 2003. "Collaborative Policymaking: Governance Through Dialogue." In *Deliberative Policy Analysis*, ed. Maarten A. Hajer and Hendrik Wagenaar, 33–59. Cambridge: Cambridge University Press.

International Monetary Fund (IMF). 2000. *Globalization: Threat or Opportunity?* International Monetary Fund Report (12 April). Available at www.imf.org/external/np/exr/ib/2000/041200.htm (accessed June 18, 2001).

Iser, Wolfgang. 1989. *Prospecting: From Reader Response to Literary Anthropology*. Baltimore, MD: Johns Hopkins University Press.

Jackson, John Brinkerhoff. 1980. *The Necessity for Ruins, and Other Topics*. Amherst: University of Massachusetts Press.

———. 1984. *Discovering the Vernacular Landscape*. New Haven, CT: Yale University Press.

Jackson, Patrick Thaddeus. 2002a. "Rethinking Weber: Toward a Non-Individualist Sociology of World Politics." *International Review of Sociology* 12: 439–68.

———. 2002b. "The West Is the Best: Culture, Identity, and the Reconstruction of Germany." In *Constructivism and Comparative Politics*, ed. Daniel M. Green, 230–64. Armonk, NY: M.E. Sharpe.

———. 2003. "Defending the West: Occidentalism and the Formation of NATO." *Journal of Political Philosophy* 11: 223–52.

———. 2004. "Hegel's House, or, 'People Are States Too.'" *Review of International Studies* 30: 281–87.

———. 2006. *Civilizing the Enemy: German Reconstruction and the Invention of the West*. Ann Arbor: University of Michigan Press.

Jackson, Patrick Thaddeus, and Daniel H. Nexon. 1999. "Relations Before States: Substance, Process, and the Study of World Politics." *European Journal of International Relations* 5: 291–332.

———. 2002. "Globalization, the Comparative Method, and Comparing Constructions." In *Constructivism and Comparative Politics*, ed. Daniel M. Green, 88–120. Armonk, NY: M.E. Sharpe.

Jacobson, Sarah, and Roy Jacques. 1990. "Of Knowers, Knowing and the Known." Presented at the Academy of Management Annual Meeting (August 10–12).

James, William. 1950 [1869]. *Principles of Psychology*, vol. 2. New York: Dover Publications.

Jennings, Bruce. 1983. "Interpretive Social Science and Policy Analysis." In *Ethics, the Social Sciences, and Policy Analysis*, ed. Daniel Callahan and Bruce Jennings, 3–36. New York: Plenum Press.

———. 1987. "Interpretation and the Practice of Policy Analysis." In *Confronting Values in Policy Analysis*, ed. Frank Fischer and John Forester, 128–52. Newbury Park, CA: Sage.

Joergenson, Joergen. 1951. *The Development of Logical Empiricism*. Vol. 2, no. 9, of the *International Encyclopedia of Unified Science*. Chicago: University of Chicago Press.

Johnson, Chalmers. 1995. "Omote (Explicit) and Ura (Implicit): Translating Japanese Political Terms." In *Japan: Who Governs?* 157–82. New York: W.W. Norton.

Jones, James H. 1981. *Bad Blood: The Tuskegee Syphilis Experiment*. New York: Free Press.

Jones, Laurence F., and Edward C. Olson. 1996. *Political Science Research: A Handbook of Scope and Method*. New York: Addison Wesley Longman.

Jordan, Birgitte. 1989. "Cosmopolitical Obstetrics: Some Insights from the Training of Traditional Midwives." *Social Science and Medicine* 28: 925–44.

———. 1992. "Technology and Social Interaction: Notes on the Achievement of Authoritative Knowledge in Complex Settings." Palo Alto, CA: Institute for Research on Learning Report No. IRL92-0027 (April).

———. 1997. "Authoritative Knowledge and Its Construction." In *Childbirth and Authoritative Knowledge*, ed. Robbie E. Davis-Floyd and Carolyn F. Sargent, 55–79. Berkeley: University of California Press.

Kahn, Ronald, and Ken I. Kersch. 2006. *The Supreme Court in American Political Development*. Lawrence: University Press of Kansas.

Kalman, Laura. 1986. *Legal Realism at Yale, 1927–1960*. Chapel Hill: University of North Carolina Press.

———. 1996. *The Strange Career of Legal Liberalism*. New Haven, CT: Yale University Press.

Kanter, Rosabeth Moss. 1977a. *Men and Women of the Corporation*. New York: Basic Books.

———. 1977b. "Some Effects of Proportions on Group Life: Skewed Sex Ratios and Responses to Token Women." *American Journal of Sociology* 82: 965–90.

———. 1993. *Men and Women of the Corporation*, 2nd ed. New York: Basic Books.

Kaplan, Abraham. 1964. *The Conduct of Inquiry*. San Francisco: Chandler.

Katz, Jack. 2004. "Subterranean Fieldworkers' Blues: Scratching Toward a Common Law of Social Research Ethics." Presented to the Center for the Study of Law and Society, Boalt Hall School of Law, University of California, Berkeley (February 17).

Kaufman, Debra R. 1989. "Patriarchal Women: A Case Study of Newly Orthodox Jewish Women." *Symbolic Interaction* 12: 299–314.

Kaufman, Herbert. 1960. *The Forest Ranger*. Baltimore, MD: Published for Resources for the Future by Johns Hopkins University Press.

Kaufman-Osborn, Timothy. 2006. "Dividing the Domain of Political Science: On the Fetishism of Subfields." *Polity* 38 (January): 41–71.

Keller, Evelyn Fox. 1985. *Reflections on Gender and Science*. New Haven, CT: Yale University Press.

Kelly, Kristin A. 2003. *Domestic Violence and the Politics of Privacy*. Ithaca, NY: Cornell University Press.

Kemper, Theodore D. 1990. *Social Structure and Testosterone*. New Brunswick, NJ: Rutgers University Press.

Kennedy, Liam. 2003. "Remembering September 11: Photography as Cultural Diplomacy." *International Affairs* 79: 315–26.

Keohane, Robert O. 1988. "International Institutions: Two Approaches." *International Studies Quarterly* 32: 379–96.

———. 1989. "International Relations Theory: Contributions of a Feminist Standpoint." *Millennium* 18: 245–53.

———. 2003. "Disciplinary Schizophrenia: Implications for Graduate Education in Political Science." *Qualitative Methods: Newsletter of the American Political Science Association Organized Section on Qualitative Methods* 1 (1): 9–12.

Keohane, Robert O., and Joseph S. Nye. 1977. *Power and Interdependence: World Politics in Transition*. Boston: Little, Brown.

Kerby, Anthony Paul. 1997. "The Language of the Self." In *Memory, Identity, and Community*, ed. Lewis P. Hinchman and Sandra K. Hinchman, 125–42. Albany: SUNY Press.

Killingsworth, M. Jimmie, and Jacqueline S. Palmer. 1992. *Ecospeak: Rhetoric and Environmental Politics in America*. Carbondale: Southern Illinois University Press.

King, Gary, Robert Keohane, and Sidney Verba. 1994. *Designing Social Inquiry*. Princeton, NJ: Princeton University Press.

Kirkpatrick, Jeane. 1979. "Dictatorships and Double Standards." *Commentary* 68 (5): 34–45.

Kirshenblatt-Gimblett, Barbara. 1998. *Destination Culture: Tourism, Museums, and Heritage*. Berkeley: University of California Press.

Kitchin, Rob, and James Kneale. 2001. "Science Fiction or Future Fact? Exploring Imaginative Geographies of the New Millennium." *Progress in Human Geography* 25: 19–35.

Klarman, Michael J. 1998. "The Plessy Era." *Supreme Court Review ##*: 303–414.

Klein, Julie Thompson. 1993. "Blurring, Cracking, and Crossing: Permeation and the Fracturing of Discipline." In *Knowledges: Historical and Critical Studies in Disciplinarity*, ed. Ellen Messer-Davidow, David R. Shumway, and David J. Sylvan, 185–211. Charlottesville: University of Virginia Press.

Klingemann, Hans-Dieter, Richard I. Hofferbert, and Ian Budge. 1994. *Parties, Policies, and Democracy*. Boulder, CO: Westview Press.

Knorr Cetina, Karin. 1999. *Epistemic Cultures: How the Sciences Make Knowledge*. Cambridge: Harvard University Press.

Kondo, Dorinne K. 1990. *Crafting Selves: Power, Gender, and Discourses of Identity in a Japanese Workplace*. Chicago: University of Chicago Press.

Konrad-Adenauer-Stiftung. 1975. *Konrad Adenauer und die CDU der Britischen Besatzungszone, 1946–1949* [Konrad Adenauer and the CDU of the British Zone of Occupation, 1946–1949]. Bonn: Eichholz-Verlag.

Kornberger, Martin, and Stewart R. Clegg. 2004. "Bringing Space Back In: Organizing the Generative Building." *Organization Studies* 25: 1095–114.

Kraft, Viktor. 1952. *The Vienna Circle*. New York: Philosophical Library.

Kraidy, Marwan M., and Tamara Goeddertz. 2003. "Transnational Advertising and International Relations: U.S. Press Discourses on the Benetton 'We on Death Row' Campaign." *Media, Culture and Society* 25: 147–65.

Kratochwil, Friedrich. 1986. "Of Systems, Boundaries, and Territoriality: An Inquiry into the Formation of the State System." *World Politics* 39: 27–52.

Krieger, Linda. 1995. "The Content of Our Categories." *Stanford Law Review* 47: 1161–248.

Kristeva, Julia. 1980. *Desire in Language: A Semiotic Approach to Literature and Art*. New York: Columbia University Press.

Kuhn, Thomas S. 1970. *The Structure of Scientific Revolutions*, 2nd ed. Chicago: University of Chicago Press.

———. 1977. *The Essential Tension*. Chicago: University of Chicago Press.

Kunda, Gideon. 1992. *Engineering Culture*. Philadelphia: Temple University Press.

Kvale, Steinar. 1996. *InterViews: An Introduction to Qualitative Research Interviewing*. Thousand Oaks, CA: Sage.

Kymlicka, Will. 1989. *Liberalism, Community and Culture*. New York: Oxford University Press.

———. 1995. *Multicultural Citizenship*. New York: Oxford University Press.

Labbé, Ronald M., and Jonathan Lurie. 2003. *The Slaughterhouse Cases: Regulation, Reconstruction, and the Fourteenth Amendment*. Lawrence: University Press of Kansas.

Labov, William. 1966. *The Social Stratification of English in New York City*. Washington, DC: Center for Applied Linguistics.

———. 1969. "The Logic of Nonstandard English." *Georgetown Monographs on Language and Linguistics* 22: 1–22, 26–31.

———. 1972. *Language in the Inner City*. Philadelphia: University of Pennsylvania Press.

Laffey, Mark, and Jutta Weldes. 1997. "Beyond Belief: Ideas and Symbolic Technologies in the Study of International Relations." *European Journal of International Relations* 3: 193–237.

———. 2004. "US Foreign Policy, Public Memory and Autism: Representing September 11 and May 4." *Cambridge Review of International Affairs* 17: 355–75.

Lagon, Mark. 1993. "'We Owe It to Them to Interfere': *Star Trek* and U.S. Statecraft in the 1960s and 1990s." *Extrapolation* 34: 251–64.

Laitin, David D. 1977. *Politics, Language, and Thought: The Somali Experience*. Chicago: University of Chicago Press.

———. 2003. "Interpretation." *Qualitative Methods: Newsletter of the American Political Science Association Organized Section on Qualitative Methods* 1 (2): 6–9.

Lakatos, Imre. 1970. "Falsification and the Methodology of Scientific Research Programmes." In *Criticism and the Growth of Knowledge*, ed. Imre Lakatos and Alan Musgrave, 91–195. Cambridge: Cambridge University Press.

———. 1976. "History of Science and Its Rational Reconstructions." In *Method and Appraisal in the Physical Sciences*, ed. Colin Howson, 41–106. Cambridge: Cambridge University Press.

Lakoff, George, and Mark Johnson. 1980. *Metaphors We Live By*. Chicago: University of Chicago Press.

———. 1999. *Philosophy in the Flesh*. New York: Basic Books.

Lakoff, Robin Tolmach. 1976. *Language and Woman's Place*. New York: Octagon.

Landau, Martin. 1968. "On the Use of Functional Analysis in American Political Science." *Social Research* 35: 48–75.

Lane, Robert E. 1962. *Political Ideology*. New York: Free Press.

Lasswell, Harold. 1950. *Politics: Who Gets What, When, How*. New York: P. Smith.

———. 1979. *The Signature of Power*. New Brunswick, NJ: Transaction.

Lather, Patty. 1993. "Fertile Obsession: Validity After Poststructuralism." *Sociological Quarterly* 34: 673–93.

Latour, Bruno. 1987. *Science in Action: How to Follow Scientists and Engineers Through Society*. Cambridge: Harvard University Press.

———. 1990. "Drawing Things Together." In *Representation in Scientific Practice*, ed. Michael Lynch and Steve Woolgar, 19–68. Cambridge: MIT Press.

———. 1999. *Pandora's Hope*. Cambridge: Harvard University Press.

Latour, Bruno, and Steve Woolgar. 1988. *Laboratory Life: The Construction of Scientific Facts*, 2nd ed. Princeton, NJ: Princeton University Press.

Laudan, Larry. 1990. *Science and Relativism*. Chicago: University of Chicago Press.

Laver, Michael J., and Ian Budge, eds. 1992. *Party Policy and Government Coalitions*. New York: St. Martin's Press.

Laver, Michael J., Kenneth Benoit, and John Garry. 2003. "Extracting Policy Positions from Political Texts Using Words as Data." *American Political Science Review* 97: 311–31.

Law, John. 2002. *Aircraft Stories*. Durham, NC: Duke University Press.

Law, John, and Peter Lodge. 1984. *Science for Social Scientists*. London: Macmillan.

Law, John, and John Whittaker. 1988. "On the Art of Representation: Notes on the Politics of Visualisation." In *Picturing Power*, ed. Gordon Fyfe and John Law, 160–83. New York: Routledge.

Lawrence, Denise L., and Setha M. Low. 1990. "The Built Environment and Spatial Form." *Annual Review of Anthropology* 19: 453–505.

Leap, William L. 1996. *Word's Out: Gay Men's English*. Minneapolis: University of Minnesota Press.

Leech, Beth L. 2002. "Asking Questions: Techniques for Semistructured Interviews." *PS: Political Science and Politics* 35: 665–68.

Leech, Beth L., Joel D. Aberbach, Jeffrey M. Berry, Kenneth Goldstein, Polina M. Kozyreva, Sharon Werning Rivera, Bert A. Rockman, Eduard G. Sarovskii, and Laura R. Woliver. 2002. Symposium: "Interview Methods in Political Science." *PS: Political Science and Politics* 35: 663–88.

Levi, Margaret. 2004. "An Analytic Narrative Approach to Puzzles and Problems." In *Problems and Methods in the Study of Politics*, ed. Ian Shapiro, Rogers M. Smith, and Tarek E. Masoud, 201–26. New York: Cambridge University Press.

Levinson, Stephen C. 1996. "Language and Space." *Annual Review of Anthropology* 25: 353–82.

Lévi-Strauss, Claude. 1969. *The Raw and the Cooked*, trans. John and Doreen Weightman. New York: Harper and Row.

Levy, Jack S. 1989. "Domestic Politics and War." In *The Origins and Prevention of Major Wars*, ed. Robert I. Rothberg and Theodore K. Rabb, 79–99. New York: Cambridge University Press.

Lewis, Bernard. 1988. *The Political Language of Islam*. Chicago: University of Chicago Press.

Lewis-Beck, Michael S., Alan Bryman, and Tim Futing Liao, eds. 2004. *Sage Encyclopedia of Social Science Research Methods*. Thousand Oaks, CA: Sage.

Lieber, Francis. 1993 [1858]. "History and Political Science, Necessary Studies in Free Countries." In *Discipline and History: Political Science in the United States*, ed. James Farr and Raymond Seidelman, 21–32. Ann Arbor: University of Michigan Press.

Liebow, Elliott. 1967. *Tally's Corner*. Boston: Little, Brown.

———. 1993. *Tell Them Who I Am: The Lives of Homeless Women*. New York: Free Press.

Lifton, Robert Jay. 1986. *The Nazi Doctors*. New York: Basic Books.

Lin, Ann Chih. 1998. "Bridging Positivist and Interpretivist Approaches to Qualitative Methods." *Policy Studies Journal* 26: 162–80.

———. 2000. *Reform in the Making*. Princeton, NJ: Princeton University Press.

Lincoln, Yvonna S. 1995. "Emerging Criteria for Quality in Qualitative and Interpretive Research." *Qualitative Inquiry* 1: 275–89.

Lincoln, Yvonna S., and Egon G. Guba. 1985. "Establishing Trustworthiness." In *Naturalistic Inquiry*, 289–331. Thousand Oaks, CA: Sage.

Lincoln, Yvonna S., and William G. Tierney. 2004. "Qualitative Research and Institutional Review Boards." *Qualitative Inquiry* 10: 219–34.

Lindblom, Charles. 1965. *The Intelligence of Democracy*. New York: Free Press.

Lindblom, Charles, and David K. Cohen. 1979. *Usable Knowledge*. New Haven, CT: Yale University Press.

Linder, Steven. 1995. "Contending Discourses in the Electric and Magnetic Fields Controversy." *Policy Sciences* 28: 209–30.

Lipschutz, Ronnie D. 2001. *Film, Fiction, and the Cold War—Popular Culture and Foreign Policy During America's Half Century*. Boulder, CO: Rowman and Littlefield.

———. 2003. "Aliens, Alien Nation and Alienation in American Political Economy and Popular Culture." In *To Seek Out New Worlds: Exploring Links Between Science Fiction and World Politics*, ed. Jutta Weldes, 79–98. New York: Palgrave.

Lipsky, Michael. 1978. "Standing the Study of Public Policy Implementation on Its Head." In *American Politics and Public Policy*, ed. Walter Dean Burnham and Martha Wagner Weinberg, 391–402. Cambridge: MIT Press.

———. 1980. *Street-Level Bureaucracy*. New York: Russell Sage Foundation.

Livingstone, David N. 2003. *Putting Science in Its Place*. Chicago: University of Chicago Press.

Locke, Karen D. 2001. *Grounded Theory in Management Research*. Thousand Oaks, CA: Sage.

Locke, Karen D., Karen Golden-Biddle, and Martha Feldman. 2004. "Imaginative Theorizing in Organizational Research." Presented at the American Political Science Association Annual Meeting, Chicago, IL (September 2–5).

Lofland, John. 1966. *Doomsday Cult: A Study of Conversation, Proselytization, and Maintenance of Faith*. Englewood Cliffs, NJ: Prentice-Hall.

———. 1969. *Deviance and Identity*. Englewood Cliffs, NJ: Prentice-Hall.

Long, David, and Brian C. Schmidt. 2004. *Imperialism and Internationalism in the Discipline of International Relations*. Albany: SUNY Press.

Longino, Helen. 1990. *Science as Social Knowledge*. Princeton, NJ: Princeton University Press.

Lorenz, Chris. 1998. "Can Histories Be True? Narrativism, Positivism, and the 'Metaphorical Turn.'" *History and Theory* 37: 309–30.

Loughlin, John, and B. Guy Peters. 1997. "State Traditions, Administrative Reform and Regionalization." In *The Political Economy of Regionalism*, ed. M. Keating and J. Loughlin, 41–62. London: Frank Cass.

Lovell, George. 2003. *Legislative Deferrals: Statutory Ambiguity, Judicial Power, and American Democracy*. New York: Cambridge University Press.

Low, Setha M. 2000. *On the Plaza: The Politics of Public Space and Culture*. Austin: University of Texas Press.

Low, Setha M., and Denise Lawrence-Zúñiga, eds. 2003. *The Anthropology of Space and Place: Locating Culture*. Oxford: Blackwell.

Luft, Joseph. 1963. *Group Processes*. Palo Alto, CA: National Press Books.

Luke, Timothy W. 1999. "The Discipline as Disciplinary Normalization: Networks of Research." *New Political Science* 2: 345–63.

———. 2002. *Museum Politics*. Minneapolis: University of Minnesota Press.

———. 2004. "The Natural Science Model in American Political Science: When Is It Natural, How Is It Science, and Why Is It a Model?" Paper presented at the Midwest Political Science Association Annual Meeting, Chicago, IL (April 15–18).

Luker, Kristin. 1984. *Abortion and the Politics of Motherhood*. Berkeley: University of California Press.

Lutz, Catherine A., and Jane L. Collins. 1993. *Reading National Geographic*. Chicago: University of Chicago Press.

Lynch, Cecelia. 1999. *Beyond Appeasement: Interpreting Interwar Peace Movements in World Politics*. Ithaca, NY: Cornell University Press.

———. 2005. "The 'R' Word, Narrative, and Perestroika: A Critique of Language and Method." In *Perestroika! The Raucous Rebellion in Political Science*, ed. Kristen Renwick Monroe, 154–66. New Haven, CT: Yale University Press.

Lynch, Kevin. 1960. *The Image of the City*. Cambridge: MIT Press.

———. 1972. *What Time Is this Place?* Cambridge: MIT Press.

Lynch, Michael. 1990. "The Externalized Retina: Selection and Mathematization in the Visual Documentation of Objects in the Life Sciences." In *Representation in Scientific Practice*, ed. Michael Lynch and Steve Woolgar, 152–86. Cambridge: MIT Press.

———. 2001. "Ethnomethodology and the Logic of Practice." In *The Practice Turn in Contemporary Theory*, ed. Theodore R. Schatzki, Karin Knorr Cetina, and Eike van Savigny, 131–47. New York: Routledge.

Lynch, Michael, and Woolgar, Steve, eds. 1990a. "Preface and Introduction." In *Representation in Scientific Practice*, 1–18. Cambridge: MIT Press.

———. 1990b. *Representation in Scientific Practice*. Cambridge: MIT Press.

Lynn, Marvin, Tara J. Yosso, Daniel G. Solorzano, and Laurence Parker, eds. 2002. "Critical Race Theory and Qualitative Research." Special issue, *Qualitative Inquiry* 5: 3–126.

MacIntyre, Alasdair. 1981. *After Virtue*. Notre Dame, IN: University of Notre Dame Press.

MacLeod, Jay. 1995. "On the Making of Ain't No Makin' It." In *Ain't No Makin' It: Aspirations and Attainment in a Low-Income Neighborhood*, 270–302. Boulder, CO: Westview Press.

MacRae, Duncan. 1976. *The Social Function of Social Science*. New Haven, CT: Yale University Press.

Mahoney, James, and Dietrich Rueschemeyer, eds. 2003a. *Comparative Historical Analysis in the Social Sciences*. Cambridge: Cambridge University Press.

———. 2003b. "Comparative Historical Analysis: Achievements and Agendas." In *Comparative Historical Analysis in the Social Sciences*, 3–38. Cambridge: Cambridge University Press.

Majone, Giandomenico. 1989. *Evidence, Argument, and Persuasion in the Policy Process*. New Haven, CT: Yale University Press.

Malinowski, Bronislaw. 1922. *Argonauts of the Western Pacific*. New York: E.P. Dutton.

Malone, Paul V., and Ronald J. Chenail. 2001. "Qualitative Inquiry in Psychotherapy." In *The Heart and Soul of Change*, ed. Mark A. Hubble, Barry L. Duncan, and Scott D. Miller, 57–88. Washington, DC: American Psychological Association.

Malone, Ruth E. 2003. "Distal Nursing." *Social Science and Medicine* 56: 2317–326.

Mangan, J.A., ed. 2000. *Superman Supreme: Fascist Body as Political Icon—Global Fascism*. London: Frank Cass.

Mannheim, Karl. 1985 [1936]. *Ideology and Utopia: An Introduction to the Sociology of Knowledge*. New York: Harcourt, Brace and Jovanovich.

Manning, Peter K. 1977. *Police Work: The Social Organization of Policing*. Cambridge: MIT Press.

———. 1987. *Semiotics and Fieldwork*. Newbury Park, CA: Sage.

Mark, Eduard. 1989. "October or Thermidor? Interpretations of Stalinism and the Perception of Soviet Foreign Policy in the United States, 1927–1947." *American Historical Review* 94: 937–62.

Marshall, Catherine, and Gretchen B. Rossman. 1995. *Designing Qualitative Research*, 2nd ed. Thousand Oaks, CA: Sage.

Martine, George, Monica Das Gupta, and Chen C. Lincoln, eds. 1999. *Reproductive Change in India and Brazil*. Oxford: Oxford University Press.

Marx, Karl. 1967. *Capital: A Critique of Political Economy*, vol. 1, ed. Frederick Engels. New York: International.

Mathes, J.C., and Dwight W. Stevenson. 1991. *Designing Technical Reports: Writing for Audiences in Organizations*. New York: Macmillan.

Mathison, Sandra. 1988. "Why Triangulate?" *Educational Researcher* 17: 13–17.

Matthew, Henry C.G. 1995. *Gladstone, 1875–1898*. Oxford: Clarendon Press.

Maxwell, Joseph A. 1992. "Understanding and Validity in Qualitative Research." *Harvard Educational Review* 62: 279–300.

Maynard-Moody, Steven, and Suzanne Leland. 1999. "Stories from the Front-Lines of Public Management." In *Advancing Public Management*, ed. Jeffrey L. Brudney, Jr., Laurence O'Toole, and Hal G. Rainey, 109–23. Washington, DC: Georgetown University Press.

Maynard-Moody, Steven, and Michael Musheno. 2000. "State-Agent or Citizen-Agent: Two Narratives of Discretion." *Journal of Public Administration Theory & Research* 10: 329–59.

———. 2003. *Cops, Teachers, Counselors: Stories from the Front Lines of Public Service*. Ann Arbor: University of Michigan Press.

Maynard-Moody, Steven, and Donald D. Stull. 1987. "The Symbolic Side of Policy Analysis." In *Confronting Values in Policy Analysis*, ed. Frank Fischer and John Forester, 248–65. Newbury Park, CA: Sage.

Mazumdar, Sanjoy. 1988. "Organizational Culture and Physical Environments." Doctoral dissertation, Department of Urban Studies and Planning, Massachusetts Institute of Technology.

McAdam, Doug, Sidney Tarrow, and Charles Tilly. 2001. *Dynamics of Contention*. Cambridge: Cambridge University Press.

McCann, Michael W. 1994. *Rights at Work*. Chicago: University of Chicago Press.

McCloskey, Donald N. 1985. *The Rhetoric of Economics*. Madison: University of Wisconsin Press.

McCloskey, Robert G. 1960. *The American Supreme Court*. Chicago: University of Chicago Press.

McClure, Kirstie. 1999. "Figuring Authority." *Theory and Event* 3 (1). Available at http://muse.jhu.edu/journals/theory_&_event/toc/archive.html (accessed November 15, 2003).

McConnell, Michael. 1995. "Originalism and the Desegregation Decisions." *Virginia Law Review* 81: 947–1140.

McCracken, Grant. 1988. *The Long Interview*. Newbury Park, CA: Sage.

McDonald, Terrence J., ed. 1996. *The Historic Turn in the Human Sciences*. Ann Arbor: University of Michigan Press.

McGrath, Joseph Edward, Joanne Martin, and Richard A. Kulka. 1982. *Judgment Calls in Research*. Beverly Hills, CA: Sage.

McGwin, Gerald, Jesse Metzger, and Loring W. Rue. 2004. "The Influence of Side Air Bags on the Risk of Head and Thoracic Injury Following Motor Vehicle Collisions." *Journal of Trauma* 56: 670–75.

McNabb, Steve. 1990. "Self-Reports in Cross-Cultural Contexts." *Human Organization* 49: 291–95.

Mead, George Herbert. 1934. *Mind, Self, and Society*. Chicago: University of Chicago Press.

Meehan, Eugene. 1965. *The Theory and Method of Political Analysis*. Homewood, IL: Dorsey Press.

Mehrabian, Albert. 1972. *Nonverbal Communication*. Chicago: Aldine.

Meinig, D.W., ed. 1979. *The Interpretation of Ordinary Landscapes*. New York: Oxford University Press.

Menand, Louis. 1997. *A Pragmatism Reader*. New York: Vintage.

———. 2001. *The Metaphysical Club*. New York: Farrar, Straus and Giroux.

Merton, Robert K. 1957. *Social Theory and Social Structure*, rev. ed. New York: Free Press.

Merton, Robert K., and Elinor Barber. 2004. *The Travels and Adventures of Serendipity: A Study in Sociological Semantics and the Sociology of Science*. Princeton, NJ: Princeton University Press.

Merttens, Ruth. 2004. "Losing the Plot." In *Defending Objectivity*, ed. Margaret S. Archer and William Outhwaite, 14–30. New York: Routledge.

Miles, Matthew B., and A. Michael Huberman. 1984. *Qualitative Data Analysis: A Sourcebook of New Methods*. Beverly Hills, CA: Sage.

———. 1994. *Qualitative Data Analysis: An Expanded Sourcebook*. Beverly Hills, CA: Sage.

Mill, John Stuart. 1865 [1843]. *A System of Logic Ratiocinative and Inductive: Being a Connected View of the Principles of Evidence and the Methods of Scientific Investigation*, 8th ed. London: Longmans.

Miller, Daniel, and Don Slater. 2000. *The Internet: An Ethnographic Approach*. New York: Berg.

Miller, Nancy K. 1986. "Changing the Subject." In *Feminist Studies/Critical Studies*, ed. Teresa de Lauretis, 102–20. Bloomington: Indiana University Press.

Miller, Richard. 1987. *Fact and Method*. Princeton, NJ: Princeton University Press.

Miller, Warren E., Donald R. Kinder, and Steven J. Rosenstone. 1993. *American National Elections Study, 1992: Pre- and Post-Election Survey*. Ann Arbor, MI: Inter-University Consortium for Political and Social Research.

Milliken, Jennifer. 1999. "The Study of Discourse in International Relations: A Critique of Research and Methods." *European Journal of International Relations* 5: 225–54.

———. 2001. *The Social Construction of the Korean War: Conflict and Its Possibilities*. New York: Manchester University Press.

Mills, C. Wright. 1940. "Situated Actions and Vocabularies of Motive." *American Sociological Review* 5: 904–13.

———. 1959. *The Sociological Imagination*. New York: Oxford University Press.

Mink, Louis. 1978. "Narrative Form as a Cognitive Instrument." In *The Writing of History*, ed. Robert Canary and Henry Kozicki, 129–40. Madison: University of Wisconsin Press.

Mitchell, Sara McLaughlin. 2002. "A Kantian System? Democracy and Third-Party Conflict Resolution." *American Journal of Political Science* 46: 749–59.

Mitchell, Timothy. 1991. *Colonising Egypt*. Berkeley: University of California Press.

———. 2002. *Rule of Experts*. Berkeley: University of California Press.

Mitchell, William C. 1958. "The Polity and Society: A Structural Functional Analysis." *Midwest Journal of Political Science* 2: 403–40.

——. 1967. *Sociological Analysis and Politics.* Englewood Cliffs, NJ: Prentice-Hall.

Modelsky, George. 1990. "Is World Politics Evolutionary Learning?" *International Organization* 44: 1–24.

Modleski, Tania. 1986. "Feminism and the Power of Interpretation." In *Feminist Studies/Critical Studies,* ed. Teresa de Lauretis, 121–38. Bloomington: Indiana University Press.

Molière. 1970. *Le Bourgeois Gentilhomme,* ed. Yves Hucher. Paris: Larousse.

Monk, Ray. 2004. "Objectivity, Postmodernism and Biographical Understanding." In *Defending Objectivity,* ed. Margaret S. Archer and William Outhwaite, 33–47. New York: Routledge.

"Monroe Doctrine Guards West." 1960. *New York Times* (July 13), A3.

Monroe, Kristen Renwick. 1996. *The Heart of Altruism.* Princeton, NJ: Princeton University Press.

——. ed. 2005. *Perestroika! The Raucous Rebellion in Political Science.* New Haven, CT: Yale University Press.

Moon, Donald. 1975. "The Logic of Political Inquiry: A Synthesis of Opposed Perspectives." In *Handbook of Political Science,* ed. Fred Greenstein and Nelson Polsby, vol. 1, 131–217. Reading, MA: Addison-Wesley.

Moore, Barrington. 1958. *Political Power and Social Theory.* Cambridge: Harvard University Press.

Moore, Mike. 2000. "In Praise of the Future." Speech to the Canterbury Employers Chamber of Commerce, New Zealand (14 August). Available at www.wto.org/english/news_e/spmm_e/spmm33_e.htm (accessed July 21, 2005).

——. 2001a. "The WTO: What Is at Stake?" European Business School: Sixth John Payne Memorial Lecture, London (12 March). Available at www.wto.org/english/news_e/spmm_e/spmm54_e.htm (accessed July 21, 2005).

——. 2001b. "The WTO: Challenges Ahead." Speech at the Conference on the Role of the WTO in Global Governance, Geneva (5 May). Available at www.wto.org/english/news_e/spmm_e/spmm52_e.htm (accessed July 21, 2005).

——. 2001c. "Promoting Openness, Fairness, and Predictability in International Trade for the Benefit of Humanity." Speech to the Inter-Parliamentary Union Meeting on International Trade, Geneva (8 June). Available at www.wto.org/english/news_e/spmm_e/spmm64_e.htm (accessed July 21, 2005).

Morgenthau, Hans. 1967. *Politics Among Nations: The Struggle for Power and Peace.* New York: Alfred A. Knopf.

Moriarty, Catherine. 1997. "Private Grief and Public Remembrance: British First World War Memorials." In *War and Memory in the Twentieth Century,* ed. Martin Evans and Ken Lunn, 125–42. Oxford: Berg.

Morrison, Wayne. 2004. "'Reflections with Memories': Everyday Photography Capturing Genocide." *Theoretical Criminology* 8: 341–58.

Morse, Janice M., and Lyn Richards. 2002. *Read Me First for a User's Guide to Qualitative Methods.* Thousand Oaks, CA: Sage.

Morton, Rebecca B. 1999. *Methods and Models: A Guide to the Empirical Analysis of Formal Models in Political Science.* Cambridge: Cambridge University Press.

Mosca, Gaetano. 1939. *The Ruling Class.* New York: McGraw-Hill.

Mosse, George L. 1975. *The Nationalization of the Masses.* New York: Howard Fertig.

Moustakas, Clark E. 1994. *Phenomenological Research Methods.* Thousand Oaks, CA: Sage.

Muppidi, Himadeep. 1999. "Postcoloniality and the Production of Insecurity: The Persistent Puzzle of U.S.-Indian Relations." In *Cultures of Insecurity: States, Communities and the Production of Danger,* ed. Jutta Weldes, Mark Laffey, Hugh Gusterson, and Raymond Duvall, 119–46. Minneapolis: University of Minnesota Press.

Murphy, Jerome T. 1980. *Getting the Facts.* Santa Monica: Goodyear.

Murray, Thomas. 1983. "Partial Knowledge." In *Ethics, the Social Sciences and Policy Analysis,* ed. Daniel Callahan and Bruce Jennings, 305–31. New York: Plenum Press.

Nakamura, Robert. 1990. "The Japan External Trade Organization and Import Promotion." In *Implementation and the Policy Process,* ed. Dennis J. Palumbo and Donald J. Calista, 67–86. New York: Greenwood Press.

Nash, Roderick. 1967. *Wilderness and the American Mind.* New Haven, CT: Yale University Press.

National Environmental Policy Act. 1969. 42 U.S.C. § 4321 *et seq.*

Nelson, Cary. 2004. "The Brave New World of Research Surveillance." *Qualitative Inquiry* 10: 207–18.

Neuman, W. Laurence. 1997. *Social Research Methods: Qualitative and Quantitative Approaches,* 3rd ed. Needham Heights, MA: Allyn and Bacon.

Neuman, W. Russell, Marion R. Just, and Ann N. Crigler. 1992. *Common Knowledge*. Chicago: University of Chicago Press.

Neumann, Iver. 1999. *Uses of the Other*. Minneapolis: University of Minnesota Press.

Nevo, Ofra. 1984. "Appreciation and Production of Humor as an Expression of Aggression: A Study of Jews and Arabs in Israel." *Journal of Cross-Cultural Psychology* 15: 181–98.

Newman, Katherine S. 1999. *No Shame in My Game: The Working Poor in the Inner City*. New York: Knopf and Russell Sage Foundation.

Newton-Smith, W.H. 1981. *The Rationality of Science*. London: Routledge.

Ng, Sik Hung. 1996. "Power: An Essay in Honour of Henri Tajfel." In *Social Groups and Identities: Developing the Legacy of Henri Tajfel*, ed. W. Peter Robinson, 191–214. Oxford: Butterworth-Heinemann.

Nicholson, Linda J., ed. 1990. *Feminism/Postmodernism*. New York: Routledge.

Nicolini, Davide, Silvia Gherardi, and Dvora Yanow. 2003. *Knowing in Organizations: A Practice-Based Approach*. Armonk, NY: M.E. Sharpe.

Nietzsche, Friedrich. 1967. *On the Genealogy of Morals*, trans. W. Kaufmann. New York: Random House.

Noakes, Lucy. 1997. "Making Histories: Experiencing the Blitz in London's Museums in the 1990s." In *War and Memory in the Twentieth Century*, ed. Martin Evans and Ken Lunn, 89–104. Oxford: Berg.

Norton, Anne. 2004a. *95 Theses on Politics, Culture, and Method*. New Haven, CT: Yale University Press.

———. 2004b. "Political Science as a Vocation." In *Problems and Methods in the Study of Politics*, ed. Ian Shapiro, Rogers M. Smith, and Tarek E. Masoud, 67–82. New York: Cambridge University Press.

Noschis, Kaj. 1987. "Public Settings of a Neighborhood." *Architecture & Behaviour* 3: 301–16.

Novkov, Julie. 2001. *Constituting Workers, Protecting Women: Gender, Law, and Labor in the Progressive Era and New Deal Years*. Ann Arbor: University of Michigan Press.

Ó Tuathail, Gearóid, and John Agnew. 1992. "Geopolitics and Discourse: Practical Geopolitical Reasoning in American Foreign Policy." *Political Geography* 11: 190–204.

O'Connor, James. 2001. *The Fiscal Crisis of the State*. New York: Transaction.

Oberweis, Trish, and Michael Musheno. 1999. "Policing Identities: Cop Decision-Making and the Constitution of Citizens." *Law and Social Inquiry* 24: 897–923.

———. 2001. *Knowing Rights: State Actors' Stories of Power, Identity and Morality*. Burlington, VT: Ashgate/Dartmouth.

Office of Environmental Project Review. 1983. Internal Memorandum (July 14).

———. 1986. Internal Memorandum (November 28).

Ohmae, Kenichi. 1995. *The End of the Nation State: The Rise of Regional Economies*. New York: HarperCollins.

———. 1999. *A Borderless World: Power and Strategy in the Interlinked Economy*. New York: HarperBusiness.

Okely, Judith. 1975. "The Self and Scientism." *Journal of the Anthropological Society of Oxford* 6: 171–88.

———. 1992. "Anthropology and Autobiography: Participatory Experience and Embodied Knowledge." In *Anthropology and Autobiography*, ed. Judith Okely and Helen Callaway, 1–28. London: Routledge.

Okely, Judith, and Helen Callaway, eds. 1992. *Anthropology and Autobiography*. London: Routledge.

Oneal, John R., and Bruce M. Russett. 1999. "The Kantian Peace: The Pacific Benefits of Democracy, Interdependence, and International Organizations, 1885–1992." *World Politics* 52: 1–37.

Onuf, Nicholas. 1998. "Constructivism: A User's Manual." In *International Relations in a Constructed World*, ed. Vendulka Kubálková, Nicholas Onuf, and Paul Kowert, 58–78. Armonk, NY. M.E. Sharpe.

Oren, Ido. 1995. "The Subjectivity of the 'Democratic' Peace: Changing U.S. Perceptions of Imperial Germany." *International Security* 20: 147–84.

———. 2003. *Our Enemies and US: America's Rivalries and the Making of Political Science*. Ithaca, NY: Cornell University Press.

Orlove, Benjamin S. 1991. "Mapping Reeds and Reading Maps: The Politics of Representation in Lake Titicaca." *American Ethnologist* 18: 3–38.

Orr, Julian. 1992. "Ethnography and Organizational Learning: In Pursuit of Learning at Work." Paper presented to the NATO Advanced Research Workshop, "Organizational Learning and Technological Change," Siena, Italy (September).

———. 1996. *Talking About Machines: An Ethnography of a Modern Job*. Ithaca, NY: Cornell University Press.

Orren, Karen, and Stephen Skowronek. 1995. "Order and Time in Institutional Study: A Brief for the Historical Approach." In *Political Science and History: Research Programs and Historical Traditions*, ed. James Farr, John S. Dryzek, and Stephen T. Leonard, 296–317. New York: Cambridge University Press.

Ortner, Sherry B. 1996. "Resistance and the Problem of Ethnographic Refusal." In *The Historic Turn in the Human Sciences*, ed. Terrence J. McDonald, 281–304. Ann Arbor: University of Michigan Press.

Owen, John M. 1994. "How Liberalism Produces the Democratic Peace." *International Security* 19: 87–125.

———. 1997. *Liberal Peace, Liberal War: American Politics and International Security*. Ithaca, NY: Cornell University Press.

Pader, Ellen-J. 1988. "Inside Spatial Relations." *Architecture & Behaviour* 4: 251–67.

———. 1993. "Spatiality and Social Change: Domestic Space Use in Mexico and the United States." *American Ethnologist* 20: 114–37.

———. 1994a. "Sociospatial Relations of Change: Rural Mexican Women in Urban California." In *Women and the Environment*, ed. Irwin Altman and Arza Churchman, 73–103. New York: Plenum Press.

———. 1994b. "Spatial Relations and Housing Policy: Regulations that Discriminate Against Mexican-Origin Households." *Journal of Planning Education and Research* 13: 119–35.

———. 1997. "Redefining the Home." *New York Times* (May 7), Op-Ed.

———. 1998. "Housing Occupancy Codes." In *The Encyclopedia of Housing*, ed. Willem van Vliet, 288–90. Thousand Oaks, CA: Sage.

———. 2002. "Housing Occupancy Standards: Inscribing Ethnicity and Family Relations on the Land." *Journal of Architecture and Planning Research* 19: 300–318.

Paley, Julia. 2001. "Making Democracy Count." *Cultural Anthropology* 16: 135–64.

Papa, Michael J., Mohammed A. Auwal, and Arvind Singhal. 1995. "Dialectic of Control and Emancipation in Organizing for Social Change: A Multi-Theoretical Study of the Grameen Bank in Bangladesh." *Communication Theory* 5: 189–223.

Park, Robert E., and Ernest W. Burgess. 1921. *Introduction to the Science of Sociology*. Chicago: University of Chicago Press.

Parsons, Talcott. 1937. *The Structure of Social Action*. New York: McGraw-Hill.

———. 1954a. *Essays in Sociological Theory*, rev. ed. Glencoe, IL: Free Press.

———. 1954b. "The Present Position and Prospects of Systematic Theory in Sociology." In *Essays in Sociological Theory*, 212–37. New York: Free Press.

Parsons, Talcott, and Edward A. Shils. 1951. "Values, Motives, and Systems of Action." In *Toward a General Theory of Action: Theoretical Foundations for the Social Sciences*, 1–189. Cambridge: Harvard University Press.

Passmore, John. 1967. "Logical Positivism." *Encyclopedia of Philosophy*, vol. 5, 52–57. New York: Macmillan.

Patomäki, Heikki, and Collin Wight. 2000. "After Postpositivism? The Promises of Critical Realism." *International Studies Quarterly* 44: 213–37.

Patton, Carl V., and David S. Sawicki. 1993. *Basic Methods of Policy Analysis and Planning*, 2nd ed. Englewood Cliffs, NJ: Prentice-Hall.

Pease, Donald. 1993. "Hiroshima, the Vietnam Veterans Memorial, and the Gulf War." In *Cultures of United States Imperialism*, ed. Amy Kaplan and Donald E. Pease, 557–80. Durham, NC: Duke University Press.

Penley, Constance. 1997. *NASA/Trek: Popular Science and Sex in America*. London: Verso.

Perri 6. 1997. *Holistic Government*. London: Demos.

Perry, William G., Jr. 1970. *Forms of Intellectual and Ethical Development in the College Years*. New York: Holt, Rinehart and Winston.

Peters, John Durham. 1990. "Rhetoric's Revival, Positivism's Persistence: Social Science, Clear Communication, and the Public Space." *Sociological Theory* 8: 224–31.

Pfeffer, Jeffrey. 1981. *Power in Organizations*. Boston: Pitman.

Pierce, Jennifer. 1995. *Gender Trials: Emotional Lives in Contemporary Law Firms*. Berkeley: University of California Press.

Pitkin, Hanna. 1972. *Wittgenstein and Justice*. Berkeley: University of California Press.

Piven, Frances Fox, and Richard A. Cloward. 1977. *Poor People's Movements*. New York: Pantheon.

Pocock, J.G.A. 1975. *The Machiavellian Moment*. Princeton, NJ: Princeton University Press.

———. 1985. *Virtue, Commerce, and History*. New York: Cambridge University Press.

———. 1987. "Texts as Events." In *The Politics of Discourse: The Literature and History of 17th Century England*, ed. Kevin Sharpe and Steven N. Zwicker, 21–34. Berkeley: University of California Press.

Polanyi, Livia. 1985. *Telling the American Story: A Structural and Cultural Analysis of Conversational Storytelling*. Norwood, NJ: Ablex.

Polanyi, Michael. 1958. *Personal Knowledge*. Chicago: University of Chicago Press.

———. 1966. *The Tacit Dimension*. New York: Doubleday.

Polanyi, Michael, and Harry Prosch. 1975. *Meaning*. Chicago: University of Chicago Press.

Polkinghorne, Donald E. 1983. *Methodology for the Human Sciences*. Albany: SUNY Press.

———. 1988. *Narrative Knowing and the Human Sciences*. Albany: SUNY Press.

Popkin, Samuel. 1979. *The Rational Peasant: The Political Economy of Rural Society in Vietnam*. Berkeley: University of California Press.

Popper, Karl. 1959. *The Logic of Scientific Discovery*. New York: Basic Books.

———. 1972a. *Conjectures and Refutations: The Growth of Scientific Knowledge*, 4th rev. ed. London: Routledge and Kegan Paul.

———. 1972b. *Objective Knowledge: An Evolutionary Approach*. Oxford: Clarendon Press.

Portes, Alejandro, and Ruben G. Rumbaut. 2001. *Legacies: The Story of the Immigrant Second Generation*. Berkeley: University of California Press.

Posner, Richard A. 2001. *Public Intellectuals: A Study of Decline*. Cambridge: Harvard University Press.

Post, Robert, and Reva Siegel. 2000. "Equal Protection of the Law: Federal Antidiscrimination Legislation after Morrison and Kimel." *Yale Law Journal* 110: 441–526.

Powdermaker, Hortense. 1966. *Stranger and Friend*. New York: W.W. Norton.

Powell, Walter W., and Paul J. DiMaggio, eds. 1991. *The New Institutionalism in Organizational Analysis*. Chicago: University of Chicago Press.

Pratt, Mary Louise. 1986. "Fieldwork in Common Places." In *Writing Culture: The Poetics and Politics of Ethnography*, ed. James Clifford and George Marcus, 27–50. Berkeley: University of California Press.

Pratt, Michael G., and Anat Rafaeli. 1997. "Vested Interests: Dress as an Integrating Symbol." *Academy of Management Journal* 40: 860–96.

Pressman, Jeffrey L., and Aaron Wildavsky. 1973. *Implementation*. Berkeley: University of California Press.

Preziosi, Donald. 1979. *Architecture, Language, and Meaning*. New York: Mouton.

Project on Disney. 1995. *Inside the Mouse: Work and Play at Disney World*. Durham, NC: Duke University Press.

Purvis, Trevor, and Alan Hunt. 1993. "Discourse, Ideology, Discourse, Ideology, Discourse, Ideology. . . ." *British Journal of Sociology* 44: 473–99.

Putnam, Hilary. 1981. *Reason, Truth and History*. Cambridge: Cambridge University Press.

———. 1983. *Realism and Reason*. Cambridge: Cambridge University Press.

———. 1988. *Representation and Reality*. Cambridge: MIT Press.

———. 1990. *Realism with a Human Face*. Cambridge: Harvard University Press.

Putnam, Linda L., and Michael E. Pacanowsky, eds. 1983. *Communication and Organizations: An Interpretive Approach*. Beverly Hills, CA: Sage.

Putnam, Robert. 1993. *Making Democracy Work*. Princeton, NJ: Princeton University Press.

Rabinow, Paul, and William M. Sullivan, eds. 1979. *Interpretive Social Science*. Berkeley: University of California Press.

———. 1985. *Interpretive Social Science*, 2nd ed. Berkeley: University of California Press.

Rafaeli, Anat, and Michael G. Pratt. 1993. "Tailored Meanings." *Academy of Management Review* 18: 32–55.

———, eds. 2005. *Artifacts and Organizations*. Mahwah, NJ: Lawrence Erlbaum.

Rafaeli, Anat, Jane Dutton, C.V. Harquail, and S. Lewis. 1997. "Navigating by Attire: The Use of Dress by Female Administrative Employees." *Academy of Management Journal* 40: 9–45.

Ragin, Charles C. 1987. *The Comparative Method: Moving Beyond Qualitative and Quantitative Strategies*. Berkeley: University of California Press.

———. 2000a. "Causal Complexity." In *Fuzzy Set Social Science*, 88–119. Chicago: University of Chicago Press.

———. 2000b. *Fuzzy Set Social Science*. Chicago: University of Chicago Press.

Ragin, Charles C., Joane Nagel, and Patricia White. 2004. *Report of the Workshop on Scientific Foundations of Qualitative Research*. Arlington, VA: National Science Foundation, Sociology Program; Methodology, Measurement and Statistics Program; Directorate for Social, Behavioral and Economic Sciences. Available at www.nsf.gov/pubs/2004/nsf04219/nsf04219_1.pdf (accessed October 25, 2004).

———, ed. 1976. *The Mutual Interaction of People and Their Built Environment*. Paris: Mouton.

Rapoport, Amos. 1982. *The Meaning of the Built Environment*. Beverly Hills, CA: Sage.

Ray, James Lee. 1995. *Democracy and International Politics: An Evaluation of the Democratic Peace Proposition*. Columbia: University of South Carolina Press.

Reed-Danahy, Deborah E., ed. 1997. *Auto/Ethnography: Rewriting the Self and the Social*. Oxford: Berg.

Rein, Martin. 1976. *Social Science and Public Policy*. New York: Penguin.

———. 1983. "Value-Critical Policy Analysis." In *Ethics, the Social Sciences, and Policy Analysis*, ed. Daniel Callahan and Bruce Jennings, 83–111. New York: Plenum Press.

Reinharz, Shulamit. 1992. *Feminist Methods in Social Research*. Oxford: Oxford University Press.

Rescher, Nicholas. 1996. *Process Metaphysics*. Albany: SUNY Press.

Reus-Smith, Christian. 1999. *The Moral Purpose of the State: Culture, Social Identity and Institutional Rationality in International Relations*. Princeton, NJ: Princeton University Press.

Review Symposium. 1995. "The Qualitative-Quantitative Disputation: King, Keohane, and Verba's *Designing Social Inquiry: Scientific Inference in Qualitative Research*." *American Political Science Review* 89: 454–81.

Rhodes, R.A.W. 1988. *Beyond Westminster and Whitehall*. London: Unwin Hyman.

Ricci, David. 1984. *The Tragedy of Political Science*. New Haven, CT: Yale University Press.

Richardson, Laurel. 1990. *Writing Strategies*. Newbury Park, CA: Sage.

———. 1994. "Writing: A Method of Inquiry." In *Handbook of Qualitative Research*, ed. Norman K. Denzin and Yvonna S. Lincoln, 516–29. Thousand Oaks, CA: Sage.

Ricoeur, Paul. 1971. "The Model of the Text." *Social Research* 38: 529–62.

———. 1988. *Time and Narrative*, trans. Kathleen Blamey and David Pellauer, vol. 3. Chicago: University of Chicago Press.

———. 1993 [1981]. *Hermeneutics and the Human Sciences*, trans. and ed. John B. Thompson. Cambridge: Cambridge University Press.

Rieder, Jonathan. 1994. "Doing Political Culture: Interpretive Practice and the Earnest Heuristic." *Research on Democracy and Society* 2: 117–51.

Riessman, Catherine Kohler. 1993. *Narrative Analysis*. Newbury Park, CA: Sage.

———. 2002. "Narrative Analysis." In *The Qualitative Researcher's Companion*, ed. A. Michael Huberman and Matthew B. Miles, 217–70. Thousand Oaks, CA: Sage.

Riley, Nancy E., and James McCarthy. 2003. *Demography in the Age of the Postmodern*. Cambridge: Cambridge University Press.

Ringer, Fritz. 1997. *Max Weber's Methodology: The Unification of the Cultural and Social Sciences*. Cambridge: Harvard University Press.

Ringmar, Erik. 1996. *Identity, Interest and Action*. Cambridge: Cambridge University Press.

Roberson, Debi. 2005. "Color Categories Are Culturally Diverse in Cognition as Well as in Language." *Journal of Cross-Cultural Research* 39: 56–71.

Roberson, Debi, Ian Davies, and Jules Davidoff. 2000. "Colour Categories Are Not Universal: Replications and New Evidence from a Stone-Age Culture." *Journal of Experimental Psychology: General* 129: 369–98.

Roe, Emery. 1994. *Narrative Policy Analysis: Theory and Practice*. Durham, NC: Duke University Press.

Rogers, Carl R. 1951. *Client-Centered Therapy: Its Current Practice, Implications, and Theory*. Boston: Houghton Mifflin.

———. 1964. "Toward a Science of the Person." In *Behaviorism and Phenomenology*, ed. T.W. Wann, 109–33. Chicago: University of Chicago Press.

Rogin, Michael. 1987. *Ronald Reagan, the Movie, and Other Episodes in Political Demonology*. Berkeley: University of California Press.

Rorty, Richard. 1967. *The Linguistic Turn*. Chicago: University of Chicago.

———. 1979. *Philosophy and the Mirror of Nature*. Princeton, NJ: Princeton University Press.

Rosen, Michael. 2000. *Turning Words, Spinning Worlds: Chapters in Organizational Ethnography*. Amsterdam: Harwood.

Rosen, Michael, Wanda J. Orlikowski, and Kim S. Schmahmann. 1990. "Building Buildings and Living Lives." In *Symbols and Artifacts*, ed. Pasquale Gagliardi, 69–84. New York: Aldine de Gruyter.

Rosenhan, David, Frank Frederick, and Anne Burrowes. 1968. "Preaching and Practicing." *Child Development* 39: 291–301.

Ross, Dorothy. 1991. *Origins of American Social Science*. New York: Cambridge University Press.

Ross, Michael A. 2003. *Justice of Shattered Dreams: Samuel Freeman Miller and the Supreme Court of the Civil War Era*. Baton Rouge: Louisiana State University Press.

Rothman, Stanley. 1971. "Functionalism and Its Critics: An Analysis of the Writings of Gabriel Almond." *Political Science Reviewer* 1: 236–76.

Royce, Edward. 2003. "Toward a Structural Perspective on Poverty and Inequality." Unpublished manuscript.

Rubin, Herbert J., and Irene S. Rubin. 1995. *Qualitative Interviewing: The Art of Hearing Data.* Thousand Oaks, CA: Sage.

Rudolph, Susanne H. 1987. "Presidential Address: State Formation in Asia—Prolegomenon to a Comparative Study." *Journal of Asian Studies* 46: 731–46.

Ruggiero, Renato. 1996. "Managing a World of Free Trade and Deep Interdependence." Address to the Argentinean Council on Foreign Relations, Buenos Aires (10 September). Available at www.wto.org/english/news_e/pres96_e/pr055_e.htm (accessed July 21, 2005).

Rule, James B. 1997. *Theory and Progress in Social Science.* Cambridge: Cambridge University Press.

Rummel, R.J. 1972. *The Dimensions of Nations.* Beverly Hills, CA: Sage.

Rupert, Mark. 2000. *Ideologies of Globalization: Contending Visions of a New World Order.* London: Routledge.

Russett, Bruce. 1993. *Grasping the Democratic Peace: Principles for a Post–Cold War World.* Princeton, NJ: Princeton University Press.

Russett, Bruce, and John Oneal. 2001. *Triangulating Peace: Democracy, Interdependence, and International Organization.* New York: W.W. Norton.

Russett, Bruce, Hayward Alker, Karl Deutsch, and Harold Lasswell. 1964. *The World Handbook of Political and Social Indicators.* New Haven, CT: Yale University Press.

Sabatier, Paul A. 1988. "An Advocacy Coalition Framework of Policy Change and the Role of Policy Oriented Learning Therein." *Policy Sciences* 21: 129–68.

———, ed. 1999. *Theories of the Policy Process.* Boulder, CO: Westview Press.

Saco, Diana. 1999. "Colonizing Cyberspace: 'National Security' and the Internet." In *Cultures of Insecurity: States, Communities and the Production of Danger,* ed. Jutta Weldes, Mark Laffey, Hugh Gusterson, and Raymond Duvall, 261–91. Minneapolis: University of Minnesota Press.

———. 2002. *Cybering Democracy.* Minneapolis: University of Minnesota Press.

Said, Edward. 1978. *Orientalism.* New York: Pantheon.

Sanjek, Roger. 1990. "On Ethnographic Validity." In *Fieldnotes,* 385–418. Ithaca, NY: Cornell University Press.

Saussure, Ferdinand de. 1996. *Course in General Linguistics.* Chicago: Open Court.

Schaffer, Frederic Charles. 1998. *Democracy in Translation: Understanding Politics in an Unfamiliar Culture.* Ithaca, NY: Cornell University Press.

———. 2002. "Disciplinary Reactions: Alienation and the Reform of Vote Buying in the Philippines." Presented at the American Political Science Association Annual Meeting, Boston (August 29–September 1).

Schafft, Gretchen E. 2004. *From Racism to Genocide: Anthropology in the Third Reich.* Urbana: University of Illinois Press.

Schank, Roger C. 1990. *Tell Me a Story: A New Look at Real and Artificial Memory.* New York: Charles Scribner's Sons.

Schatzki, Theodore R. 2001. "Introduction: Practice Theory." In *The Practice Turn in Contemporary Theory,* ed. Theodore R. Schatzki, Karin Knorr Cetina, and Eike Von Savigny, 1–14. New York: Routledge.

Schatzki, Theodore R., Karin Knorr Cetina, and Eike von Savigny, eds. 2001. *The Practice Turn in Contemporary Theory.* New York: Routledge.

Schatzman, Leonard, and Anselm L. Strauss. 1973. *Strategies for a Natural Sociology.* Englewood Cliffs, NJ: Prentice-Hall.

Scheflen, Albert E. 1974 [1966]. "Quasi-Courtship Behavior in Psychotherapy." In *Nonverbal Communication: Readings with Commentary,* ed. Shirley Weitz, 182–98. New York: Oxford University Press.

Schein, Edgar H. 1978. *Career Dynamics.* Reading, MA: Addison-Wesley.

Scheppele, Kim Lane. 1989. "Foreword: Telling Stories." *Michigan Law Review* 87: 2073–98.

Schiebinger, Londa. 1989. *The Mind Has No Sex?* Cambridge: Harvard University Press.

Schmidt, Mary R. 1993. "Grout: Alternative Kinds of Knowledge and Why They Are Ignored." *Public Administration Review* 53: 525–30.

Schmidt, Ronald, Sr. 2000. *Language Policy and Identity Politics in the United States.* Philadelphia, PA: Temple University Press.

Schneider, Anne L., and Helen Ingram. 1993. "Social Construction of Target Populations." *American Political Science Review* 87: 334–47.

———. 1997. *Policy Design for Democracy.* Lawrence: University Press of Kansas.

———. eds. 2005. *Deserving and Entitled: Social Constructions and Public Policy*. Albany: SUNY Press.

Scholte, Jan Arte. 2001. "The Globalization of World Politics." In *The Globalization of World Politics*, ed. John Baylis and Steve Smith, 2nd ed., 13–32. Oxford: Oxford University Press.

Schon, Donald A. 1979. "Generative Metaphor." In *Metaphor and Thought*, ed. Andrew Ortony, 254–83. Cambridge: Cambridge University Press.

Schon, Donald A., and Martin Rein. 1994. *Frame Reflection: Toward the Resolution of Intractable Policy Controversies*. New York: Basic Books.

Schram, Sanford F. 1995a. "Home Economists as the Real Economists." In *Words of Welfare*, 77–97. Minneapolis: University of Minnesota Press.

———. 1995b. *Words of Welfare: The Poverty of Social Science and the Social Science of Poverty*. Minneapolis: University of Minnesota Press.

Schultz, Vicki. 1990. "Telling Stories About Women and Work: Judicial Interpretations of Sex Segregation in the Workplace in Title VII Cases Raising the Lack of Interest Argument." *Harvard Law Review* 103: 1749–843.

Schütz, Alfred. 1962. "On Multiple Realities." *Collected Papers,* ed. Maurice Natanson, 3 vols., 207–59. The Hague: Martinus Nijhoff.

———. 1967. *The Phenomenology of the Social World*. Chicago: Northwestern University Press.

———. 1973. "Concept and Theory Formation in the Social Sciences." In *Collected Papers*, ed. Maurice Natanson, vol. 1, 48–66. The Hague: Martinus Nijhoff.

Schwandt, Thomas A. 2001. *Dictionary of Qualitative Inquiry*, 2nd ed. Thousand Oaks, CA: Sage.

———. 2003. "Three Epistemological Stances for Qualitative Inquiry: Interpretivism, Hermeneutics, and Social Constructionism." In *The Landscape of Qualitative Research*, ed. Norman K. Denzin and Yvonna S. Lincoln, 2nd ed., 292–331. Thousand Oaks, CA: Sage.

Schwartz, Barry. 1987. *George Washington: The Making of an American Symbol*. Ithaca, NY: Cornell University Press.

Schwartz, Richard D., and Lee Sechrest. 2000. "Introduction to the Classic Edition of *Unobtrusive Measures*." In *Unobtrusive Measures*, ed. Eugene J. Webb, Donald T. Campbell, Richard D. Schwartz, and Lee Sechrest, rev. ed., xi ff. Thousand Oaks, CA: Sage.

Schwartz-Shea, Peregrine. 2003. "Is This the Curriculum We Want? Doctoral Requirements and Offerings in Methods and Methodology." *PS: Political Science and Politics* 36: 379–86.

———. 2004. "Judging Quality: Epistemic Communities, Evaluative Criteria and Interpretive Empirical Research." Presented at the American Political Science Association Annual Meeting, Chicago, IL (September 2–5).

———. 2005. "The Graduate Student Experience: 'Hegemony' or Balance in Methodology Training?" In *Perestroika! The Raucous Rebellion in Political Science,* ed. Kristen Renwick Monroe, 374–402. New Haven, CT: Yale University Press.

Schwartz-Shea, Peregrine, and Dvora Yanow. 2002. "'Reading' 'Methods' 'Texts': How Research Methods Texts Construct Political Science." *Political Research Quarterly* 55: 457–86.

Schwarz, Hans-Peter. 1995. *Konrad Adenauer*, vol. 1. Providence, RI: Berghahn Books.

Scollon, Ron, and Suzanne B.K. Scollon. 1981. *Narrative, Literacy, and Face in Interethnic Communication*. Norwood, NJ: Ablex.

Scott, James C. 1990. *Domination and the Arts of Resistance: Hidden Transcripts*. New Haven, CT: Yale University Press.

———. 1998. *Seeing like a State*. New Haven, CT: Yale University Press.

Scott, Joan W., and Debra Keates, eds. 2001. *Schools of Thought: Twenty-Five Years of Interpretive Social Science*. Princeton, NJ: Princeton University Press.

Seale, Clive. 1999. *The Quality of Qualitative Research*. London: Sage.

Searle, John R. 1969. *Speech Acts*. Cambridge: Cambridge University Press.

Seidelman, Raymond, and Edward Harpham. 1985. *Disenchanted Realists: Political Science and the American Crisis, 1884–1984*. Albany: SUNY Press.

Seidman, I.E. 1991. *Interviewing as Qualitative Research*. New York: Teachers College Press.

Seligman, Joel. 1978. *The High Citadel: The Influence of Harvard Law School*. Boston: Houghton Mifflin.

Sellars, Wilfrid. 1963. *Science, Perception and Reality*. New York: Humanities Press.

———. 1997. *Empiricism and the Philosophy of Mind*. Cambridge: Harvard University Press.

Sewell, William H. 1992. "A Theory of Structure: Duality, Agency, and Transformation." *American Journal of Sociology* 98: 1–29.

Shapiro, Ian. 2002. "Problems, Methods, and Theories in the Study of Politics, or: What's Wrong with Political Science and What to Do About It." *Political Theory* 30: 596–619.

———. 2004. "Problems, Methods, and Theories in the Study of Politics, or: What's Wrong with Political Science and What to Do About It." In *Problems and Methods in the Study of Politics*, ed. Ian Shapiro, Rogers M. Smith, and Tarek E. Masoud, 19–41. New York: Cambridge University Press.

Shapiro, Michael J. 1988. *The Politics of Representation: Writing Practices in Biography, Photography, and Policy Analysis.* Madison: University of Wisconsin Press.

———. 1992. *Reading the Postmodern Polity: Political Theory as Textual Practice.* Minneapolis: University of Minnesota Press.

———. 1994. "Images of Planetary Danger: Luciano Benetton's Ecumenical Fantasy." *Alternatives* 19: 433–54.

———. 1999. *Cinematic Political Thought: Narrating Race, Nation and Gender.* New York: New York University Press.

———. 2001. "Sounds of Nationhood." *Millennium* 30: 583–601.

Sharp, Joanne P. 2000. *Condensing the Cold War: Readers Digest and American Identity.* Minneapolis: University of Minnesota Press.

Sheeran, Paul. 2001. *Cultural Politics in International Relations.* Aldershot, UK: Ashgate.

Shehata, Samer. 2004. "Plastic Sandals, Tea and Time: Shop Floor Culture and Politics in Egypt." Unpublished manuscript.

Shotter, John. 1993a. *Conversational Realities: Constructing Life Through Language.* Thousand Oaks, CA: Sage.

———. 1993b. *Cultural Politics of Everyday Life.* Toronto: University of Toronto Press.

Siegel, Stephen A. 1990. "Historism in Late Nineteenth-Century Constitutional Thought." *Wisconsin Law Review* 1990: 1431–547.

Silk, Michael. 2002. "'Bangsa Malaysia': Global Sport, the City, and the Mediated Refurbishment of Local Identities." *Media, Culture and Society* 24: 775–94.

Simons, Herbert W. 1989. *Rhetoric in the Human Sciences.* Newbury Park, CA: Sage.

Simpson, Brooks D. 1998. *The Reconstruction Presidents.* Lawrence: University Press of Kansas.

Singerman, Diane. 1995. *Avenues of Participation.* Princeton, NJ: Princeton University Press.

Singleton, Royce A., Jr., and Bruce C. Straits. 1988. *Approaches to Social Research.* New York: Oxford University Press.

———. 1999. *Approaches to Social Research*, 3rd ed. New York: Oxford University Press.

Skerry, Peter. 2000. "The Undercount: Some Causes and Proposed Remedies." In *Counting on the Census? Race, Group Identity, and the Evasion of Politics.* Washington, DC: Brookings Institution Press. Available at http://brookings.nap.edu/books/081577964X/html/80.html (accessed July 19, 2005).

Skinner, Quentin. 2002. *Visions of Politics. Vol. I: Regarding Method.* Cambridge: Cambridge University Press.

Skocpol, Theda. 1979. *States and Social Revolutions.* Cambridge: Cambridge University Press.

———. 1984. "Recurring Agendas and Recurrent Strategies in Historical Sociology." In *Vision and Method in Historical Sociology*, ed. Theda Skocpol, 356–91. New York: Cambridge University Press.

Skocpol, Theda, and Margaret Somers. 1980. "The Uses of Comparative History in Macrosocial Inquiry." *Comparative Studies in Society and History* 22: 174–97.

Smircich, Linda. 1983. "Concepts of Culture and Organizational Analysis." *Administrative Science Quarterly* 28: 339–58.

Smith, David Woodruff. 2003. "Phenomenology." In *The Stanford Encyclopedia of Philosophy* (Winter Edition), ed. Edward N. Zalta. Available at http://plato.stanford.edu/archives/win2003/entries/phenomenology/ (accessed December 21, 2004).

Smith, Henry Nash. 1957. *Virgin Land: The American West as Symbol and Myth.* New York: Vintage.

Smith, John K., and Deborah K. Deemer. 2003. "The Problem of Criteria in the Age of Relativism." In *Collecting and Interpreting Qualitative Materials*, ed. Norman K. Denzin and Yvonna S. Lincoln, 2nd ed., 427–57. Thousand Oaks, CA: Sage.

Smith, Rogers M. 1988. "Political Jurisprudence, the 'New Institutionalism,' and the Future of Public Law." *American Political Science Review* 82: 89–108.

———. 1993. "Beyond Tocqueville, Myrdal, and Hartz: The Multiple Traditions in America." *American Political Science Review* 87: 549–66.

———. 2003. "Progress and Poverty in Political Science." *PS: Political Science and Politics* 36: 395–96.

Snow, C.P. 1959. *The Two Cultures and the Scientific Revolution*. New York: Cambridge University Press.

Sobel, Dava. 1999. *Galileo's Daughter: A Historical Memoir of Science, Faith, and Love*. New York: Walker.

Soja, Edward W. 1989. *Postmodern Geographies: The Reassertion of Space in Critical Social Theory*. New York: Verso.

Soss, Joe. 2000. *Unwanted Claims: The Politics of Participation in the U.S. Welfare System*. Ann Arbor: University of Michigan Press.

Soss, Joe, Sanford F. Schram, Thomas Vartanian, and Erin O'Brien. 2001. "Setting the Terms of Relief: Explaining State Policy Choices in the Devolution Revolution." *American Journal of Political Science* 45: 378–95.

Spock, Benjamin. 1976. *Baby and Child Care*, rev., updated, and enl. ed. New York: Pocket Books.

Spradley, James P. 1979. *The Ethnographic Interview*. Fort Worth, TX: Holt, Rinehart and Winston.

Spradley, James P., and David W. McCurdy. 1972. *The Cultural Experience*. Palo Alto, CA: Science Research Associates.

Spruyt, Hendrik. 1994. *The Sovereign State and Its Competitors*. Princeton, NJ: Princeton University Press.

Stanley, Liz, ed. 1990. *Feminist Praxis: Research, Theory, and Epistemology in Feminist Sociology*. London: Routledge.

Star, Susan Leigh. 1988. "Introduction." Special Issue, "The Sociology of Science and Technology." *Social Problems* 35: 197–205.

———. 1989. *Regions of the Mind: Brain Research and the Quest for Scientific Certainty*. Stanford, CA: Stanford University Press.

Steele, Fritz I. 1973. *Physical Settings and Organization Development*. Menlo Park, CA: Addison-Wesley.

———. 1981. *The Sense of Place*. Boston: CBI.

Stein, Sandra J. 2004. *The Culture of Education Policy*. New York: Teachers College Press.

Stephens, Jerome. 1969. "The Logic of Functional and Systems Analyses in Political Science." *Midwest Journal of Political Science* 13: 367–94.

Stepick, Alex, and Carol D. Stepick. 1992. *Alternative Enumeration of Haitians in Miami, Florida*, Report Number 8. Washington, DC: United States Department of Housing and Urban Development.

Sterling, Bruce. 1986. "Preface." In *Mirrorshades: The Cyberpunk Anthology*, ix-xvi. New York: Ace Books.

Stevens, Jacqueline. 1999. *Reproducing the State*. Princeton, NJ: Princeton University Press.

Stocking, George. 1992. *The Ethnographer's Magic and Other Essays in the History of Anthropology*. Madison: University of Wisconsin Press.

Stockman, Norman. 1983. *Anti-Positivist Theories of Science: Critical Rationalism, Critical Theory and Scientific Realism*. Dordrecht: D. Reidel.

Stone, Geoffrey, Louis Seidman, Cass Sunstein, and Mark Tushnet. 1996. *Constitutional Law*. Boston: Little, Brown.

Stone, Lawrence. 1979a. "The Revival of Narrative: Reflections on a New Old History." *Past and Present* 85: 3–24.

———. 1979b. *The Family, Sex and Marriage in England, 1500–1800*, abridged ed. Harmondsworth: Penguin.

Storey, John. 2001. *Cultural Theory and Popular Culture: An Introduction*, 3rd ed. Harlow, England: Pearson Education.

Storing, Herbert J. 1962. *Essays on the Scientific Study of Politics*. New York: Holt, Rinehart and Winston.

Strauss, Anselm. 1987. *Qualitative Analysis for Social Scientists*. Cambridge: Cambridge University Press.

Strauss, Anselm, and Juliet Corbin. 1990. *Basics of Qualitative Research*. Newbury Park, CA: Sage.

———. 1998. *Basics of Qualitative Research: Techniques and Procedures for Developing Grounded Theory*, 2nd ed. Thousand Oaks, CA: Sage.

Suchman, Lucy, and Birgitte Jordan. 1988. "Computerization and Women's Knowledge." In *Women, Work and Computerization*, ed. K. Tigdens, M. Jennings, I. Wagner, and M. Weggelaar, 153–60. Amsterdam: North Holland Press.

———. 1992. "Validity and the Collaborative Construction of Meaning in Face-to-Face Surveys." In *Questions About Questions: Inquiries into the Cognitive Bases of Surveys*, ed. Judith M. Tanur, 241–67. New York: Russell Sage Foundation.

Summa, Hilkka. 1992. "The Rhetoric of Efficiency." In *Writing the Social Text*, ed. Richard Harvey Brown, 135–53. New York: Aldine de Gruyter.

"Summary of Editorial Content on United States Break in Relations with Cuba." 1961. *New York Times* (January 5), 10.

Sumner, William G., and Albert G. Keller. 1928. *Science of Society*. New Haven, CT: Yale University Press.

Suppe, Frederick. 1977. *The Structure of Scientific Theories*, 2nd ed. Urbana: University of Illinois Press.

Sutherland, Peter D. 1998. "Managing the International Economy in an Age of Globalization." *International Monetary Fund: The 1998 Per Jacobsson Lecture*, Washington, DC (4 October). Available at www.imf.org/external/am/1998/perj.htm (accessed June 18, 2001).

Swaffield, Simon. 1998. "Contextual Meanings in Policy Discourse: A Case Study of Language Use Concerning Resource Policy in the New Zealand High Country." *Policy Sciences* 31: 199–224.

Swartz, David. 1997. *Power and Culture: The Sociology of Pierre Bourdieu*. Chicago: University of Chicago Press.

Tanenhaus, Joseph, and Albert Somit. 1967. *The Development of Political Science: From Burgess to Behavioralism*. Boston: Allyn and Bacon.

Tashakkori, Abbas, and Charles Teddlie. 1998. *Mixed Methodology: Combining Qualitative and Quantitative Approaches*. Thousand Oaks, CA: Sage.

———. eds. 2003. *Handbook of Mixed Methods in Social and Behavioral Research*. Thousand Oaks, CA: Sage.

Tauxe, Caroline S. 1995. "Marginalizing Public Participation in Local Planning: An Ethnographic Account." *Journal of the American Planning Association* 6: 471–81.

Taylor, Charles. 1967. "Neutrality in Political Science." In *Philosophy, Politics and Society, Third Series*, ed. Peter Laslett and W.G. Runciman, 25–57. Oxford: Blackwell.

———. 1971. "Interpretation and the Sciences of Man." *Review of Metaphysics* 25: 3–51.

———. 1977. "Interpretation and the Sciences of Man." In *Understanding and Social Inquiry*, ed. Fred R. Dallmayr and Thomas A. McCarthy, 101–31. Notre Dame, IN: University of Notre Dame Press.

———. 1979. "Interpretation and the Sciences of Man." In *Interpretive Social Science: A Reader*, ed. Paul Rabinow and William M. Sullivan, 25–71. Berkeley: University of California Press.

Taylor, Charles Lewis, and Michael C. Hudson. 1972. *World Handbook of Political and Social Indicators*, 2nd ed. New Haven, CT: Yale University Press.

Teresi, Dick. 2002. *Lost Discoveries: The Ancient Roots of Modern Science—From the Babylonians to the Maya*. New York: Simon and Schuster.

Thomas, Jim. 1993. *Doing Critical Ethnography*. Newbury Park, CA: Sage.

Thomas, W.I. 1923. *The Unadjusted Girl*. Boston: Little, Brown.

Thoreau, Henry David. 1939 [1854]. *Walden, or Life in the Woods*. New York: Heritage Press.

Tickner, J. Ann. 2001. *Gendering World Politics*. New York: Columbia University Press.

Tilly, Charles. 1995. "To Explain Political Processes." *American Journal of Sociology* 100: 1594–610.

———. 1997. "Means and Ends of Comparison in Macrosociology." *Comparative Social Research* 16: 43–53.

———. 1998. *Durable Inequality*. Berkeley: University of California Press.

———. 2002. *Stories, Identities, and Political Change*. Lanham, MD: Rowman and Littlefield.

Tinic, Serra A. 1997. "United Colors and Untied Meanings: Benetton and the Commodification of Social Issues." *Journal of Communication* 47: 3–25.

Tomlinson, John. 1991. *Cultural Imperialism: A Critical Introduction*. Baltimore, MD: Johns Hopkins University Press.

Traweek, Sharon. 1988. *Beamtimes and Lifetimes: The World of High Energy Physicists*. Cambridge: Harvard University Press.

Tuan, Yi-Fu. 1977. *Space and Place: The Perspective of Experience*. Minneapolis: University of Minnesota Press.

Tuana, Nancy, ed. 1989. *Feminism and Science*. Bloomington: Indiana University Press.

Tufte, Edward R. 1990. *Envisioning Information*. Cheshire, CT: Graphics Press.

Turkle, Sherry. 2004. "How Computers Change the Way We Think." *Chronicle of Higher Education* (January 30), B26–28.

Turner, Victor. 1974. *Dramas, Fields, and Metaphors*. Ithaca, NY: Cornell University Press.

Valverde, Mariana. 2003. *Law's Dream of a Common Knowledge*. Princeton, NJ: Princeton University Press.

Van Ausdale, Debra, and Joe R. Feagin. 2001. *The First R: How Children Learn Race and Racism*. Lanham, MD: Rowman and Littlefield.

van Fraassen, Bas C. 1980. *The Scientific Image*. New York: Oxford University Press.

Van Maanen, John. 1978. "Observations on the Making of a Policeman." *Human Organization* 32: 407–18.

———. 1986. *Tales of the Field*. Chicago: University of Chicago Press.

———. 1991. "The Smile Factory: Work at Disneyland." In *Reframing Organizational Culture*, ed. Peter J. Frost, Larry F. Moore, Meryl Reis Louis, Craig C. Lundberg, and Joanne Martin, 58–76. Newbury Park, CA: Sage.

———. 1995. "Style as Theory." *Organization Science* 6: 133–43.

———. 1996. "Commentary: On the Matter of Voice." *Journal of Management Inquiry* 5: 375–81.

Vaughn, Laura. 2002. "From Panic Stations to Power Relations: UFOs and Competing Constructions of U.S. 'National (In)Security.'" M.Sc. dissertation, University of Bristol, UK.

Vickers, Geoffrey. 1983. *The Art of Judgment*. London: Harper and Row.

Vidich, Arthur J., and Stanford M. Lyman. 2003. "Qualitative Methods: Their History in Sociology and Anthropology." In *The Landscape of Qualitative Research*, ed. Norman K. Denzin and Yvonna S. Lincoln, 2nd ed., 55–130. Thousand Oaks, CA: Sage.

Viner, Jacob. 1949. "Power Versus Plenty as Objectives of Foreign Policy in the Seventeenth and Eighteenth Centuries." *World Politics* 1: 1–29.

Vivas, Eliseo. 1960. "Science and the Studies of Man." In *Scientism and Values*, ed. Helmut Schoek and James Wiggans, 70–91. Princeton, NJ: D. van Nostrand.

Vološinov, V.N. 1986 [1929]. *Marxism and the Philosophy of Language*. Cambridge: Harvard University Press.

Wallerstein, Immanuel. 1999. "The Structures of Knowledge, Or How Many Ways May We Know?" In *The End of the World as We Know It: Social Science for the Twenty-First Century*, 185–91. Minneapolis: University of Minnesota Press.

Walsh, Katherine Cramer. 2004. *Talking About Politics: Informal Groups and Social Identity in American Life*. Chicago: University of Chicago Press.

Waltz, Kenneth. 1979. *Theory of International Politics*. New York: McGraw-Hill.

Wang, Caroline C., Jennifer L. Cash, and Lisa S. Powers. 2000. "Who Knows the Streets as Well as the Homeless? Promoting Personal and Community Action Through Photovoice." *Health Promotion Practice* 1: 81–89.

Ward, Michael D., and Kristian S. Gleditsch. 1998. "Democratizing for Peace." *American Political Science Review* 92: 51–61.

Warner, W. Lloyd. 1959. *The Living and the Dead*. New Haven, CT: Yale University Press.

Warnke, Georgia. 1987. *Gadamer, Hermeneutics, Tradition, and Reason*. Stanford, CA: Stanford University Press.

Warwick, Donald. 1980. *The Teaching of Ethics in the Social Sciences*. Hastings-on-Hudson, NY: Institute of Society, Ethics and the Life Sciences.

Weart, Spencer R. 1998. *Never at War: Why Democracies Will Not Fight One Another*. New Haven, CT: Yale University Press.

Webb, Eugene J., Donald T. Campbell, R.D. Schwartz, L. Sechrest, and J.B. Grove. 1981 [1966]. *Nonreactive Measures in the Social Sciences* [orig. *Unobtrusive Measures*]. Boston: Houghton Mifflin.

Weber, Cynthia. 2001. *International Relations Theory: A Critical Introduction*. New York: Routledge.

Weber, Max. 1946. *From Max Weber: Essays in Sociology*, trans. and ed. H.H. Gerth and C. Wright Mills. New York: Oxford University Press.

———. 1976. *Wirtschaft und Gesellschaft*, ed. J. Winckelmann, 5th ed. Tübingen: J.C.B. Mohr.

———. 1978. *Economy and Society: An Outline of Interpretive Sociology*. Berkeley: University of California Press.

———. 1999a. "Die 'Objektivität' Sozialwissenschaftlicher und Sozialpolitischer Erkenntnis" [The "Objectivity" of Social-Scientific and Sociopolitical Knowledge]. In *Gesammelte Aufsätze zur Wissenschaftslehre* [Collected Essays on the Theory of Science], ed. E. Flitner. Potsdam: Internet-Ausgabe. Available at www.uni-potsdam.de/u/paed/Flitner/Flitner/Weber/ (accessed February 1, 2005).

———. 1999b. "Kritische Studien auf dem Gebiet der kulturwissenschaftlichen Logik" [Critical Studies in the Area of the Logic of the Cultural Sciences]. In *Gesammelte Aufsätze zur Wissenschaftslehre* [Collected Essays on the Theory of Science], ed. E. Flitner. Potsdam: Internet-Ausgabe. Available at www.uni-potsdam.de/u/paed/Flitner/Flitner/Weber/ (accessed February 1, 2005).

Wedeen, Lisa. 2002. "Conceptualizing Culture: Possibilities for Political Science." *American Political Science Review* 96: 713–28.

Weick, Karl E. 1969. *The Social Psychology of Organizing*. Reading, MA: Addison-Wesley.

Weisman, Leslie Kanes. 1992. *Discrimination by Design: A Feminist Critique of the Man-Made Environment*. Chicago: University of Illinois Press.

Weitz, Shirley. 1974. *Nonverbal Communication: Readings with Commentary*. New York: Oxford University Press.

Weldes, Jutta. 1999a. *Constructing National Interests: The United States and the Cuban Missile Crisis*. Minneapolis: University of Minnesota Press.

———. 1999b. "Going Cultural: *Star Trek,* State Action, and Popular Culture." *Millennium* 28: 117–34.

———. 2001. "Globalization Is Science Fiction." *Millennium* 30: 647–67.

———. 2003a. "Popular Culture, Science Fiction and World Politics: Exploring Intertextual Relations." In *To Seek Out New Worlds: Exploring Links Between Science Fiction and World Politics*, ed. Jutta Weldes, 1–27. New York: Palgrave Macmillan.

———, ed. 2003b. *To Seek Out New Worlds: Exploring Links Between Science Fiction and World Politics*. New York: Palgrave Macmillan.

Welsh, William. 1973. *Studying Politics*. New York: Praeger.

Wendt, Alexander. 1998. "On Constitution and Causation in International Relations." *Review of International Studies* 24: 165–80.

———. 1999. *Social Theory of International Politics*. Cambridge: Cambridge University Press.

White, Hayden. 1980. "The Value of Narrativity in the Representation of Reality." In *On Narrative*, ed. W.J.T. Mitchell, 1–24. Chicago: University of Chicago Press.

———. 1987. "The Question of Narrative in Contemporary Historical Theory." In *The Content of the Form*, 26–57. Baltimore, MD: Johns Hopkins University Press.

White House. 2002. *National Security Strategy of the United States of America*. Washington, DC. Available at www.whitehouse.gov/nsc/nss.html (accessed August 14, 2004).

White, Jay D. 1992. "Taking Language Seriously: Toward a Narrative Theory of Knowledge for Administrative Research." *American Review of Public Administration* 22: 75–88.

White, Stephen K. 2004. "The Very Idea of a Critical Social Science: A Pragmatist Turn." In *The Cambridge Companion to Critical Theory*, ed. Fred Rush, 310–35. New York: Cambridge University Press.

Whitehall, Geoffrey. 2003. "The Problem of the 'World and Beyond': Encountering 'the Other' in Science Fiction." In *To Seek Out New Worlds: Exploring Links Between Science Fiction and World Politics*, ed. Jutta Weldes, 169–93. New York: Palgrave.

Whitehead, Alfred North. 1932. *Science and the Modern World*, rev. ed. Cambridge: Cambridge University Press.

Whitfield, Stephen E., and Gene Roddenberry. 1968. *The Making of Star Trek*. New York: Ballentine Books.

Whyte, William F. 1955 [1943]. *Street Corner Society*. Chicago: University of Chicago Press.

Wiecek, William W. 1977. *The Origins of Antislavery Constitutionalism in America, 1760–1848*. Ithaca, NY: Cornell University Press.

Wildavsky, Aaron. 1979. *Speaking Truth to Power*. Boston: Little, Brown.

Wilderness Act. 1964. 16 U.S.C. § 1131 *et seq.*

Williams, Bernard. 1985. *Ethics and the Limits of Philosophy*. Cambridge: Harvard University Press.

Williams, Raymond. 1983. *Keywords*. London: Fontana.

Wilson, Edward O. 1998. *Consilience: The Unity of Knowledge*. New York: Alfred A. Knopf.

Wilson, Woodrow. 1889. *The State: Elements of Historical and Practical Politics*. Boston: D.C. Heath.

Winch, Peter. 1990. *The Idea of a Social Science and Its Relation to Philosophy*, 2nd ed. London: Routledge.

Wittgenstein, Ludwig. 1953. *Philosophical Investigations*, trans. G.E.M. Anscombe. Oxford: Blackwell.

———. 1968. *Philosophical Investigations,* trans. G.E.M. Anscombe, 3rd ed. New York: Macmillan.

Wolcott, Harry F. 1990. "On Seeking—and Rejecting—Validity in Qualitative Research." In *Qualitative Inquiry in Education: The Continuing Debate*, ed. Elliot W. Eisner and Allan Peshkin, 121–52. New York: Teachers College Press.

Wolin, Sheldon. 1981. "Max Weber: Legitimation, Method and the Politics of Theory." *Political Theory* 9: 401–24.

Woodward, C. Vann. 1966 [1951]. *Reunion and Reaction: The Compromise of 1877 and the End of Reconstruction*. Boston: Little, Brown.

Woolgar, Steve. 1988. *Science: The Very Idea*. London: Tavistock.

World Bank. 2001. *Globalization, Growth, and Poverty: Building an Inclusive World Economy*. Washington, DC: World Bank.

Yacobi, Haim, ed. 2004. *Constructing a Sense of Place: Architecture and the Zionist Discourse*. Burlington, VT: Ashgate.

Yanow, Dvora. 1990. "Tackling the Implementation Problem: Epistemological Issues in Implementation Research." In *Implementation and the Policy Process*, ed. Dennis J. Palumbo and Donald J. Calista, 213–27. New York: Greenwood Press.

———. 1992a. "Supermarkets and Culture Clash: The Epistemological Role of Metaphors in Administrative Practice." *American Review of Public Administration* 22: 89–110.

———. 1992b. "Silences in Public Policy Discourse: Policy and Organizational Myths." *Journal of Public Administration Research and Theory* 2: 399–423.

———. 1993. "Reading Policy Meanings in Organization-Scapes." *Journal of Architectural and Planning Research* 10: 308–27.

———. 1995a. "Editorial: Practices of Policy Interpretation." *Policy Sciences* 29: 111–26.

———. 1995c. "Writing Organizational Tales." Crossroads Symposium. *Organization Science* 6: 225–31.

———. 1995b. "Silences in Organizational Discourse: Learning from Feminist Theories." Presented at the Academy of Management Annual Conference, Vancouver, BC (August 6–9).

———. 1996. *How Does a Policy Mean? Interpreting Policy and Organizational Actions.* Washington, DC: Georgetown University Press.

———. 1997. "Passionate Humility in Interpretive Policy and Administrative Analysis." *Administrative Theory and Praxis* 19: 171–77.

———. 1998. "Space Stories; Or, Studying Museum Buildings as Organizational Spaces, While Reflecting on Interpretive Methods and Their Narration." *Journal of Management Inquiry* 7: 215–39.

———. 2000. *Conducting Interpretive Policy Analysis.* Newbury Park, CA: Sage.

———. 2001. "Learning in and from Improvising: Lessons from Theater for Organizational Learning." *Reflections* (The Society for Organizational Learning Journal) 2: 58–62.

———. 2003a. *Constructing American "Race" and "Ethnicity": Category-Making in Public Policy and Administration.* Armonk, NY: M.E. Sharpe.

———. 2003b. "Conversational Interviewing/Interrogating Texts: Feminist Methods?" Presented at the Western Political Science Association Annual Meeting, Denver, CO (March 27–29).

———. 2003c. "Interpretive Empirical Political Science: What Makes This Not a Subfield of Qualitative Methods." *Qualitative Methods: Newsletter of the American Political Science Association Organized Section on Qualitative Methods* 1 (2): 9–13.

———. 2004. "Translating Local Knowledge at Organizational Peripheries." *British Journal of Management* 15: S15–S25.

———. Forthcoming. "Evidence-Based Policy." In *Encyclopedia of Governance*, ed. Mark Bevir. Newbury Park, CA: Sage.

———. Forthcoming. "Narrative Theory." In *Encyclopedia of Governance*, ed. Mark Bevir. Newbury Park, CA: Sage.

Yanow, Dvora, Harrison M. Trice, Janice M. Beyer, Gideon Kunda, Joanne Martin, and Linda Smircich. 1995. "Writing Organizational Tales: Four Authors and Their Stories About Culture." Crossroads Symposium, *Organization Science* 6: 225–31.

Zanca, Russell. 2000. "Intruder in Uzbekistan: Walking the Line Between Community Needs and Anthropological Desiderata." In *Fieldwork Dilemmas*, ed. Hermine G. De Soto and Nora Dudwick, 153–71. Madison: University of Wisconsin Press.

Zeisel, John. 1981. *Inquiry by Design.* Monterey, CA: Brooks/Cole.

Zerubavel, Yael. 1995. *Recovered Roots: Collective Memory and the Making of Israeli National Tradition.* Chicago: University of Chicago Press.

ABOUT THE EDITORS AND CONTRIBUTORS

Robert Adcock is a Ph.D. candidate in the Department of Political Science, University of California, Berkeley. He specializes in nineteenth- and twentieth-century Anglo-American political thought, with a research focus on the history, philosophy, and methodology of social science. He has recently published on the history of political science in *History of Political Thought* (2003) and organized (along with Mark Bevir and Shannon Stimson) a conference in the area, *Historicizing the Political: Anglo-American Approaches to a Historical Political Science Since 1900* (UC Berkeley, Fall 2002). He has previously published articles (coauthored with David Collier) on issues of qualitative methodology in the *American Political Science Review* (2001) and the *Annual Review of Political Science* (1999).

Mark Bevir is a member of the Department of Political Science, University of California, Berkeley. He is the author of *The Logic of the History of Ideas* (Cambridge University Press, 1999), *New Labour: A Critique* (Routledge, 2005), and, with R.A.W. Rhodes, *Interpreting British Governance* (Routledge, 2003). He has also edited, with Frank Trentmann, *Critiques of Capital in Modern Britain and America* (Palgrave, 2002) and *Markets in Historical Contexts* (Cambridge University Press, 2004).

Pamela Brandwein is associate professor of sociology and government, and politics at the University of Texas at Dallas. Her first book, *Reconstructing Reconstruction: The Supreme Court and the Production of Historical Truth* (Duke University Press, 1999) was awarded special recognition in the Best Book Prize of 1999–2000 by the Sociology of Law section of the American Sociological Association. She is currently working on her second book, *The Supreme Court and the Lost Doctrine of State Neglect*. She holds a B.A. in Political Science from the University of Michigan and a Ph.D. from Northwestern University in Sociology.

Clare Ginger is associate professor in the School of Natural Resources at the University of Vermont. Her teaching and research interests focus on policy and planning processes in the field of environment and natural resources. She also works with colleagues on projects that integrate disciplinary perspectives in natural resource courses and curricula. Her research appears in such journals as *Administration and Society, Policy Studies Journal,* and *Society and Natural Resources.* She has also published papers on interdisciplinary teaching in the *Journal of Public Affairs Education* and the *Journal of Forestry*.

Mary Hawkesworth is professor of political science and women's/gender studies at Rutgers University. Her teaching and research interests include feminist theory, women and politics, contemporary political philosophy, philosophy of science, and social policy. Hawkesworth is the author of *Globalization and Feminist Activism* (Rowman and Littlefield, 2006); *Feminist Inquiry: From Political Conviction to Methodological Innovation* (Rutgers University Press, 2006); *Beyond Oppression: Feminist Theory and Political Strategy* (Continuum Press, 1990); and *Theoretical Issues in Policy Analysis* (State University of New York Press, 1988); co-author of *Women, Democracy and Globalization in North America* (Palgrave, 2006); editor of *The Encyclopedia of Government and Politics* (Routledge, 1992; 2nd Revised Edition, 2003) and *Feminism and Public Policy* (*Policy Sciences* 27(2–3), 1994); and coeditor of *Gender, Globalization and Democratization* (Rowman and Littlefield, 2001). She is serving as Editor of *Signs: Journal of Women in Culture and Society*, 2005–2010.

Patrick Thaddeus Jackson is assistant professor of international relations in the School of International Service at the American University in Washington, D.C. Among his publications are "Rethinking Weber: Towards a Non-Individualist Sociology of World Politics," *International Review of Sociology* 12: 439–68; "Defending the West: Occidentalism and the Formation of NATO," *Journal of Political Philosophy* 11, 223–52; and "Hegel's House, or, 'People are States Too,'" *Review of International Studies* 30, 281–87. He is the author of Civilizing the Enemy: *German Reconstruction and the Invention of the West*. He received his Ph.D. in Political Science from Columbia University.

Cecelia Lynch is associate professor of political science and international studies at the University of California, Irvine. She works at the intersection of international relations (IR) theory; social movements and world politics; peace, security, and globalization issues; and ethics and religion. She is the author of *Beyond Appeasement: Interpreting Interwar Peace Movements in World Politics* (Cornell University Press, 1999), which won the Edgar J. Furniss Prize for best first book on security from the Mershon Center at Ohio State University, and was cowinner of the Myrna Bernath Prize of the Society of Historians of American Foreign Relations. She coedited, with Michael Loriaux, *Law and Moral Action in World Politics* (University of Minnesota Press, 2000) and has written articles on the UN, the antiglobalization movement, peace movements and internationalism, religious perspectives on multiculturalism, narrative and interpretive methods, and conceptual issues in IR theory.

Steven Maynard-Moody is director of the Policy Research Institute and professor of public administration at the University of Kansas. In addition to the current chapter, he and Michael Musheno collaborated on the field research that resulted in their recent book, *Cops, Teachers, Counselors: Stories from the Front Lines of Public Service* (University of Michigan Press, 2003), which in 2005 received the Herbert A. Simon Award from the American Political Science Association and the award for Best Book of Public Administration Scholarship given by the American Society of Public Administration. He is currently completing a multi-methods study of justice norms in police stops.

Dean E. McHenry, Jr. is professor of political science at Claremont Graduate University in California. Specializing in comparative politics, with a focus on Africa and India, his research has included studies of rural development and the thwarted socialist transition in Tanzania; the creation of states and the demise of a public corporation in Nigeria; elections and state creation in India; and local-level democracy and secession in California. He taught previously in the United States at the University of Illinois and Brown University and abroad at the University of Dar es Salaam (Tanzania), the University of Calabar (Nigeria), and the University of Kerala (India). He received a B.A. from Oberlin College, a diploma in education from Makerere College (Uganda), and an M.A. and a Ph.D. from Indiana University.

Michael Musheno is professor and director of the Program in Criminal Justice at San Francisco State University. He is interested in legality, particularly the cultural force of law and other normative orders operating in and around the capillaries of the state. Recently published books on this theme are: Steven Maynard-Moody and Michael Musheno, *Cops, Teachers, Counselors: Stories from the Front Lines of Public Service* (University of Michigan Press, 2003); Lisa Bower, David Goldberg, and Michael Musheno, eds., *Between Law and Culture: Relocating Legal Studies* (University of Michigan Press, 2001); and Trish Oberweis and Michael Musheno, *Knowing Rights: State Actors' Stories of Power, Identity and Morality* (Ashgate, 2001). He is currently collaborating with Susan Ross on a field-based, interpretive study of citizen-soldiers.

Ido Oren is associate professor of political science at the University of Florida. He is the author of *Our Enemies and US: America's Rivalries and the Making of Political Science* (Cornell University Press, 2003). His articles have appeared in *International Security*, the *European Journal of International Relations, Journal of Conflict Resolution*, and other professional journals.

Timothy Pachirat is a doctoral candidate in the Department of Political Science at Yale University. In addition to his current dissertation research—an ethnographic study of industrialized animal slaughtering—he enjoys playing "Tackle," "Cooking Marshmallows by the Campfire While a Wolf Monster Creeps Up," and other such invented games with his two daughters, Parker and Mia. In the education of the imagination, they are his most persistent and passionate teachers.

Ellen Pader is associate professor of regional planning and director of the Joint Degree in Regional Planning and Law at the University of Massachusetts–Amherst. She received her Ph.D. in the Faculty of Archaeology and Anthropology at Cambridge University. She has done ethnographic fieldwork in Latin America and the United States on the relationship among domestic sociospatial relations, public policy, and housing discrimination. Her work has been published in a variety of disciplinary locales including *American Ethnologist, Rutgers Law Review Journal of Planning and Education Research,* and *Journal of Architectural and Planning Research*. She is currently at work on a book on occupancy standards.

Frederic Charles Schaffer is research associate at the Center for International Studies at the Massachusetts Institute of Technology and lecturer on Social Studies at Harvard University. His area of specialization is comparative politics, with a geographic focus on Southeast Asia and Sub-Saharan Africa. Substantively, he studies the political culture of electoral participation. He received his Ph.D. in political science from the University of California, Berkeley. He is the author of *Democracy in Translation: Understanding Politics in an Unfamiliar Culture* (Cornell University Press, 1998) and a forthcoming book on the hidden costs of clean election reform.

Ronald Schmidt, Sr. is professor of political science at California State University, Long Beach, where he has taught public policy, racial and ethnic politics, and political theory since 1972. His book *Language Policy and Identity Politics in the United States* (Temple University Press, 2000) won a Best Book Award from the American Political Science Association's Organized Section on Race, Ethnicity and Politics in 2001. Author of numerous articles on Latino politics, language policy, and immigrant political incorporation, he is currently at work on a coauthored book on the impact of recent immigration on U.S. racial politics.

Peregrine Schwartz-Shea is associate professor of political science at the University of Utah. She published her early research using experimental methods and rational choice theory in such journals as *American Political Science Review, Public Choice, Rationality and Society,* and *Journal of Public Administration Research and Theory.* While working on an article on the Seneca Women's Peace Camp (with Debra Burrington, published in *Women & Politics*), she changed her research orientation, publishing further feminist research on gendered organization in *International Encyclopedia of Public Policy and Administration* and on feminism and game theory in *Sex Roles.* This peregrination through the discipline led her to her current research focusing on methodological and epistemological practices in political science, published in *Political Research Quarterly* and *PS: Political Science and Politics.*

Samer Shehata teaches Middle East politics at the Center for Contemporary Arab Studies in the School of Foreign Service at Georgetown University. He has published articles in various journals about U.S. foreign policy toward the Middle East, Iraq, Egyptian politics, and other issues. He is preparing a book manuscript based on his dissertation at Princeton University entitled *Plastic Sandals, Tea and Time: Shop Floor Politics and Culture in Egypt.* He received the 2000 Malcolm H. Kerr Award from the Middle East Studies Association for the best dissertation in the social sciences.

Joe Soss is associate professor of political science and public affairs at the University of Wisconsin–Madison. His teaching and research focus on the politics of poverty, inequality, and social policy; political psychology and sociology; and research methodology. He is the author of *Unwanted Claims: The Politics of Participation in the U.S. Welfare System* (University of Michigan Press, 2000) and coeditor of *Race and the Politics of Welfare Reform* (University of Michigan Press, 2003).

Jutta Weldes is a senior lecturer in international relations at the University of Bristol. She is the author of *Constructing National Interests: The United States and the Cuban Missile Crisis* (University of Minnesota Press, 1999), a coeditor of *Cultures of Insecurity: States, Communities, and the Production of Danger* (University of Minnesota Press, 1999), and editor of *To Seek Out New Worlds: Science Fiction and World Politics* (Palgrave, 2003). Her main research interests currently include the critical analysis of U.S. foreign policy, the policing of neoliberal globalization, and the role of popular culture in world politics.

Dvora Yanow holds the Strategic Chair in Meaning and Method at the Vrije Universiteit, Amsterdam. Her research has been shaped by an overall interest in the communication of meaning in organizational and policy settings. She is the author of *How Does a Policy Mean? Interpreting Policy and Organizational Actions* (Georgetown University Press, 1996); *Conducting Interpretive Policy Analysis* (Sage, 2000); and *Constructing American "Race" and "Ethnicity": Category-Making in Public Policy and Administration* (M.E. Sharpe, 2003; winner of the American Society for Public Administration, Section for Public Administration Research's first Best Book Award); and coeditor of *Knowing in Organizations: A Practice-Based Approach* (M.E. Sharpe, 2003). Her articles have appeared in a variety of public policy, organizational studies, planning, and public administration journals.

INDEX